Debt Advice Handbook

....

5th edition

Mike Wolfe

with Peter Madge, John Kruse, Paula Twigg, Ceri Smith,
Fay Harris and Janet Wilson

Child Poverty Action Group

First edition 1993 by Mike Wolfe and Jill Ivison, edited by John Seargeant
Second edition 1996 by Mike Wolfe
Third edition 1998 by Mike Wolfe, with Jude Hawes, John Kruse, Peter Madge and Liz Willoughby
Fourth edition 1999 by Mike Wolfe, with Peter Madge, John Kruse, Paula Twigg, Ceri Smith, Fay Harris and Janet Wilson

Published by Child Poverty Action Group
94 White Lion Street, London N1 9PF

Charity No 294841

© Child Poverty Action Group 2002

A CIP record for this book is available from the British Library

ISBN 1 901698 47 5

Cover design by Devious Designs 0114 275 5634
Typeset and printed by William Clowes Ltd, Beccles, Suffolk

Contents

Foreword

Last year (2001), Citizens Advice Bureaux dealt with over one million debt problems. Many thousands of debt problems were handled by other free advice agencies such as National Debtline and those advice centres belonging to the Federation of Information and Advice Centres. Citizens Advice Bureaux have seen a 46 per cent increase in the number of consumer debt problems brought to them in the last five years. As the complexity of the consumer credit sector increases, so does the complexity of the debt enquiries. Ten years ago, a 'multiple debt case' might involve four or five debts. Today, it is common for advisers to report different debts that number well into double figures.

The need for high quality consumer advice on debt issues has never been greater. Figures from the Office of National Statistics show a 260 per cent increase in outstanding consumer credit from 1991 to 2001. As at December 2001, UK consumers owed £141,715 million in outstanding unsecured debt. And this figure does not include mortgage debt or the secured loans of homeowners who have consolidated their unsecured debt by cashing in on an increase in their house value. Nor does the figure include the debts owed by those having problems meeting rent, council tax or utility payments.

The continuing, and increasing, demand for advice about debt problems is, to some, a bit of a puzzle. Recent years have seen remarkably benign economic conditions facing UK consumers. Low unemployment and low mortgage rates have meant that advice agencies have, in general, faced fewer enquiries than before from those affected by the loss of their job or by an unexpected increase in housing costs.

Those working in the advice sector are sometimes criticised by the banks and finance companies for highlighting the downsides of the boom in consumer credit. Those in the finance industry point to the fact that advice agencies see only the minority of borrowers having problems with repaying credit. They highlight the way in which borrowers can take advantage of the vastly increased range of products provided by the innovative and energetic consumer credit industry. More recently, economists have suggested that the UK economy has only avoided a damaging recession through the ability and willingness of UK consumers to keep spending – using money that many do not actually have.

There is an undoubted value to consumers in having credit facilities that allow the option of bringing forward spending. A consumer able to make a confident and informed choice between a range of good credit deals can spread out spending in a way that best suits her/his needs and aspirations. Where it works well, credit gives the consumer the chance to have what s/he wants, when s/he wants it, without having to save, at a transparent cost s/he is willing to pay.

But on the whole we do not have well-informed, confident consumers. There is a general consensus that the UK faces a problem of financial illiteracy – reports for the Government have estimated that one adult in five in the UK is not functionally literate, with far more – between 30 per cent and 50 per cent – having problems with numeracy.

In the consumer credit sector consumers are often ill-equipped to get the best deal. Consumers often unknowingly choose high-cost credit agreements although lower-cost agreements would be readily available to them. They are frequently led by the nose through sophisticated and clever advertising and marketing. Consumers with existing borrowing facilities are targeted by finance companies. Anti-competitive inertia selling of credit by increasing credit limits and reducing minimum payments goes unchallenged.

And the market is failing lower-income consumers who do not appear to have benefited as much as higher-income groups from the growth of the consumer credit lending. Citizens Advice Bureaux evidence is that lower-income groups pay more for credit. On many occasions, the interest rates charged are so high that they should be open to attack if there were any effective consumer protection legislation. Unfortunately, the now badly outdated Consumer Credit Act 1974 fails to protect consumers from extortionate rates and in other respects has not kept pace with the market. The present licensing regime is woefully inadequate to the task of tackling unfair trading practices, and consumers who discover they have made a bad deal are faced with penal early settlement charges.

We therefore make no apology for continuing to suggest that there are likely to be downsides to the apparently inexorable growth in the market for credit. We make no apology because we see the distress that debt problems bring: the sleepless nights, the bailiffs at the door, the pressure on family relationships. Perhaps most frighteningly, we can see the thin line that can divide someone benefiting from the boom in consumer credit from another person who is struggling to cope with a debt problem. It is difficult to resist the conclusion that once the economic cycle revolves once more, the recent growth in consumer borrowing will lead to problems for a record number of consumers, who will face far larger debt problems than ever before.

The Government has listened to the concerns raised by advice agencies and others and is currently reviewing the Consumer Credit Act with a view to tackling loan sharks. The European Commission has launched a programme of work to revise the Consumer Credit directive and in that lies the promise of introducing responsible lending duties.

We will have to wait and see whether the Commission and the UK Government are able to bring positive and much needed changes. Irrespective of legislative reform, I have no doubt that the next few years will bring major challenges to those advising on debt. It will be vital that borrowers can obtain high quality advice that provides effective solutions to their problems. As with previous editions, this *Handbook* will be of great assistance in helping all advisers to deliver the best possible advice to their clients.

David Harker
Chief Executive of the National Association of Citizens Advice Bureaux

Acknowledgements

The production of this fifth edition has been made possible by other authors who have contributed their specialist expertise in a number of different areas and have made all the changes.

Peter Madge, from the NACAB Specialist Support Unit, has revised much of the book. Janet Wilson, also from the NACAB SSU, contributed especially to the chapter on insolvency. Paula Twigg, from CPAG, has revised the chapter on maximising income. Ceri Smith and Fay Harris, of Keele University Students' Union, have revised the chapter on student debts and John Kruse has revised the chapter on bailiffs.

Thank you to the Money Matters Unit in Newcastle-upon-Tyne, Alex Bohdanowicz from Yorkshire and Humberside Money Advice Support Unit, and Carolyn George for checking and making useful comments on the text.

I am also extremely grateful to Pauline Phillips and other CPAG staff who have produced this edition. Thanks to Kay Hart for compiling the index.

Ian Christie's contribution has been as eye-openingly minimal as his current architectural endeavours.

Thanks!

Mike Wolfe

How to use this book

This handbook is produced:
- as a guide and training aid for the new debt adviser;
- as a reference work for those who undertake debt advice alongside other sorts of advice work or other professional disciplines (eg, social workers, housing officers, etc);
- for the specialist debt adviser as a first step in accessing primary legislation and regulations, etc;
- for the manager (or purchaser) of debt advice services to help understand and evaluate debt advice.

The subjects covered within debt advice are vast and could fill many volumes. In this book much detail has deliberately been excluded in order to make it accessible to the reader and to make clear the structure of debt work. The book can best be used by different readers as follows.

Training aid

The Introduction and the first three chapters are written to assist those who are interested in debt advice and the processes and skills involved therein. These should be read in their entirety by the new debt adviser or those who have done some of this work and would like to think more about the structure that lies behind their practical experience. It may also be used by those who would commission or manage debt advice as a means of clarifying the product with which they are dealing.

The new adviser should ensure that s/he is able to identify each type of debt (this is explained in Chapter 4) because this is fundamental to using the rest of the book. S/he will wish to be familiar with the criteria to be used in prioritising debts (Chapter 7). S/he will find it useful to skim through the different strategies for priority and non-priority debts (Chapters 7 and 8); these can be examined in detail as they arise in the course of advising.

The debt adviser

Readers already familiar with the processes of debt advice may wish to use the strategy selection (Chapters 7 and 8) to help them think about the best strategy for a particular debt. The Index will enable them to find detailed information on a particular strategy, type of debt or court process. The Appendices contain examples of letters and forms, which they will need to complete, and also some of the relevant legislation. This can be accessed via the endnotes contained at the end of each chapter. Details of other useful reference material and organisations are also in the Appendices.

Introduction

Economic background

Personal borrowing has been essential to the expansion in the retail sector over the last two decades. Personal credit in 1980 was £13 billion. This had risen to £87 billion by 1997. In 2001, total UK consumer debt (including mortgages) reached over £700 billion for the first time. Figures published earlier this year (2002) showed consumer borrowing on personal loans and overdrafts increasing by more than £800 million a month, with spending on credit cards increasing by more than £350 million a month. Since 1980 mortgage borrowing has risen more than six-fold with new advances having broken through the £20 billion a month figure earlier this year. Enquiries about debt to Citizens Advice Bureaux doubled between 1979 and 1988 and have increased by almost 50 per cent in the past five years, to over 1 million enquiries a year relating to more than £1.2 billion worth of debt. Almost 23,000 people were jailed for debt in 1993 when fine defaulters accounted for a quarter of those sent to prison. Encouragingly, this figure has now fallen to under 2,500 by the use of alternatives to imprisonment for fine default.

Figures from the Council of Mortgage Lenders show that in 1980 about 13,500 mortgages were between 6 and 12 months in arrears. This figure peaked in 1995 (at 178,000) and then fell, and has continued to fall during 2002. Court figures for repossessions (although lower than in the early nineties) have continued to fluctuate and are once again rising slightly, but the number of mortgaged properties taken into possession during the first six months of the year (6,850) is reported to be the lowest number since 1984. However, the Council of Mortgage Lenders has warned that the period of improvement in arrears and possession is likely to be coming to an end.

The 'credit boom' in the 1980s fuelled a dramatic expansion in the retail sector of the economy. It was led by retailers anxious to increase their sales and also by the credit industry's own wish to expand. Traditional creditors had been comparatively small organisations, often working in a limited geographical area and lending small sums of money linked to particular purchases. Lending by banks and building societies with clearly defined markets had remained fairly static. The 1980s saw the entry into the UK market of financial institutions from abroad which brought with them new methods of marketing and sales, as well as a less conservative attitude to credit control. Many small credit companies merged or sold out to larger ones. The positive aspects of credit were emphasised, while the traditional 'evils' of 'debt' were ignored. New types of credit, notably credit cards, entered the market.

Increases in home ownership and house prices meant that more and more people were able to borrow against the increasing wealth locked up in their homes. Lenders were enthusiastic to meet a market for loans secured against property from which profit could be guaranteed, even if this involved repossession and forced sale.

The rise in interest rates at the end of the decade decreased the amount of borrowing, but also bolstered a new market for 'refinancing'. People encouraged to 'put all their eggs in one basket' often used the equity in their newly acquired property to exchange a mortgage and some debts for a single new loan. By this means, just as building societies diversified to the unsecured lending market, so the traditional loan companies gained a valuable share of the market for home-ownership loans.

The recession of the early 1990s brought about the phenomenon of 'negative equity', whereby many people owed more than their property was worth. The current rise in house prices (though still not uniform nationally) will gradually change this picture, but the effect on the repossession policies of lenders remains unclear. Many people with endowment mortgages should have been cushioned from the effects of negative equity by the value of their endowment investment. Sadly, it is now recognised that these policies have, in general, performed less well than anticipated and, therefore, offer little cushion at all. These factors have had a marked effect on debt advice strategies and practice.

Individual consequences

Credit has always led to debt in a certain number of cases. However prudently a person borrows, s/he is doing so on the basis of assumptions about the future and, where circumstances change, this must, in many cases, lead to default. Thus unemployment, separation, sickness or bereavement have all been shown to be precipitating factors in individual inability to pay. While these factors may certainly have triggered a debt crisis for a particular individual, they should not be seen as causes. Debt has always been an inevitable consequence of borrowing and is recognised by the credit industry as a necessary corollary of their lending. Lenders will always make provision in their accounts for debts that are to be written-off. This book is written on the assumption that debt is caused by lenders who predict it, but lend none the less. It should not be blamed upon the individual actions of borrowers. Individuals are led into borrowing by low wages or the paucity of benefit rates and/or the pressure to consume. They are forced into debt by factors like rises in interest rates or unemployment that are beyond their individual control.

While the causes of debt may not be individual, the effects most certainly are. Large numbers of people are still imprisoned for the crime of poverty. Bailiffs have returned in huge numbers to streets and estates. County court judgments have risen dramatically. Fuel disconnections (both formal and DIY ones caused by a person's inability to buy pre-payment tokens) are high.

The personal effects of all this are experienced by individuals and observed by advisers, social workers, healthcare professionals and other helpers on a daily basis. They include mental breakdown and illness, physical illness, stress, suicide, relationship break-up and criminality. Lives are led in fear and physical hardship.

The physical consequences are exacerbated by the negative values attached to debt, even by our consumerist society. For many years, to be in debt has been seen as to fail or to be 'wrong'. This is enshrined in language and folklore. Sayings like 'neither a borrower nor a lender be' (Hamlet Act 1 Sc3) indicate and sustain a negative image of debt.

Creditors feed negative images of 'bad payers' as those who cause prices to rise for everyone. Thus, many people finding themselves struck by the effects of the credit boom are initially overcome with negative feelings such as guilt. Similarly, advisers are not immune from often subconscious views about the morality of money or debt.

What is debt advice?

Debt advice is a series of tools and professional strategies that can be used to counter the problems so far described. Debt advice provides help to debtors by:
- enabling them to maximise their income;
- explaining the implications of the non-payment of each of their debts and on this basis deciding which are priorities;
- assisting them to plan their budgets;
- helping them to choose a strategy (usually to reduce or stop payments) that will minimise the effects of their debt on their financial, social or medical well being;
- assisting by advice or representation with the implementation of whatever strategy is chosen.

It should be distinguished immediately from 'budgeting advice'. In the 1950s and 1960s early social work practice placed much emphasis upon the need for poor people to be given advice on how to budget. Budgetary advice can only be effective where there is enough money for a person's needs to be met. Very often, due to low benefit levels or the escalation of credit charges, this is not the case. In these circumstances, budgetary advice is likely to be, at best, unrealistic and, more usually, patronising. Budgeting advice was often based upon methods which were not, in any case, open to poor people (buy in bulk or travel to distant supermarkets) or entirely unrealistic for any but the leisured classes (bake your own bread or make your own jam). Debt advice includes a comprehensive check of a person's entitlement to state benefits. However, it goes much further than welfare rights.

The past few years has seen the emergence of a new type of 'debt client' – people with substantial amounts of credit debt but also with substantial amounts of available income with which to repay them. This has coincided with the growth of so-called debt management companies – firms which arrange repayment programmes with creditors in return for a fee. At some stage a debate may need to take place as to whether the debt advice described in this book should be confined to those clients who are unable to meet their commitments instead of being available to everyone who has debts, regardless of whether or not they can service them. Concern at the activities of some debt management companies has prompted the Office of Fair Trading to issue guidance on the delivery of debt advice services and the actual content of such advice; the implications of which have not yet been fully taken on board by the traditional debt advice sector.

In the past, the words 'debt counselling' and 'money advice' have been used almost interchangeably to describe what we shall call 'debt advice'. We prefer this term to 'money advice' because this is often confused with benefit checking. 'Debt counselling', on the other hand, can appear to suggest that debt is a problem about which individuals merely need counselling. Counselling may sometimes be important in the early stages of debt advice, but is not a substitute for the work of the debt adviser.

Chapter 1

···

Debt advice – an outline

This chapter covers:
1. The adviser as a professional (below)
2. The debt advice system (p3)
3. Administrative systems (p6)
4. Computers (p8)

1. The adviser as a professional

Debt advice is a professional activity. There is a package of attitudes, skills and strategies that are necessarily part of any debt advice service. This guarantees consistency and quality assurance. Users of such services are misled if anything less than this package is offered.

Debt advice can be provided by specialists or by professionals whose job primarily involves other activities – eg, housing officers and social workers. It can be provided by paid or voluntary workers. Recent years have seen the growth of debt management companies which charge debtors a fee for setting up and handling debt repayment programmes.

A professional debt adviser needs a mixture of skills, knowledge and attitudes, which together form the basis of good practice. These are outlined below. The Money Advice Association has a code that outlines very clearly many aspects of good practice. In December 2001 the Office of Fair Trading (OFT) issued guidance to debt management companies, but made it clear that its principles applied equally to the free advice sector. The OFT subsequently issued a commentary to clarify the extent to which the guidance applies to the free sector.[1] It largely underlines what should be good practice and will be referred to where relevant below.

An unambiguous role

In any situation where money is owed there are two parties whose interests may conflict. Both parties will have a variety of legal remedies and defences, and well-established professionals know that they cannot advise both parties in such a situation. A debt adviser similarly needs to be clear that s/he is working only for the interests of the debtor. This is true even where the adviser's employment is funded by the finance industry or other creditors, such as local authorities, or if s/he works for an organisation that seeks to be impartial.

While impartiality may at different times require a worker to offer to assist both creditors and debtors, it cannot mean that a debt adviser is working towards the best interests of both parties at the same time when there is an inherent conflict of interests.

The OFT guidance and commentary make clear that all advice must be in the best interests of the debtor and should take account of:

- the nature of the debt;
- the debtor's financial position;
- the powers of the creditor.

A professional attitude

A debt adviser will be aware of experiences in her/his own past which may give her/him judgemental attitudes towards debtors and/or creditors. There exist within society well-established moral, political and religious views about debt. Debt advisers must consciously rid themselves of any personal bias and adopt a professional approach to the work.

A professional adviser must also offer an equal service to all groups within society. This requires her/him to understand attitudes towards particular groups and to appreciate those factors which mean that debt can affect working-class people, women, black people, lone parents and other groups in ways which are both different and more dramatic than for more privileged sections of the community.

A commitment to social policy

A professional debt adviser will not allow the same problem to affect adversely the lives of countless users or potential users, but will make known the lessons which can be learnt from her/his work to as wide an audience of policy makers as possible.

Sound knowledge of law and procedures

A professional debt adviser will be knowledgeable and imaginative about the ways in which the law can be applied to mitigate the effects of debt. S/he will be able to offer and explain each of these to any user.

A commitment to development of the service

A professional debt adviser will take regular opportunities to enhance her/his own skills through training, research and education, and will participate in offering this to others so that the practice of debt advice continues to be refined and developed.

A systematic approach

A professional debt adviser will apply a single systematic approach to each individual debtor. This does not, however, detract from the adviser's duty to ensure that any advice given is in the best interests of that particular debtor and is appropriate to her/his specific situation.

The ability to involve the debtor in informed choices

A professional adviser will always try to involve the debtor, ensuring that the debtor understands the implications of her/his situation and the steps that the adviser proposes to be taken. The adviser assists the debtor to make informed choices by giving her/him all her/his options and explaining their consequences before anything is done.

2. The debt advice system

The debt advice system is a structured set of procedures and activities that must be worked through if a debt adviser is to ensure that s/he is providing the best possible service to someone with a multiple debt problem. It is designed to:
- maintain the debtor's home, liberty and essential services;
- advise the debtor about her/his rights and responsibilities;
- give the debtor the information s/he needs to make informed choices in dealing with the debt situation;
- empower the debtor, where possible.

A systematic approach is essential because of:
- the large amount of information and paperwork generated by most debt enquiries;
- the need to avoid overlooking a particular strategy where advisers use a large number of options for dealing with debt, with frequent use of a range of options at the same time;
- the need to keep detailed records of the agency's work – both to ensure effective advice and to enable case material to be used for evaluating the service and for social policy development;
- the need to train new workers in a clearly-defined set of skills and knowledge;
- the need to guarantee consistency in spite of the diversity of debtors using the service;
- the need to protect the adviser from the strain of having continually to re-invent the wheel.

A system should not be seen as a straitjacket, and it does not obviate the need for individuals to operate in a creative and flexible way in the best interests of the individual debtor. Different agencies will need to develop their own paperwork and other methods based upon demand and resources, and any reporting requirements of funders – eg, the Legal Services Commission.

A debt adviser needs to perform a wide range of tasks in order to provide effective help to debtors. This section provides a list of these tasks, in the order in which they need to be performed.

Information to debtors

It is not necessary for an agency to have any written agreement with the debtor, but the adviser should provide the following information to the debtor in all cases at the outset, either verbally or, preferably, in writing:

- Adequate information about the service in plain language – ie, how the debt advice process operates.
- Warnings that:
  - creditors need not accept offers or stop interest or other charges;
  - creditors may still continue to try and collect the debt;
  - the debtor's credit rating may be adversely affected;
  - it is important to meet priority commitments (see Chapter 7);
  - correspondence from creditors should not be ignored.

Where the agency does use a form of written agreement (whatever it is called), it should:

- be fair, written in plain, intelligible language and legible;
- set out the nature of the service to be provided by the agency as above, together with the amount to be repaid or an estimate (ie, the total amount the debtor is to pay under the strategy chosen to deal with her/his debts, although it may well not be possible to provide this information to the debtor until later in the process);
- make clear that:
  - debtors are not prohibited from corresponding or communicating with creditors;
  - the agency will deal appropriately and promptly with any correspondence it receives;
  - the agency will keep the debtor informed of the progress of her/his case, including sending the debtor copies of correspondence sent to, and received from, creditors.[2]

It is good practice for the adviser to cover the following additional points with the debtor at the first interview:

- The agency's commitment to confidentiality.
- Those steps the agency will take and those steps the debtor has agreed to, or is expected to take her/himself.

- The debtor should not incur any further credit commitments without prior discussion with the adviser.
- The debtor should inform the agency of any change in her/his financial circumstances.

Fact-finding

There are many facts to be ascertained and noted in debt advice. These include details of debts, income, expenditure, property and assets, and details about the debtor and the reasons the debtor finds her/himself in financial difficulties.

Strategy selection

One or more strategies to deal with the debts must be selected and agreed to by the debtor. This must be a conscious choice based on full information and discussion with the debtor. Strategies must be clearly defined in advance and their applicability to different debt situations assessed against defined criteria.

Strategy implementation

This requires the writing of letters and/or the making of phone calls to try to negotiate agreement of the chosen strategy, and court applications or other action if this is not possible. The level of involvement of an agency must be determined in advance so that it is clear to users whether they will be expected to write their own letters or represent their own cases, or whether agency staff will be able to do this with them. An enormous number of letters are necessitated by debt advice and word processing will be essential.

Case review

The adviser needs to review cases continually in an informal way, and to have regular formal reviews with the debtor of all the strategies that s/he is using. Such reviews will take account of changes in the circumstances of the debtor and the results of negotiation.

Record-keeping

It is essential to keep detailed records of all work done. Record-keeping may be done in different styles by different agencies, but there must be a systematic way of recording information gathered from debtors and creditors.

Monitoring effectiveness

The agency should analyse in a standard way the results of the different strategies. This evaluation should include:
- debts handled;
- debts written off (fully/partially);

- debts repaid;
- homes/property saved;
- enquirer satisfaction;
- volume of work;
- rate of acceptance of each standard strategy;
- successful social policy work.

The results of evaluation should be regularly summarised and used as the basis of a review of working methods. The effectiveness of an agency's money advice work may also be used to support any funding applications.

Monitoring creditor practices

Debt advisers should keep a record of the collection techniques and tactics favoured by individual creditors. This will be useful in the future choice of strategy. In addition, they should note practices or situations that continually cause hardship to debtors and should monitor which creditors are responsible for such situations, for use in their social policy work. The effectiveness of pressure for change will often depend upon the ability of an agency to produce evidence in support of its recommendations. For this reason, case recording must not just be accurate and detailed, but must also be stored in a form which allows details of particular practices, and the hardship they cause, to be retrieved and patterns detected.

There are frequent changes in the laws and procedures that affect debt, and agencies are often in a very good position to look closely at how these are working in practice. Agencies will often carry out such exercises as part of a network of local and national debt services.

3. Administrative systems

Data

Before starting work an adviser must design systems for the collection and storage of data. Accurate debt advice depends on the accumulation of large amounts of data about enquirers, their debts and personal circumstances. This must be available to the adviser, and her/his colleagues or successors, for a period of months or even several years. If it is not held in a standard form much time and energy will be wasted each time a debtor's situation has to be considered. Systematic data handling requires the following:

- **Filing** For each enquirer a file is required in which documents (originals or photocopies) must be securely stored. Files should be designed to facilitate the efficient access to much-used documents (eg, financial statements) and the possibility of access to related data (eg, correspondence). This can be achieved by using files with two sets of clips (left and right). Whatever system is used, individual documents must be kept in order and not lost.

- **Tracers** A busy office will require a system of 'tracers' to ensure that if a file is not in its usual place (eg, gone for typing) it can be readily located.
- **Pro-formas** Data should be held on standard forms. This ensures that questions are not forgotten at interviews and also that data is always easily found. Examples of pro-formas on which to collect data are contained in Appendix 4. These can be designed to suit a particular agency's needs and may be best produced locally. The generation of pro-formas (whether by photocopy or printing) should be carefully budgeted, since the accumulated costs are likely to prove significant.

Where the agency has a Legal Services Commission (LSC) franchise or the Community Legal Service (CLS) Quality Mark, it will need to ensure that its systems are compliant with LSC/CLS requirements.

Communications
- **Letters** Debt advisers' correspondence is dominated by a limited range of forms and letters whose content is more or less identical – eg, each creditor for whom a particular strategy is chosen must be informed of the same facts. Standard letters should be designed around each strategy and to respond to other common eventualities. Experience has shown that, provided such letters contain all the information necessary for the creditor to act, they are effective. Standard letters may be:
  - pro-formas with blanks to fill in or phrases to delete;
  - held as a computer template;
  - pro-formas that are filled in but are re-typed (before despatch).

  A standard letter will take time to develop but this is time well spent if such documents can be used repeatedly. The general rules for letter writing should be followed for standard letters (see Chapter 2), but in addition such documents should:
  - avoid gender specific phrases;
  - avoid phrases that refer to debtors as only single people (or couples);
  - follow the logic of the decision the creditor is being asked to make and ensure that a blank space or deletable phrase is contained wherever variables might occur;
  - only include information that is absolutely necessary in every possible case;
  - take a format that is as similar to others as possible (this will make their completion simpler);
  - be labelled clearly with a brief descriptive phrase when they are kept for completion within an agency;

– be held in adequate stocks and be accessible to all debt advisers. If such material has to be found and copied each time it is required it is unlikely to be used;

– be copied and kept (certain letters may require photocopying if they make use of blanks to be completed according to individual circumstances).

Some standard letters designed within Stoke on Trent CABx are included in Appendix 2.

- **Standard phrases** Some agencies prefer to create letters from a list of standard phrases which are typed out, or copied into a new document if already saved on a PC, and combined in various ways as required (with appropriate links and non-standard applications).

Each phrase should be given a short label that allows it to be described. These can be made up of letters and numbers. The letter describes where the phrase will occur in a letter – eg, 'O' for opening phrases; 'S' for descriptions of strategies, and so on. The number distinguishes each of the possible phrases within a particular section.

Standard phrases give added flexibility (and sophistication) when combined with a set of standard letters. In creating standard phrases:

– avoid gender specific phrases;

– avoid phrases that refer to debtors as only single people (or couples);

– keep phrases short so that no variables occur within them (each possible variable should be covered by a different standard phrase);

– keep a note of useful phrases employed in specifically created letters and, if repeated, add these to the list of standard phrases.

- **Forms** Stocks of all necessary forms (see Appendix 3) should be monitored, maintained and updated. Such documents will be used to initiate or defend the majority of court actions, benefit claims, and so on. An index of the forms held by an agency must be created and systematically revised. Sources of forms not held in-house should also be listed. Some court forms can be reproduced by word processor (large creditors produce summonses in this way) or downloaded from the internet at www.courtservice.gov.uk.

4. **Computers**

Analysis of needs

The first stage in deciding how to use computers is to decide what need they are intended to satisfy. An analysis of advisers' needs does not require specialist computing knowledge, although it must be accepted at the outset that some of the requirements identified by a debt adviser may have technical or financial costs that cannot be met by an agency.

The analysis must be discussed among all those involved in the debt advice process. This includes clerical, administrative and managerial personnel as well as the debt adviser. The analysis should be documented and take account of at least the following points:

- Will a system of standard letters be used?
- Will standard letters be mail-merged?
- Will standard calculations (eg, equitable distribution, benefit calculations, better-off calculations) be regularly employed by advisers?
- Will a database of enquirer (client)/creditor/other information be held?
- Will statistics be maintained, calculated and analysed? Will a more complex dedicated debt advice software program be used, integrating more than one of the above elements (see below)?

Differing needs will require the use of a variety of programs and hence a more, or less, complicated (and expensive) computer. Do not underestimate what the non-computer specialist can achieve with modern software.

Assistance

In developing a computer system it is generally advisable to get specialist help to ensure that the computer (hardware) and programs (software) satisfy the needs identified in the agency's analysis. Such help should ideally be independent of both hardware and software suppliers. Help need not be expensive. In fact, volunteers can often be found in:

- university or college computer departments;
- local authorities;
- large local firms;
- councils for voluntary service, NACAB, or other umbrella organisations;
- advertising (perhaps for an enthusiastic and knowledgeable amateur, although this can be a risky option).

The market for computers and software is constantly changing. Any system purchased is likely to be surpassed almost as soon as it is installed. However, this should not be a deterrent to making a purchase. The agency that waits for the perfect (or cheapest) computer will never buy one. Once the needs have been clearly identified, it is much better to buy something that meets at least some of those needs and start learning how to maximise the benefits.

There are a number of general points to bear in mind when purchasing computer equipment. Computer experts invariably differ on the best machine or program for a particular application. Thus it is best to ensure that the consultant is confident that the system will work as predicted and that, particularly in the early days following the purchase, her/his technical support is available.

Suppliers should be acquainted with the tasks for which the machine is required, and a written statement of these should form part of the order. This will be important if systems do not live up to expectations.

If using commercial consultants or suppliers for advice, beware of choosing an over-sophisticated application. Many advice agencies have become slaves to their over-complex computer systems at the expense of service to the public.

Computer equipment – hardware

Any modern entry-level computer will run the kind of software that a debt adviser is likely to need. Sometimes old machines are available (perhaps as gifts) from local industry. Although relatively unsophisticated, these should not be rejected and if the debt adviser requires only word processing and simple database or spreadsheet applications such a computer will be quite sufficient.

Programs – software

In choosing software for a system, ensure that the computer you own has the capacity to run it – check with your dealer.

Word processing

All current word processing programs offer, as well as the standard options for producing and editing text, a mail-merge facility – a technique that allows, with minimum work, the entry of names, addresses, etc, into a standard letter.

Programs such as Word also enable users to perform simple calculations – eg, to add up income and expenditure in a financial statement and calculate the available income. They can also store standard blocks of text (eg, lists of creditors' addresses) in a manner that allows easy recall. The sophisticated design of most word processing packages means that in many situations no other software is required.

Databases

A database program assists with the handling of data. Such software allows the storage, alteration, finding, grouping and outputting of information in myriad forms and can be applied to a wide range of situations.

A database can be of particular benefit to the debt adviser because many recent programs can themselves be 'programmed' automatically to compare different pieces of data in store, and either analyse relationships between them (perhaps for statistical purposes) or prompt certain other actions when predetermined events occur – eg, suggest strategies that are applicable.

Database programs (eg, Access, dBase, Paradox) can form the basis of programs that automate the routine tasks of the debt advice process. Database programs may require more memory (RAM) and faster processors.

Spreadsheets

A spreadsheet is a program that allows numbers to be laid out in 'table form' on the computer screen. Calculations are then performed automatically on the basis of pre-set relationships (or formulas) entered in a particular place on the table (the spreadsheet).

A spreadsheet is of benefit to advisers because such programs can perform all the calculations and number storage required by the debt advice process. In particular, hypothetical changes in circumstances can easily be reviewed to determine their effect on a debt advice strategy – eg, what if I get a job paying £50 more?

Some of the most recent spreadsheet programs (eg, Excel) can be used in association with database programs to allow the full benefits of a spreadsheet to be combined with those of a database by dynamically sharing the same data – for example, when figures are changed in the database, such changes will be replicated in the spreadsheet. However, many spreadsheet programs include comprehensive database facilities.

Special programs

Special programs exist, or are being developed, that are designed specifically to help debt advisers. These may be divided into:

- Those that perform specific tasks within the debt advice process – for example, the preparation of financial statements and other forms, equitable distributions or address lists of creditors.
- Those that undertake all or most of the processes involved in debt advice. Such programs will store data about debtor's debts, income, expenditure, creditors and other relevant information. Some programs suggest strategies, and will produce letters with text and numerical inserts appropriate to a case. They may allow storage of work done and any analysis of such data.
- Those that are accessed via the internet. Although only the wiseradviser website is available at present (www.wiseradviser.org), it is likely that CABlink and other sites or 'intranets' to which advisers will have access will soon include programs to help debt advisers. In addition, the internet contains a wealth of information which the debt adviser can use for background or legal detail.

The market for specialist programs is extremely volatile. The debt advice manager is advised to view as many as possible (trial discs are usually available) and to consider with her/his consultant the costs and benefits of using one. In particular s/he should consider:

- **Features** What are the exact features of this program? These can be assessed against the stages of debt advice as outlined in Chapter 3.
- **Support** Is proper support available to users and likely to remain so?

- **Training** Is proper training available for all workers who will need to use the program?
- **Cost** What is the cost of the program along with training and support? Is there an updating cost?
- **Hardware** Does the agency have the right hardware and is it available to run a debt advice program at the time and in the place that the debt adviser will require it? The debt adviser will have to decide whether the program should be used with a debtor and if so, hardware (perhaps a laptop computer) may need to be set aside for this purpose alone.
- **Other advice** If an agency does not use computers to give other types of advice, will their use in debt advice be problematic? (This could perhaps be so if the use of computers gave debt advice a higher status or rendered it accessible to only certain advisers.)
- **Staff** Do all the staff giving debt advice have adequate computer skills to use the program? If it is proposed that only certain advisers use the program, what is the effect of this on the distribution of the debt advice caseload?
- **Future** For how long is it likely that this particular computerised system will be appropriate? Predictable changes in caseload should always be considered before investing in technology.
- **Philosophy** All computer programs have inbuilt values and philosophies. Check the criteria used for presenting or recommending strategies and see how they accord with those outlined in Chapters 7 and 8. Check the level (if any) of error prevention built into the program being considered.

Notes

1. **The adviser as professional**
   1 DMG; Note – application of debt management guidance to CABx and other independent advice agencies, OFT, April 2002

2. **The debt advice system**
   2 paras 20-21 DMG; paras 6-10 Note to agencies

Chapter 2

Key skills

1. Interviewing

This section is not a general guide to interviewing, but there are some features of an interview with a person in debt that are important to note.

- A successful debt adviser must immediately make it clear to the debtor that s/he will not be judged in this relationship.
- The debt adviser must be aware of the ways in which preconceptions or personal attitudes affect the interview process. S/he must work to expose and eradicate negative images of borrowing, debt or debtors.
- It is important that the debtor is enabled to voice her/his emotions in order that s/he can get these out of the way and concentrate on remembering, thinking and decision making as the interview progresses. For example, many people in debt fear imprisonment. For the vast majority of debts this is not currently a possibility, but this fear must be voiced if progress is to be made.
- Because of the numerous threats from individual creditors, many debtors feel hopeless about their situation. Advisers cannot afford to raise false expectations by dismissing these threats, but they should be positive and explain that it is possible to do something.
- The debt adviser must anticipate problems that the debtor may face. It is important that the debtor does not depart from decisions that have been made as part of a strategy, but the adviser is unlikely to be there when these decisions are tested. For example, an adviser and debtor may agree that, because the debtor has been paying creditors who call at the door and not paying her/his priority creditors, the best course of action is to withhold all payments to

unsecured creditors until the arrears on the debtor's priority debts have been cleared. This decision will not be tested until an unsecured creditor calls, perhaps a door-to-door collector late at night, making threats. The debtor will find it difficult to stick to her/his earlier decision unless this possibility has already been explored with the adviser.

- Partners, or other people with whom the debtor lives, will usually need to be consulted if a good decision (ie, one which is likely to be adhered to) is to be made. Many of the decisions taken involve third parties who may not be there at the interview. Even if the debt adviser considers that urgent action is required, this can generally be delayed long enough for the debtor to consult these people. Occasionally there will be compelling reasons (eg, fear of violence) for not consulting.

- A clear explanation of the tasks that will be undertaken by the adviser and which are expected of the debtor must be written down and a copy given to the debtor and one kept by the agency (see 'Information to debtors' p4).

- Performing realistic tasks can reduce the sense of hopelessness and empower the debtor. Modest tasks, such as asking a particular creditor about arrears, can help the debtor to feel involved in the processes that are being carried out on her/his behalf. While it is important for the adviser to offer expertise and services, s/he should not take over the debtor's life.

2. Negotiation

Negotiation is a process of communication between the adviser or debtor and creditor. It takes place over a period of time in which an agreement is made that both sides find acceptable. An important choice must be made as to whether it is most appropriate for negotiation to be carried out by the debtor or the adviser. Sometimes it is more empowering for the debt adviser to support a debtor by providing a financial statement, pro-formas, etc, rather than negotiating her/himself. This support should usually be mentioned to the creditor and the debtor encouraged to remain in contact with the adviser. Some creditors have a policy of refusing to deal with advice agencies. Where the debtor has authorised the debt adviser to negotiate with a creditor on her/his behalf, the Office of Fair Trading (OFT) regards it as an unfair and improper business practice on the part of the creditor to refuse without reason to do so.[1] A creditor who refuses to negotiate with an adviser without a valid reason should be challenged.

A debt adviser must only represent the interests of the debtor and should ensure that the debtor pays the minimum to extricate her/himself from the problems (and never more than s/he can afford). This does not mean that people should be encouraged not to pay their debts. It does mean that advisers should do their best to enable the debtor to regain control of her/his financial situation as quickly as possible in order to rehabilitate her/himself, as opposed to being tied in to a repayment programme which may take many years to complete (if ever) and with no light at the end of the tunnel.

A debt adviser is often in a powerful position in relation to creditors because nobody within the credit industry wants to be accused (particularly publicly) of acting illegally or oppressively. If a debt adviser from a well-respected local or national agency contacts a creditor to negotiate on a debtor's behalf, it is very likely that the creditor will want to reach a settlement. In some cases the adviser's power is increased because debt advice is likely to lead to payment and, in others, because the creditor realises that a debt cannot profitably be pursued. This does not mean that creditors should routinely be expected to agree to each and every proposal that a debt adviser puts forward. On the other hand, if the debt adviser feels that the creditor is being unreasonable or unrealistic or both, then s/he should consider referring the matter to a more senior person in the creditor organisation with a view to using the creditor's complaints procedure, if necessary (see also 'Irrational creditors' on p17).

Support arguments by referring to any relevant codes of practice. All negotiations should be conducted with the aim of resolving the debt problem and bearing in mind that the debtor's best interests are paramount.

Rational negotiation

If the creditor is a rational person seeking an outcome that maximises mutual gains, negotiation should follow six basic rules.

Separate the messenger from the message

A creditor's representative should be treated with respect, even if the message is to be rejected. Nothing will be gained by negotiating with the creditor as though s/he were simply the (unacceptable) message that s/he is trying to deliver. By recognising that the messenger is separate from the message, the adviser can treat the message with the utmost severity and reject it totally, where necessary, without allowing personal factors to enter into it.

Treating the creditor with respect does not mean pleasing the creditor by making offers the adviser thinks may evoke a pleasant response. The creditor must be tested about levels of acceptable offers. For example, it cannot be assumed that token offers are the lowest possible. A debt adviser should regularly try requesting a write-off from creditors who usually accept no less than token offers. To decide not to request a write-off on the basis of the adviser's fear of the creditor's response is to confuse personal factors with facts.

Avoid emotional involvement in the outcome

Negotiators can sometimes become emotionally involved in the outcome of their work, and losing in negotiation can seem like personal failure. Bringing such personal factors into the process will induce stress and prevent clarity.

Distinguish between aims and means

The aim of debt advice is to get the debtor out of trouble at the lowest possible cost (see above). The means of doing this lie in one of the many strategies outlined in Chapters 7 and 8. The aim remains constant, but changing the strategy is perfectly acceptable. Failure to recognise this distinction can lead to negotiations that become repetitive, inflexible or acrimonious. If the adviser is focused on a battle with the creditor from fixed positions then alternative means of reaching aims may be overlooked.

For example, insistence that a creditor accepts only an equitable distribution of the available income (see p164) would be counterproductive if s/he refuses to do so and could instead apply for, and perhaps get, a charging order (see p189) or other undesirable remedy. The adviser's aim is to satisfy the creditor at the lowest possible cost. The creditor's aim is to have an arrangement that includes an element of future security. A completely different means (eg, a voluntary charge – see p137) might achieve the aims desired by both sides, albeit through a different avenue from the one first tried.

Aims can be openly acknowledged within negotiations and indeed this is more effective and less stressful than playing power games in the dark. An adviser will be uncompromising in her/his attitude towards a response that runs contrary to the aims set for the negotiation and so does not need to be afraid of revealing such aims.

Recognise organisational constraints

A creditor's representative may be working within organisational constraints that both influence and limit the range of responses available. For example, a branch manager may refuse a request for a write-off not because s/he does not think this is sensible, but because company procedures require that all debts written off be reported to head office and perhaps be offset in some way against commission earned. The branch manager's aim may, therefore, be not so much to chase the unrecoverable as to set up token payments so that the matter does not have to go further. This will not be discovered unless s/he is questioned carefully by the adviser. It is therefore always important to know the procedures and policies for individual creditors.

Search for mutual benefit

In looking at different strategies, the adviser should seek one which will provide mutual gain. Although the aims are different, there may be occasions that lead to mutual benefit. For instance, if a building society has a possession order (see p201) and is intending to repossess and sell a property, it could be to the benefit of both sides if a reliable private sale could be arranged in advance of repossession, even if it meant the building society taking no action for some months. Even where the gains are less specific, the credit industry should see the benefits of debt advice from which is derived:

- independent advice (which is not motivated by a competitor);
- a predictable and equitable treatment of all non-priority creditors;
- the availability of full information about their customers;
- the empowerment of borrowers and the alleviation of poverty.

Establish objective criteria

Objective criteria are those which can be defined, measured and separated from the subjective feelings of the participants. They are the rules which will define what each side means by a 'satisfactory' outcome. Objective criteria might include the following:

- that a solution is reached which can be authorised locally;
- that repayments take no longer than three years;
- that repayment schedules do not reduce a person's income below benefit level.

Negotiation should not proceed until the criteria that will be used to evaluate the best options are agreed and noted by both sides. Negotiations in which criteria have not been agreed will tend to drift and it is very difficult for either side to recognise the best option. Moreover, if objective criteria are not agreed, then negotiations can turn into 'trading' – in which a debt adviser is expected to concede certain points in exchange for others conceded by the creditor. This will not give the best result for the debtor.

Irrational creditors

Most members of the credit industry can be dealt with on the basis outlined above. However, every debt adviser will come across some creditors who refuse to listen to reason or who show contempt for debt advisers and debtors alike. This section outlines some ways of dealing with such people and explains those situations where a preconceived strategy may be more effective than creating a dialogue. It should be stressed that these techniques would be counter-productive if applied to the majority of creditors who are reasonable and professional and would, therefore, see these manipulations as unnecessary. An irrational creditor is not easy or pleasant to deal with. No real solution may be possible, but these techniques might help.

An adviser dealing with an unreasonable creditor should allow her/him space to express her/his emotions. These will often be very strong and can include anger, frustration and anxiety about her/his business; they may masquerade as moralising, political views or other philosophical stances. There is no point in trying to argue with feelings, except perhaps to challenge oppressive prejudice, as they will go on being expressed however much logic is injected. Instead, after a period of listening, the discussion can be shifted to another agenda. However, to implement any of the strategies described below, the adviser needs to be able to get at least a word in edgeways and to be assertive. In this situation, the following tactics are useful.

Overbid and compromise

Start off by asking for much more than is expected (or perhaps can be justified) in order to fall back on a satisfactory compromise.

Appear to be agreeing

This is the opposite of the first tactic and it consists of making a strong statement that sounds as though it will conclude with a major concession. This lulls the listener into a false sense of security and brings her/him round to the adviser's side, but is followed by a conclusion that is different from the one s/he expected.

For example, the adviser may begin by expressing at length concern and understanding at the high level of unpaid debts within society and the large number of liquidations among small finance companies. Having appeared to understand the predicament, the adviser then says that in this case there is no money to offer and therefore it will be impossible to make a payment.

Setting up a common enemy

If creditors refuse to be rational in a negotiation then it may be possible to manipulate them into a variety of differing irrelevances. One of these is to listen for long enough to ascertain the possibility of moving their attention to something which could be seen as a 'common enemy'. In this way, the adviser ceases to be on a different side and the creditor may compromise as part of this 'battle'.

For example, in many commercial concerns there may be ways in which differences between centralised management and branch interests can be exploited.

Solve 'their' problem

If the creditor is unable to respond favourably because of factors within her/his own organisation, the debt adviser can offer to help her/him find a solution to 'their' problem – which will then also solve the debtor's problem.

For example, a creditor may say, 'I personally would like to help you but company rules just don't allow it.' The skilful debt adviser will help the creditor find a way around the problem that has been encountered with her/his own rules!

Ask the creditor to solve your problem

Asking the creditor to solve the adviser's problem can flatter her/him sufficiently to produce agreement. It may also enable creditors to see the impossibility of the demands that they are making. This tactic may work where a creditor is expressing feelings of frustration or is moralising, but the financial facts of the case offer no way out.

For example, the adviser might say something like, 'Yes, I know, it's a very low offer and I can see it must make it difficult for you, but I can't see any other way out of this. But if there's something you could suggest, which would help, I'd be pleased to discuss it. . .'

Broken record

A well-known technique of being assertive is called 'a broken record'. In this, the adviser repeats the demand and allows the other side to exhaust their opposition to it. The adviser refuses to be drawn into elaborating upon or discussing the proposal any more than is absolutely necessary and just repeats it (perhaps with a slightly different introductory phrase each time). It is important to acknowledge what the creditor says but to make it clear that any shift of position is impossible. This tactic requires patience and self-control in order to avoid the repetition beginning to sound desperate.

Responses to creditors' arguments

A debt adviser will hear many arguments from creditors and must prepare for these in advance. The most common arguments, together with effective responses, are summarised below.

We are not a charity

Creditors will often attempt to control the framework in which they negotiate by distinguishing between themselves in a hard-hearted 'real' world of business and those outside (including the debt adviser) who would wish to be 'nice' to everybody. This can lull the adviser into thinking that the creditor is actually on her/his side and would be charitable if s/he could, and the debt adviser can be made to feel like a 'wet do-gooder'.

To counter this argument it is important to shift the ground, and the easiest way to do this is to demonstrate how efficient and business-like is the proposition being put. If the adviser attempts to suggest that the creditor ought to be more charitable it will merely lead to an irrelevant argument about the relative values of people whose starting point and first principles are quite different.

> *Example*
>
> Creditor – 'I'm sorry, debt adviser, our company cannot afford to be generous just because you're asking us to be.' Adviser – 'I'm certainly not asking you to be generous but rather to accept the business realities of the situation. Your customer is insolvent. If s/he were a limited company then s/he would go into liquidation. We are acting as though we were a liquidator and would ask you to discuss what is possible on the basis of the factual evidence which we both have.'

They have got a good income coming into that house

Provided there is a good financial statement (see p47), then this argument should be relatively easily dismissed. The financial statement will demonstrate that the 'good income' is actually committed already in many ways and whatever is available is being fairly shared among the creditors.

Overspending

Sometimes a creditor will argue that a debtor is spending too much on either one particular item or things in general. This charge is most easily countered by a detailed financial statement (see p47) and individual figures.

However, the adviser must be prepared to discuss those items which may require extra justification (eg, travel or telephone), the reasons for which should have been noted on the financial statement (see p47), but should not have to justify or provide evidence for obviously routine and reasonable expenditure – eg, housekeeping. The item that probably causes most controversy with creditors is cigarettes, but these can be included within 'food and household goods'. However, where they are questioned, the reality of a person's addiction and the difficulty of overcoming it should be stressed. Arguments are often untenable if taken to their logical conclusion. For example, if the cost of pet food is challenged, the alternative of killing the pet should be made explicit.

They had no intention of repaying

If a debtor has continued to borrow money until s/he could get no more credit and faces a variety of enforcement crises, then s/he will often be blamed for being in debt or accused of deliberately misleading creditors – a 'won't pay', not a 'can't pay'. Many people who are in serious debt have created new debts in order to repay others, often on the advice of credit brokers who ignored the debtor's inability to repay the new borrowing. While it may be helpful to explain why a person borrowed money, the argument must be moved to the present, emphasising that the debtor is now getting advice and looking at her/his financial affairs as a whole. Arguments about past intent hinder a business-like approach.

Cable TV syndrome

Creditors who have visited debtors at home will sometimes complain about consumer items that the debtor has – eg, cable television. Sometimes items that are clearly not luxuries (eg, washing machines) are described as such. Many items which may have cost a lot originally will be worth very little secondhand; others will be unsaleable because they are either hired or on hire purchase. A debt adviser should dismiss discussion of a debtor's consumer goods, unless selling something non-essential would make a substantial difference to the size of the debt.

We want more

Creditors often want more than is offered without any explanation as to where the debtor is to get the extra money from. The adviser should counter this by referring to the financial statement and perhaps by asking how such a demand could be accommodated within a scheme that must treat all creditors equitably.

Sometimes this arises because the debtor has previously agreed to make higher repayments to the creditor than are now being offered. Unless the debtor's circumstances have worsened (in which case the explanation for the lower offer will be obvious), the adviser should explain that the previous arrangement was made before the debtor had obtained proper debt advice, and was unrealistic and unsustainable (eg, did not take account of other non-priority creditors) whereas the financial statement shows that the debtor can afford the repayments now proposed and is, therefore, more likely to keep to the proposed arrangement.

Majority pay more

When a debtor becomes unable to pay it is often argued that this behaviour cannot be tolerated because it means that the majority is then forced to pay more for goods or services in order to provide for these bad debts. This argument is sometimes refined, referring to the need to increase charges to pensioners, the sick and/or disabled if some people refuse to pay their fair share.

It is rarely useful to get drawn into such arguments, and the discussion should return to the strategy that has been suggested. The economic well-being of the creditor's other customers need not be discussed; it is this debtor's actual financial position that is at issue.

Floodgates

It is popularly argued that unless creditors are tough with everybody then nobody will repay anything; that examples need to be made of bad payers if the majority is to be encouraged to repay. This argument ignores the fact that the vast majority of people can, and do, pay voluntarily and can be obliged to pay by orders, such as attachment of earnings (see p194), were they to decide deliberately not to pay. The adviser should point out that this debtor cannot pay, as demonstrated by the financial statement, and that no amount of enforcement action can change that.

Administratively it can't be done

Creditors will sometimes argue that they cannot accept a nil offer or a very low offer because their administrative (or computer) systems will not allow this to be done. A debt adviser is not a business adviser and cannot suggest ways in which this could be achieved. S/he should return to the financial statement and again stress the factual objectivity of this, and explain that whatever the creditor's systems, strengths or weaknesses, there is simply no more to offer.

Secure it with a charge

Some creditors will accept reduced payments or no payment at all but will then wish to secure this by charging their debt against the debtor's home. This means that the debt will be repaid if the property is sold. If the debtor agrees, this is known as a 'voluntary charge' (see p137). A voluntary charge converts an unsecured debt into a secured one, and an adviser should almost always refuse such a suggestion, unless it is in the debtor's best interests to agree. The granting of a charge should never be seen as a mere technicality, since the debtor is at risk of losing her/his home. The adviser should argue, where appropriate, that it is both inequitable and fundamentally unnecessary to change the terms of a contract in this way, given that the loan was set up and interest charged on the basis that it was unsecured. On the other hand, where the creditor will agree to the repayments offered, to freeze interest and not enforce the charge until the property is sold, it may be in the debtor's best interests to agree.

Other debts have interest added on

Any repayment offer made will normally be conditional upon the cessation of interest and other charges. This request will sometimes lead creditors to complain that this is unfair because their competitors, to whom money is also owed, may have added interest at the beginning of the loan period and therefore will, in effect, be getting their interest within the capital sum used to calculate an equitable offer (see p164). It is important for a debt adviser not to allow a whole strategy to be questioned because of what can be seen as a relatively small matter. (For details of how to approach this problem, see p166.)

To make matters fairer the adviser may suggest that the total charges for interest over the period of each loan (which will be calculated in the agreement) is either included in each debt as part of the capital or that only a proportion of it equivalent to the proportion of the loan period which has now passed is included.

3. **Letter writing**

Much negotiation begins with a letter. While emergency applications, particularly with regard to priority debts (see p143), may have to be initiated on the telephone and confirmed in writing later, it is more effective to send a letter in the first instance so that full details can be enclosed. Important modifications to a contract should always be confirmed in writing.

It is sometimes more appropriate for the adviser to help the debtor to prepare letters and a financial statement using standard forms, but for the letters to be sent from the debtor her/himself rather than the adviser. (Letters should include a reference to the agency that is advising.) The debtor will receive the replies and must be encouraged to seek further advice as required. In this way the debtor regains control over her/his own affairs and, in the long term, may be more able to cope. In addition, the workload of the adviser may be reduced. The structure and content of the letter will be similar, whoever it is sent from.

Format of a letter

Letter writing needs to follow a basic format, which is explained below. Preparation of standard letters is advisable, and samples are included in Appendix 2.

Use simple language

Write letters in simple, clear language. 'Business language' is now a largely discredited method of communication. 'Thank you for your letter of 11 June' is just as meaningful as 'Your communication of 11 June is gratefully acknowledged'.

Assume nothing

Letters, particularly first ones, will generally be read by a person who knows little or nothing about the situation in question. A letter should, therefore, contain all the background information needed to make a decision.

Use a framework

As well as standard letters or phrases, new or unusual situations will require individual letters. These are easier to write with a framework to follow:

- **Address** The letter will begin with the address to which it is to be sent, which must appear on the adviser's copy as well as the top copy.
- **Debtor and references** Next comes the full name and address, including postcode, of the debtor and all references or other identifying numbers. Any major creditor will probably have dozens of borrowers of the same name and thus detailed identification will be essential to avoid confusion.
- **Standard opening phrase** It is easiest to begin a letter with a standard phrase because the first sentence is often the most difficult to write. This can usefully explain the agency's status. For example, 'The above has contacted us for advice about her/his financial affairs and we are now helping her/him to look at these as a whole'.
- **Outline the background** Next tell the story so far. It is essential to give all the necessary background and details. It is easiest to go through the story in chronological order. Keep sentences short and do not include any that make demands or excuses. Merely get an agreed set of facts.

Example

As you know, two years ago Mr Parkinson lost his job. Since then he has been unable to find work. His wife was until recently working part time, but she too has now given up work and is expecting a baby next month. When he first lost his job Mr Parkinson continued to make payments to yourselves on the above loan agreement, but unfortunately got behind with the rent on his council house. He is now faced with possession proceedings by the local authority and is in danger of losing his home. He has no property, assets or savings.

The statement of facts must include those on which the adviser is basing the strategy. Thus, if asking for a temporary suspension of payments and interest charges, the adviser should ensure that s/he has explained that there is at present no available income or capital and the future prospects.

- **Make the request** The next stage of the letter should be the request. This needs to be clearly and simply phrased. Use bold type if possible. Do not be apologetic or circumspect – link the request to the facts outlined and make it appear to be an inevitable consequence of them.

Example

In view of the above it is clear that Mr Parkinson must now make it an absolute priority to repay the arrears due on his rent. The council has indicated that the least it will accept is £2 a week and we believe that this is the amount that a court would order. As you can see from the enclosed financial statement, this is equivalent to the amount which he has been paying you. We therefore request that you agree to forgo any payments on this account at present. In addition, in order to ensure that Mr Parkinson's affairs do not deteriorate still further, please will you cease charging interest. We will of course be happy to review the situation in six months' time.

The letter should continue to state in what period it is proposed to review this strategy. This may be expressed either:
- as a fixed period; *or*
- with reference to other factors – eg, 'we will be happy to review this when Mr Parkinson gets a job'.

- **Add any special reasons** After outlining the request add the special reasons why this should be accepted. These may be obvious from the facts you have listed and it is certainly not worth repeating them. But if arrangements have broken down in the past or it is believed that a creditor will be resistant to the suggestion, it is useful to list whatever special reasons you can.

Example

We recognise, of course, that because Mr Parkinson has continued paying you for so long, our request may come as a surprise to you. We hope, however, that you will agree that your customer must have a roof over his head and that paying for this really has to be his first priority. We hope that you would also accept that, having continued to receive payments for so long while he has been unemployed, you have actually received more from this account than you might otherwise have expected.

- **Details of any offer** If an offer of payment (or some other offer, for example, a withdrawal of a counterclaim) is being made then this should be clearly described. For example, 'The first payment of £. . . will be made on 27 August and following payments will be made on the 27th of each month until £. . .

has been paid.' The debtor should be advised to begin making the payments in accordance with the offer without waiting for confirmation from the creditor.

- **Response expected** Your letter could then suggest the kind of reply that you expect. For example, 'We would be grateful if you could confirm, in writing, that this will be possible and send a paying-in book.'
- **To whom should the creditor reply?** It is worth considering whether or not it is desirable for creditors to reply to the agency or to debtors directly. If the volume of debt advice is great then it may be sensible to ask creditors to reply direct to their customer. It may be worth explaining to them why this is necessary.

Example

Due to the great number of people coming to us with financial problems, we are sorry that our limited resources as a registered charity prevent us from having a detailed discussion of this matter with you. Please write directly to the consumer confirming your agreement.

- **Ending** The letter can end with a conventional politeness, such as 'We are very grateful for your help in this matter' followed by 'Yours sincerely/faithfully' (by convention the former is used when the letter is addressed to a named individual and the latter when it is addressed Dear Sir/Madam).

Style and tone of letters

Avoid critical comments

Letters are written to gain agreement to a particular strategy, and this aim must be paramount. The adviser should avoid the temptation to lecture the creditor except where this is strictly necessary to achieve the aim. If a creditor appears to have broken the law or done something which requires further action (perhaps publicly), the adviser's aim is to gain more evidence or force her/him into an admission. This can be done by stating suspicions and asking for comments, rather than by accusing the creditor. For example, 'Mr Parkinson tells us that at the time he made the agreement with you he was not given a copy of it'.

Do not assume that the debtor is right in what s/he tells you as this will weaken your position if s/he has forgotten something and could also jeopardise your ability to argue on behalf of other debtors.

Avoid unnecessary legal references

It is not necessary to quote legal references to a creditor at an early stage, unless there is good reason to believe that s/he does not know them and it is relevant that s/he should. Legal information may well be considered patronising and requires not just the extra work involved in looking up references but also the possibility of an argument if the adviser or the creditor believes that the wrong reference has been quoted. If a correspondence develops, then this kind of detail may be necessary later but in a first letter it is almost certainly redundant.

A strong statement of the legal position is always required when it appears likely that the creditor is about to do something that infringes the debtor's rights. This is particularly true of cases of harassment (see p33), when the creditor should always be informed that harassment is illegal and will be reported.

Avoid unnecessary disclosure

The story told should be complete but should not contain anything that could be used against the debtor. Thus, for example, it could be dangerous to say to a building society, 'It would be particularly unfortunate if Mr Parkinson were to lose his house because this happened to him four years ago.' This is because the building society may not have been aware of such a fact and action may be taken prejudicial to his interests should it find out.

4. **Court representation**

Many debt advisers regularly represent debtors at court hearings, but if the court has not had experience of representation by lay advisers, the advice agency will need to talk to its local courts to arrange this. (For a detailed account of the workings of the courts, see Chapters 9 and 10.)

Type of hearing

Chambers

The majority of hearings at which advisers represent debtors will be in chambers.[2] This means that the hearing will usually be held in private in the district judge's office, with only the debtor and her/his representative, the solicitor or representative acting for the creditor, and the district judge present. The district judge will not wear a wig or gown, and everyone remains seated throughout the hearing. Before a hearing the debt adviser is obliged to make known all information and documents to be used at the hearing to the court and creditor.[3] (There is also a duty to reveal to the creditor and court any application which will be made at a hearing as soon as this is known.[4])

The claimant or her/his solicitor will present her/his case first to the district judge. The claimant is normally the creditor, except where the debtor has applied for something like a time order or the suspension of a warrant (see Chapter 9). After this the other side gets the opportunity to speak. The debtor's representative will have an opportunity to explain briefly the debtor's circumstances and make a proposal. A financial statement (see p47) will be essential if making an offer of payment. The solicitor or agent will be able to comment on the proposal and the district judge will make an order.

It is always worth introducing yourself to the creditor's representative at the court while waiting to be called and finding out what s/he has been instructed to ask the court for. The hearing will normally take 5 to 10 minutes, but this can be reduced if the adviser has successfully negotiated with the creditor or solicitor prior to the hearing.

The court will always need to know what powers it has to make a decision and if the district judge is unsure (or sceptical) s/he may ask an adviser to point out where in the Civil Procedure Rules 1998 (CPR) or elsewhere the proposed order is sanctioned (see Chapter 9).

Open court

Some hearings (such as appeals to judges) occur in open court and an adviser may wish to represent the debtor. At present there is still no right of audience for lay advisers (except in the small claims procedure) but most courts will welcome the assistance of a debt adviser. It is important to ask an usher or clerk to ascertain the views of the judge or magistrate in advance, if possible.

As the name suggests, such hearings are held in public, and are more formal than hearings in chambers. A circuit judge, a district judge or magistrate will hear the case. The judge will be dressed in a wig and gown. The court may be full of people waiting to have their cases heard, and solicitors or barristers waiting to represent. The creditor or a solicitor will present the case and may bring witnesses to cross-examine as part of their presentation.

The debtor may be asked to speak on oath, but the adviser may be able to present the case without the debtor needing to speak. It is customary to stand when addressing the judge.

Many magistrates' courts will not allow lay representation but the adviser may be able to be a 'McKenzie Friend (adviser)' (see p244). A refusal to allow lay representation should not be taken as final but should be taken up with the chief executive or chair of the bench who could be referred to the positive experience of tribunals (eg, social security appeal tribunals) with lay representatives.

Techniques of representation

Planning

Plan everything to be said in advance. Make sure it is logical and clear. Use notes where necessary. Rehearse presentations if possible, particularly if you are a new representative. You should inform the court if you have not had time to obtain full instructions – eg, in the case of emergency hearings or court/duty desks. It may then be in the best interests of the debtor to request an adjournment, even if this involves the debtor in increased liability for the creditor's costs.

Be brief

Local courts operate to very tight timescales (hearings are often listed for 5 or 10 minutes) and judges expect representations to be short and to the point. Avoid any repetition. Do not continue if the judge is writing down previous remarks.

Summarise

A written summary of the case will often be helpful and can be handed out at the beginning if it has not been possible to circulate it in advance (take copies for the judge and creditor's representative). This can then be amplified at presentation.

Prepare clear documents

Financial statements or other documents that are used to support a case should be clearly presented and photocopied for judge and creditor's representative.

Tell the story

Explain the background to the case clearly and concisely in chronological order. Do not assume that the judge has read the papers.

Quote precedents and powers

Give clear references and explanations of any past cases cited in support of your case if it is unusual and the legal powers upon which it depends. Have references to the Civil Procedure Rules 1998 (CPR – see Chapter 9) and any case law upon which you intend to rely (take copies for the judge and creditor's representative).

Admit ignorance

If stuck it is better to admit this and ask for help than to pretend otherwise. Provided your case appears reasonable, many judges will be helpful if they are asked. However, this should never be used as an alternative to thorough preparation of the case. The debt adviser should never pretend to be a solicitor or allow others to assume wrongly that s/he is one.

Use court staff

It is helpful before the hearing to tell the usher you wish to speak on the debtor's behalf. S/he will then inform the court clerk or the judge and tell you if anyone is there to represent the creditor.

Address

Address a district judge or magistrate as 'sir' or 'madam' and a judge as 'your honour'.

Look smart, be polite, speak clearly

Wear smart clothes (or apologise for your inability to do so – eg, emergency application). It is usually acceptable for lay representatives to dress less formally, but the dress prejudice of the judiciary should not be underestimated. Use standard English where possible; slang may not be understood and will almost certainly not further your case. Appear as confident as possible without being 'cocky'. Be respectful, but pleasant. Use eye contact and smiles to retain the attention of the judge.

Examining and cross-examining witnesses

If a case requires witnesses, it is usual for their evidence to be presented in the form of a witness statement (see Appendix 3).[5] Where the representative is required to question them in order to elicit further evidence, questions should be open and designed to facilitate the giving of the evidence in the most logical sequence.

If a witness is used by the creditor, then s/he can be cross-examined by the debtor or her/his representative. This is a fine art, but at its simplest it involves planning questions which will appear simple to a witness but whose answers will expose inconsistencies or inaccuracies in previous evidence. Cross-examination often proceeds with a series of apparently unrelated questions that are brought together in a final summary that forces the witness to appear unreliable. However, cross-examination of witnesses in debt cases is rare.

Know your own limits

Do not attempt to represent in court without being aware of all the possible outcomes. Complex representation may require lay advisers or lawyers who are not specialists to refer to lay advocates, solicitors or barristers who are.[6]

5. **Changing social policy**

If a particular law, practice, structure or policy adversely affects many debtors or affects vulnerable groups of debtors, then the adviser should work to change the policy.

In contacting individual creditors, the adviser should stress that this is a general social policy approach and not an attempt to re-open a case that has already been discussed.

Other organisations can be helpful. The ways in which creditors deal with debt may be controlled or overseen by one of a number of organisations.

The Office of Fair Trading/trading standards departments

The Office of Fair Trading (OFT) is a central government body which regulates trading or company practices and which has statutory responsibility for licensing all those who require a licence under the Consumer Credit Act 1974 (see Chapter 4).

Trading standards (or consumer protection) departments are part of a local authority. They have certain statutory functions in the field of weights and measures and consumer safety. They also have a responsibility to investigate breaches of the Consumer Credit Act and to report back to the OFT on problems encountered within their geographical area.

It is best to seek the help, first of all, of a trading standards department local to either the trader or the customer in both gathering information about a trader's practices and putting these to the OFT.

The OFT has powers to issue a number of different types of notice to traders before it actually revokes their consumer credit licence (without which they cannot operate in that field). The major one of these is a notice which declares that it is 'minded to revoke' a particular trader's consumer credit licence. In addition, since 1 June 2001, the OFT and trading standards departments can use the Stop Now Regulations to require creditors to cease engaging in conduct which breaches consumer protection legislation and harms the interests of consumers generally.[7] If the matter cannot be resolved informally, the court can be asked to make a Stop Now order to prohibit the conduct concerned. A breach of the order is punishable as a contempt of court by imprisonment or a fine.

If a local trading standards department is not helpful in pursuing a particular company then it can be reported directly to the OFT. It is important that even relatively minor infringements or bad practice are routinely reported because it is generally the volume of reported cases on a particular issue or individual which will give rise to investigation or other work by the OFT.

Ofgem, Oftel and Ofwat

The suppliers of fuel, telecommunications services and water are becoming increasingly diverse. Gas and electricity supplies are now deregulated and competition exists in all areas. However, because they were once monopoly suppliers in the public sector they can be considered a little differently from other types of business. They all have regulatory bodies (see Appendix 5) which have varying powers to investigate and comment upon their activities. The fuel regulatory bodies have a responsibility to prevent unlawful price increases or disconnections. They can also be very useful in exercising pressure in other areas.

Trade associations

Many industries have created trade associations. These are bodies that are regulated by their members, but impose upon them certain agreed standards as a membership condition. A list of trade associations is included in Appendix 5. Many of these have a code of practice or conduct and all have some kind of complaints procedure.

Trade associations exist primarily to protect their members by increasing their collective market share in comparison to that of other firms which are not members. However, provided that these limitations are understood, the trade association can be a vital tool in changing the behaviour of an individual company. Trade associations do not want the good name of all their other members lowered by the poor behaviour of one company. The peer-group pressure which they can exert, either through a complaints procedure or less formally, is probably much greater than the pressure that an advice agency acting on its own could create.

Local councillors and MPs

Much debt is payable to local or national government. This includes council tax, income tax, VAT and rent. The statutory powers which the state has given itself in order to enforce these debts are considerable and thus they all become priority debts. However, as government debts, they are subject to scrutiny by elected members – ie, councillors or MPs. This can provide a powerful method of ensuring that the state's powers are not used in too draconian a fashion.

Elected members are often not aware of the measures being used by their officers to collect debts. For instance, many local councillors are unaware of the extent to which their authority uses private bailiffs to recover debts and, once briefed by an advice agency about such situations, can make it a live political issue and change the way these debts are collected.

Ombudsmen

Where the administration of debt collection by the state is poor and leads individuals into hardship, complaints can be made to an ombudsman (see Appendix 5 for addresses). There are ombudsmen concerned with the operation of central and local government.

The Parliamentary Commissioner for Administration investigates complaints of maladministration by any central government department. Complaints have to be made via an MP. A simple statement of a complaint with dates and supporting evidence should, if possible, be sent to the MP with a request that it be forwarded to the ombudsman.

Complaints about local government matters are probably best made through a local councillor, but can also be made directly by a member of the public. Complaining to the local government ombudsman is important, even where the maladministration has been corrected in an individual case. Negative adjudications by an ombudsman are very much disliked by local government officers and will almost certainly lead to procedural changes to prevent a recurrence of the event which has been complained about. The local government ombudsman is increasingly using powers to investigate a particular department or function of an authority. The debt adviser should collect a few cases of maladministration and then discuss with staff at one of the ombudsman offices whether they will investigate in such a way. A report on the workings of a department is much more powerful than a single case.

The Adjudicator's Office deals with complaints about the way things have been handled by the Inland Revenue and Customs and Excise (but not about the amount of tax or VAT the debtor has been asked to pay) (see Appendix 5 for address). The Financial Ombudsman Service is the new body which handles complaints between debtors and finance firms (including banks and building societies) (see Appendix 5 for address).

All ombudsmen expect the debtor to give the creditor the opportunity to investigate her/his complaint and resolve the matter before referring the case to an ombudsman.

Monitoring local courts

Court procedures should be monitored on a local basis by debt advisers. Having collected information about the way in which a particular court operates, it is important to decide whether pressure for change needs to be exerted upon the court secretariat or the judiciary, or both. The secretariat is made up of the people who process the administration of the court's work and who may also, by accepting or rejecting certain procedures, have a strong influence upon the types of decisions made by the court.

Neither judges nor magistrates are open to being lobbied by groups about individual decisions or types of decisions which they are required to take and they will guard their independence jealously. However, particularly when an adviser works for a charitable organisation with a good reputation locally, it may be possible to arrange meetings with the chair of the bench (ie, the senior magistrate) or representatives of the judges in a county court to discuss ways in which the advice centre can assist the courts in their work or other issues of mutual concern. In practice, this means that it is generally possible to discuss procedures and to engage the decision makers in an analysis of the effects of their judgments.

It should not be assumed that the court system operates as a monolithic whole, and indeed there appears to have been considerable discontent among the ranks of lay magistrates with the role that the Government expected of them as rubber stampers in the collection of TV licences and other debts. In a magistrates' court the chief executive will generally discuss procedural matters and policy issues (eg, when and how they use their discretion to allow the payment of fines by instalment) and any such matter should be discussed with them where its operation causes problems.

Local liaison groups

Some public services now have liaison groups in some places. These include local court users' groups and are set up, for example, by the Department for Work and Pensions (DWP) and local authorities. The debt adviser should investigate groups which exist (and perhaps advocate their creation where they do not). S/he should use membership of these groups as a useful means of gaining credibility through networking, and changing policies and procedures that are unhelpful or oppressive. Some groups (for instance, court users' groups) may have existed for a long time with a fixed membership (perhaps solicitors, probation service and police). The debt adviser may have to invest time to secure membership, but this may be rewarded with a direct line of communication to powerful local decision makers.

Using the media

Discussion with the various bodies outlined above can often bring about useful changes that prevent continued injustice. However, it is often only when something becomes a live, public, political issue that real change can occur. It is important, therefore, to cultivate links with local and national media so that publicity can quickly be gained for particular injustices.

When considering using the media, general advice work issues, such as confidentiality, will need bearing in mind. However, even where an individual debtor does not wish to have her/his case publicised, it may be acceptable for an anonymous description of the issues involved in it to be part of a media campaign. There is an almost endless demand from media organisations – press, radio and television – to have examples of individuals who have suffered through being in debt. Many people will not wish to have their private affairs so publicly paraded, but for others this can be an important way of regaining a sense of power after the experiences they have suffered at the hands of creditors. It is certainly the way to bring an issue to public debate.

6. **Dealing with harassment**

What is harassment?

Many creditors harass debtors. Much of this goes unreported and unchallenged and indeed is expected by debtors. Section 40 of the Administration of Justice Act 1970 defines harassment as trying to coerce a person to pay a contract debt by making demands for payment that are calculated to subject a person to 'alarm, distress or humiliation, because of their frequency or publicity or manner' (see Appendix 1). In addition, any false representation that a type of non-payment is criminal or that the person is a court official or other publicly sanctioned debt collector is also regarded as harassment.

Harassment can take place in writing or orally. It can include using obviously marked vehicles, calling repeatedly at anti-social hours, calling on neighbours of debtors or places of work. Harassment occurs where a debt collector purports to be enquiring about a person but explains to neighbours why the enquiries are necessary. Harassment might also include posting lists of debtors publicly. It would include abusive or threatening behaviour and all acts of violence.

Harassment is a criminal offence and trading standards departments or local police should prosecute offenders. Your local trading standards department will probably be interested to hear of inappropriate behaviour even where this falls short of harassment.

How to deal with it

A debt adviser will rarely be told about harassment if s/he does not ask, for it is so much a part of a debtor's experience that it will not seem noteworthy. Debt advisers, therefore, should always ask exactly what was said and how demands were made, and check all written communications for evidence of harassment. It is important to take urgent action to protect the debtor from further harassment. A letter should be sent immediately outlining the facts as understood and warning the creditor off. A copy should be sent to the local trading standards department. In cases of violence or extreme harassment, the police should be informed as soon as possible.

The debtor should then be advised to have no further contact with the harassing creditor until the matter has been clarified. This may involve politely, but firmly, refusing her/him entry to property or not answering the telephone. The debtor should be advised to keep a diary recording details of any further acts of harassment. If possible, practical steps should be taken to ensure that friends, neighbours or relatives know about serious harassment and are able to provide a safe haven or support to the debtor. Some agencies give debtors a sheet of their letterhead, and advise them to show this to any creditors who call round and tell them to contact the agency.

7. Budgeting advice

Although advice on budgeting is not debt advice, a debt adviser must use the procedures and skills described in other parts of this book to assist debtors to deal with their debts. Budgeting advice is fraught with difficulties, but it can play a useful part in the debt advice process. Indeed, some people who present at advice agencies with financial difficulties may only need budgeting advice to resolve their problems and consequently should not be taken through the debt advice process.

It is important that advisers are able to identify such people. Many families living on a low income are expert at budgeting and can give the adviser some good tips. Others, especially those whose circumstances have been reduced radically, can find it helpful to discuss their budget. This gives the debtor an opportunity to consider what her/his own priorities are and to find out about ways of paying for essential items. For example, if the debtor has lost access to a bank current account, s/he may be unaware of the possibility of having a budget account for gas funded by weekly or fortnightly payments at a post office. Detailed budgeting information is privileged information between the debtor and the adviser and should not be given to creditors in detailed form, but summarised on the financial statement.

Pressure to spend can be difficult to deal with – spending can represent status, or give someone a greater sense of control, and some expenditure may be made because of problems in family relations.

There are particular problems when budgeting on a low income. Often, people on a low income only have access to the more expensive forms of credit. In the absence of credit, goods available are generally more expensive because it is impossible to buy enough to benefit from the lower unit prices charged for larger quantities. Similarly, access to the cheapest sources of goods may be denied if transport is not readily available to the large out-of-town stores. Budgeting on a low income often requires purchasing inferior goods because money is not available to buy more expensive ones which would last longer and thus be much cheaper in the long run.

Where poverty exists alongside other factors, such as disability, parenthood or the breakdown of a relationship, it is likely that budgeting is constrained by the time available, which in turn is constrained by the practical and emotional demands of these other situations.

Use the financial statement

Very often the process of producing a financial statement (see p47) will enable people to see the sources of their financial problems. It will often be clear when all items of expenditure have been listed that these cannot be met from available income. Ideally, if there is a need to cut expenditure it will occur to the debtor her/himself. If this does not happen, the debt adviser may wish to suggest ways of budgeting and put clearly to the debtor the likely results of such strategies. The adviser must be aware of vocabulary, body language and tone of voice, to avoid giving the impression that s/he is judging the debtor.

On the other hand, this exercise may establish that the 'debtor' is able to meet all her/his contractual liabilities together with any accruing charges as well as maintaining her/his essential expenditure, and consequently does not need debt advice or any of the strategies discussed in this book.

'Luxury items'

There are some items of expenditure which may, in comparison to the possible loss of other goods or services, be less essential:

- Cars are generally much more expensive than is realised to purchase, run, maintain, tax and insure. If a car is not necessary for personal mobility or work requirements, the debtor may need to consider either selling it and acquiring a cheaper one, or doing without.

- Telephones, particularly mobile ones, have often been considered a luxury. This is not always the case, and would certainly not be so if someone's health might require her/him to summon assistance in an emergency or, for instance, where someone had been subjected to racial abuse or marital violence and this could happen again. The telephone may also be an important social lifeline or a means of making emergency help available to another person outside the debtor's home. However, where no such factors exist, particularly if phone bills are large, then the possibility of doing without or changing to incoming calls only could be considered. Where a mobile phone is used the cost (which may be less than that for a landline on some tariffs and usage patterns) and appropriateness of this should be explained.
- Videos are often considered an extravagance and a cause of debt. In fact, the cost of a video would never cause serious debt and its value as very cheap entertainment (particularly where people are housebound or have children) is very high. The sale of a video will generally have a negligible effect on a debtor's current debt and the ending of a hire agreement is unlikely to do very much more.
- Cable or satellite television is more expensive than video. If a debtor has an agreement that has already run for its minimum period, the adviser could discuss whether satellite TV is more important than other items on which the money could be spent.

Non-dependants living with the debtor

A particular problem for a debtor can be the contribution made by non-dependants living in the debtor's household. The complexity of family budgeting is well demonstrated by a parent's wish to charge an adult son or daughter only a nominal amount for board. This may also be generated by a desire to keep the family together and can save money – for example, by reducing childminding costs. In some cases to challenge the amount being paid by a non-dependant could lead to family disruption.

Faced with this difficult situation, a debtor will need information and support in order to make decisions. For example, if housing benefit or housing costs are being claimed s/he will need to know by how much this is reduced by the non-dependant living with her/him. From the financial statement (see p47) a debtor can judge what might be a fair share of the total household expenditure to be attributed to the non-dependant. In addition, the adviser can provide the debtor with comparative figures such as the amounts charged by local B&Bs or hostels.

Community action on budgets

Self-help groups

These can provide support to people who need to think about their budget. They may be based on existing community facilities, advice centres or social services departments. They can provide an environment in which people can share the experience of being in debt and thereby reduce the sense of isolation.

Credit unions

A credit union may also be a useful way of creating flexibility in budgeting. A credit union is a group of people who get together and agree to pay either a fixed or variable sum of money regularly into a central pool, from which loans are made to other individuals within the group in previously agreed amounts and sometimes clearly defined circumstances.

The amount of credit available from the credit union movement does not currently make it a realistic alternative to commercial credit for most people. However, a well-organised credit union can be a real alternative to very local small-scale moneylenders, who often charge the highest rates of interest and have the worst collection ethics of the industry. It is important that groups wishing to form a credit union adopt a constitution and register this with the Registrar of Friendly Societies, and ensure that their banking and accounting procedures are carefully set up in advance.

Forming a credit union is also an important source of community empowerment. It allows ordinary people to be involved in decision making and management and it introduces people to each other as they meet to run the union. Some local authorities have credit union development officers who may be able to help with setting up a credit union. There are national organisations that provide advice and guidance to new or existing credit unions – see Appendix 5.

Notes

2. **Negotiation**
   1 para 13 DMG

4. **Court representation**
   2 Rule 39.2 CPR and Part 39 para 1 PD CPR
   3 Part 1 CPR; Part 23 para 9 PD CPR
   4 Part 23 CPR and Part 23 paras 2.7 and 2.10 PD CPR
   5 Part 32 paras 17-25 PD CPR
   6 For further information see P Madge, 'Advocacy for money advisers', *Adviser* 44

5. **Changing social policy**
   7 Stop Now Orders (EC Directive) Regs SI 2001/1422

Chapter 3
•••
Stages of debt advice

This chapter summarises the eight stages essential to debt advice and shows how the individual stages link together as a single process. It covers:
1. Creating trust (below)
2. List creditors and minimise debts (below)
3. List and maximise income (p41)
4. List expenditure (p43)
5. Dealing with emergencies (p47)
6. Dealing with priority debts (p47)
7. Draw up a financial statement (p47)
8. Choosing a strategy for non-priority debts (p49)
9. Implement and follow up chosen strategies (p49)

1. Creating trust

The adviser must create a trusting and safe environment in which the debtor can talk about her/his personal and financial affairs. This may take some time to develop but should start at the beginning of the process, as the adviser makes it clear that s/he will not judge and is on the debtor's side.

The adviser must explain what s/he will do and why. In collecting information, the adviser is not intruding unnecessarily into people's affairs but s/he needs information to decide upon a strategy and/or negotiate with creditors. It is, therefore, important to explain to the debtor that such information is confidential and how the agency's confidentiality principles operate in practice. Often, people seek advice about a specific debt and are reluctant to discuss other debts that they are managing to pay or where they feel the creditor has been particularly helpful. However, it is often impossible to deal with a particular debt in isolation. This stage assists a discussion of the whole position.

2. List creditors and minimise debts

The first facts to gather are details of the debts and the creditors. These are listed on a creditor list. This needs to show all debts, including those with no arrears or ones where the debtor has already negotiated lower payments. An example of a typical form is included in Appendix 4. The information required should be divided into four groups: the creditors; the debts; the threats posed by the recovery action so far taken; and the actions to be taken.

A debtor may not have all the necessary information with her/him on the first visit to enable the adviser to complete the creditor list. It is, therefore, important to agree how the missing information will be collected, by whom and when.

The creditors

Advisers will need to record:
- **The name, address and telephone number of each creditor** Exact company names are important, as the proliferation of credit has led to a surprising number of creditors with very similar names.
- **Account/reference numbers** Most creditors access their computers with a reference number and this must be included.
- **Letter references** If the debtor has received correspondence from the company then any letter reference should be noted together with any contact details.
- **Agents' details** Solicitors or commercial debt collectors are often used. Record details of these (and their references) separately. Record details of the one who has made most recent contact with the debtor. Check whether the agent has actually bought the debt (in which case s/he will now be the creditor) or whether the agent is acting on behalf of the original creditor (in which case s/he will be accountable to that creditor).

The debts

The following details must be noted:
- **Age of debt** Find out when the credit was first granted. The length of time for which the agreement has run or a bill has been unpaid can be a factor in negotiation. For instance, a creditor is more likely to be sympathetic where payments have been made for some time than if a new agreement is breached. The legal position with regard to some agreements will depend on when they were made (for instance, credit card debts on cards issued before July 1977, see p57).
- **Reason for debt** It is important to ask the reason for the debt. This is necessary – for instance, because certain types of repayments can attract tax relief or qualify for social security payments, or to refute suggestions that the debt was unreasonably incurred.
- **Status of the debt** Note the status of the debt. This should either be priority or non-priority (Chapter 7 explains the criteria for making such decisions). If possible, check any documents or agreements to confirm this information, as debtors can themselves be unsure or may describe debts incorrectly. (For example, 'hire purchase' is often used to mean 'credit sale agreement'.)

- **The written agreement** Check whether the debt is based on a written agreement and, if so, whether or not it has been seen and photocopied for future reference. Ensure agreements are checked for defects which may affect their enforceability (see Chapter 5). Obtain a copy from the creditor if necessary. Note the absence of a written agreement, which can render some agreements unenforceable (see Chapter 5).
- **Liability** This means checking that the debtor is actually responsible for the debt. Note in whose name(s) agreements were made. This may either be the debtor alone or the debtor and a partner, or some other friend or relative who was acting as a guarantor. This will ensure that all debts listed are properly minimised (see Chapter 5).
- **Payments** Note the amount currently owing. State whether the figure is approximate or exact. Note contractual payments under any original agreement and any subsequent amendment to them. Note the existence of arrears in payments, although initially these need only be approximate. Note the payment method. Advice may be needed about coping with doorstep collectors or about changing or cancelling standing orders or direct debit arrangements. However, debtors should not be advised to stop or reduce contractual payments to creditors unless it is clearly in their best interests to do so – for example, if the debtor has been making payments to non-priority creditors but not paying priority creditors (see Chapter 7). The date and amount of the last payment made are needed, especially for priority debts, to assess the urgency of any action.
- **Insurance cover** Many people take out insurance with a mortgage or credit agreement against sickness, death, redundancy, etc. Sometimes such insurance is given by the creditor as part of the contract. Always check whether a particular debt is insured so that this important way of minimising the debt is not overlooked (see p82).

The threats

The adviser needs to know what the creditor has done to obtain repayment of the debt and what threat is posed to the debtor by the recovery action.

- **Warnings** The first stage of recovery action will normally be a reminder letter. The date of this should be recorded. Exact details of further action should be noted. For instance, regulated consumer credit agreements (see Chapter 4) may require a default notice to be served before any further action is taken. Other creditors must issue different warnings – for example, notice of proposed disconnection of fuel or notice of intention to seek possession (of the debtor's home).
- **Court action** If court action has begun, a claim form will have been issued. The date and type of claim should always be recorded. Courts work on a system of case numbers and it is essential to record these references. If a date for a

hearing has been set, this should be noted. In many cases, a court will already have made an order and details of the judgment (see Chapter 9), including its date, the payment or action ordered and the time or amounts required, should be recorded.

- **Enforcement action** After judgment, enforcement can mean bailiffs' action (see Chapter 11), third party debt (formerly garnishee) orders, attachment of earnings, etc (see Chapter 9). Note if any of these have actually begun, with dates and full details.

Action to be taken
- **By the debtor** Any action required of a debtor relating to a particular debt should be noted on the list – eg, 'get exact balance'. This section will normally be completed once the strategy has been decided.
- **By the adviser** Record the action required on each debt. This can be crossed through when it has been carried out.

3. **List and maximise income**

The next stage is to list all possible income for the debtor (and her/his family where applicable). An example of a typical form on which to list income and expenditure is included in Appendix 4.

Whose income to include

Creditors are likely to expect that the income and debts of a heterosexual couple (particularly if they are married) should be dealt with together. There is no basis in law for this expectation and the adviser will be able to decide later which way to present things. Conversely, creditors may expect that the finances of lesbian or gay couples will be dealt with separately. The overriding consideration must be the best interests of the debtor(s).

A decision must eventually be made about whether to include the income of partners or spouses or, rarely, someone else living as part of the same household as the debtor. This depends upon several factors including:
- If all the debts are in the name of one person only (or are in the joint names of the debtor and a previous partner) and s/he has little or no income or property against which action could be taken, then the other person may be unwilling to contribute out of her/his income.
- If the same person had a number of debts that were shared with a partner then it might be more convenient to deal with both partners' debts in one set of strategies.
- If only one person has sought advice without the knowledge of her/his partner, the adviser will need to find out why and encourage both partners to be

involved when debts are in joint names. The person who seeks advice may not know details of her/his partner's income or may not want her/his partner to know about the debts.

- The type of debt. Many partners will wish to pool their income and help with each other's debts, irrespective of legal liability, where they themselves could suffer dire consequences (eg, eviction) if they failed to do so. At this stage it is, therefore, important to note the income of all household members so that a decision as to which will be used to implement any strategy can be made later.

Types of income to include

- All benefits (do not forget child benefit). Note, however, that disability benefits (including disability living allowance and attendance allowance) will not usually be offered to creditors. This view is supported by the Revised Determination of Means Guidelines (para 5.4.2) and is based on the fact that disability benefits are designed to meet only the additional costs of disability, but they must still be included in any court forms – eg, N9A (see Appendix 3). They should be included in the list of income even if they do not appear eventually in the financial statement, but (more usually) will be included and balanced by an identical item of expenditure, or mobility or care costs. If it is decided to exclude disability benefits from the financial statement, do not forget to exclude also any additional expenditure paid for out of those benefits. The fact that the debtor is in receipt of disability benefits should always be disclosed to creditors, as the fact that s/he is a disabled person is likely to be a relevant factor. Even if it is decided to exclude disability benefits from the financial statement, they should be referred to in an accompanying letter together with an explanation of why they have been excluded – for example, they have been offset by increased expenditure in meeting the debtor's needs. The decision whether or not to include/use disability benefits is ultimately for the debtor and not the adviser.
- Earnings – take-home pay from full-time and part-time work (note any deductions from wages, such as attachment of earnings orders).
- Self-employed earnings net of estimated tax and national insurance contributions.
- Maintenance payments (include what/who it is paid for).
- Investment income.
- Contributions from other household members (eg, non-dependent children living with the debtor).
- Occupational pensions.

If income has recently been unusually high or low this should be noted and the basis upon which income is assessed should be clear (eg, the average of five weeks' wage slips). Only include regular sources of income, as any offer(s) of payment must be sustainable.

The Office of Fair Trading (OFT) expects advisers to use appropriate means to verify the debtor's income (eg, wage slips) whilst recognising that advisers working at court duty desks or providing self-help advice will in practice be unable to do so.[1]

Note any impending changes/additions to income and circumstances, such as benefits recently claimed but not yet awarded, or if a member of the household is about to start or end paid employment.

Include capital

The debtor may have capital or potential capital in the form of realisable property or other assets which it would be reasonable for her/him to use and the adviser should make a separate note of any such items (see Chapter 8). Unless the circumstances are wholly exceptional, creditors are unlikely to accept that a debtor is unable to pay her/his debts where s/he has capital and may even refuse to accept nil or token offers of payment where they feel that it would be reasonable to expect the debtor to dispose of an asset.

Maximising income

Follow the advice in Chapter 6 to maximise the debtor's income. Income from benefits that have been claimed but not yet paid should be listed only where this is advantageous to the debtor. The adviser should explain that a claim is pending if it is included.

4. **List expenditure**

The next stage of the debt advice process is to list everything upon which the debtor is currently spending her/his/their income. A pro-forma, which can be used as a checklist and reminder, is included in Appendix 4. Most people spend money on different items in relation to different periods of time, and it is important to standardise everything to a particular period – generally weekly or monthly. Expenditure must include:

Housing costs
- rent;
- water charges;
- ground rent;
- service charges;
- mortgage repayments;
- other secured loan repayments (there are often several);
- an amount for household repairs and maintenance based on a full year's expenditure if possible;

- household insurance for both buildings and contents;
- any insurance linked to a mortgage, if not already included in mortgage expenses;
- the housing costs of boarders, which can simply be the amount they pay for their board and lodging (see p36).

Council tax or community charge

Fuel costs

These include charges for electricity, gas and other fuels. The conversion to weekly figures is often difficult where, for instance, coal is delivered in a greater quantity in winter than summer. Take an annual cost and divide it into weekly or monthly figures.

If payments to fuel suppliers include an amount for items other than fuel (eg, payment for a cooker), these need to be deducted and only the fuel expenditure listed here.

Furniture and bedding

Costs should be separately itemised. This item may require research by the debtor or discussion with others with whom s/he lives. (There is a likely minimum of £2 a week.)

Launderette or other washing costs

Television rental and/or licence costs

Other household items, toiletries and food

The adviser should ensure that the individual circumstances of the debtor dictate the amount allowed for these items. Other household items, toiletries and food include:

- expenditure at the supermarket;
- milk bills;
- amounts spent in specialist shops – eg, butchers or health food shops;
- other items that are regularly bought outside shops – eg, from farmers;
- expenditure at local corner shops;
- meals taken outside the home, such as school dinners or canteen meals;
- expenses related to children going to school or being given pocket money;
- nappies and sanitary protection.

Clothing and shoes

These are often bought seasonally and so costs will have to be estimated annually and divided. It is important to include small items, like tights, in this category.

Health costs

- prescriptions;
- dentistry;

- optical charges.

These are often too high and advisers need to check entitlement to reduced or free treatment, or free prescriptions.

Religious and cultural costs
- donations that are an essential part of a person's membership of a religious community;
- the cost of classes for children in religious institutions (particularly mosques).

Where a person is committed to such payments they should be protected to ensure that debt does not further exclude individuals or families from community life and support.

Transport costs
- public transport;
- the cost of owning a car or motorbike. In this case, the amount spent on tax, insurance, repairs and petrol should be included;
- if a car is essential, for instance to travel to work, then the cost of its hire purchase (but not credit sale) agreement should be included with a note to explain why the item is essential.

Hire purchase
The hire purchase or conditional sale (see Chapter 4) costs of any items which are essential for the individual family to own and whose loss would cause serious problems – eg, a washing machine.

Fines
Instalments payable on fines (see Chapter 10 for ways of reducing these).

Others
- maintenance/child support payments;
- childminding costs;
- self-employment costs not taken into account when calculating the debtor's net income;
- spending for exceptional circumstances – eg, special diets or extra heating because of illness;
- apparent 'luxury' items need to be explained. For example, for some people a telephone is an absolute necessity (eg, for health reasons) and therefore counts as essential expenditure.

Again, the Office of Fair Trading (OFT) expects reasonable steps to be taken to verify the debtor's expenditure, but says that estimates or standard expenditure guidelines can be used where there is no better indication of the debtor's expenditure and provided they are appropriate. As a guide, the Government's *Family Expenditure Survey* figures for 2000/01 show that an average family had a gross weekly income of £500 and spent the following amounts each week (excluding housing costs).[2]

	Spend £	% of total spend %
Food	61.90	16.05
Alcohol	15.00	3.90
Tobacco	6.10	1.60
Household goods & services	54.60	14.15
Leisure goods & services	70.40	18.25
Personal goods & services	14.70	3.80
Clothing & footwear	22.00	5.70
Fuel & power	11.90	3.10
Motoring	55.10	14.30
Fares & other travel	9.50	2.50
Totals	**321.20**	**83.35**

Although standard figures should not be used where actual figures or accurate estimates are available, they are useful as a 'benchmark' against which to test the debtor's level of expenditure (is s/he allowing sufficient?) and as a tool with which to challenge creditors who claim that the debtor's expenditure is too high.

At this stage, the adviser can discuss the overall income and spending with the debtor. Use Chapter 6 to try and increase income wherever possible, and discuss which, if any, items of spending could be reduced, either permanently or temporarily (see Chapter 5). This should be done in a sensitive and non-judgemental way, and any items of high or unusual expenditure should be explained to creditors in a covering letter. Debtors are not required, and should not be expected, to live on the breadline and are entitled to a reasonable standard of living. Where the adviser knows that creditors are likely to challenge an item of expenditure and it cannot be justified, it is not judgemental to point this out to the debtor and that, consequently, creditors or the court are unlikely to accept the debtor's offer based on it.

It may be necessary to advise the debtor to change the bank account into which wages are paid to prevent the bank (a non-priority creditor) taking control over income. If this is not possible immediately s/he may have to consider exercising the 'right of first appropriation'. This gives an account holder the right to earmark funds paid into the account to be used for specific purposes. This process can also be useful as a temporary measure on overdrawn accounts. In order to exercise this right the debtor should inform the bank in writing (before funds are paid in) specifically where they should be applied – ie, how much and to whom. While the bank cannot fail to honour such instructions, it will, of course, continue to charge interest on the overdraft and may refuse to undertake further transactions.

By this stage, it should also be clear why the debts have arisen, and how the debtor's circumstances have led to financial difficulties. This information will be essential when negotiating with creditors.

5. Dealing with emergencies

The adviser must next identify any emergencies (ie, eviction, repossession, imprisonment, disconnection, bailiffs) and deal with these first (see the relevant sections of Chapters 7, 9, 10 and 11).

6. Dealing with priority debts

The next stage of the debt advice process is to deal with those debts that are described as priorities (see Chapter 7). This will ensure that the threat of homelessness, the loss of goods or services or the threat of imprisonment is lifted. It is essential that any arrangements for dealing with these debts are negotiated at this stage so that any extra payments for priority debts can be included in the expenditure details before they become part of a financial statement (see next stage).

However, a financial statement may be needed when negotiating priority debts, and this stage of the process can therefore overlap with stage 7.

Each possible strategy, along with its advantages or disadvantages, must be explained to the debtor. It may be necessary for the debtor to consult with a partner or other family members, and strategy information may need to be written down. Once agreed, the adviser implements the strategy by negotiation or court application and the debtor must then carry out her/his own agreed course of action – eg, start paying rent, set up direct debit, etc. An orally agreed strategy must always be confirmed in writing with the creditor, and an acknowledgement confirming this must be requested. The debtor should be advised to start making any agreed payments immediately and not wait for confirmation from the creditor.

7. Draw up a financial statement

A financial statement is a document, which can be presented to creditors and courts, that presents a clear picture of the individual (or family) and her/his income and expenditure, details of her/his creditors and whether there is any surplus income with which to pay those creditors. It must be realistic and any offers made must be sustainable.

A financial statement based on the joint income and expenditure of the debtor and her/his partner should be fairly straightforward to prepare. A financial statement based on the income and expenditure of only the debtor needs more care. The golden rule is that the financial statement should reflect what actually happens in practice – for example, where the debtor actually pays all the household bills out of her/his own income and contributions from other members of the household, then the financial statement should be drawn up on this basis. On the other hand, in many cases it is not possible to identify who actually pays what because all income is pooled. In such a case, expenditure should be apportioned proportionately to income.

A financial statement is a vital document because it summarises information in a standard form and also allows the adviser to present this to the other side in a compelling way. A well and carefully drawn up financial statement is probably the adviser's most important negotiating tool, as it forms the justification for any repayment proposal as well as for any request for non-payment.

It is useful to devise a standard format and to prepare blank statements, using a computer.[3] The statement must be clearly and neatly presented, and must include all relevant information. Advisers should use all the facts discovered in the previous stages of this chapter when preparing the statement. Provided it is stored on computer, it is easy to amend the statement as circumstances change. A sample statement is included in Appendix 4.

The statement should include the following:

- The basis on which it was prepared. For example, 'This financial statement has been prepared on the basis of information submitted by:
  Mr A Debtor
  123 A Street
  A Town'.
- The members of the household whose income and outgoings are being considered together.
- A breakdown of all the income for the individual or unit.
- A list of expenditure under the headings used in stage 4 plus expenditure to deal with priority debts. Certain types of expenditure may best be combined: cigarettes, for instance, are probably most persuasively included in 'Other household items, toiletries and food' rather than on their own. No expenditure is shown for debts other than those that have been defined as priorities.
- Comparison of income and expenditure. In some cases, the financial statement will lead to there being more income than there is expenditure, and such excess of income over expenditure should be calculated in the financial statement and described as available income. If expenditure already equals or exceeds income, then the available income should be stated as none. In many

cases, expenditure will exceed income. This may be because amounts have been included which are not actually spent, but are what should be spent if the debtor was able to do so. Whatever the reason, the adviser should be prepared to explain if challenged by creditors.

8. Choosing a strategy for non-priority debts

From the financial statement, the adviser knows whether or not there is any available income or capital and any likely changes in circumstances. This stage involves using these factors to decide a strategy for all non-priority debts (see Chapter 8 for possible strategies). The starting point should be what the debtor wants, but s/he must be given the full range of available options so that s/he can make an informed choice of action. All advice given should be realistic and in the best interests of that particular debtor. The debtor should be advised to start making any payments offered immediately and not wait for confirmation from the creditor.

By the end of this stage, the debtor will have made an informed choice of the strategy that is likely to deal with her/his creditors at the lowest possible financial, physical or psychological cost.

9. Implement and follow up chosen strategies

Although some emergency work may have been done to prevent catastrophes, it is only when all the information is available and decisions have been made that the major work of implementing a debt advice strategy will begin. Implementation is by means of communication with creditors by letter, telephone or sometimes in person or via the courts. The strategy to be implemented may require different letters to a number of creditors or groups of creditors and perhaps court action in the case of a minority. This requires communication skills, both written and oral, as well as representational skills.

The implementation of debt advice strategies involves more than mere individual casework. In addition to this, the effectiveness of strategies used should be continually monitored and work should be done to change policies that are found to be oppressive.

The remainder of the book explains the practical knowledge and skills necessary to put into effect the strategy that has been agree by the debtor and debt adviser.

Notes

3. **List and maximise income**
   1 para 22(b) DMG; para 12 Note to agencies

4. **List expenditure**
   2 See also *Family Spending* for more detailed information; both this and the *Family Expenditure Survey* are available from www.statistics.gov.uk

7. **Draw up a financial statement**
   3 The British Bankers Association and Money Advice Trust are currently piloting a standard financial statement

Chapter 4

Types of debt

This chapter covers:
1. The Consumer Credit Act (below)
2. Consumer Credit Act debts (p54)
3. Other debts (p63)

This chapter describes, in detail, each type of credit or debt that might be encountered. It is vital to identify accurately each debt before attempting to deal with it. The chapter contains a brief outline of the Consumer Credit Act 1974, which governs most credit-related debts. Debts are therefore dealt with in two groups – those covered by the Consumer Credit Act and others. Extracts from the Act are provided in Appendix 1.

1. The Consumer Credit Act

The Consumer Credit Act is a wide-ranging piece of legislation that regulates almost all aspects of personal credit. It provides definitions of every type of credit agreement and is framed so as to cover every imaginable type of agreement. The Act brings together previous attempts to regulate credit and it uses three mechanisms to provide protection: licensing of traders; regulation of agreements; and rights of cancellation.

Licensing

The Act requires almost every credit-related business to have a licence.[1] Individuals or organisations (including non-profitmaking organisations) who undertake as part of their normal work any of the following activities are required to be licensed:
- a credit or hire business;
- credit brokerage or credit reference;
- debt collecting and debt adjusting;
- debt counselling.

This last category requires any individual or advice agency who wishes to give debt advice to gain a licence first.

The licence is issued by the Office of Fair Trading (OFT)[2] (see Appendix 5) and is granted virtually automatically, but it can be suspended or revoked if activities by the creditor lead the Director General of Fair Trading to consider that the creditor is not a fit person or organisation to hold such a licence, because s/he or it has 'engaged in business practices appearing to the Director to be deceitful or oppressive or otherwise unfair or improper (whether unlawful or not)'.[3] Unlicensed creditors cannot pursue their claims for debt through the county court without first applying to the Director General of Fair Trading for an order to validate the agreement,[4] but in practice this rarely happens. It is a criminal offence to trade without a licence. Licences currently last for five years.

Regulated agreements

The Act contains a definition of a regulated agreement. Most agreements that a debt adviser comes across will be regulated, although there are some important exceptions. A regulated agreement is an agreement which:
- provides credit of £25,000 or less (£15,000 if made before 1 May 1998); *and*
- is made with one or more individuals or consumers (who do not borrow as a limited company). The credit must be given in the course of a business. Consumers can use credit for her/his/their business provided that the business is not incorporated – ie, not a limited company.

Agreements that are not regulated include:
- agreements for more than £25,000 (or £15,000 before 1 May 1998);
- some business agreements;
- some trading checks involving small amounts;
- non-commercial agreements – ie, not made in the course of a business, eg, between friends;
- low-cost credit;
- normal trade credit – eg, payment in 30 days;
- loans taken out to purchase land or property (effectively first building society mortgages and some bank mortgages);
- charge cards (see p63).

The form of the agreement

The form of a regulated agreement is very important. If an agreement is not made in accordance with the Act then it can only be enforced with special permission of the courts and in some cases will be completely unenforceable. All regulated consumer credit agreements must be made in writing, be signed by all the borrowers and must contain the following information:
- The amount of credit (or the credit limit) and the charge for credit (where the amount of interest is fixed at the beginning).
- The rate of interest and whether it will vary (where the amount of interest is not fixed at the beginning).

- A notice of cancellation in the prescribed form (where the agreement is cancellable).
- Details of repayments (how much/how often, etc).

Otherwise, the agreement is completely unenforceable, as is any security – eg, secured loan.[5] The agreement should also contain the following:
- A prominent heading that describes the nature of the agreement.
- The names and addresses of the debtor and creditor and a signature box.
- Details of any security to be provided as part of the agreement.
- A brief description of the goods supplied under the agreement.
- The cash price of the goods or services.
- The amount of deposit/part payment.
- The annual percentage rate (APR) (see below).
- A statement about the rights of the consumer – eg, termination rights/paying off the account early.

Otherwise, the creditor can only enforce the agreement with the permission of the court and on any terms the court thinks fit, which can include reducing the amount owed by the debtor. The court will consider whether the debtor has suffered any disadvantage and the extent to which the creditor was blameworthy.

Annual percentage rate (APR)

This is a way of expressing the charges that will be added to a loan, which include not just interest but also setting-up charges, agent's or survey fees and other associated costs. These are all added to the interest payable and then distributed across the period of the loan to give customers a standardised cost for a loan which they can compare with that charged by other lenders.

Costs which can be added only when a person defaults upon a loan do not have to be shown in the APR.

Cancellation rights – the cooling-off period

A regulated credit agreement can be cancelled if it was signed somewhere other than the trade premises of the creditor or supplier of goods and following face-to-face negotiations with the creditor or supplier (including their agents or employees).

A copy of the agreement must be given to the debtor immediately s/he signs it. Unless the creditor has already signed it or signs at the same time, another copy must be sent within seven days,[6] with a notice of cancellation rights. Otherwise a separate notice of cancellation rights must be sent within seven days of the agreement being signed. The cooling-off period begins with the receipt of this second copy of the document/separate notice of cancellation rights which will also have a notice of cancellation to be used if desired. Any such agreement must be cancelled within five days.

Cancellation must be in writing and, if posted, is effective immediately even if it is never received by the creditor. Cancellation is probably best made initially by telephone but must be followed up immediately by a letter sent first class or by fax if time is short. Under such circumstances, a letter need say no more than 'I hereby give you notice that I wish to cancel the regulated credit agreement signed by me on... [date]'.[7] It should be sent to the company providing the credit, with a copy to the company supplying the goods, if appropriate. Any goods already supplied under the agreement should be returned or await collection by the trader. Any deposit or advance payment for the goods must be refunded to the debtor.

Joint liability

A great advantage of the Consumer Credit Act is that when credit is provided as part of an agreement to supply goods or services, then both the credit provider and the supplier of the goods or services are jointly and severally (see p77) liable for ensuring that the goods or services are properly represented and the contract is not broken.[8] This means that if goods or services supplied were not fit for their purpose or were of a sub-standard quality, then the consumer is afforded greater protection than cash buyers. In the absence of action by the original supplier (or if the supplier is in liquidation), the debtor can take action against the creditor and will have a valid defence or counter-claim against any action to recover monies due under the agreement.

Linked agreement

The right to a cooling-off period (see above) also applies to any sale that was linked to the supply of the credit. In other words, if someone ordered double glazing at home and at the same time applied for credit to a company recommended by the seller, then s/he would have the right not just to cancel the credit application but also the order for double glazing.[9] In addition, the creditor is jointly and severally liable with the supplier for the refund of any deposit or advance payment following cancellation of the credit agreement.[10]

2. Consumer Credit Act debts

Types of debt covered by the Consumer Credit Act are listed here in alphabetical order.

Bank overdraft

A bank overdraft is a type of revolving credit (see p61). The bank will allow a customer with a current account to overdraw on the account up to a certain amount. Repayment of the overdraft is made as money is paid into the account.

The legal position

Bank overdrafts are regulated under the Consumer Credit Act, provided the credit is for no more than £25,000 (or £15,000 before 1 May 1998). It is immaterial whether the overdraft is authorised or unauthorised. No written agreement is required.

Special features

Interest is charged usually on a daily basis and repayment in full can be requested at any time. When the agreed overdraft limit is reached, cheques drawn against the account will usually be stopped.

If the overdraft is not approved by the bank, a higher rate of interest will usually be charged and additional service charges may be made at the bank's discretion (though see 'extortionate credit', p84).

When a customer has both a current account with overdraft facilities and a loan account with the same bank, it is common for banks to make payments to the personal loan account from the current account. This may be done even if there are no funds in the current account so that the higher overdraft rate of interest will apply to the payments that have become due on the personal loan account.

Similarly, if someone has her/his wages paid directly into a current account, this will always be applied initially to reduce any overdraft on that account even if debts such as mortgage arrears ought to be accorded a higher priority for repayment.

Emergency action may therefore be needed to ensure income is not swallowed up as it becomes available. It may be necessary to open a current account with another bank so that wages can be paid into the new account or, if this is not possible, exercise the right of first appropriation (see p46). A bank overdraft should be considered a non-priority debt (see Chapter 8) unless it has been charged to a debtor's home.

Bill of sale

A bill of sale is also known as a chattel mortgage and is a way of raising money by offering an item of personal property as security for the loan. The mortgaged item remains in the possession and use of the debtor but it would become the property of the creditor if the debt were not repaid.

The legal position

This type of agreement is regulated by the Bills of Sale Acts of 1878 and 1882 and partially regulated under the Consumer Credit Act, provided the credit is for no more than £25,000 (or £15,000 before 1 May 1998). The formal agreement, known as the bill of sale, must be set out in the way specified by the Schedule to the Bills of Sale (1878) Amendment Act 1882. The credit part of the agreement is covered by the Consumer Credit Act. There will be a separate agreement detailing the credit and repayment arrangements, which will refer to the security required by the creditor as a bill of sale.

Special features

All bills of sale must be independently witnessed and registered at the High Court in London within seven days. A copy of the registered document is then forwarded to the local county court. If a bill of sale is not registered in this way then it is unenforceable.

Emergency action may be needed if there is a risk of repossession of the goods. This is likely to be a priority debt (see Chapter 7).

Budget account

A budget account is a type of revolving credit (see p61) provided by shops. The consumer can spend up to an agreed credit limit and makes regular repayments.

The legal position

This type of account is regulated by the Consumer Credit Act.

Special features

Many large stores offer budget account facilities which, by requiring consumers to pay a monthly amount even when they have not recently purchased anything, can be a powerful incentive to continue shopping at that store. Instant credit is often available, including interest-free credit (see p59) on larger purchases.

These debts are not priority debts (see Chapter 8).

Conditional sale agreement

A conditional sale agreement is a sale made subject to conditions that give the consumer the use of goods during a period in which regular payments for these are made. The goods only change ownership when the last payment has been made. Conditional sale agreements are mostly used for motor vehicles (and are very similar to hire purchase agreements – see p58).

The legal position

Agreements are regulated under the Consumer Credit Act, provided the credit is for no more than £25,000 (or £15,000 before 1 May 1998).[11]

Special features

Conditional sale has a number of special features. These are the same as those for hire purchase (see p58) and the two types of credit operate in just the same way.

The goods belong to the seller until the end of the agreement. The consumer must not sell the goods during this period without obtaining the permission of the seller. The consumer can choose to return (surrender) the goods to the seller at any time during the lifetime of the agreement. The consumer must, however, give written notice to the seller.

The amount payable on return depends on the amount already paid.

- If less than half the total purchase price (as stated on the agreement) has been paid, the consumer must pay the difference between the payments made and half the price plus any other payments which had become due by the surrender date.
- If more than half the total purchase price has already been paid, the consumer may return the goods and will owe nothing further except any arrears on payments due.

If the consumer defaults on payments, the seller can repossess the goods, but will need to obtain a court order unless:

- the consumer gives informed permission;
- less than a third of the total purchase price has been paid and the goods are on public ground.

Advisers should:

- check liability and that the goods purchased were as described and of satisfactory quality (see Chapter 5);
- be prepared to take emergency action to prevent repossession and choose a strategy from Chapter 7, as this may be a priority debt.

Credit cards

A credit card (eg, Mastercard, Visa) is a form of revolving credit (see p61) and allows the consumer to buy goods or services from a trader by signing an authorisation slip. The trader then invoices the credit card company and the consumer receives a monthly account showing all transactions made during that period. A minimum monthly repayment is required – usually 5 per cent of the total balance or a nominal amount, such as £5. Interest is added to balances outstanding after a specified payment date, or immediately for cash withdrawals using a credit card.

The legal position

Transactions made by credit card are linked agreements under the Consumer Credit Act. Consequently, credit card companies can be held responsible for misrepresentation and for defective goods or services which cost between £100 and £30,000 if the trader is unwilling to remedy the situation. This could include a claim for damages due as a consequence of the misrepresentation or other breach. This section of the Act came into force in 1977 and there are differing views as to whether it applies to credit cards taken out prior to 1 July 1977. This has not been tested by the courts, but both Mastercard and Barclaycard have told the Director General of Fair Trading that they would be willing to accept limited liability up to the actual cost of the goods or services purchased with pre-1977 cards.

Special features

The use of a credit card is the cheapest way to obtain short-term credit (up to about six weeks) for specific items. This is because on most cards no interest is charged at all if the account is cleared at the first due date after a purchase is added to it. However, interest is charged immediately for cash withdrawals and there is often an annual charge for cardholders. Advisers should:

- check liability and that the goods purchased were as described and of satisfactory quality (see Chapter 5); *and*
- choose a strategy from Chapter 8, as this will not be a priority debt.

Credit sale agreement

Goods bought on credit sale are owned immediately by the consumer. Regular payments are due in accordance with a regulated agreement. The creditor is often the supplier of the goods and this type of credit is used extensively for selling furniture and cars and by fuel suppliers for cookers, fires, etc.

The legal position

The agreement is regulated by the Consumer Credit Act provided the credit is for less than £25,000 (or £15,000 before 1 May 1998).

Special features

With a credit sale agreement the creditor has no rights over the goods. The consumer simply takes the goods, signs the agreement, and starts to make payments. Sometimes interest-free credit (see p59) is given in the form of a credit sale agreement. Advisers should:

- check liability and that the goods purchased were as described and of satisfactory quality (see Chapter 5); *and*
- choose a strategy from Chapter 8, as this will not be a priority debt.

Hire purchase (HP) agreement

A hire purchase (HP) agreement hires goods to the consumer for an agreed period. At the end of this period the consumer has the option to purchase them (usually for a nominal amount). Hire purchase is predominantly used for motor vehicles. The creditor (who is the hirer) owns the goods, generally having bought them from the supplier who introduced the consumer to the hirer.

The legal position

Hire purchase agreements for up to £25,000 (or £15,000 before 1 May 1998) are regulated under the Consumer Credit Act. The contract is between the consumer and the hirer of the goods, rather than the supplier – ie, in the case of a car, between the consumer and the finance company, rather than with the garage. Therefore the hirer is liable for compensation for misrepresentation and faulty goods (see p81).

Special features

The goods belong to the hirer until the end of the agreement. The consumer must not sell the goods during this period without obtaining the permission of the hirer. The consumer can choose to return (surrender) the goods to the hirer at any time during the lifetime of the agreement. The consumer must, however, give written notice to the hirer. The amount payable on return depends on the amount already paid.

- If less than half the total purchase price (as stated on the agreement) has been paid, the consumer must pay the difference between the payments made and half the price plus any other payments which had become due by the surrender date.
- If more than half the total purchase price has already been paid, the consumer may return the goods and will owe nothing further except any arrears on payments due.

If the consumer defaults on payments, the hirer can repossess the goods but will need to obtain a court order unless:

- the consumer gives permission;
- less than a third of the total purchase price has been paid and the goods are on public ground.

Advisers should:

- check liability and that the goods purchased were as described and of satisfactory quality (see Chapter 5);
- be prepared to take emergency action to prevent repossession and choose a strategy from Chapter 7, as this may be a priority debt.

Interest-free credit

This is a type of credit sale agreement in which money is loaned to buy goods without any interest being charged. It is usually offered by larger stores. Some agreements will offer interest-free credit provided the total balance is paid off within a specified period and thereafter will become ordinary credit sale agreements.

The legal position

These agreements are regulated by the Consumer Credit Act, provided the credit is for no more than £25,000 (or £15,000 before 1 May 1998), even though the annual percentage rate (APR) will be 0 per cent. They must contain all the details required by a regulated agreement (see p52) and details of the circumstances in which interest could become chargeable. Interest can be charged on late payments if the agreement contains a clause allowing it.

Special features

Interest-free credit is offered as an inducement to buy particular goods in a particular place and, therefore, will be a linked agreement (see p54). Advisers should:
- check liability and that the goods purchased were as described and of satisfactory quality (see Chapter 5);
- choose a strategy from Chapter 8, as this will not be a priority debt.

Mail order catalogues

Mail order catalogues offer a way of buying goods by post and spreading payment over a period of weeks by instalments. Payments are sometimes collected by an agent – often a friend or neighbour of the consumer.

The legal position

Catalogue debts are covered by the Consumer Credit Act whether or not there is a charge for credit, provided the credit is for no more than £25,000 (or £15,000 before 1 May 1998).

Special features

Often consumers do not receive a copy of an agreement to sign. This means that the consumer's liability for the debts is unenforceable.[12] Under such circumstances, the consumer is not legally obliged to settle the debt, although s/he may choose to do so.

Mail order purchases can be cancelled by returning the goods within seven days of receipt.

Catalogues are often particularly important to people on low incomes as the only way of affording essential items such as bedding or clothing and charges for their delivery. Advisers should:
- check liability by asking the creditor to supply a copy of the agreement signed by the consumer and that the goods were of satisfactory quality and as described (see Chapter 5);
- choose a strategy from Chapter 8, as this will not be a priority debt.

Pawnbrokers

Money is lent against an article left with the pawnbroker as security – a pledge. The goods can only be reclaimed (redeemed) if the loan is repaid with interest.

The legal position

Pawnbrokers must be licensed and lending is covered by the Consumer Credit Act, provided the credit is for no more than £25,000 (or £15,000 before 1 May 1998).

Special features

The pawnbroker must keep the goods for at least six months, during which time interest will be charged on monies borrowed. If the goods are not redeemed then the debtor will have to review the pledge to prevent the goods being sold. Advisers should:

- check liability (Chapter 5);
- choose a strategy from Chapter 8 (or Chapter 7 unless the pawned item is essential).

Personal loan

A personal loan is a loan offered at a fixed or variable rate of interest over a set period.

The legal position

Personal loans are regulated under the Consumer Credit Act, provided the credit is for no more than £25,000 (or £15,000 before 1 May 1998).

Special features

Personal loans are widely available from banks, building societies and other finance houses, including small moneylenders. Some personal loans have fixed interest rates and the total interest charged is set at the beginning of the period of the loan. Repayments are then made in equal instalments. Sometimes a personal loan is part of a linked transaction (see p54). Sometimes the amount to be loaned is paid direct to the supplier rather than the borrower. With smaller moneylenders repayments are often collected at the door by a representative. Advisers should:

- check liability (see Chapter 5);
- choose a strategy from Chapter 8 as personal loans are generally not a priority.

Revolving credit

Revolving credit is a type of personal loan in which the creditor agrees to a credit limit and the consumer can borrow up to that limit, provided s/he maintains certain previously agreed minimum payments. Revolving credit takes a number of different forms – eg, credit cards (see p57); budget accounts (see p56); and bank overdrafts (see p54).

Second mortgage (secured loan)

A second (or subsequent) mortgage allows a homeowner to take out a (further) loan using the property as security. There has to be sufficient equity (see pp151 and 122) in the property. The lender takes a legal charge on the property giving rights of repossession similar to those of a building society or bank holding the first charge on the property. However, if a house is repossessed and sold, the proceeds will be distributed to meet claims of secured lenders in the order in which loans were given.

The legal position

Second mortgages for £25,000 or less (£15,000 prior to 1 May 1998) are regulated agreements under the Consumer Credit Act if not exempt (usually because the lender is a building society lending for the purpose of acquiring or improving a home).

Special features

Interest rates on second mortgages with finance companies are much higher than those charged by building societies or banks for first mortgages. Loans are often repayable over a much shorter term than for first mortgages and this, together with higher interest rates, means it is an expensive form of borrowing. However, it is extremely difficult to persuade courts that such loans are extortionate credit agreements purely on the basis of the interest rate alone (see p84).

There are special rules for entering into secured loans under the Consumer Credit Act. The borrower must be given a copy of the agreement, which is not to be signed for seven days. Then s/he must be sent a copy for signing and left for a further seven days. If the borrower does not sign, there is no agreement. If the agreement is signed and returned, the borrower has entered the agreement and it cannot be cancelled. The lender should not contact the prospective borrower during either of the seven-day 'thinking' periods unless asked to do so in writing. If these rules have not been followed the loan is not enforceable without a court order.

Advisers should:
- consider whether emergency action is necessary; *and*
- choose a strategy from Chapter 7, as this will be a priority debt.

Trading cheques/vouchers

Finance companies may supply a voucher or cheque to the consumer, which can be used at specified shops in exchange for goods. Repayments, which include a charge for the credit, are then made by instalments to the finance company. The shop is paid by the credit company.

The legal position

Agreements are regulated under the Consumer Credit Act, provided the credit is for no more than £25,000 (or £15,000 before 1 May 1998), although if the voucher is for £50 or less the creditor is not obliged to comply with the form and content rules considered on p52.[13]

Special features

This is normally an expensive way of borrowing and limits the consumer to shopping in a limited number of outlets where prices may be high. This will not be a priority debt – see Chapter 8 for details of how to deal with it.

3. Other debts

Business debts

It will often be necessary to advise people with business debts (see Chapter 13). If a business is still trading but is facing financial difficulties, specialist advice should be sought from an accountant, insolvency practitioner, local business centre or small firms advisory service as to the viability of the business.

The legal position

If the business has already ceased trading, then debts should be dealt with like any other case of multiple debt, using the same criteria to decide whether they should be treated as priority or not (see Chapter 7).

Liability for the debts must be ascertained and the adviser needs to check whether the debtor was a sole trader, in a partnership or a limited company. A sole trader will be personally liable for all the debts; in a partnership, all partners will be jointly and severally liable. In limited companies only the directors can be held liable for any debts, and then only if they have personally guaranteed a loan or, under company law, if there has been wrongful trading or neglect of their duties as directors.

Charge cards

A charge card (eg, Diners Card) is not a credit card. Purchases are made and the amount is charged to the account, but the balance must be cleared in full at the end of each charging period (usually monthly).

The legal position

Charge cards are exempt from the Consumer Credit Act because there is no extended credit.

Special features

In order to obtain a charge card it is necessary to pay an annual fee and show proof of a high income. The upper spending limit for these cards is usually very high (eg, £5,000-£10,000). This will not be a priority debt (see Chapter 8).

Child support payments

The Child Support Agency (CSA) collects payments from non-resident parents to parents with care if the caring parent is in receipt of income support or income-based jobseeker's allowance. In addition, it may collect payments from other non-resident parents where the parent with care/applicant requests this.

The legal position

Child support payments are governed by the Child Support Acts 1991 and 1995, the Child Support, Pensions and Social Security Act 2000 and subsequent regulations and amendments. Enforcement of payment can be made through a deduction from earnings order, or a liability order in the magistrates' court. The CSA can seize goods using bailiffs if a liability order is granted. Where all other enforcement action fails the CSA may seek the debtor's imprisonment or disqualification from driving.

The Child Support scheme is being reformed; this is likely to happen in late 2002. The main changes relate to:

- how maintenance is worked out; *and*
- internal case administration.

The powers to collect and enforce maintenance payments remain unchanged.

Special features

Child support payments are worked out according to set rules. The pre-reform scheme (old rules) is a complex and rigid formula, although sometimes a 'departure' from this is allowed. It is vital to check the calculation (although it is difficult to do this because it often requires information about the other parent and her/his family which may not be available to the debtor). Some debt advisers will require the assistance of a specialist to do this. The reformed scheme is simpler to calculate, although variations from it may still be possible to reflect special circumstances.

Under the pre-reform scheme the CSA's power to collect maintenance is based upon an authorisation to act, given to the CSA by the parent with care. In some circumstances this can be withheld or revoked and the CSA must stop acting. However, in certain circumstances some arrears may remain due to the Secretary of State. The circumstances of a parent with care should be investigated when the other parent is unable to make child support payments. The parent with care might be prepared to consider withholding/revoking authorisation (pre-reforms) or opting-out. However, the parent with care may face a reduction in benefit of £21.58 if this is done without good cause.

The CSA has been subject to continual media scrutiny and political volatility. The rules are changing continuously and MPs and others may be interested in cases of particularly serious hardship caused by it. It is probably not prudent to base a long-term debt advice strategy upon an expectation that money will be received or required under this legislation.

The enforcement powers of the CSA are potentially draconian. The first step in enforcement is to make a deduction of earnings order. This is made, in practice, by a member of the CSA staff. If this cannot be implemented and there are arrears of more than £25 and there is no arrears agreement (or one has been broken), then a liability order will be sought from the magistrates' court. Following the granting of this, distress may be used (see Chapter 10) or the powers of the county court used to make a charging order or third party debt order (see Chapter 9). If one of these fails, the CSA can apply to the magistrates' court to commit a person to prison (maximum six weeks) or disqualify the person from driving (maximum two years). The court must decide whether the debtor has 'willfully refused or culpably neglected' to pay (see p258).

Further information

The child support legislation is complex and onerous. Specialist independent help must be sought if an adviser is unfamiliar with it. The *Child Support Handbook* (see Appendix 6) is an essential reference work for the adviser.

Community charge (poll tax)

Community charge (poll tax) replaced domestic rates in April 1990, and was replaced itself by council tax in April 1993. The main type of community charge was called personal community charge. This was set by the local authority and was payable by every individual in England and Wales (not Northern Ireland) over 18 unless they were exempt. Heterosexual couples who were either married or living together could be held responsible for each other's community charge if either of them did not pay.

The legal position

The community charge was payable under the powers of the Local Government Finance Act 1988 and the regulations based on that Act. It is recoverable for six years after it became due but this period is extended indefinitely if a liability order was obtained within the six-year period.

Special features

Despite its abolition, local authorities are still committed to the recovery of millions of pounds worth of unpaid community charge (and are often under pressure from the District Auditor to do so).

All outstanding community charge is likely to be subject to a liability order (see Chapter 10). This means that bailiffs can be used, followed by further court action. It is a sensitive political area and magistrates are increasingly unhappy about dealing with it because of the legal complexities. In the event that any local authority did apply to commit a debtor to prison for unpaid community charge, the magistrates should be invited to remit the whole sum on the grounds of undue delay.[14]

Council tax

This replaced the poll tax (community charge) in April 1993 in England and Wales. It is a tax administered by local authorities, and is composed of two equal elements – a 'property' element and a 'people' element.

Property element

All domestic properties have been valued and placed in one of eight valuation bands.

The valuation is based on what the property would have sold for on the open market as at April 1991. It assumed that the property was sold freehold (99 years' leasehold for flats), with vacant possession and in a reasonable state of repair. Under some circumstances, an appeal against this valuation can be made – advisers should consider this if it appears to be a problem. Certain properties are exempt, and advisers should check to make sure that exemption has been applied for if appropriate.

Assuming the property is not exempt, the level of council tax is set annually by the local authority with occupants of Band H properties paying approximately three times as much as those in Band A.

People element

The tax assumes that two adults aged 18 or over live in each household. Nothing extra is payable if there are more than two adults. One adult living on her/his own receives a 25 per cent discount, and if there are no adults there is a 50 per cent discount. If the latter applies, it may be that the property is exempt and advisers should check whether this is the case.

When counting the number of adults in the household, certain people can be disregarded. Once again, this should be checked. Additionally, in certain cases there are reductions for people with disabilities whose homes have been modified. There is also a transitional relief scheme which partly compensates people who otherwise would have suffered a substantial increase compared with their poll tax.

Liability

A council tax bill is sent to each domestic property. The person(s) nearest the top of this list will be the council tax payer(s):

- resident freeholder (owner);
- resident leaseholder;
- resident statutory/secure tenant (including a council tenant);
- other resident(s);
- non-resident owner.

If there is more than one person resident in the house who has the same interest in the property (that is, joint owners or joint tenants) then they will be jointly and severally liable. This means that all the people concerned can be asked to pay the full charge, together or as individuals.

Married couples and heterosexual couples who live together will also be held jointly and severally liable. A single bill will be sent, either in the name of one of the persons concerned, or in both names.

Bills should be issued less any discounts, transitional relief, deductions and council tax benefit, and must arrive at least 14 days before the first instalment falls due. The local authority must offer the option of paying by monthly instalments. As discount is not a benefit, provided a claim is made the appropriate discount(s) can be backdated indefinitely.

Special features

The local authority's recovery powers are very similar to those used for community charge (see p65), except that it has an additional power to apply to place a charging order on a property if the debt is more than £1,000. This is a priority debt (see Chapter 7).

Fines

Fines are the most common form of punishment imposed by the magistrates' or crown courts for criminal offences. Many of the offences for which people are fined are minor and are often related to individual poverty. Such offences can include not having a television licence or motor insurance, or doing casual work while claiming jobseeker's allowance.

The legal position

Magistrates' courts are empowered to impose fines for criminal offences by a wide variety of legislation. They are bound to consider the means of the defendant 'as far as they are known to the court'.[15] Maximum amounts are laid down for each offence.

Special features

Fines should be distinguished from costs or compensation, which are often also awarded against defendants in criminal actions. Fines are also much more serious than civil court orders, money judgments, etc. However, fines can be imposed in the county court (eg, for non-payment of maintenance) and these are normally collected by the magistrates' court. Fines are often imposed in the absence of the defendant and, in such cases, a 'fine notice' is sent to her/him. This shows the amount of the fine (and cost or compensation, if any) and whether payment by instalments is ordered.

Advisers should consider emergency action if payment of fines is difficult for a debtor. This is a priority debt (see Chapter 7). Court procedures and enforcement are explained in Chapter 10.

Gas and electricity charges

Gas and electricity suppliers charge for their fuel in a number of ways. The most common way is by quarterly account sent out at the end of each quarter on the basis of a meter reading carried out either by the company's own staff or by the consumer. Coin and token meters and budget schemes are also common payment methods. Recent changes have given consumers a choice of supplier for fuel although a supplier to whom debt is owed can usually object to a transfer.

The legal position

Electricity supply is regulated by the Electricity Act 1989, as amended by the Competition and Services (Utilities) Act 1992, and gas by the Gas Acts 1986 and 1995 and the Utilities Act 2000. Detailed references to the legislation are available in the *Fuel Rights Handbook* (see Appendix 6).

Fuel bills may include payments for goods sold by the supplier – eg, cookers, freezers, etc. These non-fuel debts will generally be credit sale agreements (see p53). A consumer cannot have her/his fuel supply disconnected for arrears on a credit sale agreement.

Many bills are based upon estimated meter readings. If these are higher than the actual reading, the debtor should ask for the true amount to be used.

The name and address of the consumer as well as the address to which fuel was supplied should be noted from the bill, as the prioritisation of the debt will depend upon the customer's continued need for that fuel at her/his present address.

Fuel supplies may be disconnected if there are arrears and this is likely, therefore, to be a priority debt (see Chapter 7). In the case of electricity, the supply can only be disconnected at the address to which the bill relates, but in the case of gas, the customer can be disconnected at her/his current address even though the arrears may relate to a previous address.[16]

These are usually priority debts (see Chapter 7).

Income tax arrears

Most income above certain fixed limits is taxable. Employees are taxed by direct deduction from their income by their employer (the pay-as-you-earn or PAYE scheme). PAYE taxpayers will rarely owe tax on their earned income unless mistakes have been made in the amounts deducted. Self-employed people receive their earnings before tax is deducted, and are responsible for paying their own tax directly to the Inland Revenue. Arrears are therefore more likely to occur with self-employment (see Chapter 13).

The legal position

Income tax is payable under the Taxes Management Act 1970 and the Income and Corporation Taxes Act 1988 and subsequent Finance Acts and regulations.

Special features

The amount of tax that a tax inspector assesses as due should rarely be accepted at face value. There are many ways of reducing liability for tax, unless it is deducted under PAYE. Self-employed people in particular will require detailed advice on how to complete their tax returns since the introduction of self-assessment in April 1997. They will also need detailed advice on any arrears that the Inland Revenue may be claiming. Self-employed people should always consider appealing against an assessment but should seek specialised help from an accountant to do so.

This is a priority debt (see Chapter 7).

Maintenance payments

Before April 1993 either the magistrates' court or county court made orders to require a parent or married partner to make maintenance payments to the other partner and/or children.

From April 1993, child maintenance payment powers passed to the CSA (see p63) under the Child Support Act 1991, but arrears due under court orders still exist. The only new court orders are applications not covered by child support regulations (eg, applications for additional maintenance over and above the maximum awarded on CSA assessment) and for spousal maintenance.

The legal position

Magistrates' courts made orders on application from a parent.[17] If income support had been claimed, the Secretary of State for Social Security also applied.[18] Magistrates also collect and review maintenance orders made by the county court, divorce registry or High Court.[19]

Special features

If a maintenance order is unpaid, the magistrates' court has powers similar to those used where fines are unpaid (see Chapter 10). Maintenance payable under a court order should be distinguished from voluntary maintenance payments, even where these are written as a legal agreement. See child support payments above.

This is a priority debt (see Chapter 7).

Mortgages

A mortgage is a legal way of linking repayments due to the ownership of property. Commonly, the term is used to describe a loan used for the purchase of a house. If repayments are not kept up, the lender has the right to recover the money lent by repossessing the property and selling it. A 'charge' is registered on the property to safeguard the rights of the lender.

The legal position

First mortgages from building societies and the major banks are exempt from regulation by the Consumer Credit Act (see p51). Most are regulated by the Law of Property Act 1925 as amended.

Special features

There are a variety of different mortgages:

- **Capital repayment mortgage** The capital is repaid gradually over the term of the mortgage. At the beginning, repayments consist of virtually all interest, but towards the end of the term of the mortgage they are virtually all capital.
- **Endowment mortgage** Repayments cover the interest on the capital borrowed and separate payments are made to an insurance company for the endowment premium. The capital is repaid at the end of the term of the mortgage in one lump sum from the proceeds of the insurance policy. Endowment policies should at least pay off the mortgage capital when they mature; in addition they aim to produce extra capital for the borrower to use as s/he wishes.
- **Pension mortgage** The borrower pays interest only to the lender and a separate pension premium which attracts tax relief. When it matures, the cash available from this pension pays off the capital on the mortgage and the rest funds a personal pension plan.
- **Low start/deferred interest mortgage** These mortgages were introduced during a period of high interest rates. Reduced interest was charged for some of the first two to three years. In some schemes interest remitted during this period is paid over the remainder of the term of the mortgage. They are only helpful for people who expect their income to increase in order for them to afford the rise in repayments after the first few years.
- **Fixed rate mortgage** The interest rate is fixed for a number of years at the beginning of the loan. They are obviously more attractive during a period when interest rates are rising.

Most mortgages will be the liability of all the property owners ('jointly and severally' – see p77). However, in some cases, one co-owner will have taken a loan with a mortgage on only her/his share of the property. Specialist legal advice will be required to ascertain liability in such a case.

A mortgage is a priority debt (see Chapter 7). See p215 for the position with regard to mortgage shortfall after repossession of a property.

National insurance contributions

National insurance contributions are a compulsory tax on earnings and profits above certain levels (set annually).

The legal position

National insurance contributions are payable under section 2 of the 1975 Social Security Act as amended by the Social Security Contributions and Benefits Act 1992.

Special features

Employed people pay class 1 national insurance contributions directly from their wages and thus arrears do not build up. Class 2 contributions must be paid by self-employed earners unless they have a certificate of exemption on the grounds of low income. Self-employed people have to pay class 2 national insurance contributions by monthly direct debit or quarterly bill. In addition, self-employed people may have to pay class 4 contributions, calculated as a percentage of their profits above a certain level (set annually). After the year-end, the Inland Revenue sends out demands to self-employed people from whom it has not received the required class 2 contributions.

If a self-employed person has also employed someone else, then s/he may be liable for class 1 national insurance for their employee as well as class 2 and perhaps 4 for themselves.

Demands for payment should be distinguished from the notice sent to people whose contribution record is insufficient to entitle them to use it towards a retirement pension or bereavement benefits. In such cases, the Inland Revenue sends a notification that gives the insured the opportunity to make up the deficit for a particular year with voluntary (class 3) contributions. This is not a demand for payment.

This should usually be regarded as a priority debt (see Chapter 7).

Rent

Rent is payable by tenants to landlords in exchange for the use of their property. A landlord may be either a private individual or property company, or a public sector landlord, such as a local authority or housing association.

The legal position

Rent is payable under a tenancy agreement (whether written or oral), and it can be modified by the decisions of a rent officer or rent assessment committee. For more details, see *Manual of Housing Law* (see Appendix 6).

Special features

After the termination of a tenancy (eg, because a notice to quit is served), a tenant is still allowed to remain in possession of the home because of the protection given by legislation. In these circumstances, the landlord may refer to the money due in exchange for possession of the home as 'mesne profits'. For practical purposes, this is the same as rent. Similarly, where a person is a licensee rather than a tenant (see Manual of Housing Law), what s/he pays will not strictly be rent but will be a charge for use of the property. Arrears of payment due under a licence are treated in the same way as rent when giving debt advice.

Rent due for a person's current home is a priority debt (see Chapter 7).

Social fund repayments

Social fund loans are mainly for income support and income-based jobseeker's allowance claimants who need to borrow money for essential items. They are normally repaid by a direct deduction from the claimant's weekly benefit. However, when a person stops getting benefit before having repaid the entire loan, s/he will still owe money to the fund.

The legal position

Social fund repayments are required by section 78 of the Social Security (Administration) Act 1992. The Social Fund Guide lays down the procedures that the Department for Work and Pensions (DWP) will use to collect loans from claimants.

Special features

The DWP will tell the debtor how the loan is to be repaid. Claimants on income support or income-based jobseeker's allowance will have a fixed proportion of their benefits deducted, depending on their other commitments. The debt adviser should consider asking for these deductions to be reduced or the loan rescheduled, especially if the DWP was unaware of the financial problems. See the *Welfare Benefits Handbook* (see Appendix 6) for further details. The DWP can take court action to recover the money if no arrangement is made. If the debtor is unable to afford repayment, it may be that it will consider writing off the debt. The debt should be treated as a normal unsecured loan and is not a priority (see Chapter 8).

Uniform business rate

This is a charge levied on all commercial property. It is based on a national valuation and fixed amounts are charged across England and Wales in proportion to this value.

The legal position

The rate is payable under the Local Government Finance Act 1988.

Special features

Recovery of arrears is through a liability order in the magistrates' court. Bailiffs have the power to seize any goods belonging to the ratepayer once a liability order is made, so (non-exempt) goods at the home address could be seized in addition to business assets. Unlike community charge/council tax, there is no exemption for goods, etc, which are necessary for use in the debtor's business.[20] Once a business ceases trading, no rates are payable for the first three months; after that half rates are payable.

Local authorities have power[21] to reduce or write-off arrears of business rates in situations of severe hardship. This is most appropriate in cases of business failure and should always be sought before considering payment.

This may or may not be a priority debt, depending on the risk of loss of essential goods by the debtor.

Value added tax (VAT)

Value added tax (VAT) is a tax charged by the Customs and Excise Department on most transactions of businesses with an annual taxable turnover of more than a certain limit, set annually. A business must be registered for VAT unless its turnover is below the limit.

The legal position

VAT is payable under the Finance Act 1972 and the VAT Act 1983 and subsequent regulations and amendments. Its scope and level is reviewed each year and changes are often made to the Act following the budget.

Special features

VAT is a tax on the value added to goods and services as they pass through the registered business. Thus, although VAT is payable on purchases, this amount can be offset against the tax on the company's own sales. For example, if the total purchases in a year were £100,000 and the total sales were identical, there would be no value added and no tax payable.

A debt adviser will generally encounter VAT debts after a business has ceased trading and the partner or sole trader is left responsible for VAT (see Chapter 13). Some goods are exempt and the calculation of the amount of VAT is complicated. Help should normally be sought from an accountant specialising in VAT. If VAT is overdue, a surcharge – which will be a percentage of the VAT owed – will be added to the debt. This amount can be appealed.

This is a priority debt (see Chapter 7).

Water charges

Water companies charge for water, sewerage and environmental services on the basis of either a meter or the rating system, which was abolished as the basis of a local tax in April 1990 in England and Wales. Under the rating system, every dwelling was given a rateable value. Each year, water companies set a 'rate in the pound', which converts this rateable value into an annual charge. For example, a rate of 20p in the pound converts a rateable value of £300 to an amount of water rates payable of £60.

Where a water meter is installed, a consumer pays for the actual amount of water used. Charges are per cubic metre at a rate set by the water company. A standing charge is also payable. Separate charges are levied for sewerage and environmental services. These charges are based either on the rateable value of the property or on the amount of water used as recorded by the meter.

The legal position

Water charges are payable under the Water Industries Act 1991. Water companies will initially use county court action to recover arrears. They have no discretion to waive charges if there is an ongoing supply.

Special features

Bills for water charges are sent out in April. Payment can be made in eight to ten instalments or weekly/monthly in cases of financial hardship. It is important to check that the bill refers to a property in which the consumer actually lives, or lived, and that the dates of occupation and name(s) shown on the bill are correct. The occupier of the property is the person liable to pay the bill. Where there is a meter, there may be installation and inspection charges. Bills are issued every three or six months based on meter readings carried out by the company's staff or the consumer. If this is not possible, an estimated bill will be issued. Bills should be checked and queried if they seem too high as there may be a hidden leak or the meter may be faulty.

Since 30 June 1999 water companies no longer have the right to disconnect for arrears of domestic water charges and, therefore, this is a non-priority debt (see Chapter 8), but the realistic cost of current water charges must be in the financial statement to avoid on-going enforcement action.[22]

Ofwat may be able to help (see Appendix 5).

Notes

1. The Consumer Credit Act
1 s21(i) CCA 1974
2 s1(i)(a) CCA 1974
3 s25(2)(d) CCA 1974
4 s40 CCA 1974
5 ss113 and 127(3) CCA 1974
6 s63 CCA 1974
7 s7 CCA 1974
8 s75 CCA 1974
9 ss57(i) and 69(i) CCA 1974
10 s70(3) CCA 1974

2. Consumer Credit Act debts
11 s8 CCA 1974
12 s127(3) CCA 1974
13 ss14 and 17 CCA 1974

3. Other debts
14 *R v Warrington Borough Council ex parte Barrett,* 18 November 1999, unreported; *R v Gloucestershire Justices ex parte Daldry,* 12 January 2000, unreported
15 s35 MCA 1980
16 Sch 6 para 1(6)(a) Electricity Act 1989; Sch 2B paras 7(1) and 3 Gas Act 1986
17 s2 DPMCA 1978
18 s26 SSA 1986
19 s1 MOA 1958
20 Reg 14(1A) Non-Domestic Rating (Collection and Enforcement) (Local Lists) Regs 1989
21 s49 LGFA 1988
22 s1 and Sch 1 Water Industry Act 1999

Chapter 5

Minimising debts

This chapter covers:
1. Using the law of contract to avoid or reduce liability (below)
2. Using the Consumer Credit Act to avoid or reduce liability (p83)
3. Reducing gas and electricity charges (p87)
4. If money is owed to the debtor (p92)

Advisers must check that the debtor is legally liable to pay the debts claimed by her/his creditors. In general, a debt will be owed only if there is a valid contract between the debtor and creditor; or money is owed because of particular legislation; or if the debtor has been ordered by a court to make payments to someone else, or to the court itself, and there are no grounds to challenge the court order. Sometimes nothing will be payable because a contract has not been made in the correct way or the rules governing the ways in which public authorities can demand money have not been complied with. Even if the adviser has established that a debt does exist, it is still possible that the debtor is not liable for it, either because liability actually falls on someone other than the debtor, or because the contract is not enforceable.

The adviser must also check that the amount of any debt is correct – both by checking the accuracy of calculations and by looking for any amounts that the debtor is entitled to offset against the debt.

The situations in which someone else may be liable, or in which an agreement involving payments may not be valid, or in which a debt may be reduced, are outlined below.

1. Using the law of contract to avoid or reduce liability

A contract is an agreement between two parties (individuals, companies, etc, or a mixture of these) that becomes binding – ie, legally enforceable – because it specifies that goods or services are to be exchanged by one of the parties in return for a 'consideration', usually money, from the other party. There are a number of circumstances in which monies claimed under a contract may either not be due at all or can be reduced. For further detail on this see the Law of Contract.

There are also important ways in which consumer, housing or other legislation can reduce the amount a debtor owes. These are listed below.

Joint and several liability

If more than one debtor enters into a credit agreement, they will each be liable for the whole amount of the debt. This is known as 'joint and several liability'. If relevant, the agreement must be signed by all parties in the form required by the Consumer Credit Act (see p51). If all the debtors have not signed such an agreement, none of them is liable.

Joint and several liability can also apply to rent arrears on joint tenancies, or arrears on joint mortgages, to community charge payments for heterosexual couples, to water/sewerage charges and to council tax on properties which are jointly owned/occupied.

Guarantors

A creditor will sometimes ask for a guarantee before agreeing to lend money or provide services. The guarantor agrees to make the necessary payments should the actual customer or borrower fail to do so, and is bound by the terms of the guarantee that s/he has given. Where these terms are part of a regulated consumer credit agreement, they will be governed by the Consumer Credit Act, and the guarantee must be in writing and signed by the guarantor. Sometimes creditors ask for people to act as second purchasers, who are asked to sign the original agreement as purchasers and become jointly and severally liable for the debt. Guarantors should be given copies of the original agreement and also any notices required to be sent to the debtor on default.

If the creditor has not properly explained to a guarantor that s/he is equally liable for the total debt, there may be a way out of liability if it can be shown that the guarantor has been either misled or coerced. In any case where there is a non-commercial relationship between the debtor and the guarantor, for example cohabitees, the creditor is required to take reasonable steps to satisfy itself that the guarantor understands the transaction and the risks s/he is taking by entering into it. The creditor can either do this itself or require the guarantor to see a solicitor.

If the creditor fails to take these steps and the guarantor's consent to the transaction has been improperly obtained, then the creditor may be unable to enforce the guarantee.[1] This commonly arises where one of a couple applies for a loan for her/his own purposes, which the creditor requires to be in joint names so that it can be secured on jointly owned property. If it appears that agreement was only given to a joint loan because the first borrower used undue influence (see p81) — by saying, for instance, 'we'll lose our home if you do not sign', or by misrepresenting the effect of the transaction — then the second borrower may be able to escape liability. S/he should always seek specialist help in doing this. However, in the Etridge case the House of Lords pointed out that in the typical husband–wife surety case, undue influence will be difficult to establish.

Agents

An agent sells goods or collects money on behalf of somebody else – for example, with mail order catalogues the agent shows or distributes catalogues to her/his friends, neighbours, etc, and then takes orders and passes them on to the supplying company. S/he collects money from the customers over a number of weeks, and is liable to pay over any money collected from customers, regardless of whether or not the creditor can enforce the agreement against the customer, for example because s/he has not signed a contract. An agent is obliged to create a separate account for each customer. If s/he does not do this, then s/he can become liable for monies not paid by customers for whom s/he has failed to create an account. If there is a separate account, the agent will not be liable for monies that customers do not pay.

An agent may lose commission with which s/he has already been credited (and thus her/his own personal account may go into arrears) if someone does not keep up the payment on items bought and supplied. However, an agent is not liable for the customer's default.

When advising an agent about liability, it is important to check whether the amount owed includes other customers' debts. If so, provide the creditor with a clear breakdown of the accounts and names and addresses of customers in arrears and ask the creditor to invoice them separately.

Wrong person

An account may be sent to the wrong person or the wrong address, and the person who receives the request for payment is not actually liable. If there is any doubt about this, check any documents relating to the debt and ask the creditor to produce original invoices, agreements and details of goods or services supplied. Full initials and addresses are obviously important in this process, as are reference numbers.

Using the wrong name, however, does not invalidate a debt and, if a name is shown incorrectly, particularly if it has always been inaccurate but both parties know who is intended, then the debt can still be valid.

Forgery of signatures

If a signature on an agreement has been forged, then the person whose name has been forged will not be liable for any debt arising from that agreement. A signature may have been forged with knowledge. For example, a woman who wants a loan but has reached her credit limit with a particular creditor uses her sister's name to obtain the loan, receives the monies and makes repayments. The sister knows and agrees. In such cases, the adviser should proceed as though the signature was valid and the beneficiary of the loan should continue to maintain repayments.

A partner or close relative's signature may be used without her/his consent – for example, obtaining credit by using a parent's name and signature without the knowledge of the credit company or the parent. If there is any accusation of fraud, the debtor should obtain legal advice.

In some cases the use of a more creditworthy relative's name may have been sanctioned by the credit company. If a representative of a creditor has allowed a false name to be given knowingly, then that representative may be either conniving with a fraud or – if the signing occurred on her/his advice – creating a situation in which the creditor accepts that the borrower is allowed to use another name. However, a broker is not usually regarded as a representative of the credit company for this purpose.

In all cases where signatures may have been forged a criminal offence may have been committed, and so it is important to say nothing that might incriminate the signatory. The adviser should explain the right to remain silent if interviewed by the police, although noting that such a silence can be used to challenge any subsequent defence.[2] Fraud is a serious criminal offence and a solicitor specialising in criminal law may be required.

When advising the person whose name has been used, the debt adviser need only state to the creditor that the signature is not hers/his and advise the person that s/he does not owe the money because s/he has not signed the agreement. The adviser should be aware of the possible repercussions for the actual signatory and should explain these to the person being advised as s/he may prefer to accept liability for the debt rather than risk a prosecution of the actual signatory.

Liability after the death of a debtor

An individual's debts usually die with her/him, although creditors may be entitled to make a claim against the deceased's estate – ie, money, personal possessions, property, etc, if any. It is, however, possible that creditors will attempt to hold partners or close relatives responsible for an individual's debts, particularly if they lived with the deceased. If someone is dealing with a deceased's estate s/he has no personal liability for any debts that cannot be paid from the deceased's own property. There are several possible exceptions to this rule:

- Debts for which someone had joint (and several) liability with the deceased (see p77).
- Where the deceased's estate has been handed over to beneficiaries without first paying her/his creditors, the person dealing with the estate will be personally liable (as will the beneficiaries), but only up to the value of the estate handed over/received. This includes the situation where the person handling the estate is also the only beneficiary. The risk of creditors making claims after the estate

has been disposed of can be eliminated by advertising for creditors in accordance with s.27 of the Trustee Act 1925 and waiting for two months to see if any claims are received.

- The deceased's share in a jointly owned property is not part of her/his estate and passes directly to the other co-owners – regardless of whether the deceased made a will or died intestate – and so is not available to creditors (unless the owners were tenants-in-common – eg, where a creditor obtained a charging order on the beneficial interest of one of the owners (see p193)). However, since 2 April 2001, if a creditor presents a bankruptcy petition against the deceased's estate and an order is made, the court can require the surviving owner(s) to pay the value of the deceased's share as at the date of death to the trustee. The petition must be presented within five years of the deceased's death. A client faced with this possibility may be well advised to make a payment arrangement with the creditor(s) rather than risk a sale of the property. Advice should be sought from a specialist.
- A mortgage remains on a property even if this passes to a new owner by inheritance (although it may be paid off by an insurance policy at death).
- Taking over a tenancy from the deceased by succession, which may involve taking over rent arrears if these cannot be paid by the estate. A tenant by succession can lose her/his home if s/he does not pay off arrears.[3]
- For married couples, there is joint liability for council tax and community charge. Although liability ceases at the date of death, the surviving partner remains jointly liable for any arrears. Local authorities have the usual powers to pursue a surviving partner (see pp65–66), but in practice they will not normally seek repayment of community charge arrears from the surviving partner unless s/he has inherited money from the deceased.

When a person has died and someone continues to live in her/his home and use services for which the dead person previously paid (eg, fuel, water charges, etc), it is important that the survivor opens a new account in her/his own name as soon as possible after the death. In this way s/he is stating a willingness to pay for future goods or services used and also demonstrating that s/he was not hitherto liable. It is important to ensure that s/he does not agree to take responsibility for the deceased person's debt when s/he opens the new account (although the deceased person's estate, of which the house may be part, will be liable).

Some debts are paid off on death by insurance policies or life insurance. Many mortgages, and some consumer credit agreements, will be covered, and advisers must check this in each case.

Money owed by under 18-year-olds

If a debtor was under 18 (a 'minor') at the time a contract was made, check whether it was for 'necessaries' and, if not, a court may decide it is not enforceable. **'Necessaries'** are defined as 'goods suitable to the condition in life of a minor and her/his actual requirements at the time of sale and delivery' and examples would be fuel or clothing. The debtor would have been expected to pay no more than is 'reasonable' for such goods. Young people under 18 are often asked to provide a guarantor who would be liable to pay if the debtor could not (see p77). If there were no guarantor and the goods were not 'necessaries', the debtor need not pay and the creditor would have to use the court to claim repayments. However, a court could also order any goods to be returned if the supplier had suffered loss.

Contracts made under undue influence

If a contract has been made under 'undue influence' – that is, where a person has taken unfair advantage of her/his influence over another person – it may not be enforceable. Undue influence may be actual – for example, where a person has been subjected to oppression. It may also be presumed – ie, if a person is persuaded to enter into a contract, by someone else on whom s/he relies for advice and guidance, and the transaction is explainable only on the basis that undue influence was used, because it puts the person at a substantial disadvantage. For example, if a creditor persuaded a debtor that unless s/he borrowed more money from her/him to clear arrears, the creditor would seize the debtor's home, such a contract might be unenforceable and, in such cases, the advice of a specialist solicitor should be sought.

Misrepresentation of the terms of the contract

If one party misrepresents the terms of a contract to another – ie, inaccurately explains the transaction – the latter party may be able to avoid the transaction. For example, if a creditor persuaded a debtor to sign a legal charge by stating that a secured loan does not put the debtor's home at risk, the loan may not be enforceable as the debtor would have the right to cancel the legal charge.

The debtor can seek compensation for any loss suffered in consequence of a misrepresentation. It is very difficult to prove oral misrepresentation, and so it is important that the adviser obtains copies of all relevant correspondence. Alternatively, if the misrepresentation can be established, the creditor may decide not to pursue the debt for fear of bad publicity.

In the case of agreements regulated by the Consumer Credit Act 1974 where the finance is arranged through the supplier or dealer, the lender is jointly and severally liable with the supplier or dealer for any misrepresentations made by the supplier or dealer both in relation to the goods or services supplied as well as the credit agreement (see Chapter 4).

Capacity to make a contract

A contract is only valid if someone has the 'capacity' to make it. This means that if someone is unable to understand what s/he is doing through, for instance, the influence of alcohol or drugs or because of mental ill health or a learning disability, then the contract may not be enforceable provided the creditor either knew or ought to have known of the person's incapacity. Advice from a specialist solicitor should be sought.

Housing disrepair

In many cases where there are rent arrears landlords have not always fulfilled their obligations in connection with repairs. The amount of rent arrears claimed by the landlord can then be reduced either by a 'set off' or a 'counterclaim' by the tenant. 'Set offs' are amounts of money that have been spent by the tenant to carry out repairs required by law and are, therefore, owed to the tenant by the landlord. 'Counterclaims' are amounts of money claimed by the tenant in compensation for a failure to repair and the resultant loss of rights (under the tenancy contract).[4] The services of a specialist housing lawyer may also be required.

Faulty goods/services

If a debtor owes money on faulty goods or unsatisfactory services, s/he may be able to avoid paying all or part of the bill. A debtor may be able to obtain a refund on goods that are not of satisfactory quality or not as described.[5] The goods must be rejected immediately or very soon after purchase. Similarly, services should be carried out with reasonable care and skill and within a reasonable time.[6] In addition, faulty goods or services may entitle the purchaser to claim for whatever expenses s/he has incurred as a result of the fault(s). Dangerous goods should be reported to the local trading standards department.

Insurance

Many loans are covered by insurance against sickness, unemployment, etc, and, if the terms of the insurance policy are met, the policy will pay for any repayment towards contractual instalments. However, in some cases insurance companies refuse to pay – eg, if the debtor is suffering from an illness that started before the insurance policy began (a 'pre-existing condition').

The adviser must check the terms of the policy and the debtor's circumstances carefully, and negotiate with the company. It is always worth pursuing a claim and, if the insurance company is unreasonable, it should be sued (consult a specialist solicitor). Alternatively, a complaint can be made to the Association of British Insurers, the Office of Fair Trading (OFT) or the Financial Ombudsman Services (see Appendix 5).

Inaccurate calculation

Advisers must take care not to assume that the amounts owed by debtors have been accurately calculated. Advisers must check the debtor's own records of payments and that all payments have been credited to the account, and request a full statement to check this if in any doubt.

The adviser should also request that any recovery action be suspended while the matter is being investigated. It may be necessary to contact a regional or head office if negotiations with the local branch are unsuccessful. Where the creditor is not being co-operative in supplying information and the debt is regulated by the Consumer Credit Act 1974, the adviser should accompany the request for a full statement of account with a payment of £1. If the creditor fails to comply with the request within two weeks, the debt will be unenforceable until the information is supplied.[7]

2. Using the Consumer Credit Act to avoid or reduce liability

The Consumer Credit Act (see p51) regulates the ways in which most credit agreements can be set up. It gives the borrower certain rights and, if these are denied, a court may decide that the agreement is unenforceable and, therefore, the creditor will not be able to demand repayment.

Creditors must be licensed

If a creditor enters into a regulated agreement (see p51), but does not hold a current consumer credit licence, s/he cannot enforce that agreement without permission from the Director General of Fair Trading and s/he also commits a criminal offence.[8] If a creditor appears to be unlicensed – because the company is clearly new, badly organised and unprofessional, or its documentation is of a poor standard, or the adviser has not heard of it before – the adviser can check whether the creditor does have a licence by phoning the Office of Fair Trading (OFT) on 0207 211 8608. Creditors who are not licensed will sometimes withdraw at this point when the need for a licence is pointed out to them. In the meantime, the debtor should be advised that s/he need not pay and informed of her/his rights concerning harassment (see p33).

A consumer credit licence is not needed when credit is granted otherwise than in the course of a business or only occasionally – for instance, where workmates lend each other money. Nor is it needed if a shop arranges informal deferred payment, perhaps by allowing someone to come back and pay for goods the following week or at the end of the month, but does not charge interest.

The local trading standards department will usually know whether a particular creditor is licensed. If not, contact the OFT.

Early settlement of a credit agreement

If a regulated agreement is ended early, the borrower should pay less than the total amount that would have been payable if the agreement had run to full term.[9] There is a formula (the Rule of 78) laid down in regulations appended to the Consumer Credit Act.[10] This formula is a means of ensuring that the creditor can recoup those costs associated with setting up an agreement and, therefore, a lower percentage rebate will be given for settlement during the earliest parts of a credit agreement.

Checking the settlement figure is important where one agreement has already been settled early and replaced by another. (A local trading standards or consumer protection department probably has a computer program to do this.) Although generally not advisable, often people in debt have been persuaded to replace a number of debts with a single loan. If a regulated agreement has been settled early and replaced by a new one with the same company, but the correct rebate has not been given, ensure that the lender reduces the amount of the second loan by an amount equal to the underpayment of rebate, and removes all interest charged on this unnecessary portion of the second loan.

If the second loan was taken out with another company, the first company should be asked to pay the full rebate and interest on it. The adviser should consider reporting the creditor (perhaps via the local trading standards department) to the OFT. If a credit broker was used to arrange the second loan, then it too could be held responsible and should also be reported either to the trade association (see Appendix 5) and/or to the OFT.

It is generally accepted that the Rule of 78 operates unfairly to the debtor where the loan is taken out for more than 10 years. However, unless the agreement itself provides for a more generous rebate, the creditor is entitled to insist on using the statutory formula to calculate any rebate. Nevertheless, where the actual outstanding balance is apparently less than the settlement figure, it may be worth trying to negotiate for the lower figure, particularly where a high rate of interest has been charged from the start of the loan.

Extortionate credit

The Consumer Credit Act 1974[11] gives a court the power to decide that any credit agreement which is 'extortionate' can be reopened 'so as to do justice between the parties'. It specifies the factors that should be taken into account when deciding if credit is extortionate:

- The risk the creditor was taking having regard to the value of any security provided by the debtor.
- The age, health and experience of the debtor.
- Whether the debtor was under any financial pressure at the time the credit was taken out.

- Interest rates prevailing in the particular sector of the lending market at the time the credit was granted.
- Any relationship between creditor and debtor.
- Whether the credit charges were made to appear reasonable by inflating the cost of any goods/services.

If a court decides that an agreement is extortionate, it can:
- require the creditor to repay money to the debtor; *and*
- alter the terms of the agreement – eg, reduce the interest rate; *and*
- set aside either part or the whole of the agreement.

Unfortunately the courts' interpretation of extortionate is very different from most people's interpretation. This is because the Consumer Credit Act defines 'extortionate' as involving either *grossly* exorbitant payments or *gross* contravention of the ordinary principles of fair dealing. Interest rates of up to 50 per cent have generally been considered reasonable. If unsecured loans are for short periods of weeks, or for small amounts (and thus the setting-up costs have to be included in a very short period), even higher rates of up to 300 per cent have not been considered extortionate. Unsecured loans justify higher interest rates than secured loans.

Prior to the Consumer Credit Act, the Moneylenders Act 1927 defined extortionate interest as being anything over 48 per cent, but in 1981 it was ruled that this guideline should no longer apply.[12] Instead, each case should be judged only according to the criteria listed above. Subsequent case law is not particularly helpful in determining new guidelines, but the Court of Appeal has made it clear that there should be a substantial imbalance of power of which the creditor has taken advantage and that interest and security should be high. This case describes interest of 44.17 APR on a secured loan as 'bordering on the extortionate' (see p211).[13]

If a debtor believes that the credit is extortionate s/he can apply to the county court to ask for the credit agreement to be reopened under Para 3 of Part 7B PD CPR (s139 CCA), outlining as many of the above factors as are relevant. Unfortunately, although an application can be made validly within 12 years of the original loan agreement, if the debtor is seeking repayment of sums already paid, the application must be made within 6 years.[14] If judgment has already been given it may be too late to challenge the rate of interest because the Consumer Credit Act prevents an order that is inconsistent with an existing judgment.[15] So long as the debtor is still living in the property, a possession order is not necessarily a bar to an application, as the court can always review such an order.[16]

The courts are unlikely to assist a debtor who has made a bad bargain, or entered into an unwise transaction, or on the basis of a high interest rate alone. But where a creditor has imposed a particularly unfair or oppressive agreement on a vulnerable debtor, an application stands some chance of success and may at least provide a valuable negotiating tool.

Although the courts appear to accept that extortionate credit provisions are a failure of the Consumer Credit Act's aim of protecting consumers, the remedy appears to lie with Parliament.

Dual interest rate schemes (DIRS)

Sometimes a lender will attempt to apply a different rate of interest once an account is in arrears. The Consumer Credit Act prohibits creditors from increasing the rate of interest on default.[17] These attempts will often be disguised by the use of terms like 'concessionary rate' for the (lower) ordinary rate and 'standard' for the (higher) one charged once problems arise. Guidelines produced by the OFT describe these practices as 'unfair and oppressive' and recommends that their use be discontinued.[18] These guidelines make it clear that the OFT will consider revoking a credit licence if such dual interest rate schemes (DIRS) are imposed, unless:

- the additional interest charges can be shown to be realistically linked to the extra administration costs of an account in arrears;
- their existence was pointed out to the borrower in advance;
- the creditor undertook proper credit checks in advance of borrowing.

Loan agreements signed after 1 July 1995 are subject to the Unfair Terms in Consumer Contracts Regulations 1994-1999 and the OFT regards DIRS with large differentials between ordinary and penalty interest as unenforceable.

Debtors should, if necessary, use this as a defence in possession proceedings, and also complain to the OFT via their local trading standards department. However, the Court of Appeal has recently upheld a concessionary payment that provided a 'modest incentive' to the debtor as unobjectionable.[19]

Procedural irregularities in making regulated agreements

The Consumer Credit Act[20] specifies procedures that must be followed for a regulated agreement to be properly executed (see p52). Further provisions are contained in the Consumer Credit (Agreements) Regulations 1983, the Consumer Credit (Cancellation Notices and Copies of Documents) Regulations 1983, and the Consumer Credit (Guarantees and Indemnities) Regulations 1983.

An improperly executed regulated agreement is enforceable only on the order of the court.[21] Such an order can only be made where the court has considered both the creditor's culpability for the improper execution and its effect on the debtor.[22] The court has no power to order enforcement where:

- the agreement has not been signed by the debtor(s);
- the agreement does not contain certain prescribed information (see p52 for details);

- in the case of a cancellable agreement, the consumer was not given a copy of the agreement before the creditor took court action, or told of her/his cancellation rights.[23]

It is always up to the creditor to apply to the court to enforce an improperly executed agreement. The court can allow enforcement on such terms as it thinks fit – eg, reduce the amount owed by the borrower and make a time order (see p211).[24]

Mail order catalogues

A debtor may not be liable for a mail order catalogue debt if the catalogue company has failed to provide a copy of the agreement and details of the account upon request. Catalogue debts are regulated by the Consumer Credit Act 1974. The creditor must supply:

- a 'true copy of the executed agreement';[25] *and*
- a 'statement signed by or on behalf of the creditor showing the total sum paid by the debtor, the total sum which has become payable and the total sum which is to become payable' if these are requested in writing by the debtor.[26]

The only exception to these requirements is if less than five payments were required under the agreement, but in practice, most debts to catalogue companies are repayable over more than four instalments.

The adviser should write by recorded post to the catalogue company requesting the information required under the Act, together with the prescribed fee of £1. If the information is not sent out within 12 working days, the creditor is not entitled to enforce the agreement and, therefore, the debtor could cease making payments. If the company has already started legal action in the county court, the debt could be disputed on the reply to the claim – see Chapter 9.

The creditor may send a sample form, but not a signed copy. This meets the requirements of the Consumer Credit Act. However, in order to enforce through the courts, the creditor will still have to prove the debt by showing a signed copy of the agreement to the court. If the creditor is unable to do this, the court should decide not to grant an order. By failing to provide the required information, the catalogue company may be committing an offence and the adviser should report this to the local trading standards department if the information is not forthcoming after one month.

The above may be a useful tactic in any other case where the adviser has good reason to suspect that the debtor may not have signed a regulated agreement.

3. **Reducing gas and electricity charges**

Debts for the supply of gas or electricity are regulated primarily by the Gas Acts 1986 and 1995, as amended, and Electricity Act 1989, as amended. Gas and electricity suppliers, although now private companies, in the past have been in the public sector and tend to assume that their own procedures are identical with the law and that customers and advisers are legally obliged to fit in with these. This is not the case and their procedures should be challenged, when necessary, as with any business. The *Fuel Rights Handbook* (see Appendix 6) provides full details and legal references for advisers dealing with complex fuel debts.

Arrears of gas or electricity payments may be as a result of high bills. While high bills may be caused by high consumption, they may also be caused by faulty meters or estimated bills based on wrong assumptions about the amount of fuel used.

With the deregulation of fuel supplies, it may be increasingly possible to reduce charges by changing supplier. Although any bills which have been unpaid for less than 28 days are usually transferred to the new supplier, if the debt has been outstanding for longer, the old supplier may object to the transfer or impose conditions unless the arrears are paid. However, if the transfer goes ahead without objection, the arrears cannot be transferred to the new supplier.

Estimated bills

If the bill is estimated and the estimated reading is higher than the actual reading, it will be possible to reduce the amount owing. The bill will explain (often by means of an 'E' next to a reading) whether an estimated reading has been given. The adviser should ask the debtor to read the meter and request an amended bill.

Liability for electricity and gas bills

Electricity

A person is liable to pay an electricity bill if:

- s/he is the owner/occupier of the premises supplied with electricity; *and*
- s/he has either given written notice requiring a supply of electricity or has requested a supply of electricity over the phone; *or*
- s/he has signed a contract for the supply of electricity; *or*
- no one else is liable for the bill and s/he has in practice been supplied with electricity.

A person will no longer be liable to pay an electricity bill where:

- s/he has terminated any contract in accordance with its terms (but s/he will still be liable if s/he continues to be supplied with electricity); *or*
- s/he ceases to be the owner/occupier of the property, starting from the day s/he leaves the property, provided s/he has given at least two days' written notice of leaving; *or*
- in a situation where written notice was not given, on the earliest of:
  - two working days after s/he gave written notice of ceasing to be an owner/occupier; *or*

– on the next day the meter is due to be read; *or*
– when any subsequent occupier either requires/requests a supply, or signs a contract for, the supply of electricity to those premises.

Gas

A person is liable to pay a gas bill if:

- s/he was a British Gas 'tariff customer' prior to 1 March 1996 and has continued to be supplied with gas after that date; *or*
- the liability of the former tariff customer has ended or been terminated and s/he has continued to occupy the premises supplied with gas; *or*
- s/he entered into a contract for the supply of gas on or after 1 March 1996 and is being supplied under the terms of that contract; *or*
- her/his contract has come to an end or been terminated, but s/he has continued to be supplied with gas; *or*
- s/he is a new owner/occupier of premises on or after 1 March 1996 and has not entered into a contract for the supply of gas to those premises.

A person was a tariff customer of British Gas if:

- s/he was the owner/occupier of premises supplied with gas; *and*
- s/he either gave written notice requiring a supply of gas or requested a supply of gas over the phone; *or*
- no one else was liable for the bill and s/he was in practice supplied with gas.

The liability of a tariff customer ended when:

- s/he left the premises, provided s/he gave at least 24 hours' written notice that s/he intended to leave; *or*
- in a situation where written notice was not given, on the earliest of:
  – 28 days after s/he gave written notice that s/he had left; *or*
  – on the next day when the meter should have been read; *or*
  – on the day when any subsequent occupier of the premises required a supply.

A person currently liable will remain liable until:

- s/he terminates the contract by giving 28 days' notice (but if s/he remains in occupation of the premises and continues to be supplied with gas, s/he will still be liable to pay for the gas supplied); *or*
- s/he ceases to occupy the premises, provided s/he has given at least two working days' notice that s/he intended to leave; *or*
- if notice was not given, the earliest of:
  – 28 days after s/he informs the supplier that s/he has left the premises; *or*
  – the next date the meter was due to be read; *or*
  – the date when another person requires a supply of gas.

The 'beneficial user' argument

In the past, fuel suppliers have often argued, as a matter of policy, that where a consumer lives in a property with other adults, those other adults are liable for some of the cost of the fuel used if the registered consumer defaults, because they are 'beneficial users' of this fuel. Although some county courts have held in favour of fuel companies, this has never been taken to appeal and a Sheffield County Court case dismissed claims based on this argument.[27]

Where a spouse, partner or joint occupier (eg, joint tenant) has left a property and either there is no contract or it is not clear who actually required/requested the fuel supply, the liability of the remaining occupier will be a question of fact. However, if no one else is liable under the rules discussed on p88, the occupier will be liable under the terms of a deemed contract for the supply of electricity or gas.[28]

In the case of joint occupiers, provided the supplier has the address(es) of the former occupiers, the remaining occupier could argue that the arrears should be apportioned. In the case of spouses/partners where the spouse/partner had control of the household finances, s/he could argue that s/he should not be treated as liable for any fuel supplied while the spouse/partner was living in the premises. Otherwise, the supplier could be asked to apportion the arrears.

The *Fuel Rights Handbook* explains, in detail, the views of suppliers and of Ofgem (previously the Office of Gas Supply (Ofgas) and Office of Electricity Regulation (Offer)). Either Ofgem or Energywatch (previously the Gas Consumers' Council and the electricity consultative committees) should be consulted if a supplier is demanding payment from someone other than the registered consumer.

Non-fuel items

Debtors may owe money for items other than fuel, such as repairs or credit sale agreements. The adviser should reduce repayments by arranging to pay for fuel costs only and treating non-fuel items alongside other non-priority debts.

Meter faults

If a gas or electricity meter is registering fuel consumption at too high a rate, then the consumer will receive a bill that is higher than it should be. If the debtor believes a meter is faulty, the fuel supplier will check the accuracy of the meter if requested to do so.

Electricity suppliers will (usually for a charge) check the accuracy of a meter themselves and, if a dispute is not resolved by this check, a meter examiner from Ofgem (see Appendix 5) can be asked to check the meter at the premises, or by removing it. Ofgem makes no charge for this service, but a waiting period of several months is not unusual.

British Gas will first look at all appliances but will then arrange an independent test on the meter by the Department of Trade and Industry if the consumer wishes. If the consumer requests this test, s/he has to pay for it if it shows the meter is accurate. The results are legally binding. Ofgem does not normally become involved in disputes over meter accuracy except in providing advice.

If a meter has been malfunctioning, then any bill submitted is an estimate of the fuel used. This will often be reduced after representations from an adviser. If agreement cannot be reached, the supplier should be forced to prove its case in court by suing for the amount claimed. The local gas consumers' council or electricity consultative committee (see Appendix 5) may also be able to help with negotiation. If disconnection is threatened, Ofgem has the power to intervene.

Theft from coin meters

If a coin meter has been broken into and coins taken from it, the fuel supplier may claim the missing money from the consumer. The law is not clear in this area and is unlikely to become clarified, as coin meters rapidly become obsolete. However, cases in county courts have sometimes been resolved in favour of consumers where suppliers have claimed money that had disappeared from the meter.

If consumers have coin meters on their property, they have a duty of care towards both the meter and the coins inside. This means that, for example, doors and windows should be locked during the consumer's absence. The coins become the property of the fuel company as they pass into the meter.[29]

The supplier has no right to claim that money stolen from a meter should be repaid unless it can prove that the consumer failed to care for, or took, the money. If this were proved, it would be likely to take criminal action. The supplier has no right to disconnect the supply for non-payment following a theft because the fuel was paid for by the consumer. The adviser should help the consumer to present the available evidence to the supplier and use the evidence to dispute liability for repayment of the stolen money.

Meter tampering

Fuel suppliers may allege that a meter has been tampered with and, in some cases, they will disconnect the supply. Reconnection will then only be agreed if the debtor pays arrears to cover fuel estimated by the supplier as used while the meter was being tampered with. This may give rise to very high bills, as suppliers are generally unsympathetic in such cases and will overestimate the amount of fuel used during the 'tampering period'. An adviser should ask for a detailed breakdown of how such amounts have been calculated and challenge them, where appropriate, in order to reduce the amount owing.

In order to challenge the amount claimed, it is advisable immediately to take new meter readings of actual consumption, look at the number of appliances and seek help from Energywatch or Ofgem (see Appendix 5).

If high repayments or no supply are likely to cause hardship because there are old, young, sick or disabled people in the home, this should be explained to the supplier, which may agree to install a token meter in order to recover arrears gradually.

If a debtor has been prosecuted for tampering, the amount repayable to the supplier is generally not set by the criminal courts, which will probably consider only specimen charges relating to quite small amounts. It may be difficult (though not impossible) to challenge the supplier's estimate in the civil courts (eg, by defending an action for debt or seeking a declaration in the county court). Legal aid should be available for this, but judges are unlikely to be sympathetic.

If it is a gas debt and there are safe, affordable, alternative forms of cooking and heating, then it may be preferable to choose these rather than reconnection (although it should be noted that gas is often the cheapest fuel).

It may be possible to ask another member of the household to become the registered consumer in order to regain the supply quickly. However, the supplier may then try to insist on payment from the new consumer as a beneficial user (see p88).

If the supply has been disconnected, but the circumstances of the household make reconnection a matter of urgency, the best solution may be to accept the terms of reconnection offered and then consider the best strategy for paying (see Chapter 7). For further details, see the *Fuel Rights Handbook* (see Appendix 6).

Deliberately tampering with a meter in order to gain free fuel is a criminal offence. Anybody who is charged with such an offence should get good legal advice immediately. Evidence relating to who actually tampered with the meter and whether s/he intended to use fuel without paying for it needs to be examined. As in all criminal matters, people should be advised of their right to remain silent (while noting that such a silence can be used to challenge a defence which is subsequently proffered – see *Legal Action*, April 1995).

4. **If money is owed to the debtor**

There are a number of situations in which the amount being claimed can be reduced because money is owed to the debtor.

Debts to benefits providers

The Department for Work and Pensions (DWP) or a local authority may be a creditor if it is seeking to recover an overpayment of benefit, and it may be possible to reduce or cancel the amount in one of the following ways:
- check whether a claim can be backdated so that extra benefit is paid;
- claim unclaimed benefits;

- check if there are underpayments of existing benefits – for example, income support premiums.

See Chapter 6 for ways of checking benefit and always ensure that this is done thoroughly.

When a local authority is the creditor for rent or council tax arrears, a check should be made to ensure that it has paid the debtor all the relevant housing benefit or council tax benefit and backdated claims as far as is permissible.

If a private landlord is seeking possession on the grounds of rent arrears, advisers should check on unpaid housing benefit. The adviser should ask the local authority for an interim payment of housing benefit if necessary. If the rent arrears are solely due to unpaid housing benefit and the landlord issues a possession summons, the adviser should argue against any award of court costs on the basis that the action was unnecessary since the arrears had arisen due to unpaid housing benefit and it would have been reasonable for the landlord to wait for payment. (See Chapter 9, especially if the tenant is an 'assured' tenant and there are more than 13 weeks' arrears.)

Notes

1. Using the law of contract to avoid or reduce liability
1 *RBS v Etridge (No.2)* [2002] HLR 37, HL
2 *Legal Action,* April 1995
3 *Sherrin v Brand* [1956] 1 QB, 403
4 A Arden, *Manual of Housing Law,* and *Defending Possession Proceedings* (see Appendix 6)
5 s14 SGA 1979
6 s13 SGSA 1982
7 ss77-79 CCA 1974

2. Using the Consumer Credit Act to avoid or reduce liability
8 ss 39 and 40 CCA 1974
9 ss94-95 CCA 1974
10 CC(RES) Regs
11 ss137-40 CCA 1974
12 *Ketley v Scott* [1981] ICR 241
13 *Southern and District Finance v Barnes and others,* 23 March 1995, CA, *Adviser* 50 abstracts
14 *Rahman v Sterling Credit,* 20 July 2000, CA, *Adviser* 82 abstracts
15 s139(4) CCA 1974

16 *Rahman v Sterling Credit,* 20 July 2000, CA, *Adviser* 82 abstracts
17 s93 CCA 1974
18 *Office of Fair Trading Guidelines for Non-status Lenders and Brokers 1997*
19 *Broadwick Financial Services v Spencer,* 30 January 2002, CA, *Adviser* 91 abstracts
20 ss60-64 CCA 1974
21 s65 CCA 1974
22 s127(1) CCA 1974
23 ss127(3) and (4) CCA 1974
24 *National Mortgage Corporation v Wilkes,* LAG, October 1991
25 Reg 3 CC(CNCD) Regs
26 ss77 and 78 CCA 1974

3. Reducing gas and electricity charges
27 *Faulkner v Yorkshire Electricity,* October 1994, *Adviser* 50, July/August 1995
28 Sch 2B para 8 Gas Act 1986 as inserted by Gas Act 1995; Sch 4 para 3 Electricity Act 1989 as inserted by Utilities Act 2000
29 *Martin v Marsh* [1955] Criminal Law Review 781 Divisional Court

Chapter 6

. . . .

Maximising income

This chapter covers:

Maximising income is more than merely checking benefit entitlement. It should also ensure that:
- wages or other monies are raised as high as possible. This includes ensuring that all possible income disregards are applied for those claiming benefits and tax credits alongside wages;
- tax liability is as low as possible;
- a debtor is in receipt of all the possible state benefits.

If a debt adviser is not a welfare rights specialist, s/he should consult with colleagues who are, or refer cases for checking to someone who is able to undertake such a comprehensive task. Maximising income is not the same as increasing it. Maximisation means that income is not only increased, but that it cannot be increased any more.

The debt adviser's approach to income maximisation must be systematic in order to be comprehensive. Advisers must be familiar with the benefits system and the books on income maximisation in the booklist (Appendix 6). Many terms are not described fully here and the adviser who is unfamiliar with them is invited to look them up in the relevant CPAG benefits guide. Pointers to further reading are included in each section.

This chapter cannot explain all the possible ways in which income can be maximised. Instead, it points towards some common ways of increasing income for particular groups of people in debt. It assumes general advice training. It does not explain everything about each benefit or allowance but highlights issues which can give rise to extra income. Many of the ideas listed will be appropriate for groups other than those under which they are described. Many people will fit into more than one of the categories.

Some of the categorisations may appear stereotyped, but the aim of the chapter is not to compartmentalise debtors, but to provide the debt adviser with a systematic tool to ensure that individuals do not suffer unnecessarily as a result of low income.

Listed below are different types of debtor followed by a list of some significant benefits, organisations and tactics to use in maximising their income. At the end is a miscellany, 'the safety net', which includes other ways of increasing income. Note that, although arranged under convenient headings, these lists are not mutually exclusive and you should cross-refer in most cases.

Note: From April 2003 a new tax credit system comes into effect that will fundamentally change the current benefit and tax credits scheme.

1. Parents

Child benefit[1]

Child benefit is paid to people who have a child living with them, or to those who contribute to the maintenance of the child at a rate of at least the child benefit rate. Advisers must always check that a debtor with children is receiving the correct amount of child benefit. Child benefit is not normally paid for the children of new residents in Great Britain until the residents have been here for six months.

Educational maintenance allowance (EMAs)

People aged 16 to 19 living in one of the EMA pilot areas may qualify for an EMA if they stay on in full-time education. EMAs are expected to be introduced on a national basis from September 2004. Meanwhile the debt adviser should check the local position with the local education authority, careers service or the relevant college. Applications are made to the local education authority.

Other local authorities will pay means-tested awards to young people who remain at school after the school-leaving age. They are awarded at the discretion of the local authority and will not affect other family benefits. Educational maintenance allowance provision has been cut dramatically in many parts of the country over the past few years, but such benefit is often worth applying for, particularly if each application is assessed by a panel of councillors or there is an appeals procedure from officers to such a panel. A full letter of support from the debt adviser should always be submitted with such an application, explaining perhaps how the family's debt situation will prejudice the student's education if an award is not made.

Free school meals

Young people whose parents are on income support (IS) or income-based jobseeker's allowance (JSA) or are asylum seekers, and IS claimants of 16, 17 or 18 years of age who are still at school are entitled to free school meals.[2]

Students with dependent children aged 3 to 16 can apply to their local education authority for a means-tested grant to pay for their children's school meals.

For further details, see CPAG's *Welfare Benefits Handbook*.

Uniform grants

Local education authorities have a discretionary power to give grants for school uniforms or other clothing needed for attendance at school (eg, sportswear). Policies vary enormously across the country but funds for these grants have been cut greatly over recent years. The grant could be in the form of cash or vouchers. There are probably no authorities which have sufficient funds to meet all the need for school uniforms. The debt adviser should become familiar with the decision-making cycle and put in applications at the time when it is most likely that funds will be available.

For further details, see CPAG's *Welfare Benefits Handbook*.

Tax allowances

Married couples allowance was abolished from 6 April 2000 and now only applies to those aged 65 or over before 6 April 2000 (see section on retired people on p108).

The children's tax credit can be claimed by married or unmarried couples or lone parents. In the case of a heterosexual couple where neither pay taxes at the higher rate, either partner can claim or they can share the credit equally between them. Any unused credit can be transferred to the other partner. Where both partners pay higher rate tax, the credit must be claimed by the partner with the highest income and no sharing or transferring of the credit is possible.

Means-tested benefits

Family premium within some means-tested benefits[3]

Family premium is included in the applicable amount for housing benefit (HB), council tax benefit (CTB), IS/income-based JSA of any claimant who has a dependent child living with her/him.

Where such a child is in the care of the local authority and comes home for part of a week, a proportion of the family premium should be included in the applicable amount.

Starting work

Parents starting work may be entitled to one-off lump sum payments. See child maintenance bonus (p101) and back to work bonus (p112). They may be also entitled to extended payments of HB/CTB or mortgage interest run-on (see p112).

Working families tax credit[4]

Working families tax credit (WFTC) can be paid to people who have responsibility for a child(ren) and who work for 16 hours a week or more in low-paid work. The adviser should always check whether a wage earner with children is entitled. WFTC is normally awarded for six months and in most circumstances the amount paid will not change during the period of an award, even if benefit rates or individual circumstances change. WFTC will end before the six months if the youngest dependent child becomes 19 or ceases to be a dependant (eg, s/he leaves school and gets a job).

Sometimes a claim for WFTC should be delayed if circumstances are about to change (eg, hours are expected to be reduced) in order to increase the amount paid. Similarly, it may be advantageous to claim during the first week in April rather than in late March because claims received on the later date will be calculated on the basis of increased benefit rates. A careful calculation can check whether benefit lost is outweighed by any gain from an award at the new rate. Some parents might be worse off working and claiming WFTC than claiming IS/income-based JSA. This is more likely to be the case if they have mortgage costs as only IS and income-based JSA can help with these costs. Registered childminders working from home over 16 hours a week can claim either IS or WFTC. Advisers should check how parents would be better off.

See also disabled person's tax credit (DPTC) on p103.

Note: WFTC and DPTC will be replaced by a new tax credits system from April 2003.

Childcare costs[5]

The following can receive a childcare tax credit (CCTC) as part of their WFTC or a disabled person's tax credit (DPTC) award and/or have some childcare costs disregarded from their earnings for the purposes of calculating HB and CTB (see p99) to offset some of the costs of childcare:

- lone parents who work over 16 hours a week;
- couples where both partners work over 16 hours a week;
- couples where one partner works over 16 hours a week and the other is incapacitated.

The CCTC is 70 per cent of the actual cost of care by a registered childminder, school scheme or similar specified schemes, up to a maximum of £135 for one child (£94.50 CCTC) or £200 for two or more children (£140 CCTC). The credit applies to the care of children up to the age of 15, or 16 if they have a disability.

Up to £94.50 of childcare costs for one child, or up to £140 for two or more children, are disregarded as earnings in the calculation of HB and CTB for parents working 16 hours a week or more. Again, only costs of certain types of childcare, such as registered childminders, for children up to the age of 15, or 16 if they have a disability, are allowed.

For further details, see CPAG's *Welfare Benefits Handbook*.

Housing benefit[6]

Housing benefit (HB) is paid by local authorities to tenants on a means-tested basis, and must routinely be checked for all tenants. There may be particular problems for private tenants who may be unaware of the scheme. Some non-dependants living with the claimant can affect the amount of HB paid. It is therefore vital that correct details of the non-dependant's income are disclosed to ensure that the maximum HB entitlement is paid. Claims can be backdated for a maximum of 52 weeks if a claimant can show continuous 'good cause' for claiming late. Changes in circumstances should be reported immediately to avoid underpayments and overpayments.

Eligible rent

Sometimes the amount of 'eligible rent' upon which the HB is based is reduced because the local authority considers a rent is too high. The procedure which authorities have to follow before they are allowed to reduce HB in this way is complex.

Most claimants living in privately rented accommodation are subject to stringent rent restriction rules. The rules do not apply to local authority tenants. In general, claimants will have their benefit restricted unless they are paying a reasonable market rent for their accommodation, it is not too large for their basic needs and it is in the bottom half of the property market. Decisions on reasonableness and average market rent levels are made by the rent officer and the local authority is bound by a rent officer's decision. Safeguards for certain vulnerable claimants have disappeared and have been replaced with a general, cash-limited local authority discretionary power to be used in cases of exceptional hardship.

Single claimants under 25 may be subjected to even harsher rent restrictions under the 'single rent' rules.

Different rent restriction rules may apply to tenants who claimed benefit before January 1996. For claimants affected by these old rent restriction rules, rents cannot be restricted where a claimant or someone living with her/him is incapable of work (ie, satisfies the tests for incapacity for work), or is aged 60 or over, or has a child or young person living with her/him for whom s/he is responsible, unless the local authority can show that:

- cheaper accommodation is actually available to the claimant; *and*
- it is reasonable to expect her/him to move.

Income support housing costs[7]

These are paid as part of the applicable amount for IS and income-based JSA where a person has housing costs as a result of owning or buying her/his home. There are harsh waiting periods which depend upon when the housing costs began. Some claimants, however, qualify for immediate help, such as those over 60.

Council tax benefit[8]

Council tax benefit (CTB) is paid by local authorities to people who have a council tax liability and are on a low income. It is means-tested and may be payable to people in work or out of work. It is not the same as a discount or disability reduction, which is applied before CTB is calculated. It is important to initially check that any relevant discount or reduction has been applied to the council tax liability.

Earnings disregards[9]

For HB, CTB, IS and JSA, some of the money that a claimant earns can be disregarded when calculating her/his income. These amounts include income tax and national insurance contributions, as well as half of any contributions to a personal or occupational pension. However, in addition to those amounts which are individually calculated there are also standard 'earnings disregards' which apply to different groups of claimants.

Social services departments

Social services departments are empowered to give direct financial assistance, or assistance in kind (eg, food parcels), to families who have a child(ren) who has been assessed as being in need. This power is contained in section 17 of the Children Act 1989 and these payments are known as 'section 17 payments'. Although empowered to make these payments, local authority practice differs widely. In some areas, it is accepted that the disconnection of fuel supplies or an eviction could present a child with the danger of being taken into care and thus payments may be made. If a local authority refuses to make any payments, fails to follow its own procedures or decides perversely or arbitrarily about these grants, then a challenge by way of judicial review should be considered (see Legal Action Group, *Judicial Review*).

Maternity payments

Four types of payment should be checked for a woman who is about to have, or has just had, a baby. These are listed below.

Social fund sure start maternity grant[10]

For details, see CPAG's *Welfare Benefits Handbook*.

Statutory maternity pay[11]

Employees who earn above the national insurance 'lower earnings limit' and who will have worked for the same employer for more than 26 continuous weeks by the date their baby is expected – including at least part of the 15th week before the expected week of childbirth – are normally entitled to statutory maternity pay (SMP) from their employer. SMP is paid at a higher rate for the first six weeks (90% of her average weekly earnings). After this period, SMP is paid at a standard lower rate, £75 (2002/2003 rates), for another 12 weeks.

SMP does not depend upon a woman deciding to return to work (although there are certain formal notifications she needs to give about her expected date of confinement – see CPAG's *Welfare Benefits Handbook*).

If an employer refuses to pay SMP, see CPAG's *Welfare Benefits Handbook* for how to challenge this.

Contractual maternity pay

Some employers have maternity pay schemes which are much more generous than SMP. These have generally been negotiated by a trade union and should be included in the statement of terms and conditions of employment.

Maternity allowance[12]

This is a national insurance benefit, available to women who meet the national insurance contribution conditions for at least 26 weeks out of 66 before the baby is due, but whose employer is not obliged to pay SMP to them (perhaps because they have recently given up or changed their job). Self-employed women can also claim if they meet the national insurance contribution conditions. Maternity allowance has to be claimed from the Department for Work and Pensions (DWP) and is payable for 18 weeks at a standard or variable rate, depending upon whether the average earnings are more or less than the lower earnings limit (and at least above the maternity allowance threshold).

There are strict time limits for all maternity payments and recipients need to claim at the right time.

For further details, see CPAG's *Welfare Benefits Handbook*.

---

2. Lone parents

Means-tested benefits

Higher rate of family premium within some means-tested benefits[13]

The higher rate of family premium, which is an amount included in the calculation of income support (IS)/income-based jobseeker's allowance (JSA), housing benefit (HB) and council tax benefit (CTB) for lone parent claimants, was abolished for new claimants from 6 April 1998. Existing claimants will continue to receive the higher rate of the premium if:

- they remain entitled to income support; *and*
- they have not ceased to be a lone parent; *and*
- neither a pensioner nor disability premium has become applicable.

Income disregards

The earned income used to calculate HB/CTB for lone parents should be reduced by a £25 disregard,[14] and for IS/income-based JSA by a £20 disregard.[15]

Working families tax credit/disabled person's tax credit[16]

If a lone parent works 16 or more hours a week, s/he may be able to claim working families' tax credit (WFTC) (see p97) or disabled person's tax credit (DPTC)(see p103).

Childcare costs[17]

Lone parents who work more than 16 hours a week and need to pay a childminder or a childcare scheme for looking after their child(ren) can offset some of this cost. They will receive a childcare tax credit (CCTC) as part of their WFTC or DPTC award. Additionally, childcare costs, subject to a maximum, are disregarded as income for calculating HB and CTB (see p99).

See CPAG's *Welfare Benefits Handbook* for further details.

Starting work

Extended payments of income support, housing benefit and council tax benefit and back to work bonus

Lone parents who find employment may be entitled to up to two weeks of IS when they start work[18] and up to four weeks of extended payments of HB and CTB[19] (see p112) or up to four weeks of income support mortgage interest run-on.[20]

Lone parents starting work may also be entitled to a back to work bonus (see p112).[21]

Child maintenance bonus[22]

A lone parent who comes off IS/income-based JSA as a result of taking a job or increasing her/his hours may be entitled to a child maintenance bonus. For each week that the lone parent's IS/income-based JSA was reduced by an amount of child maintenance s/he will receive £5, or the actual reduction if this was less.

A lone parent who comes under the child support scheme 'new rules' and qualifies for a child maintenance premium (see below) will not be entitled to a bonus.[23] See CPAG's *Welfare Benefits Handbook* for further details.

Child support maintenance premium

A lone parent who receives child support under the 'new rules' scheme is entitled to have £10 of that child support disregarded for IS and income-based JSA. The new child support scheme was due to come into force in April 2002 but has been delayed due to problems associated with the IT system.

Tax allowances

The additional personal allowance for children was abolished from 6 April 2000. In addition to a parent's own personal allowance s/he can claim children's tax credit where there is responsibility for a child. Extra children's tax credit can be claimed for the first year of the child's birth if this is on or after 6 April 2002.

For further help, contact the children's tax credit helpline on 0845 300 1036.

Note: The children's tax credit will be abolished from April 2003 and replaced by a new tax credits scheme.

Lone parent rate of child benefit[24]

The lone parent rate of child benefit was abolished from 6 July 1998. Some claimants will be able to continue to receive this rate.

For further details see CPAG's *Welfare Benefits Handbook*.

3. Sick and disabled people

Disability living allowance

Disability living allowance (DLA) is a non-means-tested benefit. It is paid regardless of savings and any other income. It is not counted as taxable income. It is not taken into account as income for the purposes of calculating means-tested benefits in almost all circumstances.

DLA consists of a care component,[25] payable at three different rates, and a mobility component,[26] payable at two different rates. It is paid to those who are eligible who claim under the age of 65. The mobility component is for people with difficulty getting around. The care component is for people with attention and/or supervision needs.

A claimant who is 'terminally ill' (ie, suffering from a progressive disease from which it would not be unexpected for her/him to die within six months) will qualify automatically for the higher rate care component. These are known as claims under the 'special rules'.

Many DLA claimants can increase their income by claiming a higher rate of one of the components than they already receive. Advisers should be aware that in trying to claim a higher rate of one of the components, there is a risk that the component already being paid may be taken away. The debt adviser should get specialist help, if necessary, but should never assume that a claimant is receiving the correct rate.

Entitlement to DLA may give rise to an entitlement to income support (IS), income-based jobseeker's allowance (JSA), housing benefit (HB) and council tax benefit (CTB) (or higher amounts if they are already paid) and these should, therefore, also be checked/claimed.

For further information, see CPAG's *Welfare Benefits Handbook*.

Disabled person's tax credit[27]

Disabled person's tax credit (DPTC) is a means-tested benefit for people who work more than 16 hours a week, earn low wages and have a disability. Take-up is low partly because there are a number of disadvantages associated with claiming DPTC.

The 'better-off' problem means that certain people may be worse off claiming DPTC. Recipients of incapacity benefit (IB) or severe disablement allowance (SDA) should investigate whether they are better off continuing to claim these benefits and working under the permitted work rules which replaced the therapeutic earnings rules from 8 April 2002. Some claimants with disabilities can work more than 16 hours a week and remain on IS. Again, check if it would be better to take this option rather than claim DPTC. Those in receipt of incapacity benefit and SDA prior to receiving DPTC can go straight back on to that benefit if they stop working within two years. In practice, it is unlikely to be as simple as this. Those who work for anything other than a very short period of time may be declared fit for work.

For further information, see CPAG's *Welfare Benefits Handbook*.

Attendance allowance[28]

Attendance allowance (AA) is a benefit for people who are aged over 65 and who need either attention from another person in connection with their bodily functions, or supervision in order to avoid substantial danger to themselves.

There are two rates of benefit, the higher of which requires a claimant to need attention or supervision during both the day and the night. Advisers should always check that the higher rate is awarded where appropriate.

A claimant who is 'terminally ill' (ie, who is suffering from a progressive disease from which it would not be unexpected for her/him to die within six months) should be awarded the higher rate of AA immediately, as in the case of the higher rate care component of DLA.

For further information, see CPAG's *Welfare Benefits Handbook*.

Invalid care allowance[29]

Invalid care allowance (ICA) is paid to people who devote substantial time (35 hours a week or more) to caring for someone who is in receipt of AA or the middle or higher rate of the DLA care component. Changes to ICA rules come into effect from October 2002, which will remove the upper age limit. From April 2003 ICA will be renamed 'carer's allowance'. Advisers should note:

- Those getting ICA may be entitled to a carer premium if they claim IS/income-based JSA, HB or CTB. However, ICA is taken into account in full for the purposes of these benefits.
- A major reason for failure to claim ICA is that claimants who receive an 'overlapping benefit' are told that ICA will not improve their position and do not reclaim when the overlapping benefit ends. Overlapping benefits are those that are also intended to provide a basic income (incapacity benefit, retirement pension, etc).
- If someone cares for a person who is not a member of her/his household, s/he can still claim ICA if s/he meets the conditions. It is worth remembering that ICA recipients receive a Class 1 national insurance contribution credit.

Note: Receipt of ICA prevents the person being cared for receiving a severe disability premium with her/his IS, income-based JSA, HB and CTB. Therefore, careful consideration must be given, or specialist advice sought, to ensure that the client is aware of all the implications.

For further details, see CPAG's *Welfare Benefits Handbook*.

Premiums included in the applicable amount for IS/income-based JSA/HB/CTB

Carer's premium[30]

This premium is included in the applicable amount of claimants who either get ICA or would do so but for their receipt of an 'overlapping' benefit. Many people who do not live as part of the same household as the AA/DLA claimant may not realise that they would be eligible for ICA in respect of the care that they provide. The possibility of carer's premium may make a new claim beneficial.

Disabled child premium[31]

This is not payable if a child has her/his own capital of more than £3,000. It is important to inform the Department for Work and Pensions (DWP) if the child's capital falls below £3,000 so benefit can be reassessed.

One of the qualifying conditions for this premium is blindness. The premium is also payable if a child receives DLA.

Disability premium[32]

This is added to the applicable amount of people who are in receipt of a 'qualifying benefit' (DLA, incapacity benefit long-term rate, an invalid car, etc). Claimants who have been incapable of work for one year are also eligible for the premium, as are those who are registered blind. Claimants may be able to get backdated medical certificates from their GP. A claim for incapacity benefit should be made to establish incapacity for work, even if there is no entitlement to incapacity benefit.

Change claimant

If a heterosexual couple live together as husband and wife, only one of them can be the claimant for means-tested benefits. The choice of which partner makes the claim can affect a couple's entitlement to the disability premium which may be part of their applicable amount for IS (for income-based JSA, the claimant must be capable of work). One way of qualifying for this premium is for the claimant to have been continuously incapable of work or treated as incapable of work for 364 days. To qualify for this premium through this route the person incapable of work must be the claimant.

For further details, see CPAG's *Welfare Benefits Handbook*.

Severe disability premium[33]

This is included when the person receives a 'qualifying benefit' (AA, middle rate care or higher rate ca. ˙ of DLA) and has no non-dependant over 18 normally residing with her/him and no one gets ICA for looking after them.

Enhanced disability premium[34]

This can be paid in addition to the disability and severe disability premiums where a person is under 60 and receives the higher rate care component of DLA.

Civil compensation for damages

There are many circumstances in which a claim in a civil court for damages (ie, compensation for a wrong done or an obligation not carried out) can arise. Most common of these are personal injury claims, which are made against an individual or organisation if that person or organisation has been negligent in causing damage, either by doing something or by failing to do something. Injury caused by negligence can be an issue in road traffic accidents, accidents at work or in the street and other public places. Damages for personal injury can be very substantial.

Refer to a solicitor

Claims for personal injury should normally be made within three years of the injury becoming known, but the law in this area is very complex. If it is possible that a debtor has suffered in a way that could give rise to a claim for compensation, s/he should be referred without delay to a solicitor or advice agency specialising and experienced in personal injury work. Some solicitors offer a free interview to personal injury claimants so that they can examine the likelihood of a claim succeeding, usually through a personal injury referral scheme, such as Accident Line. Legal action for compensation can be costly. Publicly-funded legal services are only available (in England and Wales) for certain categories of personal injury claims and only then if the person is financially eligible and the case is deemed as having sufficient merit by the Legal Services Commission. If a person is not eligible for publicly-funded legal services, solicitors might help with such cases on a conditional fee basis if it is likely that s/he is going to win something, because their costs will be awarded in addition to damages.

Minor personal injury claims (eg, for a sprain suffered in a fall over an uneven paving stone) should never be settled on the basis of accepting what the insurers of the person responsible for the injury offer, as though this were a fixed amount or as though the insurers were offering disinterested advice. The debtor must be referred to a specialist.

For more information contact:

- The Law Society for details of members of The Law Society's personal injury panel on 0207 242 1222;
- Accident Line on 0800 19 29 39 or, alternatively, visit its website www.accidentlinedirect.co.uk.

Industrial injuries benefits[35]

If a debtor has suffered a personal injury at work s/he may be entitled to an industrial injury benefit. S/he will have to satisfy the industrial injury condition. For more details on this see CPAG's *Welfare Benefits Handbook*.

Health benefits

IS and income-based JSA give automatic entitlement to free prescriptions, dental treatment, optical vouchers and fares to hospital. WFTC and DPTC recipients are entitled to these benefits if they earn below £11,250 net a year. Other people qualify for free or reduced-cost treatment on the grounds of age, pregnancy (and for one year after childbirth), certain illnesses and disabilities and low income. Certain war pensioners also qualify.

Charges for some NHS treatment are now very high in relation to a low weekly income and these health benefits must be claimed if debt is to be avoided. It is important to check whether a debtor requires, or is likely to require, any health benefits and to claim in advance (particularly if the claim is made on low income grounds which may take some time to settle). The claim on low income grounds is made on form HC1 or HC1(RC) if in a care home (available from the DWP, post offices, some CABx, etc). People claiming free prescriptions on the grounds of age or because they are in receipt of a qualifying benefit will merely need to state this on the reverse of the prescription.

Those who do not qualify for free prescriptions and who need them frequently can purchase a prepayment certificate which reduces the overall cost. The form for England is FP95, for Wales FP95W, and for Scotland EC95.

For further details, see CPAG's *Welfare Benefits Handbook*.

Housing benefit[36]

Housing benefit (HB) is paid to tenants on low incomes. Claimants who are sick and/or disabled may qualify for premiums within their applicable amount which will increase their potential to receive HB and/or CTB (see p104).

Council tax benefit[37]

A client who has a liability to pay council tax may qualify for council tax benefit (CTB) (see p99).

Incapacity benefit[38]

Incapacity benefit is payable (subject to national insurance contributions) during the first 28 weeks of illness to those who cannot get statutory sick pay and thereafter to others who are incapable of work.

Claimants will periodically be required to fill in a questionnaire (form IB50). A decision will be made, based on this, about whether or not to send them for an examination by the DWP's medical service. The completion of the IB50 is, therefore, crucial and the debt adviser should ensure that it is well filled in and a copy is kept.

Where a person suffers from both mental and physical illnesses, the calculation of her/his incapacity (which is done according to supposedly objective 'points' awarded against descriptors) will be more complex. Specialist advice should be sought if necessary.

Many people have days on which their incapacity is greater than others. The debt adviser should ensure that they do not exaggerate their abilities but rather tell the DWP's medical service doctor, or list on the IB50, the worst case and then explain how often this applies.

Certain people are exempt from the personal capability assessment. These include people with a severe and progressive immune deficiency state, severe mental illness, severe learning disability, progressive neurological or muscle wasting disease, dementia or people registered blind. Sometimes people with these (and/or the other diseases which bring exemption) are unaware of their right to exemption, or their doctor's diagnosis is either not specific enough or does not concur with the medical service doctor. In these cases, specialist help will be required. People who are terminally ill should always be exempt.

For further information, see CPAG's *Welfare Benefits Handbook*.

Tax allowances

A person who is registered blind, or satisfies the Scottish or Northern Ireland equivalent, can claim a blind person's allowance for the whole tax year. Any unused allowance can be transferred to a spouse. Where both spouses are registered blind, the allowance can be claimed for each of them. It may be possible for this allowance to be granted for the previous tax year if the person has provided proof of blindness at the end of that year, even where s/he is not registered at that time, perhaps due to registration delays.

Council tax disability reduction

A disabled person may be entitled to a reduction in her/his council tax where the dwelling in which s/he lives has features which are, due to the nature of her/his disability, essential or of major importance. An application must be made in writing to the local authority. See CPAG's *Council Tax Handbook* for more details.

4. Retired people

Retirement pension[39]

A few months before retirement age (men aged 65, women aged 60), the Department for Work and Pensions (DWP) normally sends out a claim form (BR1). The final award is calculated from a person's national insurance contribution throughout her/his working life. If s/he is offered only a reduced retirement pension the situation should be examined carefully. In some cases, this is correctly based upon an incomplete contribution record (as a result of periods spent not working, abroad, in prison, etc). However, in some cases employers have deducted national insurance contributions and have not paid these over to the national insurance fund. In such cases, any available evidence (which may not be as formal as P60s or pay slips) should be gathered to support someone's claim that s/he did pay contributions in a particular period.

A claim for retirement pension can only be backdated up to three months so it is important to claim in time.

A male retirement pensioner whose wife does not have a pension of her own will be awarded a lower rate (category B) retirement pension for her. Widows and widowers may also qualify for a category B pension if certain conditions are met.

There is also an addition payable with retirement pension for any dependants a person has. However, the Government intends to abolish the child dependency increases from April 2003 as part of the new tax credits system.

For further details, see CPAG's *Welfare Benefits Handbook*.

Income support – for those over 60, known as the minimum income guarantee (MIG)

Pensioner premium[40]

This is paid for people aged 60 to 74 years old and for people aged 75 to 79, when it is sometimes referred to as enhanced pensioner premium, and a higher pensioner premium for people over 80, or others (see below).

The pensioner premiums are now paid at the same rate, with a higher amount for a couple. However, it is important to identify entitlement to the higher pensioner premium as this brings more generous earnings disregards and may help to satisfy entitlement to disabled person's tax credit (DPTC) (as one of the qualifying conditions).

Higher pensioner premium[41]

This is added to the applicable amount of:
- people aged 80 and over;
- people eligible for the pensioner premium who receive one of the qualifying benefits described under disability premium (see p105);
- anyone getting the disability premium just before her/his 60th birthday who has continued to be eligible for it ever since. Qualifying via this third route is more complicated than the others and it should always be checked.

For further details, see CPAG's *Welfare Benefits Handbook*.

Tax allowances

A higher personal allowance can be claimed by those aged 65 to 74 and an even higher amount by those over 75.

People aged 65 or over before 6 April 2000 may still be entitled to married couple's allowance. It is paid in addition to the personal allowance and is given to the husband, unless the couple choose for the wife to receive half or all the allowance. Any unused married couple's allowance can be transferred to the other partner. There is a lower amount where either partner is aged 65 to 74 and a higher amount for those 75 or over.

Housing benefit/council tax benefit[42]

Retired persons on a low income may qualify for housing benefit (HB) (p107) and/or council tax benefit (CTB) (see p99). The limitation on a local authority's rights to restrict 'high' rents, described above under the section on people with disabilities, also applies to households in which someone aged 60 or over lives, unless the pre-January 1996 rules apply.

Income support housing costs[43]

The stringent waiting period for income support housing costs payments does not apply where the claimant or their partner is over 60.

5. Unemployed people

Jobseeker's allowance[44]

Jobseeker's allowance (JSA) is a benefit payable to unemployed people who register with the Employment Service and who are available for work and actively seeking work. JSA may be income-based (means-tested) or contribution-based (paid if national insurance contribution conditions are satisfied and for a maximum of 182 days).

Some principal problems which arise with JSA are outlined below.

Sanctions[45]

If it is decided that a person has left her/his job voluntarily, or lost it through misconduct, or has failed to apply for a job, then a decision maker is empowered to disqualify that person from JSA for up to 26 weeks or, in the third case, to refuse JSA payments if this happened repeatedly. Such curtailments or sanctions should always be challenged and, in particular, the 26-week period of disqualification should be seen as a maximum to be used only in cases where a job was given up in a wholly premeditated and voluntary fashion. A sanction may be applied for other reasons – eg, not agreeing a jobseeker's agreement or refusing to carry out a 'jobseeker's direction'. The sanction period for the latter is two or four weeks.

Hardship payments[46]

If benefit has been refused, the claimant may be able to claim hardship payments from the Department for Work and Pensions (DWP). There is no automatic right to hardship payments and not all claimants will be eligible. People with children or with a partner who is sick, who has a disability or who is pregnant are more likely to qualify. The payments are discretionary and subject to a restrictive means test. If payments are refused, the claimant can challenge the decision by appealing.

For further details, see CPAG's *Welfare Benefits Handbook*.

Tax rebate

A person who is unemployed or is laid off (where an employer fails to provide work for an employee) may be entitled to a tax rebate at the end of the tax year. However, this will be reduced or may be cancelled out if s/he receives JSA, as this is taxed.

Money in lieu of notice

If someone is dismissed (including redundancy) and either cannot work the notice period because of illness or the employer does not wish her/him to do so, s/he should be paid money in place of the wages that s/he would have earned during that period. Notice rules are laid down and these are dependent upon age and length of service. Some employees may be entitled to a longer period of notice under the terms of their contract with the employer. The contract may be written or unwritten.

For further details, see the Department of Trade and Industry's Rights to Notice and Reasons for Dismissal (PL707), available from www.dti.gov.uk.

Private pensions

Debtors who are members of an employer's (occupational) pension scheme or a private pension plan may be entitled to take benefits from these plans before the normal retirement age if, for instance, they become permanently incapable of work. Benefits available from pension schemes should be closely examined and independent financial advice should be sought.

Redundancy payments

An employee who is not in an excluded occupation, and is under 65, or below the normal retirement age for her/his occupation if this is less than 65, and loses her/his job through redundancy will be entitled to a statutory redundancy payment. If a statutory redundancy payment has not been made or has been based upon lower wages than the person's normal pay, this should be referred to an employment tribunal, but there is a strict six-month time limit from the date of termination for making such an application.

In addition to these statutorily required redundancy payments, some workers are also entitled to larger payments under their contract (generally negotiated by the trade union).

For further details, see the Department of Trade and Industry's Redundancy Payments (PL808) available from www.dti.gov.uk.

Guarantee payments

If an employer fails to provide work for (lays off) an employee, then s/he must pay a guarantee payment for the first five days of lay-off in any six-month period. These payments are commonly overlooked, particularly by small employers and especially where lay-off is caused by bad weather or other occasional but unavoidable causes. Sometimes the employer does not know about guarantee payments and will pay when they are pointed out. Guarantee payments can be enforced through an employment tribunal. Specialist help should be sought, particularly where a debtor has worked for the employer for less than one year. A debtor should be advised about joining a trade union. Advice can be obtained from the Advisory, Conciliation and Arbitration Service (ACAS).

For further details, see the Department of Trade and Industry's Guarantee Payments (PL724) available from www.dti.gov.uk.

Starting work

Claimants starting work may be entitled to one-off lump sum payments – see child maintenance bonus (p101) and back to work bonus (below) or extended payments of out-of-work benefits (see p101 for extended payments of income support (IS) for lone parents and below for housing benefit (HB)/council tax benefit (CTB)).

Back to work bonus[47]

If an IS or income-based JSA recipient has had part-time earnings and consequently received a reduction in her/his benefit, s/he can receive up to half the amount of reduction in her/his benefit as a lump sum when s/he comes off benefit and enters full-time work.

Housing benefit and council tax benefit extended payments[48]

Claimants on IS or income-based JSA whose entitlement ends because they start work or increase their hours may be entitled to a four-week extension in the payment of their HB or CTB or their IS housing costs.[49]

6. The safety net

This final section contains ways of maximising income that apply to several types of debtor and which have not been covered above.

Charities

There are thousands of charities in England and Wales, many of which have substantial income that they distribute directly to individuals in need. Charities all have very strict rules that govern to whom they can give money (or other benefits). Many will have a committee that sifts applications and meets on a cyclical basis. Some of the very large charities will receive thousands of applications in a year and may place limits on people from whom they are prepared to accept applications – eg, from social workers only.

It is worthwhile investigating less well known charities to approach, in addition to major charities. These will be either locally based or will specialise in helping particular people. There are many very small local charities that rarely receive any applications at all, and if a debt adviser can identify these and build a relationship of trust with the secretary or trustees, it may be possible to gain a steady stream of donations, albeit modest. Some charities will expect a person to have exhausted other statutory provision before approaching them – eg, the social fund. The publication *A Guide to Grants for Individuals in Need* provides a list of local and national charities, advises on the most appropriate charity and gives guidance on how to make a successful application.

Lump-sum payments or regular payments of up to £20 per week will not count as income for the purposes of income support (IS), housing benefit (HB) and council tax benefit (CTB).

Armed services charities

Various charities exist specifically for ex-service people or their dependants. These are well organised, with national networks of contacts, and often have very considerable funds. If someone has served in the armed forces (perhaps as part of their 'national service'), these charities can be approached to help with debt. See *A Guide to Grants for Individuals in Need* for details of national headquarters of these groups, or try the local phone book. In addition, many regiments will have their own benevolent funds and these can usually be contacted through a request to the regimental or unit headquarters.

Trade unions

Many trade unions will have central hardship funds for members or ex-members. Branch funds are sometimes voted for this purpose if a request is made. Unions may also be involved in various benevolent funds and charities associated with particular industries. If someone has been a member of a union it is worth approaching the union for lump-sum payments or, in some cases, ongoing support.

Equal pay rules

The equal pay rules mean that a woman should not be paid less than a man for work of equal value. Where a working woman is in debt, it is always worth checking whether these rules might help increase her income. Specialist help from the Equal Opportunities Commission, a law centre or trade union may be necessary to pursue a claim.

For further details, see Equal Opportunities Commission briefing papers.

Overpayments

If an amount of benefit to which a claimant is not entitled has been paid, this is an overpayment. The rules on overpayments of HB and CTB differ from those for other benefits. For the latter, an overpayment is recoverable if the Department for Work and Pensions (DWP) or tax credit office can show it has been caused by a claimant's misrepresentation or failure to disclose a material fact.[50] If there is any doubt about whose fault the overpayment was, the claimant should appeal to a tribunal.

Overpayments of HB/CTB are recoverable unless caused by official error and no relevant person caused the official error and no relevant person could reasonably have been expected to realise s/he was being overpaid.[51]

Even if a recoverable overpayment has occurred, the adviser should always check the amount being recovered in great detail. Ensure, for example, that the correct earnings disregards and any offsets have been applied on a weekly basis. If a claimant's circumstances have altered during the period of overpayment, the calculation may be complex. Rates of recovery of overpayments are negotiable and the debt adviser should always consider this. There is a discretionary power to waive recovery in exceptional circumstances.

For further details, see CPAG's *Welfare Benefits Handbook*.

Capital

If a claimant has capital of more than £3,000, or £6,000 if aged over 60 (£10,000 if s/he is living in residential care), this will be assumed to generate a tariff income which will be offset against any IS, income-based jobseeker's allowance (JSA), HB or CTB payable.[52] This is known as the lower capital limit. For working families' tax credit (WFTC)/disabled person's tax credit (DPTC) the lower capital limit is £3,000 in all circumstances.[53] There is also an upper capital limit. If a claimant has more than this amount s/he will not be entitled to any benefit at all. If a person deliberately disposes of this capital in order to become entitled to benefit, the DWP may decide that s/he can be treated as still being in possession of it.

This rule is often used with no real evidence that the spending was linked to a desire to be able to claim benefit. This is particularly so where a large amount of money has been spent in a short period and on items which are judged by the DWP to be frivolous – eg, holidays. Unless there is clear evidence of a positive intention to spend in order to be able to claim benefit, then the decision should be challenged.

For further details, see CPAG's *Welfare Benefits Handbook*.

Social fund[54]

The social fund comprises two separate elements. Some payments (ie, maternity grants, funeral expenses, winter fuel payments and cold weather payments) have specific mandatory rules, and if the claimant satisfies these s/he will be entitled to a payment.

Decisions on the rest of the social fund are largely at the discretion of local DWP officials. There are some basic rules that must be satisfied. The claimant must:

- be in receipt of IS or income-based JSA. This does not apply to crisis loans. In the case of budgeting loans, s/he must have been receiving the benefit for 26 weeks;
- not have too much capital;
- not be applying for certain excluded items.

From 6 April 1999 the budgeting loan scheme has changed, making it less discretionary and more focused on legally binding factual criteria when making determinations.

Assuming the claimant satisfies the basic entitlement rules, s/he should apply to the social fund. S/he should not be put off by what DWP officials might suggest about low chances of success. If s/he is refused a grant or a loan, or s/he does not consider the amount offered is sufficient, the decision can be challenged by asking for a review. If the claimant is still dissatisfied, s/he should ask for a further review by a social fund inspector. There is nothing to lose by taking such action because the fund is discretionary.

For further details, see CPAG's *Welfare Benefits Handbook*.

Tax reliefs

Tax reliefs are amounts that are deducted from taxable income in recognition of money necessarily spent by the taxpayer in working. Tax reliefs for the self-employed should be calculated by a specialist adviser.

For employed people, it is possible (though it requires arguing in every case) to claim relief on any money that is spent to enable a job to be done, but which is not refunded by the employer.

Tax reliefs should be claimed on a tax return form, accompanied by a covering letter and any supporting evidence – eg, an itemised phone bill.

Items for which tax relief is commonly claimed include:
- membership of professional bodies;
- special clothing for work;
- using heating/lighting or the telephone at home for work;
- buying tools;
- buying a car (paying interest on a car loan).

Tax reliefs are important because they are neglected by the majority of taxpayers.

War pensions

There are a number of different schemes providing benefits for those disabled, or for the dependants of those killed, in either the First World War or any conflict since 3 September 1939. Some of these schemes only cover members of the armed forces but there are others that apply to auxiliary personnel, civil defence volunteers, merchant mariners and ordinary civilians.

Who qualifies and what payments they can receive are complicated. For who may be eligible, contact the veterans helpline on 0800 169 2277 or write to the Veterans Agency, Norcross, Blackpool, FY5 3WP.

Bereavement benefits

The old system of widows' benefits was replaced on 9 April 2001 by bereavement benefits which can be claimed by both men and women whose spouse died on or after 9 April 2001. For details if a spouse died prior to this date see CPAG's *Welfare Benefits Handbook*.

There are three main types of bereavement benefits, all of which are based on national insurance contributions. These are:
* bereavement payment (a lump-sum payment of £2,000);[55]
* widowed parent's allowance – a weekly benefit paid to widows or widowers who have children or widows who are pregnant at the time their husband dies;[56]
* bereavement allowance – a weekly benefit paid to widows or widowers who were 45 or over when their spouse died.[57]

These benefits are not contributory if a spouse dies as a result of an industrial accident or disease. The contribution conditions are different for each of the benefits.

Bereavement allowance and widowed parent's allowance cease when the claimant remarries and are suspended during any period of cohabitation. The exact circumstances should be examined to see whether or not a couple's relationship actually consists of living together as husband and wife.

Problems can also arise if the DWP doubts the existence or validity of a marriage. This is most often the case where a marriage took place abroad.

For further details, see CPAG's *Welfare Benefits Handbook*.

Notes

1. **Parents**
 1 s141 SSCBA 1992
 2 s512 Education Act; Sch 14 para 117 IAA 1999
 3 Sch 2 para 3 IS Regs; Sch 1 para 4 JSA Regs; Sch 2 para 3 HB Regs; Sch 1 para 3 CTB Regs
 4 s128 SSCBA 1992
 5 Regs 46 and 46A FC Regs; Regs 51 and 51A DWA Regs; Regs 21(1)(c) and 21A HB Regs; Regs 13(1)(c) and 13A CTB Regs
 6 s130 SSCBA 1992
 7 Sch 3 IS Regs; Sch 2 JSA Regs
 8 s131 SSCBA 1992
 9 Sch 8 IS Regs; Sch 6 JSA Regs; Sch 3 HB Regs; Sch 3 CTB Regs
 10 Reg 5 SFM&FE Regs

11 ss164 and 165 SSCBA 1992
12 s35 SSCBA 1992

2. **Lone parents**
13 Sch 2 para 3 IS Regs; Sch 1 para 4 JSA
     Regs; Sch 2 para 3 HB Regs; Sch 1 para 3
     CTB Regs
14 Sch 3 para 4 HB Regs; Sch 3 para 4 CTB
     Regs
15 Sch 8 para 5 IS Regs; Sch 6 para JSA Regs
16 s128 SSCBA 1992
17 Regs 46 and 46A FC Regs; Regs 51 and
     51A DWA Regs; Regs 21(1)(C) and 21A
     HB Regs; Regs 13(1)(c) and 13A CTB
     Regs
18 Regs 6(2) and 6(3) IS Regs
19 Sch 5A para 1 and Reg 62A HB Regs; Sch
     5A and Reg 53 CTB Regs
20 Regs 6(5)-(8) IS Regs
21 Reg 7 SS(BTWB) Regs
22 Reg 3 SS(CMB) Regs
23 Reg 4 SS(CMPMA) Regs
24 Reg 4 CB&SS(FAR) Amdt Regs

3. **Sick and disabled people**
25 s72 SSCBA 1992
26 s73 SSCBA 1992
27 s129 SSCBA 1992
28 s64 SSCBA 1992
29 s70 SSCBA 1992
30 Sch 2 para 14ZA IS Regs; Sch 2 para
     14ZA HB Regs; Sch 1 para 16 CTB Regs;
     Sch 1 para 17 JSA Regs
31 Sch 2 para 14 IS Regs; Sch 1 para 16 JSA
     Regs; Sch 2 paras 14 and 15(6) HB Regs;
     Sch 1 paras 15 and 19(7) CTB Regs
32 Sch 2 para 11 IS Regs; Sch 1 paras 13
     and 14 JSA Regs; Sch 2 para 11 HB Regs;
     Sch 1 para 12 CTB Regs
33 Sch 2 para 13 IS Regs; Sch 1 paras 15
     and 21 JSA Regs; Sch 2 para 13 HB Regs;
     Sch 1 para 14 CTB Regs
34 Sch 2 para 13A IS Regs; Sch 1 paras 15A
     and 21A JSA Regs; Sch 2 para 13A HB
     Regs; Sch 1 para 14A CTB Regs
35 s94 and Sch 7 SSCBA 1992
36 s130 SSCBA 1992
37 s131 SSCBA 1992
38 s30A SSCBA 1992

4. **Retired people**
39 ss44, 44A, 48A, 48B, 48BB, 48C, 51 and
     78 SSCBA 1992; Reg 10 SS(WB&RP)
     Regs
40 Sch 2 para 9 and 9A IS Regs; Sch 1 paras
     10 and 11 JSA Regs; Sch 2 paras 9 and
     9A HB Regs; Sch 2 paras 9 and 10 CTB
     Regs

41 Sch 2 para 10 IS Regs; Sch 1 para 12 JSA
     Regs; Sch 2 para 10 HB Regs; Sch 1 para
     11 CTB Regs
42 ss130 and 131 SSCBA 1992
43 Sch 3 IS Regs; Sch 2 JSA Regs

5. **Unemployed people**
44 s1 JSA 1995
45 ss19(5) and (6), 20 and 20A JSA 1995
46 Regs 140 and 146 JSA Regs
47 Reg 7 SS(BTWB) Regs
48 Sch 5A para 1 and Reg 62A HB Regs; Sch
     5A and Reg 53 CTB Regs
49 Reg 6(5)-(8) IS Regs

6. **The safety net**
50 s71 SSAA 1992; s1 and Sch 1 TCA 1999
51 Regs 98 and 99 HB Regs; Reg 83 CTB
     Regs
52 Reg 53 IS Regs; Reg 116 JSA Regs; Reg
     45 HB Regs; Reg 37 CTB Regs
53 Reg 36 FC Regs; Reg 40 DWA Regs
54 SFM&FE Regs; SFCWP Regs; SFWFP
     Regs; Social Fund Directions; ss138 and
     140 SSCBA 1992; s66 SSAA 1992
55 ss36 and 60 SSCBA 1992
56 ss39A and 60 SSCBA 1992
57 ss39B and 60 SSCBA 1992

7

Chapter 7

Dealing with priority debts

This chapter covers:
1. Deciding on priorities (below)
2. The general approach to priority debts (p121)
3. Strategies for dealing with priority debts (p123)
4. Emergency action (p143)
5. Penalties for non-payment of priority debts (p148)

1. Deciding on priorities

Advisers need to identify which debts must be dealt with first – ie, which debts are priority debts. The criteria for deciding which debts are priorities are for the most part 'objective' – the severity of the legal remedies available to creditors determines the degree of priority. If non-payment would give the creditor the right to deprive the debtor of her/his home, liberty, essential goods and services, then that debt will have priority.

Debtors often believe that priorities must be decided on the basis of the amount owed, or that any debt that is subject to a court order should be a priority. But the existence of a court judgment does not automatically accord priority status to a debt and there are millions of judgments given by courts in England and Wales each year for debts that remain unpaid. These debts would only become a priority if the enforcement methods open to a creditor through a court posed a serious threat to the home, liberty or essential goods of a debtor.

Recognising priority debts

Using the criteria outlined above, the following are priority debts.

Secured loans

Mortgages and all other loans that are secured against a debtor's home are priorities because non-payment can lead to possession action by the lender and homelessness. One of the strategies outlined in this chapter must be adopted immediately for any secured loan in arrears.
- Immediate contact should be made with the lender.

- If it is not possible to make a definite offer of payments immediately, ask for more time (eg, 14 or 28 days) and for the lender to take no further action during this period. If possible, the debtor should be advised to pay at least the contractual instalments in the meantime.
- If the lender has already begun possession action, see Chapter 9.

Rent arrears

Rent arrears are a priority because they can lead to possession action by the landlord and homelessness.

- Immediate contact should be made with the landlord, even if further detail is required before an offer can be formulated. If possible, the debtor should be advised to pay at least the weekly/monthly rent in the meantime.
- If rent arrears are owed to a local authority or housing association as providers of 'social housing', these landlords may have policies on seeking repossession which allow tenants to repay arrears at a level they can realistically afford.
- Any outstanding housing benefit claim should be urgently pursued.
- If the landlord has begun possession action, see Chapter 9.

Council tax (or community charge)

Council tax and community charge arrears are a priority because non-payment allows local authorities to use bailiffs to seize a debtor's property and could ultimately lead to imprisonment.

- Immediate contact should be made with the council, even if further details are required before an offer can be formulated. If possible, the debtor should be advised to pay at least the monthly instalments towards the current year's council tax bill in the meantime.
- Any outstanding council tax benefit/discount/exemption claim(s) should be urgently pursued.
- If bailiffs are dealing with the collection of arrears, see Chapter 11.
- If the magistrates' court has issued a liability order (which allows the council to use bailiffs) or a committal warrant (which orders imprisonment), see Chapter 10.

Fines, maintenance and compensation orders

Unpaid fines, maintenance and magistrates' court compensation orders are a priority because non-payment could lead to a loss of essential items to bailiffs or, ultimately, to imprisonment. A distress warrant allowing bailiffs to seize goods can be issued once payments due are in arrears (see Chapter 10).

A committal warrant ordering imprisonment can be issued if bailiff action is unsuccessful and arrears are unpaid due to 'wilful refusal or culpable neglect' (see p258).

- Immediate contact should be made with the magistrates' court and a request for lower instalments made as soon as possible. It is much easier to arrange low

instalments before enforcement action has begun because such an arrangement can be agreed by clerks with power delegated from magistrates.
• If bailiffs are dealing with the collection of arrears, see Chapter 11.

Gas and electricity charges

Payment for gas and electricity are priorities because suppliers have powers to disconnect for non-payment of bills. Such sanctions do not apply to arrears on non-fuel items (eg, cookers or the cost of central heating installation) purchased from gas and electricity suppliers, and thus debts for such items are not a priority.

Until the passing of the Water Industry Act 1999, water companies also had powers to disconnect for debt and so were considered priorities. This is no longer the case and attempts by water companies to retain priority status should be resisted as this would be inequitable to other creditors. Obviously a realistic amount for current consumption of water must be included in the financial statement but not for arrears. Help with arrears may be available from one of the water industry's trust funds.
• If disconnection is threatened, make immediate contact with the supplier to challenge this and discuss ways of paying for the supply.

Tax and VAT

These debts are a priority – particularly where the debtor is still trading – because Inland Revenue and Customs and Excise officials can seize goods from the debtor to cover unpaid tax without requiring a court order.

Both creditors instigate bankruptcy proceedings even when they are unlikely to receive any payment and the Inland Revenue can take court action in the magistrates' court as well as in the county court. If the debtor does not keep to the terms of the order, but can afford to do so, s/he can be imprisoned. A debtor can only be imprisoned for VAT arrears if there has been a fraudulent evasion.
• Immediate contact should be made with the tax/VAT inspector to ask for time to pay or to make a repayment proposal.
• If bailiffs are involved, see Chapter 11.
• If action has been started in the magistrates' court, see Chapter 10.
• If action has been started in the county court, see Chapter 9.

Hire purchase/conditional sale

Some hire purchase (HP) or conditional sale agreements will need to be treated as priority debts if they are for goods that are essential for the debtor to retain (eg, a car for work in the absence of suitable public transport), because the creditor would have powers to repossess the goods if payments were not kept up – see Chapter 4.

National insurance contributions

Class 4 national insurance contributions for self-employed earners are a priority as they are assessed and collected by the Inland Revenue along with unpaid income tax.

2. **The general approach to priority debts**

Once identified, priority debts must be dealt with quickly and effectively. General rules about how this should be done are listed below. There are also specific ways of dealing with particular types of debts.

Advisers should work through the following list of tasks.

- Ring the creditor as soon as possible, even if the adviser does not have all the necessary information on which to base a strategy. This will help prevent further action and alert the priority creditor to the involvement of an independent agency.
- If necessary, take emergency action to prevent the immediate loss of home, liberty, essential goods or services (see p143).
- Negotiate the amount, manner and time of repayments.
- Ensure the debtor is clear about whom to pay, when to pay and how much to pay.
- Encourage the debtor to seek further assistance from the adviser if s/he is facing practical difficulties with repayment arrangements.
- Monitor the initial strategy with the debtor. If the debtor's circumstances change or the original strategy is unsuccessful, the adviser and the debtor will need to decide whether to adopt a new strategy or whether the details of the original strategy can be modified.

Consider carefully the amount of income included as 'available' to the debtor. The fact that a debt is priority may influence the way in which a partner's income is treated. A partner may not wish to pool her/his income and liabilities if only non-priority debts have been accrued (and there is no need to – see p41). However, where serious consequences – such as loss of home – could be suffered by the debtor's partner, s/he may wish to contribute towards repaying a debt for which s/he is not legally liable. This situation can also occur when a debt arose whilst someone was with a previous partner.[1]

Points to note

- Although many priority creditors will have their own collection policies which act as guidelines for their officers, these are not above negotiation.
- It may be necessary to contact someone in a position of authority within the relevant organisation before policies can be changed.

- Accounting periods, such as local authority financial years or other periods between quarterly bills, should not be taken as absolute dates by which current liabilities must be met.
- Secured lenders often argue that arrears should be repaid in quite short periods. However, in an important decision the Court of Appeal suggested that a reasonable period to clear arrears might be the whole of the remaining term of the mortgage.[2] Thus, if a possession action were started halfway through a 30-year mortgage, it would be possible for the court to suspend an order on payment of an amount which would repay the mortgage together with the arrears over the next 15 years.

The debtor should be advised to:
- start making payments immediately the strategy has been decided, as this will encourage the creditor to accept the arrangements; *and*
- where possible, set up a direct debit or standing order to ensure a payment arrangement is kept.

Creditors should be asked to:
- confirm the agreed strategy in writing. They may often require a financial statement (see p47), list of debts and written proposal from the adviser before providing such confirmation.

'Negative equity'

Negative equity occurs when the value of a debtor's property falls below the amount due under her/his mortgage or other loans secured on it. This means that, even if her/his property were sold, the debtor would not be free of debt and would still owe an amount (the negative equity) to the creditor.

The strategies that follow depend on the housing market. If houses cannot be sold easily, then creditors will not want to repossess and a sale by the debtor may be undesirable or impossible. When property values fall, creditors try everything they can to avoid taking possession of homes for which they would become responsible and which could not easily be sold. However, advisers should not necessarily rely on this as lenders will sometimes decide to cut their losses and repossess regardless.

Where there is only negative equity, a creditor could probably be persuaded to allow a debtor to remain in possession on generous terms. However, if house prices are on the rise, the debt adviser must be aware of the risk that creditors will want to repossess property on which arrears still exist. If possible, it is important to reach an agreement in advance to avoid such a situation.

Negative equity will alter the applicability of a few of the strategies that follow. However, in most circumstances the approach remains the same, either because a lender is prepared to ignore the negative equity or because it becomes an unsecured and non-priority debt (see Chapter 8).

The 'mortgage shortfall' on the sale of the property

For what to do where there is a 'mortgage shortfall' or a claim from a mortgage indemnity insurer, see Chapter 9. These debts, though non-priority at present, need to be dealt with because by nature of their size they represent a potential future problem if an attachment of earnings order, bankruptcy or charging order were to be used at some future date.

3. Strategies for dealing with priority debts

'Interest only' payments (for mortgages and secured loans)

A large proportion of secured borrowing is repaid by means of monthly payments that combine interest with a repayment of capital. In such cases, a debtor can reduce the payments if the creditor will agree to accept payment of the interest alone without any capital repayment. Creditors will need to be persuaded that a request to make interest-only payments is not just a delaying tactic or an excuse for being unable to pay anything. If a debtor can afford to pay the interest which is accruing on an agreement, advisers are not asking for anything that is either out of the ordinary or generous.

Payments towards the capital can be resumed if the debtor's financial circumstances improve in the future. Some creditors are prepared to wait until property is sold for the capital to be repaid. Creditors will need to be satisfied either that the arrangement is a temporary one and that the debtor will be able to resume making the full contractual payments or that repayment of the capital by some other method is adequately assured.

When applicable

The payment of interest only is applicable to repayment of mortgages and other secured loans where payment of the interest and capital cannot currently be afforded. Interest-only payments cannot be used for:
- any agreement where the total interest has already been added at the beginning of the loan period and the whole amount secured against the property, because no interest is accruing on a daily basis (but see 'Reduced payments' below); *or*
- an endowment mortgage, because payments are already for interest only and the capital is repaid in a lump sum at the end of the period of the loan by an endowment insurance policy (see p70).

Advantages
- It is easily accepted by priority creditors.
- It prevents further action.
- It may avoid a bad credit rating.

Disadvantages

- The debt will take longer to clear than it would if either full payments were maintained or a reduction in capital charges could be negotiated.
- A court could not suspend a possession order for mortgage arrears on this basis. The Administration of Justice Act 1973 requires the arrears to be cleared in a 'reasonable time'.[3] However, the court could use its powers to order an adjournment instead of a suspended possession order, to allow payments of interest only.[4] This would only be possible for a short period (eg, six months), after which time an increased payment would be necessary to clear the arrears in a reasonable time (see p127). Similarly, the court could not make a time order on this basis as it would not provide for payment of the loan (see p136).

Useful arguments

Most building societies or other secured lenders will have policies that allow local managers to accept interest-only payments for a fixed period (perhaps six months). These can often be arranged over the telephone (although any such arrangement must be confirmed in writing and a financial statement may be required).

For debtors in receipt of income support (IS)/income-based jobseeker's allowance (JSA) that does not yet cover the whole mortgage interest, many creditors will accept half the interest until the debtor becomes eligible to have the full interest met by the Department for Work and Pensions (DWP).

Checklist for action

- Telephone/write to the creditor to propose the strategy and request written confirmation that the strategy is accepted.
- Explain the cause of the debtor's inability to pay – through a change of circumstances or economic factors such as high interest rates.
- Advise the debtor of how much to pay and when.
- Consider direct payments for debtors on IS/income-based JSA (see p139).
- Consider advising the debtor to set up a direct debit/standing order to ensure payments are kept up.

Reduced payments

A creditor can be asked to renegotiate the contract that has been made so that a debtor can afford the payments. There are three principal ways in which payments can be reduced:

- Ask the creditor to charge a lower rate of interest, either for a period of time (eg, the next year) or for the rest of the loan, even if interest has already been added to the amount payable over the whole period of the loan.
- Ask the creditor to agree to reduce the amount outstanding on a loan so that future charges (perhaps of interest only) are affordable by the debtor.

- Ask the creditor to allow repayments to extend over a longer period, thereby reducing the capital portion of the repayments. There would need to be enough equity to allow this – the amount of equity can be calculated by deducting the total amount of all loans secured on the property from the market value of the property.

When applicable

- If the debtor cannot possibly meet her/his original contractual obligations.
- If interest rates have risen significantly since the contract was taken out, or if the interest originally charged was significantly higher than available elsewhere or if, despite a general fall in interest rates, a high rate of interest continues to be charged. This is particularly true where a time order would be appropriate (see p211).
- If the outstanding balance includes capitalised arrears of interest/charges, particularly where these have accrued at a high rate.
- If the property against which the loan is secured is worth less than the capital outstanding, some lenders will reduce their capital outlay rather than continue to chase something which is effectively no longer a fully secured debt.
- If there is another secured loan against the same property, the first mortgagee may reduce the amount outstanding on its loan in order that the debtor can borrow enough to be able to pay off the second mortgagee and then have one remaining loan. This might be a likely option if the second mortgagee is considering repossession, and the first mortgagee wishes to continue with the business it has with its customer.
- Where adverse publicity would be attracted by a repossession.
- Where the property market is slow and, therefore, repossessed properties are unlikely to be saleable.

This strategy is not applicable to endowment mortgages.

Advantages

- It reduces the amount payable and protects the debtor's home and essential goods.

Disadvantages

- It will be difficult to gain acceptance of these strategies from creditors, particularly where the loan is more than fully secured.
- Repaying an interest-bearing debt over a longer period may result in additional interest being paid, unless the payments are sufficient to cover this or the rate of interest is reduced accordingly.
- It is sometimes better to allow the home to be lost if it will end indebtedness and ensure appropriate rehousing by a local authority or housing association (see p168).

- If the capital outstanding is to be reduced, it may require changes to the legal charge (see p151) which is registered on the property.

Useful arguments

- If a time order would be possible (see p211), a creditor may prefer to negotiate changes voluntarily rather than have them imposed by the court, especially if adverse publicity is likely to be attracted by a case.
- Point out any failure by the creditor to prevent the build up of arrears, to send the debtor regular statements of account or to inform the debtor of the need to increase payments to cover the ongoing arrears/charges. If the alternative for the creditor is repossession of a house, point out that the strategy being offered may be cheaper, as possessing and reselling a property is a time-consuming, and therefore expensive, way of making a profit.
- Payments are more likely to be maintained if set at a lower level, affordable by the debtor.
- The sums already paid by the debtor have given the creditor a more than adequate return on the loan.

Checklist for action

- Telephone/write to the creditor to propose the strategy and request written confirmation of acceptance of the strategy.
- Advise the debtor of how much to pay and when.
- Consider a time order in Consumer Credit Act cases (see p211).

Capitalise arrears

Where arrears have built up (particularly on a repayment mortgage), a creditor can be asked to add these to the capital outstanding and simply charge interest on the new capital amount. This effectively draws a line under the arrears and allows the debtor to repay them along with the sum originally borrowed at an affordable rate.

When applicable

- This strategy is particularly useful when there is an improvement in the debtor's circumstances following a period in which arrears have built up. For example, if a debtor has recently become employed after a period of unemployment or returned to work after a long strike or period of sickness, then, provided her/his payment record was previously satisfactory, most creditors will agree to capitalise the arrears.
- Creditors will only capitalise arrears if the market value of the property is significantly greater than the amount of capital currently outstanding. They will not usually do so if it would lead to the capital outstanding being more than the value of the property.

Advantages
- It regularises the situation.
- It prevents further action.
- It can avoid a bad credit rating as the debtor will no longer have arrears.
- The repayments are affordable.

Disadvantages
- The repayments on the loan will be increased if the loan is to be repaid within the original contractual period.
- The debt may take longer to pay off, in which case the debtor would pay more.
- If interest charges rise, the effect is greater than when capital was less.
- Tax relief may not be available for the extra interest payments on the capitalised arrears. However, if the amount of arrears to be capitalised is less than either £1,000 or 12 months' interest, whichever is the greater, the total loan will remain within the MIRAS (mortgage interest relief at source) scheme.[5]
- Interest is in effect paid on the arrears throughout the term of the mortgage.
- For IS/income-based JSA claimants, the DWP will not usually meet the cost of additional interest due to capitalising arrears.

Useful arguments
- Some creditors will only consider capitalising arrears after a trial period in which a debtor makes regular repayments, particularly where there is little prospect of an improvement in circumstances.

Checklist for action
- Telephone/write to the creditor to propose the strategy and request written confirmation that this is agreed.
- Advise the debtor of any change in repayments.
- For debtors on IS/income-based JSA, advise them to notify the DWP of changes in repayments.

Scheduled payment of arrears

On secured loans

Arrears may be repayable over a period of time. This may be a set amount each month, calculated to repay the arrears over a period of time acceptable to the creditor/lender and/or court. Proposals to clear arrears over three years are regularly accepted.

However, advisers should be imaginative in their suggestions for repayment schedules. Staggered offers, where initially a smaller amount is offered towards the arrears, followed by increased payments, are very useful for repayment in anticipation of improved circumstances. Such arrangements may be made directly with the creditor or may need to be ratified by the court if proceedings have already started.

If there is no spare income immediately available, so that only the normal contractual payment can be met, creditors can sometimes be persuaded to accept no payments towards the arrears for several months, particularly if there is plenty of equity (see p151) in the property. In extreme circumstances, they may be persuaded to accept no payments at all for one or two months where inability to pay is clearly temporary.

Many creditors will have their own internal rules about over how long they will spread the repayment of arrears for secured borrowing, but two years is increasingly acceptable, and some companies are willing to accept repayments over four years. These periods can generally be increased by contacting regional or head offices when necessary.

Rescheduling rent, fuel, council tax or community charge debts

Creditors will use various criteria to decide whether the repayments are acceptable, including the level of arrears, the debtor's previous payment record and the likelihood of the debtor remaining as a tenant, consumer or council tax payer in the same location.

When applicable

- After there has been an improvement in financial circumstances (as described above for capitalising arrears).
- After a debt adviser has helped the debtor to prioritise payments of debts.

Advantages

- Provided the income is available to repay both contractual payments and something towards the arrears, this should be readily acceptable to creditors.
- It prevents further action.

Disadvantages

- It increases the debtor's outgoings at a time when financial shortage may not be over.
- In the case of loans, interest will be accruing not only on the capital outstanding but also on the unpaid arrears so that, unless the creditor agrees to freeze interest and other charges, the repayments will continue beyond the original contractual period (sometimes, on unregulated agreements, at a penalty rate which is higher than that normally charged; check the agreement to find out if this is the case).

Useful arguments

- Creditors will need to understand why payments have not been made in the past and why they are now possible.
- Advisers must explain any changes of circumstances and the fact that the debtor has now reorganised her/his financial affairs to give priority to these debts.

- Advisers will need to explain to creditors that ability to pay needs to be the guiding factor in deciding on repayment of arrears. A carefully drawn up financial statement will be the adviser's most useful tool.
- The strategy is considered sensible by a reputable money advice agency.
- Where the creditor/court is reluctant to accept that payments will be increased, the arrangement can be made subject to a review after a set period – eg, six months – so that the creditor's position is not prejudiced.

Checklist for action
- Telephone/write to the creditor to propose the strategy and request written confirmation of the repayment schedule.
- Advise the debtor of how much to pay and when.
- If necessary, make the appropriate application to court.

Change to repayment mortgage

An endowment mortgage is a secured loan on which only interest is payable, accompanied by an endowment life assurance policy which will pay off the capital borrowed either at the end of the agreed term or on the death of the borrower (whichever is the sooner).

There are many potential problems with endowment mortgages. In broad terms, they will only be to the borrower's advantage where (as pre-1990) the return on the investment made by the insurers on the stock market exceeds the cost of borrowing money. These general problems (described by the Financial Services Authority (FSA) in its press release 'Endowments – The FSA's conclusions and actions' issued December 1999) affect all endowment mortgages. The FSA estimates that as many as 500,000 households have endowment policies that will not cover their loans.[6]

For the borrower in debt there is a particular problem because it is essential that the full amounts of both the endowment insurance payments and the interest on the loan itself are repaid on, or shortly after, the due date. The creditor relies on the insurance company to repay the capital amount lent at the end of the loan period and, if payments to the insurance company stop, the creditor is likely to call in its loan on the basis that its security is at risk, unless acceptable proposals for repayment of the capital at the end of the loan can be made. If, on the other hand, payments to the creditor are not kept up, then the amount outstanding on the loan rises and is likely to become more than the amount which will be produced by the insurance policy at its maturity. Thus, endowment mortgages are less flexible than repayment ones.

To have flexibility to capitalise arrears, extend the period of a loan or negotiate repayment of arrears over several years, an endowment mortgage would have to be changed to a repayment mortgage. For some debtors, the creditor will do this automatically once the endowment premium is significantly in arrears.

7

Chapter 7: Dealing with priority debts
3. Strategies for dealing with priority debts
• •

However, to cease paying, surrender or sell an endowment policy is a major financial decision and should not be taken without specialist advice from an independent financial adviser. In particular, where a person's poor health means that s/he may not get another endowment policy in the future, s/he should carefully consider her/his options.

When applicable
- When a debtor is in arrears with an endowment mortgage, or likely to go into arrears, and therefore a renegotiation on the terms of the mortgage is necessary.
- When a debtor is unable to maintain the payments on the endowment policy.
- When the debtor is facing a substantial period of low income and needs to achieve more flexibility.
- When the endowment policy has been running for several years – in which case it may be beneficial to cash it in or sell it and use the lump sum to pay off arrears. Advice from a number of independent financial advisers should always be taken before surrendering an endowment policy. Some insurers charge significant fees for early surrender and, in addition, the value of the policy depends on the state of the stock market. The surrender value of a policy is frequently much less than the amount of the payments made into it to date. A sale of the policy usually produces a better return. Therefore, even if changing to a repayment mortgage, it is probably better if possible to keep the endowment policy (without making any new payments into it) until such time as it matures.

Advantages
- Increased flexibility in the long term.
- Ensures that the home is not lost.
- Reduced monthly outgoings.

Disadvantages
- There may be an arrangement fee to convert the mortgage to a capital repayment type.
- The debtor will have to arrange separate life insurance cover.
- Some or all of the money already invested in the endowment policy may be lost (especially if it is relatively new).
- If a policy is 'assigned' to the lender, then the surrender/sale value may be taken by it in full (though negotiation is possible).

Useful arguments
- Creditors will be sympathetic if this is the only way of paying the mortgage as it does ensure that the loan is repaid.

Checklist for action

- Get independent advice from a specialist in this field (but not from a broker who was involved in setting up the endowment mortgage as s/he may be motivated by the knowledge that s/he will probably lose commission if a recently taken out endowment policy is cancelled).
- Telephone/write to the creditor to propose the strategy and request details of new instalments and the surrender/sale value of the endowment policy.
- Advise the debtor of how much to pay and when.
- If disposing of the endowment policy, ensure the full surrender value of the policy is paid to the debtor. Selling it rather than merely surrendering may produce a larger sum.
- Advise the debtor to arrange new life assurance cover for the mortgage, if necessary.
- For debtors on IS/income-based JSA, advise them to notify the DWP of changes in repayments.

Mortgage rescue schemes

This is the name given to schemes that allow a borrower to become a tenant (wholly or partly) in a home when s/he has become unable to meet the mortgage repayments. The finance industry, local authorities and housing associations were all encouraged to offer these as part of a government package to meet the 'repossession crisis' at the start of 1992.

Rescue schemes are offered by individual creditors to debtors of their choice. They are usually financed by a housing association or local authority, which will buy the home from the debtor, clear the mortgage and then allow the debtor to remain in the home as a tenant. A variant is the shared-ownership scheme, which involves a housing association buying part of the home and allowing the householder to remain in possession as a part-owner/part-tenant with the right to buy back the entire property.

Despite encouragement, such schemes are very rare. However, they do exist and debt advisers should find out what is available locally.

When applicable

- A rescue scheme, if available, will be worth consideration if arrears are not too high (and thus the creditor will be paid in full on a sale), if the debtor wants to remain in a particular house (perhaps to keep children in a school) and rehousing by the local authority is either impossible (eg, because the debtor is not in 'priority need') or undesirable (because the local authority uses bed and breakfast accommodation).
- A rescue scheme could be useful if the debtor expects her/his circumstances to improve in the mid-term. If outgoings can be reduced for a few years, s/he might be able to buy her/his home back again.

Advantages
- It will be acceptable to priority creditors.
- It maintains housing stability.
- Capital (if there is equity) can be released for other purposes (perhaps to pay off debts).
- It may be possible to combine with a partial write-off so that the mortgage lender accepts settlement of its loan at a reduced amount.

Disadvantages
- The debtor ceases to be a homeowner.
- Such schemes are rare.
- Legal costs will reduce equity (particularly if it is seen as a short-term strategy and buy-back is anticipated).
- It will not assist debtors who expect to be long-term IS/income-based JSA claimants (who can get mortgage interest paid anyway).

Useful arguments
- Where schemes exist, creditors and housing associations or local authorities will want to use them if they will reduce outgoings and are deemed to be appropriate. It should not be difficult to argue for a scheme. However, at certain times of the year money allocated to scheme budgets may be low and debt advisers should argue for a delay in possession proceedings if a creditor would accept one of these schemes but for the timing of the application.

Checklist for action
- Become familiar with schemes available locally (particularly if not tied to one lender).
- Contact the creditor and/or 'rescuer' as early as possible.
- Ensure that the debtor receives independent legal advice prior to sale.
- Ensure that the terms of sale and tenancy are understood.

Sale of property

There are a number of circumstances in which it may be advisable to sell a home in order to repay priority creditors.

When applicable

To advise someone to give up her/his home may appear to be conceding defeat. However, there are circumstances in which the loss of a home may be inevitable and indeed the best option. These include:
- if a debtor has somewhere else to live as well as the home in question;
- if a debtor has considerable equity in the home but now the property is too large or in the wrong place for her/his current requirements and a more suitable home could be purchased at a lower price;

- where repossession is inevitable. For example, where the debtor's available income is too low to make an acceptable repayment proposal, a better price may be paid to an owner-occupier than a mortgagee in possession. This can give a debtor equity but her/his need for a suitable home must be paramount (see disadvantages below).

This strategy, although superficially tempting, is not generally applicable merely to repay priority debts. But when other circumstances make the sale of the home inevitable or even desirable, then the clearing of the debts can be achieved in this way and there may even be sufficient capital to make a full and final offer to non-priority creditors (see p158). As it is such a major decision, it is important that the debtor and her/his family reach it for themselves. The debt adviser must ensure that the advantages and disadvantages of this strategy are understood and that the debtor has time to consider all the implications.

For former local authority tenants who have exercised their right to buy, it is worth checking if the local authority or a housing organisation to whom their stock is now transferred operate a 'buy back' scheme, whereby the owner could sell the house back to the local authority and remain as tenant. It is, however, necessary to check whether the debtor is still within the discount-repayment period – ie, a proportion of the purchase price will have to be repaid to the local authority.

Advantages
- It is easily accepted by priority creditors and courts. (Time will be given for the sale to go through if necessary.)
- It prevents further action.
- It may avoid a bad credit rating.
- It may release capital for other purposes.
- A better price will generally be achieved by a voluntary sale than by a financial institution selling the house after it has repossessed it.
- It is an alternative to bankruptcy proceedings either as part of an individual voluntary arrangement (see Chapter 12) or an informal arrangement with creditors.
- It may avoid court costs if the strategy is agreed prior to repossession action (see p201).
- It can be seen by the debtor as an opportunity for a fresh start.

Disadvantages
- The debtor is forced to move home. This is costly and disruptive.
- Unless the debtor actually has a buyer, it may be seen by the creditor and the court as a way of delaying possession/eviction proceedings.
- If rehousing by a local authority is required, it may be difficult to persuade it that the debtor has not made her/himself intentionally homeless.

- It may not be possible to find alternative housing which is ideally suitable.
- The debtor may lose money if the housing market is depressed and s/he has only recently bought the house.

The debtor or adviser must explain the circumstances to the local authority in advance and gain its approval of the strategy, in writing, and its acceptance that homelessness is inevitable rather than intentional. For further details, see *Manual of Housing Law* (Appendix 6).

The Housing Act 1996 has reduced the help given to homeless people. Advisers will have to decide as circumstances change whether or not the offer of only temporary accommodation or a probationary tenancy make this strategy inadvisable.

Useful arguments

- Creditors prefer to avoid repossessing and selling property and so can be persuaded of the advantages to themselves of being relieved of having to sell an empty property. A house is likely to sell more quickly if inhabited.
- The loan will be repaid in full, or if not, and the creditor is unreasonably refusing to agree to a sale, the court can override the creditor's objections.[7]

Checklist for action

- Ensure that the debtor will have suitable alternative accommodation.
- Inform the creditors of the proposed strategy.
- Advise the debtor to put the house on the market. If a quick sale is required, the debtor should explain this to the estate agent.
- Discuss with the debtor how much to pay, if anything, towards the mortgage until the house is sold, particularly if there is negative equity.

Refinancing

Refinancing means taking an existing loan or loans and negotiating a new loan to cover them.

When applicable

When a priority debt (often a second mortgage) has terms that are very expensive, then it can be worth refinancing it. It is common for possession of homes to be sought by second mortgagees (who may have lent money for double glazing or other home improvements) from debtors who had always managed to pay their first mortgage. The repayments on a medium-term loan from a finance company may be greater than those on a standard building society mortgage – a debtor could typically be required to pay as much per month on a home improvement loan of £10,000 as s/he was required to pay on her/his main mortgage of £50,000.

In these circumstances, the first mortgagee will generally be sympathetic to the debtor and will not want to lose the business that it is doing with her/him simply because the debtor has become unable to repay the very high rate of interest charged by the second mortgagee.

Even though possession action is not threatened, it may be obvious that a debtor's financial problems are caused by excessive repayment on a particular priority debt. Refinancing may, therefore, be more appropriate than asking the creditor to capitalise arrears as this could result in higher repayments than if the loan were refinanced.

Refinancing should be used when a cheaper form of borrowing is available to replace a priority debt. Debt advisers need to ensure that refinancing is arranged with building societies or banks and not with finance companies which may charge higher rates over shorter terms.

Advisers could consider a maturity loan for debtors approaching retirement age (see p167).

When refinancing is not applicable

- For unsecured debts. Refinancing is often suggested by mortgage brokers and financial advisers as a means of 'putting all debts in one basket' and consolidating unsecured debts such as credit cards or loans. Unsecured loans should never be replaced by secured loans unless it reduces the debtor's monthly outgoings and the debtor can make the repayments as well as servicing her/his other essential expenditure and any other financial commitments.
- When either substantial setting-up charges have already been added to a loan account and are not refundable, or the interest payable over the period of a loan was added to the capital sum at the beginning and the rebate available on this is not substantial (see Chapter 5).

Advantages

- Outgoings to priority creditors can be reduced.
- Credit rating is maintained.
- It prevents further action.

Disadvantages

- The amount required to pay off an existing secured loan may be higher than the equity in the home, particularly where the early settlement provision is onerous.
- Once refinanced, payments may be required over a longer period.
- Debtors may find it difficult to obtain refinancing if they have existing arrears.
- There is often a higher rate of interest charged for the first year of the loan.
- There will be charges for setting up the new loan.
- It may involve converting non-priority debts into priority debts.

Useful arguments

- If the first mortgagee is being asked to refinance a second secured loan, whenever possible emphasise the debtor's good payment record.
- Point out the business advantages to the creditor of refinancing the loan rather than allowing another secured lender to take possession.
- If they will not agree immediately, it is worth advising creditors to review their decision after three to six months of regular payments.

Checklist for action

- Advise the debtor to take independent financial advice and obtain full details of the refinancing, including new monthly instalments, arrangement fees, interest rates, annual percentage rate (APR), etc.
- Inform the existing creditor of the proposed action.

Time orders

A time order is granted by the county court and sets new terms for a loan if the court believes that the original terms should be altered (see p211 for further details).

When applicable

- A time order can only be granted for loans regulated by the Consumer Credit Act 1974.[8]
- Time orders are most likely to be granted if the original terms of the contract were particularly disadvantageous to the borrower, or if the borrower's circumstances have changed radically during the period of the loan. Time orders will usually be granted if the change in circumstances is expected to be temporary but can be made for a longer period where the court accepts that it is just to do so.[9]

Advantages

- The agreement of the creditor is not required if the courts can be persuaded that an order should be made.
- The order is backed by the force of the court.
- Once made, the creditor can take no further action as long as payments are maintained.
- It can reduce interest rates and set payments at an affordable level.

Disadvantages

- Time orders are difficult to get. The court is required to draw a distinction between the 'deserving' and the 'undeserving' debtor.

- For secured loans regulated by the Consumer Credit Act, the debtor will have to wait until the creditor either issues a default notice or takes court action before applying for a time order.
- Creditors' costs may be added to the mortgage debt.

Useful arguments
- See Chapter 9.

Checklist for action
- See Chapter 9.

Voluntary charge

Most unsecured debts are not priorities. However, very occasionally they fall into this category and in these rare cases it may be advisable to offer to turn an unsecured debt into a secured one. This is achieved by offering the creditor a 'voluntary charge' secured on the debtor's property.

When applicable

It cannot be stressed too strongly that, although often requested by creditors, a voluntary charge is only very rarely in the debtor's best interests. The only circumstances in which it may be advisable are:
- if it is the only means of stopping the Inland Revenue or Customs and Excise from taking action to commit a person to prison;
- if it is the only means to stop someone issuing undesirable bankruptcy proceedings (note that although many creditors threaten bankruptcy proceedings, including issuing a statutory demand – see Chapter 12 – this very rarely results in an actual petition for bankruptcy);
- if it is essential to the debtor that no county court judgment is made – for example, because s/he would lose her/his job if this happened (note that a time order may be a more appropriate way of stopping a county court judgment);
- where the creditor refuses to accept the debtor's repayment offer and/or freeze interest/charges and the repayments the debtor can afford are not sufficient to cover these;
- if the creditor has an automatic right to impose a charge – eg, Community Legal Service funding debts – which will incur higher costs than a voluntary charge;
- if it is known that when a person's current home is sold s/he will not need the proceeds of sale – eg, if s/he is terminally ill. In this situation, a voluntary charge could reduce the stress of lengthy negotiations with creditors.

It is essential that the debtor seeks legal advice before signing a voluntary charge in order to safeguard her/his position should the creditor decide to enforce the charge and apply for an order for sale. In addition, the debtor must ensure almost always that the creditor will agree to freeze interest so that the charge is against a fixed sum that will not swallow up the equity.

Agreement also needs to be reached about whether any instalments are required by the creditor in addition to the charge. All these issues need to be agreed before a voluntary charge is made, and must be part of a written agreement.

Advantages
- A voluntary charge is likely to satisfy a creditor and therefore mean that no further action is taken.
- Once their capital outlay is secured by a voluntary charge, many creditors will agree to add no interest until the property is sold and to accept the debtor's repayment offer or even no (or only token) payments.
- Some lenders can be persuaded not to enforce their charge – ie, not to force a sale.

Disadvantages
- By changing the status of a debt, a debtor may be ensuring that her/his liberty is not threatened, but s/he is potentially putting her/his house under threat.
- There may be costs incurred by the debtor seeking legal advice to ensure a watertight agreement is drawn up.
- If the debtor has a partner who is a co-owner of the property, the partner will have to sign the charge document and thereby make her/himself liable for the debt.
- The creditor may still insist on payments being paid in addition to having the charge.

Useful arguments
From the debtor's point of view the voluntary charge is only ever the lesser of two evils. To the creditor, the adviser may need to argue that:
- it is the only way in which it will practically ever get any money;
- making people bankrupt does not often produce money, but a voluntary charge will do so;
- if house prices increase then so will the equity against which the charge is made.

Checklist for action
- Consider whether any other strategy would be more appropriate – eg, a time order.
- Advise the debtor to obtain full details of the terms of the charge in writing from the creditor.
- Ensure the debtor receives legal advice about the agreement before signing.
- Check that interest is frozen and all the other terms are acceptable.

Direct payments from income support/income-based jobseeker's allowance

Certain priority arrears can be paid directly from an income support (IS)/income-based jobseeker's allowance (JSA) claimant's benefit at a set weekly amount.[10] If this is done, then the creditor concerned can demand that payments for current liabilities also be met in full from benefit.

Direct payments are commonly used to pay off arrears of gas and electricity charges as an alternative to disconnection, or rent arrears as an alternative to eviction. In some circumstances, direct payments can be made without the claimant's consent – eg, council tax arrears (see below).

When applicable

- Direct payments are useful if the alternative is either the disconnection of a fuel supply, or an impending eviction.
- Because of the statutory maximums on the amount that can be deducted for arrears, they are often a cheaper method of paying off arrears than a repayment schedule, or than token or slot meters that have been recalibrated to recover arrears along with current consumption. Gas and electricity suppliers will often seriously overestimate current use and request an amount from the DWP far in excess of the amount actually required to cover consumption. If they do, advise the debtor to take daily or weekly meter readings. It is the appropriate decision maker at the DWP who decides how much to deduct for current consumption, so the debtor can ask for a lower deduction to be made based on her/his own readings. The joint statement of intent on direct payments for fuel allows for regular reviews and, if the DWP refuses, the debtor can appeal to an appeal tribunal.
- Some gas and electricity suppliers insist on installing a token meter to cover current consumption and will only collect arrears through direct payments.
- For an IS/JSA claimant, full help with the cost of home loans is not available until s/he has been claiming for a period. Interest on mortgage payments will be paid automatically to the creditor as soon as the claimant qualifies for full interest, even if there are no arrears. Lenders may agree to adjourn a claim for possession if they are receiving interest direct from the DWP. If they have already obtained a possession order, they can be asked not to enforce it so long as direct payments are maintained.

Advantages

- If the debtor fits the criteria for direct payments, it is a simple and quick way to ensure that no further action will be taken by the creditor and that arrears are paid at a relatively modest rate – 5% of the IS/JSA personal allowance of a person aged 25 or over, £2.70 per week in 2002/03 – particularly if money is owed to several creditors (but see below).
- Creditors are assured of payments.

Disadvantages

- Only debtors claiming IS/income-based JSA are eligible.
- Only debts for rent, community charge, council tax, fines, water, gas and electricity can be paid for in this way (and community charge/council tax only at the request of the council, fines at the request of the magistrates' court). However, where the debtor has more than one such debt, direct payments might not be made for all of them. If this happens, there is a set order of priority.[11]
- By reducing subsistence level benefits, they reduce the flexibility with which a claimant can juggle her/his weekly budget.
- Fuel suppliers may demand a large amount for current consumption.
- If the debtor is likely to cease claiming benefit in the near future (particularly if only for a temporary period), direct payments will have to be replaced with another strategy. The debtor may be faced with a demand for the full amount when her/his benefit ends.
- The DWP often pays amounts collected on a quarterly basis. This can mean long delays for creditors in receiving their money.
- If the debtor is getting help with her/his mortgage (or loans for repairs or improvements) via IS/income-based JSA, payment is usually made directly to the lender under a mortgage payment scheme. If the debtor's lender is participating in this scheme, no amount for mortgage arrears can be deducted from benefit and paid to the lender.

Checklist for action

- Telephone the creditor to obtain agreement to direct payments and to establish how much will be required.
- Assist the debtor in her/his request of the DWP to arrange direct payments.

Gas and electricity pre-payment meters

Both electricity and gas companies must provide a pre-payment meter to a customer to prevent disconnection of her/his supply, if it is safe and practicable to do so.[12] If someone has arrears on fuel bills, a pre-payment meter will collect money not just for the fuel actually used, but also towards the arrears. There are two types of pre-payment meter:

- Coinless pre-payment meters, including token meters, card meters and credit key meters. These meters are sometimes set to collect the arrears over a period of time, irrespective of whether fuel is being used currently, and will, therefore, require the debtor to continue to insert tokens/cards/credit keys, even when no fuel is used. After a period of absence from home, such a meter may well require feeding to make up for the arrears which have become due for payment during the consumer's absence.
- Coin meters, which are calibrated so that a percentage of the money put in (often 40 per cent) is used for arrears. Thus, someone who had not been able to

pay a bill in the past would receive only 60 per cent as much gas for her/his money as a consumer without arrears. These meters are being replaced by card or token meters.

When applicable
- Pre-payment meters allow arrears to be collected over a period of time, and are therefore a way of avoiding disconnection.

Advantages
- A debtor continues to have some access to fuel supplies and will not be pressed further for the debt.
- Pre-payment meters can assist budgeting.

Disadvantages
- A pre-payment meter is often a do-it-yourself disconnection kit, because it may not be possible to keep it running at all times.
- In some cases, the amount of money recovered towards the arrears varies in relation to the amount of fuel used and thus, in the winter, not only does a debtor have to spend more money on fuel, s/he also has to contribute more towards her/his arrears.
- With token meters the debtor has to remember to buy enough tokens. There may be costs incurred (eg, bus fares) in buying tokens/cards or charging credit keys, or it may be difficult for the debtor to get to a charging point or point of sale (eg, in the case of illness), and such places may be closed.
- Fuel is more expensive per unit if paid for in this way. It should, therefore, be considered very much as an option of last resort.
- A pre-payment meter is not always technically possible. This applies where gas appliances have pilot lights that could go out when the pre-payment ends and are not protected by a fail-safe device when payment is resumed.
- Coin meters have to be positioned somewhere safe, which normally means they cannot be placed in buildings that do not have inside meters.

Useful arguments
Fuel suppliers are required to offer pre-payment facilities if this is the only means of avoiding disconnection, and therefore arguments about providing them are not necessary. However, it may be necessary to argue with a fuel supplier about the level at which the arrears will be collected through the pre-payment meter. The codes of practice and conditions require that ability to pay should determine the way a meter is calibrated to collect arrears. Most suppliers have one or two levels, depending on factors like the level of arrears or past payment record. Other special social factors (eg, illness or old age which make the need for heating or light particularly acute) should, therefore, be pointed out. If a debtor is on IS/

income-based JSA, the DWP direct payment amounts should be used as a maximum level of recovery.

Checklist for action
- Check exactly what type of meters are available locally.
- Contact the fuel supplier to request installation of a meter.
- Advise the debtor to monitor fuel consumption to check the calibration of the meter. This will involve taking a meter reading each week and comparing the number of units with the amount paid.

Remittance of debts

Both the magistrates' court (in respect of fines, community charge and council tax) and the local authority (in respect of non-domestic and general rates) have powers to remit (ie, write off) amounts owing in cases of hardship. The Inland Revenue can also remit taxes.

When applicable
- **General rates** Any remaining arrears of general rates are now debts that are a number of years old. In most cases the reason for non-payment will have been low income and it will be appropriate to request remittance.
- **Non-domestic (ie, business) rates** The local authority can reduce or remit payment where it is satisfied that the debtor would otherwise suffer hardship and it is reasonable to do so having regard to the interests of other taxpayers.[13] Guidance suggests that the authority should consider each case on its merits and take account of all relevant factors, not just financial hardship. The cost of granting relief should not be the only consideration in determining reasonableness.
- **Fines/maintenance arrears** If a debtor's financial circumstances have deteriorated since the fine was imposed, or if the fine has been ongoing for over 12 months, magistrates should be asked to remit all or part of the remaining fine. Maintenance arrears can be remitted where there is a drop in income or rise in expenditure and any arrears more than 12 months old are usually remitted as a matter of course.
- **Community charge** Magistrates may be sympathetic to the plight of those who still owe community charge and should be asked to remit in all cases of hardship.

Advantages
- It reduces or removes the debt.

Disadvantages
- The debtor will often need to attend a means enquiry (see Chapter 10).
- The magistrate will need to consider whether there has been 'wilful refusal or culpable neglect' and may therefore look at other alternatives to remittance, such as imprisonment (see Chapter 10).

Useful arguments
- **Non-domestic rates** The closure of a business may adversely affect the amenities or employment prospects of an area. Only 25% of the cost of relief is borne by the authority; the remainder is borne by central government.
- **Fines** Magistrates need to see how the debtor's circumstances have changed since the fine was imposed. Guidelines state that fines should be paid in a reasonable period, and that two years would be exceptional.
- **Rates and community charge** Local authorities and magistrates' courts are anxious to clear old debts off their books. Any collection of instalments is costly to the council.
- **Tax** The Inland Revenue will need to see that there is no means of clearing the debt and little likelihood of further liability.

Checklist for action
- Write to the creditor to request remittance.
- Enclose a financial statement.

---

4. **Emergency action**

The necessity for debt advice very often arises as a result of a threat from a priority creditor to take immediate action against someone's gas, electricity, property or liberty. In such circumstances, a debt adviser must always be prepared to take emergency action. In some cases, enough information and time will immediately be available to use one of the strategies outlined above. In other cases, neither time nor information is immediately available and, therefore, action by the creditor needs to be halted or delayed. This may be possible by a telephone call to a creditor explaining that the debtor has approached the agency seeking advice and assistance, and indicating when an offer will be made. However, particularly when adjournments or delays have already been granted, this is unlikely to be the case. In such situations other emergency action will have to be taken.

To prevent fuel disconnection

The legislation governing the supply of gas and electricity states that supplies should not be disconnected while there is a genuine dispute about the amount due.[14] When there is any question about the amount claimed, such a dispute should immediately be registered with the relevant supplier and confirmed in writing. The supplier should be asked not to disconnect the supply until the dispute has been resolved.

Codes of practice for the fuel industry also require that suppliers do not disconnect pensioners during winter months and do not disconnect households with pensioners, people with disabilities or children under 11 until social services have been informed and given at least 14 days to sort things out. For this reason, a telephone call to the social services department may be a useful way of gaining time.

If negotiation with the fuel supplier is proving to be unsuccessful, then the adviser should contact Ofgem (see Appendix 5), which has the power to intervene when disconnection is threatened.[15]

To prevent loss of home

When a possession order has already been granted and followed by a warrant of possession (see p226), an immediate application may need to be made to the court on form N244 to suspend the warrant. If the eviction is not due to take place for several days, then the debt adviser should attempt to negotiate directly with the lender, or the lender's solicitor, or the landlord, to try and obtain a binding agreement that the property will not be repossessed. If this is not possible or appears unlikely, or the eviction is due to take place that day or the following day, then form N244 will need to be submitted to the court. Form N244 needs to state the grounds of the application and, if possible, include an offer of payment. (For further information about a warrant of possession and how to complete an N244, see Chapter 9.)

In the case of council or registered social landlord tenants, there will usually be an internal procedure that must be followed before a warrant is applied for, which may involve considering representations from the tenant, therefore the adviser should check that procedure has been complied with and challenge the landlord if it has not.

Such an application will always stop county court bailiffs executing (ie, carrying out the instructions of) a warrant until the court has heard the application, although the court is usually very quick in arranging a hearing. The success of an application depends largely on:
- whether several arrangements have already been made but not kept to;
- the adviser's and the debtor's ability to present the case;
- how many previous warrants have been suspended;
- how long the debtor has been seeking help from an advice agency.

If it is too late to make the application to the court because the bailiffs are already on their way to carry out the eviction, the adviser will need to ring the creditor immediately and negotiate, on the doorstep if necessary, with the bailiff for more time. Bailiffs will normally have a mobile telephone with them and so can be contacted right up to the point of eviction.

To prevent seizure of goods by magistrates' court bailiffs

Bailiffs working for the magistrates' court cannot act without the authority of a distress warrant. This is a document issued by the court allowing the bailiffs to take goods belonging to the debtor, that can then be sold and the money used to pay for the unpaid debt. (See Chapter 11 for details of bailiffs' powers.)

If a distress warrant has been issued by a magistrates' court because of arrears in the payment of fines and bailiffs are about to seize goods, an application could be made to the court to give further time to pay.[16] However, there is some doubt as to whether magistrates are entitled to hear such an application and it is to be hoped that a debtor will subject it to judicial review in the near future (see p248). Meanwhile, their policy on this is negotiable and it could be discussed with the local chair of the magistrates or the chief executive. Occasionally, bailiffs will agree to give a debt adviser a few days in which to produce an offer of repayment. This is always worth trying, but success is limited.

The debtor does not have to let bailiffs in to seize goods if they have not previously gained entry to the property, but s/he should be advised to ensure that no goods are left outside (including motor vehicles) and that all doors, windows, etc, are carefully locked. S/he can also, providing walking possession has not been obtained (see p269), remove goods from her/his home to avoid seizure if the bailiffs have not already visited.

Community charge and council tax

Private bailiffs (see p261) will be used by a local authority after a liability order has been granted to collect council tax or community charge owing. Different local authorities give different instructions to their bailiffs. In some areas a clear code of conduct exists in the authority's contract with its bailiffs, which prevents the seizure of goods from people on benefit or in certain other circumstances. An adviser must know what rules (if any) her/his own local authority uses. If an action by bailiffs breaches these, the relevant section in the local authority should be contacted immediately so that its order to the bailiffs can be withdrawn.

Even where there is no clear policy, the adviser should contact the local authority and ask it to consider withdrawing the warrant from the bailiffs or, if that is not possible, instructing the bailiffs to accept a lower payment offer. Bailiffs themselves may occasionally agree to delay action, but this is unlikely. There may be no need for the debtor to let the bailiffs in. (See p267 for rules about bailiffs' powers to enter property.)

To prevent seizure of goods by county court bailiffs

The bailiffs used by the county court to collect debts are employed by the court. They cannot act without the authority of a warrant of execution. This is a document issued by the court allowing the bailiffs to take and sell goods belonging to the debtor and use the money to pay the unpaid debt. (See Chapter 9 for further information about warrants of execution.)

If a creditor has instructed the court to issue a warrant of execution for an unpaid county court judgment, the debtor always has the right to make an application to the county court to suspend the execution of the warrant. This is done on form N245. (See p229 for details of how to do this and Chapter 11 for details of county court bailiffs' powers.)

To prevent seizure of goods by sheriff's officers from the High Court

Sheriff's officers enforce High Court judgments (including county court judgments transferred to the High Court for enforcement). They are private bailiffs employed by the court to act on the instruction of the sheriffs, who are court officers responsible for the enforcement of debts in the High Court.

It may be possible to negotiate with the sheriff's officer to prevent seizure of goods, or with the creditor directly. However, if this is unsuccessful, the debtor will have to apply for a stay of execution on form N244 (which means that the sheriffs will be unable to take further action if the debtor can make some payment). The court will arrange a hearing to consider the application. (See Chapter 9 for details of how to make such an application and Chapter 11 for details of the powers of sheriff's officers.)

To prevent seizure of goods by tax bailiffs

Officials from the Inland Revenue and Customs and Excise have the powers of bailiffs to take and sell goods to pay for unpaid tax debts.[17] If they are unable to gain access to a property they can apply for an order to force entry. Normally a private bailiff would accompany the collector on such visits.

It is possible to negotiate with the collector directly and either suggest a repayment arrangement or submit a late return if the debtor does not agree with the amount of the debt and is out of the normal time limit for appealing (see Chapter 13). If the debtor has no goods, the collector is likely to seek an alternative means of enforcement, such as court action or bankruptcy.

To prevent imprisonment

Magistrates' courts have the power to imprison people who refuse to pay financial penalties, maintenance, community charge, council tax or rates. (See Chapter 10 for the exact circumstances in which they can use this power and the arguments to deploy against them.)

Warrant with bail

When a debtor has failed to attend a court hearing, or sometimes just failed to keep up the payments, then a warrant can be issued for her/his arrest by magistrates. In most cases this will be a warrant with bail which requires the debtor to surrender her/himself and be given a time and date for a court hearing.

Warrant without bail

Occasionally (usually where previous warrants have been ignored) a warrant without bail is issued. This requests the police to arrest the debtor and hold her/him in custody until a court hearing can be arranged (within 24 hours). Such warrants have a very low priority for the police and are often left for weeks or months before being discovered when the adviser rings the court.

If a warrant without bail has been issued the debtor should report to the court at a time, depending on local circumstances, when it is likely not to be too busy so that s/he will not be held in the cells for too long. This may be after lunch if the court sits then or first thing in the morning before other prisoners have been brought from police stations. Some courts will demand that people surrender themselves to the police station rather than the courts, but there is no legal foundation for this and advisers should ensure that police and other court staff accept a debtor's surrender in court buildings.

Committal hearing

Most courts will not imprison people until they have been given a number of opportunities to pay by instalments (see Chapter 11). Whenever someone is brought before court after the issue of an arrest warrant, s/he should be represented, if possible. S/he cannot lawfully be imprisoned if legal representation has not been made available to her/him. If a solicitor (perhaps from the Duty Solicitor scheme) is to provide representation, then an advice agency should brief her/him first and provide a full financial statement, as it is common for unrealistic offers to be made by solicitors, which then cause the debtor to be brought back before the court and treated with even less sympathy because s/he has broken a previous undertaking to pay. In some courts, probation officers are able to obtain adjournments so that they can produce a statement of the debtor's means for the courts. For further information about committal hearings, see p255.

After imprisonment

If magistrates have imprisoned someone for debt, it is possible that they have done so improperly and thus an application for judicial review should be made immediately. An application for bail pending a hearing can also be made (to a High Court judge in London). The applications will always have to be made by a solicitor or barrister specialising in this field. The most likely improprieties are procedural irregularities (eg, the court failed to consider the question of wilfulness/culpability/alternatives to imprisonment) or unreasonableness (eg, the court expected someone on income support to pay £20 a week towards a fine), natural justice (eg, legal representation was denied to the debtor) or acting *ultra vires* (eg, the resolution setting council tax was not signed by the appropriately authorised officer of the council).

To prevent the issue of a county court claim form

Although the issue of a claim form is not in itself of great importance, it may be important to take emergency action to avoid the issue, particularly of a possession summons, so that court costs are not added to a priority debt. The court cost for the issue of a possession summons is currently £120 (2002) and this is an extra burden on someone in rent or mortgage arrears. Solicitors' costs will increase this amount. If a debtor is faced with the imminent issue of a summons, then the creditor should be contacted immediately and asked to withhold action until an offer has been made. If the creditor fails to withhold, then the fact that such a request was made may sometimes be enough to persuade the court not to award the creditor the costs of the action.

5. Penalties for non-payment of priority debts

Debt	Ultimate penalties
Mortgage arrears	Repossession/eviction
Rent arrears	Goods seized
	Eviction
Community charge arrears	Goods seized
	Imprisonment
Council tax arrears	Goods seized
	Imprisonment
Unpaid fine/maintenance	Goods seized
	Imprisonment
Gas/electricity arrears	Disconnection
Income tax/VAT arrears	Goods seized
	Bankruptcy
Hire purchase arrears	Goods repossessed

Notes

2. **The general approach to priority debts**
   1 See P Madge, 'Till debt do us part',
     Adviser 71
   2 *Cheltenham & Gloucester BS v Norgan*
     [1996] 1 All ER 449

3. **Strategies for dealing with priority debts**
   3 s8(2) AJA 1973
   4 s36 AJA 1970
   5 s357(6) ICTA 1988
   6 FSA press release, 3 November 1999;
     see FSA Factsheet 'Your endowment
     mortgage – time to decide', February
     2002, available on www.fsa.gov.uk
   7 *Palk v Mortgage Services Funding,* 31 July
     1992, CA, *Adviser* 34 abstracts
   8 s129 CCA 1974
   9 *Director General of Fair Trading v First
     National Bank* [2001] UK House of Lords
     52, *Adviser* 89 abstracts
   10 Reg 35 and Sch 9 SS(C&P) Regs 1987
   11 See CPAG's *Welfare Benefits Handbook
     2002/2003,* p1023
   12 Condition 18 ESL; condition 19 GSL
   13 s49 Local Government Finance Act 1988

4. **Emergency action**
   14 Sch 6 EA 1989; Sch 2B GA 1986
   15 CPAG's *Fuel Rights Handbook,* 12th ed,
     p107
   16 s75(2) MCA 1980
   17 s61 TMA 1970

8

Chapter 8
. . . .
Dealing with non-priority debts

This chapter covers:
1. The criteria (below)
2. Should all debts be treated the same? (p152)
3. The strategies (p153)

1. The criteria

The majority of debts are likely to be non-priority ones. Non-priority debts are those where non-payment will not result in the loss of the debtor's home, liberty, essential goods or services. They will vary from an unpaid bill of a few pounds to a loan of several thousand pounds. They will not generally include any of the debts listed in Chapter 7. Six criteria are important in deciding which strategy will be the most appropriate for dealing with each of these debts. The six are as follows.

Availability of income

Once the financial statement (see p47) has been produced, the adviser will know whether there is any income left over for non-priority debts after payments have been arranged with priority creditors and all the other essential items of expenditure have been met. In many cases, there will not be enough income even to meet essential expenditure, but in others a significant amount may be available.

Availability of capital

It will have been ascertained at the initial interview whether a debtor has any significant capital or savings available. These can include:
- bonds, savings certificates, shares that have been bought (or been given – eg, under an employee share option scheme);
- money put aside for specific items (eg, a holiday);
- capital that will become available in the near future – for example, expected redundancy pay and proceeds from the sale of a house or business;
- legacies under a relative's will.

Realisable assets

A debtor may have assets that it would be reasonable to realise. These will be valuable items that could be sold to raise money – for example, antiques or works of art, cars and life assurance policies with a considerable surrender value. Such a list should only include items of a non-essential nature. For example, a recently acquired and fairly new car that is only used for weekend trips may be a realisable asset, while one that is necessary for work is not. The debtor must be adequately advised about her/his options before coming to a decision about disposing of assets – for example, to ensure that a car is not subject to a hire purchase (HP) or conditional sale agreement, or that sale or surrender of an insurance policy is in the client's best interests.

Is there equity in the home?

The equity in a person's home is the total value of the property less the amount required to pay any loans or debts secured against it, including any 'charges' and the costs of a sale. 'Charges' include mortgages and secured loans, charging orders and statutory charges owed to the Legal Services Commission in connection with publicly funded legal work. For example, to calculate the equity on a property saleable for £45,000:

Deduct solicitor's fee on sale	£200
Deduct estate agent's fee	£700
Deduct first mortgage (building society)	£25,000
Deduct second mortgage (after early settlement discount)	£15,000
Total deductions	**£40,900**

Total equity = £45,000 – £40,900 = £4,100

Where the property is jointly owned, then the equity is shared in proportion to the amount each person owns (usually equally). However, the value of the equity of a joint owner is complicated by the rights of the co-owner and specialist help should be sought.

In many cases, particularly when a property was purchased mainly or totally with borrowed money towards the end of the 1980s, there may be no equity at all in the property (see p122), and indeed the amount owed may exceed the now lowered value of the property. In the case, however, of even the most modest property acquired in the early 1970s and not remortgaged, it is likely that the 'equity position' will be very favourable.

It is important to make clear to the debtor that enquiries about equity are not a prelude to a recommendation that s/he sells her/his house. However, advisers should bear in mind that, unless the circumstances are wholly exceptional, creditors are unlikely to agree to, for example, writing off a debt (see p154) where there are realisable assets or equity in the home, even if a creditor is not suggesting that these be made available immediately. For example, a creditor may accept a token offer (see p162) on the basis that the amount due will be repaid out of the sale of the asset/property in due course.

Are circumstances static?

It is important to know whether the debtor's current circumstances are likely to change. For example, if a debtor's income was until very recently quite high, but has now been reduced by a period of illness that is not expected to last very long, then this must be taken into account. Similarly, if someone were either about to retire or begin a new job with higher wages, then these factors would be vital to the strategy selection.

The amount owed

The choice of strategy is affected by the amount owing because, firstly, some strategies cost money to set up (eg, a voluntary charge (see p137)) and would be too expensive for a small debt. Secondly, large companies often have policies to write off small amounts owed if they are not paid after a final warning. Very large debts may also be written off. Debt advisers should not assume that very large debts 'simply must be paid'. Creditors do write off sums of several thousand pounds.

It will sometimes be obvious to a debt adviser, particularly where a small debt is concerned, that a large company has already written off an amount owed because it has not communicated with the debtor for several years and the debtor has not been contacted by a collection agent acting on behalf of the creditor. In such circumstances, it is probably best to take no action and assume that the creditor has decided not to pursue the debt. If there has been no contact for more than six years, the debt is most probably unenforceable anyway.

If the debtor subsequently intends to apply for an administration order (see p170) or is made bankrupt (see Chapter 12), the adviser would need to contact the creditor to clarify this.

2. Should all debts be treated the same?

If the strategy suggested is to be accepted by creditors, it is important that it is based on a consistent set of criteria and that all creditors are treated alike. The credit industry is competitive and individuals within it are likely to reject any strategy that appears to favour a competitor. The strength of a debt adviser's negotiating position lies in the ability to present a strategy that is empirically based and businesslike, and in line with the way courts would treat creditors and debtors. Thus, all offers to creditors must be made on the same basis, using the same criteria when making choices with regard to their debts.

If a debt has a special importance to the debtor, there may need to be an exception to this. Some debts that may be treated differently are:

- Debts created by a loan from a family or community member, or an employer. These may, on strict legal criteria, be no different from monies owed to a finance company. However, if failure to repay this debt will lead to serious financial or personal problems elsewhere in the family or at work (eg, dismissal), then it may be necessary to treat it as a priority debt.
- Unsecured debts that have been guaranteed (see p77). These may need to be treated as a priority in order to protect the guarantor, or family or work relationships generally.
- Mail order catalogues, because they are essential to someone on a low income as a way of budgeting for essentials such as household items and clothing, so long as they maintain a low balance.
- A debt incurred through the fraud of the debtor or her/his partner or a relative, where s/he could face prosecution if the debt is not paid.

3. **The strategies**

This section describes the recommended strategies for non-priority debts. They are not mutually exclusive. The adviser may use several strategies to deal with each of a person's debts – for example, a moratorium of three months followed by a partial write-off and the freezing of interest/charges with instalments by equitable distribution. Alternatively, different strategies (or combinations of strategies) may be needed for individual debts – for example, some requests for write-offs, some token offers and one voluntary charge.

Strategy selection often is not a single process, but will be done on first contact and then reviewed later. The criteria described here should be equally applicable to initial or review strategies. The strategy chosen for each debt will need to be reviewed:

- if a creditor refuses to accept a particular strategy; *or*
- at the end of the time agreed by the creditor. For example, the creditor may agree to accept no payments for six months and then review the position; *or*
- if the debtor's financial circumstances change.

Often strategies will not be accepted on first application, and debt advisers should always re-urge creditors several times to accept a realistic strategy. Second and third letters can be strengthened by details of how other creditors have come to agree with a particular strategy.

Debtors should not routinely be advised to stop payments to all their non-priority creditors while negotiations are taking place. In most multiple debt cases it will be appropriate for the debtor to reduce payments to non-priority creditors or even stop them altogether. Where the debtor is able to maintain contractual payments to non-priority creditors (whilst still servicing her/his essential commitments, including priority debts) s/he should be advised to do so. Where s/he is unable to do so, the adviser should point out that the debtor's default will be registered with credit reference agencies and may eventually lead to court action by the creditor, but that it is still in the debtor's best interests not to make those payments because there is no, or very little, available income after meeting essential expenditure and payments to priority creditors. A long period without any payments at all to creditors is undesirable, unless a strategy involving non-payment has been proposed in the meantime. On the other hand, a short period where no payments are made may be inevitable while the adviser works out a strategy with the debtor.

Request a write-off

When there is no available income or capital and a debtor's circumstances are unlikely to improve in the foreseeable future (or may even worsen), then a request should be made for a debt to be written off by creditors. This means that the creditor agrees not to collect the debt and removes the account from its records. The debtor makes no further payments. If the debt is large, then any realisable assets or equity in the debtor's home will have to be considered, as it is probable that, if the creditor took court action and the debtor could not make payment as ordered by the court, the creditor could either apply for a charging order against the equity in the home (see p189) or ask the court to make a bankruptcy order (see p297) so that goods owned by the debtor or the home could be sold.

A write-off could also be requested where either the size of the debt or the payments the debtor can afford make it uneconomical for the creditor to collect the debt – eg, where the pro rata payment would be less than £1.

The question of write-offs has generated much discussion among debt advisers. Every creditor recognises the need to write off some debts (and makes provision for this in its accounts and the interest rates it sets). Advisers, exposed as they are to a society whose prevalent moral code is one which lays emphasis on the importance of repaying one's debts, may well have personal anxieties about requesting a write-off. These should not be allowed to prejudice advice. Debtors, too, may be anxious about the consequences of this strategy, so the adviser may need to explain the reasoning behind the suggestion and that it is being proposed to the creditor as the most economic solution available.

Advantages

- It removes the financial and emotional stress caused by that debt.
- It enables the debtor to make a fresh start.
- The creditor may be able to offset the loss against profit for tax purposes.

Disadvantages

- Creditors will not agree easily to write off debts, particularly if the debt has been incurred recently.
- When creditors write off debts, they often report this to a credit reference agency. This is an agency that collects evidence, such as county court judgments or evictions, and sells details of individuals who have suffered these to creditors. If a debt is reported as written-off, then it may be difficult for a debtor to get credit in the future.
- Many creditors never formally agree to write off a debt, even when they have received a request to do so. They will take no further action on it and at some point convenient to themselves will write it out of their accounts. This can mean that the debtor is left uncertain as to whether or not the creditor has agreed to her/his request, and s/he can be vulnerable either to a change of company policy or to pursuit of a debt if her/his circumstances do improve.

Useful arguments

- The circumstances of the debtor will need to be outlined carefully and attention drawn to the fact that the debtor has no property or goods of significant value, no income except benefits/low wages and no prospect of improvement in the foreseeable future. This will help creditors to see that court action is unlikely to be successful. Explain that if bankruptcy were pursued, then the outcome would be the same. Medical evidence confirming, for example, the nature of any disability or that the debtor is unable to work may also be persuasive.
- Inform the creditor of the total amount of debt owing to all creditors to show how hopeless the debtor's situation is.
- Most creditors will have a set of criteria for deciding when to abandon debt recovery, which will be determined by the cost of recovering the money. The adviser should suggest that writing off a debt is likely to be the most economic solution for the creditor.
- Creditors may be more willing to write a debt off after withholding action on the account for three or six months (see p161).
- It will be easier to get smaller debts written off.

Checklist for action

- Write to the creditor(s) proposing the strategy and request written confirmation that the strategy is agreed.
- Advise the debtor to stop paying.
- A creditor may not accept a write-off at first, but the adviser should not give up and should ask the creditor to reconsider after, say, three to six months.

Partial write-off

If there is some money available to meet a creditor's demands, but this will not pay off the whole debt in a realistic period of time (in line with what a court would consider reasonable), then creditors can be asked to reduce the balance owing immediately or to accept agreed instalments for two to three years, after which the balance will be written off.

Partial write-off should be seen as a means of coming to an arrangement similar to an individual voluntary arrangement and which accords broadly with what a court would order if an income payments order in bankruptcy application were being considered (see p304). A request should be made that further interest is stopped (see p157). A request for a partial write-off can also be important in reducing the amount of debt to below the limit for an administration order (see p170).

Partial write-off is appropriate when:
- there are no realisable assets or substantial equity that could be charged;
- the debtor's circumstances are such that s/he cannot repay the whole debt within a reasonable period of time;
- there is no expectation of capital or extra income becoming available soon.

Advantages
- It reduces the amount owed and gives the debtor a realistic target to aim for and, therefore, a framework in which s/he can regain a sense of control over her/his financial affairs.
- The debtor repays less money.
- Creditors may be able to offset the loss against profit for tax purposes.

Disadvantages
- When creditors write off debts they often report this to credit reference agencies and thus it may be difficult for a person to get credit in the future.
- It may be difficult to get all creditors to agree to the strategy.

Useful arguments
- It can be argued in support of a partial write-off that the creditor will receive more than if the debtor were made bankrupt, and thus it is quicker, cheaper and less stressful to the debtor for the creditor to limit demands to that amount now.
- A partial write-off is also very similar to a composition on an administration order (see p170) or an individual voluntary arrangement (see p290) and so creditors are only being asked to take a similar course of action to that taken by the courts, but on an informal basis.
- The creditor may be persuaded that it is better going for something shorter term and realisable, rather than longer term but potentially expensive to collect and unlikely to be paid. Unless creditors reduce their demand to

something that the debtor can pay within the foreseeable future, then the debtor is likely to lack the motivation to keep up with payments. It is completely unrealistic for both sides to set up repayment schemes which will last more than about five years and the likelihood is that such monies will eventually be written off.

- If the creditor refuses to agree to this strategy initially, it is worth requesting it again after, say, 12 months of regular payments if there is still no improvement in the debtor's circumstances.

Checklist for action

- Agree with the debtor the amount of income available to creditors.
- Calculate offers and decide a payment period (two or three years).
- Write to the creditor(s) proposing the strategy, with details of the offers and requesting written confirmation that this is accepted.
- Advise the debtor to start making payments. Consider direct debits or standing orders if the debtor has a current account.
- Unless the arrangement is time-limited, ensure that interest is stopped. (If not, consider advising the debtor to withhold payments until agreement is given to stop interest.)

Freeze/reduce interest

If a debtor is unable to pay the contractual payments due under an agreement, then to go on adding interest and other charges, especially if s/he is not even repaying any capital due, will only increase the total balance and the debt will never be repaid. This fact has long been recognised by the county court where interest is not charged after judgment on debts regulated by the Consumer Credit Act. (See p187 for when interest can be charged after judgment.)

Whenever there is income or capital available (or is likely to be in the future) and a repayment schedule of less than the original contractual payments is envisaged, or if no payment can be afforded at present, then a request should be made that all interest or other charges accruing on the account be stopped (or frozen). This strategy will always be used in conjunction with another strategy.

The request to stop interest will be made in most cases immediately the debtor contacts a debt adviser. However, the adviser will need to explain to the creditor why it is considered necessary – eg, the payments the debtor is likely to be able to afford will not cover the ongoing interest.

Advantages

- Realistic repayment schedules can be created under which debts will be repaid in a known time.
- All payments made will reduce the debt. The debtor will be able to see that s/he is repaying her/his debts.

- The creditor can sometimes offset the unrecovered interest against profit for tax purposes.

Disadvantages
- Creditors may not accept the strategy, particularly if there is substantial equity in a property or the debtor has realisable assets.
- It is not appropriate for loans where all interest is added at the beginning of the loan. In these cases a partial write-off may achieve the desired result.

Useful arguments
- If a county court judgment were awarded, then in practice interest would be stopped for all regulated consumer credit agreements (see p52).
- It is a necessary incentive to the debtor because otherwise s/he will not be prepared to lose valuable income in pursuit of a completely hopeless goal.
- Many other creditors are being asked (or have agreed) to stop interest and, therefore, equity demands that this creditor does too.
- Make any offer of payment conditional upon interest stopping.

Guidance on the Banking Code suggests that creditors should consider such requests on a case-by-case basis and that the seriousness of the debtor's situation may make it appropriate.

Checklist for action
This strategy will always be used with another strategy.
- Write to the creditor and include a request to freeze interest and other charges together with some justification for the request.
- Request written confirmation that this has been done.
- If the strategy is not successful initially, ask the creditor to reconsider; it may be useful to provide evidence of other creditors' agreement to freeze/reduce interest and other charges.

Offering a reduced capital sum in full and final settlement

If there is available capital or saleable assets, or if the debtor will have such assets in the near future (for instance, because s/he intends to sell a house for reasons unrelated to the debt), then it may be that an offer of an amount less than that which is actually due as early settlement under the agreement will be acceptable to a creditor. This is particularly likely where there is no available income and the financial position is unlikely to improve or may even worsen. Creditors are likely to recognise that the existence of a cash lump sum is a way of making either a modest but certain profit or at least cutting their losses. When the debtor's income is low and unlikely to improve, it would probably be an attractive alternative to waiting to see if they get more over a long period.

Ask the debtor if there are essentials s/he needs to purchase, or essential repairs that need to be carried out, before the lump sum is allocated to creditors.

The key to using this strategy successfully is to ensure that the lump sum payment is not made until the creditor has agreed in writing to accept this in full and final settlement of all monies owed. It is argued that contractual obligations, once taken on, cannot be removed by mere agreement and a new contract is required to replace the old. However, there will be a legally binding agreement where either an arrangement is made with all the debtor's unsecured creditors or the funds are made available by a third party (eg, a relative) and the offer is made by her/him on the debtor's behalf. If there is any doubt about the trustworthiness of a particular creditor, then specialist legal help should be sought to draw up a binding agreement to give effect to this strategy.

Advantages
- The debtor pays less than s/he would if repaying over a longer term.
- The debtor has the opportunity of a fresh start.
- It is a more immediate and convenient solution than setting up a repayment schedule over a number of years.

Disadvantages
- The debtor loses the advantage of having a lump sum which could have been used to avoid the need for future credit.
- Once aware of the existence of a lump sum, the creditor may attempt court action.

Useful arguments
- Contact the creditor before the money is available and suggest that this is the only chance that the debtor will have of paying a substantial amount and that because the debtor wants to pay her/his debts, s/he is prepared to hand all (or if there are several debts to be treated in this way, a proportionate share) of the money over to the creditor.
- It is worth pointing out that the creditor is not going to get more by refusing the offer and taking enforcement action and that acceptance of the offer makes more commercial sense than the debtor continuing to make small payments over a long period of time. Note that such an arrangement may have to be made with quite senior staff in a creditor organisation and the adviser should ensure that s/he is writing or speaking to senior credit control managers.

Checklist for action
- Write to the creditor(s) with details of the offer and request acceptance in full and final settlement to be confirmed in writing.
- Consider specialist legal help to draw up the agreement.

- Once written confirmation is received, advise the debtor (or third party) to send the payment(s).
- Any covering letter sent with a cheque should explain exactly what it is for and state that it is in 'full and final settlement'.
- If money is being made available from the sale of a house, it may be necessary to obtain a solicitor's undertaking that the money will be paid to the creditor once the house is sold.

Offering payment of a capital sum with instalments

When a debtor has capital or assets together with stable available income, but there are substantial arrears, the threat of further action often can be avoided by paying a single capital sum towards the arrears and then paying instalments towards part or all of the contractual payments. This often needs to be linked to another strategy, particularly the freezing of interest/charges (see p157) or partial write-off (see p156) or administration order (see p170). This is different from paying a capital sum in full and final settlement in that the payments will have to continue.

Advantages
- The creditor is no longer pressing.
- Weekly income has been maintained to a greater extent than otherwise.

Disadvantages
- The flexibility to use the capital sum elsewhere is lost.

Useful arguments
- If this tactic is being used to prevent imminent court action, the adviser can argue that the creditor will obtain its money more quickly than by going to court, and more money will be available to repay the debt as there will be less cost. An agreement such as this will have to be made in writing.

Checklist for action
- Telephone/write to the creditor proposing the strategy and request acceptance in writing.
- Calculate the instalments (see p164).
- Once written confirmation is received, advise the debtor to send payment of the capital sum, followed by regular instalments (set up a direct debit/standing order for these if possible).
- Ensure that interest is stopped. If not, consider advising the debtor to withhold instalments until agreement is given to stop interest.

Holding tactics

It may sometimes be important for the adviser to gain time for the debtor when:
- there is some available income, but this is immediately required to deal with priority debts;
- there is no available income, but shortly there will be some;
- available assets are being sold;
- the full situation is not yet known.

There are two types of holding tactic:
- **Asking creditors for a short delay** It may be useful to request a short delay if the adviser needs to check a credit agreement or its enforceability. Some agencies write automatically to all creditors asking them to withhold action for a short period when their advice is first sought. This is not necessary if a strategy can be formulated quickly or if the debt adviser will be asking the creditor to write off the debt or to accept no payments for three months. It is wasteful of resources to employ this device automatically and can increase the stress faced by the debtor, as it lengthens the time before agreement with creditors about a long-term strategy is reached, and may lead to creditors routinely refusing requests. If a delay is needed because balances are required before a strategy can be implemented, ask the debtor to obtain these where possible.
- **Asking creditors to accept no payments for a specified period** If no money is available at present to pay any non-priority debts, the creditor should be asked to accept no payments for three or six months and then review the situation.

This may be used as part of another strategy – for example, to ask a creditor to withhold for three months and then follow this up with a request for a write-off. This can be useful where it is known that the creditor is unlikely to accept a write-off immediately. If a request is made to a creditor to withhold any action and accept no payments, the creditor must always be asked, at the same time, to stop interest/charges in order to prevent the debt increasing even further.

The length of time for which the adviser requests no payments will depend on:
- any known future changes in the debtor's financial position which might allow payments to begin;
- the length of time needed to repay priority debts;
- the stress faced by the debtor and whether s/he needs a long or short breathing space.

The creditor may be more likely to agree to a request to write off a debt after withholding for six months, and it is obviously doubling the work for the adviser if three months is requested initially, followed by a request for a further three-month withholding period.

If the creditor agrees in the first instance to withhold action and collect no payments for six months, it gives the debtor a substantial period of relief.

However, as this strategy can never be a permanent solution, it does mean that a request for a six-month delay is prolonging the process of reaching one.

Advantages
- Time can give the adviser space to gather all the necessary facts and work out the best strategy.
- It removes the immediate pressure from the debtor, and enables payments to be made for priority debts.
- It gets creditors used to the idea that there are problems, but does not leave them in the dark.
- Many creditors will accept a request to withhold action for a short period from a debt advice agency almost as a matter of routine.

Disadvantages
- It does not actually solve anything. Some creditors will refuse to stop interest and thus the debt grows while no action is taken.
- It can create extra work for the adviser.

Useful arguments
- Explain that considerable debts have arisen and outline the debtor's circumstances.
- Explain that time is required for professional debt advice.

Checklist for action
- Telephone/write to the creditor to explain the situation and request written confirmation that the account will be held in abeyance. Enclose a financial statement where withholding more than a month's payments is requested, unless a debtor receives means-tested benefits.
- Ensure that interest/charges will be stopped.
- Advise the debtor not to make payments.

Token instalments

When there is no available income, assets or capital and the situation is unlikely to change, but it is impossible to get agreement to any other strategy, then payment by instalments of a nominal or token nature may be necessary. This will sometimes satisfy either the pride or the administrative systems of a creditor and may be the only way to prevent it from taking further action.

Debtors initially seeking advice often want to make token payments rather than withholding payments or asking creditors to write off, out of fear or ignorance of enforcement action, or because of previous harassment by creditors, or even because they want to make some payment, however small, towards their debts. The adviser needs to ensure that debtors do not make payments they cannot actually afford or at the expense of making payments towards priority debts. It should be stressed that a nominal payment need not be more than 50p a month (although it is usually £1).

The strategy need not be used for all creditors owed money by the debtor and should only be offered as a last resort where the creditor has refused to either write off the debt or accept no payments, and where court action by the creditor would be undesirable. It is imperative that the creditor is asked to agree to take no further action and to stop interest in return for token payments being made. It is obviously important to review the strategy at a later date to choose a more suitable long-term option.

If a creditor has already taken court action, but there is no available income and the court is unwilling to order no payments (see p161), the debtor will need to make a token offer to pay by instalments (eg, 50p a month) in order to prevent further enforcement action (see Chapter 9 for more detail).

Advantages
- Paying a token amount may be the only way to obtain a creditor's agreement to taking no further action and stopping interest.

Disadvantages
- It is using up income that is not really available.
- It is encouraging creditors to take an unrealistic view of people's ability to pay.
- It can be expensive for the debtor as it may cost as much in postage and other charges to make the payment as the payment is worth.
- The debt will never be repaid at this rate and it hangs over the debtor.
- Creditors can continue to apply pressure on debtors to pay more, particularly where money is paid to a collector who comes to the home.

Useful arguments
- A request for token payments should be made by the creditor after the adviser has made clear there is no (or only a nominal amount of) available income as shown by the financial statement. The adviser should explain that, in fact, the payment is only possible because the debtor is cutting back on essential spending, such as food or fuel, in order to make the payment.
- Where creditors are threatening court action, draw their attention to any recent low judgments awarded by the local county court in similar cases and suggest that even if they go to the trouble of going to court they will actually get no more than a nominal amount (or a general stay).

Checklist for action
- Telephone/write to the creditor and await written confirmation of the strategy.
- Ensure that further action and interest and other charges are stopped.

- Advise the debtor to make payments (ask for a payment book if this facilitates payments without cost).
- Review at an agreed date with the debtor.

An equitable distribution of the available income

If there is available income and a number of debts, and no capital or realisable assets, this income should be distributed amongst all the non-priority creditors in a fair way. Apportioning the available income fairly is best done by a method known either as 'equitable distribution' or 'pro rata payments', where the amount of each instalment is directly proportionate to the total amount owing to that particular creditor. Thus, if there are ten creditors, of whom five are owed £1,000 and the rest are owed £500, then those owed the larger debt will be paid twice as much each week or month.

Some creditors seek a distribution that is proportionate to the payments due under their agreement rather than the capital outstanding. This is popular with those creditors which lend smaller amounts over short periods at very high rates of interest. Such arrangements should be rejected because:

- this is not the way in which a court would define an equitable offer if an administration order (see p233) or other insolvency procedures were being considered;
- the creditors which are owed large sums are unlikely to agree to it and thus they will go to court and probably obtain an order for repayments based on capital outstanding;
- short-term lenders of small sums have already allowed for the high risk associated with such lending and this is reflected in the rates of interest charged.

The adviser will have to calculate the amount due to each creditor per week or month. The calculation will be based on the following formula:

Amount owed to creditor ÷ total amount owed x total income available for distribution

Example
The debtor owes money to three creditors:

Creditor A	£1,000
Creditor B	£800
Creditor C	£250
Total amount owing	£2,050

(the debtor's total available income is £12 a month)

Calculation:

Creditor A	1,000 ÷ 2,050 x 12 = £5.85 a month
Creditor B	800 ÷ 2,050 x 12 = £4.70 a month
Creditor C	250 ÷ 2,050 x 12 = £1.45 a month

Total of repayments to creditors = **£12.00 a month**

(amounts may be rounded up or down for convenience, but not if this results in payments which the debtor cannot afford)

If the adviser does not have a programmable calculator or computer (see Chapter 1), this sum will have to be worked out for each creditor. Even if you do not know the exact balances, it may be worth calculating a distribution on the basis of good estimates as the weekly variation will probably be very small and may be acceptable to creditors.

If the calculation gives rise to a very low payment to a particular creditor (eg, less than £1 per month) you may wish to include in your letter offering this to the creditor a request that, in view of the high collection costs for such a small sum, the creditor should consider writing off the debt (see p154). There is an example of this request in Appendix 2.

In calculating the amount of available income on offer to creditors, the adviser should ensure some leeway in the financial statement to cope with unexpected events (eg, short periods of sickness) so that payments can still be maintained.

The Office of Fair Trading (OFT) points out that advisers should not assume that pro rata offers to non-priority creditors on outstanding balances are always in the debtor's best interests, and that debtors should not usually be advised to make payments that do not cover ongoing interest or other charges. Instead, they should take into account that some loans may lose the benefit of a reduced rate of interest and consider paying off loans with a higher rate of interest before loans with a lower rate.[1] Although this appears to conflict with the principles of money advice discussed elsewhere, unless the debtor has sufficient available income to be able to maintain the contractual payments on these debts as well as servicing her/his other debts, it will be in the client's best interests to offer pro rata payments provided this is accompanied by a request for any ongoing interest to be stopped so that each payment made by the debtor actually reduces the debt. On the other hand, if the creditor refuses to stop interest or reduce it sufficiently, pro rata payments will almost certainly not be in the client's best interests and the creditor will have to be urged to reconsider or the strategy reviewed with the debtor.

Advantages
- Equitable distribution is widely accepted by the credit industry (indeed, many creditors think that it is the only strategy that money advisers should use).
- It ensures that all non-priority debts are dealt with together.

• It is based on court practices, as this is how money is distributed to creditors when an administration order is granted (see p233).

Disadvantages
• A debtor may be left with little financial flexibility and money only for basics.
• Unless coupled with a partial write-off (see p156), many debts may take years to clear.

Useful arguments
• The strongest argument in favour of this strategy is its fairness. It can be presented as a business-like response to a difficult situation which ensures that every creditor will be treated in a way which will give them the maximum possible amount.
• It is exactly what would happen if a court were to grant an administration order or in bankruptcy and is the kind of order which a court should be making every time it makes an instalment order. The creditor cannot expect to do better.
• Some creditors will argue against the stopping of interest, particularly if the capital sums upon which the equitable distribution is based include some sums where interest was added at the beginning of the loan. This is a reasonable argument and does lessen the fairness of this method. However, it ignores the fact that interest is often lower if applied at the start of the loan. It may be possible to discuss with creditors whose claim is for an amount which includes interest added to the beginning of the loan the option of claiming only that part of the interest due by the date of the equitable distribution.
• This strategy has often been used successfully where it can be shown that the person is starting to pay her/his creditors and wishes to treat them all fairly. In addition, consideration should be given to asking for a partial write-off where offers will be paid for two or three years only (see p156 for details).

It is usual to send to each creditor details of the amounts owed to all creditors together with the offers made. This should not be done if the debtor wishes confidentiality to be maintained. However, it will be helpful for the creditors to know that they have been given the whole financial position of the debtor as they would in an administration order or bankruptcy. If the creditor has already obtained a court order that is higher than the offer calculated, the debtor will need to apply to the court on form N245 to vary the order if s/he cannot obtain the creditor's written agreement to accept the offer made and to take no further action to enforce the debt (see Chapter 9 for how to do this).

Checklist for action
• Agree with the debtor the amount of income available for creditors.
• Calculate offers to creditors – consider a partial write-off (see p156).

- Write to the creditors with offers; suggest a write-off where offers are low.
- Ensure that interest and other charges are stopped.
- Advise the debtor to make payments (consider direct debit or standing order if the debtor has a current account); ask for a payment book if this allows payment without cost.

Maturity loan

A maturity loan is available from most building societies and occasionally from local authorities for homeowners approaching retirement age. It is secured on their property and is a way of raising capital to repay debts. The term of the loan will be either the person's lifetime or until s/he sells the property, at which point all the capital becomes due. Only payments of interest are made during the term of the loan. Some maturity loans do not even require interest payments to be made – the creditor depends on the capital and accrued interest being met from the proceeds of the house sale.

This type of loan involves the conversion of unsecured borrowing into secured borrowing, which makes it a risky and drastic step to consider. It is only appropriate if there is plenty of equity in the property. It will be most useful if the debtor is finding it particularly stressful owing money to a number of different creditors, or if creditors are proving difficult to negotiate with. Building societies will advise on the type of loan available, but debtors should always be advised to obtain independent financial advice.

Advantages
- The maturity loan prevents further action by the creditors.
- It may be a means of releasing equity from the house to use for other purposes, such as insulation or heating, which in turn can reduce living costs.

Disadvantages
- If payments of interest are not maintained then the home is at risk.
- The equity in the home is reduced by the value of the maturity loan and will be steadily eroded if arrears arise.

Useful arguments
- Local authorities will often have existing contacts with a number of building societies which have agreed to provide maturity loans in their area. These may be a good start. Otherwise a debtor should approach the building society with which s/he has or had her/his mortgage, or with whom s/he has held a savings account. The implications for debtors claiming benefits will often need explaining to building societies and the debtor will have to persuade them that s/he is in fact able to repay the loan, or find a creditor which can offer a loan with no repayments required.

Checklist for action

- Ensure that the debtor obtains full details about repayments, conditions and the cost of the loan before signing any agreements.
- Inform creditors of the proposal and ask them to take no further action to enable the loan to be set up.

Sale of home

When there is no available income or capital or realisable assets other than a home, sale may be considered. It should not be considered if the financial situation is likely to improve or if the sale of the home would result in homelessness. It is only appropriate as a way of dealing with non-priority debts if there is sufficient equity to satisfy most creditors' demands and cover the costs of selling and moving, and when the stress of debts is creating unacceptable problems for the household.

The sale of a house is often recommended to people who are in debt as an easy way out of the situation, but it should be remembered that courts will very rarely order a property to be sold to satisfy unsecured borrowing and only, of course, after a charging order (see p189) has been made and an order for sale subsequently applied for (see p192), or a bankruptcy order made. It is generally much worse to be homeless than to be in debt. If, however, an expensive house can be sold and a more modest one, which would nonetheless satisfy the debtor's needs, can be purchased, then this can be an acceptable way of coping with a debt problem and perhaps having money left over for other purposes as well.

A debtor may have been advised (sometimes by family or friends) that s/he has no alternative other than to sell her/his house and s/he will, therefore, approach an adviser at a stage where this process has already begun. By examining the other strategies outlined here, it should be possible to demonstrate that the sale of the house in these circumstances is not the only option and would certainly not be ordered by the courts. The state of the housing market may also mean that this strategy is not easily achievable.

If a local authority or housing association rehouses people following a sale of their home, it will normally only do so where it is clear that the sale is the only means to prevent eviction. Some local authorities still consider that the sale of a house makes someone intentionally homeless and, therefore, not eligible for rehousing under homelessness legislation. However, the code of guidance for local authorities states that a person should not be treated as intentionally homeless if her/his house was sold due to real financial difficulties, and advisers should draw attention to this if necessary.[2]

After two years as a secure tenant of the local authority, the debtor will acquire the right to buy. S/he will then be able to acquire a minimum of 32 per cent stake in the equity of the new rented home for nothing and get a mortgage to assist with buying the rest.[3] If this factor is taken into account, it can sometimes tip the balance in favour of deciding to sell the home.

Advantages
- It can clear the debts.
- It may raise capital for other purposes.
- The debtor may see it as providing the opportunity for a fresh start.

Disadvantages
- It releases equity held in property to satisfy unsecured creditors in a way that a court would be unlikely to order.
- It may not be possible to find alternative housing which is ideally suitable.
- Moving house is a major disruption and costs a lot of money.
- The debtor may lose money if the housing market is depressed.
- The sale may take a very long time or, in the midst of a recession, prove impossible, and the benefits of choosing this strategy may be lost.

Useful arguments
- Once it has been decided to put the house on the market, letters should be written informing the creditors of this and asking them to withhold interest charges or any other action until sale prices are available. Creditors may require a letter from an estate agent, and if a confirmation of a request to sell a property is available, this can be photocopied and sent. They may also want a letter from the debtor's solicitor confirming that her/his share of the proceeds of sale will be forwarded directly to them.

Checklist for action
- Discuss the pros and cons of selling a house with the debtor.
- Telephone/write to creditor(s) to inform them of the strategy and get written confirmation that they will take no further action.
- Ensure that the house is put on the market with a reliable estate agent.
- Ensure that suitable alternative accommodation is available.

General stay

If a court order has been made, or is about to be made, for an instalment order and there is no available income nor available capital or assets, then the county court can make an order for a general stay of judgment or enforcement. (See p229 for an explanation of the court's power to make such an order and how the adviser can assist the debtor to make an application for no instalments.)

Voluntary charge

Occasionally, but only as the 'lesser of two evils', it is advisable to turn an unsecured loan into a secured one in order to prevent any further action being taken. This is a very high-risk strategy and should not be undertaken lightly. It is described in detail in Chapter 7.

Administration order

If a debtor already has at least one county court (or High Court) judgment against her/him and her/his total debts do not exceed the limit for an administration order (£5,000 in 2002), then s/he can apply to the county court for the court to 'administer' payments to all her/his creditors. The debtor will make one monthly payment to the court which will divide it equitably among all creditors (see p233 for details).

Bankruptcy

Bankruptcy is a legal procedure in which the inability of a debtor to pay her/his debts is acknowledged and the majority of unsecured creditors can no longer pursue their debts, which are eventually written off, usually after two or three years. Bankruptcy is a suitable strategy for a debtor if:
- debts have arisen which creditors will not write off;
- the debtor does not own a home;
- the debtor does not have any available assets or capital;
- the debtor has a low income;
- the debtor is not intending to be in business on her/his own in the next few years.

See Chapter 12 for further details, particularly of the proposed reforms, including the advantages, disadvantages and procedures involved in bankruptcy.

Individual voluntary arrangements (IVAs)

Individual voluntary arrangements (IVAs) are a means whereby a debtor can protect her/himself from further action by creditors by entering into a legally binding arrangement with them, which is supervised by an insolvency practitioner. IVAs are often described as an informal bankruptcy and should be considered before bankruptcy itself. See Chapter 12 for further details.

Notes

3. **The strategies**
   1 paras 22(e)-(g) DMG
   2 s15.6 Code of Guidance on parts 6 and 7 of HA 1996 (Department of the Environment)
   3 s132 HA 1985

Chapter 9

•••

The civil courts

1. Introduction

Most non-criminal cases in England and Wales are dealt with by the High Court and county courts. The High Court is the superior civil court and is divided into 'divisions'. The Queen's Bench Division deals with most debt cases and the Chancery Division deals with bankruptcy and actions for possession of land. The High Court is located in the Royal Courts of Justice in London and at 126 District Registries around the country. Cases are heard by High Court judges and by masters (in London) and district judges (outside London).

The majority of cases involving debt are dealt with by a network of around 220 county courts throughout the country. Cases are heard by district judges and circuit judges, assisted by part-time judges, with some decisions being delegated to court staff (see p182). Judges are drawn from the ranks of experienced barristers and solicitors. The county court was originally intended to provide a cheap and simple system for the recovery of small debts, but its jurisdiction has gradually been increased. Nearly two million court actions are entered in the county courts every year (1,871,923 in 2000).

The High Court and county courts derive their powers from the Supreme Court Act 1981 and County Courts Act 1984 respectively as amended in particular by the Courts and Legal Services Act 1990 and the Civil Procedure Act 1997. Prior to 26 April 1999 each court also had its own set of rules to govern its procedure – the Rules of the Supreme Court (RSC) and the County Court Rules (CCR). Since 26 April the procedures have been unified and are contained in the Civil Procedure Rules (CPR) 1998.

These comprise:

- Numbered rules, some of which also have practice directions. In general terms the rules deal with the principles, and the practice directions the details, of the particular court procedure. The rules and practice directions have equal authority and apply to both the High Court and county courts.
- Schedules containing those orders of the RSC and CCR that still apply (in debt cases these relate mainly to post-judgment matters). These apply only in the High Court and county courts respectively.
- Pre-action protocols. These are codes of practice that the parties are expected to follow prior to commencing court action. Although there are now six such protocols (relating to personal injury, clinical and professional negligence claims, construction and engineering disputes, defamation and judicial review, with consultation taking place on a general protocol), regardless of whether there is a protocol relating to the specific type of case, the parties are expected to act reasonably in their pre-action conduct in exchanging relevant information and documents and generally in avoiding the necessity of court proceedings.[1]

The CPR are intended to enable courts to deal with cases 'justly' by:

- ensuring that the parties are on an equal footing;
- saving expense;
- dealing with cases in proportion to the amount of money involved, the importance of the case, the complexity of the issues and the financial position of each party;
- ensuring that cases are dealt with expeditiously and fairly;
- taking account of the courts' resources and their availability (the 'overriding objective').

The CPR are published in *The Civil Court Practice 2001* (Butterworth). This is an expensive two-volume publication (plus a separate volume containing prescribed forms) which, like its predecessor, is known as the 'Green Book' and is published annually with supplements. In addition to the rules, the Green Book contains annotations, tables summarising various common procedures, details of court costs and fees, the pre-action protocols and excerpts from relevant legislation.

The Lord Chancellor's Department and the Court Service are the government agencies responsible for the courts. The Court Service publishes various leaflets and guides to court procedure and these are available free from court offices and on the Court Service's website (www.courtservice.gov.uk). There is also a Courts Charter, a series of leaflets covering all the courts and offices run by the Court Service, which sets out the standards of performance court users can expect and how to complain. All forms of discrimination should be challenged and taken up with the court as part of the debt adviser's social policy work.

The court manager and her/his staff are responsible for carrying out the court's administrative functions – for example, issuing proceedings, processing applications and fixing hearing dates. It is a good idea for debt advisers to establish a working relationship with their local court. Many courts operate users' groups and/or court desks for unrepresented parties. Debt advisers have no right to represent their clients in courts (as opposed to tribunals) except at hearings allocated to the small claims track, but judges have increasingly recognised the value of such representation and rarely refuse to allow debt advisers to speak on behalf of their clients. However, only legal representatives[2] can sign court forms on behalf of clients or allow their addresses to be used for service of documents.

The procedures described in this chapter apply equally to the High Court and the county court unless stated otherwise.

Court fees

Most steps taken in court proceedings attract a court fee to cover administrative costs, which must be paid to the court before the step can be taken. The fees are set annually by statutory instrument and details can be obtained from any court office or the Court Service website.

A person is exempt from paying a fee if s/he is in receipt of income support, income-based jobseeker's allowance (JSA), working families tax credit or disabled person's tax credit (provided that the amount to be deducted from the weekly maximum tax credit does not exceed £72.70) and is not Legal Services Commission (LSC) funded for the proceedings in question.

Someone who is not exempt can nevertheless apply for the remission or reduction of a court fee if the exceptional circumstances of the case involve undue financial hardship. The application should be made on Form EX160, together with evidence of eligibility. Court Service guidance (available from any court office) points out that 'hardship' should not be confused with 'inconvenience'. If payment of the court fee in whole or in part would reduce the applicant's income below income support (IS) levels, full or partial remission should be granted. A refusal can be appealed within 14 days.

If the application is not made at the same time as the court action is taken, any fee can be refunded retrospectively provided an application is made within six months of the fee being paid. This time limit can be extended for good cause. There is no space on the form to give details of debts or exceptional circumstances, so a supporting letter may be required. Exemption/remission cannot be applied for in the case of consolidated attachment of earnings orders (see p196) or administration orders (see p233).

2. Types of court action

The person who or organisation that brings court action is called the 'claimant'. The person against whom or organisation against which court action is brought is called the 'defendant'. Most forms used in court proceedings are prescribed and can be identified by their number and title in the bottom left hand corner. It is important for debt advisers to familiarise themselves with these forms. Some examples of the forms debt advisers most commonly encounter are in Appendix 3.

Cases can be classified as follows:

- Money only claims – eg, for goods supplied and delivered (see p174).
- Claims relating to agreements regulated by the Consumer Credit Act 1974 – eg, for possession of goods supplied under a hire purchase (HP) agreement (see p199).
- Claims relating to land – eg, for possession of a house by a mortgage lender (see p201).
- All other claims – eg, a claim for the return of goods supplied under an agreement not regulated by the Consumer Credit Act 1974. These differ from money only claims in that, if the debtor does not respond to the claim, the creditor must make a formal application to the court for judgment and submit supporting evidence. The court will decide whether the creditor is entitled to judgment.

3. **Action to recover money only**

Court proceedings start when the court issues a 'claim form' at the request of the creditor (claimant). In order for a claim form to be issued in the High Court the creditor must expect to recover more than £15,000. The claim must be started in the county court if the creditor is unable to state this.[3] Even if the claim is for more than £15,000 the creditor should not issue proceedings in the High Court unless s/he believes that one or more of the following justify the matter being dealt with by a High Court judge:[4]

- the financial value of the claim and the amount in dispute;
- the complexity of the facts, legal issues, remedies or procedures involved;
- the importance of the outcome of the claim to the public in general.

These factors will rarely, if ever, be present in the ordinary debt case, and so there should be no reason for creditors to issue proceedings in the High Court.

Debts regulated by the Consumer Credit Act 1974

The High Court cannot deal with claims related to agreements or secured loans regulated by the Consumer Credit Act 1974, or actions linked to such agreements, regardless of the amount of the claim. If action that is based on a regulated agreement is started in the High Court it should be transferred to the county court.[5] The High Court can 'strike out' (ie, dismiss) an action if the creditor knew, or ought to have known, that the county court should have been used.[6] The debt adviser should immediately request that the creditor withdraws or transfers the action and, if s/he refuses to do so, should acknowledge the service of the proceedings (see p177) but apply at the same time to have it struck out or transferred to the county court. Unless the creditor has deliberately ignored the rules, the court is likely to transfer the case and penalise the creditor in costs.

A judgment made in the county court with regard to a regulated credit agreement cannot be transferred to the High Court for enforcement.[7]

Default notice

A default notice is a form which must be issued by a creditor for all debts regulated by the Consumer Credit Act 1974 before court action can start for early payment of monies due under an agreement. It is usually required in debt cases where arrears are claimed along with the monies which would become due if the agreement ran its course. It is not required if the time allotted to an agreement is already over but arrears remain or only arrears are claimed.

The default notice must contain the following details:
- the type of agreement, including the name and address of creditor and debtor;
- what terms of the agreement have been broken;
- for fixed-sum credit, the early settlement figure;
- what action is necessary by the debtor – eg, pay arrears in full by a certain date;
- what action the creditor intends to take if the debtor is unable to comply with the default notice – eg, refer to debt collection, start court action.

The debtor must be given at least seven days to carry out the required action, and if the default notice requests payment it must contain a statement about time orders (see p211) and about seeking advice from a Citizens Advice Bureau, solicitor or trading standards department.

Upon issuing a default notice a creditor is entitled to:
- terminate the agreement;
- recover any goods or land which form part of the agreement;
- demand earlier payment of money due under an agreement.

Creditors will not always automatically initiate court action if a default notice is not complied with, and even if the time limit has expired it is always worth negotiating with a creditor in order to prevent possible court action. Debtors often claim not to have received default notices and so advisers should bear in mind that a default notice is treated as served for this purpose if it is sent by post to the debtor's last known address.[8]

Venue

Claims for the recovery of money only can be started by creditors in any county court (or High Court District Registry or the Royal Courts of Justice, where relevant). This may not be anywhere near to where the debtor (defendant) lives. Large creditors which issue county court claims in bulk and prepare claims on computer can use the Claims Production Centre (CPC) at Northampton County Court which charges a lower court fee (see p173). The court that issues the claim (the originating court) will deal with the matter by post unless it is transferred to another court. The case will automatically be transferred to the debtor's 'home court' (ie, the county court for the district in which the debtor lives, or in High Court cases, the district registry for the district in which s/he lives or, if there is no such registry, the Royal Courts of Justice) if one of the following applies:[9]

- the debtor defends the action (see p185);
- there is a request for redetermination of a decision by court staff relating to an instalment order (see p184);
- the district judge decides to dispose of a request for an instalment order at a hearing;
- there is an application to set aside a default judgment (see p226);
- there is an application by a creditor to increase the amount payable under a judgment (see p227);
- there is a request for reconsideration of a decision by court staff relating to a debtor's application to vary the amount payable under a judgment or to suspend a warrant of execution (see pp227 and 229).

If the debtor's defence is that s/he paid the debt before the claim was issued, then this will be checked with the creditor before the case is transferred. In Northampton CPC cases, all defences are checked with the creditor before the case is transferred. Automatic transfer is only available where the defendant is an individual. The court has a discretion to transfer the case where:

- it would be more convenient or fair for a hearing to be held in some other court; *and/or*
- the facilities available at the court where the case is currently being dealt with are inadequate because a party or witness has a disability.

The claim form

The claim form (N1) must contain a concise statement of the nature of the claim and a 'statement of value'. This states the amount the creditor is claiming and whether s/he expects to recover (i) not more than £5,000; (ii) more than £5,000 but not more than £15,000; or (iii) more than £15,000. The amount claimed will include the court fee paid by the creditor to issue the proceedings and, if a solicitor has been instructed, an amount for the solicitor's costs. The court fee and solicitor's costs vary with the amount claimed. There may also be a claim for interest (see p187).

Details of the court of issue and of the unique reference number allocated to the case appear in the top right corner of the claim form. Appendix 3 contains an example of a claim form.

The claim form must be served on the debtor within four months. This will usually be done by the court and will be by first class post. The claim form is deemed to have been received on the second day after it was posted – ie, if posted on Monday it is deemed to have been received on Wednesday (Saturdays, Sundays, Bank Holidays, Christmas Day and Good Friday are not counted)[10] (in Production Centre cases, the claim form is deemed to be served five days after issue).

Particulars of claim

The claim form must either be accompanied by 'particulars of claim' or these must be sent to ('served on') the debtor by the creditor within 14 days of the claim form being served. The particulars of claim must include a concise statement of the facts relied on by the creditor (including the details of any contract) and must be verified by a statement of truth – ie, that the creditor believes the facts stated are true. A copy of any written agreement should (but not must) be attached (unless the claim form and particulars of claim are issued from the Production Centre).[11]

Where the claim form includes particulars of claim (as will usually be the case), it must be accompanied by:

- a response pack, including an acknowledgement of service (N9);
- a form for admitting the claim (N9A);
- a form of defence and counterclaim for use when the debtor disputes the claim (N9B);
- notes for the debtor on replying to the claim form (N9C).

Where the particulars of claim are served separately from the claim form, the forms must be served with the particulars of claim. This may be important as the debtor's time for responding to the claim runs from the date of service of the particulars of claim.

Responding to the claim form

The debtor must respond to the claim form/particulars of claim within 14 days of service – that is, the response must be received on or before the 16th day after the date of posting – in one of the following ways:

- send ('file') a defence or counterclaim to the court (see p185);
- file an acknowledgement of service within the 14-day period if s/he is unable to file a defence in time or wishes to dispute the court's jurisdiction – for example, if a creditor has issued proceedings for an amount due under a regulated consumer credit agreement in the High Court rather than, as required, in the county court (see p174). Once an acknowledgement of service has been filed, the debtor must file the defence within 28 days of the date of service of the claim form/particulars of claim;

- send ('serve') an admission to the creditor admitting the whole of the claim (see p178). There is no provision for filing an acknowledgement of service where the debtor admits the whole claim, but the debtor may still send the admission to the creditor outside the 14-day period provided the creditor has not requested a default judgment (see p184);
- file an admission and defence, admitting part of the claim but disputing the balance or making a counterclaim (see p185).

The flowchart in Appendix 3 illustrates the usual procedure following the issue of a claim form for money only.

The admission and statement of means form (N9A)

The admission and statement of means form provides the creditor and the court with information about the debtor's financial circumstances and allows the debtor to admit the amount owing and make an offer to pay the debt (see p185 where the debtor only agrees that part of the amount claimed is due).

Importance of form N9A

The statement of means accompanying any admission is a vital document. It may be all that the creditor knows of the debtor's ability to pay. Apart from any information provided by the creditor, it will be the sole basis for the court officer's decision about the rate of payment if the creditor does not accept the offer made by the debtor.

Court officers use a purely mechanistic way of working out an instalment order to allow the debtor to make monthly payments (see p182). They have no powers to penalise those whose borrowing they consider excessive or ill advised and will generally make a decision purely on the basis of the debtor's 'available income'. However, the guidance given to court officers allows wide scope for the use of discretion, which means that judgements can undoubtedly creep in (see p182).

Using financial statements

Much of the information required on form N9A is contained in the financial statement and list of creditors (Chapter 3). Courts may be willing to accept a financial statement attached to form N9A, together with a list of creditors with balances and offers (if there are any) instead of the debtor completing form N9A in full. This certainly saves time, and is permitted by the Civil Procedure Rules (CPR),[12] but may not be acceptable to court officers who need to extract certain information from the specific boxes on the form. Debt advisers should check with the court before submitting financial statements separately to the N9A. If in doubt, complete N9A and attach a financial statement.

The following section explains in detail how to complete form N9A, but it is also relevant to completing form N245 (Application to Suspend a Warrant of

Execution or Reduce an Instalment Order) or form N56 (Reply to Attachment of Earnings Application) – see pp229 and 195.

Completing form N9A

An example of a form N9A can be found in Appendix 3.

1 **Personal details** This section should show the name, address and age of the debtor. If there are joint defendants, either can complete the form, but it should be made clear if any offer is made jointly and both should sign the N9A.

2 **Dependants** This information is needed to explain the level of expenditure. A heterosexual partner should be entered as a dependant even if s/he has an independent source of income. If a heterosexual partner does not wish to be considered as a dependant, then this fact should be noted either in the box or in an accompanying letter. S/he must, however, be included on the N9A (because s/he is a member of the household) and her/his presence may affect the level of instalment payments.

3 **Employment** Every employment status of the debtor should be shown (s/he may have more than one). The question about annual turnover for self-employed people appears unnecessary. Take-home pay is entered in the income section 6. Court officers do not take account of information provided by self-employed debtors in section 3 when determining a rate of payment. The information may, however, influence the decision the creditor may make. However, if the information is not easily available, it will be sufficient to indicate employment status only. Details of any tax or national insurance arrears should be included in sections 8 or 9. Other business debts should be included in sections 8, 9 or 10, although the N9A is not really suitable for a business which is still trading to use to make payment offers. Indeed, guidance to court staff suggests that, unless the creditor is prepared to accept the debtor's payment offer, the papers should be referred to the district judge.

4 **Bank account and savings** Court officers are instructed to see whether sums are available to pay either a large lump sum towards a debt or a regular amount. They should ignore any amounts that are less than one and a half times a debtor's monthly income or seven times her/his weekly income.

If the amount shown is more than the ignored amount and some, or all, of the money in an account is needed to pay a priority creditor, it is important that the money is paid before form N9A is completed so that it is not shown as being available for a non-priority debt. If the amount is intended to meet the expenses detailed in section 7, this should be made clear as otherwise the court officer will assume that it is available to pay the debt. If the debtor has a joint bank account, only her/his share of any savings need be declared.

5 **Property** This section provides background information to the creditor and may indicate whether the debt could ever be enforced by a charging order in the event of default on the judgment (see p189).

6 **Income** This section requires details of the debtor's income from all sources. See p41 for how to treat debtors who are couples to help decide whether to show joint income and expenses (see notes to section 7) on the form.

The decision is further complicated by the instruction at the top of section 7. If, for example, a partner (or any other member of the household) pays all fuel bills, then those items should not be included as an expense unless that person's contribution is included at 6, 'Others living in my home give me'. Court officers are instructed to convert all figures to either weekly or monthly amounts for consistency.

7 **Expenses** Unless joint income and expenditure figures are being used, only include items of expenditure actually paid for by the debtor out of her/his income disclosed in section 6 (see notes for section 6). A major problem with this section is the absence of many categories of essential expenditure. These can be added in the space marked 'Others' and need not be limited to the three lines given there – eg, telephone or mobile phone bills, insurance premiums, childcare costs. Always explain what 'other' expenditure is and use a covering letter to explain its importance if necessary. The expenses figure at the end of section 7 should be accurate and the items that a court may consider 'non-essential' should be included, where necessary, in one of the named categories listed on the form.

Travelling expenses need to cover either fares or vehicle running costs plus petrol. Mail order catalogues are often used to budget for clothing, bedding and small household items and so expenditure for these items can be listed in that section if the debtor pays for these items this way.

Section 7 should include details of payments to meet the regular cost of ongoing services provided by priority creditors, including water charges (any arrears should appear in section 10, regardless of the instruction in section 8). Expenditure figures need to reflect accurately the actual spending as far as possible.[13]

8 **Priority debts** This section requires information about offers which have already been accepted to prevent action by priority creditors in pursuit of arrears. Thus, it is desirable before submitting form N9A that arrangements with priority creditors have been made. If an arrangement has not yet been made with one or more priority creditors then state the total arrears outstanding to that priority creditor. If the total arrears figures are given, court officers are advised to assume repayment of arrears in three months, except for hire purchase (HP) and mortgage arrears which might be spread over one to two years. If offers have been made but a reply is awaited, they should be included on the form. Include priority business debts, such as VAT or income tax, here.

Debtors may be uncertain about what proportion of payments to priority creditors are to cover arrears. In this case, to save time, total payments, including arrears, could be entered in section 7 'Expenses' and a note written in box 8 to indicate this.

9 **Court orders** Only existing court orders should be listed here, but not the one subject to the present action. If another creditor has agreed to a temporary cessation of payments on an existing court order, this should be noted, especially if the debtor intends to ask this creditor to do the same. Use a separate sheet or financial statement if there is not enough room on the form.

10 **Credit debts** This section requires details of payments already arranged with other non-priority creditors who have not obtained a court order. The three spaces provided for such debts are unlikely to be adequate and another sheet may be needed. Only the amounts currently being paid should be included, but an accompanying financial statement is useful information to indicate the level of indebtedness and offers made to other creditors, as well as indicating how the offer on the N9A has been calculated.

11 **Offer of payment** If there is available income, an offer should normally be made on a pro rata basis, but some offer should always be made even if it is only a nominal figure – eg, 50p or £1 a month.

The creditor's response

When the creditor receives form N9A s/he will decide whether to accept or reject the offer of payment. If s/he accepts, s/he will request the court to enter judgment on form N205A/225 for the sum claimed to be paid as offered and the court will send the debtor a copy of the judgment – N30(1) Judgment for Claimant (Acceptance of offer). 'Judgment' is the formal term for the court's decision in a case. Prior to judgment the creditor is trying to establish that the debtor owes the money. After judgment, liability cannot be denied unless the debtor appeals (see p237) or applies to set the judgment aside (see p226).

The court can order the debtor to pay in one of three ways:

* by monthly instalments; *or*
* in one instalment, for example, within 14 or 28 days; *or*
* immediately. This means that the debtor is inevitably unable to comply with the order and is automatically in arrears with the judgment.

The creditor is not required to send a copy of the N9A to the court when accepting the offer and so the court has no information as to the debtor's ability to pay the judgment.

If the debtor fails to comply with the judgment and takes no steps to change its terms (see p227) the creditor can decide whether or not to use a means of enforcement in order to obtain payment of the money (see p189). Some creditors request orders for immediate payment as a matter of course so that they can take enforcement action quickly. The debt adviser should argue that this is not a valid objection to the debtor's offer of payment (see below).

If the debtor does not 'request time to pay' (see below) the creditor may specify the terms of the judgment (s/he could specify immediate payment) and the court will enter judgment accordingly. If no terms are specified, the court will enter judgment for immediate payment.[14] A 'request for time to pay' is defined as a 'proposal about the date of payment or a proposal to pay by instalments at the times and rate specified in the request'.[15] Thus, if the debtor wishes to avoid a judgment for immediate payment, s/he must make an offer of payment – however small – in order to trigger the next step in the procedure (see below).

If the creditor rejects the offer s/he must inform the court and supply reasons for the refusal and a copy of the N9A. The court will then enter judgment for the amount admitted and 'determine' the rate of payment. In doing this, the court must take into account:

- the debtor's statement of means;
- the creditor's objections;
- any other relevant factors.[16]

How court staff calculate instalment orders (determination)

Where the amount involved is not more than £50,000, the rate of payment may be determined by a court officer who must do so without holding a hearing. The Lord Chancellor's Department provides guidance on how to do this.[17] It is useful to obtain a copy of the guidelines (available free from the court office) to refer to when completing the N9A. The total income (box 6) is the starting point. To this may be added any savings (box 4). From this total income the following are deducted:

- expenses (box 7);
- priority debts (box 8);
- court debts (box 9);
- credit debt repayments (box 10).

Court officers are instructed to use common sense when assessing essential items of expenditure and to allow a reasonable amount for items which are not listed in box 7 but which are essential to the debtor's household (eg, payments for a vehicle or childminder to enable the debtor to work, or the cost of travelling to and from work). Although court officers are not expected to assess whether any of the amounts are too high, 'frivolous' and 'non-essential' items will be disregarded. These are specified as:

- children's pocket money;
- money for gambling, alcohol or cigarettes;
- money for newspapers or magazines (unless essential to the debtor in her/his work);
- holiday money.

The guidance does, however, give the court officer discretion to allow £10 a week for 'sundries' (presumably per household).

The debtor should be allowed sufficient resources and time to pay priority debts, although court staff are instructed to make certain assumptions about what is a reasonable period for clearing such arrears (see above). Although court officers are instructed to take a common sense approach to credit debts, the guidance also states that 'there is no logical reason why these debts should take precedence over a county court judgment'.

The guidance reminds court officers that creditors must state reasons for rejecting offers. Rejecting an offer because of the amount of the debt or the length of time it has been outstanding or because the offer is 'too low' is not sufficient unless the creditor can demonstrate inaccuracies in the information provided by the debtor.

The resulting figures are then transferred to a 'Determination of Means Calculator' (EX120) and the court officer works out the rate of payment based on the amount of 'disposable (available) income'. If the disposable income is:

- higher than the offer but lower than the figure the creditor is prepared to accept, the instalment order should be for the amount of disposable income;
- higher than the figure the creditor is prepared to accept, the instalment order should be for the amount the creditor is prepared to accept;
- lower than the offer, the instalment order should be for the amount the debtor has offered unless this is 'unrealistically high';
- nil or a negative figure, either the instalment order should be for the amount the debtor has offered (unless unrealistically high) or the matter should be referred to the district judge for advice or a decision.[18]

The guidance recognises that the N9A is designed for individual rather than business debts and that, unless a business has provided information about its financial position, it will be difficult for court officers to make a decision on the rate of payment. If the creditor has indicated the terms upon which s/he will accept payment by instalments, the court officer can enter judgment accordingly. Otherwise, s/he is instructed to refer the matter to the district judge.

Where the amount involved is more than £50,000, the rate of payment must be determined by a district judge who may decide the matter with or without a hearing. In some courts, claims for less than £50,000 are referred to the district judge for determination. The district judge is not required to follow the guidelines issued to court staff. If the district judge decides to hold a hearing, the case will be automatically transferred to the debtor's home court.

The court will notify both creditor and debtor of the order made – N30(2) Judgment for Claimant (Determination without a hearing) – and either party may apply to the court for a reconsideration of this decision, known as redetermination (see below).

Redetermination by a district judge

Where the rate of payment has been decided without a hearing, either the creditor or the debtor can ask for a reconsideration (redetermination) by a district judge within 14 days. No court fee is payable.[19] The debtor can request redetermination regardless of whether the original determination was made by a court officer or the district judge (provided there was no hearing).

District judges are not bound by the determination of means guidelines and can make whatever order they think fit. Accordingly, where there is available income, the N9A should be carefully completed so that a decision can be made from the form alone, which is likely to be upheld by a district judge if the creditor asks for a redetermination. This is particularly important where large amounts are owed or a creditor feels particularly aggrieved for some other reason – eg, no payments have so far been made on an agreement. However, there is an increasing trend for district judges to reject low or nominal offers of payment and make an order for immediate payment instead to enable the creditor to enforce it, if possible. Such offers are seen as unrealistic and the creditor is not regarded as being unreasonable in refusing to accept an offer of payment which will take many years to pay off the judgment, if ever. Where the debtor is on a low income and has no property, assets or savings then this is purely academic, but otherwise that income, etc, may be at risk.

A debtor whose position is unusual may benefit from the wider discretion of a district judge if, for instance, payment could be made from monies which s/he expects to receive in time or if s/he is seriously ill and likely to gain sympathy. All such arguments should be made clearly, and the application should be made by letter (or on form N244 – see p232) giving reasons why the debt adviser thinks the matter should be reconsidered. The court will arrange for the case to be transferred to the debtor's local court.

If the original determination was made by a court officer, the redetermination may take place without a hearing unless one is requested. If the original determination was made by a district judge, the redetermination must be made at a hearing unless the parties agree otherwise. Difficulties may arise because there is no pro forma application and sometimes courts fail to recognise a written request. The request should always refer to redetermination under para 14.13 of the Part 14 practice direction, specify whether or not a hearing is required and set out why the original determination should be reconsidered. If the determination was made by a district judge at a hearing, there is no right to request a redetermination. If circumstances change, either party can apply for a variation in the rate of payment ordered (see p227).

Default judgment

If the debtor fails to reply to the claim form (including a 'nil' or no offer of payment, see above), the creditor can request the court to enter judgment in default on form N205A/225. Default judgment cannot be entered where the debtor has, within the specified time limits:

- filed a defence; *or*
- filed an acknowledgement of service; *or*
- filed or served an admission together with a request for time to pay.[20]

The creditor must specify the date by which the whole of the debt is to be paid (which may be immediately) or the rate at which it is to be paid by instalments. If none is specified, the judgment will be for payment immediately.[21]

A debt adviser who thinks that default judgment has been entered, or is about to be, should check with the court of issue. If it has not been entered, the debtor can still respond (see above). However, if judgment has already been entered s/he should apply either to vary the judgment (see p227) or to set it aside (if appropriate, see p226).

If the creditor does not apply for judgment within six months of the expiry of the debtor's time for responding to the claim, the action is 'stayed' and the claimant must apply to the court for permission to proceed with it.[22]

After judgment, if the amount required is not paid within a month, details are entered in the Register of County Court Judgments. This information is publicly available and is used by many credit reference agencies. Entries are cancelled after six years, but not until the end of the calendar year.

Completing the defence and counterclaim (form N9B)

Form N9B provides the debtor with an opportunity to explain the circumstances and facts of any dispute, which should be stated clearly and in sufficient detail. A defence should be submitted where there is one – eg, if the debt has already been paid. It is not a defence that the debtor cannot afford to pay the debt. In these circumstances the debtor should follow the admission procedure described above. A counterclaim should be made if the debtor has lost money because the creditor has failed to carry out her/his legal obligations.

Where some of the claim is admitted and time is required to pay that amount, but some is disputed, then both forms N9A and N9B should be completed and returned to court. These may be used to challenge the creditor's costs where it is felt that para 4 of the pre-action protocols practice direction has not been complied with. This imposes a general obligation to act reasonably in negotiations and avoid unnecessary court action. Advisers should beware of substituting what they consider reasonable for what a district judge is likely to consider reasonable, as it is the debtor who will have to pay any additional costs incurred. As a general rule, district judges do not consider it unreasonable for a creditor to seek a judgment which the debtor appears to be unable to pay. On the other hand, the district judge may well consider it unreasonable of a creditor to refuse to negotiate at all, or to agree to a payment arrangement and then sue the debtor anyway, or possibly to refuse an offer of payment accepted by the debtor's other creditors.

An example of an N9B is in Appendix 3. It should be returned to court within 14 days of service. If the defence cannot be prepared within that time the debtor should return the acknowledgement of service (N9) to the court and will automatically have a further 14 days in which to file a defence – ie, 28 days from the date of service of the claim form/particulars of claim. The debtor may need to obtain specialist consumer or legal advice before completing the N9B.

Where the debt is disputed on grounds other than that it was paid before the issue of the claim form (see p176) the case will be automatically transferred to the debtor's home court on the filing of the N9B and the court will send both parties an allocation questionnaire (N150). This must be returned to the court within 14 days, together with a fee of £80 payable by the creditor (unless the claim is for £1,000 or less). The purpose of the questionnaire is to enable the court to allocate the case to a 'track'. On receipt of the questionnaire the court will:

- allocate the case to a track (see below); *or*
- set a hearing date to consider allocation; *or*
- make orders as to the future conduct of the case ('case management directions'); *or*
- summarily dispose of the case (see p187); *or*
- (if requested on the questionnaire by both parties) suspend further action for up to one month to enable the parties to try and settle the case.

Tracks

The 'small claims track'[23] is the normal track for cases with a financial value of not more than £5,000. On allocating the case the court gives standard directions for its future conduct and fixes a hearing date at least 21 days ahead. The case is normally heard in private by a district judge. Debt advisers have the right to represent clients at the hearing.

The 'fast track'[24] is the normal track for cases with a financial value of no more than £15,000, which the court estimates can be tried in a day. On allocating the case, the court gives case management directions and sets a timetable in which those steps are to be taken. At the same time the court also fixes either a hearing date or a period within which the hearing is to take place. The hearing of the case should take place within 30 weeks.

The 'multi-track'[25] is the normal track for all other cases – ie, cases with a higher financial value that cannot be heard in a day or more complex cases requiring individual directions. On allocating the case the court will either give case management directions with a timetable in which those steps are to be taken (although no trial date or period is fixed) or fix a hearing to consider the issues in the case and the directions that will be required.

Summary disposal

One of the key features contained in the CPR is the duty of the court to actively manage cases, with greater scope to act on its own initiative. The court can strike out the particulars of a claim or defence where:

- no reasonable grounds are disclosed in the particulars of the claim (eg, 'money owed £1,000') or defence ('I do not owe the money') for either bringing or defending the claim; *or*
- it is an abuse of the court's process – eg, where it raises issues which could or should have been dealt with in a previous cases involving the same parties; *or*
- the court is satisfied either that a case has no real prospects of success on the facts or is bound to succeed or fail on a point of law and there is no other compelling reason for the matter to go to trial.

This means that it cannot be relied on and the party will be unable to proceed. The court can then enter 'summary judgment' for the other party.[26] The court can take this step either on its own initiative or on the application of a party. Courts are now more proactive in this area than in the past and debt advisers should, therefore, exercise great care in the preparation of defences and counterclaims. Defences which lack detail are likely to be struck out – ie, the defence must set out the relevant facts and reasons for disputing the claim.

Interest

In most of the cases which will be dealt with by a debt adviser, no interest will be chargeable after a county court judgment (but not a High Court judgment, see below). This is important, not only because it means that any payments that the debtor is able to make will reduce the amount outstanding, but also because, if the creditor knows that interest charges will have to stop once the matter is taken to court, s/he may be persuaded to stop charging interest once a debtor begins to experience difficulties in repaying.

The court can include in any judgment simple interest, at such a rate as it thinks fit, from the date the debt fell due to:

- in the case of a debt paid before judgment, the date of payment; *or*
- in the case of debt for which judgment is entered, the date of judgment ('discretionary interest').[27]

Interest must be claimed specifically by the creditor in the particulars of claim and cannot be claimed in addition to any other interest, nor can it be awarded so as to run after the date of judgment. Provided the creditor restricts her/his claim to the rate of interest payable on judgment debts (currently 8 per cent a year, see below), the claim for interest can be included in a default judgment or judgment on admission.

High Court judgments carry simple interest from the date of judgment to the date of payment at the rate specified from time to time (currently 8 per cent a year since 1 April 1993, 15 per cent prior to that date). This is known as 'statutory interest'.[28]

Since 1 July 1991 county court judgments for £5,000 or more have carried statutory interest unless:

- under the terms of the judgment payment is either deferred to a specified date or is to be made by instalments (when interest does not accrue until either that date or on any instalment until it falls due); *or*
- the judgment arises out of a consumer credit agreement regulated by the Consumer Credit Act 1974; *or*
- a suspended possession order is made; *or*
- an administration order or attachment of earnings order is in force.[29]

Interest ceases to be due when enforcement proceedings (other than by way of a charging order) are started, but if these do not recover any money then interest accrues as if those proceedings had never started. It seems that, if the debtor defaults under the terms of the original judgment and then obtains a variation or suspension of the judgment (see p227), interest does not accrue.

The above covers most debts with which debt advisers are likely to be involved. Loan agreements, however, contain provisions for lenders to charge interest on the amount borrowed and additional interest in the event of default by the debtor ('contractual interest'). The general rule is that once the lender obtains judgment, the right to any further contractual interest ceases, but this can be, and invariably is, excluded by the agreement itself. The House of Lords has recently ruled that such a clause is 'fair'.[30] Following the judgment in *Forward Trust v Whymark*,[31] which allowed lenders to obtain judgment for the outstanding balance of a loan without giving credit for any early settlement rebate, many lenders issue proceedings for the full sum owed (including interest pre-calculated to the end of the agreement). Other lenders (where the interest rate is variable) limit the claim and the judgment to the principal amount outstanding plus accrued interest to the date of judgment, whilst reserving the right to issue separate proceedings for the ongoing interest.

Debtors who are paying off the judgment can be confused and alarmed to receive statements showing the debt increasing and demands from the creditor for additional payments. The judgment is satisfied once the amount sued for (plus costs) has been paid. Creditors who claim to be able to 'add' contractual interest to the judgment should be challenged. If creditors wish to include ongoing contractual interest in a judgment, they should seek a judgment for the amount of interest to be decided by the court.[32] Although the House of Lords in the First National Bank case declared that this situation was unacceptable, and that judgments should take account of accruing contractual interest so that courts could consider making time orders (see p211), they declined to decide whether the current rules allow this to happen. If a creditor threatens to pursue additional interest by taking further proceedings, the debt adviser should take specialist advice.[33]

Enforcement of a judgment (what the creditor can do)

Once judgment has been given it is the responsibility of the creditor (and not the court) to collect payments. It is, therefore, important for the debtor to record all payments made and obtain receipts. If the debtor fails to pay in accordance with the judgment, the creditor can attempt to enforce payment through the court. Debt advisers should always explain to clients that, provided they keep to the terms of the judgment, the creditor cannot take enforcement action however unhappy s/he may be with the terms of the judgment. The creditor can use any available method of enforcement, and can use more than one method of enforcement either at the same time or one after the other.[34]

Following consultation about changes to enforcement procedures with a view to making them more 'effective', a number of amendments have been made to several of the procedures discussed below with effect from 25 March 2002.

See p226 for how to prevent enforcement.

Warrant of execution

The warrant of execution is a document that allows the county court bailiff to take and sell goods belonging to the debtor to pay a judgment debt plus the court fees and costs. If the debtor does not keep to the payments ordered by the court the creditor can ask the court to issue a warrant of execution once a payment is missed. The warrant can be for the whole amount of the judgment outstanding or just the arrears, which must be at least £50. Goods can be taken unless the amount shown on the warrant plus costs are paid. Certain goods are exempt from seizure (see p270). The debtor has an opportunity to apply for the warrant to be suspended (see p229).

A county court judgment may be transferred to the High Court for enforcement by sheriff's officers if the judgment is between £600 and £5,000. It must be transferred to the High Court for enforcement if it is for more than £5,000.[35] The judgment then becomes a High Court judgment for the purpose of statutory interest (see p187) and it will be necessary for the debtor to apply for a stay of execution (see p229). Judgments relating to agreements regulated by the Consumer Credit Act 1974 cannot be transferred regardless of the amount of the judgment.

The warrant of execution remains the preferred enforcement method for most creditors. In 2000, 470,270 warrants were issued.

Charging orders

A charging order is a court order that secures the amount owed, usually against the debtor's interest in a property in which case an entry is made on the Land Register to this effect. When the property is sold the judgment debt, together with court fees/costs plus any statutory interest (but not contractual interest) (see above),[36] must be repaid out of the balance of the proceeds of sale after payment of any prior mortgages or charges. A charging order can be made only if judgment has been given but has not been complied with. Even if only one instalment under a judgment has been missed, the creditor can apply for a charging order. The effect of a charging order is, therefore, to turn an unsecured debt into a secured one.

Many creditors request the court to make judgments for immediate payment simply so that they can apply straight away for a charging order. Unfortunately, some district judges regard this as reasonable, especially in cases where it appears that the debtor's offer of payment will not clear the debt for many years (if at all). Advisers should, therefore, follow through the admission procedure as far as redetermination (see above), if necessary, in order to demonstrate to the district judge that the debtor cannot afford to pay higher instalments and that it would be unreasonable in the circumstances to make a charging order (see below).

Charging orders are governed by the Charging Orders Act 1979. The High Court can only make a charging order where the judgment is a High Court judgment for more than £5,000, but the county court has jurisdiction in all cases.[37] In 2000, the number of charging orders applied for rose to 16,357, a fifth more than in 1999.

Charging orders are normally made against a person's home (including a part share in a home) or business premises, but could be made against shares or the debtor's interest under a trust.

There are two stages in the charging order process, which are now dealt with by Part 73 CPR.

Interim charging order

The creditor must apply to the court to obtain an interim charging order on form N379. This must be sent either to the court which made the judgment or, if the case has subsequently been transferred to a different court, to that court. The application must demonstrate that the debtor is in arrears with payments due under a judgment. The creditor will also have to provide details of the debtor's interest in the property to be charged and details of all other creditors known to the creditor with their addresses, if known.[38] Provided the papers are in order, the court will send the debtor a copy of form N379 and the interim charging order together with notice of the date and time of the court hearing to consider making the order final. These must be sent at least 21 days prior to the hearing. Copies will also be served on such creditors as the court directs, so that they can have the opportunity to object.[39]

The creditor will also apply to the Land Registry to register a 'caution' on the property. This is a warning that an application is about to be made for a final charging order and means that if the debtor attempts to dispose of the property, or her/his interest in it, the creditor will be informed and will be able to object to the transaction. The Land Registry will send a copy of the registered caution to the debtor as soon as it is received. This effectively 'blocks' any transfer or sale of the property by the debtor made with the intention of avoiding the charge.

Once an interim charging order has been made against shares or other securities a 'stop order' will come into force. This is a court order that stops the sale or transfer of the shares and also prohibits the taking of dividends or other income from them.

Final charging order

The second stage in the charging order process is for the creditor to obtain a final charging order. At the hearing, the district judge will decide whether to make the interim charging order final, or to discharge it. S/he should take into account both the personal circumstances of the debtor and whether any of the creditors would 'be likely to be unduly prejudiced by the making of the order'.[40]

If the debtor wishes to object to the making of the final order, s/he can apply to have the hearing transferred to her/his local court.[41] The debtor must also file at court and serve on the creditor written evidence stating the grounds of objection not less than seven days before the hearing.[42] Any relevant documents (including a financial statement) should be attached. In many cases, debt advisers will want to present a defence, but in practice most district judges appear to make final charging orders automatically. However, if the debtor does wish to defend the charging order the following arguments could be used:

- Some creditors believe they can apply for a charge at any time, so check if any of the instalment payments due under a judgment have been missed. If not, the court cannot grant a charging order.[43]
- Check if an application to redetermine/vary the judgment was submitted before the interim order was applied for. If it was, the redetermination/ variation should be dealt with before the charging order and, so long as the redetermination/variation is granted and the new payments maintained, the application for a charging order could fail. However, an instalment order made after the date of the interim order is no bar to the making of a final order.[44]
- Check if other creditors have been notified of the charging order application, as the charging order could unduly prejudice their rights and, therefore, should not be made final. District judges may accept this argument if an arrangement has already been made for an equitable distribution to other creditors, which will be overturned if a charge is made for this debt (to prevent an order for sale following failure to make payments). If the court has not directed that other creditors be notified of the charging order application, it could be argued that the debtor has been denied a fair hearing, as prejudice to creditors is one of the matters which the Charging Orders Act specifically requires the court to take into account. Alternatively, the district judge may adjourn while other creditors are notified; if none of the creditors lodge an objection this defence may fail.

- The defendant is technically insolvent and thus a charge in favour of one creditor prejudices the rest. This would be the case if there were insufficient equity in the property to cover all the debts in full.[45]
- The debt is small compared with the amount of equity in the property.

Conditions attached to a charging order

A charging order can be made either with or without conditions.[46] A debtor could apply at the charging order hearing for a condition to be imposed to prevent the charging order being used as a basis for an order for sale, or for it only to be used as such in certain circumstances – eg, after the youngest child of the family has reached the age of 18. If a court is clearly determined to impose a charging order, such conditions can mitigate the worst effects of its decision. Debt advisers should point out to the court that when making a final charging order, it should consider the possibility of enforcement by the creditor and should attach conditions to the order on that basis.

Payment of instalments may be ordered as a condition under which the final charging order is not to be enforced.[47] The debtor can apply for these payments to be suspended or varied if her/his circumstances change. If an instalment order is attached to the charging order and payments are missed, this might strengthen the creditor's case for an order for sale; some district judges are, therefore, very reluctant to make an instalment order. In some cases creditors will ask for a charging order as a condition of accepting payment offers.

If the debtor is going to ask the district judge to attach conditions to the final order, written evidence should be submitted as above. If a final order has already been made, it is still possible to make an application to the court to vary or discharge the order if it seems the court did not consider the debtor's circumstances at the time the order was made or the circumstances have since changed. A co-owner or a joint occupier who is a spouse can also apply.[48]

Order for sale

Note: An application to sell a charged property is both serious and legally complex. The inexperienced adviser should always consider referral to a qualified legal practitioner.

An order for sale is a court order to sell a property that is the subject of a charging order so that the debt can be paid out of the proceeds of the sale. It is only possible after a charging order has been made final and if any conditions attached to the order have not been met. However, the Charging Orders Act requires a district judge to use her/his discretion to decide whether to order a sale as though this were a charge, like a mortgage, which the debtor has entered voluntarily.[49] This means s/he could decide what is reasonable and fair in a particular case (see p204).

In the past, orders for sale have been very rare, but there appears to be a worrying trend towards them at present.

The creditor must apply using the procedure under Part 8 CPR. This requires a hearing in all cases. The debtor should complete and return the acknowledgement of service not more than 14 days after service of the claim form, together with any written evidence, indicating that s/he intends to oppose the order for sale and her/his reasons for doing so. It is vital that debtors attend and are represented at this hearing.

All the factors that should have been considered at the time the charging order was made should be reconsidered (see above). In particular, if there is now very little equity in the property or if there are other, more substantial, debts than when the order was made, an application could be made for the original charging order to be set aside on the basis that it is now prejudicial to the rights of other creditors. The debt adviser will need to discuss with the debtor a way of ensuring that the charging order creditor is paid and this debt will now have to be treated as a priority (see Chapter 7). A full financial statement should be completed and an offer of payment made if at all possible. Always re-check income maximisation, especially payment of interest by the Department for Work and Pensions (DWP) for home improvement loans.

If an order for sale is made, the debtor will normally be given 28 days to pay the debt or leave the property. If this does not happen, the creditor can apply for a warrant of possession (see p226). An order for sale can be suspended on terms.

Joint ownership of property

A charging order can be made against a debtor's 'beneficial interest' (her/his share) in a property. If a debtor owns only a part share of a property, then a charge can still be made but it will apply only to her/his part share.

In considering whether a part owner is insolvent, the district judge should look at the equity represented by her/his part share, not that of other owners.

If a charging order is made, the creditor becomes a party with an interest in the property and can apply for an order to sell the property so that the creditor's interest can be realised.[50] The court is required to have regard to the following matters:

- the intentions of the owners at the time of the original purchase – ie, the purpose for which the property was bought;
- the purposes for which the property is held. For example, it may be that a court should not order the sale of an asset, which was bought for a specific purpose, until the need for it has ceased to exist. If this is a correct interpretation, then a family home should not be sold until all members of the family have ceased to need it;
- the welfare of any minor who occupies the property as her/his home;
- the interests of any secured creditor.[51]

Pre-1997 case law suggests that, in the absence of exceptional circumstances, the wishes of the creditor should prevail (loss of the home not being regarded as 'exceptional' in this context). However, it appears that these cases are no longer good law as a result of the statutory provisions quoted above.[52]

The personal circumstances of the debtor and other occupiers should be explained to the court in detail and the following points drawn to the attention of the district judge about the other owners:

- it is not equitable (or fair) for a whole family or group of occupants to be evicted for the debt of one of their members;
- any special factors – eg, age, disability, illness, need for stability at work or school, availability of alternative housing, effect on children;
- the history of the loan.

If an application for an order for sale is made, a claim form will be sent to all co-owners of the property. This may include someone who owes no money to the creditor who has obtained the charging order. However, because that person owns part of the property against which the debt is secured, the court must treat her/him as a joint defendant in the case.

Where a divorce petition has been served, an application for a charge (or order for sale) should normally be considered along with the finances and property of the couple.[53]

Some creditors argue that a charging order allows them to enforce payment of accrued contractual interest even though it forms no part of the judgment. If a creditor tries to argue this, the debt adviser should seek specialist advice.

Attachment of earnings

An attachment of earnings order requires an employer who is paying wages, statutory sick pay or an occupational pension to a debtor to deduct some of it and make payments to the court to meet the debt. It cannot be used to attach state benefits. Attachment of earnings orders can be made either by the magistrates' or the county courts. They are governed by the Attachment of Earnings Act 1971. The following information relates to county court judgments, not to magistrates' court judgments.

The county court can make attachments to cover default on any judgment debt or administration orders and maintenance orders made in the county court or referred to it by the High Court. Statutory interest can still be applied in the case of High Court judgments. A creditor can request an attachment of earnings order for any unpaid judgment debt over £50. The debtor will receive a notice of the application (form N55) together with form N56 to complete showing a statement of her/his means. If s/he does not return form N56, the court can order the debtor to complete a statement of means and the debtor's employer can be ordered to supply a statement of earnings. An example of form N56 can be found in Appendix 3. This must always be filled in and returned to the court, as failure to do so can lead to a summons for a personal appearance and failure to comply with that can lead to imprisonment for contempt.

Suspended attachment of earnings order

The N56 is similar to the N9A considered on p178 except that there is provision to include a heterosexual partner's income. There is also space on the form to request that only a suspended attachment order is made. This allows the debtor to agree to make regular payments; an attachment of earnings order will not be made unless the debtor fails to keep up with the agreed payments. A debtor should always be advised to request that only a suspended order be made initially, particularly where an attachment order may lead to, for example, dismissal of the debtor by her/his employer.

A court officer will use the information supplied on the N56 together with a formula – contained in the Protected Earnings Calculator (EX119) – to make an attachment of earnings order and set a 'protected earnings rate' in accordance with the Determination of Means Guidelines considered on p182. This is an amount that the court considers is the minimum the debtor, and any dependants, needs to live on. The income support level is considered the minimum that is required plus housing costs, essential work-related expenses and other court orders. If, after taking into account any heterosexual partner's income or other sources of income, the debtor has less than this amount (the protected earnings rate), then the order will not be made. The guidance instructs court officers to disregard disability living allowance (both components) and attendance allowance when calculating means. The guidance suggests that deductions (the 'normal deduction rate') are set at between 50 per cent and 66 per cent of the debtor's 'disposable income' – that is, the difference between the debtor's net earnings and the protected earnings rate. The guidance recommends that a suspended attachment of earnings order should only be made if the debtor requests one, but that the request should be granted unless an attachment of earnings order is already in force. If the debtor does not give enough information on form N56, the court officer will refer the matter to the district judge to make an order.

Both the debtor and the creditor have 14 days to give notice to the court that they object to the terms of the attachment of earnings order, whether the order has been made by a court official or a district judge. If an objection comes from either side, then a hearing will be arranged in the debtor's local court at which the district judge can make any order s/he thinks appropriate.

Disadvantages of an attachment of earnings order

There are two principal problems with an attachment of earnings order. Firstly, it reduces a debtor's flexibility to manage her/his own affairs, and secondly, it may endanger her/his employment because it notifies the employer of debts. Certain employers (eg, security firms or those where money is handled) have policies of dismissing anybody against whom a judgment is made. If this happens, the debtor should seek the advice of an employment specialist.

The legislation allows a court to make an order rather than requiring it to do so and, therefore, if a debtor's livelihood is threatened by the making of an order the debt adviser should always argue that it is unreasonable to do so.

If made, an attachment of earnings order tells the employer of the total due under the judgment(s) concerned, and gives the normal rate to be deducted each week or month and states the protected earnings rate. If the debtor's earnings are insufficient to enable the full, or any, deduction to be made without breaching the protected earnings rate, the employer can only deduct from any earnings in excess of the protected earnings figure. Any resulting shortfall is not carried forward to the next pay day unless the attachment of earnings order was made by a magistrates' court.

Even if the principle of an attachment is accepted, the adviser could argue against the normal deduction figure suggested. An offer could be made on a pro rata basis if the debtor has more than one non-priority debt. A good financial statement is the basis of this argument, showing how repayment of priority creditors represents essential expenditure and that amounts to cover these should be included in the protected earnings rate.

If an attachment order is made, a fee (currently £1) can be added to each deduction by the employer to cover administrative costs. If a debtor leaves a job s/he must notify the court within seven days of any new employment and income; failure to do so is an offence which could be punishable by a fine. If the debtor becomes unemployed or self-employed s/he should write to the court immediately.

An attachment of earnings order made under the 1971 Act does not take priority over an attachment of earnings order made to recover local taxes or a deduction from earnings order made to recover child support arrears, even if made earlier. The combined effect may be to reduce the debtor's resources to a very basic level indeed. In such a case the debtor should be advised to apply to vary the attachment of earnings order under the 1971 Act (see p227).

Consolidated attachment of earnings

Where there are two or more attachment of earnings orders for debt, or one attachment is in force and a second one is applied for, the debtor can ask the court to consolidate these two debts and all other debts on which there is a judgment. The court can also make such an order on its own initiative.[54] No procedure is specified, but the debtor should provide the court with details of the other judgments and a financial statement. There is no limit on the number of judgments or the amount owed. The advantage of this procedure is that there is only one protected earnings rate and one deduction figure. Some debtors welcome this opportunity to save having to make several payments each month themselves.

A court can also decide to make an administration order (see p233), when considering an attachment of earnings, if the total indebtedness is below the administration order limit.[55] The court should always consider this if there are other debts. If an attachment of earnings is to be accepted by the debtor, then its conversion into an attached administration order can simplify repayments.

In 2000, the number of applications for attachment of earnings orders rose by nearly 50 per cent to 81,309.

Third party debt orders

Formerly 'garnishee' orders, a third party debt order instructs someone (the 'third party') who owes money to the debtor to pay it instead to the creditor (eg, a bank which holds savings belonging to the debtor). A third party debt order may only be given to a creditor who has already obtained a judgment that is not being complied with.[56] The procedure is now contained in Part 72 CPR.

The order is given in two stages. An interim third party debt order is made on application by the creditor on form N349 either to the court which made the judgment or, if the proceedings have since been transferred, to the court being used. This temporarily prohibits the third party from making any payment which reduces the amount s/he owes the debtor to less than the amount specified in the order – ie, the balance of the debt plus the costs of the application. This is followed by a final order after a hearing in front of a district judge, which must be not less than 28 days after the making of the interim order. If the debtor wishes to object to the making of the final order, s/he can apply to have the hearing transferred to her/his local court. The debtor (and also the third party) must file at court and serve on the creditor any written evidence setting out the grounds of objection not less than three days before the hearing. In making a final order, the district judge has a full discretion and should consider the position of both the debtor and any other creditors (if known).[57] If, for instance, an attempt were made to seize a person's only monthly income, then the debt adviser should argue that this would be unreasonable and would cause hardship to the debtor and her/his family, as well as preventing payments to other (possibly priority) creditors.

Where the third party is a bank or building society, on receipt of the interim order it must carry out a search for all accounts held in the name of the debtor and inform both the court and the creditor within seven days. Similarly, the bank or building society is required to inform the court within seven days if the debtor has no account. If, because of an interim order, a debtor finds her/his account frozen and s/he or her/his family is suffering 'hardship in meeting ordinary living expenses' through not being able to withdraw money from the account, s/he can apply to her/his local county court for a 'hardship payment order'. The debtor must produce written evidence to prove both her/his financial position and the need for payment. Two days' notice of the hearing must be given to the creditor, but the court can dispense with this in cases of 'exceptional urgency'. The court can permit the bank or building society to make one or more payments out of the account either to the debtor or some other specified person.[58]

Garnishee orders were most often used to instruct banks or building societies to pay over monies in a debtor's account to a creditor. Benefit payments cannot be made subject to a third party debt order, nor can an order be made against funds in a joint account in respect of a debt owed solely by one of the account holders. However, a third party debt order could be used if, for example, a debtor had told a creditor that an amount of capital would shortly be due from the maturing of an endowment insurance policy. The creditor could obtain a third party debt order against the insurance company after the amount became due but before it had been paid out. For this reason, it is important for a debt adviser not to reveal details of future monies available to a debtor if they are required to pay priority creditors or to be shared out among a number of creditors.

Orders to obtain information

Formerly oral examinations, an order to obtain information from a judgment debtor (or information order) is an order for the debtor to attend the court, in person, to be interviewed by a court official about her/his means or any other matter about which information is needed to enforce a judgment. It is not strictly a way of enforcement, but more an information gathering process. It can be used at any time, not just when payments have been missed. The procedure is now contained in Part 71 CPR.

A creditor who has obtained a judgment against someone can apply to court on form N316 for an information order requiring that person to attend a hearing at her/his local court before either a district judge (where there are 'compelling reasons) or more usually a senior court official. The order is in form N39 and must be served personally on the debtor at least 14 days before the hearing. Within seven days of service the debtor can require the creditor to pay her/his reasonable travel expenses to and from the court. The N39 contains a list of documents which the debtor is required to bring to court (eg, pay slips, rent book, credit agreements, outstanding bills) and the creditor can ask the court to add further documents to that list.

At the hearing the court officer asks the debtor a set of standard questions contained in form EX140. This is a 12-page questionnaire designed to find out what money, goods, property or other resources the debtor has to satisfy the judgment, in order for the creditor to decide what action to take next. The creditor can ask additional questions. The debtor must answer on oath. The debtor must attend the hearing and, if s/he does not appear, or if s/he refuses to take the oath or to answer any questions or, possibly, if s/he fails to bring any document listed on form N39 to the hearing, the court can make a suspended order committing her/him to prison unless s/he attends a further hearing and complies with the other terms of the original order – ie, produces documents, takes the oath, etc. If s/he again fails to comply, s/he will be arrested and brought before the judge to decide whether or not s/he should be committed to prison. In practice, the debtor will not be sent to prison so long as s/he co-operates in the process.

The adviser can help the debtor who has been served with an information order by providing a financial statement and a list of other debts and capital resources (including any equity in a house) in accordance with the information required by form N39, together with the documents referred to, where appropriate. An information order will almost certainly be followed by further action if any is possible. For example, the creditor may apply for an attachment of earnings order or a charging order. It is therefore important to pre-empt this if possible by submitting the above information to the creditor, implementing the most appropriate strategy for all the debts, and agreeing this with the creditor who has requested the information order before the hearing, which may no longer need to take place. If this cannot be agreed then it nevertheless may be appropriate to offer the strategy to all the other creditors and then this fact (along with any responses that are available) can be reported at the hearing. The court can also treat the hearing as an application for an administration order (see p170).[59]

Bailiffs

Chapter 11 discusses bailiffs' powers in detail.

---

4. **Action to recover goods on hire purchase or conditional sale (the Consumer Credit Act procedure)**

A court order is required to repossess goods on hire purchase or conditional sale if more than one-third of the total cost has been paid (see p59) or if the debtor has paid less but has refused to allow the creditor to enter private property in order to take back the goods. The creditor must first serve a default notice (including, in the section on what action may be taken, that goods can be repossessed). See p175 for further information about the default notice. In these cases the so-called 'Consumer Credit Act procedure' applies:

- The claim must be started in the county court for the district in which the debtor either lives or carries out her/his business (or did when s/he made her/his last payment for hire purchase/conditional sale cases) (or where the goods are situated for other cases).
- The court fixes a hearing date when it issues the claim form (N1) and notice of the hearing date is given when the claim form is served.
- The particulars of claim (containing the information prescribed by paragraph 7 of the Part 7B practice direction) must be served with the claim form.
- The claim form/particulars of claim are accompanied by forms N1(FD) (Defendant's Notes for Guidance), N9C (Admission and Statement of Means)

and N9D (Defence and Counterclaim). There is no acknowledgement of service.

Response

The debtor is not required to file either an admission or a defence, although s/he should do so as the court can take account of a failure to do so when deciding on its order for costs in the case. The creditor cannot request a default judgment. The N9C enables the debtor to admit the claim and make an offer upon which the court can make an order for the return of the goods suspended, so long as the debtor makes payments in accordance with her/his offer (a 'time order').[60] The statement of means is similar to the N9A. The debtor should indicate whether or not s/he still has the goods in her/his possession, admit liability for the claim and offer to pay the unpaid balance of the total price (this figure is contained in the particulars of claim). The admission is returned to the court and not sent to the creditor. A copy is sent by the court to the creditor and, if s/he accepts the offer, s/he informs the court, which enters judgment accordingly and sends a copy to the debtor (N32(2) HP/CCA). No one need attend the hearing. If nothing is heard from the court, the debtor should attend the hearing. If either the creditor does not accept the offer or the debtor does not respond, the hearing proceeds.

Negotiating prior to the hearing

An adviser should always try to negotiate with the creditor to reach an agreement before the court hearing. Most creditors will prefer to continue to receive payments rather than repossess the goods. Resuming the contractual payments will often be enough to persuade the creditor to withdraw or adjourn the court action. If no agreement can be reached the hearing will take place and the debtor should attend, with a financial statement indicating her/his ability to pay. A court is unlikely to accept a long-term substantial reduction in payments, for example £20 per month when the contractual agreement is for £120, but may accept a short-term reduction – eg, £20 per month for three months, then £120 per month. Unless a time order application is made (including completing form N9C, see above) or the hearing is adjourned, the court appears to have no power to make an order for payment of less than the contractual instalments.

If the agreement is regulated under the Consumer Credit Act 1974 then a default notice must have been issued in the correct format (see p175).

Decisions the court can make

The court has a general power to adjourn for a short period if required, but will only exercise this power if it has compelling reasons (see p238). If the debtor can make an offer of payment for the contractual instalments plus something off the arrears which the court finds acceptable, it will award possession but suspend the order so long as the payments are maintained.[61] If there is no acceptable payment offer the court will order that the goods be returned. The judgment will be on form N32(1) and give the date for delivery – ie, for the debtor to return the goods. If the goods are no longer in the possession of the debtor, the court cannot order their return;[62] the creditor will have to obtain a judgment for the total balance due under the agreement.

Alternatively, the debtor could make an application for a time order once the default notice has been issued (see p211).

If the debtor fails to make payments or return the goods as ordered, the creditor does not need any further court order and may repossess the goods provided it is possible to do so lawfully – eg, without trespassing on private land. Otherwise, the creditor can ask the court to issue a warrant of delivery (see p201).

Note that returning the goods to the creditor is not the end of the matter. The creditor will sell the goods and set the proceeds of the sale against the remaining balance due under the agreement. There may well be a shortfall that the debtor will be liable to pay. Although the claim is for money only, the Consumer Credit Act procedure still applies (see p199) and the creditor would need to apply to the court for a further hearing date to obtain an order for payment of the money.[63]

If the debtor's circumstances change, s/he can apply to vary the order. If the debtor disputes the claim, the court will either:

- deal with the case at the hearing; *or*
- allocate the case to a track and make directions; *or*
- give directions to enable it to make a decision as to allocation (see p185).

Warrant of delivery

A warrant of delivery is a document that allows the county court bailiff to seize goods which are the subject of a hire purchase or conditional sale agreement where the court has ordered the return of those goods to the creditor. It is issued by the court following a request from the creditor, if the debtor does not return the goods described in the judgment to the creditor as ordered by the court or is in breach of a suspended return of goods order (see p200). The warrant may allow the debtor to pay the value of the goods as an alternative to allowing them to be taken by the bailiffs. The debtor can apply for this warrant to be suspended and for delivery of the goods to be postponed (see p230). It is always worthwhile approaching the creditor to negotiate an agreement before applying back to the court.

5. **Action to recover property (possession action)**

A landlord or a mortgage lender can start an action in the county court for possession of a tenant's or owner occupier's home by completing a claim form (N5) and particulars of the claim (on form N119 for tenants and N120 for mortgagees). The creditor cannot request a default judgment or apply for summary judgment in this type of action; there must be a hearing to consider the merits of the claim. Since 15 October 2001, the procedure has been contained in Part 55 CPR. Possession claims are normally brought in the county court for the area where the property is situated. A claim may only be brought in the High Court in 'exceptional circumstances'. Neither the value of the property nor the amount of any financial claim on its own can normally justify starting a claim in the High Court. Circumstances which may justify it are if:

- there are complicated disputes of fact;
- there are points of law of general importance; *or*
- the claim is against trespassers and there is a substantial risk of public disturbance or of serious harm to persons or property which requires immediate determination.[64]

An occupier never should be advised to leave against her/his will unless a court order has been obtained.

This section covers only those possession actions that are taken on the grounds of unpaid rent or payments due under a mortgage (or other secured loan). The law relating to either of these areas is much greater than can be encompassed here and advisers should have to hand specialist books (see Appendix 6) and be prepared to refer to a housing specialist where necessary.

In 2000, 239,957 actions were started – a slight fall from the 1999 figure of 240,020 – of which 73,045 were mortgage possession actions. Although the number of mortgage possession actions fell by more than 10% from the previous year, the number of rent possession actions increased from 157,406 in 1999 to 166,912 in 2000.

Negotiating prior to the court hearing

The debt adviser should always try to negotiate with a creditor and reach a satisfactory agreement before going to court. This is preferable to relying on the decision of a district judge and avoids the possibility of things 'going wrong' at the hearing. In addition:

- tenants are usually ordered by the courts to pay landlords' costs;
- most mortgages allow the creditor to charge all her/his costs to the debtor in the event of a default or repossession;
- it is important to avoid unnecessary court hearings or delays;
- ideally both parties will apply for the matter to be adjourned generally (that is, without a future hearing date).

Often creditors will insist on a suspended possession order (see below) being made even though there is already an informal agreement in place. This puts the home at risk, but it may result in a better order for the debtor than if the matter had been left to the discretion of the district judge. If the creditor agrees to a suspended possession order, the debt adviser should check that the solicitor representing the creditor has been informed and obtain written confirmation of the terms of the proposed suspended order so that this can be produced at the hearing if there is any dispute. See Chapter 7 for possible strategies. It is rarely a good idea to agree to a 'consent order' (ie, where a suspended possession order is made at the request of both parties and confirmed by the court) because these are almost impossible to overturn later.

On the other hand, where the agreement to clear the arrears was made before the landlord/lender issued court proceedings and the debtor has not defaulted under the agreement, the adviser should ask the court to adjourn the matter and disallow the landlord's/lender's costs. This is because the overriding objective and paragraph 4 of the Pre-actions Protocol PD require people to act reasonably in trying to avoid the necessity for court proceedings (see p172).

Mortgages and secured loans

If the loan was a regulated agreement under the Consumer Credit Act (see Chapter 4) a default notice (see p175) must first have been issued. In addition, many mortgage lenders have their own policies – eg, a special letter may be sent warning borrowers of impending court action, or the mortgagee will not seek possession until payments of mortgage interest are three months in arrears. The Council of Mortgage Lenders has published a code of practice for its members, stating that 'possession of your property will be sought only as a last resort when attempts to reach alternative arrangements with you have been unsuccessful.'[65] The claim form (N5) will include the date and time of the hearing. It must be accompanied by a particulars of claim (form N120), although the lender can use its own particulars of claim provided it contains all the information prescribed by Part 55 paragraph 2 PD CPR as follows:

a.
- The identity of the property to be recovered.
- Whether the claim relates to residential property.
- The grounds on which possession is claimed.
- Full details of the mortgage or charge.
- Details of every person in possession of the property (to the best of the lender's knowledge).

b. Whether any charges or notices have been registered under the Family Law Act 1996 or Matrimonial Homes Acts 1967-1983.

c. The state of the account between the borrower and lender, including the following:
- The amount of the advance of the periodic payments and any repayment of interest required to be made.
- The amount which would have to be paid, taking into account any allowance for early settlement rebate, to redeem the mortgage at a stated date not later than 14 days after the commencement of proceedings, including solicitor's costs and administrative charges.

- If a regulated consumer credit agreement, the total amount outstanding under the terms of the mortgage.
- The rate of interest payable originally, immediately before any arrears accrued and at the commencement of proceedings.
- A schedule of arrears showing all amounts due and payments made together with dates and a running total of the arrears.
- Details of any other payments required to be made as a term of the mortgage, such as: insurance premiums, legal costs, default interest, penalties, administrative and other charges; whether any of these payments are in arrears; and whether or not they are included in the periodic payment.

d. Whether or not the loan or loans are regulated consumer credit agreements and the dates on which the appropriate notices under the Consumer Credit Act have been served.

e. Such relevant information as is known by the lender about the borrower's circumstances and, in particular, whether s/he is in receipt of benefits and whether direct mortgage payments are being received from the Department for Work and Pensions (DWP).

f. Any previous steps taken by the lender to recover either the money secured under the mortgage or the property itself, including dates of any court proceedings and the terms of any orders made.

All the above requirements with regard to the particulars of claim are covered within 'paragraphs' 1 to 9 on form N120.

Para 10 will be deleted unless the lender and borrower have entered into any tenancy agreement.

Para 11 is for details of the order that the lender is seeking, which will normally be:

- an order for possession of the property; *and*
- an order for payment of the total amount outstanding under the mortgage (see challenging the shortfall debt on p216).

The lender will not normally be seeking:

- an order for costs,

as the mortgage normally allows for these to be added to the outstanding balance automatically.

The particulars of claim must be verified by a statement of truth.

Replying to the claim

The hearing (which takes place in private) will normally be fixed for not less than 28 days or more than eight weeks after issue of the N5. The claim form and particulars of claim must be served on the borrower not less than 21 days before the hearing. Not less than 14 days before the hearing the claimant must send a notice to the property addressed to 'the occupiers' containing details of the claim. The purpose of this is to alert anyone living at the property who is not the borrower but who may be in a position to oppose the claim for possession. There is no acknowledgment of service.

There is a form of defence (N11M) which should be completed and filed at court within 14 days but may be filed at any time before the hearing. The questions are all fairly straightforward although they are not cross-referenced to the numbered paragraphs in the particulars of claim. It is not really a defence as such but a reply to the claim. It is not essential to respond at all but it is advisable to do so, as any delay caused by the borrower's failure to file the defence may involve her/him in further liability for costs. Although there will be a hearing, it is helpful if the district judge has been prepared for the borrower's circumstances and argument by the submission of a well-completed reply form. A copy of the form will also be sent by the court to the lender.

Question 2 relates to paras 2 to 4 on form N120 which should either be confirmed as correct or particulars given of any disagreement.

Question 3 – check the level of arrears as carefully as possible. The court may not make an order if it is unsure that the arrears figure is correct.

Question 4 needs completing only in cases where possession is sought (perhaps partly) on grounds other than arrears.

Questions 5 and 6 are addressed to borrowers whose loans are regulated agreements. Question 5 asks whether they want the court to consider whether the terms of the loan agreement are 'fair'. This appears to be applicable to the extortionate credit provisions of CCA 1974 as well as to unfairness, for example under the Unfair Terms in Consumer Contracts Regulations 1994–1999, and applies to all agreements, not just regulated agreements. Question 6 asks whether the borrower intends to apply for a time order (see p211). Any applications will need to be supported by written evidence setting out the grounds.

Question 7 – if the arrears have been paid in full by the date of the hearing, the case should be adjourned.[66]

Question 8 – if an agreement has been reached, details should be included and in this case the reply should ideally be accompanied by a letter requesting a general adjournment. If the lender agrees, it too should write to the court indicating its agreement to a general adjournment. If the agreement has been running since before the action started, the borrower may argue that there was no need to take court action, and ask for the matter to be adjourned generally and challenge any costs the lender seeks to charge.[67] Send proof of payments. Alternatively, include a written request from the lender that an order be made and suspended on payment of whatever sum has been agreed.

Question 9 should be completed in the affirmative where agreement has not been reached. Note that borrowers who fail to ask the court to consider instalments might later find this used against them if a local authority is considering the question of the intentionality of their homelessness.

Question 10 asks for the amount, in addition to the contractual payments, which is being offered. This question may not be relevant where the borrower is applying for a time order (see p211). In other cases, if money is not available yet for the arrears, then the court can be asked (probably on a separate sheet) to make an order suspended on payments of £x extra each month, with the first payment on a specified date in the foreseeable future. Alternatively, a token offer could be suggested for the first months, followed by something more realistic.

Questions 11-13 relate to income support and income-based jobseeker's allowance. It is important to check with the DWP what payments have been made before attending court, so that any misunderstandings with the lender can be resolved. Remember to convert weekly benefit amounts to calendar monthly amounts to compare with monthly mortgage payments.

Questions 14-25 relate to dependants (and non-dependants), bank accounts and savings, income and expenditure, priority debts, court orders and credit debts similar to those required on form N9A (see p179) and should be filled in similarly.

Question 26 – the borrower should not answer 'yes' to question 28 (If an order is made will you have somewhere to live?) unless the accommodation is absolutely certain. The date given, even in such cases, should always be realistic.

Question 27 is important because it gives the borrower the opportunity to explain:
- the circumstances in which the loan was made if relevant – eg, to refinance unsecured borrowing in response to high pressure selling;
- why the arrears arose;
- what circumstances were beyond her/his control;
- why it would cause particular hardship if eviction were ordered.

Powers of the court in dealing with possession action

Any evidence to be given at the hearing may be in writing and should be filed at court and served on the other side at least two days before the hearing date. Evidence of the arrears (including interest on the arrears) should be up to the date of the hearing, by reference to a daily rate, if necessary.

If a court is considering an action for the possession of a private house then it has wide powers in relation to non-regulated agreements under section 36 of the Administration of Justice Act 1970 and section 8 of the Administration of Justice Act 1973 to either:
- adjourn the proceedings; *or*
- suspend a possession order; *or*
- postpone the date for the delivery of possession.

Adjournment

The court has a general power to adjourn any proceedings for a short period.[68] For example, if the borrower needs more time to seek money advice or the lender is required to clarify the arrears, the court may well adjourn the matter, commonly for 28 days. The court may attach terms to the adjournment – eg, that basic instalments are paid or that no further interest is added to the loan. The court will send out a written notice giving the date and time of the next hearing. If the property is about to be sold or the arrears cleared in full in some other way the court may adjourn with liberty to restore. There will not be another hearing so long as the expected action happens. However, if the expected action fails the lender can ask for a hearing to be restored.

Advisers may wish to argue that the matter should be adjourned in preference to the granting of a suspended possession order, in one of the following ways:
- Adjourn with liberty to restore – eg, because the arrears have been, or are about to be, paid in full, or the property is in the process of being sold or an agreement to pay the arrears has already been agreed.
- Adjourn for a fixed period (eg, 28 days or 3 months) for the borrower to get further advice or for the lender to produce correct particulars of claim.
- Adjourn generally because there is a repayment plan agreed and working.

Terms may be attached to an adjournment, commonly that basic payments be maintained. District judges can adjourn on DWP payments, which are commonly less than basic payments, temporarily. An adjournment is preferable because no further action, including enforcement, can be taken without a further court hearing. For borrowers who are vulnerable through age or infirmity, this can be a valuable tactic. Alternatively, advisers can request that a suspended possession order is not to be enforced without the court's permission. This will mean that a court hearing will have to be set before a bailiff's warrant can be issued.

Suspended possession orders

Under section 36 of the Administration of Justice Act 1970 a court can suspend possession so long as the mortgage arrears can be cleared in a 'reasonable period'. The terms of the order will usually be for basic instalments plus £x towards the arrears. In 1996, in the case of *Cheltenham and Gloucester v Norgan*,[69] the Court of Appeal said that a starting point for 'reasonable period' should be the remaining period of the mortgage.

This valuable precedent strengthens the money advice case for setting repayments at a level the debtor can afford. In exceptional cases a 'reasonable period' could be longer than the remaining mortgage. The decision also guides the court on points it should take into consideration, including the means of the borrower and the security for the lender. A clear financial statement is an essential tool. Identify the basic mortgage instalment separately from the payment towards the arrears so that the court can see clearly what order it is being asked to make. Initially, advisers worried that borrowers would have to demonstrate the value of their property at the time of the hearing, but this does not appear to have happened. On the whole, the judiciary appears satisfied that for a long-term agreement, such as a mortgage, the security is safe. Tactically, advisers should still look for an affordable sum rather than spreading the arrears over as long a period as possible, just in case further difficulties arise in the future. Do not be intimidated by creditors and solicitors who say they want the arrears cleared in a shorter fixed period – eg, three years. The court will make its own decision and it should be familiar with the Norgan case.

Where the arrears cannot be paid by instalments but only out of the proceeds of sale of the property, then the 'reasonable period' for a suspended order could be the time it will take to effect the sale. Factors the court could take into account are:

- the extent to which the balance of the mortgage as well as the arrears are secured;
- where there is little equity, so that the value of the security is at risk, only a short period of suspension might be appropriate;
- where there has already been delay and/or there is negative equity or insufficient evidence of the property's value, an immediate possession order might be appropriate.[70] A court should grant a suspended possession order where the proceeds of the sale will fully cover the first mortgage.

Creditors have challenged suspended orders made to allow time for sale of properties in negative equity. The Court of Appeal has held that if the arrears cannot be cleared from the proceeds of the sale then the court has no jurisdiction to suspend the order.[71]

It is beyond the court's powers to suspend a possession order on any other terms (but see below). Although courts have been known to suspend on, say, DWP payments only, there is no jurisdiction to do this but the court could adjourn on such terms.

Order for possession

If there is no real chance of clearing the arrears the court will make a possession order, usually effective in 28 days. If the debtor has special reasons (eg, ill health or a new home not yet available) the court may extend this to 56 days. At the end of the 28/56-day period the creditor can apply back to the court for bailiffs to execute a warrant of possession (also known as a warrant of eviction) (see p226). The order points out that if the borrower does not leave the property, the lender can ask the court to instruct the bailiff to evict the borrower without a further hearing (although it also points out that the borrower can apply to the court to postpone the eviction).

A warrant of possession allows the county court bailiff to evict the occupants from their home. The homeowner or tenant will receive notification that a possession warrant has been obtained on form N54 and it will state the exact date and time the bailiffs will call to carry out the eviction. The bailiffs are empowered physically to remove the occupants from their home, if necessary, and hand over possession of the property to the landlord or mortgage company. This is usually followed by the creditor's agent changing the locks to prevent the occupier moving back in. The N54 informs the borrower that:

- a possession warrant gives the bailiff authority to remove anyone still in the property when the eviction takes place;
- the borrower should act immediately to get advice about the eviction or re-housing from an advice agency, solicitor or local Housing Department;
- the borrower can apply on an N244 (see p232) for the court to suspend the warrant and postpone the date for eviction;
- the borrower must attend the hearing of the application or it may simply be dismissed, incurring further costs;
- if the borrower can pay off any arrears, s/he should contact the borrower or the borrower's solicitor immediately;

The N54 must also contain details of the bailiff and the borrower or the borrower's solicitor.

In dealing with a warrant of possession, the debt adviser should either negotiate directly with the lender or landlord or help the debtor make an application to the court to suspend the warrant (see p231 for how to do this). County court bailiffs acting for a mortgage company or landlord who has issued an eviction warrant can change the locks and evict the debtor if no application has been made to suspend the warrant. They can use necessary reasonable force to carry out the eviction.

The granting of a possession order should not, however, be seen as the end of the line. Even where this has occurred, creditors still do not want to repossess homes unnecessarily and it may be possible to negotiate terms directly with the creditor which are more acceptable than those imposed by the court. Such variations should at least be agreed in writing and the court should be asked to vary the relevant order, with the consent of the other party if possible (see p227). Alternatively, it may be possible for the borrower to remain in her/his home while it is sold. In *Cheltenham & Gloucester v Booker* it was said that if the court was satisfied that:

- possession was not required by the lender pending the sale but only by the purchasers on completion;
- the presence of the borrowers would enhance the sale price (or at least not depress it);
- the borrower(s) would co-operate with the sale in every way;
- they would give up possession on completion to the purchasers;

then, in theory, they could be allowed to remain in occupation and conduct the sale.[72]

Regulated secured loans

Where a secured loan agreement is regulated under the Consumer Credit Act 1974 (see Chapter 4) (usually called a second mortgage), the court should consider making a time order. This can be also specifically requested by the debtor and may give a better outcome. See p211 for separate consideration of time orders.

Arguing against a possession order (mortgage)

In some cases, the situation when the loan was made is relevant. In particular, if a borrower was clearly badly advised to take on a new secured loan by a financial adviser (perhaps the lender itself), then the court should be acquainted with the facts. If there is any question of a claim for negligence against the adviser, then help from a specialist solicitor should be sought. The early history of the loan can be vital in enlisting the sympathy of the court.

If mortgage interest should have been paid by the DWP but has not been, or if a claim is pending, this should be brought to the court's attention. Similarly, if penalties have followed slow payments from the DWP these should be challenged (and compensation sought from the DWP with the help of an MP if necessary).

Debt advisers sometimes agree to a suspended possession order on the ground that this is a technicality and does no more than safeguard the lender's position. This is a very dangerous view and means that any future default in payment or the accruing of further mortgage arrears puts the borrower at serious risk of losing her/his home. If a suspended order is clearly going to be made, then the amount of instalments towards arrears should be set at a level that provides some leeway for the borrower faced with an unexpected and essential item of expenditure.

It will be unnecessary to argue against a possession order if a time order is made instead (or as well), in which case the order for possession should be suspended as long as the time order is complied with. A time order should, therefore, always be considered (see below) in cases of regulated agreements.

Some secured lenders have fallen foul of the Office of Fair Trading (OFT) in recent years because of so-called 'dual interest rate schemes'. Under these schemes, provided the borrower makes the contractual payments on time s/he is charged a 'concessionary' rate of interest. However, if s/he defaults on just one payment a substantially higher rate of interest becomes payable for the remainder of the loan. In November 1997 the OFT ruled that such schemes were 'unfair and oppressive and should be discontinued' unless:

- the differential between the concessionary and default rates of interest was 'reasonable' and reflected the lender's loss as a result of the borrower's default – eg, 2.5 per cent; *and*
- the borrower could return to the concessionary rate once the arrears were cleared.

A 1998 county court decision ruled that such schemes can 'grossly contravene the ordinary principles of fair dealing' under the Consumer Credit Act extortionate credit provisions and also the Unfair Terms in Consumer Contracts Regulations 1999 (for agreements made after 1 July 1995).[73] So-called 'arrears charges' and 'fines', legal charges unreasonably incurred and/or unreasonable in amount,[74] and interest penalties on early settlement are also possible areas where the terms of a loan could be challenged so as to reduce the amount payable by the borrower.

Time orders

A time order is an order under sections 129-136 of the Consumer Credit Act 1974 by which the court changes the terms of a regulated credit agreement. A time order provides for the payment by the debtor of any sum owed under a regulated agreement by instalments, payable at whatever frequency the court thinks 'just', having regard to the means of the debtor and/or any surety.[75] In the case of possession actions the 'sum owed' is the outstanding balance of the loan. The provisions of the Administration of Justice Acts 1970 and 1973 (see above) do not apply to regulated agreements[76] and debt advisers should challenge district judges who still insist on making orders for payment of contractual instalments plus arrears instead of time orders.

When appropriate

A debtor can apply for a time order if monies are owed under a regulated agreement and one of the following conditions applies:
- a default notice; *or*
- a notice of intention to recover goods or land; *or*
- a notice requiring payment early due to default; *or*
- a notice seeking to terminate an agreement has been served by the creditor; *or*
- enforcement action has been taken by the creditor (including an application for an enforcement order).[77]

A time order application is appropriate where:
- current circumstances make payments due impossible, but the borrower's income is likely to increase – eg, short-time working, a period of unemployment, benefit disqualification, reduction in income support during early months of a claim, illness (although a time order can still be considered in exceptional circumstances where there is no foreseeable improvement in circumstances);
- the agreement originally reached was harsh on the borrower and s/he was disadvantaged in negotiations for it or ignorant of its implications (but was not actually misinformed or forced – for these see Chapter 5). In these circumstances the court may well be sympathetic to using a time order in the interest of justice;

- an application might persuade the creditor to negotiate realistically and reduce the payments due under a regulated agreement.

In *Southern and District Finance v Barnes* the Court of Appeal made it clear that a court 'must first consider whether it is just to make a time order' in all possession cases involving regulated agreements.[78] This accords with the Consumer Credit Act 1974's grant of discretion to award a time order in such cases 'if it appears to the court just to do so'.[79] To use this discretion properly the court must consider the justice of an order in each case. The circumstances and terms of the loan, the reasons for default and the borrower's payment record will be relevant circumstances.

There is usually no advantage to the debtor in obtaining a time order for an unsecured loan since, once judgment is obtained, interest is frozen in practice and affordable instalments can be requested. (It may be a way to prevent judgment and this can be useful where, for instance, people work in the security industry.) However, in *Director General of Fair Trading v First National Bank*[80] the House of Lords recommended that a time order application could be made where a creditor was continuing to charge contractual interest after judgment. This can be done by adding in Box 11 of the N9A:

> I ask the court to (1) make a time order in the terms of my offer and (2) amend the loan agreement in consequence so that no further contractual interest accrues after the date of judgment.

If the applications are granted, the debtor's full liability to the creditor will be discharged on completion of the payments ordered. If a hearing is required, the court should transfer the hearing to the debtor's local court on its own initiative.[81]

The application

Application can be made by the debtor after receiving a default notice using form N440. A fee of £120 is payable (see court fees on p173 for fee exemption/ remission). The borrower will be the claimant and the lender will be the defendant. This can be most useful when a lender is demanding very high payments towards the arrears, or in other ways pressurising the borrower, but does not start court action itself and refuses to negotiate. It is much more common for an application for a time order to be in response to a claim for possession. Application can be on form N244 or in the borrower's defence.[82]

The application will need to show that it is just to both lender and borrower and indicate the terms of the time order that are required. Include:

- the circumstances of the borrower at the time s/he took out the loan, the situation now and her/his likely prospects for the future;
- the borrower's payment history to date;
- the amount of the loan, the interest rate charged and any extra charges due to default;

- the value of the security;
- the payments that can be made now and if and when these can be increased in the future, including a financial statement;
- the implications the time order will have on any changes that are required to the original agreement, particularly the extra time required and the reduction in interest rate required.

The scope of the order

The court is required to be just to both parties, thus it will consider the borrower's position with some care. Was s/he able to afford the agreement when s/he entered into it? Is the cause of the arrears a temporary one? Will s/he be able to afford to resume at least contractual payments at a foreseeable future date? Positive responses to these questions suggest it is just to the borrower. The court will also consider if there is adequate security for the lender and how the interest rate charged compares with other lenders. Adequate security and a higher interest rate will support an argument that a time order will not be unjust to the lender.

Example

A couple took a secured loan at 28 per cent APR to pay for double glazing and maintained payments for 18 months. The wage earner then had a serious accident and was unable to work. He should be fully recovered in about 9 months when he will resume employment and contractual payments. The loan is secured against the couple's home, which has adequate equity. On these facts a court should grant a time order.

'The sum owed'

A time order can be made for 'the sum owed'. This phrase has been the subject of much dispute but has now been clarified by the Court of Appeal. It means 'every sum which is due and owing under the agreement'. Where possession proceedings have been brought, this is the total indebtedness, and this was confirmed in the Barnes case. In the case of unsecured regulated loans, it will also usually be the total amount due.

The amount due (and subject to a time order) is therefore the sum of:
- the amount borrowed;
- the total charge for credit (early settlement rebates should not be applied to this);
- any default interest properly charged up to the hearing date;
- less all payments made to date.

The lender should make clear to the court the total sum owed and the present arrears as well as the contractual instalments. The debt adviser should, if possible, check these calculations.

How much to offer

The offer of payment will, of course, be according to the borrower's ability to repay and personal circumstances. In Barnes, an order was made for £25 per month for 6 months, then nearly £100 per month for the remaining 174 months.

Varying other terms

Having decided what the instalments and their timing should be, the court is left 'inevitably', according to the Court of Appeal, with the need to make consequential amendments to either the rate of interest or the length of the loan. It is empowered to do this by section 136 of the Consumer Credit Act 1974 provided that it is 'just to both parties and a consequence of the term of the order'. It is, therefore, important for the debt adviser to demonstrate that a reduction in interest is a necessary consequence of a reduction in payments in order to prevent a loan running for too long. This may simply be a reduction in interest on the arrears, or a reduction in interest on the arrears and principal during the period of reduced payments, or a longer-term reduction. The court will not have the facilities to calculate interest charges. Advisers may consider approaching their local trading standards office for assistance calculating interest rates or asking the court to include in the order that the lender adjusts the interest rate for payments to be completed in a fixed period.

Reviews

A time order can be varied or revoked by the court on the application of creditors or debtors.[83] This power to review should be sufficient to persuade district judges who still resist time orders on principle that one can safely be granted because it can later be reviewed.

Policy

Time orders are unpopular with the credit industry. It is easy to see why. They give the court wide powers to vary existing agreements. Some lenders will prefer to negotiate out of court rather than have a time order, so the threat of an application can be part of the negotiating tactics.

Although Barnes clarified the court's powers in relation to time orders, it suggested that:

When a time order is made it should normally be for a stipulated period on account of temporary financial difficulty. If, despite the giving of time, the debtor is unlikely to be able to resume payments by at least the amount of the contractual instalments, no time order should be made. In such circumstances it will be more equitable to allow the regulated agreement to be enforced.

However, the House of Lords decision in the First National Bank case suggests that the fact that the borrower's difficulties are not temporary may no longer be an obstacle to making a time order: '. . . the broad language of s129 should be so construed as to permit the county court to make such an order as appears to it just in all the circumstances' (including any amendment to the loan agreement – eg, freezing/reducing interest as it considers just to both parties).

Lenders are likely to continue to oppose time orders, so advisers must be well prepared and, if required, take further advice before making an application.

After repossession for mortgage default

A warrant of possession is executed on the date and time stated in the warrant. A court bailiff will come to the property accompanied by a locksmith and a representative from the lender. The bailiff may use force to enter the property and evict all occupants. If opposition is expected, the bailiff may be accompanied by a police officer to prevent a breach of the peace (not enforce the eviction). The locksmith will change the locks. Any of the borrower's property left in the home will therefore be locked in. The borrower can ask the lender for access to the home to remove her/his property within a reasonable period, considered to be two weeks. Otherwise there is little to be done after execution except apply for the judgment to be set aside if there is a strong legal case – eg, papers had not been served at all. The property will then be sold by the lender (see below).

Execution of the warrant can be suspended in certain circumstances while the lender or borrower sells the property. In the case of *Cheltenham & Gloucester v Booker*,[84] the judge took the view that the borrower could remain in occupation so long as the court was satisfied that the property would not be required by the lender before passing to the purchaser on completion, that occupation would improve (or at least not depress) the purchase price, that the borrower would co-operate with the sale and that the borrower would give up occupation on completion of the sale. Lord Justice Millet could not envisage a situation that would satisfy these conditions, and as the court was satisfied that the Bookers would not co-operate in the sale, they were evicted. Nonetheless, the guidelines are now set and advisers may encounter appropriate cases. For example, where a family is to be re-housed and is totally reconciled to repossession they may well be prepared to co-operate in preference to going into temporary accommodation.

After the sale of the property the lender will balance the payments and proceeds of the sale against the outstanding mortgage (the 'account'). The sale proceeds are applied first of all to any arrears of interest and are usually sufficient to extinguish these so that any shortfall is likely to be principal.

There is no duty on the lender to give details of the sale. If the mortgage is less than the payments and proceeds of sale, the balance will be paid to the borrower. If the mortgage is more than the payments and proceeds, the borrower will be asked to make up the difference, usually referred to as a 'mortgage shortfall' debt. In order to recover any debt, the lender must produce an account to show all payments made and proceeds of the sale versus the amount of the mortgage and its other costs to show the balance outstanding (see below). The borrower will be bound by law and contract to repay the mortgage and all the costs associated with recovering the debt. Once the property has been sold, the shortfall debt will be unsecured. Some lenders have a policy of not seeking to recover the shortfall for a year or two; in other cases borrowers have moved and it may take some time to trace them. It is not unusual for borrowers to remain unaware of the shortfall debt for several years.[85]

To lose a home is not necessarily the end of the line for the borrower and the debt adviser must ensure that action is taken to protect the borrower from future attempts to recover this money. Many lenders will not take any action immediately following a forced sale because they recognise that the borrower is likely to be suffering from the financial problems which caused the arrears and therefore could not afford to pay anything anyway. However, many lenders will keep records of repossessed borrowers and are likely to attempt to recover any shortfall at a later date when either the borrower's situation is known to have improved or the general economic situation is better. It is also possible that such lenders could sell these debts at a later date to companies whose standards of collection would be very much more draconian than those of the original mortgage lender. It is, therefore, vital that the debt adviser seeks ways of advising any borrower whose home is sold by a secured lender, following that sale.

Challenging the shortfall debt

There are few court precedents that relate to mortgage shortfall debts. Actions for negligence against professionals involved in the original purchase (eg, surveyors and solicitors) have not proved particularly successful. However, during the late 1980s there was some evidence of mortgage fraud involving professionals. If there is any possibility of a claim against a professional involved in the purchase, valuation or financial advice so far received, this will certainly require a specialist solicitor, possibly from outside the area in which the professionals involved practice. Under no circumstances should a debt adviser alert the potentially negligent party to the possibility of action.

In most cases, once the borrower has described circumstances that could give rise to a claim against one of these people, then s/he should be referred directly to a specialist solicitor. This should not be the firm involved in the original purchase unless there are reasons to know that it could not have been involved in earlier bad practice and that it is determined to take action (this could be the case, for instance, where a solicitor has alerted a borrower to the likely need for action against a particular developer and is already taking other claims against that developer). What follows is a brief summary of the responsibilities of the lender, properly called the 'mortgagee in possession'. Advisers can help borrowers to compare the lender's figures with this list to see if there are any items which could be challenged – eg, if the property was sold for well below its market value. These arguments may then contribute to the negotiating process.

- The lender must take proper care of the property. This will include making essential or emergency repairs (eg, a leaking pipe) and may include simple maintenance (eg, mowing the lawn, painting the windows) but will not include improvements (eg, refitting the kitchen).
- The lender must sell the property at a proper market price. It need not be the best possible price. Most lenders will get at least two valuations to ensure the price is fair and sell through an estate agent in the usual way. Sale by auction is usually considered to achieve a fair market price.
- The lender can decide when to sell. The lender is not under an obligation to sell quickly and, indeed, may delay the sale and let the property if it wishes. However, where there is already a potential shortfall, the lender should not delay marketing the property if, by so doing, the mortgage debt increases and puts the borrower in a worse financial position.[86]
- The lender must account to the borrower for money received and charged in respect of the property (the account, as above).
- The lender may appoint a receiver. Where a property is let as a business the lender may appoint a receiver to manage the property. It is unlikely that a domestic residence would be affected.

Mortgage indemnity guarantee

Most, but not all, mortgage lenders have a normal lending limit of 70-80 per cent of the property value. If a borrower wants to borrow a higher proportion, say 95-100 per cent, these lenders will ask the borrower to pay for an insurance policy to protect the lender against a fall in the value of the property. This is the mortgage indemnity guarantee (or indemnity insurance or building society indemnity). The insurance premium is usually, but not always, paid as a lump sum of several hundred pounds at the time of purchase. Note that the mortgage indemnity guarantee (MIG) is to protect the lender not the borrower. The only value to the borrower is that s/he will not be given the amount of mortgage s/he requires without agreeing to pay the insurance premium. Some financial advisers have offered, for a fee, to argue that the MIG will benefit the borrower. There is no indication that this will succeed. Two court cases have failed.[87] The Council of Mortgage Lenders and *Which?* magazine agree with this interpretation.

The MIG will not meet the full shortfall. The amount paid will be a proportion of the shortfall relative to the lending risk. There will, therefore, still be a shortfall owing to the lender. The lender's account should include payment of the proceeds of a MIG claim.

In addition, the insurance company that provides the MIG can pursue the borrower for the money paid out on her/his behalf, under a process known as 'subrogation'. In some cases the borrower may receive a demand for money from the insurer, even though the lender has agreed not to pursue the shortfall. Alternatively, some insurers appoint the lender to act on their behalf to collect the entire shortfall. Commonly, the borrower can expect to receive a demand from the insurer and the lender for their respective proportions of the shortfall. The Court of Appeal will probably make some decisions on this matter in the near future. Meanwhile, claims should be resisted and advice sought from a specialist. Unfortunately, however, claims cannot be ignored and must be dealt with if they are not to remain a threat to the debtor's financial security for years to come.

Time limits for action

There are time limits in which to take court action to recover debts. These are contained in the Limitation Act 1980. So long as the loan remains secured, the lender has 12 years in which to take action to recover the principal amount (ie, the capital sum borrowed) and 6 years to recover arrears of interest (the limitation period).[88] The position is complicated by the fact that the limitation period for the principal (but not the interest) starts again every time the borrower makes a payment to the lender or admits in writing that s/he owes the debt (known as an acknowledgement). Once the limitation period has expired it cannot be started again by further payments or acknowledgements.

Until 1997, it was generally believed that the limitation period for mortgage shortfall debts was still 12 years for the principal and 6 years for the interest, even though the debt was no longer secured by the mortgage. Then a judge in the Court of Appeal suggested that it was 'seriously arguable' that the 6-year limit applied to the principal as well as to the interest.[89] After a period of considerable uncertainty, the Court of Appeal has now resolved the issue:

- The limitation period for the principal sum borrowed is 12 years from the date when the sum became payable under the terms of the mortgage deed, usually after the borrower failed to pay 2 or 3 monthly instalments.[90]
- The limitation period for the interest is 6 years from the date when the lender had the right to receive that interest.[91]
- The fact that the mortgage deed contained an express provision under which the borrower agreed to pay any shortfall to the lender does not give the lender a fresh right of action starting on the date of sale.[92]

In the majority of cases, the shortfall will comprise principal only because the interest has been paid off out of the proceeds of sale (see above) and the whole debt will be subject to a 12-year time limit. This should, however, be checked with the lender.

As a concession, where:

- the lender is a Council of Mortgage Lenders member (or the MIG insurer is an Association of British Insurers member); *and*
- no contact has been made by the lender/insurer with the borrower prior to 11 February 2000,

the lender/insurer has agreed not to pursue the claim unless the borrower is contacted within six years of the date of sale of the property. 'Contact' here includes letters or telephone calls received but ignored by the borrower, but should not include letters sent to a previous address, unless these have been forwarded, or failed attempts to trace the borrower. This concession does not apply where the borrower was contacted prior to 11 February 2000 or had entered into a payment arrangement with the lender/issuer prior to that date, even if the contact was made more than six years after the property was sold.

Strategies

A mortgage shortfall debt is, in many ways, no different from any other unsecured debt since once the property has been sold it is no longer a priority debt. The strategies, tactics and principles of good money advice described throughout this book still apply. However, the debt is often disproportionately high compared with the borrower's normal income and lifestyle. For borrowers it can be very distressing to be faced with such a huge debt. However, it is becoming apparent that lenders and insurance companies are exercising a greater degree of flexibility in their approach to recovery.

Some lenders will already have a county court judgment for money. This does not prevent the borrower from using any of the strategies detailed, but in addition the adviser may need to protect the borrower's interest by applying to vary or suspend the judgment. This will be essential if the lender is attempting to enforce the judgment (eg, by attachment of earnings) as the Limitation Act does not apply to enforcement action. Borrowers who have acquired assets, particularly another property, may be especially vulnerable. If possible, the borrower should try to resolve the shortfall debt before acquiring further assets such as a house or flat.

It is not unusual for borrowers to fail to tell the lender of their new address. Some may hope that they will not be found. The Council of Mortgage Lenders has indicated that its members will vigorously pursue borrowers with shortfall debts, using tracing agents if necessary.

Before entering into negotiations, always check whether the Council of Mortgage Lenders/Association of British Insurers concession (known as 'the CML Agreement') applies and then use the preceding paragraphs to check the account and, if appropriate, note any points which may be used to challenge the extent of the debt. Otherwise consider the following strategies:

- **Write-off** A total write-off is likely to be the most appropriate strategy where it can be demonstrated that the debtor has no available income or assets and that the position is unlikely to improve (see p154). In other cases, pressure should be brought (perhaps by using publicity or local politicians) to highlight the manifest unfairness of both seizing a person's home and also expecting repayment of the shortfall.

- **Individual voluntary arrangements** (see Chapter 12) An individual voluntary arrangement (IVA) will usually only be appropriate where the shortfall is modest and in proportion with other unsecured debts, and the borrower can afford substantial repayments and/or owns a home that would be at risk in bankruptcy proceedings, or if the lender obtained a charging order (see p189).

- **Bankruptcy** (see Chapter 12) If all else fails, personal bankruptcy will legally and finally end the shortfall debt recovery process. It will usually be appropriate when the lender/insurer insists on pursuing the claim but the borrower has no property or assets, little income and needs the peace of mind and fresh start that follows bankruptcy.
- **Full and final settlement** Most lenders and insurance companies will agree to accept a smaller sum than the full outstanding shortfall debt. How much will be acceptable varies according to individual circumstance. Settlements in the region of 10 per cent to 50 per cent are not uncommon. The offer should be made in writing in a letter from the borrower(s) (drafted by the adviser if necessary). It must be made absolutely clear that payment is offered in full and final settlement of the borrower's liability (and/or any other parties to the mortgage). The lender must confirm in writing that payment will be accepted on these terms (see p158). Advisers should ensure that any full and final settlement covers the claims of both the lender and any insurer.
- **Instalment payments** Many lenders will accept modest monthly payments towards a substantial debt, where personal circumstances show this to be reasonable. The borrower may find it extremely daunting to be asked to pay, say, £20 a month towards a debt of £35,000 because s/he cannot see an end. On the other hand, many lenders see token payments as a tacit recognition that the borrower is being responsible about the shortfall. Debt advisers should suggest that provided the borrower keeps up the payments for, say five years, the lender should accept this in full and final settlement and agree to write off the balance. If the borrower has other non-priority debts and the mortgage shortfall is to be included in a pro rata payment arrangement, the debt adviser should attempt to agree a total figure that the lender is prepared to accept for inclusion in the financial statement on the basis that the balance will be written off on completion of the payment arrangement.

When preparing a strategy bear in mind that if there was an MIG there may be two separate demands to negotiate, one from the lender and one from the MIG insurer.

Implications for the future

In 1991 the Council of Mortgage Lenders instigated a Central Register of Repossessions. Subscribers report repossessions to two credit reference agencies, CCN and Equifax. Borrowers can ask to see their credit reference in the normal way. As with all credit, no one has a right to a mortgage and lenders will have their own individual policies on whether to offer a mortgage to someone who has been repossessed in the past. The Council of Mortgage Lenders has indicated that its members are more likely to consider applicants who admit their previous repossession and can show that their circumstances have improved.

Rented property

The particulars of claim, on form N119, in a possession action for rented property must contain information prescribed by Part 55 para 2 PD CPR as follows:
- what land is to be recovered;
- whether the claim relates to a dwelling house;
- full details of the tenancy agreement;
- the grounds on which possession is claimed;
- details of every person living in the property (to the best of the landlord's knowledge);
- the amount due at the start of proceedings;
- a schedule showing all amounts of rent due and payments made, including dates and a running total of the arrears;
- the daily rate of rent (and any interest);
- any previous steps that the landlord has taken to recover the arrears, including dates of any court proceedings and the dates and terms of any order made;
- any relevant information as is known about the tenant's circumstances, including whether s/he is in receipt of benefits and whether any direct payments are being made to the landlord.

Replying to the claim

The reply will be on a form N11R.

Question 2 relates to paragraphs 2 and 3 of form N119 and should either be confirmed as correct or particulars given of any disagreement.

Question 3 asks about the service of the 'notice to quit' or equivalent. The debt adviser should always ensure that this has been done in the prescribed manner. (See Appendix 6, Defending Possession Proceedings, LAG, or similar.)

Question 4 asks the tenant to check the rent arrears as stated by the landlord. This should be done most carefully.

What counts as rent arrears

In many cases, particularly when the local authority is landlord, some of what is claimed as rent arrears may not, in fact, be so. For example, amounts of overpaid housing benefit that an authority wishes to recover may be added to a tenant's rent account as though they were arrears. In fact, even where such an amount has properly become payable (and the tenant has been given the rights of appeal, etc),[93] such amounts do not constitute unpaid rent. It is permissible for them to be included in a tenant's rent account provided they are clearly distinguished from rent that is owed to the authority. They should not appear on a claim form as rent arrears. However, in non-local authority tenancy cases, where housing benefit has been paid direct to the landlord and the local authority has exercised its right to recover any housing benefit overpayment direct from the landlord, the amount recovered can be treated as rent arrears.[94]

In some cases tenants may also have amounts of rates (from before April 1990), water charges, rent arrears from a previous tenancy or other non-rent charges included in their rent arrears. These amounts should not appear on a claim form.

Question 5 only needs completing where possession is sought on grounds other than rent arrears – eg, nuisance.

Question 6 asks for any counterclaims that the tenant may have. There are a series of counterclaims or 'set-offs' that can be made by a tenant when a landlord claims possession. These include:

- Under a tenancy created before 15 January 1989, a landlord may be charging more than the fair rent set by the rent officer. In such cases, not only is the excess over the fair rent not recoverable or counted as arrears for the purposes of seeking possession of the property but the tenant can claim back all the overpaid monies for up to two years.[95]

- A counterclaim can be made for disrepair, if a landlord has failed to keep her/his statutory obligations to repair the exterior or main structure of the property or facilities for the supply of water, gas, electricity or removal of sewage. The tenant can claim that the rent arrears should be reduced by an amount to compensate her/him for this loss, which can be done by completing the defence part of the reply to the possession claim form. However, in order to safeguard their rights, tenants should either pay the rent or open an account into which to pay it. In a recent case, a county court judge still made an order for possession because of rent arrears despite awarding an amount for damages for disrepair that was greater than the actual arrears. The decision to order possession was subsequently overturned by the Court of Appeal.[96]

Consider seeking the advice of a specialist housing adviser if a landlord has failed in some contractual obligation – eg, has not provided furniture as agreed or redecorated a property as regularly as promised. In such cases, it is often wise to refer the matter to a solicitor before proceeding.

Question 7 is self-explanatory and asks for details of payments made since the claim form was issued.

Questions 8 and 9 – if an agreement has been reached, details should be included in **question 8** and in this case the reply should ideally be accompanied by a letter requesting a general adjournment (and a similar one from the landlord sent separately) or a request from the landlord that an order be made and suspended on payment of whatever sum has been agreed. If an unrealistic offer was previously made (perhaps under pressure) and broken, this should be made clear.

Question 9 should be completed in the affirmative where agreement has not been reached. Note that tenants who fail to ask the court to consider instalments might later find this used against them if a local authority is considering the question of the intentionality of their homelessness.

Question 10 asks for the amount in addition to the rent that is being offered. If money is not available for the arrears yet, then the court can be asked (probably on a separate sheet) to make an order suspended on payments of £x extra each week or month with the first payment on a specified date in the foreseeable future. Alternatively, a token offer could be suggested for the first months followed by something more realistic.

Questions 11-15 are self-explanatory and relate to income support or housing benefit. In preparation for any hearing, it is important for the debt adviser to know the up-to-date position on these (particularly if rent is paid directly to a landlord or if non-dependant deductions vary with the movement of non-dependants).

Questions 16-27 relate to dependants (and non-dependants), bank accounts and savings, income and expenditure, priority debts, court orders and credit debts similar to those required on form N9A (see p178) and should be filled in similarly.

Question 28 – the debtor should not answer 'yes' to question 28 (If an order is made will you have somewhere to live?) unless the new accommodation is absolutely certain. The date given, even in such cases, should always allow for 'slippage'.

Question 29 is important because it gives the debtor the opportunity to explain:
• why the arrears arose;
• what circumstances were beyond her/his control;
• why it would cause particular hardship if eviction were ordered;
• why an expensive property was rented (if applicable).

The powers of the court in dealing with a possession action

There are a number of grounds on which possession may be sought when rent is unpaid and these differ slightly according to whether the tenant has a private or public landlord and whether her/his tenancy commenced before or after 15 January 1989. A debt adviser must be certain about the status of the debtor's occupancy before giving advice about a possession claim. For example, some occupiers who consider themselves tenants may be, in fact, licensees.

A debtor may receive a possession claim form on grounds that are not connected to a debt. This book does not attempt to cover these matters at all. For an excellent and detailed explanation of all the grounds upon which possession might be sought, see Defending Possession Proceedings, LAG (see Appendix 6), or consult a specialist housing advice service such as Shelter.

The court's role in every case of arrears, except those of some assured tenants who are more than 13 weeks in arrears (see p225), is to decide whether or not it is 'reasonable' to make an order for possession and then to decide whether or not to suspend this upon particular terms (usually payment of the normal rent plus an amount towards the arrears). This means that, as long as the tenant keeps to the payment ordered by the court, the landlord cannot regain possession of the property. If the tenant does not attend the hearing or there is no application from her/him, the order may be made absolutely – ie, for possession to be given up in a certain period of time, usually 28 days.

Since 25 March 2002 the court has been able to award fixed costs (instead of assessed costs) in all cases where a possession order is made and not just in cases where the possession order is suspended.

Arguing against a possession order (rent)

An outright possession order is not necessarily a breach of the tenant's human rights (Article 8: respect for family and private life).[97] A variety of arguments can be used to demonstrate that it is 'unreasonable' to make a possession order. It should be noted, however, that courts take into account the view that a landlord is entitled not only to the increase in capital value of her/his property but also to revenue from rent. A debt adviser should argue that the existence of a reasonable offer to clear arrears makes a possession order unnecessary (and, therefore, unreasonable). Arguments can be based upon the tenant's circumstances (eg, s/he has children or is sick or disabled) or her/his finances (eg, s/he has been dependent on benefit for some time). If an improvement in circumstances can be shown (for instance, s/he has just got, or is about to get, a job) then this will probably help to convince the court that it is unreasonable to make a possession order. Other arguments could be based upon the position of the landlord – eg, the landlord's identity was unknown or s/he had failed to collect rent.

Any defence that the tenant offers may be assisted if s/he has begun to pay the contractual rent and something towards the arrears by the time the hearing takes place. Such payments should have been recorded by the landlord or, if the landlord has refused to accept payments prior to the court hearing, the money should have been paid into a separate account. Proof of payment made should be taken to the hearing.

If a tenant should have been getting housing benefit but was not, or is awaiting the outcome of a claim, this can be a powerful argument for saying it is unreasonable to make an order, particularly if a local authority is the landlord (except for assured tenants, see p225). Indeed, para 5.3 Part 55 PD CPR encourages tenants to give evidence about any outstanding benefit claims (including claims subject to review or appeal). The adviser should ask the court not to award costs if arrears are solely due to unpaid housing benefit as possession action was unnecessary.[98] Where the landlord is not a local authority, the tenant can ask the court to consider making a third party costs order against the local authority – ie, an order that the local authority pay the landlord's costs. This can only be done if the local authority is:

- made a party to the proceedings for the purposes of costs only; *and*

- given a reasonable opportunity of attending the hearing for the court to consider the question.[99]

This obviously requires action to be taken prior to the possession hearing itself. A threat to seek an order for costs may prompt the local authority to expedite the housing benefit claim and clear the arrears. Otherwise, if possible, the debtor should obtain a letter from the local authority explaining when housing benefit will be paid and take this to the hearing.

Debt advisers sometimes agree to a suspended possession order on the ground that this is a technicality and does no more than safeguard the landlord's position. This is a very dangerous view and means that any future default in payment of rent or arrears puts the tenant at serious risk of losing her/his home. If a suspended order clearly is going to be made, then the amount of instalments towards arrears should be set at a level that provides some leeway for the tenant faced with an unexpected and essential item of expenditure.

Assured tenants – a special case

The 1988 Housing Act created a new mandatory ground upon which a court must make a possession order. This applies only to assured tenants (eg, of housing associations and private landlords) and thus to nobody except previously protected shortholders whose tenancy began before 15 January 1989. It requires a court to grant a possession order to a landlord if at the date of the hearing at least eight weeks' or two months' rent (three months' if paid quarterly) is unpaid. The landlord has to prove that there was two months' rent in arrears (or three months' if paid quarterly) both at the time when the notice of seeking possession was served and at the date of the hearing, which need be only two weeks later.

There is no requirement for the court to consider reasonableness when this ground is used. Therefore, even if delays in the payment of housing benefit caused the arrears, this could nonetheless lead to a possession order being granted, as the court has no power to adjourn where the mandatory ground has been made out. In such a case, the adviser should pressure the local authority to make an emergency payment before the hearing and, if it fails to do so, local politicians and the local government ombudsman should be informed. This ground will fail if the arrears are reduced by the date of the hearing to even a nominal amount (for example, £1) below two or three months' rent. It may occasionally be worthwhile borrowing money, particularly from family or friends, to ensure that the tenant does not become subject to this mandatory ground. (See also Chapter 6 for ways of maximising income.)

If possession is granted, it may still be possible to set aside a warrant of possession (see p231) before bailiffs actually evict if payment has by then been made. For further details, see *Manual of Housing Law*.

Warrant of possession/eviction

Advisers should carefully check the wording of any suspended possession order to see whether it provides for the order to cease to have effect once the borrower/tenant has paid the arrears in accordance with its terms. In such a case, if the borrower/tenant then falls into arrears again, the lender/landlord will need to obtain a further order and will not just be able to issue a warrant of possession.

A warrant of possession gives county court bailiffs the power to evict the occupiers and change the locks (see Chapter 11). It is issued by the court following a request from the mortgagee or landlord if the defendant has not voluntarily left the property by the date ordered by the court at a possession hearing or has not kept to the terms of a suspended order for possession. In order to prevent eviction, an application must be made for the warrant to be suspended (see p231). The notice of eviction (form N54) informs the tenant/borrower about this (see p208). A challenge to the procedure whereby the warrant is issued without a further court hearing based on Article 6 of the European Convention on Human Rights (right to a fair trial) failed on the ground that a fair hearing would have taken place when the possession order was originally made, and that obtaining the warrant was part of the process and not a separate issue.[100]

The number of warrants actually executed in 2000 fell from 71,256 in 1999 to 63,239.

6. **Preventing enforcement**

Setting aside judgment

If a judgment is set aside, its effect is cancelled and the debtor and creditor are put back to the position they were in before judgment was obtained. This includes the cancelling of any enforcement action by the creditor.[101]

Part 13 Civil Procedure Rules deals with setting aside (or varying the amount of) a default judgment. The court must set aside a judgment where:

- judgment was entered before the debtor's time for filing an acknowledgement of service or a defence had expired (see p177); or
- the debtor served an admission on the creditor together with a request for time to pay before the judgment was entered (see p177); or
- the debtor paid the whole of the claim (including any interest or costs due) before judgment was entered. (If the debtor paid the whole of the claim before the claim form was issued, s/he should have filed a defence – see p185.)

The court may set aside a judgment where:

- the debtor has a real prospect of success in the claim; or
- the court is satisfied that there is some other good reason why the judgment should be set aside/varied or the debtor allowed to defend the claim; or

- there has been an error of procedure, such as a failure to comply with a rule or practice direction.

These provisions could be used, for example, where the proceedings were served on the debtor by post but s/he did not receive them or judgment has been entered for too much. The court must take into account whether or not the debtor acted promptly in making the application. In applying for a judgment to be set aside, the defendant should always try to find an argument based on the facts or law of the case (eg, 'I do not owe the money because the goods supplied under a linked agreement were of unsatisfactory quality'), rather than personal circumstances (eg, 'I did not know how to reply to the summons').

Unless the debtor wishes to defend the claim or the creditor has already taken enforcement action (which would also be cancelled), it may be preferable for the debtor to apply to vary or suspend the terms of payment of the judgment (see below). Applying to set aside a judgment does not automatically prevent or delay any enforcement action by the creditor. The application to set aside should also contain an application for a stay of execution pending the hearing quoting CCR Order 37r8(2) Civil Procedure Rules. Application is made on form N244 and must be supported by evidence (see below). A fee of £50 is payable (see court fees on p173 for applying for fee exemption/remission). The case will be transferred to the debtor's local court.

Where there has been a hearing in the county court, the debtor can apply to have the order set aside and the matter re-heard if:

- the debtor did not attend the hearing and an order was made in her/his absence. The court will want to know why the debtor did not attend and whether there has been a miscarriage of justice. The court is unlikely to order a re-hearing if the debtor deliberately fails to attend;[102] *or*
- there has been a miscarriage of justice resulting from an error or misconduct of a court officer, for example, advising the debtor that there was no need to attend the hearing; *or*
- new evidence has been discovered which was not available at the time of the original hearing; *or*
- there has been default or misconduct by the other party, for example, misleading the court.[103]

Varying payments due under an order for money

Where the decision on the rate of payment was made by the court, the procedure on p184 should be followed if there has been a change of circumstances. In other cases the following procedures apply.

If the creditor believes that s/he can persuade the district judge that the debtor can afford to increase her/his payments, s/he can apply for the rate of instalments to be increased. Application is made on an N244 (see p232) and the case will be automatically transferred to the debtor's home court for a hearing (the determination procedure on p182 does not apply).[104]

Once an order for payment has been made either in default or on acceptance of the debtor's offer of payment, the debtor can apply to the court that made it to have it varied at any time. S/he does not need a particular reason for making this application, although it will normally be because a change in circumstances means that the original instalment order no longer can be afforded or because the original order was made in ignorance of some material fact.

The variation can include changes either to the amount of instalments or their frequency and in the county court is made on form N245, which is very similar to the form N9A (see p179 on how to complete this). The N245 should be sent to the court that made the judgment (but if it is also being used to apply to suspend a warrant of execution it should be sent to the enforcing court – see p229). A fee of £25 is payable (see court fees on p173 for applying for exemption/remission).

The court sends a copy of the N245 to the creditor and if s/he does not respond within 14 days the variation must be granted in the terms applied for.[105] If the creditor objects within 14 days, a court officer will use the determination of means guidelines to decide what the order should be.

Once the variation order has been made, either the creditor or defendant has 14 days to apply to the court for a reconsideration if they do not agree with the terms (see p184). The case will automatically be transferred to the debtor's local court and a hearing arranged there. At the hearing, the district judge can make whatever order s/he thinks just. When helping a debtor to apply for a variation order, it is helpful to send a letter to accompany the N245, with a copy to the creditor, outlining the reasons for the application, especially if this is the first contact the debt adviser has had with the creditor.

Not all courts follow the above rules for dealing with an N245 (for example, some have failed to follow up the application, because for instance the creditor has applied for a charging order, or allowed considerably more than 14 days for the creditor to send objections). Advisers should keep a copy of the N245, applicants may wish to ask the court for a receipt and advisers should follow up applications which are not dealt with in 21 days.

If the order for payment was made by a court officer or the district judge without a hearing and the debtor is out of time to apply for redetermination, or was made by the district judge at a hearing, the debtor can only apply to vary the order on the ground of a change of circumstances (including information not previously before the court). The application is made on an N244 in both the High Court and the county court (see p232).[106] A fee of £25 is payable (see court fees on p173 for applying for fee exemption/remission). The case will not be transferred to the debtor's local court.

If the order for payment was made in the High Court either in default or on acceptance of the debtor's offer of payment, the debtor must apply for a stay of

execution under RSC Order 47 Civil Procedure Rules on an N244 (see p232) on the ground that:
- there are special circumstances which render it inexpedient to enforce the judgment; *or*
- the debtor is unable, from any source, to pay the money.

The application must be accompanied by a witness statement substantiating the grounds and disclosing the debtor's income, assets and other debts. For an example of a witness statement in support of an application for a stay of execution, see Appendix 3. A fee of £25 is payable (see court fees on p173 for fee exemption/remission). The case will not be transferred to the debtor's local court.

Variations to nothing – suspensions or stays

Applications on an N245 must include an offer of payment. If even a nominal sum cannot be found then the debtor can apply for the judgment to be suspended or stayed (see also p178 on N9A). A suspension is usually on terms – for example, so long as payments are made – and a stay is usually until an event occurs – for example, until a particular date. In practice, the terms seem to be interchangeable. Application should be on form N244 (see p232) in the county court, or for a stay of execution in the High Court (see above). Applications are more likely to be accepted if there are compelling reasons, for example serious ill health (mental or physical) or the debtor being in prison or an institution, or otherwise temporarily unable to make any payment. A fee of £25 is payable (see court fees on p173 for fee exemption/remission). The case will not be transferred to the debtor's local court. Where a debtor is submitting multiple applications, the debt adviser should argue that remission should be considered on the basis of the total fees payable rather than individual applications.

Suspension of a warrant of execution (for money) – county court

If payments are missed and the creditor applies to the county court for bailiffs to enforce the debt, the debtor will receive a notice from the court warning that a warrant for the seizure of goods has been issued and giving a date after which it will be executed. Bailiffs may call at the home to try and take goods to sell. Form N245 should be completed in order to suspend the warrant. Note that the bailiffs can continue to attempt to seize goods until the application has been heard and a decision given. In many cases the debtor may also want to vary the judgment and this application can be included on the same form. The N245 should be sent to the enforcing court, which will be the debtor's local court. A fee of £25 is payable (see court fees on p173 for applying for fee exemption/remission).

The debtor could apply to have the matter stayed (see above). However, in order to prevent seizure of goods an offer of payment must be made on the N245 but this need only be a token amount (eg, £1 per month) if the defendant is realistically unable to afford payments. The debt adviser should write to the creditor to explain the circumstances of the debtor and if payments cannot be afforded explain why such enforcement is not appropriate.

An offer of payment may not be appropriate when the debtor has no goods that could be seized (see p270 for excluded items) and there are no other methods of enforcement open to the creditor (eg, charging orders, attachment of earnings – see pp189 and 194). In these circumstances, the debt adviser should ask the creditor to consider writing off the debt.

Once the court receives form N245, a copy is sent to the creditor who has 14 days to agree to the debtor's proposal or not. If the creditor agrees with the proposal, the warrant is suspended and the debtor is ordered to pay the amount offered. If the creditor does not agree to suspension on any terms, then a hearing will be arranged at the debtor's local court, where the district judge will decide whether or not to suspend the warrant and on what terms. If the creditor agrees with a suspension but not the proposed terms, then the determination procedure described above for varying an order will be followed.

Suspension of a writ of fi-fa – High Court

In the High Court, the sheriff's officer will carry out execution against goods using private bailiffs (see Chapter 11). The instruction to the bailiffs is known as a 'writ of fi-fa'. In some cases county court judgments may – and in others, must – be enforced in the High Court (see p189). Once the debtor is aware that bailiffs have been instructed, an application for a stay of execution should be made (see p229) and the bailiffs informed.

Suspension of a warrant of delivery (hire purchase or conditional sale)

If the debtor wants to keep goods that are the subject of a hire purchase or conditional sale agreement, an application can be made on an N244 (see p232) to suspend the warrant, with a financial statement supplied as well. The N244 should be taken to the enforcing court. A fee of £25 is payable (see court fees on p173 for applying for fee exemption/remission). An offer of payment must be made which will realistically repay the agreement and arrears. A court is unlikely to agree to very small payments compared with the original contractual sum. If this is not possible, the debt adviser should try and re-negotiate with the creditor the payments due under the agreement or consider a time order (see p211).

Varying the terms of a suspended/postponed possession orderi

If the repayments under a suspended order, or any other terms of an order, require a change, the borrower can apply back to the court for the order to be changed or varied. Application is on form N244 (see p232). A fee of £25 is payable (see court fees on p173 for applying for fee exemption/remission). See the following section on suspension of a warrant where the arguments and process are similar. It is always better to apply to vary an order if circumstances have changed, rather than be served with a warrant and have to apply to suspend it. For example, if the borrower is on maternity leave, and therefore has a reduced income, for a period she could apply for a reduction in payments, or if the borrower unexpectedly finds employment s/he can apply for a possession order to be suspended because s/he can now make payments.

Suspension of a warrant of possession

Following the issue of a warrant, a notice of eviction in form N54 will be sent or delivered from the court which will state a date and time when the bailiffs will evict the debtor from her/his property (see p208). The debtor can apply for a warrant of possession to be suspended at any time before the date and time specified on the warrant, although it is preferable to apply as early as possible in case further negotiations are necessary.

An N244 should be completed (see below), showing:

- how the debtor's circumstances have changed since the possession order (see p208) was made;
- that the equity or rental revenue of the creditor is not threatened by the delay;
- a well-supported offer of payment of current charges and arrears, and a lump sum (or first payment) if at all possible;
- if the debtor does not wish to remain in the property, that arrangements are in hand for sale of the property or re-housing, but that this will take time.

Form N244 should be accompanied by a financial statement. A fee of £25 is payable (see court fees on p173 for applying for fee exemption/remission). If possible, take the form to the court in preference to posting as there will be little time available.

A hearing will be granted almost immediately and the debtor must attend. A debt adviser should always try to negotiate directly with the creditor prior to the hearing and ensure that if an agreement has been reached the details are communicated to the solicitor or agent who will be representing the creditor at the hearing. If possible, arrange for confirmation in writing so that the debtor can take this to the hearing in case there is any dispute. If no agreement can be reached then the matter must be presented clearly before the district judge using similar arguments to those covered in the sections on mortgage arrears and rent arrears. It may be necessary to ask for the payment order to be varied (reduced) to a level that the borrower can afford, at the same time.

In theory, there is no limit to the number of applications to suspend a warrant, but if the debtor persistently applies and then fails to make payments the application may be refused and s/he may be told that s/he cannot make any further applications without leave of the court. In this case, assuming that the application is realistic, the debtor must ask for leave of the court to apply, on an N244, before continuing on the same application to explain the reasons. The court will usually consider granting leave to apply first then, if granted, continue in the same hearing to consider the application for suspension.

If the application is refused the eviction will usually take place on the date and time on the warrant. The debtor may ask for a short suspension, say two weeks, to find alternative accommodation. Alternatively, in mortgage cases, if repossession is granted, the borrower could ask to stay in the property while the mortgagee sells it (see p208).[107] After the execution of a warrant (eviction), then no order for suspension can be made unless:

- the possession order itself is set aside (see p226); *or*
- the warrant was obtained fraudulently; *or*
- there had been an abuse of the process or oppression in the execution of the warrant.[108] It appears that 'oppression' is not limited to conduct by the creditor but can extend to conduct by the court – eg, misleading information from court staff as to the procedure for suspending a warrant.[109]

Applications – N244

Part 23 Civil Procedure Rules deals with applications. Form N244 is prescribed for making applications (there is an example in Appendix 3). It contains:

- A box in which the applicant can request a hearing and provide information about it. The applicant must indicate whether or not s/he wants the court to deal with the application with or without a hearing. If a hearing is requested, the court will fix a time and date and notify the parties at the same time as it serves the N244. Debt advisers should use their experience to estimate hearing times. If no hearing is requested, the application is referred to a district judge to consider whether the application is suitable for consideration without a hearing. There is no advantage in asking the court to deal with the application without a hearing since (i) the district judge may disagree and order a hearing anyway and (ii) the other party can apply to set aside or vary any order made without a hearing.[110] Debt advisers should only ask the court to deal with an application without a hearing if the application is one that will not automatically be transferred to the debtor's local court, and should also ask the court to exercise its discretion to transfer the case to the debtor's local court if it decides that a hearing should take place.
- A section (Part A) in which the applicant sets out (a) what order s/he is seeking and (b) briefly, why s/he is seeking the order (this information must be supplied).[111] The following are suggested wordings for some common applications:
  - **Redetermination/reconsideration:** the judgment be paid by instalments of £x per month because I cannot afford to pay at the rate determined.
  - **Variation:** payment of the judgment debt be varied to £x per month because my circumstances have changed and I can no longer afford to pay at the rate ordered.

- **Suspension:** payment of the judgment debt be suspended under section 71(2) of the County Courts Act 1984 on the ground that I am no longer able to pay it because. . .
- **Stay of execution:** execution on the judgment be stayed for as long as I pay instalments of £x per month because. . . or execution on the judgment be stayed on the ground that I am unable to pay it because. . .

- A section (Part B) in which the applicant indicates whether s/he is relying on (a) a witness statement or affidavit; or (b) the applicant's statement of case – ie, the claim form, particulars of claim or defence; or (c) the matters contained in Part C (which is on the other side of the form) as evidence in support of the application. Evidence is required in certain cases (eg, set-aside applications) and the court can always ask for evidence of facts in support of an application. The debtor will not usually have served a defence and so any facts that the debtor wishes the court to consider should be set out in Part C and any written evidence referred to and attached – eg, a financial statement. The debtor should sign the statement of truth (see particulars of claim on p177) at the foot of Part C. There is no need for a financial statement to contain a statement of truth.

Applications should be made as soon as the debt adviser realises that one is going to be necessary. Applications can be made at a hearing that has already been fixed (eg, for an application by the creditor) and can be made without an N244 being used, but the creditor and the court should be informed (if possible in writing) as soon as possible.[112]

Administration order

An administration order is a county court order which prevents individual creditors taking enforcement action without permission from the court and which requires that all a person's debts be treated together.[113] It is applied for by the debtor, who must have at least one judgment against her/him in either the county or High Court. The debtor makes a single monthly payment into the court, which then distributes it equitably among the creditors. Chapter 8 describes when an administration order is appropriate. An administration order is applied for on form N92. There is no fee payable on application, but costs will be added to the sum the debtor repays at 10p per pound repaid.

In spite of the low financial limit for administration orders, the number of orders made in 2000 increased by nearly 10 per cent to 7,916.

Making the application

Form N92 requires a list of all the proposed debts to be subject to the order. These must not exceed £5,000. This limit has been the subject of much criticism and changes were proposed in 1991. To date, the proposed changes have not been implemented and there is no timetable for their future implementation.

Administration orders can only be given to individuals, but debts that are jointly owed must be included. Where a person is jointly and severally liable, s/he should include the whole value of such a debt. Even if finances are shared, couples cannot apply together and should make individual applications if both want to repay their debts in this way. Where a couple make applications for an administration order at the same time and there is a joint debt it may be acceptable to divide the debt between the two applications.

The N92 requires the applicant to list arrears of:

- rent/mortgage;
- council tax (community charge);
- maintenance;
- hire purchase;
- consumer credit debts (including cards).

This requirement does not appear to fit with the legal requirement that the administration order should cover the 'whole indebtedness'. Courts' practice on this matter appears to differ and it may be advantageous (for instance, to stay within the £5,000 limit) to apply for an order on the basis of arrears alone if this will be granted by a local court (and another strategy is available for the rest of the indebtedness).

In most cases, the whole indebtedness should be included on the form. Some courts have queried the inclusion of some debts (eg, council tax arrears and fines) but, following *Preston Borough Council v Riley*,[114] these debts should all be included. The only debts that cannot be included on an administration order are social fund loans and benefit overpayments, where the debtor is still in receipt of a benefit from which deductions can be made.

For employed applicants an attachment of earnings order will be made unless the debtor indicates otherwise on the N92 form. See p194 for further discussion of the pros and cons of attachment of earnings orders. Most debtors prefer not to have an attachment of earnings.

The proposed order

It is intended that most administration orders should be decided by court officers without a hearing. A notice of the application and a calculation are sent to creditors explaining what they can expect to receive (the proposed order). The involvement of a district judge becomes necessary only if the amount offered is insufficient to repay the debts in a 'reasonable time'. Guidance to court staff suggests this is three years.

Where court staff cannot make an order, a district judge will decide the matter. S/he can either propose a longer repayment period or make a composition order (see below). S/he can do this with or without a hearing. Debt advisers should explain in a covering letter what they are requesting in an N92 if a straightforward administration order is not possible. If a court hearing is required the debtor and all the creditors will be sent notice of the hearing and the creditors will be advised of the balance owing and the proposed terms of the order. The creditors must send a corrected balance to the court, if required. See below for details about the hearing.

If the court staff prepare the order a copy is sent to the debtor and all the creditors who then have 14 days in which to object to the grant of an administration order. This is an opportunity for the debtor to object to the level of instalments as well as for the creditors to object to being included. If no objections are received, a 'final order' is made. If objections are received a hearing will normally be set to consider the objections.

Composition order

A district judge can order that a debtor pays only a proportion of her/his debts (a composition order). This should be considered where the debts cannot be cleared in a 'reasonable time' (as above, about three years).

The debt adviser should help the debtor to work out what monthly amount is available to satisfy unsecured creditors. If this amount will not clear the debts in three years, s/he should suggest a composition order in a letter accompanying the N92.

The percentage of each debt offered is calculated by ascertaining the total time available for payments (ie, 36 – the number of months in three years) multiplied by the monthly payment, dividing this by the total owed and then showing this as a percentage.

Example
A person has £75 a month available income and owes a total of £4,500. A sensible composition would be to offer:
36 x £75 = £2,700 total amount to be paid (less 10% handling) = £2,430
2,430 divided by 4,500 = 0.54 (the proportion to be paid)
0.54 = 54% (the percentage to be paid)

In many cases, the actual order will not be opposed but a composition may be. However, provided the debt adviser is prepared with facts and figures to justify the financial necessity of what s/he argues, such orders are increasingly acceptable to courts. An application for a composition order can only be decided by a district judge (and not court officers) and cannot be rejected without a hearing.

The court hearing

There will be a court hearing if a composition order is requested or if a creditor objects. Creditors may attend the hearing (but rarely do), at which a district judge will decide whether or not to grant the order. The court will normally grant an administration order unless the information given is incorrect or it appears that the order would unreasonably deny a creditor another type of remedy. If creditors object merely because they want to take action in pursuit of their debt the debt adviser should argue that this would result in other creditors being treated less fairly. Some local authorities object to the inclusion of community charge/council tax arrears in an administration order on the ground that they have an attachment of earnings order and that this will continue regardless. This is incorrect and should be challenged.[115]

Once an administration order is granted, it is unlawful for any creditor to approach the debtor for individual payment. Interest is frozen on all debts included in the order. The court charges a percentage handling fee (currently 10 per cent) for all monies collected and distributes these quarterly. Provided the debtor makes all the payments required by the administration order, s/he is discharged from all the debts in it.

Reviewing an administration order

An administration order can be reviewed at any time by the court. The defendant, any creditor included in the order or the court itself can request a review. Some orders contain provision for periodic reviews. If the defendant applies, a letter should be used explaining why the review is being requested (usually because of a change in circumstances) and enclosing a financial statement. The court will then arrange a hearing.

On review the court may do any of the following:
* reduce the payments;
* suspend all payments for a specified amount of time;
* add or vary a composition order, including theoretically varying it to 0 pence in the pound;
* reinstate a revoked order (but see below);
* make an attachment of earnings order to secure payments due under the order.[116]

Although creditors are allowed to apply to be added to an administration order, there is no specific provision allowing debtors to do so. New creditors can sometimes be included by a review on the basis of a 'material change of circumstances', although some courts apply the rules strictly and only allow the creditors to apply. Once made, an administration order is not invalidated because the debts are found to exceed the £5,000 limit, but the court can cancel the administration order. The court might take this step if it felt that the debtor had 'abused' the protection of the administration order by obtaining further credit.[117]

If a debtor misses two consecutive payments or persistently fails to pay on time, then the court should send a notice requiring either:
* payment;
* an explanation;
* an application for a variation;

• a proposal for payment of arrears.

If the debtor fails to do one of these, then the administration order is revoked in 14 days. If the debtor replies, then the matter is referred to the district judge who may either order a hearing or revoke, suspend or vary the administration order. Where no hearing takes place, creditors or the debtor can object within 14 days and a hearing must be held.

At a hearing, the district judge will consider all circumstances of the case and make one of the decisions listed above.

If the district judge decides to revoke the order, the court will no longer collect and distribute payments. The creditors will then be informed that they are free to pursue their debts individually. In practice, only a small proportion of creditors contact debtors following the revocation of an administration order.

For many creditors an administration order seems to represent the 'end of the line' and they do not expect to receive any payments thereafter. This can make it a useful tactic and if one is revoked it is not advisable to contact creditors unless they first contact the debtor. Administration orders are registered at the Registry Trust and will probably affect a person's ability to get credit.

Appeal to a judge

The debtor may appeal to a circuit judge against any decision made in a county court by a district judge (unless it was made by consent) on the ground that the decision was:

• wrong – for example, the district judge wrongly decided a legal issue or wrongly exercised her/his discretion by reaching a decision which no reasonable judge could have made; *or*
• unjust – ie, there was a serious procedural or other irregularity in the proceedings before the district judge.[118]

An appeal must be made on a point of law, not on such things as a change in the debtor's circumstances. If new evidence becomes available, then this may be a reason for having a decision set aside (see p226) but it does not constitute a point of law.

The debtor must obtain permission to appeal:

• verbally from the district judge at the end of the hearing; *or*, if permission was refused or not applied for,
• to the circuit judge in the notice of appeal.

However, permission will only be given where:

• the court considers that the appeal would have a real prospect of success; *or*
• there is some compelling reason why the appeal should be heard – eg, a test case.

The district judge must give written reasons for the grant or refusal of permission to appeal.[119]

Time limits

The notice of appeal must be filed:
* within the time specified by the district judge when granting permission verbally; *or*
* within 14 days of the date of the decision being appealed.[120]

An appeal must be made on a form N161. Grounds for the appeal should be set out clearly, together with a summary of the arguments in support of the appeal, and the decision that the appeal court is being asked to make should also be stated clearly. A fee of £150 (£100 on the small claims track) is payable (see court fees on p173 for applying for fee exemption/remission), unless permission is granted by the district judge after the hearing, when it is £100 (£50 on the small claims track).

All appeals will be heard by a circuit judge. If possible, the debtor should be represented at the hearing by the adviser or solicitor. The hearing will normally take the form of a review of the district judge's decision rather than a re-hearing and the circuit judge will not normally hear oral evidence or consider any new evidence. Where new evidence becomes available, the adviser should consider an application for a re-hearing rather than an appeal (see p227). If the appeal is allowed the judge will either make a new judgment, or order that there be a re-hearing before a district judge.

Adjournments

An adjournment is a court order that a hearing be delayed either for a specified amount of time or indefinitely. The county court can, at any time, either adjourn or bring forward the date of a hearing. It can decide to do this itself or because one or both of the parties have applied.[121]

An application for an adjournment on the grounds of illness should be accepted, provided it is backed up by a sick note, unless there is evidence that the illness or medical evidence is not genuine. Similarly, if an important witness cannot be present a district judge should adjourn a hearing. It is reasonable to grant an adjournment where there would otherwise be a miscarriage of justice. Thus, for example, if a debtor comes into an advice agency at 10am to ask for representation at a possession hearing a quarter of an hour later, then it should be argued that there are (or may be) legal points which the court will need to hear and which cannot be adequately presented without further preparation. However, there will need to be some explanation of why the debtor has left it until the last minute to obtain advice or representation.

It is not a sufficient reason to adjourn a hearing simply because one (or even both) party is not yet ready. Judges will often be impatient or suspicious of applications to adjourn which they believe are merely means to prolong an action in which they believe the creditor should succeed.

A district judge should consider the merits of an adjournment, whether or not one or both parties are requesting one. However, it is clearly much easier to get an adjournment if the creditor agrees and it is always worth contacting her/him or her/his representative before applying for one. This may be appropriate where the creditor is persuaded that a debtor will not be able to pay anything whatever judgment is given.

It is important, if possible, to attend court to make the application just in case it is not granted. One of the main aims of the Civil Procedure Rules (CPR) is to avoid delays in the hearing of cases. Judges can, therefore, be expected to be more reluctant to adjourn cases than previously. In a recent case the Court of Appeal upheld the trial judge's refusal to grant an adjournment on the basis of the unavailability of an expert witness on the ground that another expert should have been instructed.[122] If the adjournment is being sought precisely because no one is available to represent the debtor and it is not opposed by the creditor, then a letter (or fax) should be sent to the court explaining that this is the case and that nobody will be attending. In such circumstances, if a court did proceed to make a decision other than to adjourn, an application should be made to set it aside (see p226) on the grounds that both sides had not been properly heard.

A matter can be adjourned either:
* to the next available date after a certain period (eg, 28 days); *or*
* generally, with liberty to restore.

Notes

1. Introduction
1 para 4 Protocol PD CPR
2 Barristers, solicitors and their employees, and people authorised by the Lord Chancellor to conduct litigation under s11 of the CLSA 1990

3. Action to recover money only
3 Part 7 para 2.1 PD CPR
4 Part 7 para 2.4 PD CPR
5 s141 CCA 1974
6 s40(1) CCA 1984 as amended; *Restick v Crickmore, The Times,* 3 December 1993
7 Order 8(1A) High Court and County Courts Jurisdiction Order 1991
8 ss176(2) and (3) CCA 1974; *Lombard North Central v Power-Hines* [1995] CCLR 24
9 Rule 2.3(1) CPR
10 Rules 2.8(4), 6.2 and 6.7 CPR
11 Part 16 para 7.3 PD CPR; Part 7C para 1.4 PD CPR
12 Part 4 para 1.2 PD CPR
13 For a discussion on drafting separate financial statements, see P Madge, 'Til debt do us part', *Adviser* 71
14 Rule 14.4(6) CPR
15 Rule 14.9(2) CPR
16 Part 14 para 5.1 PD CPR
17 *Determination of Means – Guidelines for Court Staff,* Lord Chancellor's Department, Revised December 1998
18 Rule 3.2 CPR
19 Advisers should refer court staff who query this to item 3.4.5, 'What happens next?', in *Determination of Means – Guidelines for Court Staff,* Lord Chancellor's Department, Revised December 1998
20 Rule 12.3 CPR
21 Rule 12.5 CPR
22 Rule 15.11 CPR
23 Part 27 CPR
24 Part 28 CPR
25 Part 29 CPR
26 Parts 3 and 24 CPR
27 s69 CCA 1984; s35a SCA 1981
28 s17 JA 1838
29 CC(IJD)O 1991

30 *Director General of Fair Trading v First National Bank* [2001] UKHL 52, 25 October 2001 (unreported), *Adviser* 89 abstracts
31 [1989] 3 All ER 915, CA
32 Rules 12.6, 12.7 and 14.14 CPR. In the First National Bank case the House of Lords assumed that the creditor could take further court action, but the point was not argued and so the issue remains unclear.
33 For further discussion of these issues, see P Madge, 'Interest after judgment under regulated consumer credit agreements', *Legal Action,* December 1990; P Madge, 'A point of interest', *Adviser* 59; P Madge, 'No further interest', *Adviser* 79; P Madge, 'Full circle', *Adviser* 89; R Rosenberg, 'Interest after judgment – is it the end of the road?', *QA* 62
34 Rule 70.2(2) CPR
35 Order 8 HCCCJO 1991 as amended
36 see also P Madge 'Charging interest', *Adviser* 76
37 s1(2) COA 1979
38 Part 73 para 1.2 PD CPR
39 Rule 73.5 CPR
40 s1(5) COA 1979
41 Part 73 para 3 PD CPR
42 Rule 73.8 CPR. 'Written evidence' is a person's evidence set down in writing and signed to the effect that the maker of the statement believes the facts stated are true. See Part 32 PD CPR for the formalities of witness statements. Unless specifically required, an affidavit should not be used in preference to a statement.
43 *Mercantile Credit Co Ltd v Ellis, The Times,* 1 April 1987, CA
44 *Ropaigealach v Allied Irish Bank,* 12 November 2001, CA (unreported), *Adviser* 90 abstracts. By the same token, an application for redetermination/variation made after the date of the interim order would not prevent the order being made final.
45 *Rainbow v Moorgate Properties* [1975] 2 All ER 821
46 s3(1) COA 1979

47 s71(2) CCA 1984; there is no corresponding High Court provision, but an application for a stay of execution should have the same effect, see p000

48 s3(5) COA 1979; Rule 73.9 CPR

49 s3(4) COA 1979

50 Under s14 Trusts of Land and Appointment of Trustees Act 1996

51 s15 Trusts of Land and Appointment of Trustees Act 1996

52 *Mortgage Corporation v Shaire, The Times,* 21 March 2000, Chancery Division

53 *Harman v Glencross* [1986] 1 All ER 545, CA

54 CCR Order 27 Rules 18-22

55 s4(2) AEA 1971

56 *Mercantile Credit Co Ltd v Ellis, The Times,* 1 April 1987, CA

57 *Rainbow v Moorgate Properties* [1975] 2 All ER 821

58 Rule 72.7 CPR

59 CCR Order 39 Rule 2

4. Action to recover goods on hire purchase or conditional sale (the Consumer Credit Act procedure)

60 s130(1) CCA 1974

61 s135 CCA 1974

62 s135(2) CCA 1974

63 Part 7B para 3.3 PD CPR

5. Action to recover property (possession action)

64 Part 55 para 1 PD CPR

65 *The Code of Mortgage Lending Practice ('The Mortgage Code'),* Council of Mortgage Lenders, July 1997

66 *Halifax Building Society v Taffs, Legal Action,* April 2000, CA

67 See C Evans 'The new rules are working!', *Adviser* 79

68 Rule 3.1(2)(b) CPR

69 [1995] 28 HLR 443, CA

70 [1996] 29 HLR 282, CA

71 *Cheltenham & Gloucester Building Society v Krausz* [1996] 29 HLR 597, CA

72 [1996] 29 HLR 634

73 *Falco Finance Ltd v Gough,* Macclesfield County Court, 28 October 1998 (unreported), *Adviser* 73 abstracts

74 Part 48 para 1 PD CPR

75 s129(2)(a) CCA 1974

76 s38a AJA 1970

77 s129(1) CCA 1974

78 *The Times,* 19 April 1995, CA

79 s129(1) CCA 1974

80 *Director General of Fair Trading v First National Bank, The Times,* 1 November 2001, *Adviser* 89 abstracts

81 Rule 3.1(2)(m) CPR

82 Part 55 para 7 PD CPR

83 s130(6) CCA 1974

84 [1996] 29 HLR 634

85 For a full discussion of this issue, see D McConnell, 'No equity?', *Adviser* 53

86 *Palk v Mortgage Services Funding plc* [1993] 2 All ER 481, CA

87 *Household Mortgage Corporation v Abbott & Collins,* June 1994, Northampton County Court (unreported); *Woolwich Building Society v Brown,* 14 December 1995, QBD, *Adviser* 55 abstracts

88 s20 LA 1980

89 *Hopkinson v Tupper,* 30 January 1997 (unreported), *Adviser* 63 abstracts, CA

90 s20(1) LA 1980

91 s20(5) LA 1980

92 *Bristol & West plc v Bartlett,* 31 July 2002, CA (unreported), *Adviser* 94 abstracts. For a full discussion of the issues, see P Madge, 'Out of the blue', *Adviser* 61; P Madge, 'About face', *Adviser* 94.

93 CPAG's *Welfare Benefits Handbook 2002/ 2003*

94 Reg 93(2) HB (Gen) Regs 1987 as amended by SI 1997/65 from 7 April 1997

95 ss57 and 44 RA 1977

96 *Trevantos v McCullogh* [1991] 19 EG 18, CA

97 *Lambeth LBC v Howard,* 6 March 2001, *Adviser* 88 abstracts, CA

98 *Brent London Borough Council v Marks,* 21 May 1998 (unreported), *Adviser* 73 abstracts, CA

99 Rule 48.2 CPR; Part 19 contains the procedure for adding parties

100 *St Brice v Southwark LBC,* 17 July 2001, *Adviser* 88 abstracts, CA

6. Preventing enforcement

101 Rule 70.6 CPR

102 Rule 23.11 CPR

103 CCR Order 37 Rule 1

104 CCR Order 22 Rules 10(3) and (4)

105 CCR Order 22 Rule 10(7)

106 Part 14 para 6 PD CPR

107 *Cheltenham & Gloucester Building Society v Booker, The Times,* 20 November 1996, CA

108 *Hammersmith & Fulham LBC v Hill, The
    Times,* 25 April 1994, CA; see also
    *Cheltenham & Gloucester Building Society
    v Obi* [1994] 28 HLR 22, CA
109 *Hammersmith & Fulham LBC v Lemeh,* 3
    April 2000, *Adviser* 83 abstracts, CA;
    Lambeth LBC v Hughes, 8 May 2000,
    Adviser 84 abstracts, CA
110 Part 23 para 2.4 PD CPR
111 Rule 23.6 CPR
112 Part 23 paras 2.10 and 3(5) PD CPR
113 s112 CCA 1984
114 *The Times,* 19 April 1995, CA; see also
    Various v Walker, Walsall County Court,
    3 January 1997, *Legal Action,* May 1997;
    Various v MM, HW & CE, Birmingham
    County Court, 23 October 1997, *Legal
    Action,* January 1998
115 *Various v MM, HW & CE* (ibid); *A v
    Fenland District Council,* Kings Lynn
    County Court, August 1997, *Adviser* 64
    abstracts. The decision to the contrary in
    Lane v Liverpool City Council, Liverpool
    County Court, 19 May 1997, *Adviser* 69
    abstracts, appears wrongly decided in
    the light of the decision in *Re Green*
    [1979] 1 All ER 832 that an attachment
    of earnings order is not an assignment of
    the debt.
116 CCR Order 39 Rule 14
117 s112(5) CCA 1984
118 Rule 52.11(3) CPR
119 Rule 52.3 CPR
120 Rule 52.4 CPR
121 Rule 3.1(2)(b) CPR
122 *Rollinson v Kimberley Clark Ltd, The Times,*
    22 June 1999, CA

Chapter 10

The magistrates' court

This chapter covers:
1. Financial penalties (p244)
2. Compensation orders (p253)
3. Council tax and community charge (p254)
4. Maintenance (p256)
5. Domestic rates (p257)
6. Tax debts (p258)
7. Wilful refusal and culpable neglect (p258)

The magistrates' court is best known as the first tier of the criminal justice system. Its decisions are made by magistrates (also called Justices of the Peace). Magistrates have traditionally been lay volunteers – that is, unpaid and not legally qualified, although it is increasingly common for them to be full-time and paid, particularly in London and urban areas. Paid magistrates are called District Judges (Magistrates' Courts) (previously, stipendiaries) and are appointed from either barristers or solicitors. Lay magistrates do not receive very much training and are, therefore, very dependent upon their legally qualified clerks in much of their decision making. A justices' clerk, who is a qualified barrister or solicitor, will be present at all hearings in order to direct the way the hearing proceeds and to advise the magistrates on the law and procedure, on the penalties available and any guidance on their use, but should not otherwise take any part in the proceedings.

A justices' chief executive must make arrangements for the efficient and effective administration of the magistrates' court. This includes allocating responsibilities to the justices' clerks and other magistrates' court staff, such as issuing summonses, timetabling hearings, collecting payments (eg, fines) and conducting means enquiries. S/he is required to arrange for the justices' clerks to discuss matters of law (including practices and procedures) in order to secure consistency in the advice given to the magistrates themselves. Some decisions are specifically delegated to court staff, such as:
* considering requests for further time to pay fines;
* varying payment arrangements;
* making transfer of fines orders;
* ordering a debtor to furnish a statement of means prior to a means enquiry;
* re-arranging means enquiries;

• dealing with applications for financial penalties to be paid by deductions from a debtor's social security benefit.

This chapter looks at how the magistrates' court operates as a creditor, or collector of other people's debt, and discusses how the debt adviser should proceed when advising on such debts as:
• financial penalties – eg, fines;
• local taxes – eg, council tax;
• maintenance;
• civil debts, particularly Crown debts.

The debt adviser's role is predominantly to prepare a financial statement and list of debts for the debtor to take to court hearings and perhaps a letter explaining her/his circumstances.

The adviser may be involved in representation or in acting as a 'McKenzie friend' (ie, a person who accompanies the debtor to the hearing, advises her/him, suggests what s/he should say and makes notes of the proceedings), but more often will be liaising with probation staff or solicitors, particularly in respect of unpaid fines. It will be very helpful to form links between the debt advice agency and the probation service so that once the debt adviser has produced the financial statement and details of debts the debtor can be put in touch with the probation service for assistance and support at the court hearing. Probation officers and assistants will normally be based at the court. Some advice agencies now staff help desks at their local magistrates' courts.

If a committal warrant has been issued for the debtor to be imprisoned (see p146), it is usually advisable to obtain good legal representation for the debtor. Free legal representation is now available at committal hearings.

The circumstances in which a debt adviser will come across magistrates' courts are likely to be as follows.

1. **Financial penalties**

A fine is the most common penalty imposed by magistrates' courts in criminal cases. In 2000 nearly 75 per cent of all offenders were fined. Magistrates can also make costs and compensation orders (see p253). These are all known as 'financial penalties'. Although in setting financial penalties the court must take account of the offender's financial circumstances, when setting a fine the court must also take into account the seriousness of the offence. Where both cannot be paid, the court should order compensation (see p253) rather than a fine. Costs are at the discretion of the court, but are usually ordered and fixed at the time.

When imposing a financial penalty the court can order:
• immediate payment; *or*

- payment within a fixed time; *or*
- payment by instalments.

Magistrates' courts are discouraged from inviting applications for time to pay and will usually ask the debtor how much can be paid immediately. The court can search the debtor for any money that can be used to meet the financial penalty, but this power is rarely used. Where the court allows the debtor time to pay, it can fix a day when it will consider the matter again if the financial penalty has not been paid by then or, where instalments were ordered, there has been default. If immediate payment is required but is not made, the court can:

- order the issue of a distress warrant (see p247); *or*
- order the debtor to be detained for the remainder of the day either within the court building or at the police station (see p250).

The court can only order imprisonment in default of immediate payment if:

- the offence is imprisonable and the debtor appears to have sufficient means to pay immediately; *or*
- the debtor is unlikely to remain long enough in the UK to enable other enforcement methods to be used; *or*
- the debtor is already serving a prison sentence (known as 'lodging' the financial penalty); *or*
- the debtor is sentenced to imprisonment by the court for the same, or another, offence.[1]

The debt adviser is likely to be concerned with the debtor's difficulty in paying financial penalties after they have been imposed rather than with the conditions attached on the day of sentence.

Payment by instalments

Where time has been allowed for payment the debtor can apply in writing to the magistrates' clerk for:

- further time to pay; *or*
- payment by instalments; *or*
- variation of the instalments.[2]

Many clerks will be reasonable in their decision but will normally require a financial statement produced by a debt adviser as evidence of income and expenditure upon which to base a realistic payment schedule. The debtor can make an application at any time before the issue of a distress warrant (see p247) or summons in the case of maintenance arrears (see p256) if s/he cannot afford to comply with the original order. Some courts may ask the debtor to attend a means enquiry, which will look afresh at her/his financial situation, before making a decision. Financial penalties should generally be capable of being paid within 12 months, but this is not a fixed rule and the period can be longer, provided it does not exceed two to three years, or even longer in the case of particularly serious offending.[3] If the debtor is unable to do this then it suggests that either there has been a change of circumstances since the penalty was imposed or that it was fixed without adequate financial information.

The High Court has expressed concern at the level of fines imposed on benefit claimants. Recognising that (i) income support is only sufficient for the necessities of life and (ii) a small but regular payment towards financial penalties might be possible over a short period of time, but (iii) contingencies might occur which would stretch a tight budget to breaking point, Lord Justice Staughton recommended that fines on people of limited means should be lesser in amount so that they could be paid in a matter of weeks.[4] In either case the debt adviser should consider asking for all or part of the financial penalty to be remitted at a means enquiry (see p248). However, in making any applications – whether for further time to pay or remission – debt advisers should bear in mind not only that financial penalties are a priority debt but also that they were imposed as a punishment and are meant to cause some inconvenience.

Payments are applied by the court in the following order:

- compensation orders;
- costs;
- fines.

This will be relevant to any term of imprisonment the debtor is ordered to serve in default of payment and also to the question of remission. It is also relevant to the collection of Crown court fines in the magistrates' courts, since the Crown court will already have fixed the term of imprisonment the debtor is to serve in default of payment of the fine, but not of any costs or compensation. Although the sentence can be reduced proportionately by part payment or remission, the magistrates have no power to vary the actual sentence.

Problems can also arise if a debtor has more than one fine or compensation order. Courts do not always make it clear to debtors how their payments will be applied, which can lead to enforcement action being taken in respect of one matter, even though regular payments are being made in respect of another. Financial penalties can be paid either:

- consecutively, where the debtor will be allowed to clear the oldest first with no enforcement action being taken on later ones; *or*
- concurrently, and payments credited to each outstanding financial penalty.

This second method should always be requested, as a proportion of each financial penalty is then cleared.

Once a debtor has defaulted on the payment ordered, it is good practice to send a reminder (although this is not a statutory requirement), giving her/him a further short time to pay and warning the debtor that enforcement action will be taken if s/he fails to comply. If the court has ordered payment by instalments, enforcement action can only be taken if the debtor defaults on payment of an instalment, but once the debtor has missed a payment, enforcement action can be taken in respect of the whole outstanding balance. If no payment is made following the reminder (depending on local practice) the court will either issue a distress warrant (see p247) to bailiffs (see Chapter 11), or a warrant to the police to arrest the debtor (with or without bail) for the purpose of holding a means enquiry, or will summons the debtor to attend a means enquiry (see p248). Repeated missed payments could have the same result. Debt advisers should encourage a debtor to make some payment while waiting for the means enquiry in order to prevent the magistrates deciding that s/he is guilty of 'wilful refusal' or 'culpable neglect' (see p258).

Debt advisers should always contact a magistrates' court immediately if there are arrears on an order. This is because, although the court can make arrangements for time, or further time, to pay before a distress warrant is issued and can postpone the issue of a distress warrant, it appears to have no power to suspend or cancel the operation of a distress warrant after it has been issued until it is returned by the bailiffs (see p279).[5]

Enforcement procedure

When enforcing financial penalties, magistrates' courts are encouraged to follow guidance issued by the Home Office, which aims to bring good practice and consistency to courts.

Distress warrants

The court can issue a distress warrant against the debtor's money and goods if s/he fails to pay as ordered by the court.[6] The issue of distress warrants by magistrates' courts has become more prevalent since a government efficiency scrutiny in 1989 recommended the use of private bailiffs as an efficient means of collecting fines and other magistrates' court orders. Most courts employ private bailiffs to execute distress warrants. Most magistrates' courts appear to use this power almost automatically once a person is in default with her/his payments. This policy has been commended by the High Court on the basis that it is essential that there is effective machinery for fines enforcement. There is no requirement to hold a means enquiry before issuing a distress warrant[7] but, where there is evidence that the debtor has sufficient assets to pay the debt, the magistrates should use distress rather than committal.[8] Where the court is conducting a means enquiry and has it in mind to issue a distress warrant, the debtor should be given the opportunity to make representations.[9] The issue of distress warrants can be delegated by the magistrates to a court official provided checks exist within the system to ensure warrants are not issued inappropriately.

No hearing is required before a distress warrant is issued, although the court can postpone the issue of the warrant if it wishes.[10] The bailiff executing the warrant may not seize bedding or clothes belonging to the debtor or any member of the debtor's family, or the tools, books, vehicles or other equipment which the debtor personally needs to use in her/his employment, business or vocation (Reg 54(4) of the Magistrates' Court Rules 1981 lays down a more restrictive list of exempt goods than applies to most other debts). The debtor must receive specific notice that a distress warrant may be issued on either:

- the original notice of fine or compensation order; *or*
- a reminder, final demand or other similar document.

A debtor may want to apply to the court to reduce the instalments after a distress warrant has been issued. Although the High Court has held that the magistrates' court is not able to suspend or cancel such a warrant after it has been issued,[11] it has been pointed out in another High Court case that magistrates may be able to review the situation under s142 MCA 1980 on the basis that it is 'in the interests of justice to do so' (see p252).[12] However, many courts refuse to consider a matter further once a distress warrant has been issued, until that warrant is returned by the bailiffs to the court. It may be possible for the debt adviser to discuss local policy with the justices' chief executive or the chair of the magistrates, either in principle or in connection with a particular case. (For more details on bailiffs, see Chapter 11.)

Means enquiry

Before the court can take certain types of enforcement action it must enquire into the debtor's ability to pay the financial penalty and reason(s) for default at a hearing at which the debtor is present. For example, unless a person was sentenced to a term of imprisonment in default of immediate payment, there must be a means enquiry before imprisonment can be considered.[13] The questioning of the debtor can be conducted by the magistrates' clerk.[14]

Debtors are often required to complete a statement of means, which may be similar to a debt adviser's financial statement. Magistrates may have little knowledge of the benefits system and of many items of ordinary expenditure, and advisers should ensure that a full financial statement is prepared and given to the magistrates, even if this means adding considerably to the court's own form. This should include explanations for any essential expenditure which the debt adviser feels may be questioned by the court. In addition, magistrates may not take into account items of expenditure to which the debtor has given priority over payment of the financial penalty, but which the magistrates regard as non-essential. Magistrates usually take account of expenditure on housing (including fuel), clothing and feeding the debtor and her/his dependants, water charges and council tax. However, there is no consistent approach and debt advisers should establish local practice. Information should also be made available on the reason(s) for non-payment, the financial position at the time of the previous order and future prospects, as appropriate.

At a means enquiry, or at any other hearing, the court has the power to do the following.

Remit a fine

To remit a fine means that the fine is cancelled, either in full or in part. Provided that circumstances have changed since the fine was imposed or, when the court is considering issuing a committal warrant that was suspended on a previous occasion, since the date of suspension, the court can remit all or part of the fine.[15] Where information is available to the means enquiry that was not before the court at the earlier hearing(s), the debt adviser should argue that this should be regarded as a change of circumstances.

Debt advisers should always argue for full remission of a fine where a person is on benefit or in serious debt (although the court may well take account of the financial position at the time the financial penalty was imposed, or warrant suspended, and any other resources available to the debtor). The magistrates should be urged to consider partial remission where the guidelines on the time for payment of a financial penalty have not been observed. Unfortunately, the magistrates do not have power to remit costs and can only remit compensation orders in limited circumstances (see p253).

Fix a return date

Magistrates may also order payment of the amount due by a certain date or fix an amount to be paid periodically and give a date when the debtor must return if s/he has not paid either the amount due or all the instalments then due. If the debtor fails to appear, a warrant of arrest can be issued. Debt advisers should try to ensure that the order is one with which the debtor can realistically comply or, if s/he defaults, that they will be able to show that this was not due to the debtor's 'wilful refusal' or 'culpable neglect' (see p258).

Money payments supervision order

The court can also make a money payments supervision order (MPSO), appointing someone to 'advise and befriend the defendant with a view to inducing him to pay the sum adjudged to be paid' – ie, supervise the debtor during the payment of the financial penalty.[16] This would normally be a member of the probation service or court staff, but theoretically could be anyone appointed by the court – eg, a debt adviser. The court is not required to hold a means enquiry before making an MPSO nor is the debtor's consent required but, since the debtor's co-operation is essential to the working of the order, it is normally required and should always be considered as an alternative to imprisonment. As a matter of good practice, the MPSO should specify the terms of payment.

Attachment of earnings order

An attachment of earnings order can also be made under the Attachment of Earnings Act 1971 (see p194). The fact that the debtor's earnings fluctuate is no bar to making an attachment of earnings order as no deductions will be made if the debtor's earnings fall below the protected earnings rate.[17]

High Court/county court orders

The clerk may also apply to the High Court or a county court for orders that are only available in these courts – eg, third party debt order, charging order or appointment of receiver.[18] A means enquiry must be held and such an application is unlikely to be made unless the clerk is of the opinion that none of the other methods open to the magistrates' court are likely to be successful but a High Court/county court remedy is.

Deductions from benefits

The court can apply to the Secretary of State to deduct a financial penalty from the debtor's income support or jobseeker's allowance following a means enquiry. For income support and income-based jobseeker's allowance, the maximum deduction is currently £2.70 a week and for contribution-based jobseeker's allowance the maximum deduction is one-third of the single person's applicable amount for a person of the same age as the debtor (but £2.70 a week if there would otherwise be entitlement to income-based jobseeker's allowance). Fines have low priority and no deductions can be made from contribution-based jobseeker's allowance if deductions are already being made for community charge or council tax. Deductions can only be made in respect of one application at a time. If the debtor is likely to suffer hardship as a result of the deduction being made, the debt adviser should consider making representations to the Secretary of State not to enforce the court's application.

Imprisonment

If a debtor falls into arrears with payment of a financial penalty the court may order her/his imprisonment.[19] There is a similar power to detain under-21-year-olds in a young offenders' institution, but there are additional restrictions.[20] The minimum term of imprisonment is 5 days and the maximum term that can be imposed by a magistrates' court is 12 months.

The court can only issue a warrant to imprison someone:
- if a distress warrant is returned to the court by the bailiffs because there are insufficient goods or money to cover the amount owing; *or*
- instead of issuing a distress warrant.[21]

Once a distress warrant has been issued, imprisonment cannot be considered unless the warrant is returned with an endorsement stating that there were no goods. Debt advisers should consider asking solicitors to argue that if a warrant has been returned because the bailiffs were unable to gain access to the debtor's property then imprisonment is not an option open to the court, but this argument has not been tested in the higher courts.

The power to imprison for default is further limited as there must be a means enquiry.[22] At the means enquiry the court must be satisfied either:

- if the original offence was punishable by imprisonment, that the debtor appears to have sufficient means to pay the sum forthwith; *or*
- that the default is due to the debtor's 'wilful refusal' or 'culpable neglect' (see p258); *and also*
- that all other methods of obtaining payment have either been considered or tried but have been inappropriate or unsuccessful (including a money payments supervision order (see p249)).

The Divisional Court has stressed to magistrates the mandatory nature of this second part of the requirement.[23] In practice, the court will often assume that if a person has paid nothing then this is deliberate. Debt advisers should encourage solicitors and other representatives to argue strongly the impossibility of finding money, even for priorities like financial penalties, from a debtor's low income. However, even where the court has expressed itself 'satisfied' that the debtor had the means to pay, a sentence of imprisonment will be quashed unless the court can demonstrate that it has considered all the non-custodial alternatives discussed above. Over the past few years there has been considerable publicity over the number of wrongful committals. This has generally been due to inadequate means enquiries and/or failure to follow the above rules (see p258). In 1996, more than 8,500 debtors a year were being imprisoned for non-payment of financial penalties. In 2000, that figure had fallen to 2,480.

Any term of imprisonment must be proportional to the size of the financial penalty (the period is determined in accordance with a statutory scale depending on the amount of the financial penalty outstanding) and a stay in prison can be avoided by immediately paying the outstanding balance. Any costs of unsuccessful bailiff action can be added to the amount the debtor must pay to obtain her/his release. The length of any period of detention (whether actual or suspended) can be reduced by paying a proportion of the outstanding balance.[24] The financial penalty and any costs are wiped out if the prison sentence is served.

If the court decides to impose a period of imprisonment, it can be postponed upon certain conditions, for example, if the debtor keeps to a payment arrangement.[25] This is known as a 'suspended committal'. The conditions can be varied if, for example, the debtor's circumstances change and s/he can no longer comply with the terms of the suspended committal. A suspended committal order cannot be combined with any other enforcement order, since by implication they have all been considered inappropriate, and any attempt to do so could be challenged on the basis that no period of imprisonment should have been imposed in the first place. If the debtor fails to comply with the conditions of postponement, another hearing must be held before the debtor can actually be sent to prison. The debtor must be given the opportunity to attend the hearing in order to make representations as to why the committal warrant should not be issued. This will involve attempting to persuade the magistrates that circumstances have changed since the previous hearing (including new facts). The court can still consider remission at this stage. Although the rules state that notice of the hearing is deemed to be served if sent by registered post or recorded delivery to the debtor's last known address, the High Court quashed a sentence of imprisonment where a notice of hearing had been returned to the court as undelivered. The High Court said that the magistrates should have adjourned the hearing until the debtor had actually been served with notice of the hearing.[26]

Short local detention

Instead of imposing imprisonment, the magistrates can order the debtor to be detained for the remainder of the day, either within the court building or at a police station up until 8pm. S/he must be released in time for her/him to get home on the same day. The magistrates can also order the debtor to be detained overnight at a police station until 8am in the morning.[27] This is not imprisonment and so the restrictions on imposing imprisoning debtors do not apply, but as with imprisonment, the financial penalty is wiped out (see p250).

This might be appropriate where the magistrates have the financial penalty to be paid forthwith, but the debtor is unable to do so and the magistrates are not prepared to allow time to pay.

Attendance centre order

If the court has an attendance centre available to it and the debtor is less than 25 years old, the magistrates can order the debtor to attend an attendance centre for at least 12 hours but no more than 36 hours.[28] Attendance can be required for 2 to 3 hours at a time, usually on Saturday afternoons.

Re-opening a case

A magistrates' court may vary or even rescind any sentence or other order imposed or made by it when dealing with an offender when it appears to be in the interests of justice to do so.[29] Although discretionary, this could be a speedy and effective means of cancelling or reducing a financial penalty that has been wrongly imposed or is demonstrably too high as there is no time limit on making the application and the debtor does not have to show any change of circumstances since the financial penalty was imposed.

In addition, where the case was dealt with in the debtor's absence and s/he had no knowledge of the summons or the proceedings, s/he can make a statutory declaration to this effect, which will result in the conviction being rendered void and the financial penalty being set aside. There will need to be a new hearing and so this option needs to be carefully considered.[30] The statutory declaration must be delivered to the magistrates' court within 21 days of the proceedings first coming to the debtor's knowledge. There is discretion to extend the time limit where it appears to the court that it was not reasonable to expect the debtor to comply with it.

If neither of the above applies and the debtor maintains her/his innocence of the offence(s), s/he should be referred to a solicitor for a possible appeal or application for judicial review. There are time limits.

Transfer of fines

If a debtor moves to a different magistrates' court's area but still has a financial penalty to pay at the magistrates' court where s/he used to live, it may be advisable to apply to the original court for a fine transfer order to the new local court.[31] This should make payments easier to arrange.

2. Compensation orders

A magistrates' court can impose a compensation order alongside a fine or other sentence and must give reasons for not making an order in cases where it is empowered to do so.[32] The compensation order is intended to be a simple way for the injured party in a criminal case to get compensation without having to sue in the county court. Compensation orders are often made in cases such as criminal damage or petty theft. They are collected by the court and paid to the victim exactly like fines, with one important exception. The powers to remit a fine (see p249) do not apply to compensation orders. The only circumstances in which a compensation order could be altered are:

- if a person appeals against either the conviction or the compensation order. A solicitor would need to assist with this and there are strict time limits; *or*
- if subsequent civil proceedings demonstrate that the loss in respect of which the order was made was less than stated in the order; *or*
- if a compensation order is made for stolen goods which are later recovered; *or*
- the defendant has suffered a substantial reduction in her/his means which was unexpected at the time the order was made and her/his means seem unlikely to increase for a considerable period.[33]

Because compensation orders are difficult to change, it is very important for a debt adviser to ensure that if someone is appearing in a criminal court on a charge which might result in a compensation order s/he is advised to take with her/him a clear statement of means and that any representative is prepared to argue that in view of her/his other debts s/he should not have a compensation order awarded against her/him. The court must consider a debtor's financial statement and debts in making a decision.[34]

Costs awarded along with a fine or compensation order are treated in exactly the same way as the compensation order – that is, they cannot be remitted by the court.

---

3. **Council tax and community charge**

Magistrates' courts have two distinct roles in relation to the collection of council tax and community charge. These are:
- to decide about the issue of a liability order;
- to decide about committal to prison.

The first should already have taken place in any remaining community charge cases.

Issue of a liability order

The court can issue a liability order against an individual at the request of a local authority. The debtor is summonsed to attend a hearing. The summons must be served at least 14 days before the hearing date.[35] The order states that an amount of tax is due from the debtor, that s/he has not paid it and is therefore liable. Issues regarding, for example, liability for, or exemption from, the tax cannot be raised at the hearing, but must be dealt with through the appropriate appeals procedure, although the court would probably adjourn if an appeal were pending.[36] Failure by the local authority to follow the rules on billing and reminder notices can be raised as a defence, as can the fact that the demand has actually been paid. Although the fact that a claim for council tax benefit or rebate is pending is not a defence, the magistrates could adjourn the matter. If payment is made after the liability order has been applied for, the local authority is entitled to ask for an order for payment of its reasonable costs.[37] The magistrates cannot be asked to allow time to pay at this stage.

The order allows the authority to pursue collection of the debt by way of:
- a payment arrangement; *or*
- distress warrant (see p247); *or*
- attachment of earnings in accordance with the scales set out in the regulations (see p250); *or*
- a deduction of income support or jobseeker's allowance (see p250); *or*
- a charging order (see p189); *or*
- bankruptcy (see Chapter 12)

as well as enabling it to require information about the debtor's means to be supplied.

Enforcement of a liability order is done by the local authority unless it chooses to return to the magistrates' court in order to seek the imprisonment of the debtor.

Committal to prison (council tax or community charge)

If an application to commit someone to prison is made, the court must arrange a hearing and hold a means enquiry.[38] These proceedings can only begin once a distress warrant has been issued and returned because insufficient, or no, goods of the debtor could be found (for whatever reason, including because the bailiffs could not gain entry).[39]

The adviser should not rely on the court to produce paperwork and must prepare a full statement of income, expenditure and debts as well as a clear explanation of any particular difficulties facing the debtor.

The court must decide whether the debtor has shown 'wilful refusal' or 'culpable neglect' in failing to pay (see p258). For community charge, the magistrates should consider the issue only up to the date of the liability order, but for council tax, the magistrates can consider the whole period up to the date of the committal hearing. In all cases, the magistrates must also consider the debtor's ability to pay at the date of the actual committal hearing. The court normally assumes that if somebody has been warned several times then, however poor they are, they have at least 'culpably neglected' to pay. In community charge cases this viewpoint was exacerbated by people who sought to make high-profile refusals to pay as a part of a campaign of non-violent civil disobedience. For this reason a debt adviser who acts as a representative in the magistrates' court should ensure that the bench understand that poverty, rather than politics, is the cause of the non-payment, by producing evidence about the debtor's income and spending and other priority debts. Free legal representation is available to assist debtors at these hearings as well as at committal hearings regarding financial penalties.

Committal hearing

If the court decides that there has not been either wilful refusal or culpable neglect then it can either remit (write off) all or some of the arrears,[40] or make no order at all. Although there is no time limit within which a local authority must enforce a liability order, the High Court has said that magistrates should consider remitting the debt on their own initiative where more than six years has elapsed between the date of the original default and the committal hearing.[41]

If the magistrates decide that there has been wilful refusal or culpable neglect they can issue a warrant committing the debtor to prison for up to three months. They can (and usually do initially) suspend this warrant on payment of regular instalments. This means that so long as the agreed payments are kept to, the debtor will not be imprisoned; but, unlike in the case of financial penalties, the court no longer has the option to remit the debt. Where the debtor fails to comply with the terms of the suspended order, the magistrates must satisfy themselves that s/he had the ability to pay before they can activate the committal order.[42]

If a debtor is committed to prison no further enforcement action can be taken against those particular arrears. They are still owed, but would cease to be priority debts.

The High Court has repeatedly advised magistrates that the purpose of committal in such cases is to obtain payment and not to punish the debtor. Therefore, although there is no statutory obligation to do so, local authorities, as well as magistrates, should consider alternative viable methods of enforcement and not refuse reasonable offers of payment.[43] However, a suspended committal order is regarded as a method of enforcement in its own right.[44] Orders should not be suspended for more than two to three years and partial remission should be considered in order to reduce the sum in respect of which the order is being made.[45] The magistrates must have regard to the principle of proportionality, with the maximum term being reserved for the most serious cases. The magistrates should use the tables of sentences provided for fines as a guide to the appropriate level of sentences (see *Anthony and Berryman's Magistrates' Court Guide,* Appendix 6).[46] The magistrates must consider the question of wilfulness/culpability separately from the question of how they are going to deal with the case.

When representing a council tax or community charge defaulter it is helpful to begin with the presentation of a financial statement and evidence relating to debts and social circumstances before asking the court to make a specific decision on the question of wilfulness or culpability. After the court has decided this, the debt adviser can argue about an affordable instalment arrangement, if necessary. It is useful to secure the court's agreement to conduct proceedings in this format because it encourages the court to think about wilfulness and because it allows the debt adviser to rescue something if the initial decision is unfavourable. The financial argument about the payment of a weekly amount by the debtor should be based on the scales laid down in the regulations for attachment of earnings, although as these make no allowances for dependants or other commitments they will often require modification.

Many magistrates' courts will not allow lay representatives in council tax or community charge hearings. If the magistrates will not accept a debt adviser as a representative, then s/he can act as a 'McKenzie friend' (see p244).

4. Maintenance

If a maintenance order is made by the magistrates' court for a child or adult dependant or is registered by a magistrates' court for collection after being made in the county court or High Court, the debt is collected by the court exactly as though it were a financial penalty.[47] The court is likely to be sympathetic to varying a maintenance order as soon as financial problems arise, or to remitting unpaid maintenance, if this has not been paid as a result of a change in circumstances since the order was made. An application to vary an order should first be made in writing to the clerk, stating the reason for the application and providing financial details. The application should explain any change in the debtor's circumstances and give details of reduction in income or increase in spending. The clerk informs everyone named in the maintenance order, and the whole matter can be dealt with without the need for a hearing. If the clerk does not agree to vary the order, then an application must be made to the court.[48] A debt adviser should always ensure that the debtor makes an immediate application for the variation of a maintenance order if debts arise. If there are existing arrears the court can be asked to remit these, although the person entitled to the maintenance must be given the opportunity to make representations. It is usual to remit all but the previous 12 months' arrears.

Once a maintenance order is in arrears then either a summons or warrant can be issued for a means enquiry. If the debtor is required to attend a means enquiry, the debt adviser should prepare a financial statement, list of debts and a supporting letter to request a variation in the order and remission of the arrears. The court can adjourn the hearing to enable the debtor to clear the arrears, but otherwise can issue a distress warrant (see p247). It can also consider making an attachment of earnings order (see p250) if the debtor is employed (but not a deduction from benefits order). If the court is satisfied that an attachment of earnings order is not appropriate and that the debtor has failed to pay the arrears because of wilful refusal or culpable neglect, it can issue a committal warrant, either suspended or for the debtor's immediate imprisonment. The maximum period of imprisonment is six weeks. Serving a term of imprisonment does not discharge the arrears, but the debtor cannot be imprisoned again in respect of the same arrears.[49]

5. **Domestic rates**

Some magistrates' courts are still dealing with unpaid domestic rates which were payable before the introduction of the community charge in April 1990. However, most local authorities would probably be quite pleased to use their powers to remit old rates so as to allow them to concentrate on the collection of council tax/ community charge, and a debt adviser should always approach them first (even where a magistrates' court hearing is pending) and persuade them to adjourn any court action and consider remitting the rates bill in full. If this request is refused, the court should be asked to use its powers to remit.

6. Tax debts

Magistrates' courts have powers to deal with some tax debts. These include amounts of income tax and national insurance contributions of less than £2,000. The Department for Work and Pensions (DWP) or Inland Revenue will make a 'complaint' to the magistrates' court, which will issue a summons to a hearing. There is either a 6-month or 12-month time limit depending on the type of debt. At the first hearing the court may make an order for payment if satisfied that the tax is due. The order for payment can be by instalments, but it will be necessary for the debtor to attend court and apply for this and so a financial statement will be required.[50] As these authorities have the power to use bailiffs without a court order, a distress warrant will not usually be applied for. If the initial order for payment is not obeyed the authorities may issue a judgment summons for the debtor to 'show cause why s/he should not be sent to prison'. At this 'committal hearing' the court will proceed exactly as for unpaid financial penalties by conducting a means enquiry then assessing whether or not the debtor has 'wilfully refused' or 'culpably neglected' to pay (see below). Although the court could decide not to imprison the debtor it cannot remit these debts.

7. Wilful refusal and culpable neglect

There are a number of situations in which magistrates acting as debt collectors are required to decide whether a non-payment is due to 'wilful refusal' or 'culpable neglect'.

Although magistrates' courts have been making decisions based on their interpretation of this important phrase for many years, the two phrases are not defined by statute or regulation. There is little guidance as to what factors should be taken into account when making a decision, but the debtor's conduct must be 'blameworthy' in some way.

The debtor should only be found guilty of wilful refusal if s/he has made a deliberate decision not to pay the amount due even though s/he is able to do so – eg, on a point of principle. However, a finding of wilful refusal does not automatically justify a sentence of imprisonment; the two questions must be considered separately.

'Culpable neglect' is more difficult. It means a reckless disregard of the court order and usually involves the situation where the debtor applies any available income to non-essential items rather than the payment of the financial penalty, etc. It is not sufficient for the magistrates to find that the debtor had available income and did not pay; they must also make findings as to why it has not been paid.[51] Where a couple are in receipt of benefits intended for them both, the non-claimant debtor can be found guilty of culpable neglect where there has been a 'household' decision not to pay.[52] To prove 'culpable neglect', the prosecuting authorities must show that:

- money was available but was not paid to the court or local authority; *and*
- this was due to a failure which demonstrates an avoidable choice to use the money for other purposes.

Evidence in the form of a financial statement should demonstrate to the court how impossible were a debtor's choices and thus that a failure to pay was not culpable.

Most courts assume that if a person has ignored reminders or suspended committals, then they have culpably neglected payment. This assumption should be challenged by debt advisers who should argue that a person:

- did not have any money available after paying for essential items; *or*
- was too stressed to be culpable; *or*
- did not understand the need to pay; *or*
- was not skilful enough to balance a very difficult budget; *or*
- was wrongly advised not to pay.

Notes

1. **Financial penalties**
   1 ss75, 76, 80, 82, 86 and 135 MCA 1980
   2 ss75 and 85A MCA 1980
   3 *R v Olliver & Olliver* [1989] 11 Cr App R (Sentencing) 10
   4 *R v Newark Justices ex parte Keenaghan, The Times,* 3 January 1997
   5 s77(1) MCA 1980; *Crossland v Crossland* [1992] 2 FCR 45; confirmed in *R v Hereford Magistrates' Court ex parte MacRae, The Times,* 31 December 1998
   6 s76 MCA 1980
   7 *R v Hereford Magistrates ex parte MacRae, The Times,* 31 December 1998
   8 *R v Birmingham Justices ex parte Bennett* [1983] 1 WLR 114
   9 *R v Guildford Justices ex parte Rich* [1997] 1 Cr App R 49
   10 s77(1) MCA 1980
   11 *Crossland v Crossland* [1992] 2 FCR 45; confirmed in *R v Hereford Magistrates' Court ex parte MacRae, The Times,* 31 December 1998
   12 *R v Sheffield City Justices ex parte Foster, The Times,* 2 December 1999
   13 s82 (3)(b) MCA 1980
   14 *R v Corby Magistrates' Court ex parte Mott, The Times,* 12 March 1998
   15 s85 MCA 1980
   16 s88 MCA 1980 and s56(2) MCA 1980
   17 *R v York Magistrates' Court ex parte Grimes, The Times,* 27 June 1997
   18 s87(1) MCA 1980
   19 s76 MCA 1980 restricted by s82
   20 s88(5) MCA and ss1(5) and 5A CJA 1982
   21 s76(2) MCA 1980
   22 s82 MCA 1980
   23 *R v Stockport Justices ex parte Conlon, The Times,* 3 January 1997
   24 s79 MCA 1980
   25 s77 MCA 1980
   26 *R v Doncaster Justices ex parte Harrison* (1998) 163 JP 182
   27 ss 135 and 136 MCA 1980
   28 s60 Powers of Criminal Courts (Sentencing) Act 2000
   29 s142 MCA 1980 as amended by CAA 1995
   30 s14 MCA 1980
   31 s89 MCA 1980

2. Compensation orders
32 ss1(1) and 35(1) PCCA 1973
33 s37 PCCA 1973
34 s35(1)(a) PCCA 1973

3. Council tax and community charge
35 Reg 35(2A) CT(AE) Regs 1992 as
    amended
36 *R v Bristol Justices ex parte Wilson and
    Young* (1991) 156 JP 409
37 Regs 34(5)(b) and (8) CT(AE) Regs 1992
38 Reg 41(2) CC(AE) Regs; reg 44(2)
    CT(AE) Regs
39 Reg 41(1) CC(AE) Regs; reg 44(1)
    CT(AE) Regs
40 Reg 42(2) CC(AE) Regs; reg 48(2)
    CT(AE) Regs
41 *R v Warrington Borough Council ex parte
    Barrett,* 18 November 1999,
    unreported; *R v Gloucestershire Justices ex
    parte Daldry,* 12 January 2000,
    unreported
42 *R v Felixstowe Justices ex parte Herridge*
    [1993] Rating Appeals 83
43 *R v Sandwell Justices ex parte Lynn,* 5
    March 1993, unreported; *R v Alfreton
    Justices ex parte Gratton, The Times,* 17
    December 1993
44 *R v Preston Justices ex parte McCosh, The
    Times,* 30 January 1995
45 *R v Newcastle upon Tyne Justices ex parte
    Devine,* 23 April 1998, QBD; *R v
    Doncaster Justices ex parte Jack &
    Christison, The Times,* 26 May 1999
46 *R v Warrington Borough Council ex parte
    Barrett,* 18 November 1999, unreported

4. Maintenance
47 s76 MCA 1980
48 s60 MCA 1980 as amended by s4 MEA
    1991
49 s94 MCA 1980

6. Tax debts
50 s58 MCA 1980

7. Wilful refusal and culpable neglect
51 *R v Watford Justices ex parte Hudson,* 21
    April 1999, unreported
52 *R v Ramsgate Magistrates ex parte
    Haddow* (1992) 157 JP 545

Chapter 11

Bailiffs

This chapter covers:

A bailiff is someone who acts on behalf of creditors or courts to collect debts, repossess homes or goods, or execute certain arrest warrants. This chapter will look mainly at the role of bailiffs in the seizure of goods to enforce debt and will also outline their new powers of arrest (see section 4). Advisers should constantly bear in mind two points. Firstly, bailiffs are employed to seize goods, not to collect debts by instalments. Arranging affordable repayments on behalf of a client in multiple debt may, therefore, be very difficult. Secondly, bailiffs seldom have to actually remove or sell goods, as it is the threat of this that is effective in eliciting payments from a debtor.

---

1. Types of bailiff and the seizure of goods

There are several different types of bailiff operating in England and Wales. The most meaningful distinction that can be made between them is on the basis of their powers to seize goods ('distress' or 'distraint'). This determines both their duties and their liabilities as enforcement agents, and their powers as bailiffs. The categories of seizure of goods can be classified as follows.

Common law distress

There has always been a power in English law for a landowner to levy distress in respect of certain liabilities arising from, or associated with, her/his land. The surviving forms today are as follows.

Distress for rent

Arrears of unpaid rent can be collected by means of distress, either by the landlord personally or by using a private 'certificated' bailiff. Many private bailiffs hold a certificate, though firms described as certificated bailiffs will often employ other staff who are not certificated to undertake the vast majority of their work.

In order to become certificated, an individual bailiff must make application to a county court. Applicants must have a bond of £10,000 lodged either with the court or in a bank, or indemnity insurance for the same amount, must know the law of distress sufficiently, and must be a 'fit and proper person to hold a certificate'. A certificated bailiff cannot be part of a firm whose business is to buy debts.

In practice, certification means very little as the courts do not investigate a person's suitability or check the information submitted on the application form. There is no monitoring of certificated bailiffs, and though most certificates are renewable every two years, this process is largely regarded as a formality. The certification system does, however, allow for complaints to be heard by the court (see p277).

'Distress damage feasant'

'Distress damage feasant' is a remedy that permits the seizure and impounding of 'trespassing chattels'. The power was generally regarded as obsolete until recently, when it was revived to provide a legal justification for the practice of private wheel clamping of wrongfully parked cars.

Execution

Execution is the enforcement of civil court judgments by the seizure and sale of goods. There are three different types of execution that the adviser may encounter. Readers should note that, in regard to execution, only in the civil courts may a court suspend the enforcement of a warrant.

High Court execution

The High Court uses bailiffs (sheriff's officers) to enforce the following judgments by seizing and selling the defendant's goods:
- High Court judgments of any amount;
- any county court judgment of over £5,000 where the debt has not arisen from an agreement regulated by the Consumer Credit Act 1974;
- county court judgments of between £600 and £5,000 which do not arise from an agreement regulated by the Consumer Credit Act 1974 if the creditor chooses to transfer them.

Sheriff's officers are private bailiffs, organised on a county basis. Their day-to-day instructions come from the county's undersheriff, who can be a useful contact for negotiation. Sheriff's officers have similar powers to county court bailiffs, but are preferred by some creditors because, being private bailiffs, they are considered more effective.

County court execution

The Court Service employs bailiffs in each county court who are responsible for enforcing all warrants in that court's area. The bailiff may enforce the following judgments by seizing and selling the defendant's goods:

- all judgments based on agreements regulated by Consumer Credit Act 1974;
- all judgments for under £600;
- any other judgment for up to £5,000, unless the creditor chooses to transfer to the High Court for enforcement by execution.

Road traffic penalties

Local authorities (primarily in London) may use private bailiffs to enforce unpaid orders for road traffic penalties (decriminalised parking fines). Any sum payable for a parking offence is recoverable by a new form of warrant of execution as if payable under a county court order. Road traffic execution is a complex amalgam of county court execution, distress for rent and special provisions of its own, but is essentially execution levied by a private certificated bailiff.

Statutory distraint

Many public bodies have a statutory power to seize and sell goods if money is owed to them. There are many forms of such 'statutory distraint', but debt advisers will most often encounter the following.

Local taxes

Both council tax and business rates are enforceable by seizure and sale of goods. Distraint may be levied by either local authority officers or by private bailiffs, provided in either case they are certificated.

Income tax

The Inland Revenue can levy distraint to collect any unpaid taxes and class 1 and 4 national insurance contributions. A private bailiff may attend a levy, but only to assist and advise the Inland Revenue's staff. The power of distraint is generally only used against businesses that are still trading, although occasionally it is used to collect tax or national insurance contributions from someone who is no longer trading, but has property in the home against which to levy.[1]

VAT

Customs and Excise may use its own officers or private bailiffs to levy for arrears of VAT. About 75 per cent of its collection work is now is private hands.

Magistrates' court orders

Private bailiffs may be used by magistrates' courts to collect unpaid civil debts (ie, tax and national insurance contributions), damages, compensation orders and fines, including those from the Crown court, Court of Appeal and House of Lords. Many courts restrict distress for fines to fixed penalty offences (eg, fines for motoring offences) or to sums under £100 to £150. Though it is not a legal requirement, many courts prefer to use only certificated bailiffs. The bailiffs will be appointed by the court in line with the new tendering and authorisation procedure created in respect of their new powers to execute arrest warrants, in force since April 2001 (see section 4).

Child support maintenance

The Secretary of State for Social Security is empowered to levy distraint to collect arrears of maintenance due to the Child Support Agency under a magistrates' court liability order. Private bailiffs are employed.

---

2. How bailiffs become involved

Whatever the type of bailiff or debt involved, the process of seizure is initiated by the issue of a warrant to the bailiff for the specific sum due from the debtor. The details of how warrants are issued (and how they may be stopped, if that is possible) differ from form to form.

Distress for rent

The process by which a warrant is issued will depend on the tenancy of the person against whom the levy is to be directed. Landlords of assured and protected or statutory tenants cannot levy distress without first obtaining permission from the county court. Generally the courts will be reluctant to grant permission. In addition the court has, at this stage, the power to suspend or adjourn the order (see Chapter 9).

Landlords of secure or commercial tenants or of long leaseholders can seize goods without a court order. If the landlord is not an individual a certificated bailiff must be used, although this could be a member of staff of a local authority.

A warrant may be issued, and distress levied, the day after a rent payment falls due. There need be no prior demand. The remedy can be used only for the collection of rent and sums collectable as rent, such as service charges. Housing benefit overpayments or council tax arrears which may, in some cases, appear on a tenant's rent account should not be enforced in this way.

County court warrants of execution

A warrant of execution (see p189) may be issued by a creditor when a person has defaulted on the terms of payment of a judgment debt. A warrant may be issued for the whole of the balance due under the judgment, or it may be a part warrant. If the judgment was payable by instalments, the bailiff may be asked to levy for one monthly instalment (or four weekly instalments, as appropriate) or for not less than £50, whichever is the greater. Consumer credit lenders often prefer to issue part warrants as these are considered more likely to be effective. As a result, lenders may repeatedly use execution to threaten the debtor following default upon an instalment order.

The debtor does not have an opportunity to oppose the issue of a warrant, but the bailiff must deliver a warning notice telling the debtor that a warrant has been issued. Levy upon the warrant is then delayed for seven days to allow payment to be made. A warrant is valid for 12 months and may be executed at any time within that period.

At any time after the issue of the warrant the court can suspend or 'stay' its execution. The debtor should apply to the court on form N245 (see p229).

High Court execution

If a judgment of the High Court (and some county court judgments – see p189) is unpaid, it may be enforced by execution by the issue of a writ of *fieri-facias* (commonly known as 'fi-fa'). This instructs the sheriff's officers to seize sufficient goods to cover the full amount of the judgment debt, plus interest and the costs of execution. Unlike in the county court (see above), no part warrants are possible. The debtor should receive a warning note from the sheriff's officer that the writ has been issued, though this is not compulsory and does not always happen.

The debtor should apply immediately on N244 for a stay of execution in order to suspend the writ (see p232 for how to do this).

Road traffic penalties

If a penalty imposed by a parking attendant is not paid, the relevant local authority can obtain an order in Northampton County Court, confirming liability. The local authority can enforce this by issuing a warrant to private certificated bailiffs with whom it has a contract.

It can often be difficult to negotiate, as the bailiffs' instructions will usually be to collect the whole debt and not to accept instalments. Although the order is made by the county court, it cannot intervene to suspend the warrant. Normally the only way of challenging the warrant is to challenge the original charge or order. Various means of appeal exist, initially through the county court Parking Enforcement Centre in Northampton, and then through the Parking Appeals Service in London.

Income tax

The use of distraint for income tax arrears does not have to be sanctioned by a court. Initially, demands for payment will be made from the computer collection centres and then by the local collector. If the taxpayer is still seen to be 'neglecting or refusing' to pay, a warrant is issued internally by a senior Inland Revenue officer. If dealing with the threat of bailiffs for an unpaid tax, the debt adviser should contact the relevant tax office. The collector will probably accept a reasonable offer to clear the debt (though possibly only over a period of 6 to 12 months) and stay the warrant, if the offer is accompanied by a financial statement. The collector may also be persuaded to take no action where a debt is clearly unrecoverable.

VAT

Customs and Excise may use distraint for two reasons – to recover the debt and to close down a business to prevent the problem reoccurring. Little warning is given once the final demand for payment has been ignored, and it is often difficult to negotiate anything but the severest terms of repayment.

The distraint process is activated when a VAT return is made by a trader without enclosing full payment of the VAT due or, if a return has not been made, s/he has been assessed as owing over the prescribed figure of £200. At this stage the Customs and Excise collector will often try to negotiate directly with the debtor. If this fails, a final demand notice will be issued. If the trader still neglects, or refuses, to pay and at least £200 is still due, a warrant will be issued. In either case, the adviser may be able to agree a stay on enforcement whilst instalment payments are made, though the timescale allowed to negotiate may be quite short.

Magistrates' court orders

If a debtor defaults on a magistrates' court order for payment, the whole sum ordered to be paid will fall due and may be enforced by distraint. In respect of fines, which are most commonly enforced by distraint, if the court allowed time to pay or set instalments, or if the defendant was absent at the hearing, a warrant cannot be issued until the court serves written notice upon the debtor stating the total balance due, the instalments ordered and the date when payment begins. Once these conditions have been satisfied a warrant may be issued on default.

If there is a hearing before the issue of a warrant, either because a review date has been set by the court or because, as with maintenance, an opportunity for the debtor to appear is required by the legislation, the debtor may have a chance to prevent distraint. S/he can apply to have the warrant postponed by the magistrates' court at the hearing. This may be done upon further terms of payment. It is, however, almost impossible to suspend or withdraw a warrant once it is with the bailiffs (see p279). However, the bailiff has the power to postpone the sale of goods.

To make matters harder for the debtor and adviser, the bailiffs are normally instructed to collect the whole debt forthwith and not to agree to instalment payments.

Local taxes

Prior to enforcement, the magistrates' court issues a 'liability order' that enables the local authority to use a variety of enforcement measures (see p254) including distraint. The court has no power to intervene in the enforcement, either at this stage or later, nor can it set terms of payment.

A warrant is then issued by the local authority to bailiffs to levy the sums due. The debt adviser can either come to an agreement directly with the bailiffs or persuade the local authority to withdraw its warrant. Many local authorities will wish to come to reasonable arrangements with debtors if these result in regular payment (see p128). Bear in mind the council's own code of practice on local tax enforcement (see p276) when negotiating over these debts, especially when seeking to have the warrant withdrawn.

3. Bailiffs' powers

To enter

The first crucial stage in the procedure is for the bailiff to enter the debtor's premises. In most cases, it is upon this that success hangs. The debtor has a number of legal rights. If the bailiff breaches one of these basic principles, the whole levy may be rendered illegal. See p276 for remedies.

Time

Distress for rent cannot be carried out between sunset and sunrise, nor on a Sunday; and court execution cannot take place on Sundays, Good Friday or Christmas Day. Most other forms of distraint and execution can be at any time of day and on any day of the week. Codes of practice may restrict when distraint may be levied (eg, the Child Support Agency's code of practice). VAT distraint has its own rules about times of levy: in general, levies may only be begun between 8am and 8pm. Where the debtor trades partly (or wholly) outside these times, the levy may be commenced at any time and on any day when the business is trading. Bailiffs will tend to call at varying times and on different days in order to have a good chance of finding a person at home.

Place

In general, bailiffs may go anywhere within England and Wales where the debtor's goods may be found. In practice, of course, they will only have either a business or home address on the warrant and this will be the only place they will visit. Matters are more restricted for landlords, who may only levy at the rented premises for which the arrears are due (though there is a right to pursue goods they know have been removed to avoid distress).

Method

Most bailiffs do not have the right to force their way in to execute a warrant. The only exception is that bailiffs from the Inland Revenue can obtain a warrant to force entry, but this is very rare. In theory at least, a well-informed debtor may simply deny the bailiff access and that is the end of the matter.

Bailiffs are, of course, well aware of the limitations on their powers and will, therefore, try various tactics to get round a determined debtor. They will visit at different times over a period of a few weeks, they may attempt to walk straight into a house as soon as a door is opened to them, or they may simply decide not to try to enter the house itself but to seize goods outside, such as a car parked on the driveway. Another solution to an obstructive debtor would be to use one of the wide range of entry rights that bailiffs enjoy. They can enter through doors, windows and skylights that are left open, and can use ladders to climb in upstairs windows or over back walls. Normally it is not necessary for them to use these powers – they are frequently admitted by debtors to avoid embarrassment or confrontation.

Once entry has been gained, a bailiff may break open internal doors. This may be to open cupboards or attics or, if they have entered a house which is shared by a group of people with no single 'householder' (ie, in multiple occupation), the bailiff is entitled to use force to enter parts of that house which may be exclusively used by the debtor even if they are locked. Once again, the exercise of these powers is usually unnecessary.

Note that bailiffs cannot call the police to assist them to enter a debtor's home. The police can only be called to prevent a breach of the peace. The breach may, of course, be caused by the bailiff or the debtor. In the latter case, the bailiff may summon police support in advance if s/he has a genuine expectation of difficulty, or may call for help whilst conducting the levy. A bailiff acting unlawfully may well be in breach of the peace and could be arrested by the police. A bailiff acting lawfully will not be liable to arrest.[2] The police should only enter a property where a breach of the peace is occurring or is a real risk.[3]

Identification

Bailiffs levying distress for rent and for road traffic penalties must produce their certificate to the tenant or other person responsible for the house. A bailiff collecting local taxes must carry written authority from the collecting council. Enforcement agents acting for magistrates' courts in the execution of warrants of distress and arrest (see section 4) must carry identity cards at all times. These must be shown to the debtor when executing the warrant and to any other person on demand. Warrants should also be shown to the defendant upon request. No rules are laid down for other bailiffs, though it would be normal to expect them to produce the warrant.

To levy

The power to levy is the power of bailiffs to seize, secure and, if necessary, sell goods in order to discharge the debt due. The levy process, however, can generate many disputes and requires close examination by the adviser.

Seizure

Seizure involves a bailiff selecting certain specified goods with a view to taking and selling them later. If the goods to be seized are household items, it is essential that the bailiff has first entered the home (see earlier). However, once this has been achieved little in the way of a physical act of seizure will be necessary for the bailiff to assert the creditor's rights. A mere verbal declaration of intent may be enough. Usually, though, an inventory is taken. This lists the goods that have been seized. Ideally it should specify items individually, but a statement of 'all goods on the property', though unsatisfactory, is legal. Inventories which seize 'all goods except those exempt' (see later) are illegal.

Sometimes bailiffs claim to be able to levy without entry and formal seizure. This process is sometimes known as a 'constructive levy'. Often a notice is put through a person's door saying that certain goods have been levied, presumably merely by looking through the window. The courts have rejected levies of household goods by such means. Advisers should proceed on the assumption that seizure requires the bailiff who wishes to levy distress to be physically capable of removing the goods. The emphasis on having at some time had this physical ability indicates that seizure without being in the building in which goods are kept is a nonsense.

Impounding

Impounding is when goods are placed in the 'custody of the law'. This legal custody is important as it gives the bailiff the right to return at a later date (forcing entry to the debtor's premises if necessary) and remove and sell them. It also protects the goods from seizure or interference by another party, whether this is the debtor or another bailiff seeking to levy upon the goods.

There are a number of ways in which the goods may be impounded. The most common is when the bailiff takes the goods away immediately or leaves them with the debtor subject to a 'walking possession agreement'. Removal is most common with vehicles or with easily disposable business assets. Walking possession is preferred in almost every other case. In the case of magistrates' court distraint, unless the warrant specifies otherwise, household goods can only be removed from the debtor's property on the day of sale, having been seized and impounded by means of a distinct mark. There is no provision for 'walking possession' in magistrates' court cases.

A walking possession agreement is an agreement in which the debtor acknowledges that the property is now in the control of the bailiff and is liable to be removed if the debt is not paid. However, the debtor will be allowed to continue to use the property while s/he arranges payment, provided s/he keeps it carefully. A nominal daily fee is usually charged for walking possession. Bailiffs will prefer to have a written agreement to secure their rights and fees, though a verbal agreement could be adequate just to impound the goods. In local tax distraint an agreement must be signed in the presence of the bailiffs, and the signatory must be the debtor; in other cases any 'responsible person' in the property would do – for example, a spouse or adult dependant.

If the bailiff is claiming 'constructive seizure' it is never advisable to sign any 'walking possession agreement'. In other cases, if the bailiff has gained entry, the debtor will have no choice but to sign a walking possession order if s/he does not want the goods to be removed immediately. In addition, county court bailiffs will often require an agreement to walking possession as a security before they will allow time for an application to suspend the warrant and to vary a payment order to be made (see p229). In these cases, although this procedure may not be strictly correct, it may be advisable to agree to walking possession if it is the only way to avoid seizure of property. In either case, signing the agreement gives the debtor a few days to try to negotiate instalments, to raise a lump sum of money to pay the debt, or to try to have the warrant withdrawn or suspended.

Bailiffs will frequently seek to impound motor vehicles by using wheel clamps. Some seek to justify this as an intermediate stage between seizure and removal, to merely 'immobilise' the vehicle while waiting for a removal truck. It is highly debatable whether this practice has any legal justification. Clients faced with such a situation need urgent specialist advice to consider their options.

Advisers will always need to check any walking possession agreement signed by the client and investigate the circumstances in which seizure and impounding took place in order to satisfy themselves that a legal levy has occurred.

Goods

The general rule is that a bailiff may seize any property belonging to the debtor. Certain goods are exempt from seizure and it is therefore very important for advisers to go through any inventory with the client to establish which goods (and whose goods) have been seized.

The following basic tools and household goods cannot be seized, except by magistrates' court and VAT bailiffs:

- 'such tools, goods, vehicles and other items of equipment as are necessary to that person for use personally by him in his employment, business or vocation'; *and*
- 'such clothing, bedding, furniture, household equipment and provisions as are necessary for satisfying the basic domestic needs of that person and his family'.

There is little case law to guide the interpretation of these categories. It seems that a self-employed trader's essential and basic tools will be protected, but only so long as these are not used by any employee or partner. The Lord Chancellor's Department has indicated to county court bailiffs that cars will rarely be exempt, while in the home a three-piece suite may be seized if dining chairs remain, or a microwave may be taken if an oven is also available.

In VAT distress a different list of exemptions applies, which is very generous in protecting the home but exempts little at a business:

- **Household items** which are reasonably required to meet the domestic needs of any person living there are exempt. The exempt goods are beds and bedding; household linen; chairs and settees; tables; food; lights and light fittings; heating appliances; curtains; floor coverings; furniture, equipment and utensils used for cooking, storing and eating food; refrigerators; articles for cleaning, pressing and mending clothes; articles for cleaning the home; furniture used for the storing of clothing, bedding or household linen, cleaning articles or utensils for cooking and eating food; articles used for safety in the home; toys for the use of any child in the household; and medical aids and equipment.
- **In business premises** the only exempt goods are fire fighting equipment and medical aids for use on the premises.

In magistrates' court distraint the following goods are exempt:
- clothing, beds, bedding;
- tools of the trade.

In distress for rent a very wide range of goods is exempt, including the following:
- things in use at the time of distress (eg, electrical goods which are turned on);
- perishable items.

These categories of exemptions (known as 'privileges' in distress for rent) are very lengthy and in some cases complex. If dealing with a client facing distress for rent, especially at business premises, it is important to consult either more detailed materials (see Appendix 6) or seek specialist advice.

Fixtures and fittings from a property cannot be seized in either distress or execution because these are part of the property itself. The definition is difficult, and is complicated by modern building techniques and materials, but basically a fixture is not merely something fixed, but something that has become part of the property and without which the home becomes incomplete – light fittings would be fixtures, whereas shades would not; kitchen units would be, but shelf units may not.

Goods belonging to third parties cannot generally be seized (again, distress for rent is a complicated exception – see above). In practice, many bailiffs will attempt to seize any goods at a particular property, irrespective of their ownership, and will deal with adverse claims to ownership later. If receipts of purchase can be produced, this should certainly be good enough to prove the ownership of goods. If there is a possibility that another person's goods may be seized, the debtor or the owner of the goods could draw up an inventory and tell the bailiff that s/he will be liable for the costs of legal action if any goods are wrongly taken and retained. Bailiffs may decide not to risk seizing goods where it is clear from a well-produced inventory (perhaps on the headed notepaper of a local advice agency) that there is serious doubt about the ownership of the goods. Such an inventory could also be drawn up as a statutory declaration, made on oath by the owner in the presence of a commissioner for oaths. Items which are hired, or subject to hire purchase or conditional sale agreements, are certainly not the property of the debtor and should not be seized – a copy of the relevant agreement should be sufficient to satisfy the bailiff.

If goods have been seized wrongfully, the owner of the goods has a number of remedies. Initially, the matter should be taken up informally with the bailiff or creditor (as described above). If this approach is not successful the owner may take court action (though the threat may be sufficient). See p276 for further information on remedies.

To sell

The purpose of seizure is to give the creditor security over the debtor's goods and to put the debtor under pressure to settle the debt. The ultimate conclusion of the process is to sell the goods, but this is seldom reached because of the costs, inconvenience and low returns of the procedure. Except perhaps for motor vehicles, most second-hand goods are of no, or negligible, value and it is the threat of sale that is effective, not the remedy itself.

If sale becomes necessary the bailiff will need to remove the goods seized previously and can, at this stage, use force to re-enter the debtor's property. Prior warning is generally given of an intended visit to remove, and entry may only be forced if the debtor has received such prior notice. If this is the case, failure to permit access may be construed as deliberate obstruction. The goods will then be stored for a few days while the sale is arranged. It will be clear from these stages worked into the process that the debtor is, once again, being given the chance to pay the sums due. This is preferable for all parties, releasing the seized goods and producing a better rate of return for the bailiff.

Normally there is a statutory delay of at least five days before sale, which in most cases must be by public auction. The bailiffs are expected to raise the best price possible, but at the same time returns from auction sales tend to be very low. In most forms of distress and execution the debtor may request that the goods be 'appraised' or valued before the sale. This may lead to a slightly higher reserved price being set, but as fees are charged for the process, any gain may be offset by the extra expense incurred.

It is usual for the bailiff to deduct her/his fees from any sale proceeds (or payments made to her/him) before passing the sums on to the instructing creditor. Goods cannot be sold merely to cover the bailiffs' fees if the debt is paid direct to the creditor. The bailiff would presumably have to sue the debtor in the county court to recover her/his money in such a situation.

If the bailiff damages the goods whilst removing or selling them, or can be shown to have mishandled the sale so that the goods were sold for too little, s/he can be sued for damages in the county court (see p278).

To charge fees

Bailiffs are allowed to recover money from the debtor to cover the cost of their action. The charges can inflate the sum due considerably and are naturally the cause of much complaint. These understandable grievances are aggravated by the fact that legally recoverable charges are often substantially increased by charges of disputable, or no, legality. Advisers should give bills close attention to ensure that the burden of debt upon a client is not being added to improperly.

The rules for charging for distress are varied, but in most cases the amount bailiffs are allowed to charge is regulated by statutory instrument (see Appendix 1 for copies of the statutory scales for rent and council tax). The exception to this is magistrates' courts in which no scale is laid down. Fees will have to be negotiated separately between each magistrates' court and its bailiffs. Advisers will need to request a copy of the scale in operation. It is recommended that, in every case, an adviser checks the fees being levied against the appropriate scale.

All scales, whatever their source, tend to include the same sorts of elements. Fees will be charged for certain actions such as visits, seizure and removal, and reasonable disbursements for storage and advertising are permitted. Charges tend to be a mixture of flat rate fees, sums calculated as a proportion of the sum due, and 'reasonable' amounts. Note that the fees charged in the county court, though set by statute, are much lower than those found in the private sector. There is a standard charge for the issue of the warrant, which is added to the debt. This will cover all visits made by bailiffs, plus seizure and possession. Only if the matter reaches the stage of removal and sale are any other fees charged. Any unreasonable charges of any description may be reviewed by the county court.

Disputed fees

The county court has a power to examine and reassess, if necessary, disputed charges arising from a number of sources. This includes solicitors' bills, but also covers fees charged by tribunals and by bailiffs. The process was formerly called 'taxation', but under the new CPR is known as 'detailed assessment'. The debtor disputing the fees can apply to the court under CPR part 8 for a district judge to review the sums demanded by, or paid to, the bailiff. Note that this power only extends to charges made under the scales set by statute. Magistrates' bailiffs charges are established by their contract with the court – these fees are not taxable, though the legislation permits the magistrates' court to punish bailiffs whose fees are 'improper or undue'.

Another remedy could be for the debtor to pay the disputed fees and then use the county court to recover the balance. This would be by issuing a small claim in the county court. The debtor would protect her/his costs, but would have to be able to pay up front the whole sum due.

A 'reasonable' fee recoverable by a bailiff may be described as one that is calculated correctly, is applied at the correct stage of the process, is for a fair amount and is legal. Some bailiffs' bills contain fees that may be questioned on all these points. Again, close comparison should be made between the sums demanded and the sums permitted on the statutory scale. Fees to watch out for are those that are made too early in the process, before the proper point for making them has been reached (eg, a levy fee before the property has even been entered); those that are for a sum disproportionate to the work done or expense incurred; and those which are simply not allowed for at all on the scale (eg, fees for administering accounts or for contact with the debtor).

The meaning of 'reasonable' charges was subject to scrutiny in a case in Birmingham County court. Although this case considered charges made by a firm of private bailiffs who were recovering general rates, the definition of 'reasonable' is applicable generally. The bailiffs in this case were allowed to charge 'reasonable expenses' for the removal and storage of goods. The judge's decision noted that any question about 'reasonableness' should be resolved in favour of the payer. A reasonable charge must be related to the value of goods taken. Thus, it cannot be reasonable to remove goods if their sale value is unlikely to cover the costs of removal and sale. The amount charged for bailiffs' general services and availability must be spread across all the debtors against whom they hold warrants from this particular creditor. Most bailiffs still seek to charge all their costs to those debtors from whom they actually take goods, but this argument was rejected by the Birmingham court. In the case in question a charge for a removal van was 'taxed down' on the basis that a van could be hired privately for considerably less than the billed sum, and any overheads incurred by the bailiffs could be spread across all those subject to removals on that day.

Codes of practice

The powers described so far in this section are those laid down in law. In addition, some creditors (mostly local authorities) operate codes of practice for their bailiffs. These regulate the conduct of their bailiffs (exempting additional goods, etc), as well as specifying the circumstances in which it will be considered inappropriate to levy distraint – eg, if a debtor is on means-tested benefits, has a disability or is recently bereaved.

As warrants are often issued against those whom the local authority has voluntarily exempted from distress, it is important for advisers to be familiar with any code their local council operates and to lobby strongly for warrants to be withdrawn in cases where they should not have been issued. Some local authorities, however, are reluctant to release their codes, stating that they are part of their contract with their bailiffs and are therefore confidential. This argument should not be accepted. Compliance with the European Convention on Human Rights requires that any measure governing the interference with individuals' rights should be made accessible to them. Codes dealing with bailiffs' rights to enter property and seize goods clearly fall into this category and must be released. The Child Support Agency operates a very comprehensive code of practice which gives extensive additional protection to debtors facing distraint. Other creditors, though not having explicit codes, will often be prepared to withdraw warrants in cases of severe personal and/or financial hardship.

In addition to these specific or local codes, in April 2002 the Lord Chancellor's Department produced a National Standard for Enforcement Agents.[4] This provides a statement of minimum standards of business management and best practice in enforcement work. For example, it requires enforcement agents to ensure that all information and documentation supplied to debtors is clear and unambiguous, to act without any form of discrimination, to be aware of potentially vulnerable individuals, taking special care when proceeding against them, and to treat debtors' information confidentially. Levies should generally not occur outside the hours of 6am and 9pm, or on Sundays or public holidays, and goods belonging to or used by a child should not be taken. Bailiffs' firms are required to operate complaints procedures and to make details of these readily available.

4. Powers of arrest

Since April 2001 private bailiffs have been given the power to enforce a range of magistrates' court warrants previously executed by the police. These include warrants of arrest to ensure attendance at means enquiries following default in payment of fines and local taxes, and warrants of commitment made following such means enquiries.[5]

A new and relatively rigorous system of appointment has been introduced to accompany these changes. When choosing the firm to work for the court, possession of a distress for rent certificate from a county court, convictions and being the subject of complaints, damages claims and insolvency proceedings will all be considered. Advisers should note that as part of this scheme there is now a requirement for both bailiffs and courts to operate and publish complaints procedures.

Bailiffs' powers when executing these warrants are broadly similar to those already described for distress. Warrants may be executed anywhere in England and Wales at any time of day. There is no power to force entry to premises (except perhaps where the warrant has been issued in respect of a breach of a non-financial penalty such as a community service order). Excessive force should not be employed in making the arrest. A person may be physically seized or touched and informed that s/he is under arrest, or arrest may be effected by words alone (provided that the person submits to these). As soon as possible after being arrested, a person must be given full and clear details of the reason for her/his arrest and how to complain. Defendants are not liable for any fees for the execution of these warrants.

Resisting a lawful arrest can be an offence. Whilst it may be lawful to resist an unlawful arrest, it will generally be more advisable for clients to make a civil claim for damages for false imprisonment and/or assault after the event, and they should be encouraged to seek legal advice.

5. **Complaints against bailiffs**

In recent years, the action of bailiffs has been subject to increasing public scrutiny. It is possible that this may lead to changes in certification and regulation. Meanwhile, media interest remains high and such pressure may be effective. It is true to say, however, that the media often want stories of gross wrongdoing, especially physical violence, by bailiffs – which are actually rare.

Complaints to creditors

While it is always worthwhile contacting the bailiffs to complain about their actions, it may be unproductive if the point at issue is whether they should have been instructed at all or if the terms of repayment, set by the contract with the creditor, are impossible for the debtor to meet (a common example is that council tax contracts often require the bailiff to collect within three months). In such cases the bailiffs will be bound by the contract with the instructing creditor to enforce the warrant issued to them, and other than asking them to stay the action whilst negotiations are conducted, little else may be possible.

Creditors should be notified about wrongful acts by their agents, as this may help to bring pressure to bear in individual cases and may lead to improved monitoring more generally, but direct contact with a creditor is most important where matters such as the personal circumstances of the debtor are at issue. Complaints may be made about either the incorrect use of legal powers or a failure to follow a code of practice (see section 3 earlier). A supporting financial statement will be a vital tool in negotiating these cases.

If the complaint is not properly dealt with it may be possible to use the organisation's internal complaints procedure, and if this is unsatisfactory, there is often the option of complaining to an independent adjudicator, such as the local government ombudsman or the parliamentary ombudsman.

Complaints to trade/professional bodies

If a complaint to a firm of bailiffs is not dealt with satisfactorily, a complaint could be made to the bailiffs' professional or trade organisation. When making such a complaint it should be borne in mind that these bodies ultimately exist to promote their members' interests and are not entirely independent or impartial. Several bodies may be responsible, depending on the type of enforcement agent involved. The relevant bodies to which advisers may turn are the Sheriff's Officers Association, the Under Sheriff's Association, the Certificated Bailiffs' Association and the Association of Civil Enforcement Agencies. All operate disciplinary codes linked to complaints procedures. Serious breaches of professional ethics or of procedure may lead to investigation and the imposition of penalties, such as being excluded from membership and, as a result, from the profession (though this is rare). A complaint can also lead to at least an apology and perhaps compensation, such as a refund of fees, for the complainant. See Appendix 5 for addresses. The Certificated Bailiffs' Association also has a code of practice regulating members' business practices, which may be of some assistance.

Court proceedings

If non-judicial action or pressure fails, the fall-back is to initiate court proceedings against the bailiffs in order to recover seized goods or gain financial redress. The form of action suitable will depend upon the bailiff's offence (see below), though it should be noted that in most cases the value of the claims involved will be well within the small claims limit, and therefore will be cases that can be conducted – for relatively little expense and at little risk of legal costs – by the client in person, with the adviser's assistance as necessary. It may be that, when the threat of court action is made by a determined adviser or when the claims form is received, in order to avoid the expense of small claims litigation or the scrutiny of the court, the bailiffs will choose to settle the matter.

Bailiffs' offences

Broadly speaking, the law recognises three categories of bailiffs' offence:
- **Illegal levies**, where the bailiffs do something (generally at the outset of the levy) that they have no power to do – for instance, to force entry on a first visit or to seize exempt goods. Because the whole action is rendered unlawful as a result, the debtor can often recover appreciable damages, and the bailiff will have to give up and start again.
- **Irregular levies**, which are seizures where something is done wrong later in the process. Most forms of enforcement have regulations that state that such mistakes are not to be treated as illegalities. In other words, in contrast with the above paragraph, an error in the conduct of a sale or in leaving a required notice will not invalidate the whole procedure and will only entitle the client to recover any loss that s/he can prove to have suffered.

- **Excessive levies**, where the bailiff takes far more than is necessary to cover the debt and costs by sale at auction. The debtor can sue to recover the value of the excess.

Normally it is only really worthwhile pursuing illegal acts, and this will be assumed in the following paragraphs.

County court claims

The debtor or owner of the seized goods may be able to start one of the following claims (though readers should recall that there are detailed procedural requirements for all of these, plus court fees to pay and the risk of substantial legal costs if the claim is lost):

- Sue for wrongful interference with goods. The owner may be able to get an order for the return of the goods illegally seized – though an award of damages for their value is more likely – plus an award of damages for any other losses incurred, such as loss of use.
- Sue for the recovery of money paid out, either to prevent an illegal seizure of goods or in respect of disputed fees.
- Start 'replevin'. This is an obscure and ancient remedy whereby the goods are immediately ordered to be returned to the debtor, who then takes court action to prove that the levy was illegal and that s/he was consequently entitled to have her/his goods back.
- Challenge the certificate. If the bailiffs are certificated, it is possible for an application to be made to the court that granted the certificate for it to be revoked. No form is prescribed for the complaint but the proper officer at the court is required to send written details to the bailiff. The bailiff must respond within 14 days and, if the judge is then dissatisfied that the bailiff remains fit to hold a certificate, s/he is summonsed to show why the certificate should not be cancelled. At this hearing the judge can decide a procedure as s/he thinks fit – generally the court would allow the complainant to make representations. If a certificate is revoked the debtor may also be awarded compensation for any wrongful acts suffered. There is very limited experience of complaints against certification. The only recent reported case was in Manchester, in which a landlord was certificated on condition (amongst others) that he did not levy distress at any property from which he collected rent. Although he broke that condition, used a pass key to illegally enter the property and left outdated forms for the tenant, his certificate was not removed.

  Another problem that advisers may encounter is that the rules on certification complaints relate solely to distress for rent. Some judges therefore question whether they have any jurisdiction either to hear complaints at all, or to award any compensation, where the complaint relates to the activity of the bailiff in other fields, whether or not they require a certificate. Nonetheless, the procedure is under-used and can provide a quick and effective means of redress for an aggrieved person.

If unsure whether a particular bailiff is certificated, the adviser should consult the local county court. If the bailiff is not certificated there, a check can be made on the central register of certificates, held by the court service.

- If a third party's goods have been seized in a county court or High Court execution, a special remedy know as 'interpleader' exists to enable the third party to prove ownership and recover them. Specialist help should be sought.

6. **Emergency action**

People often seek advice only when the 'crunch' comes, such as a visit from a bailiff. In order to buy time at this stage for a debtor's finances to be investigated and an overall repayment strategy devised, it may be necessary to consider some of the emergency measures described here.

Refuse the bailiffs access

Often a debt adviser is first consulted when a debtor hears from bailiffs. The best advice to protect goods from seizure is to ensure that bailiffs are not given access to property and for the debtor to remove any goods that are outside the home (especially cars) to a place where they will not be seen. However, in cases of distress for rent, removing goods in this way is an offence.

Bailiffs will try to visit more than once to gain access, so debtors should be advised to be vigilant and keep doors and windows locked. If the bailiffs are unable to gain entry, they will eventually return the warrant to the court and should indicate whether or not there are sufficient goods to satisfy the debt. They will rely on what they can see through a window to decide this. If the bailiff fails to raise the sums due, this will, of course, not be the end of the debt's recovery; other means will be tried. With fines and local taxes the debt often goes back to the court for committal to prison to be considered (see p250). A person may be committed for 'wilful refusal or culpable neglect' to pay, and it is often threatened that failure to give access to the bailiffs will be construed by the court as wilful refusal. All that can be said about this is that there are no reported instances of a person being committed on this ground.

If bailiffs have already gained access, they can subsequently force their way in for the same debt (see p272).

Get the warrant withdrawn from the bailiffs

In every case the aim of the debt adviser should be to remove the matter from the hands of the bailiffs and place it back for consideration by the creditor.

In the civil courts the debtor should make an immediate application to suspend the warrant. For county court action this is done on form N245 (see p229). For High Court action, an application for a stay of execution should be made (see p229). Magistrates' courts do not have such a power (see p247). However, since April 2001 magistrates' court bailiffs have had the power to postpone the removal and sale of seized goods from the previous period of 6 days to a maximum period of 60 days where instalment payments have been agreed. This is approved by a court clerk without the need for a hearing to take place.

In situations where there is no power to suspend through the courts and the debtor cannot afford to pay a lump sum or sums, the only option may be to try to persuade the issuing creditor that the warrant should be withdrawn because of the personal or financial circumstances of the debtor. This may also be because the person falls into one of the categories of people exempted from distraint by the code of practice operated by that creditor (see p276). In many cases terms of payment will have to be negotiated at the same time, and often these will be for instalments of sums much lower than it would have been economic for the bailiff to collect.

Threaten court action

If an error in procedure can be detected, a lever for negotiation or withdrawal may be to threaten court action (see p277). Bailiffs may be reluctant to have their procedures tested in court and may, in any event, find it more advantageous to settle the matter than be involved in the expense of litigation.

Raise a lump sum to clear the debt

If the above tactics have been unsuccessful, or if the goods have been seized already, it may be necessary for the debtor to pay the debt to avoid goods being sold (see Chapter 6 for ways of maximising income). This may be in violation of certain basic principles of money advice, but will often be the only option that the client is prepared to consider and may make financial sense in that the replacement cost of the items in question may be much more than the total required by the bailiffs. Note that the Court of Appeal has recently clarified a debtor's rights to make payments to a bailiff. This may occur either before a levy (or removal) takes place, or afterwards, but payment cannot be offered during a levy or removal, as the sums due cannot be calculated.[6]

7. Reform

At the time of writing the Government is involved in a process of review of the whole field of bailiffs' law. A number of important reforms are under consideration:

- creation of an 'Enforcement Services Commission' to appoint, monitor and discipline all bailiffs. It will also advise on good practice and further changes to the law;
- harmonisation and modernisation of the law on bailiffs' powers, by the creation of a single Act dealing with the process of seizure of goods;
- creation of a single, fair scale of fees;
- abolition of distress for rent against domestic tenants.

If these proposals are all brought into effect, many of the problems that advisers have with the process of distraint, and which this chapter seeks to address, will become things of the past and a well regulated and accountable bailiffs profession will have been created. A White Paper is promised in early 2003.

Notes

1. Types of bailiff and the seizure of goods
1 See article by TaxAid in *Adviser* 85, pp42-51

3. Bailiffs' powers
2 *Bibby v Essex Police* [2000] *Adviser* 81, p25
3 *McLeod v UK*, 1998
4 J Kruse, 'Bailiff Standards', *Adviser* 92, pp45-7

4. Powers of arrest
5 This subject is discussed more fully in 'Privatising the power of arrest', J Kruse, *Adviser* 85, pp7-9

6. Emergency action
6 *Wilson v South Kesteven District Council* [2000]

Chapter 12
··
Bankruptcy and individual voluntary arrangements

This chapter covers:

1. Last resort or fresh start?

A person is 'insolvent' if s/he is unable to pay her/his debts at the time they fall due for payment. In many cases, people are able to resolve their financial problems by coming to an informal arrangement with their creditors – ranging from temporary suspension of repayments to writing the debts off altogether. Bankruptcy has often been seen by people who are in debt for the first time as the only possible way of 'escaping' from their debts, and by debt advisers as a last resort.

Using the courts to formalise insolvency should probably not be regarded as being at either of these extremes. There are times when bankruptcy can be very useful and the only viable option, but there are also times when it represents a very serious mistake. Bankruptcy has in the past been used by some creditors as a punishment for debt and it continues to be so to some extent. Debt advisers need to be aware that their own views of bankruptcy may be governed by apprehension. Debtors should not consider bankruptcy as an option unless the debt adviser has explained the advantages/disadvantages and consequences (see pp283 and 284) and after all other options have been considered.

There are three ways in which a debtor can ask the court to acknowledge and act upon her/his insolvency. These are:
- **Administration order** Administration orders are dealt with on p233. For someone with total unsecured debts exceeding £5,000 they are not a viable option under current legislation.
- **Individual voluntary arrangement** An individual voluntary arrangement (IVA) is a formal arrangement made between the debtor and the majority of

Chapter 12: Bankruptcy and individual voluntary arrangements
1. Last resort or fresh start?

12

her/his creditors that creates a legally binding agreement between the debtor and all her/his creditors (although secured creditors cannot be included unless they agree). The arrangement provides either for the debtor to defer payment of her/his debts and/or for the creditors to accept less than 100p in the pound. The arrangement is set up by a nominee – an insolvency practitioner who is an approved solicitor or accountant – who is likely to be appointed as a supervisor to oversee the arrangement (see p293). No further action can then be taken by any unsecured creditor or any secured creditor who has agreed to take part in the IVA.

- **Bankruptcy** Someone (either the Official Receiver, a government official employed by the Insolvency Service (an Executive Agency of the Department of Trade and Industry) or a 'trustee in bankruptcy') is appointed to take over the handling of a debtor's financial affairs for the benefit of her/his creditors. This can be done either on the basis of a request from the debtor or from one or more creditors (see p294). This chapter deals only with the law relating to bankruptcy in force since 1987. The law is contained in the Insolvency Act 1986 and the detailed rules and forms in the Insolvency Rules 1986. The Civil Procedure Rules do not affect insolvency proceedings, although there is a practice direction.

Legislation currently going through Parliament will have a significant impact on insolvency law and practice (see p311).

Bankruptcy or IVAs are only available to individuals. The number of individual insolvencies is on the rise again and increasingly involves consumer debt rather than debtors facing business failure. In 2000, there were 21,550 bankruptcy orders and 7,978 IVAs. Company and partnership insolvencies are outside the scope of this book.

Bankruptcy

Advantages

There are a number of advantages to bankruptcy. It can remove the uncertainty and anxiety that is caused by negotiating with a large number of creditors simultaneously. Once an order is made, a third party takes over the decision making and makes any payments; often the officials with whom the debtor deals will be helpful and matter of fact about her/his debts. Furthermore:

- The debtor pays less. Bankruptcy usually forces creditors to acknowledge that they must accept less than all the money owed and, in most cases, nothing at all.
- It can be a fresh start. The aim of the Insolvency Act 1986 was to free the debtor from an overwhelming situation and then enable her/him to carry on with her/his life. There is an emphasis in the legislation on the rehabilitation of the debtor. Discharge releases the debtor from the status of a bankrupt and from the restrictions of bankruptcy (see p310). If a decision is made quickly to

12

Chapter 12: Bankruptcy and individual voluntary arrangements
1. Last resort or fresh start?

become bankrupt, or not to oppose bankruptcy, then the two or three years which are likely to elapse before discharge are actually quite short and may compare favourably with a more sophisticated strategy negotiated by a debt adviser over a longer period.
- The process is certain. Unlike strategies worked out by a debt adviser, those sanctioned by the courts give the debtor the security of knowing that creditors cannot change their minds. An order for bankruptcy must be recognised by creditors and will often encourage them to take very little further interest in the debt.
- After discharge most debts are written off and cannot be pursued by creditors (see p310).

Disadvantages

There are also many disadvantages, including:
- The debtor will almost certainly lose any realisable property of value.
- If the debtor owns equity in the family home, this will probably be sold, unless her/his share is bought by another family member (see p306).
- If the debtor has a business that employs people or is itself of value, then the employees may have to be dismissed and the business sold.
- If the debtor has mortgage or rent arrears, the home may be at increased risk. This is because the mortgage lender or landlord may consider that bankruptcy indicates that the arrears are unlikely to be paid and they should therefore commence possession action on the grounds of those arrears (see Chapter 9).
- The debtor cannot obtain credit of more than £250 (including ordering goods and then not paying for them on delivery) without disclosing that s/he is an undischarged bankrupt and it may be difficult to maintain/obtain her/his bank or building society account. Although the major banks and building societies are supposed to provide basic bank accounts (allowing customers to pay in and withdraw money but not become overdrawn or make use of a cheque guarantee card) without carrying out credit reference checks, there is evidence that people are not able to access these accounts.[1]
- The process can be very expensive. The courts, insolvency service and any trustee will charge fees. There is a 15 per cent levy on all sums received by the Official Receiver/trustee. All these are payable out of the debtor's assets.
- The debtor must allow all her/his financial affairs to be scrutinised by officials who may take (criminal) action for irregularities discovered.
- The debtor cannot hold certain public offices (eg, MP, magistrate or councillor) or practise certain professions (eg, accountant, solicitor) and bankruptcy can affect job security if employed.
- The debtor's credit rating will continue to be adversely affected and this will probably make running a business or buying a home in the future very difficult and/or expensive, if not impossible, even after discharge. A record of the bankruptcy order will remain on the Insolvency Service's register for five years

Chapter 12: Bankruptcy and individual voluntary arrangements
1. Last resort or fresh start?

12

from the date of the order and will be kept on the files of credit reference agencies for six years.

- The debtor may feel judged and humiliated. There is still a stigma attached to bankruptcy.
- A bankrupt cannot be a company director (without leave of the court), nor can s/he trade under any other name than the one used at the time of bankruptcy.
- Bankruptcy might in some cases jeopardise an application for naturalisation as a British citizen, or prevent a person acting as sponsor, or put at risk the immigration status of an independent business person.
- Names of those made bankrupt are published in the *London Gazette* and also in the local press, so friends and neighbours may find out about the debtor's financial difficulties.
- Any changes in circumstances during the bankruptcy must be reported to the trustee – eg, the receipt of a legacy. Even after discharge from bankruptcy, the debtor may still have to co-operate with the trustee and the Official Receiver who will continue to administer the debtor's assets.
- Not all debts may be written off by bankruptcy and discharge (eg, fines, maintenance/child support payments) (see p309).
- The debtor may still have to make payments to the trustee if her/his income is high enough throughout the period of bankruptcy (see p304).
- The rights of secured creditors are not affected by bankruptcy and they can still enforce their security both during the bankruptcy and subsequently. Joint debts are not written off in the sense that creditors can still pursue the non-bankrupt debtor. If s/he is the bankrupt's partner, the family will still be in financial difficulties.
- The debtor's employment may be put at risk.

Individual voluntary arrangements (IVAs)

Advantages

The advantages of an IVA include:

- There is not the stigma or publicity that surrounds bankruptcy.
- A business can continue to trade and generate income to fund the arrangement (even if only to sell it as a going concern).
- The arrangement can be tailored to the individual's situation (eg, property such as the family home can be excluded with the agreement of the creditors) so long as creditors are no worse off than if bankruptcy had been pursued.
- Administration costs should be lower than in bankruptcy, which means creditors should get higher payments and so regard the arrangement as a preferable option.
- Creditors can still claim tax relief against a bad debt as in bankruptcy.
- Unsecured creditors who voted against the IVA are still bound by it (as long as 75 per cent of the creditors in terms of amounts owed accept the IVA), so can

12

Chapter 12: Bankruptcy and individual voluntary arrangements
1. Last resort or fresh start?

take no further action against the debtor and must accept less than all the money owed.

- The debtor is not subject to the restrictions of bankruptcy – for example, s/he can still be a company director and use any business name.

Disadvantages

Disadvantages include:

- IVAs are not generally suitable unless the debtor has at least three unsecured creditors and unsecured debts of at least £10,000 to £15,000 (although there will be cases where an IVA is appropriate for less).
- Payments will generally be higher and go on for longer than in bankruptcy (generally three to five years), where there are few income payment orders.
- The costs of paying an insolvency practitioner are high and may have to be paid in advance (although it should be possible to find an insolvency practitioner who does not require upfront fees).
- The family home and any other assets will still be at risk if creditors do not agree to exclude them.
- If the IVA fails, the debtor may still be made bankrupt and the costs of the IVA will be added to the debts.
- There will be close supervision of the debtor by the insolvency practitioner during the period of the IVA.
- All IVAs are recorded in a public register, which may jeopardise future applications for credit. A record of the IVA will remain on the Insolvency Service's register for a further two years after the arrangement has been completed (or terminated).

2. When to use bankruptcy and voluntary arrangements

Debtors often have no choice over whether or not to go bankrupt. On the other hand, debtors are often faced with deciding whether or not to oppose bankruptcy. The possibility of obtaining an IVA should always be considered before deciding on bankruptcy, particularly where the debtor has to keep her/his business running in order to pay creditors or has property which s/he needs time to sell. An IVA is only likely to be an option if the debtor has income and/or property and is able to make a substantial offer, but for some reason cannot persuade her/his creditors to accept an informal arrangement. In view of the costs involved (see below) it is not likely to be appropriate unless the debtor has debts of at least £10,000. However, an IVA does not end in automatic discharge, unlike bankruptcy (usually after two or three years). A debtor may pay more for the 'privilege' of avoiding bankruptcy (a typical fee charged by an insolvency practitioner for arranging an individual

Chapter 12: Bankruptcy and individual voluntary arrangements
2. When to use bankruptcy and voluntary arrangements

12

voluntary arrangement is £2,500 to £3,000 plus VAT and expenses, but it could be significantly more).

Bankruptcy is likely to be the preferred option if the debtor has multiple debts, no property (or no equity in her/his home), a low income, and it is unlikely that this situation will change. S/he must also have no need for credit in the short or medium term, nor want to hold any of the offices described above.

In deciding whether to use bankruptcy and IVAs, the following factors should be considered.

Risk to current assets

Bankruptcy is most likely to be appropriate where the debtor does not own very much. If bankruptcy is used as a strategy to cope with non-priority debts, then all of a debtor's property is put at risk for those debts.

Only property owned by the debtor is directly put at risk in bankruptcy. In practice, many things which are used by a person may be owned by someone else (eg, a partner). These goods cannot be touched. However, jointly-owned property (eg, the family home) may be indirectly at risk if the trustee can sell it in order to realise the value of the debtor's share. Any gifts or undervalued sales made in the past five years can be investigated by the trustee if a person is bankrupt. If a gift was made or goods sold at a price lower than the real value of those goods at a time when the debtor was actually insolvent, then the trustee can take steps to claim the value of the gift, or the undervalued part of the goods, from the recipient.[2]

With an IVA, there is more flexibility because creditors are normally being offered regular payments.

Future assets

Before considering bankruptcy or an IVA, the debtor should consider the possible risk to any future assets, particularly if s/he expects to inherit money or already owns property which may increase in value during the bankruptcy. Sometimes it is possible to arrange matters so that this does not happen (eg, by ensuring that potential donors change their wills), but not by transferring assets (see above).

Effect on future credit

Both bankruptcy and IVAs are a matter of public record. It is very unlikely that anybody would give credit to a bankrupt person and it is likely to be more expensive to obtain credit after discharge (some lenders specialise in this area). It is an offence[3] for an undischarged bankrupt to fail to disclose her/his status to anybody from whom credit of more than £250 is sought (including hire purchase or conditional sale agreements). This also includes ordering goods and then failing to pay for them. For people who want to run their own business, the need to make this declaration may be an insuperable barrier because they are unlikely to be given further credit. They are also forbidden to be company directors

12

Chapter 12: Bankruptcy and individual voluntary arrangements
2. When to use bankruptcy and voluntary arrangements

without special leave from the court. Although utilities cannot insist on payment of pre-bankruptcy arrears as a condition of continuing to supply a service, often they will require a security deposit or insist on the installation of pre-payment meters and so it may be beneficial to transfer accounts to another non-bankrupt member of the household. With an IVA, the debtor is unlikely to face such problems.

Effect on employment or office

Being an undischarged bankrupt limits not just a person's financial prospects but also prohibits her/him from being an MP, a councillor, a magistrate or an estate agent. The professional rules of solicitors and accountants make it virtually impossible for people who have been bankrupt to work in these professions. Other employers (eg, civil service, security firms) may not wish to employ a bankrupt person, especially if s/he is responsible for money. Charity law limits the ability of people who have been bankrupt to serve on management committees. A bankrupt usually cannot be a school or college governor.

The fact that a sole trader has been made bankrupt does not necessarily mean that the business will close, but it will be difficult for it to continue in view of the following factors:

- If there are items of business equipment used by the debtor's employees rather than by the debtor personally, the debtor will not be able to claim exemption for them (see p304) and the trustee may insist that these be sold. Stock in trade is not exempt from sale by the trustee for the benefit of the bankrupt's estate.
- If the business can only survive on credit, the debtor will have to disclose that s/he is an undischarged bankrupt to anyone from whom s/he obtains goods or services on credit and they are unlikely to give credit in such circumstances, particularly as they may well be creditors whose debts are included in the bankruptcy.
- The bankruptcy order will be advertised locally and this may damage the reputation of the business as well as of its proprietor.
- An undischarged bankrupt cannot be a director of a limited company or be concerned (directly or indirectly) in the management of a company without the court's permission.
- The debtor will be unable to carry on certain professions (see above) and cannot trade under a name other than that under which s/he was made bankrupt.
- The debtor will find it extremely difficult to operate a business bank account, not only because of the credit restrictions, but also because of the possibility of the trustee making a claim against any credit surplus in the account.

These restrictions do not apply where the debtor has an IVA.

Chapter 12: Bankruptcy and individual voluntary arrangements
2. When to use bankruptcy and voluntary arrangements

12

Effect on housing

Although the debtor could consider paying any rent arrears before being made bankrupt, because rent arrears are a 'bankruptcy debt' (see p310), the trustee might claim that the payment was a 'preference' (see p308). The effect is that the trustee could re-claim the payment from the landlord and so jeopardise the debtor's tenancy. Additionally, some tenancy agreements contain a clause to say that an undischarged bankrupt cannot be a tenant. In these cases, the debtor should seek specialist housing advice. It might be advisable to contact the landlord to see if s/he is willing for the tenancy to continue provided the current rent is paid. Many social landlords are prepared to do so. An IVA avoids this risk and the rent arrears can be repaid as part of the IVA.

Once a tenant is made bankrupt, the trustee can take steps to claim certain types of tenancy. This rarely happens and would be most likely where there was income available from the sub-letting of rooms in a large property. More likely, the trustee would want to 'disclaim' the tenancy, that is, refuse to pay the rent (so as to reduce expenditure) (see p303). The debtor would then have no right to remain in the property and the landlord could take 'summary possession proceedings' (see Chapter 9). This provision (designed to rid the bankrupt of 'onerous property') would not, however, be used to terminate the tenancy on an ordinary home required for living purposes, unless the trustee considered that the home was too large or luxurious for the needs of the debtor and her/his family.[4] This does not happen where the debtor has an IVA.

Where the debtor owns her/his own home (either in her/his sole name or jointly with, for example, a partner) her/his interest automatically passes to her/his trustee in a bankruptcy. In order to realise the debtor's interest for the benefit of creditors, the trustee will almost certainly insist on the home being sold at some stage in the future unless the debtor's partner or some other family member can buy out the trustee and so preserve the home (see p306). In the case of an IVA (assuming the creditors agree to the debtor keeping her/his home), the value of the debtor's share can be taken into account in the level of payments made under the IVA.

Even if a debtor does not own her/his own home, the effect of bankruptcy could be to limit her/his freedom because it reduces her/his ability to borrow money which s/he may have needed to move home and buy property elsewhere. It does not prevent her/him exchanging local authority or housing association properties (unless local rules prohibit this). The restrictions on obtaining credit may, however, cause difficulties in renting a new property as a deposit and/or rent in advance may have to be found.

Effect on reputation and stress

Bankruptcy can still be a very humiliating experience for many people. Although there is no legal justification for it, and it appears increasingly rare, people who are involved in bankruptcy will sometimes be treated as though they are criminals.

12

Chapter 12: Bankruptcy and individual voluntary arrangements
2. When to use bankruptcy and voluntary arrangements

There is a possibility that there may be a public examination of the debtor's conduct and financial affairs in open court, but this does not happen to the majority of debtors, and even then only where there has been either a failure to co-operate with the Official Receiver or if 50 per cent of the creditors request one. There will be an advertisement in a local paper to notify creditors of a person's bankruptcy and invite claims from them.

The effect of bankruptcy can add considerably to a debtor's stress, although the finality of it may also reduce this.

Individual voluntary arrangements carry less stigma, but can be time-consuming to draw up and gain agreement for, and could therefore add to the stress being faced by the debtor.

Are there resources available?

If a debtor wishes to petition for her/his own bankruptcy, s/he will be required to pay a certain amount (currently a deposit of £250 plus the £120 court fee, unless this can be waived – see p173). Lack of resources sometimes prevents this. Most insolvency practitioners will require at least £750 in advance of setting up an IVA, although an initial interview to discuss options is often free. A debtor may well pay more for the 'privilege' of avoiding bankruptcy.

3. Individual voluntary arrangements

Who can make individual voluntary arrangements?

Normally only a debtor can institute an individual voluntary arrangement (IVA). However, where s/he is an undischarged bankrupt, either the trustee or the Official Receiver may also do so, and bankruptcy courts sometimes refer people to insolvency practitioners so that IVAs can be set up. At the hearing of a debtor's petition the court is required to consider whether an IVA might be more appropriate than bankruptcy (see p293).

The process of individual voluntary arrangements

An IVA should always be considered in cases where the debtor has a reasonable level of available income (eg, £100 to £200 a month) and an informal repayment programme is likely to last more than 10 years, as an IVA would be time limited. This can be considered even if s/he has property.

In these cases, it is usually worth an early referral to an insolvency practitioner to discuss whether an IVA is the best solution. The proposal should provide greater benefits to creditors than would be the case if the debtor were to be made bankrupt and should provide similar benefits to the debtor.

It is most helpful if the debt adviser can help the debtor to prepare a financial statement and list of debts and assets (with their value) to take to the first appointment with the insolvency practitioner, as this will save the debtor time and money. Many debt advisers have found it useful to develop contacts with local insolvency practitioners who are willing to give free first appointments. There are also several companies that now operate without an upfront fee and instead recoup the fee from the debtor's monthly repayments.

The proposal

The first step is to prepare a 'proposal' for the debtor's creditors and the court. In theory, the debtor is supposed to prepare her/his own proposal, but the insolvency practitioner who will ultimately supervise the arrangement will assist her/him. The insolvency practitioner becomes the debtor's 'nominee' and will, in effect, vouch for the reasonableness of her/his proposals to the court and other creditors. S/he is acting within a statutory framework, which requires very full investigation and disclosure of the debtor's affairs, and s/he may refuse to recommend certain courses of action. The debtor should take to the insolvency practitioner sufficient information to be able to create a 'proposal'.

Information that must be contained in the proposal includes the following:[5]

- Details of the proposed arrangements, and why an IVA is considered appropriate and is likely to be accepted by creditors. Normally, IVAs do not provide for repayment of the debtor's debts in full, but for a pro rata distribution of available income and the proceeds of any assets sold, along with a partial write-off, so that only a percentage of each pound is paid – ie, a composition.
- Anticipated level of the debtor's income during the proposed IVA.
- Details of all assets (including an estimate of their value and of any assets being made available by third parties) and whether the debtor has either her/his 'centre of main interests' or an 'establishment' in another EU Member State (see p294).
- Details of any charges on property in favour of creditors and of any assets that the debtor proposes to exclude from the IVA.
- Whether, in the event of bankruptcy, there are any circumstances giving rise to possible claims in relation to transactions at undervalue, or payments to creditors in preference to others (see p118) or under the extortionate credit provisions of the Consumer Credit Act.
- Whether there are any preferential creditors who would be paid in priority in a bankruptcy (see p308), or secured creditors, and how it is proposed to deal with them.
- Details of the debtor's debts and any guarantees given by third parties for them.
- The proposed arrangements for conducting any business run by the debtor during the IVA.
- The proposed duration of the IVA (usually no longer than five years) and the estimated amounts, and frequency, of payments to creditors.

• Details of the supervisor and of the fees to be paid to the nominee/supervisor.

This proposal must then formally be served on the insolvency practitioner, who only becomes the debtor's 'nominee' when s/he accepts and returns one signed copy of this proposal. S/he will not do this unless satisfied that the proposal is reasonable and viable, and is one that is likely to be acceptable to creditors and the court. After making the proposal the debtor must prepare a statement of affairs.

Interim order

Once the insolvency practitioner has agreed, then the debtor can apply to the court for an interim order.[6] An application for an interim order is made to the county court for the insolvency district in which the debtor resides (in London, to the High Court). It must be accompanied by an affidavit (sworn statement) and the signed copy of the notice of the proposal sent to the insolvency practitioner endorsed with her/his consent to act. There is a fee. The insolvency practitioner will help the debtor to make the application. The court will set a hearing date with at least two days' notice, and give notice of this to any creditors who have already presented bankruptcy petitions and to the debtor.

If the debtor is an undischarged bankrupt, then the Official Receiver and the trustee in bankruptcy will also be notified. Once this application has been made, the court may, and usually does, stay any execution or other enforcement action against the debtor pending consideration of the interim order.[7]

Provided the court is satisfied that:
• the debtor 'seriously' intends to make a proposal – ie, it is viable and has not been made just to delay bankruptcy proceedings;
• the insolvency practitioner is prepared to act;
• there has been no other application within the previous 12 months; *and*
• the debtor is either an undischarged bankrupt or could petition to be made bankrupt;

it will make an interim order.

This stops the presentation of new bankruptcy petitions or the action on existing ones and prevents the execution of distress warrants or other enforcement measures without the court's permission. Creditors who do not need a court order to levy distress are not affected by the interim order – eg, Inland Revenue, landlord of a business tenancy. An interim order initially lasts for only 14 days but is normally extended to allow sufficient time for the creditors' meeting to take place and for the nominee to report back to the court.

During the period of the interim order, and at least two days before it expires, the nominee must submit a report to the court, evaluating the proposals by saying whether or not they merit being put before a meeting of creditors. In most cases, this is presented at the hearing for the interim order and the insolvency practitioner will recommend the arrangements to the court and give a date for the proposed meeting (between 14 and 28 days after the report is submitted). Provided it is satisfied that the proposals are worthy of being put to creditors, the court will usually endorse the recommendation and extend the interim order for seven weeks after the proposed date of the meeting (where the matters are dealt with together the order is known as a 'concertina order').

The court can reject the recommendation of the insolvency practitioner (in which case the interim order is discharged and enforcement action can continue) or, if s/he fails to make a report, replace her/him if the debtor so requests.[8]

Creditors' meeting

The insolvency practitioner must inform all creditors of the meeting.[9] The debtor and (if possible) debt adviser should attend. The meeting will normally be held in the offices of the insolvency practitioner and s/he will also chair it. The meeting has to consider the proposal. This can be amended, but the debtor must consent to each modification. The meeting will eventually vote on the proposal, with creditors' votes being counted as a proportion of the unsecured debts owed to them. In other words, if a debtor's total debts are £35,000 and a particular creditor is owed £3,500 then her/his vote will count for 10 per cent of the total vote. To gain approval, the proposal must be supported by 75 per cent in value of the creditors voting. The meeting cannot approve a proposal that would affect the rights of preferential or secured creditors without their consent.[10] A creditor with an interim charging order will be a secured creditor for this purpose and the debtor would need to apply to the court to discharge the interim order to prevent the creditor from obtaining an advantage over other unsecured creditors, although the fact that an IVA is being considered may be good grounds for challenging the order being made final.

After the meeting, the insolvency practitioner must report the result to the court within four days,[11] and at the same time write to all creditors. If s/he is approved by the meeting, s/he becomes known as the 'supervisor' at this stage.

The Inland Revenue and the debtor's bank are usually the main creditors and so their support will be essential in obtaining the required majority. If approved, the arrangement takes effect immediately and is binding on every creditor who received notice of the meeting and was entitled to vote.[12] If the debtor is already an undischarged bankrupt then the court can either:

- annul the bankruptcy order (this can only be done after the 28-day appeal period ends); *or*
- use its powers to act under that order (see below) to facilitate the agreement reached.

The creditors or debtor have 28 days in which to appeal to the court against the IVA.[13] This can only be on the grounds that:

- there were irregularities in the way the meeting was held – eg, the proposal contained misleading or inaccurate information; *or*
- the arrangements unfairly prejudiced the rights of that creditor.

The court will consider this challenge and may:
- revoke (or suspend) the agreement made; *or*
- order that a new creditors' meeting be held to consider either a new arrangement or reconsider the old.

After an individual voluntary arrangement is made

The supervisor will take charge of ensuring that the debtor complies with the proposals. S/he will arrange the sale of any assets to be sold under the terms of the proposal (including houses, business, etc). S/he must prepare accounts at least annually and send these to all creditors.[14] In practice, a debtor is usually left to carry on business and make regular payments to the supervisor, who distributes them. Provided these are maintained, there should be little problem and the debtor will be discharged from all liability for the debts covered by the IVA. Whether or not any joint debtor (eg, the debtor's spouse or partner) will be released from her/his joint and several obligations will depend on the express terms of the IVA and so must be specifically considered and included.[15] However, if the terms of the IVA are not kept to, then the supervisor will probably petition for bankruptcy (if the creditors do not). If the debtor's circumstances change, the original proposal can be modified. Any modification would have to be discussed and agreed at a meeting of creditors.

4. Bankruptcy

Who can become bankrupt?

A debtor who is insolvent can be the subject of bankruptcy proceedings. A person can petition for her/his own bankruptcy (debtor's petition). Creditor(s) can also apply (alone or jointly) where someone owes at least £750, as can a supervisor of an individual voluntary arrangement (IVA) where the debtor has defaulted.

People who are 'domiciled' or 'normally resident' in England or Wales (or have lived or carried on business in England and Wales in the three previous years) are subject to bankruptcy law. People who conduct the administration of their financial affairs on a regular basis in another EU Member State (ie, that State is their 'centre of main interests') are not subject to bankruptcy law unless they also have somewhere in England and Wales where they carry out economic activities on a non-temporary basis (ie, an 'establishment').[16] Bankruptcy is normally used only for unsecured debts.

The bankruptcy process

The process can be started either by a debtor or creditor.

Debtor's petition

A debtor who decides to go bankrupt must 'petition' the county court for the insolvency district where s/he resides (in London, the High Court) on the ground that s/he is unable pay her/his debts. This is done on form 6.27 together with an affidavit and statement of affairs (form 6.28) (see Appendix 3).

The debtor must pay the court fee (currently £120) and deposit (currently £250). The court has some limited powers to waive the fee (see p173) but not the deposit. This anomaly has been unsuccessfully challenged on the ground that it is a barrier to a debtor's access to justice and a breach of Article 6 of the European Convention on Human Rights (right to a fair trial).[17] In practice, therefore, this money either must be raised by borrowing from friends or relatives or, alternatively, some charities will help (see Chapter 6).

Completing the debtor's petition (form 6.27)

See Appendix 3 for an example of this form.

The petition is primarily designed for people who have been in business as these make up the majority of bankruptcies.

The petition must be presented to the debtor's local court with bankruptcy jurisdiction (not all county courts have bankruptcy jurisdiction) unless s/he has lived and/or traded in the area of another county court for most of the previous six months, in which case it can be presented in that court.

The petition must state:
- the debtor's full name, current address and occupation, together with any other names by which s/he is, or has been, known and details of any current or previous business names and addresses;
- either the address in England and Wales of the debtor's centre of main interests or that the debtor's centre of main interests is not in an EU Member State;
- that s/he is unable to pay her/his debts;
- either that s/he has not previously been bankrupt or details of any previous bankruptcies;
- either that s/he has not entered into any voluntary arrangement with her/his creditors or been subject to an administration order; or, if s/he has, give details.

Completing the statement of affairs (form 6.28)

See Appendix 3 for an example of this form.

A considerable amount of information is required on this form and the debtor may not have this immediately available – eg, Page A requires details of mortgages, secured loans and the value of any property. Guidance notes (form B44.24) are supplied with the court forms but they are not comprehensive. The following points should be noted.

- **Page B** All creditors need to be listed in alphabetical order and all unsecured debts (including joint debts) must be included. Do not include any shortfall due to secured creditors, as this will be covered by the information on Page A.

- **Page C1** Care needs to be taken when completing this page. Any money in bank/building society accounts which will be needed to cover living expenses should be withdrawn before the petition is taken to court and, therefore, should not be included in this section. Do not include the value of any equity in property listed on Page A.

- **Pages C2/3** Ensure that the value of any vehicle is not set too high by using bottom book value as a guide. If it is subject to hire purchase (HP) or conditional sale, the owner is the creditor. When calculating the value of furniture and belongings, use the figure they would sell for at an auction, not their price when new or their replacement cost. Any valuables entered here risk being taken. Cash in hand should be entered at C3(e).

- **Page D** If any creditor has a prior claim on goods because of distress action already taken, this should be noted here. The creditor will only be allowed to keep the benefit of the distress if it has been 'completed' before the making of the bankruptcy order – ie, by the seizure and sale of the goods.

- **Page E** Any ongoing court action taken by creditors needs to be noted here. Action will usually be stayed – ie, no further steps can be taken once the petition has been filed at court.

- **Page F** The court will use this information to decide whether to ask an insolvency practitioner to examine the appropriateness of an IVA. Only attempts to make arrangements with creditors generally should be included here, not attempts to make separate arrangements with individual creditors.

- **Page G** Only 'regular' income should be included (as well as any contributions from other members of the debtor's household). The debtor is not expected to restrict her/his expenditure to income support levels and in practice Official Receivers are more generous in the items of essential expenditure that they will allow. The form suggests that any available income will be taken for creditors, but in practice, offers of less than £100 to £200 per month can cost more than this amount to administer and there is, therefore, little benefit to creditors.

- **Summary page (Form B44.28)** Some courts require the debtor to complete a summary page stating whether or not:
  - s/he owes unsecured creditors less than £20,000 in total;
  - her/his available assets are worth £2,000 or more;
  - s/he can afford to make monthly payments to her/his creditors.

This allows the court to determine:
- whether an IVA should be considered (see below); *and*
- whether a certificate of summary administration should be issued (see p301).

Once the forms are completed, the debtor needs to take them to the court to be sworn, with the fee (or application for exemption/remission on form EX160) and deposit (see p295).

Upon receipt of the petition, the court will arrange for the matter to be put before a district judge. In many cases this does not result in a hearing. Otherwise a hearing, which the debtor is expected to attend, will be arranged, probably on the same day. At the hearing, the court should refer the matter to an insolvency practitioner for consideration of an IVA if:

- the debts are below £20,000;
- assets are at least £2,000;
- the debtor has not been subject to bankruptcy proceedings in the last five years; *and*
- it seems appropriate to appoint an insolvency practitioner to report on whether it would be possible to make an IVA. No guidance is given about this.[18] (If the debtor does not want an IVA s/he should make this known to the court.)

The debtor does not have to pay for this report. If an IVA is not applicable (as is usually the case), the court either will make a bankruptcy order or can dismiss, adjourn or stay the petition – for example:

- if it appears that the debtor has only a single debt; *or*
- her/his assets exceed liabilities; *or*
- the debts are not legally enforceable; *or*
- an alternative method of dealing with the debts would be more appropriate – eg, an administration order – see p233.

If a bankruptcy order is made, with or without a certificate of summary administration (see p301), then the procedure thereafter is similar to bankruptcy under a creditors' petition (see below).

Creditors' petition

An individual creditor must be owed £750 or more to petition for bankruptcy. Creditors can join together to petition to meet the £750 requirement. Proceedings will normally be in the debtor's local county court with bankruptcy jurisdiction but Crown departments (eg, VAT, Inland Revenue) can use the High Court in London.

Creditors can only ask to make someone bankrupt if the debt is unsecured and for a fixed sum which the debtor 'appears unable to pay'. The debt can be payable immediately or at some time in the future. This can only be established in one of two ways:

- when they have served a 'statutory demand' on the debtor with which s/he fails to comply (see below); *or*
- if they have been unable to enforce a judgment debt by means of execution against goods by a bailiff.[19] For example, if a warrant of execution is returned

unsatisfied partly or completely, it can be seen as evidence that the debtor 'appears to be unable to pay' and the creditor can proceed to petition for bankruptcy without issuing a statutory demand. However, the bailiff must have made serious attempts to levy execution; a mere visit to the debtor's property and a report of the bailiff's failure to gain access is not sufficient.[20]

A creditor who has a judgment is not required to use bailiffs to try and enforce the judgment before resorting to a statutory demand.

Statutory demand

A statutory demand requires the debtor to:
- pay the relevant amount; *or*
- offer to secure it against property; *or*
- offer to repay the debt in a way that is satisfactory to the creditor (eg, by instalments).

The creditor does not need a judgment in order to serve a statutory demand.

A statutory demand is made on form 6.2 (form 6.3 if the creditor has a judgment) and does not have to be issued by a court. Some creditors use statutory demands as a means of debt collection to try to persuade debtors to pay them, for example, by borrowing elsewhere, but with no intention of actually applying to make the debtor bankrupt. The debt adviser should ensure, however, that all statutory demands are taken seriously, for after 21 days the creditor can ask for a bankruptcy order without further warning. It is usually worth a telephone call to the creditor to ask what the next step will be. Although there is no requirement for a statutory demand to be served personally on the debtor, if it is not, it is unlikely that the creditor intends to petition for bankruptcy.

The debt adviser should always consider whether an application for an administration order (see p233) is appropriate or, in the case of debts regulated by the Consumer Credit Act 1974 where a default notice has been served by the lender, an application for a time order should be made. If a time order is made, the debt will not be 'due' (see below). If there is any doubt about the amount of the debt (see Chapter 5), which could reduce it to below £750, this should be pursued with vigour so that bankruptcy ceases to be possible. If the debt is subject to a judgment, the debtor should consider applying to the court to vary the judgment by making an instalment order before the creditor can apply for a bankruptcy order.

Ignoring a statutory demand might encourage a creditor to present a petition, thus saving the debtor the fee if bankruptcy were to be the debtor's preferred option.

Otherwise the debt adviser should advise the debtor to consider:
- making payment(s) to reduce the debt to less than £750; *or*

- making an offer to secure or compound (ie, payment by instalments or a reduced amount in full and final settlement of) the debt. The debt adviser should treat the creditor like any other unsecured creditor at this stage and explain the debtor's social and financial situation. Where the debtor has little property or income, it is worth pointing out to the creditor that s/he is unlikely to receive anything in a bankruptcy and so should consider the alternatives on offer. Obviously, full or partial write-offs or reduced payments with a freeze of interest are preferable if these can be negotiated, but if bankruptcy would have serious consequences for the debtor, a voluntary charge on the debtor's property may be appropriate; *or*
- applying to set aside the statutory demand (see below).

Setting aside a statutory demand

Twenty-one days after the statutory demand has been served the creditor can apply for a bankruptcy order unless the demand has been 'set aside' by the court. A debt adviser should help the debtor make an application to set aside:

- if there is a substantial dispute about the money owed;
- if there is a counterclaim of more than the money owed;
- if the creditor holds security that equals or exceeds the debt in value;
- on 'other grounds'. These are not defined but could include: the demand was issued in error (eg, for less than £750, or after the relevant limitation period expired, or for a secured debt); failure by the creditor to comply with the rules, where this has prejudiced the debtor; execution has been stayed on a judgment; or the debtor is complying with an instalment order (in which case strictly the debt will not be 'due').

It is not appropriate to apply to set aside a statutory demand as a means of making an offer of payment by instalments: this must be done by direct negotiation with the creditor.

The application to set aside must be made within 18 days of service of the statutory demand. Forms 6.4 (application) and 6.5 (affidavit) must be completed and taken to the court specified in the statutory demand (there is a £50 court fee, but the debtor can apply for exemption/remission). The paper will be put before a district judge who can dismiss the application if there are not sufficient grounds. Otherwise, a hearing is arranged where the court decides whether or not to set the statutory demand aside.[21] If the debt is disputed, the court must be satisfied that the debtor has a 'reasonable prospect' of establishing her/his case. The court will not enquire into the merits of any judgment upon which the creditor relies, unless it was obtained by default. If the creditor refuses the debtor's offer of payment or security (or even to consider it) the court will not investigate at this stage the 'reasonableness' of the creditor's refusal.[22] However, if the debt is regulated by the Consumer Credit Act 1974 the court should consider any relief available to the debtor under the Act, including a time order application.[23] The

12

Chapter 12: Bankruptcy and individual voluntary arrangements
4. Bankruptcy

. . . .

fact that the demand is for an excessive amount is not, in itself, grounds for setting it aside. The correct procedure in such a case is for the debtor to pay the amount admitted and apply to set aside the demand only as to the remainder.[24] A statutory demand cannot be set aside subject to conditions, for example, if the debtor makes a payment on account.[25]

Bankruptcy hearing

The debtor will receive a copy of the petition with a hearing date and an affidavit outlining the circumstances. It is not too late to stop the bankruptcy but the debt adviser should go to the court with the debtor if this is to be attempted. In this event the debtor must give notice to the court and to the creditor at least seven days before the hearing that s/he intends to oppose the petition. In addition, payment, or an offer of payment, can still be made or an IVA applied for (see above). Failure to set aside a statutory demand (or to apply to do so) does not prevent the debtor from raising the same arguments at the hearing of the creditor's petition that were, or could have been, raised at the earlier hearing.

At the hearing the court may only make an order if:

- the conditions above (see pp294 to 299) are met; *and*
- the statutory demand has expired without being set aside by the court. The petition must be dismissed if the debtor has either paid or provided security for the debt or made a payment arrangement with the creditor.

The court can reject a petition if:

- the debtor can demonstrate an ability to pay all her/his debts (ie, is not insolvent);
- the creditor has 'unreasonably' refused to accept an offer to pay by instalments, an offer of a reduced sum in full and final settlement, or an offer to secure the debt. At this stage it is the court which determines the reasonableness of the debtor's offer. The test is whether any 'reasonable hypothetical creditor would have refused the offer in the circumstances'.[26] The onus is on the debtor to demonstrate this. A petition can be adjourned for payment of the debts by instalments, but repeated adjournments should not be granted unless there is a reasonable prospect of payment within a reasonable time;[27]
- execution on a judgment has been stayed (including an instalment order for payment) or an appeal (or application to set aside the judgment) is pending;[28] *or*
- the debt is disputed on substantial grounds (ie, the court is satisfied there is a bona fide defence[29]) or the debtor has a previously unlitigated cross claim which exceeds the creditor's claim – ie, strong evidence of a solid claim that would reduce the debt below £750.[30]

If an IVA supervisor is the petitioner s/he must show that:
- the arrangement was based on false or misleading information from the debtor;[31] *or*
- the debtor has not complied with the IVA.

After a bankruptcy order is made

Certificate of summary administration
If a bankrupt:
- owes less than a certain amount (currently £20,000); *and*
- has not been either bankrupted or subject to an IVA in the previous five years; *and*
- petitions for bankruptcy her/himself,

then the court will, where it appears appropriate, also issue a 'certificate of summary administration'.[32]

In many cases the district judge will automatically issue a certificate if the above criteria are met. Otherwise, the debtor must ask the district judge to consider issuing the certificate at the actual hearing as it is too late to raise the matter later on. A certificate of summary administration simplifies the procedure. It means that the Official Receiver will administer the bankrupt's affairs. The Official Receiver will normally proceed without investigating a debtor's affairs (although s/he does have power to do so).[33] There will not need to be a creditors' meeting or an examination in open court, although the Receiver must inform all creditors of the order.[34] The Official Receiver will act as trustee in cases of summary administration. Crucially, the debtor will be automatically discharged from bankruptcy after two years instead of the usual three years.[35] A certificate of summary administration can be revoked if it subsequently appears to have been wrongly issued.

Where summary administration cannot be used (eg, because debts exceed £20,000) the Official Receiver will decide, on the basis of whether available assets merit it, whether to call a meeting of the creditors. If a meeting is called, a trustee will be appointed. This person must be an insolvency practitioner and is usually an accountant from one of a small number of large firms. A creditors' committee may also be formed to 'assist the trustee'. The main difference between this procedure and 'summary administration' is that the creditors' meeting guides the trustee and it can, consequently, be slower and more expensive. If no creditors' meeting is held, or no trustee appointed, the Official Receiver becomes trustee.

There is no need to call a creditors' meeting if bankruptcy comes as a result of failure to keep to an IVA (and the supervisor agrees to be trustee) or if a debtor petitions her/himself and the possibility of an IVA is referred for investigation by an insolvency practitioner and the court appoints that insolvency practitioner as trustee.[36]

Procedure after a bankruptcy order

On the making of the bankruptcy order, the court will immediately inform the local Official Receiver. The Official Receiver's main functions are to:

- investigate the debtor's conduct and financial affairs, and report to the court (except in summary administration cases);
- protect the debtor's assets by taking control of her/his property and any relevant documents.

On the day of the bankruptcy order, or as soon as possible afterwards, the debtor will usually be summoned to the Official Receiver's office. Due to the volume of work, Official Receivers now ask debtors to complete form B40.01, Bankruptcy Preliminary Information Questionnaire, to take to the meeting (a 40-page document). This booklet replicates many of the questions in the debtor's statement of affairs and the debtor should keep a copy of this document in order to assist in completion of the questionnaire. The debtor must also make a full statement to the Official Receiver at the meeting.[37] In summary administration cases, this interview is usually conducted by telephone.

The bankrupt is required to co-operate with the Official Receiver. Failure to do so could result in the debtor's discharge from bankruptcy being delayed. The Official Receiver can require a bankrupt to produce any documents, books, certificates, etc, relating to her/his finances. The debtor's bank account will be frozen. S/he can summon the debtor to court for an examination under oath (although this is very rare in ordinary debt cases). Either the Official Receiver or trustee can ask the court to order the examination of a third party and order her/him to surrender the bankrupt's property,[38] and can have mail redirected[39] if it is appropriate.

The debtor must give up possession of all her/his assets except protected goods (see below). This can be a humiliating and stressful experience. At this stage, the debt adviser's role will be predominately one of support and income maximisation.

The Official Receiver will report the making of the bankruptcy order to local authorities, utilities, courts, bailiffs, the Land Registry, relevant professional bodies, banks, building societies, pensions and insurance companies, and the debtor's landlord (if any). The Official Receiver will also advertise the order in the *London Gazette* and another local paper (only the court can dispense with this). The advert will invite creditors not notified individually of the bankruptcy to write and 'prove' their debts.

From the statement and documents submitted by the debtor and others, the Official Receiver will investigate the conduct and affairs of the bankrupt. Any criminal offences revealed must be reported to the authorities (see below for the so-called 'bankruptcy offences'), but this rarely happens in practice. An examiner from the Official Receiver's office may visit the debtor's home and complete an inspection report and remove any valuables which can be sold (see below for protected goods). Visits are invariably made to business premises, but visits to a debtor's home are increasingly rare.

Appointing a trustee

Once a trustee is appointed, or the Official Receiver becomes trustee, the debtor is deprived of ownership of all her/his property (comprising the 'bankrupt's estate') except certain items (see below) which then 'vest' in the trustee – ie, ownership passes automatically to the trustee. The debtor cannot sell anything, but if arrangements have already been made to sell (eg, the home) then the trustee will almost certainly approve these, provided it is a proper commercial deal. The proceeds would then be used to satisfy creditors. The trustee becomes responsible for handling the debtor's affairs and getting as much money as possible for her/his creditors. The trustee is charged with gathering together and selling all of the property previously owned by the debtor and distributing it amongst her/his creditors.

The debtor may have property which either cannot be disposed of and/or is subject to obligations which would involve expenditure to the detriment of the bankrupt's estate, and hence creditors. The trustee can dispose of such 'onerous property' – eg, a business lease.[40] If the debtor attempts to give away or sell 'their' property after the petition but before it vests in the trustee then this transfer is void – ie, of no effect. The court can ratify a sale, but, in the absence of this, the property still forms part of the bankrupt debtor's estate and can be recovered and sold by the trustee, unless the purchaser either did not know of the petition or bought the property for full value or otherwise acted 'in good faith'.[41]

Jointly owned property requires the consent of the co-owner or a court order. The trustee will not sell property unless it is economic to do so. If a debtor acquires any property before discharge, s/he must inform the trustee within 21 days. The trustee then has 42 days (during which the debtor must not dispose of the property) in which to claim the property for the estate.[42]

It is an offence for the debtor to do anything that intentionally conceals information or property from the Official Receiver or trustee, or to deliberately mislead the Official Receiver or trustee about such property which s/he had either before or after the bankruptcy. Criminal charges can be brought against a bankrupt, leading to a fine and/or imprisonment. However, if the debtor can show that there was no intention to mislead or defraud, this counts as a valid defence. Other so-called 'bankruptcy offences' include obtaining credit of £250 or more and trading under a different business name.[43] The majority of convictions are for these two offences. Self-employed debtors may be guilty of an offence if they have failed to keep proper accounting records of the business in the two years prior to the presentation of the petition.

Protected goods

Some goods cannot be taken and do not vest in the trustee (see above):[44]

- Tools of the trade, including a vehicle, which are necessary and used personally by the debtor for work (this protection does not extend to the stock in trade of the debtor's business, if any, which will almost certainly mean that the business has to close down).
- Household items necessary to the basic living of the debtor and her/his family. These should include all furniture, bedding and household equipment, except perhaps particularly valuable items (eg, antiques/works of art) or new and resaleable goods (eg, video cameras or expensive hi-fi systems).

A motor vehicle will generally be sold unless its age and condition mean it is worth only a minimal amount. If a car is essential for work, then the debtor may be allowed to keep it, although if it is particularly valuable the trustee may order that it be sold to allow a cheaper replacement to be bought, with the profit used to pay creditors. Any other asset can be treated in the same way if the trustee regards it as a 'luxury' item. The trustee must claim the asset within 42 days of becoming aware of it.[45] The trustee can visit bankrupted people and remove such goods or close businesses, etc, although this is, in practice, mainly done in cases of businesses or domestic properties where there may be valuable goods. In general terms, trustees do not dispose of items worth less than about £500, as it is not usually economical to do so.

Assured, protected and secure tenancies do not automatically vest in the trustee, but can be claimed within the 42-day period, if they have a value, but this is relatively rare.

Earnings

The trustee may suggest a weekly or monthly payment from a debtor's earnings during the period of the bankruptcy. If payment is not agreed, s/he can apply for an order called an 'income payments order' from the court. An order can last for a maximum of three years, including after discharge. The court must leave sufficient money for the reasonable domestic needs of the debtor and her/his family – the debtor is not restricted to income support levels. These payments will be ordered to be paid to the trustee by the court and can be required of either the debtor or employer under an attachment of earnings order.[46] Many courts appear to be more generous to a bankrupt person than they would be under attachment of earnings rules (see p194) and income payment orders are not common. In *Re Rayatt* the court allowed private school fees as a necessary expense, holding that the test is 'reasonable' and not 'basic' domestic needs.[47] Because of the administrative costs, monthly payments of less than £100 to £200 mean that most of the money is swallowed up by expenses and hardly any will go to the creditors. In other words, the debtor must be able to offer a substantial monthly amount for the trustee to consider it worthwhile.

For the purpose of recovery of benefit overpayments and social fund loans, a debtor's income support or jobseeker's allowance is not treated as the debtor's 'property' and so the Secretary of State can carry on making deductions from the debtor's income support or jobseeker's allowance to recover those debts.[48] If the debtor is not entitled to income support or jobseeker's allowance, the Secretary of State must 'prove' for the debt in the usual way (see below). However, if the debtor becomes entitled to either of these benefits prior to her/his discharge, then deductions can be made until the debtor is discharged and released from the debts.

Pensions

Where the bankruptcy order was made on a petition presented to the court before 29 May 2000, personal pensions are part of the bankrupt debtor's estate and must be paid to the trustee by the pension company whether the payments fall due during or after the bankruptcy.[49] The position with occupational pensions depends on whether or not the scheme contains a 'forfeiture clause' – ie, the pension is forfeited on bankruptcy and payments are at the discretion of the scheme, usually to another member of the debtor's household. If there is no forfeiture clause, it appears that the pension vests in the trustee.[50] Trustees may assert that pensions vest in them as a matter of course and so the position should be checked with the pension company direct. However, although an occupational pension cannot normally be claimed directly by the trustee, the income could be made the subject of an income payments order in appropriate cases. In *Kilvert v Flackett* it was held that a lump-sum payment made to the debtor out of his occupational pension scheme during the bankruptcy was income and could be made the subject of an income payments order where the debtor already had sufficient other income.[51]

Where the bankruptcy order was made on a petition presented on or after 29 May 2000, all rights under an 'approved pension arrangement' are excluded from the debtor's estate (ie, they do not vest in the trustee), including personal pension plans. However, if the debtor becomes entitled to the pension (including a lump sum) during the period of the bankruptcy, it could be made the subject of an income payments order, as above.[52]

Since 6 April 2002 the debtor has been able to either:
- apply to the court for an order (an 'exclusion order'); *or*
- agree with her/his trustee in bankruptcy (a 'qualifying agreement')

that part or all of her/his rights under an unapproved pension arrangement should be excluded from her/his estate. In deciding whether or not to make an exclusion order and, if so, on what terms, the court is required to have regard to:
- the future likely needs of the debtor and her/his family; *and*
- the extent to which those needs are likely to be adequately met out of any other pension (other than retirement pension or an income-related benefit).

A qualifying agreement must be made by deed and can be revoked by the trustee if:

- the debtor fails to make full disclosure of all material facts relating to the pension; *and*
- the debtor has done so for the purpose of enabling her/his rights to be excluded where otherwise they would not have been.

The debtor must apply to the court for an exclusion order:

- within 13 weeks of the bankrupt's estate vesting in the trustee – ie, the date of her/his appointment; *or*
- within 30 days of a qualifying agreement being revoked.

The court can extend the above time limits for good cause.[53]

Student loans

Loans under the Student Loans Act 1990, whether made before or after the bankruptcy order, are not part of the debtor's estate and so cannot be claimed by the trustee. On the other hand, they are not bankruptcy debts and so the debtor is not released from liability to repay the loan on discharge (see p310).

Loans made under the Teaching and Higher Education Act 1998 are again not part of the debtor's estate and cannot be part of an income payments order, but they are bankruptcy debts and so the debtor is released from liability on discharge (see further, Chapter 14).

Owner-occupied homes

The debtor's interest in the home automatically vests in the trustee. If it is solely owned by the debtor, the legal title vests in the trustee and the debtor's interest is the whole value of the property. If the home is jointly owned, it is only the debtor's share which vests in the trustee, but this does not prevent the trustee from taking action to realise that share. A debtor's home is, therefore, at risk from bankruptcy if there is equity in it. The trustee will not, of course, sell a property where no benefit could accrue from its sale (although s/he will register a caution and may order a sale in the future, including after discharge).

If another person shares ownership of the home, the trustee will try to sell the debtor's share to that person. S/he will have to obtain an up-to-date valuation, plus details of any outstanding mortgages or secured loans, and pay her/his own legal costs (at least £250). If the property is jointly owned, the trustee will require 50% of the equity plus her/his legal costs, but will allow some discount to take account of the savings made from not having to take possession of the property and conduct the sale. Where there is negative, or very little, equity it will usually be possible to buy out the trustee for a nominal sum (£1) plus her/his legal costs (typically £250). Similarly, where the property is solely owned by the debtor, s/he may be able to buy back her/his interest from the trustee. If there is equity, the purchase money will have to come from a third party – eg, a friend or relative. Mortgage lenders are reluctant to agree to people buying an interest in property, unless they take some responsibility for the mortgage.

If the debtor lives in the home with a husband/wife, then the spouse has a right to residence even where s/he is not a co-owner.[54] The Insolvency Act 1986 allows an application to the bankruptcy court to sell such properties.[55]

The trustee will probably seek a court order for the sale of a jointly owned property if the non-bankrupt owner will not/cannot purchase the whole. If children live in the home a court order is essential.[56] If there is a partner and/or children, then their interests should be considered, but after a year these are overridden by the interests of the creditors. This means that, in practice, homes are not sold for at least a year after the bankruptcy.

In deciding whether to order the sale of a house, the court must consider:

- the creditors' interests;
- whether the spouse contributed to the bankruptcy;
- the needs and resources of the children and spouse;
- other relevant circumstances (but not the bankrupt's needs).[57]

If the debtor is discharged without the property being sold, the trustee may obtain a charging order over the debtor's interest. This means that the trustee retains an interest in the property and could apply for an order for sale many years after discharge. Otherwise, the debtor's interest will continue to belong to the trustee, together with the benefit of any increase in the value of that interest. It is, therefore, in the interests of the debtor and her/his family to enquire about buying out the trustee as soon as possible.

If property is sold, the trustee will send monies due to the co-owner or other house-sharer to them on completion. It is very important that people who share homes with a bankrupt debtor (lesbian, gay or heterosexual partners and others) should be properly independently advised by a solicitor, particularly where they have made direct contributions to the purchase price, because they may have an equitable or beneficial interest in the property for which they should be paid, even if they are not an 'owner' on the deeds.

Under value

A transaction is said to be made 'under value' if it is an exchange at less than the market value. This may be quite innocent (eg, a birthday present), but if a trustee considers that such a transaction has reduced the assets available to creditors, s/he can apply to the court, which can set the transaction aside and order the parties to revert to their starting point.[58]

The trustee can apply to the court to have any transaction set aside if:

- it was carried out in the five years before the date of the bankruptcy order; *and*
- the debtor was insolvent at the time; *or*

- the transaction was carried out within two years of the date of the bankruptcy order, regardless of whether or not the debtor was insolvent.[59]

Such transactions could be:
- gifts;
- working or selling goods for nothing;
- working or selling goods for an amount significantly less than the value of the labour or goods;
- giving security over assets for no benefit in return;
- transferring an interest in property to a former spouse or even under a court order on divorce.

Preference

Where prior to the bankruptcy the debtor has paid an unsecured creditor whose debt would otherwise have been included in the bankruptcy, this may be a 'preference'. The following conditions must be satisfied:
- the effect of the payment was to put the creditor in a better position than s/he would have been in the bankruptcy; *and*
- the debtor had this intention; *and*
- the debtor was insolvent at the time;[60] *and*
- the payment was made within six months before the date of the bankruptcy order (or within two years, where the preference was to an 'associate' – ie, spouse or other relative, business partner or employer/employee).[61]

In the case of either transactions at under value or preferences, the court can restore the position of the parties by, for example, requiring any property or money to be returned to the trustee, ordering the release of any security, or payment to the trustee for goods or services. Protection is given to third parties who act in good faith without notice of the circumstances.[62]

If an owner occupier or business owner makes a statement that is clear and supported by bank statements, etc, and is prepared to allow a sale of the assets demanded, s/he will almost certainly not be subjected to any further scrutiny. It is only if other creditors submit evidence that leads the trustee to suspect fraud or deliberate disposal or hiding of assets that the trustee will investigate.

A creditor who has attempted to enforce a judgment debt prior to the bankruptcy will be allowed to retain the benefit of that enforcement only where:
- in the case of execution against goods, the goods have either been sold or money paid to the creditor to avoid execution before the date of the bankruptcy order;
- in the case of attachment of earnings, the payment has actually been received by the creditor before the date of the bankruptcy order;
- in the case of charging orders, the order was made final before the date of the bankruptcy order.

How money is paid

Once a bankruptcy order is made, the trustee will take over many of the functions of the debt adviser. The debtor may need considerable personal support, and the debt adviser may be required to ensure that the trustee acts correctly. However, until discharge, the debt adviser is largely powerless to affect decisions.

The statutory advertisement requests creditors to contact the trustee. They will be required to 'prove' their claims – ie, demonstrate that they are really owed the money. This must be done on a prescribed form.[63] The court can prevent any creditor who is entitled to prove in the bankruptcy from attempting to recover the debt in any other way. This power arises as soon as the bankruptcy petition is presented and continues until discharge.[64]

The only debts which cannot be proved are:[65]

- fines;
- maintenance orders (and Child Support Agency orders);
- student loans under the Student Loans Act 1990;
- debts arising from certain other orders of the criminal courts.

There are rules that regulate the despatch of forms to creditors.[66]

Secured loans do not need to be proved because the right of a secured creditor is not affected by bankruptcy.

Secured creditors can, theoretically, remove their security and ask to be included in the list of creditors. If they have already forced a sale of the home, they can be included as creditors for any balance due.

The trustee will work out the value of the assets and debts. S/he will list the following, which are priorities to be paid first:[67]

- Bankruptcy expenses (including amounts due to the trustee, the court or the Insolvency Service, which charges for the services of the Official Receiver). Research has shown that this often accounts for over 50 per cent of payment.
- Expenses of estate agents, etc, in realising assets.
- PAYE tax due for a year before the bankruptcy.
- Tax payable for sub-contractors due before the bankruptcy.
- VAT due for six months before the bankruptcy.
- Other taxes (road tax, betting tax, etc) due for 12 months before the bankruptcy.
- National insurance contributions due for 12 months before the bankruptcy.
- Arrears of wages to employees for four months before the bankruptcy (up to a maximum of £800 each).
- Other ('ordinary') creditors. These creditors receive nothing until the other 'preferential' creditors have been paid in full. If paid at, all these creditors generally receive only a percentage of the value of their debt.
- Deferred debts, for example, debts due to the debtor's spouse.
- Interest on any of the above from the date of the bankruptcy order.

Any surplus will be returned to the debtor.

Discharge

- If a bankruptcy order was made under summary administration, then discharge is automatic after two years.
- If a previous bankruptcy had been undischarged within 15 years of the start of this one, then a court order is required for discharge. This will not be granted within five years of bankruptcy.
- In other cases (ie, all 'ordinary' bankruptcies), discharge is automatic after three years. The trustee can ask the court to delay this if s/he believes that the bankrupt debtor has failed to carry out her/his obligations.[68] The debt adviser should be present at hearings to consider this. If unsuccessful, the court will suspend the automatic discharge and the debtor must then apply for discharge and persuade the court that s/he has now complied with all reasonable requirements.

After discharge, the court will issue a certificate to the debtor on request and payment of a £50 fee. More importantly, all the bankruptcy debts remain unenforceable, except the following:[69]

- secured creditors (if the home was sold, but insufficient equity was raised to pay the secured lender, that debt is no longer secured, but the unsecured part will remain unenforceable provided the mortgage or secured loan was taken out prior to the bankruptcy even if the home was not sold until after discharge; any jointly liable person will remain liable for the whole debt);
- fines;
- maintenance orders and other family court orders;
- debts from personal injury claims;
- debts incurred through fraud;
- debt arising from certain other orders of the criminal court;
- student loans made under the Education (Student Loans) Act 1990.

Occasionally the trustee is still working on something (eg, the sale of a home) when discharge is granted. In this case, that asset will still be realised and distributed after discharge despite the fact that the recipients of funds could not otherwise pursue payment. The duties to co-operate with, and to provide information to, the Official Receiver and/or trustee continue after discharge for so long as it is reasonably required.[70] The Insolvency Service has now set up a Protracted Realisations Unit in order to deal with such long-term matters.

Credit reference agencies will record bankruptcies but it is not necessarily impossible to get credit again after discharge.

Annulment

A bankruptcy order can be annulled (cancelled) at any time by the court if the debtor has either repaid the debts and bankruptcy expenses in full, or has provided full security for them, or if there were insufficient grounds for making the order in the first place.[71] The debtor then becomes liable once again for all the bankruptcy debts. A bankruptcy order can also be annulled where a creditors' meeting has approved an IVA proposal (see p293).[72]

Reform of insolvency law

When the Enterprise Bill becomes law (not now expected until April 2004), the Insolvency Act will be amended in the following respects:

- **Discharge** The bankruptcy discharge period will be reduced to a maximum of one year (the power to suspend discharge where the debtor fails to co-operate will remain). The summary administration procedure will no longer be available. Transitional provisions will enable debtors who are undischarged on the date the legislation takes effect to be automatically discharged one year after that date or at the end of the two-year or three-year discharge period, if earlier. Undischarged bankrupts who are not currently eligible for automatic discharge will be automatically discharged five years after the date the legislation takes effect, unless the court makes an order for earlier discharge under the current arrangements.

- **Bankruptcy restrictions and offences** Certain automatic bankruptcy restrictions (eg, appointment as a magistrate) and offences will no longer apply. Failure to keep proper accounts and gambling will no longer be bankruptcy offences. However, debtors whose conduct is regarded as dishonest or otherwise culpable may be made the subject of Bankruptcy Restriction Orders (BROs) on the application of the Official Receiver which will impose restrictions on the debtor for between 2 and 15 years. As an alternative to a BRO, the debtor will be able to agree to be subject to restrictions without the need for a court order (Bankruptcy Restriction Undertakings (BRUs)). A BRU will have the same effect as a BRO. Examples of the conduct of which the court is required to have regard include:
  - failure to keep records to account for transactions;
  - entering into a transaction at an undervalue or giving a preference;
  - failure to supply goods or services which were already paid for;
  - trading at a time the debtor knew or ought to have known that s/he would be unable to pay her/his debts;
  - incurring a debt which the bankrupt had no reasonable expectation of being able to pay;
  - gambling;
  - fraud;
  - failure to co-operate with the Official Receiver or trustee.

The Official Receiver must apply for a BRO within 12 months of the date of the bankruptcy order. Restrictions which will continue to apply to the debtor during bankruptcy and where a BRO (or BRU) is in force include:

– obtaining credit above £250 without disclosing that the debtor is an undischarged bankrupt or subject to a BRO/BRU;
– trading in a name other than that in which the debtor was made bankrupt;
– disqualification from acting as a company director.

If the debtor breached any of these restrictions (including a BRO/BRU) it will be a bankruptcy offence.

- **Official Receiver's duty to investigate** The Official Receiver's duty to investigate every case (although currently not where a certificate of summary administration has been issued) will be replaced by a duty to investigate only those cases where s/he considers it necessary (including cases which would have been covered by the Summary Administration procedure).
- **Income payments orders** Income payments orders (IPOs) will run for three years from the date of the order irrespective of discharge. Provision is made for the debtor to make a written payment agreement with the trustee (an income payments agreement (IPA)) which will have the same effect as an IPO.
- **Debtor's home** The debtor's interest in the home will revert back to the debtor unless within three years of the date of the bankruptcy order the trustee:
  – sells the debtor's interest; *or*
  – applies for an order for sale or possession; *or*
  – applies for a charging order; *or*
  – enters into an agreement with the debtor regarding the interest.

  The trustee will be unable to claim the debtor's interest where its value is below a figure to be prescribed in secondary legislation.
- **Post-bankruptcy IVAs** The Official Receiver will be able to act as nominee/supervisor for a post-bankruptcy IVA. Creditors will be invited to agree/disagree with the proposal by post: there will be no meeting of creditors and no possibility of modifying the proposal. The creditor majority required for approval will remain unchanged and, if a post-bankruptcy IVA is made, the court may be asked to annul the bankruptcy order.
- **Disqualification** MPs, members of the House of Lords and members of devolved assemblies will only be disqualified where a BRO (or BRU) is made.
- **Crown preference** Crown preference will be abolished in all areas (except in relation to road tax and certain other duties, and levies on coal and steel production). However, the Secretary of State will retain preferential status where s/he has made payments from the Redundancy Fund to cover preferential payments to employees.

Notes

1. Last resort or fresh start?

1 Basic Banking Research, Financial Services Consumer Panel, April 2002; for details of available accounts see the British Bankers Association website (www.bba.org.uk)

2. When to use bankruptcy and voluntary arrangements

2 ss339 and 341(1) IA 1986
3 s360 IA 1986
4 s308A IA 1986 as amended by s117(2) HA 1988

3. Individual voluntary arrangements

5 Rule 5.3 IR
6 s253(1) IA 1986
7 s254 IA 1986
8 s256(3) IA 1986
9 Rule 5.13 IR
10 s258 IA 1986 and Rule 5.18 IR
11 Rule 5.22 IR
12 s260(2) IA 1986
13 s262(ii) IA 1986
14 Rule 5.26(2) IR
15 *Johnson v Davies, The Times,* 31 March 1998, CA

4. Bankruptcy

16 Council Regulation (EC) No.1346/2000 of 29 May 2000; see P Madge, 'Centre of interest', *Adviser* 93
17 *R v Lord Chancellor, New Law Journal,* 14 August 1998, QBD
18 s273 IA 1986
19 s268 IA 1986
20 *Re a debtor* (No.340/92), *The Times,* 6 March 1995, CA
21 Rule 6.5 IR
22 *Re a debtor* (No.415/1993), *The Times,* 8 December 1993, Chancery Division
23 *Mills v Grove Securities Ltd,* unreported, 24 April 1996, CA, *Adviser* 64 abstracts
24 *Re a debtor* (No.490/1991), *The Times,* 9 April 1992; Rule 6.25(3) IR
25 *Re a debtor* (No.32/1991)(No.2), *The Times,* 3 May 1994
26 *Re a debtor* (No.32/1993), *The Times,* 1 March 1994
27 Rule 6.29 IR; *Re Williams (a bankrupt), The Times,* 16 July 1997
28 Rule 6.25(2) IR

29 *London & Global v Sahara Petroleum, The Times,* 3 December 1998, CA
30 *Re Greenacre Publishing, The Times,* 17 December 1998
31 s276(1) IA 1986
32 s275 IA 1986
33 s289(5) IA 1986
34 Rule 6.49 IR
35 s279(2) IA 1986
36 ss297(4)-(6) IA 1986
37 s288(1) IA 1986
38 s366(1) IA 1986
39 s371 IA 1986
40 s315 IA 1986
41 s284 IA 1986
42 s307 IA 1986
43 ss350-362 IA 1986 deal with 'bankruptcy offences'
44 s283(2) IA 1986
45 ss308 and 309 IA 1986
46 s310 IA 1986
47 *The Times,* 4 May 1998, Chancery Division
48 s32 JA 1995; *R v Secretary of State for Social Security ex parte Taylor and Chapman, The Times,* 5 February 1996
49 *Re Landau (a bankrupt), The Times,* 1 January 1997
50 *Re Stapleford,* 1 April 1998, Chancery Division, *Insolvency Intelligence,* August/ September 1998
51 *The Times,* 3 August 1998
52 s11 and Sch 2 Welfare Reform and Pensions Act 1999
53 Regs 5 and 6 Occupational and Personal Pension Schemes (Bankruptcy) (No.2) Regs SI 2002/836
54 s30 Family Law Act 1996
55 s336(2) IA 1986
56 s337 IA 1986
57 s335A IA 1986 as inserted by the TLATA 1996
58 s342 IA 1986
59 ss339 and 341(1) IA 1986
60 s340 IA 1986
61 s341 IA 1986
62 s342 IA 1986
63 Rule 6.93 IR
64 s285 IA 1986
65 Rule 12.3 IR
66 Rules 6.97 and 6.108 IR

67 Sch 6 IA 1986
68 s279 IA 1986
69 s281 IA 1986
70 ss291(5) and 333(3) IA 1986
71 s282 IA 1986
72 s261(1) IA 1986

Chapter 13
· ·
Business debts

This chapter covers:
1. Types of small business (below)
2. Stages of debt advice (p318)

This chapter deals with certain types of debt which arise during or after the running of a business. It also looks at ways in which the debts or strategies covered elsewhere in the book need different consideration for the small business person.

This chapter must be used in conjunction with the rest of the book. It sets out exceptions to the rules outlined elsewhere. Provided the adviser is familiar with the processes of debt advice outlined throughout the book, this chapter will often be a starting point when dealing with someone who has recently run, or is running, a business.

This chapter is not a guide to business credit or business viability, which are both specialist areas in their own right.

Debt advisers often declare themselves unable to deal with a person's debts while s/he is still running a business. The need for referral to other professional specialists (for instance, tax or business advisers) cannot be overstressed. However, this chapter assumes that some limited involvement with the debts of a trading business person is possible. In addition, of course, it will be apparent that many ancillary debts (particularly after a person has ceased trading) can be handled by the debt adviser.

1. Types of small business

It is important to understand what type of business a debtor is involved in because this governs the question of her/his liability. There are several types.

Sole trader

A person who is self-employed without business partners is described as a sole trader. Typical sole traders might include people like joiners, electricians or solicitors (who are sole practitioners) and also sales people who work their own patch on a purely self-employed basis. Sole traders can work either in their own name or using a business name.

Sole traders are legally responsible for their business debts in exactly the same way as they (or other debtors) are responsible for personal debts.

Partnership

A partnership is the relationship that exists when two or more people carry on a business together in order to make a profit. The law of partnerships was codified by the Partnership Act of 1890, which has been clarified by many decided cases. In the absence of a partnership agreement, this legislation regulates many of the activities and liabilities of a partnership. A partnership can be very informal, as, for instance, where musicians perform together in the evenings and share their expenses and payment. No formal written agreement is required for a partnership to exist, but this will always be useful where disputes or problems arise. Partnership agreements should cover questions like distribution of profits (which will be equal unless stated otherwise) and how the partnership can be dissolved.

A partnership is considered a single legal entity. Unless the partnership rules state otherwise, contracts can be entered into by any one of the partners and bind them all. A partner is normally responsible only for those debts accrued during the period in which s/he was a member of the partnership (although sometimes new partners will agree to take responsibility for any partnership debts accrued by their predecessors). Partners continue to be responsible for debts accrued during their membership, unless they all formally agree otherwise, and also gain the agreement of creditors to a transfer of their liability (perhaps to the remaining partners). Partners may even be held liable for debts incurred by the partnership after they have left, unless notice was given to the creditors. Outgoing partners should ideally seek legal advice when leaving a partnership to ensure that they take all necessary action to avoid this happening.

Partnerships may trade under a particular business name or the names of the partners.

Partners are normally jointly and severally liable (see Chapter 5) for all their partnership debts. However, this is no longer the case with tax debts, where the liability for tax falls personally on each partner according to their share of the profit.

Limited companies

A limited company is a means whereby a separate legal body is set up to trade and make a profit (which is either kept in the company or distributed to its owners – ie, shareholders). Losses fall to the company rather than the individuals who have set it up. A limited company can be public (ie, where the shares can be bought or sold on the stock market) or private (where shares are owned and transferred among a limited number of people as allowed by the company's rules). Companies are owned by their shareholders. They are run by their directors who may also be shareholders (and in most small companies they are) but they need not be.

Directors are elected by shareholders and are employees of the company. Companies are governed by a great deal of legislation, much of which is administered by Companies House, where records of directors and accounts are kept. Company law is complex and outside the scope of this book – it is vital to advise debtors to get specialist advice where appropriate.

Unlike in a partnership, the directors are not personally responsible for the debts of a company unless:

- they have agreed to act as guarantor for some, or all, of the company's debts; this is often the case with bank loans to small companies; *or*
- they have acted fraudulently and the company has been liquidated, or they have continued to trade while the company was insolvent and the company subsequently goes into insolvent liquidation.

Companies legislation is intended to encourage entrepreneurship by protecting unsuccessful business people from the individual consequences of corporate debts.

Credit arrangements made in the name of a limited company cannot be regulated under the Consumer Credit Act 1974.

Co-operatives

Some businesses are run by co-operatives, which are governed not by the Companies Acts but by the Industrial and Provident Societies Acts of 1965-75. These allow companies to trade for a profit without distributing profits to shareholders. As with a limited company, a co-operative trades as an independent legal entity and, therefore, protects its members from responsibility for its own debts (unless, as with a company, they have acted fraudulently or have agreed to take responsibility for some or all of the debts).

Some co-operatives are not registered under the above Acts and are, therefore, merely partnerships whose partnership agreement has co-operative aims. Other organisations described as co-operatives may actually be incorporated as ordinary limited companies.

In order to establish whether a client in a co-operative is personally liable for its debts, legal advice may be necessary.

Franchises

A franchise is a renewable agreement which allows the person buying the franchise the right to run a branch of a business that someone else has already set up.

The person buying the franchise (the franchisee) is the owner of her/his individual branch and not an employee of the franchisor.

A franchisee can choose which way s/he wants to trade – either as a sole trader, in partnership or as a limited company. This choice governs the franchisee's liability for the business debt.

Specialist advice may be needed in connection with legal and/or tax issues – contact the British Franchise Association, Franchise Chambers, Thames View, Newtown Road, Henley-on-Thames, Oxon, RG9 1HG.

Limited liability partnerships

A new kind of business known as a limited liability partnership (LLP) was introduced in April 2000, which has some of the characteristics of a partnership and some of a company. The liability of the 'members' (not partners) to contribute to the debts of the LLP are limited to the assets of the LLP. There is no recourse to personal assets unless the member has been personally negligent.

Queries relating to LLP debts should be referred to a legal specialist or an accountant with expertise in this area.

2. **Stages of debt advice**

The rest of this chapter highlights factors to be taken into account in the debt advice process, as outlined in Chapter 3, when advising someone who either runs, or has run, her/his own business, whether as a sole trader, a partner or a company director.

Create trust

People who have run their own business may pose particular challenges to the debt adviser's trust-building skills. Being self-employed requires self-confidence and independence, which may make it difficult for a person to ask for help. If an employee becomes unable to pay her/his debts after being made redundant, then at least s/he can see that the causes are beyond her/his control. However, someone whose indebtedness arises after the collapse of her/his own business may have to face feelings of personal failure in addition to the ordinary problems associated with serious debt.

Over the past decade much political and media hype has been given to the rejuvenation of the economy via the growth of small businesses. This can have the effect of further increasing a person's sense of responsibility and, therefore, failure. The entrepreneur in debt may, therefore, require time to unburden her/himself of these feelings.

The debt adviser should also ensure that as much responsibility as possible for undertaking the tasks necessary to sort things out is carried by the business person. If s/he has already run a business (often for many years), s/he will feel both de-skilled and disempowered if the debt adviser takes over simply because the business is no longer successful.

List creditors and minimise debts

Minimising debts by ceasing trading

Where a person is still running a business but is seriously in debt, then s/he should consider whether or not to continue trading. There is clearly no point in doing so if this is just increasing indebtedness and the situation is unlikely to alter. This is a highly complex area and specialist help should be sought from a small business adviser, perhaps via the local Learning and Skills Council or the business's own accountants. The process may be helped by drawing up a business plan for a reasonable period ahead (business advisers often recommend a period of between one and five years). This plan is similar to the financial statement that is drawn up for the debtor, except that it deals with income and outgoings of the business, not an individual. The plan should include:

* **All the business's assets.** This should include equipment or machinery with its approximate resale value (which will be different from amounts shown in professionally produced accounts, where the 'book value' is based upon the original cost of an item and its theoretical life). The greatest asset of a business may be the work that it has in hand and the debts owed to it. These are notoriously difficult to value. The likelihood of a debt owed to the business actually being paid must be assessed and the contractual status of work in hand measured. For instance, a painter and decorator may have agreed in the autumn to paint the exterior of an existing customer's house the following spring. If the customer loses her/his job during the winter then in the (usual) absence of any binding agreement the work may not materialise.

  A realistic value for any premises or leases on premises that are owned should be estimated, perhaps by a local estate agent, although it should be borne in mind that valuations of business premises are not usually free (as they are for domestic premises). The client's estimate of value may therefore have to be sufficient for now. Business premises are particularly susceptible to a fall in value caused by developments elsewhere in the locality. (For instance, the opening of a supermarket nearby is likely both to cause a collapse in the business of a corner shop but also a fall in the value of its premises.) In this way a reduction in the market which causes a business to flounder can also reduce the value of its assets, which would otherwise have been its major protection from financial problems. The value of a lease is a complex matter which can only be accurately assessed by a professional. Leased business premises are not valued in the same way as domestic premises. The shorter the period that the lease has left to run, the less likely it is to be of any value. Advisers should note that if there is no one prepared to take over the lease then this might represent a liability rather than an asset (because the client/tenant otherwise remains liable for the rent until expiry of the lease).

  Items like cars should always be valued at the price likely to be obtainable at auction rather than a price that an optimist might expect to get from a private sale. There are various used car price guides available from newsagents (and updated monthly) which will give a trade price for reasonably modern cars, and this can be used as a guide.

- **Likely income to the business.** Draw up a list of payments that the business might expect to receive based on a conservative, but realistic, assessment. Note the dates when payments can be expected. The debt adviser can demonstrate respect for the debtor's business skills by asking her/him to prepare these figures her/himself.

- **Expenditure by the business.** A similar, dated list of payments that the business is required to make must be drawn up next. This must include, for example, bank interest and charges, lease or rental charges for both property and equipment, regular bills for fuel and other services (eg, telephones and waste disposal), payments required by suppliers, value added tax (VAT) payments, wages to any staff, estimated tax and national insurance.

The excess of income over expenditure will give a rough idea of how much is available for the business person to pay her/himself in 'drawings'. If there is no foreseeable likelihood of anything being available then an end to trading is strongly indicated. However, it should be stressed again that the client and/or debt adviser must seek expert assistance before taking such a major step, because items like liability for tax or payments due under a lease, which can be very complex, could make the difference between viability and insolvency. A lay adviser will not generally be qualified to make this decision.

If a person is trading as a partner, then the decision to cease trading may not be hers/his alone. Where one partner wants to cease but others do not, then s/he should ensure that s/he has formally severed her/his partnership agreement in order to limit her/his liability to those debts that have accrued at that time. S/he should try to gain the agreement of creditors and ex-partners, preferably in writing, that s/he will not be liable for any debts which subsequently come to light, but which relate to the period of her/his membership of the partnership. Where a partnership is informal and there is, therefore, no prescribed way of leaving it, legal advice should be sought so that an agreement can be drawn up terminating the informal partnership. If possible, this should include an agreement that those remaining in the business will indemnify (that is, agree to pay instead of) those leaving against claims against them for past actions (or bills).

Sometimes informal business partnerships exist between people who have personal relationships, such as married or co-habiting couples. It is often the custom that either party can enter into contracts on behalf of the partnership (for which both partners become jointly and severely liable). In such a case, it is most important that suppliers are informed that the partnership no longer exists if this is desired. This is often the case when a personal relationship ends and thus a couple cease trading together.

Minimising other debts

Business borrowings are often secured by banks against a person's home. Sometimes such a security is not enforceable if the agreement was entered into as a result of undue influence or misrepresentation by the creditor or another debtor (see p102). This more commonly occurs where a person who is not the debtor is required to agree to a charge being made on a property in which s/he is either a joint owner or has another interest (perhaps because s/he lives with the owner). In one case, it was decided that a charge was not enforceable where a debtor's wife had signed it, but had not been recommended to take separate legal advice and had been told that her husband's business would be closed down by the bank if she did not do so.[1]

If it is thought that undue influence or other wrong doing occurred at the time the security was signed, specialist or legal advice should be sought, as the law is complex in this area.

The debts owed by a person who has run a business may include tax debts. See below for ways in which these might be minimised.

List and maximise income

The scope for improving the income of a person running her/his own business is often greater than that of an employee. Specialist business advice can improve profitability, for instance, through better marketing, the lowering of production costs or overheads, or diversification. The debt adviser should, therefore, refer the debtor to someone who can help with this.

In addition, there are many grants and other facilities (cheap loans, etc) available to small businesses which should be investigated. The local Learning and Skills Council or Business Link are probably the best places to start looking for these. The payment of tax may represent a substantial proportion of income and, therefore, the need to claim all the relevant individual tax allowances, reliefs and expenses that a business can offset against tax should be noted – see below.

Business people with children may benefit from the working families' tax credit or, from April 2003, the new tax credits. They should always apply unless the earnings from the business have been untypically high just before a claim is made. They should ensure that they make their claim, where possible, at a time when recent earnings have been low (see p97). Council tax benefit (CTB), housing benefit (HB), income-based jobseeker's allowance (JSA) and occasionally income support (IS) may also be available, as well as disability benefits.

List expenditure

In drawing up a financial statement for a business person, the debt adviser will need figures from the business plan (see above). However, the personal financial statement is a quite different document and should be kept separate. The expenditure required by the business (even of a sole trader) should be separately listed from personal or household expenses. Sometimes this is not easy, particularly with a sole trader, where, for instance, a car might be necessary for work and to provide family transport. The debt adviser may send the draft business plan along with a household financial statement to creditors.

In such cases, the debt adviser should be careful not to double count items which are shown as outgoings on the business account (and, therefore, reduce the available income) which may also be paid as part of the household accounts. Thus, for instance, where a car is used for both domestic and business purposes it should be apportioned partly to the business account before the drawings from the business are shown and then only the remaining (domestic) portion should be shown on the financial statement.

Deal with priority debts

Services

If a business has ceased trading and utility debts on commercial premises are outstanding, then the gas and electricity bills may need to be treated as a priority. This is because the power to disconnect home premises for non-payment of commercial bills exists for gas and electricity supplies[2] where those supplies are in the same name and provided by the same supplier. It follows that, if someone traded from home, gas and electricity arrears would be priority debts. If s/he traded from part of the same building (for example, from a shop above which s/he lived), s/he should separate the suppliers to the two premises before arrears accrue to avoid the risk of disconnection of the domestic premises.

Water companies cannot disconnect a supply to any premises other than those to which the water was supplied, and since 30 June 1999 can no longer disconnect the supply to residential premises.[3]

Business rates

Business rates should not be charged upon premises that are empty for the first three months and thereafter should be charged at only half the relevant rate. If the ratepayer has a lease on the premises, s/he will be liable for the business rates for as long as her/his tenancy exists, even if the premises are empty. Business rates are collected and enforced in the same way as council tax, except that tools of the trade etc are not exempt. Advisers should note that this means that bailiffs can seize a ratepayer's property from anywhere (including her/his home address) once a liability order has been made. Another difference is that attachment of earnings orders and charging orders are not allowed for business rates, nor are deductions from benefit.

In practice, many local authorities will write off large amounts of unpaid business rates. Unlike council tax, they have the power to remit, or write off, unpaid business rates where there is 'severe hardship' and where it is reasonable to do so. Most local authorities will, in practice, use this power to write off unpaid rates where a business has ceased trading and those responsible for the rates are dependent upon benefit, or where a business may close with job losses if rates are pursued. Local councillors should be approached to put pressure on officers if this is not done.[4]

Distress for rent

Distress for rent (see p262) is a possibility that should be borne in mind where a business is behind with its rent. If a person is continuing to trade, then it is probably impossible to stop bailiffs from making a peaceful entry to her/his premises (since they are likely to be open to the public). Some landlords will see the seizure of the whole of a business's stock as the easiest way of recovering rent arrears but this will almost certainly have the effect of forcing the debtor to cease trading. The possibility that the bailiffs will arrive unannounced, therefore, means that the utmost priority must be given to securing an arrangement with a business's landlord if the debtor wishes to continue trading.

Leased premises

Many businesses lease their work premises. Such arrangements are governed by the Landlord and Tenant Act 1954. In some cases, the unexpired part of a business lease can be a valuable asset that can be realised if the debtor decides to cease trading or trade from other premises. Professional advice should always be sought as to the valuation of such leases. Where a lease is to be 'assigned' to another person, legal advice should be sought and the permission of the landlord will be required. Unfortunately, if the new tenant fails to pay her/his rent, then, in certain circumstances, the earlier tenant can still be held responsible. In order to protect against this future liability, it is sometimes better to agree with a landlord the surrender of a lease, even where the lease may be saleable for a premium.

Landlords may be prepared to accept the surrender of a lease (which ends the tenant's contractual obligations, such as rent and therefore rates) where it is clear that they are unlikely to get any more money from this particular tenant. If they wish to sue for unpaid rent, landlords should be able to show that they have mitigated their losses. In the circumstances where a debtor has ceased trading and is likely to remain unemployed for some time, and has responsibility for a lease, the debt adviser could approach the landlord directly. S/he should explain that the tenant is unlikely to meet her/his contractual obligations and, in some cases, landlords will agree to a surrender. It is important, however, for the adviser to ensure that s/he is not dealing with a lease which is of value (perhaps because it forms a small part of a redevelopment site or because the rent has been fixed at a low rate for many years to come) before s/he gives it away – specialist advice should be sought.

Other leases

Many businesses will have equipment like photocopiers, electronic scales or games machines which are held on a lease from owners. The debt adviser should first check whether or not the lease is a regulated agreement under the Consumer

Credit Act (see Chapter 4). Many lease documents are complex and specialist help may be required.

A business lease will run for a number of years, during which time the owner of the goods (which may be a finance company) simply charges rent for the business to use them. At the end of the period there can be no automatic transfer of the goods to the lessee but, in practice, items are often not taken back by lessors. A lease will usually contain provision for early settlement. However, in many cases this figure will be almost as high (usually 95 per cent) as continuing to pay rental until the end of the lease period.

Once a lessee is in arrears with the rental, however, the courts can intervene under common law and alter any clause that is designed to penalise a lessee who is in arrears. Because the courts have this power only when arrears arise, it may be useful to allow business leases to go into arrears if a debtor has decided to cease trading.

It should be stressed that business leases are very complex and, as the sums of money involved can be substantial, expert advice should be obtained before reaching any agreement with a lessor about early settlement (trading standards departments may be equipped to provide such advice).

In calculating the amount that should be paid by the lessee who is in arrears, the courts will ensure that the lessor receives only the actual amount of money that they have lost as a result of the termination. This should include either the goods or their full value at the time of termination. Additionally, lessors should receive the amount that would have been paid in interest less an amount (usually 5 per cent a year) in recognition of the fact that they are receiving this money early. Where a lease contains charges for service to equipment leased out, then the courts may reduce the future service charges which will not be required after the goods are returned.

VAT debts

Value added tax (VAT) is a tax on the increase in the value of most goods or services (some are exempt) between the time they are bought by a business and when they are sold. Businesses with a turnover of less than £55,000 per annum (2002/03) do not have to register for VAT. All others have to submit quarterly returns to show the difference between the VAT they pay to other suppliers (input tax) and the VAT they charge their customers (output tax). If they have collected more VAT than they have paid, they must enclose this with their return and submit it by a 'due date' (usually a month after the end of the relevant quarter). If a return is late, then the amount due is increased by an automatic surcharge. If a return is not made, Customs and Excise can estimate the amount due and issue its own assessment, which becomes payable immediately.

Local customs officers who collect VAT vary greatly in their approach to struggling or failed businesses. In general, it should be noted that they consider themselves as collectors of a tax which has already been paid by a third party to the debtor and of which the debtor is only a custodian. While this may bear little relation to the realities of running a small business, it is an attitude that makes them assertive and swift in their recovery process.

Once payment is outstanding, the Customs and Excise officer at a local office will usually use the threat of distress to force payment. This may initially consist of a visit, phone call or letter to state that distress will be used. A formal notice (VAT 879) will then warn the debtor that immediate payment is required and bailiffs will be used in default.

A distress warrant is then signed by a customs officer (recourse to the courts is not necessary).[5]

The warrant will usually be executed by a firm of private bailiffs with a customs officer in attendance. Although they have no right to force entry (see Chapter 11), most business premises are necessarily accessible to the public (including bailiffs) and therefore negotiation is essential. A debtor who is still trading should always try to give the bailiffs some money and treat this debt with utmost priority. Unfortunately, distress can provoke or escalate the collapse of a business, both by removing necessary stock or equipment and also by reducing confidence in the business.

The adviser who is faced with unpaid VAT should:

- contact Customs and Excise, explain the position and request a short time to organise the person's affairs;
- get an accountant to check the amount claimed (particularly if it is an assessed amount);
- explain the seriousness to the debtor – use a small business adviser if necessary to look at the viability of the business, its credit control procedures, etc.

See Chapter 11 for details of how to deal with the bailiffs. Advisers should note the detailed list of exempt goods contained in the Distress for Customs and Excise Duties and Other Indirect Taxes Regulations 1997.

Where distress is not appropriate, Customs and Excise will often use bankruptcy as a means of collection (see Chapter 12).

Income tax debts

The self-employed and businesses are responsible for making a return to their local inspector of taxes upon which tax bills are based. In April 1996 a new system of self-assessment was introduced and taxpayers are now invited to calculate their own tax and send in a payment to accompany their return for a particular year. A small business should always get specialist help in claiming all the allowances against tax to which it may be entitled and in treating its profits and losses in the most tax-efficient way. The tax bill will be based on simple 'three-line accounts' for small businesses with a turnover of less than £15,000 per year. These are required to show:

- total turnover;

- total expenses and costs of purchases;
- net profit (which is gross profit less all the business expenses).

In addition to the tax due on its profits, a business may also owe tax (and national insurance contributions) on wages paid to employees.

The actual assessment process is outside the scope of this book and the adviser should, where necessary, get specialist help to check the amount of tax demanded.

If a debtor is required to pay tax on the basis of an estimate made by the inspector of taxes (known as a 'determination') because s/he has not submitted returns or these are not believed, it is no longer possible to appeal these to a tax commissioner. A determination is enforceable immediately and can only be overturned by the filing of a return. The return can be amended within 12 months, although errors and mistakes can be corrected outside this period. The Inland Revenue can impose penalties and surcharges for late filing of returns and/ or non-payment of tax. If the debtor is unable to persuade the Inland Revenue to waive or remit these impositions, the debtor can appeal on the ground that s/he had a 'reasonable excuse' for the failure. It is also possible to ask the collector of taxes (not, as might be expected, the inspector) to accept a lesser amount in settlement of a tax bill, where this lesser amount can be shown to be all that should have been due in respect of the relevant period. This type of (partial) write-off is known as accepting 'equitable liability'. It is sometimes useful where the patience of the debt adviser has uncovered figures relating to income for a particular period which were not found by other professional advisers. However, as the debtor has up to five years from the date when the return should have been filed to challenge the determination by filing a completed return, the Inland Revenue expects to make less use of 'equitable liability'.

If a tax bill is unpaid, then the collector of taxes may:
- use distress (without a court order) – see p265;
- use the magistrates' court – see p258;
- use the county court – and follow judgment with a third party debt order, attachment of earnings, distress, charging order, instalment order, etc – see p174;
- seek a bankruptcy order (see Chapter 12).

As with VAT, the collector of taxes is likely to be particularly strict where the money owed includes tax already collected by a business from employees and not passed on to the Inland Revenue. It should be noted that the Inland Revenue makes no secret of taking exemplary action, such as bankruptcy proceedings, against some debtors, even where this is unlikely to lead to a payment being made.

The **collector of taxes** does not require a court order to execute **distress** (seize goods). S/he usually takes a bailiff to assist with valuation of goods to be seized, but it is the collector who is empowered to seize them (see Chapter 11).

A **summons** to the **magistrates' court** is usually used to collect unpaid tax of up to £2,000 where the debt is less than 12 months old. This is a potentially dangerous action for the debtor because of the inconsistent (and often unrealistic) decisions of these lay adjudicators. The debtor will be summonsed to appear at a hearing at which the magistrates will make an order that s/he pays the tax (unless s/he can demonstrate that it is not due or is someone else's liability). After this, although the Inland Revenue can use distress, if payment is still not made, magistrates are more likely to issue a summons for the debtor to show that s/he has not 'wilfully refused or culpably neglected' to pay this tax (see Chapter 10). To avoid this, the debtor should attend the initial hearing and ask the magistrates to order the unpaid tax to be paid by instalments. The debt adviser can assist by preparing a detailed financial statement.

The **county court** is probably the best outcome for the debtor unable to pay tax because the county court is likely to make a more realistic **instalment order** (based on its greater experience of debt). The Inland Revenue is entitled to claim interest under the Taxes Management Act 1970, currently at 6.5 per cent a year on any unpaid tax until payment, and enforces this even after a county court judgment. Once a judgment has been made, the possibility of an administration order exists if the debts are below £5,000 (see Chapter 9).

It is possible to **negotiate** with both **Customs and Excise** and the **Inland Revenue**. Although it is generally easier to negotiate after the debtor has ceased trading, as with all negotiation, the outcome will depend on the circumstances of the individual case. Sometimes the intervention of an MP can help. If the taxpayer has been caused problems by maladministration the parliamentary ombudsman can be used. There is also an Inland Revenue adjudicator who may intervene in cases of particular hardship or unreasonableness.

Draw up a personal financial statement

The creation of a financial statement for a person who is running her/his own business is no different from that of an employed person, except that expenses may need apportioning, as explained above, and the amount of her/his income may be less predictable. Both these things should be made clear on the financial statement. The figure for earnings ('drawings') net of tax and national insurance contributions should be taken from the business plan produced to help decide the viability of the business.

Choose a strategy for non-priority debts – bankruptcy and individual voluntary arrangements

These are discussed in Chapter 12. Bankruptcy may often be the most satisfactory way out of the large debts that can arise after the failure of a business. Bankruptcy in itself does not necessarily mean the business must cease trading, particularly where there are no assets of significant value. However, it should be remembered that although discharge from bankruptcy may occur after one to three years (depending on the date of the bankruptcy), a person's credit rating will be affected for considerably longer, and if s/he wishes to run a business which will require credit in the future, then bankruptcy can be a serious obstacle to this. The person with an otherwise viable business but serious debts may be well advised to consider an individual voluntary arrangement (IVA).

Notes

2. Stages of debt advice
1 *Barclays Bank plc v O'Brien* [1993] 4 All ER 417, HL
2 Sch 6 para 1(6) EA 1989; Sch 2B paras 7(1) and (3) GA 1986
3 s1 and Sch 1 Water Industry Act 1999
4 s49 LGFA 1988
5 Sch 11 para 5(4) Valued Added Tax Act 1994

Chapter 14

··

Students in higher education

This chapter covers:

1. Introduction

In September 1999 the Government introduced the Education (Student Support) Regulations. These consolidated funding arrangements for students who entered higher education after September 1998, and appeared to mark the end of the transition from publicly-funded local education authority (LEA) support through grants and fees to substantially self-funded education through student loans and tuition fees. Since this date both the 'old' and 'new' systems have run concurrently, the old one applying to those students who are excluded from the new regulations. The system of undergraduate support is currently undergoing further review and subsequent revisions are anticipated. For more details see p345.

The changes already implemented have precipitated a major shift in the financial position of students. Before the introduction of the 1999 Regulations surveys indicated that undergraduates could expect to leave their courses with an average debt of £3,000. While this level of indebtedness appeared high, the situation facing today's students is staggering. The Student Living Report 2002 (commissioned by Unite and conducted by MORI) showed that, on average, students anticipated owing £8,133 once they had completed their studies. However, the level of debt anticipated varied depending on social class, the highest level of predicted indebtedness being from students from the lower socio economic groups (C2DE) at £9,376. In the same study, 35 per cent of those who took part stated that they were seriously worried about the debts they were incurring as a result of attending university. Interestingly, concerns about debt do not extend to student loans in the same way, 59 per cent preferring not to worry about loans now, but rather to worry about them later, when they begin working.

Higher education is set to expand further in the light of current policy – the Government aims to achieve 50 per cent participation by 18 to 30-year-olds by 2010.

As a consequence of the introduction of national quality standards, more thorough regulation and increased expectations of clients, the field of advice work has undergone major changes. Student debt has become a real issue due to the nature of student funding and debt advisers are required to have more specialised knowledge, as well as being licensed by the Department for Trade and Industry.

When advising students and ex-students about debt, the adviser may need to adopt some different strategies in order to assist students and needs to be aware at all times that students expect to owe money prior to, and on completion of, their studies. Most creditors (banks and the Student Loans Company) have structured repayment programmes for 'normal' student debt once the student starts earning. Such indebtedness should not adversely affect the student's creditworthiness (eg, for obtaining a mortgage), though any repayments made (or due to be made) will be listed as outgoings in affordability calculations in future credit applications.

Definitions and structure of this chapter

Home student

This chapter covers only home students in higher education or further education. A **'home student'** is defined in Schedule 1 of the Education (Student Support) Regulations 1999 or the Education and Mandatory Awards Regulations 1999, Part II, para 7 and 8, as:

> a person settled in the UK within the meaning of the Immigration Act 1971 and the person is ordinarily resident in England and Wales on the first day of the first academic year of the course and has been ordinarily resident throughout the three-year period preceding the first day of the course. The residence must not have been wholly or mainly, for the purpose of receiving full-time education.

Ordinary residence was defined by Lord Scarman's judgment in the case of *Akbaraly and others v Brent and others* (1982) as: 'habitual and normal residence in the United Kingdom from choice or settled purpose throughout the prescribed period apart from temporary or occasional absences.'[1]

In addition, a student may be regarded as a home student if s/he, or a certain member of her/his family:

- has refugee status;
- is an European Economic Area (EEA) migrant worker;
- has been granted leave to enter or remain in the UK.

The financial position of international students is not discussed in this chapter. Advisers should contact UKCOSA – see Appendix 5 for details.

The majority of this chapter follows the structure of the rest of the book. Issues are discussed only where the position of the students differs from that of other debtors. Therefore, if not covered in this section, advisers should refer to the main text.

---

2. **Stages of debt advice**

The stages of debt advice described in Chapter 3 need to be applied when working with students just as with anyone else. There are, however, some additional issues to be considered at each stage. These are highlighted below.

Stage 1: Create trust

Most higher/further education institutions and students' unions/guilds/ associations offer money advice services. The majority of these will be experienced in dealing with student debt and have student specific information resources, and therefore many students will prefer to use the more convenient 'student aware' service. There can, however, be very real issues of impartiality, independence, confidentiality and trust arising when advisers work for the educational institution. This situation is further complicated when the institution is the creditor – see p340. It may not always be appropriate or ethical for an adviser employed by the institution to assist a student in this position. Even when the adviser works for the students' union/guild/association the student may need reassurance that the service is confidential and/or impartial.

In order to create a position of trust with a student in need of debt advice it is important for the adviser to have an awareness of the different causes of student debt and not to make a judgement about the position clients finds themselves in. Very often the student will not seek help for causes of problems, but their effects.

There are many reasons why a student may be in debt. In addition to the causes of indebtedness that apply to the general population, this can be due to: above-average course costs; local education authority (LEA) assessments not being a true reflection of parental disposable income; debts incurred prior to the client becoming a student; aggressive marketing towards the student group; tuition fees; coping with an income paid in irregular instalments.

Some students can cope with increased levels of debt, accepting that a certain level of indebtedness is inevitable and part of the student experience. For others it can have a more negative impact. The adviser could be faced with a student who may be extremely anxious, ashamed, desperate, worried and confused. The stage at which the student presents may also have an effect on her/his emotional state, as many wait until the situation can no longer be dealt with without external assistance before seeking help. The impact of all of this can be that the student may be experiencing poor health, mental ill-health, relationship difficulties and difficulties with her/his course – eg, low marks, missed deadlines and exam failures. Some students may feel forced to withdraw from their course completely.

Stage 2: List creditors and minimise debts

When noting the status of the debt on the creditor list it is important to consider the sanctions connected with non-payment in order to determine whether the debt should be recorded as a priority or non-priority. In addition to the criteria referred to in Chapter 7 (if non-payment would give the creditor the right to deprive the debtor of her/his home, liberty, essential goods and services or place in the community, then that debt will have priority) the adviser needs to consider the sanctions available to and used by the institution where it is the creditor. It is generally accepted that outstanding tuition fees correctly attributable to the student can be listed as a priority debt. For some ex-students outstanding tuition fees can remain a priority debt as the majority of institutions will withhold the award until the debt is cleared. Students entering some professions (eg, teaching) need their degree conferring before they can take up employment. Prioritisation needs to be discussed with the student. See also p335.

The adviser needs to be aware of the threats posed to the debtor by the recovery action, and whether they are appropriate – p343 details what sanctions should be imposed on the different types of debt the student may have with the institution.

Stage 3: List income

Many students rely wholly or mainly on student loans for their income. These are taken into account as income for benefit purposes and it is therefore important that loans are listed as such. Most creditors will otherwise suggest that they are used as a means of making repayments. Without them the financial statement will show a hugely unrealistic deficit. However, advisers need to explain that this source of income is a loan used only for living expenses, that interest is accruing, and that repayment will be required at a future date.

Students with disabilities can receive non-means-tested additional allowances to their loan/grant. These allowances are to help the student with the extra costs of being on a course of study – they are not to help with living expenses. It is not necessary to include them as income as they will have been already allocated.

Students with dependants and those who have two homes may also be entitled to additional allowances. These should be included, but need to be balanced by the expenditure needed to maintain both homes.

Where a grant or any other additional allowance is paid it must be listed as an income.

Parental contributions, if paid regularly, should be listed as income. These are intended to make up for any shortfall in the grant/loan. The LEA will assess how much the parent(s) should pay, although it is not able to enforce payment. In reality many students do not receive the prescribed parental contribution.

Period to be used

Students, institutions and advisers tend to think of students' income within the framework of the instalment periods for which it is paid – ie, termly, quarterly or annually. Creditors are more likely to understand income expressed in weekly or monthly periods. Breaking down income into these periods is also a helpful exercise for students, as the irregular payment periods often reduce their budgeting ability or financial control.

If a maintenance grant is paid to a student the adviser will need to establish the period which it is meant to cover. Where extra weeks' allowances are paid, the payment period should include the total number of weeks.

For final year students this income will cease to be taken into account once the course has finished.

How income from a student loan is listed will depend on the student's personal circumstances. It can be spread over 52 weeks if it is likely to be the student's main source of income over this period, or if the student has an alternative income during the summer vacation it can be listed as spread over the length of the course. The adviser must consider the financial benefit to the student when deciding how to show this income to creditors. The client should be made aware of the distinction between the income calculation for benefit purposes and that shown on a financial statement or part of a budget plan.

Stage 4: List expenditure

In addition to the items outlined in Chapter 3, students will have additional expenditure, which must be included and which may be required by the course. At this stage the adviser can help the student identify areas where it may be possible to reduce expenditure – eg, by claiming help with health costs. This area is where the adviser can be of most use to the student, as many students will have little or no experience of budgeting and financial planning. This process should also highlight from where debts have arisen and therefore help prevent further financial difficulty. The adviser should also help the client deal with irregular income, and both regular and irregular expenditure.

Cost	Period to be attributed	Ways of reducing cost
Tuition fees	This needs to mirror the period of time over which the student loan/main source of income is attributed – eg, over the length of the course (43 weeks).	Ensure that liability is correctly attributed to the student. Ensure no (further) assistance is available.

Books/reading packs	Advisers should, through experience, be able to attribute a realistic figure for particular courses within the institution. If this figure cannot be quantified the adviser can use the annually set figure for books included in the student loan.	Suggest using the university library; sharing resources with students on the same course; second-hand book stalls or schemes; local libraries. Students in the year above can advise on books that are absolutely necessary. Some universities have departmental libraries.
Stationery	To be attributed over the length of the course.	Printing facilities should be provided by the institution. Cost needs to be measured against individual printing costs.
Materials – eg, fabrics, photographic equipment, costs related to field trips	As above.	As above. Bulk purchasing may reduce costs if possible.
Room insurance	Over the rental period, which can differ from the length of the course.	Advisers should check if this is necessary as some policies held by parents can cover items temporarily removed from the family home. The amount of cover can be too little or too much depending on the student's personal effects.
Transport costs	Any transport costs that the student may have may vary depending on time of year, personal circumstances and whether s/he has any dependants. If these costs cannot be attributed, use the annually set figure for travel in the loan, plus the cost of at least four journeys home per year.	Season tickets are often available, as are student travel cards.

Telephone	As above.	Eighty-six per cent of students own a mobile telephone. Some creditors may need convincing why this is a necessity rather than a luxury. However, the student will need guidance on how to ensure telephone costs are kept to a minimum – eg, on the type of contract and service (and internet) providers, and alternatives such as using telephones in rooms, university-provided internet links and landlines.

Advisers will often have local knowledge (for example, shops and services that offer NUS-related discounts) that may help students who are new to the area reduce their expenditure.

If the student and adviser decide to use a period of 43 weeks to list the main student income and expenditure it will usually be necessary to draw up a new financial statement showing revised figures for the remaining 12 weeks, the long summer vacation. This statement will generally not need to include study-related costs and related funding.

3. **Types of debt**

This section lists some types of debt which are peculiar to students (and ex-students) and which are not included in Chapter 4.

Bank overdrafts

For a definition and the legal position, see Chapter 4.

Special features

Student overdrafts have certain features that are different to other debtors. All the high street banks offer most undergraduate, and some postgraduate, students special interest-free overdrafts up to a set limit. The limit may be increased in the later years of the course. The special facility is only available on student accounts. Packages will therefore vary – eg, students in different academic years may have different overdraft limits. If the overdraft limit is exceeded, interest should be charged on the excess only. In these circumstances the adviser should inform the bank that the student is seeking assistance with her/his finances. The adviser should try to negotiate an increase in the limit at least to reflect the new overdrawn figure. If the bank refuses, challenge on what basis the bank can say it is unauthorised – ie, if cheques have been honoured or funds have been released, this would have been authorised.

Chapter 4 outlines the strategy of opening a new account in order to prevent an existing bank overdraft swallowing income. In the short term advisers should also advise on the use of 'first right of appropriation'. This is where the client has the right to state how a deposit made into an overdrawn account should be used. The student should inform the bank, preferably in writing, what specific amounts are to be paid and to whom. The bank must carry out these directions from the client. However, the bank may still charge the client for the use of the overdraft. This facility should only be used on a short-term basis and the adviser should discuss the overdraft with the client in terms of debt advice and maximising income (see p351).

Students may not be allowed an interest-free facility on any new account until they can show a closing balance on an existing account. However, this is happening less frequently. If a student is unable to open an account (eg, due to low credit scoring) the adviser could contact the Financial Services Authority (see Appendix 5) for information about 'introductory accounts' where basic facilities are available even if overdrafts are not.

Most banks allow students terms that continue for a period after they have graduated. The length of time varies between banks and can often be extended by negotiation. This is preferable and advisers should negotiate this option rather than requesting that overdrawn accounts be 'converted' into graduate loans, as it will be more beneficial to the student. Most banks offer preferential graduate terms – eg, free currency exchange and lower mortgage rates for limited periods.

Graduate loans

Personal loans are available to students after they graduate to cover costs related to graduation and starting work (eg, clothing, relocation costs) and to consolidate student debts. They are only usually authorised if the bank has evidence that the student has secured employment.

Legal position
Graduate loans are regulated by the Consumer Credit Act 1974 – see Chapter 4.

Special features
Graduate loans attract a preferential interest rate. Some banks offer a deferred period of repayment.

Postgraduate loans

Postgraduate loans are personal loans offered by certain high street banks to students undertaking postgraduate studies. As with all other personal loans, they are offered at a fixed or variable rate of interest.

Legal position

Personal loans are regulated under the Consumer Credit Act 1974 – see Chapter 4.

Special features

The terms of these loans vary between the different banks and according to the type and duration of the course the student is taking. The most significant common feature of these loans is deferred repayment. Interest usually accrues during this period. Some loans allow for repayment to be deferred until after the course has ended. In other cases, repayment begins partway through the course.

Career development loans

For the legal position and definition, see the section on personal loans in Chapter 4.

Special features

Repayment is deferred during the course and for up to one month afterwards. During the deferment period the Department for Education and Skills (DfES) pays the interest on the loan. This period can be extended, on application to the bank, for a further five months if, after completing training, the borrower is registered unemployed and claiming benefit, or if s/he is receiving certain welfare benefits (the adviser should check which currently apply), or if for reasons beyond the student's control s/he is required to continue attending her/his course or training. There may be other circumstances where the period of repayment can be further extended – the terms and conditions of the loan should be checked.

Student loans –mortgage-style loans

In 1990 the Government froze the mandatory grant to students in higher education and introduced student loans to 'complement' grants as a source of income. These loans are not means-tested. The maximum student loan increases each year. The Student Loans Company is the creditor, even though applications will have been administered by the institution. These are now known as mortgage-style loans.

Bankruptcy will not prevent a student from getting a loan; however, bankrupt applicants must declare their status when they apply. Student loans (mortgage-style) cannot be included in bankruptcy proceedings (England, Wales and Northern Ireland). Legal action should not be taken against the student while s/he is bankrupt. Deferment forms should be completed to inform the Student Loans Company of the student's situation.

Legal position

Agreements are regulated under the Consumer Credit Act 1974 – see Chapter 4.

Special features

Repayment is not required until the April after the student has finished her/his course, either because s/he has completed or abandoned it. Repayments are monthly and are usually by direct debit from the borrower's bank account. The student will have signed an agreement to repay by direct debit at the time of borrowing. If the student begins another eligible course at the same college immediately after the first course ceases, repayment will not start until the April after the latter course finishes but s/he may have to apply for deferment (see below).

Repayments are expected to be made over five years (seven years for those who borrow for five years or more). If more than one loan is outstanding, they are repaid concurrently. The amount owed (including interest) is totalled and divided by the number of months (either 60 or 84) to arrive at the monthly repayment. This is reviewed annually.

Repayment can be deferred if the debtor's gross income is below 85 per cent of the national average earnings. Only the income is taken into account in this calculation; no account is made of the individual client's expenditure/financial commitments. An application for deferral should be made when repayment is due to start and a fresh application for deferral must be made each year. Proof of income should be submitted with this. Interest continues to be charged during any period of deferment.

As long as repayments are not in arrears, any amount still due will be cancelled after 25 years, or when the borrower reaches the age of 50 (whichever is earlier). If s/he last borrowed at the age of 40 or over, the outstanding amount will be cancelled when the borrower reaches the age of 60.

As with other agreements regulated under the Consumer Credit Act, repayment of student loans is enforceable through the county court and the Student Loans Company has been quick to take court action against large numbers of borrowers. Problems may arise where students have closed the bank account from which the Student Loans Company expects direct debit repayment and have not made alternative arrangements, or where that account is so overdrawn that the bank will not honour the direct debit arrangement.

The Student Loans Company has sold off some loans to private companies for recovery but this should not affect the collection of outstanding loans.

Advisers should:

- check the borrower's gross income and assist her/him to apply for deferment where appropriate;
- otherwise treat this as any other non-priority debt (see Chapter 8).

Student loans – income-contingent loans

In July 1997 the Government announced a package of measures, including the replacement of grants by loans. In 1998 the Teaching and Higher Education Act introduced income-contingent loans (for students who normally live in England or Wales). The amount a student can borrow depends on the year of study, the course the student is studying and where. The maximum available is set by the local education authority (LEA) (or by the DfES if s/he is an eligible European student). Once the student has made arrangements with the Student Loans Company for the loan to be paid, the amount will stay fixed for the rest of the year. If the student has not borrowed all of the amount to which s/he is entitled s/he can alter the amount of the loan by completing a loan adjustment form. The Student Loans Company is the creditor, repayments are made via the Inland Revenue.

Legal position

Income-contingent loans are not regulated by the Consumer Credit Act. Repayment arrangements are governed by the Education (Student Support) (Repayment) Regulations 1999, from the April 2000 start date.

Special features

At the same time as the Government announced the above package of measures it also announced that loan repayments would be linked to the individual graduate's income. Section 22 of the Teaching and Higher Education Act 1998 enables the loans to be collected through the tax system and allows the Secretary of State to make regulations requiring employers to deduct the repayments from borrowers' earnings. Unearned income will also be taken into account when calculating repayments. Income of the ex-student's partner/parents/spouse is not taken into account. No repayments are due during the course.

An income threshold has been set at £10,000 gross per year from April 2000. (Though this might change depending on economic conditions, it has remained at this figure since the introduction of this type of loan.) Once the income threshold is reached, repayment must be made at a percentage of the difference between the ex-student's total income and the threshold. Students whose earnings are below the threshold will not be asked to make payments.

Repayments will begin from the April after the student graduated or left the course, regardless of earning levels before then. In general, loans will be repaid over five years. Refunds will be payable if there are special circumstances, for example, if the ex-student only works for a few months during the year. Interest will be charged at the rate of inflation.

Loans cannot be transferred to an ex-student's estate if s/he dies – the liability dies with her/him. Loans will be cancelled if the ex-student reaches 65 years without repaying her/his loan. Loans made under the Student Support Scheme (income contingent) cannot be excluded from being a bankruptcy debt and therefore should be listed on the petition. They will be released when the bankrupt is discharged. Student loans can be included in an individual voluntary agreement (IVA) or administration order (England and Wales).

Borrowers with disabilities

Any disability benefits received will not count towards the threshold income (even if they are taxable). If a student has a disability at the time s/he takes out the loan and is receiving a disability-related state benefit, s/he can have ten years to repay the loan if s/he can show that s/he is unfit for full-time work and that s/he is unlikely to be fit for at least the next three years. The Regulations state that if the Secretary of State is satisfied that, because of her/his disability, the ex-student is permanently unfit for work and s/he is receiving a disability-related benefit, liability for the loan is cancelled. There is no further guidance on how this is done and no definition of 'permanently unfit for work'. If the client complies with other welfare benefit definitions of permanently unfit, advisers can use this when negotiating to have the debt cancelled.

Debts to the institution

Students are often in debt to their institutions for a wide variety of items, such as library fines, hardship loans, rent, tuition fees, accommodation and disciplinary fines. University regulations govern the circumstances in which fines may be imposed and fees are due. Liability should always be checked and appeal mechanisms used, where appropriate.

The main sources of students' indebtedness to their institutions are discussed below.

Accommodation charges

Most institutions provide some accommodation for their students. Charges are made for the rent and services provided. Services usually include items such as fuel and cleaning. These charges may be called 'residence' or 'accommodation' fees.

Legal position

Rent is payable under the tenancy agreement or licence. The terms of these agreements may be in an individual's contract or in university regulations.

Special features

The amount of accommodation provided directly by institutions to students varies a great deal. Some of this accommodation is within halls of residence, some will be in houses/flats in the locality owned by the university or leased to it by private landlords for the purpose of accommodating students.

The length of tenancies may vary but are rarely longer than 52 weeks. Especially in halls of residence, many tenancies will be for the academic year only – excluding the summer vacation. Some tenancies exclude all vacations. The usual practice is to charge three instalments. There may be a financial penalty for late payment. As in the case of tuition fees, students in financial difficulties may be able to negotiate delayed payments or a more flexible instalment arrangement.

The accommodation charge due for a student's current home is a priority debt. Whilst institutions are often reluctant to evict or take/precipitate court action against their own students, they do try and enforce the repayment using other means, for example by refusing to allow the student to return to university-managed accommodation in subsequent years.

Fines/other charges

Certain costs incurred by students arise from fines or charges. If an appeal procedure exists to resolve disputes about liability or amounts, students should be encouraged to use it. Advisers may be able to assist by providing supporting information or representing students where this is allowed. In some cases, institutions will take into account extenuating circumstances and may waive or reduce certain fines or charges.

The consequences of non-payment will differ both between institutions and according to the circumstances of each student. For instance, where a debt for tuition fees could legally prevent the student from graduating, it could also prevent her/him from progressing to a course of further study or employment and, therefore, needs to be treated as a priority debt. However, where withholding the qualifications would not impede the student's progress, the debt should be treated as non-priority. A student may consider any outstanding debts to an institution where s/he wishes to continue studying to be a priority. Advisers need to discuss this carefully with her/him, especially if the student has mistaken notions of the consequences of non-payment.

Tuition fees

As from 1998/99 the majority of full-time students have been means-tested for a contribution to their tuition fees. However, the legislation surrounding tuition fees is under review in devolved parts of the UK. The 'Review of Student Support' set up in November 2001 had yet to report at the time of writing. Changes are already being implemented in Wales and Northern Ireland. Further information and guidance about the changes will need to be sought from the relevant assemblies/executives and from the DfES website (see Appendix 5).

Most students will be asked to supply their LEA with their (parents', spouse's, own) financial details. This information will then be used to assess any contribution towards tuition fees. If the LEA deems that the student is to make a contribution and s/he subsequently does not make a payment, this will be a debt to the respective university (not to the LEA).

Part-time undergraduate students who are studying at least 50 per cent of a full-time course are eligible for help with tuition fees if they:

- are on income-related benefits; *or*
- receive tax credits due to low income; *or*
- earn less than £10,000 net; *or*
- lose their job after the course begins.

There is no age limit on help for tuition fees.

Colleges can use their discretion to support students who are studying full time despite having a degree. However, tuition fee help will only be available if a student falls into the final category – ie, s/he loses her/his job after the course began.

Some students will have a mixed award, where some of the fees are paid and they have to make up the remainder. Problems can arise for students who start university not knowing how much they will have to pay towards their fees because of delays in the applications process. Institutions are aware of these delays and should be sensitive and receptive to reasonable requests for delays in payment – however, unless informed of the delays, a late payment can be added to the debt. The student must therefore communicate the difficulties to the university in order to avoid late charges.

Students who begin their studies having been assessed to make a contribution and then subsequently leave should be given a date by which they can do so without having to pay anything towards their fees. This date is fixed by the university. Where tuition fee support is to be paid by the LEA, the date is fixed at 1 December. Advisers should argue with the institution that the date should also be the same for the fee-paying student, though the institution is under no obligation to do so. Beyond that date there is some scope for negotiation to allow the fee to be divided over the academic year minus holidays, with the student only paying for the period s/he has actually attended. Where students who have to pay fees subsequently transfer from one university to another, the two institutions must negotiate with each other regarding the transfer of the payment. For students who transfer before 1 December, no fees should be paid to the first institution.

Transfers where local education authority contributes to fees

The most important aspect about transferring support when a student transfers, is the date s/he is required to start, not the date s/he expects to begin attending. LEAs determine this date (eg, 1 September is a common start date).

If a student transfers at the end of the first year and secures the transfer before the required start date, s/he can transfer her/his eligibility for full support.

If a student wishes to transfer after studying for more than one year s/he will be eligible for support for a number of years equal to the length of either the first or the second course, whichever is longer.

Example
A student studies for two years on a three-year course, then transfers to a four-year course. She will receive a total of four years' support – equivalent to the length of the new course as this is the longer. This means that the student has to pay the fees for the two years during which the LEA does not offer support.

Regardless of support for fees, the loan and supplementary grants will be available (where eligible) provided normal requirements are met and the transfer has been made in accordance with the regulations.

Students who are not exempted from the attendance rule for fees (see p355) are not eligible for future fee support, though other forms of assistance may be available (see p346).

Recovery of debts to the institution

Methods of recovery vary between institutions. Many will not allow a student to continue into the next year of study if debts are outstanding. Where the debt is for tuition fees, this procedure is probably perfectly legitimate. However, some institutions will not permit continuation where other charges are outstanding (eg, accommodation fees and library fines). This practice is probably unlawful and should be challenged. Similarly, where debts remain at the end of the student's course, most institutions refuse to give the student a certificate of qualification or allow her/him to collect her/his results. Questions arise as to the legality of this position. As yet, the practice has not been tested in the courts, but refusal to award a degree certificate for non-payment of charges other than tuition fees is unlikely to be legitimate.

Institutions may make threats that are not legally permissible in order to ensure payment. These practices put students under considerable pressure to pay outstanding charges and may constitute harassment under the Administration of Justice Act 1970 (see p33). However, most students are anxious not to jeopardise their future and are most reluctant to take any action other than to clear their debts in full.

Recent legislation, such as the Freedom of Information Act and the Data Protection Act 1998, may force institutions to re-evaluate these practices and gives the adviser more options to explore when assisting clients who owe debts to the institutions. Advisers directly employed by the institution need to be aware of the potential conflict of interest when advising a student with debts to the same institution.

Overpaid mandatory awards

See also Chapter 6.

Students are required to repay some, or all, of their LEA grant for living costs if it has either been overpaid or if they leave their course (both temporarily or permanently) during a period for which a grant instalment has been paid in advance. In this latter case, the amount of grant for the weeks after the student has left her/his course will be calculated and repayment of only this amount is required.

Legal position

LEAs have a statutory duty to recover overpaid awards. The legislation requires them to do so during the period of the award – ie, before the student completes her/his course.

Special features

Practices vary between LEAs, but normally the authority will attempt to recover the amount – in full – by deducting it from the next instalment.

Advisers need to negotiate with the LEA in the usual way, arriving at an affordable level of repayment. However, where a student continues to receive a grant, the LEA is in an extremely powerful position as it holds the instrument of recovery in its own hands – the next instalment. Advisers should be aware that whilst it is the LEA's statutory duty to recover during the period of the award, reductions of each future grant instalment are permissible within the legislation. If the LEA remains unwilling to extend the repayment period, evidence of hardship needs to be presented, perhaps to elected members of the authority concerned as well as officers. The Regulations state that the recovery action to be taken should be appropriate to the circumstances and so the adviser should ensure that the LEA is fully aware of the student's situation.

Overpaid student loans – mortgage style

See p338 for the definition and legal position.

These loans are regulated under the Consumer Credit Act. Repayment arrangements will vary depending on negotiations between the student/adviser and the Student Loans Company. Advisers should suggest to the Student Loans Company that the time period for repaying the overpayment should reflect the period of time allowed for repayment.

Overpaid student loans – income contingent ('new' students)

See p339 for definition and legal position.

Special features

This type of student loan is not regulated by the Consumer Credit Act. If the loan has been made properly (ie, the student is eligible but the amount is classed as an overpayment) it can be recovered from the amount of loan for which the student is eligible for the following academic year. If the student has completed her/his studies recovery should be through the normal repayment process, though advisers may need to negotiate with the Student Loans Company for this to happen.

Overpaid hardship loans

Most students are eligible for hardship loans, which are means-tested by the institution. It should be argued that as the need for this additional loan was assessed by the institution, its authorisation means that there cannot have been an overpayment. Hardship loans are added to the student loan – see above.

4. Minimising debt

See also Chapter 5.

Reducing council tax bills

Advisers must examine the student's liability for council tax. Any dwelling solely occupied by students is exempt for council tax purposes. Where a student lives with non-students, s/he may be liable to pay council tax, but the bill may be reduced because full-time students attract a status discount. Thus, where the number of people living in the dwelling is less than two, not counting any person who may be disregarded for discount purposes, a discount should be awarded. That is, where a full-time student lives with one other 'visible' person, the council tax bill should be reduced by 25 per cent.

Institutions may provide local authorities with lists of full-time students attending courses and, where requested, will issue a letter to a student establishing her/his status. Some institutions charge the student for this letter. Advisers should argue that this is not appropriate. Students should inform council tax offices of their status in order to obtain exemption from, or reduction of, council tax.

See also CPAG's *Council Tax Handbook* for more information.

5. Maximising income

Student support in the UK is undergoing a review. The current funding arrangements are extremely complex, with student entitlement depending on a range of variables. There are now a number of funding arrangements in place or about to be introduced. It will be necessary for advisers to check eligibility using regulations and guidance issued by the appropriate funding body. The system of funding for Scottish students has always differed from the rest of the UK and this has changed further with the abolition of up-front tuition fees and the introduction on non-repayable bursaries.

The Northern Ireland Assembly has announced its intention to re-introduce means-tested non-repayable grants, and to extend the number of students who are exempt from paying tuition fees. The Welsh Assembly has launched a new means-tested, non-repayable Assembly Learning Grant.

Entitlements will vary depending upon where the student is domiciled and where s/he is studying. Regulations are not yet available and so it is not possible to anticipate the details of these new arrangements. The student funding covered in this section is therefore limited to that which is currently in payment.

Local education authority mandatory awards (pre-1998 students)

The 1962 Education Act established the local education authority's (LEA's) duty to bestow an award on a student in respect of her/his attendance on a designated course if s/he was 'ordinarily resident'. The Act, under which regulations were made was repealed on the 1 January 1999. The Education (Mandatory Awards) Regulations are, therefore limited to ensure that students who began their courses before September 1998, and certain other exceptions, continue to receive awards until the end of their course. There will only be a tiny minority of students in receipt of such an award. If an adviser needs to check eligibility, s/he should use The Education (Mandatory Awards) Regulations Notes for Guidance.

Help with tuition fees

Help is available to meet the cost of tuition fees – this is assessed on the student's income and that of her/his family (if s/he does not qualify for independent status.) The LEA will assess eligibility and income. The student may be liable for all, part or none of the tuition fee. Advisers need to check the assessment has been done correctly. If the student has had a change of circumstances or the family income has decreased s/he may be able to request that the LEA reassess the level of help given.

Previous attendance on a higher education course will rule out the student from help from the LEA with tuition fees.

Previous attendance

Students are not eligible for support for fees for a second course (some students are exempt – see below), but are eligible for loans for living costs – ie, loans and any appropriate supplementary grants.

There are exceptions to the previous study rules:
• False starts. Students who wish to make a fresh start can do so, provided the previous course was for one academic year or the student only attended for

one academic year. The student must have completed or withdrawn from the course by the day before the start of the next academic year.

- There are special rules for students who have attended courses for less than two years, though the LEA may not allow full support. There are three scenarios where they are entitled to full support:
  - an additional year in higher education;
  - the final year of a subsequent course of two years' study;
  - the total number of years of a subsequent course which is two years less than its duration, when support is given for the latter years of the course.
- Students on courses of initial teacher training of not more than two years are exempt from the previous study rule, unless they have already studied for a teaching qualification.

Student loans – income contingent

Students are required to meet the personal eligibility requirements, detailed in the Education (Student Support) Regulations 1999 to be able to receive support. In order to support themselves students are able to get support from loans, grants (for certain groups of students), access bursaries and hardship funds. Full-time, sandwich and part-time initial teacher training students who are aged 55 or under are eligible for a student loan.

In addition to the basic (75 per cent) non-means-tested loan, students can get an extra amount, equivalent to 25 per cent of the maximum loan available. This element of the loan is means-tested on parental/spousal income (or, on the student's own income if s/he fulfils the independent status requirements). Students apply to their LEA, initially to see how much they are able to borrow and then their application is made to the Student Loans Company. Rates depend on the year of study, whether the student is living in the parental home, away from home, or in London.

Students aged 50 to 54

Students who are eligible and who are aged 50 to 54 and intend to enter employment after they complete their studies can take out an income-contingent loan. Applicants must state that they plan to work after their course when they apply.

Extra weeks

Students can apply for a set amount for each additional week they have to attend the course on top of the basic academic year. The amount of extra weeks' allowance depends on whether the student is living in the parental home, away from home or in London. The allowances are made in addition to the student loan and so have to be repaid in the same way.

Students studying abroad

Additional support is available to students who spend time studying abroad as part of their course (the period abroad does not have to be a compulsory part of the course). The extra amount is paid at different rates depending upon the country. Repayment arrangements are the same as for the basic loan.

Change in circumstances

If a student has a change in circumstances during the year s/he should inform the LEA in order to obtain a reassessment of the level of loan s/he can take out.

Members of religious orders

These students are currently eligible for support for living costs, but if the student lives in the house of the order the support will be at the parental home rate.

Additional grants

These additions, although part of the 'new' arrangements, are non-repayable grants.

Disabled student's allowance

Part-time, full-time, postgraduate or undergraduate students who have a disability which makes it more expensive for them to take their course, may be entitled to a number of extra allowances. These will be in the form of non-repayable grants. These are the same as for students receiving mandatory awards under the 'old' system. For full details, see the Education (Student Support) Regulations 1999.

Dependant's grant

Students with dependants are entitled to a dependant's grant which consists of a dependant's allowance (means-tested), a books, travel and equipment grant (means-tested), and a childcare grant (means-tested). There is also a school meals grant (see below).

The dependant's grant is payable if the student has another member of the family who depends on her/him for financial support. The amount of help is means-tested and based on the number of dependants. The Student Loans Company pays the dependant's grant, even though it is not repayable. Advisers need to recognise the potential difficulty the student may have with budgeting when in receipt of the dependant's allowance, as it is paid in three instalments.

Childcare grants are for children under the age of 15 at the start of the academic year (or if the child has special needs under 17). Help is only for 'formal' care by registered and approved childcare providers. The student will receive help with 85 per cent of her/his childcare costs during the semester and short Christmas and Easter vacations and 70 per cent of the costs during the long summer vacation. Students under the previous mandatory system have the option of switching from the old lone parent's grant to the childcare package. Advisers need to do a better-off calculation in order to ascertain which would be better for the student.

The childcare funding system is complicated and confusing for all involved. This system is also currently under review by the Department for Education and Skills (DfES) with the aim of making it easier to understand, the administration more streamlined and consequently enabling more students to take up the package. It is not clear whether the amount of help students will receive will increase.

Travel allowances

Students with disabilities, students who attend an institution outside the UK for at least eight weeks (whether obligatory or optional) and those who must attend a place in the UK away from their main college as part of a medical, dental or nursing course, are entitled to help with their travelling expenses above the normal allowance paid in their loan.

Care leaver's grant

This is an allowance that is intended to help students who have been in care with their accommodation costs during the long vacation. It applies to students who are under 21 on the first day of the course, where the parental contribution does not apply, and where in the opinion of the LEA the student is subject to greater financial hardship because of previously being in care. These students usually do not have access to parental home and/or support during the long vacation and many institutions' accommodation is only available during term time. Payment is not automatic. It is paid for each week of the long vacation and cannot be paid for any week in which the student attends her/his course, even for one day. This provision is not available to those students who have independent status as a result of being estranged from their families.

School meals grant

This grant is available to all students to meet the cost of school meals for dependent children. It is not means-tested. Payment is made through the LEA.

Hardship loans

Additional loans can be added to a student's main loan account if the student is in serious financial difficulty during her/his course. To be eligible the student must have applied for her/his full loan entitlement and be in receipt of the first instalment. The institution decides how much the student could receive based on a means test. Loans are payable in amounts from £100 to £500.

NHS bursaries

These are paid for health professional courses including: nursing, midwifery, physiotherapy, radiology, chiropody, dental hygiene, dental therapy, dietetics, occupational therapy, orthoptics, prosthetics and orthotics (England only), speech and language therapy. There are two types of NHS bursary. Students studying for a diploma are paid a non-means-tested bursary covering 45 weeks. Additional allowances include a dependant's allowance for the first child; a single parent addition; and older students' allowances (for students aged 26 and over). These students cannot apply for student loans, hardship loans, NHS hardship grants or institutions' hardship funds. Students following a degree course receive a means-tested bursary. Additional allowances include those for older students, dependants and lone parents. They are also eligible for student and hardship loans, and both NHS and institutions' hardship funds.

From 2004 childcare grants will be available for both diploma and degree level students.

Teacher training incentives

There are incentives available for those undertaking postgraduate courses that lead to qualified teacher status. Home and European Union (EU) national students can apply to have their fees paid by the LEA.

In England, training bursaries are paid as well (except to those who already are qualified as teachers or are employed as teachers). These do not need to be applied for and are paid by monthly instalments (usually over nine months).In addition to these bursaries there is a 'Secondary Shortage Subject Scheme'. This scheme is eligible to home and EU graduates on Key Stage 2/3 or secondary level courses in maths, science, modern languages, design and technology, information technology, geography, music and religious education which leads to qualified teacher status at institutions in England. It is subject to an assessment of income and the award made depends upon the level of student need with an upper limit set centrally (2002/03: up to £5,000 for trainees under 25; up to £7,500 for trainees over 25). As with the hardship fund (see p357) the maximum awards are only made in cases of exceptional hardship. The scheme is administered by the institution.

In Wales, home and EU graduates on postgraduate courses leading to qualified teacher status at institutions in Wales (except those already qualified as teachers or employed as teachers) receive a training grant (2002/03: £6,000). The institution arranges for this to be paid. It is paid by monthly instalments (usually over nine months). In addition, for those studying maths, science, modern languages, information technology or Welsh at secondary level and receiving the main teaching grant there is an additional teaching grant payable on successful completion of the first year (2002/03: £4,000). Application is to the National Assembly for Wales and payment is by lump sum directly into a bank account.

Undergraduates can apply for secondary undergraduates placement grants, paid by the institution in two instalments. The rate payable depends on whether the subject is a shortage subject or not. Additional hardship funding (see p357) can also be available to both undergraduate and postgraduate students who experience financial difficulties which could prevent them finishing their course. Some students studying in Welsh can apply for Welsh medium incentive supplements. Application is to the institution.

Bank overdrafts

The major banks and some building societies offer interest-free overdraft facilities on students' current accounts, up to a set limit. These limits change each year and vary between banks. The special facility is essential to most students in maximising income, both to cover temporary periods of cash-flow shortage, for example, between payments of grant instalments, and for long-term financial management.

Prospective students with existing bank accounts should change to a student account with either their own or a different bank, in order to benefit from the facilities offered. When choosing which bank to open or transfer an account, students need to consider the following factors, rather than any 'free gifts' on offer:

- Which bank offers the largest interest-free overdraft, and the period for which it is offered – generally these extend beyond the end of the course, but can vary.
- The proximity of the bank to where the student lives or studies.
- Whether there are reciprocal cashpoint facilities to avoid charges on transactions.
- The interest rates and charges imposed for exceeding the interest-free facility.
- The attitude of campus bank managers or student advisers in local banks – debt advisers in institutions or students' unions can be consulted on these matters.

Managers of campus banks are usually more conversant with the intricacies of student finance and, therefore, more sympathetic and realistic when difficulties arise.

A student's credit rating will be checked when s/he opens a new account. S/he may be refused the usual student deal if there is a recorded history of credit problems. A student requires an account that will accept direct credits in order to receive her/his student loan. If a student has no bank account and is refused one because of her/his credit rating, the money adviser in the institution or students' union may be able to negotiate with the local or campus bank manager.

Bank loans

Banks will sometimes offer loans to students at competitive rates. A student should be advised, however, that the interest rates on loans from the Student

Loans Company make them a cheaper form of long-term borrowing. A bank loan is usually offered towards the end of the student's course. If overdraft facilities appear no longer appropriate, the bank may offer to convert the overdraft to a loan. This offers the advantages of a lower interest rate than the excess overdraft and allows the student access to additional funds. However, unless the loan has a deferred repayment arrangement, the repayments are usually much greater than can be met from the student's income, and may create an overdraft in the student's current account that will result in her/him paying interest on two accounts. In this way, it can become a very expensive, usually unmanageable, option. Advisers should be aware that most banks will now allow students terms on their overdraft to extend to graduation and beyond (in some cases for a number of years) and may, therefore, be a cheaper option.

Students often feel pressured into accepting loan arrangements, as the banks present them as a positive alternative and are reluctant to allow further borrowing on any other terms. The student will often be better off by ceasing to use the existing bank account and using an ordinary building society savings account. Advisers can then negotiate with the bank as with any other creditor. This strategy will, however, result in the loss of the interest-free overdraft facility to the student.

See also information on postgraduate loans on p353.

Career development loans

Career development loans (CDLs) are deferred repayment personal loans available through a partnership between the DfES and four high street banks. Interest on the loan is paid by the DfES during the period of the course and for up to one month after. Repayment is deferred for the same period – longer periods of deferment are available (see p337).

In practice, CDLs are usually only available for certain types of postgraduate courses (full time or part time). This is because the course must last no longer than two years (although CDLs can be considered for up to two years of a longer course or a three-year course that includes work experience). Applicants must be over 18 and must not have reasonable and adequate access to funds for their course or mandatory funding. There are rules regarding the student's intentions after completion of the course – the student must live or plan to train in the UK or European Economic Area. While non-EU nationals are eligible to apply for a CDL they must seek special permission from the Home Office in order to study, train or work in the UK after their studies. Refer to UKCOSA for advice (see Appendix 5). CDLs are only available for vocational courses. Students can borrow between £300 and £8,000 to pay for up to 80 per cent of course fees, plus the full cost of books, materials and other related expenses. If the student has been out of work for three months or longer s/he can apply for 100 per cent of the course fees and, if the course is full time, living expenses. Banks will consider applications after the course has already started.

Further information about CDLs can be obtained from participating high street bank.

Advisers can assist students to make a realistic assessment of all non-course costs to ensure that an adequate loan is requested. Also, students should be advised to compare CDLs to postgraduate loans from banks (see below), as the interest rates and repayment terms of the latter can be more favourable. Where a student who receives means-tested benefits obtains a CDL to fund her/his course, the CDL is treated as income. If this reduces benefit entitlement, the student should consider paying her/his tuition fees in full at the beginning of the course instead of the more usual instalment methods.

Postgraduate loans

Some of the major banks make personal loans available to postgraduate students to cover their course fees and living costs. The loans usually offer deferred repayments, which begin only after the course has finished. Some of these loans are available for specific courses, especially those leading to professional qualifications. The terms and amounts of loans vary between different banks and students need to check which is most suitable for them, and how the terms offered compare with those available from a CDL if they are pursuing a course for which either might be payable. Students also need to consider whether they can afford the amount of indebtedness involved, which could exceed £5,000 a year.

Postgraduate students can apply to the Arts and Humanities Research Board or to other research councils (see Appendix 5 for details). Disabled postgraduate students considering applications to research councils or who are receiving bursaries will not be eligible for disabled student's allowance (see p348), so the adviser should do a better-off calculation to assess which would be the better option for the particular student.

Postgraduate bursaries

A variety of bodies make awards, but usually only one is appropriate to a particular area of study. It can be difficult to obtain an offer of grant aid to fund postgraduate study, especially in the arts and social sciences. A student can obtain appropriate information and assistance from the departments in which s/he intends to study and the university careers service. Students should begin their enquiries well in advance of the start of their course – applications may need to be made at the start of the academic year before the year in which they intend to study. There are numerous research councils that offer postgraduate funding and other organisations which offer awards for vocational courses. A limited number of companies offer assistance to postgraduates. Sponsorship is usually linked to particular courses and institutions, rather than individual students. Students should be advised to contact the appropriate careers/advice centres at the relevant institution.

Benefits

This section is intended as a general guide to eligibility. Advisers should refer to CPAG's *Welfare Benefits Handbook* for full details. The National Union of Students released a survey in February 2002[2] that said that 'Students Would be Better off on Benefits'. It went on to say that thousands live below the poverty line. Despite this, most full-time students are not eligible to claim welfare benefits. There are a few groups which are not excluded from the means-tested benefits system. These are:

- lone parents (if the child is under 16 years old);
- students with disabilities;
- pensioners;
- students from abroad who are temporarily without funds (seek further advice on this from UKCOSA – see Appendix 5);
- people who have refugee status and who are learning English;
- two full-time students with responsibility for a child under 16 years old (though only eligible for help during the long summer vacation).

Some students will be eligible for non-means-tested benefits and, therefore, means-tested elements at certain times of the year.

Advisers need to highlight the rules regarding entitlement to benefit, and to advise students not to accept Department for Work and Pensions (DWP) or local authority statements that students cannot claim benefit.

The DWP and local authorities find the calculation of students' entitlement highly complex. In many offices it is rare for the first decision to be correct. Students must be advised to have their claims checked by an expert in the institution, students' union, or local advice centre.

Advisers need to check that decision makers do not include the student loan as income for students who are ineligible for loans. Advisers also need to inform students who are entitled to benefits, but who are reluctant to take out a loan or a full loan, that the full loan will be taken into account whether or not it is taken out.

Career development loans are also taken into account as income. However, most of this income is ignored. Only that part of the loan paid and used for certain living costs is taken into account (for full details, see CPAG's *Welfare Benefits Handbook*).

Where a student receives allowances towards extra expenses due to disability (see p348), these are disregarded in full when calculating her/his benefit entitlement.

Council tax benefit

Full-time students are not liable for council tax if they live in accommodation occupied solely by students (or other persons who are exempt).

Those who are liable for council tax are entitled to council tax benefit (CTB) during their period of study only if they fall into one of a small number of categories. Advisers need to check whether their client falls into one of these categories, or if s/he has a partner who is eligible to claim CTB on her/his behalf. Further, the period of study applicable in each case should be checked as, in most cases (and unlike income support (IS)), this excludes the summer vacation and, therefore, the enquirer may be eligible to claim during that period.

For further details, see CPAG's *Welfare Benefits Handbook*.

Health benefits
See also Chapter 6.

Students under 19 and those on IS, income-based jobseeker's allowance (JSA) and some tax credit claimants qualify for health benefits. Otherwise, students must apply for assistance on the grounds of low income using Form HC1. These forms are often held by student services departments in institutions, students' unions/guilds/associations or health centres.

For further details, see CPAG's *Welfare Benefits Handbook*.

Housing benefit
Advisers need to check whether their client is exempt from the rule that full-time students are not entitled to housing benefit (HB), or whether s/he has a partner who is eligible to claim on her/his behalf. Even those students who are not disqualified by the full-time student rules may still fail to be entitled during their period of study where they pay rent to their own educational establishment. (This does not apply, however, where the institution itself rents the accommodation from a third party – for certain exceptions, see CPAG's *Welfare Benefits Handbook*.)

The period of study applicable should be checked as, in most cases (and unlike IS), this excludes the summer vacation and, therefore, the student may be eligible to claim during that period.

Some students who need to maintain two homes may be eligible for payment of housing costs on both (see CPAG's *Welfare Benefits Handbook*).

In most instances, HB is reduced by the 'student rent reduction' during the period of study (ie, the first day of each academic year until the day before the start of the summer vacation). Advisers may need to re-check entitlement to HB for students to whom this reduction should not be applied. The parental contribution will be disregarded.

For further details, see CPAG's *Welfare Benefits Handbook*.

Income support
Advisers should check whether their client is exempt from the rule that full-time students are not entitled to IS, or whether s/he has a partner who is eligible to claim on her/his behalf.

Particular caution with regard to vacation employment needs to be exercised by students who receive payments for housing costs/mortgage interest as part of their entitlement to IS. Advisers need to check that the hours and/or level of earnings do not result in a loss of entitlement to IS for any period exceeding the 12-week linking period for payment of housing costs/mortgage interest.

Under certain circumstances, a student or her/his partner may be entitled to housing costs/mortgage interest for two homes.

For further details, see CPAG's *Welfare Benefits Handbook*.

Income-based jobseeker's allowance

If the student has a partner who is able to claim income-based JSA, the same precautions with regard to vacation employment and housing costs as with IS need to be observed.

For further details, see CPAG's *Welfare Benefits Handbook*.

Students taking time out (intercalating students)

For a number of reasons, some students need to leave their course temporarily, for example, because of ill health, suspension due to exam failure, family or personal problems. Benefit regulations state that full-time students are excluded from IS, HB and CTB for the whole duration of their period of study. For precise definitions of this period in relation to each benefit, see CPAG's *Welfare Benefits Handbook*. Students who are exempt from the full-time student rule are entitled to those benefits during a period of temporary absence from their course.

Students who take time out because of sickness may be able to claim IS once they become classed as a 'disabled student', that is, where they have been sick for 28 weeks. Whilst students cannot get IS or JSA while they are ill (unless they are classed as a 'disabled student') they can however claim JSA, HB, and CTB once the illness or caring responsibilities have come to an end. They can claim from this point until they restart the course or up to the day before they start the new academic year. They can only qualify if they are not eligible for student support during this period.

For others the definition of the meaning of student in the regulations results in intercalating students still being treated as though they were on a full-time course and therefore not entitled to IS, HB and CTB.

Charities

See also p112.

There are many charities whose terms of reference are directed at providing assistance to students. However, most of these are unable to meet the level of demand placed upon them since the reduction in mainstream funding to students.

Applications are more likely to succeed if the student is close to completing her/his course, and/or where funding arrangements have broken down. There are a number of fund-finding vehicles specialising in helping students access money from trusts and charities, such as the Educational Grants Advisory Service and Funderfinder. These can make the process less time-consuming for students.

Hardship funds

Hardship funds are cash-limited allocations made annually to higher education institutions by central government (via the funding councils). Hardship funds can only be used to help students from the following groups:

- all home students on a full-time or part-time course of higher education at a level above first degree;
- all home students on a full-time (including sandwich but excluding a year out) or part-time course of higher education, other than postgraduates;
- all home students following full-time (including sandwich but excluding year out courses) or part-time courses of further education, who are aged 16 or over.

Students who have temporarily suspended their studies are still eligible to apply for hardship funds.

Students on a part-time course are only eligible for hardship funds if their course is a minimum of 60 credit points in an academic year where the full-time time equivalent is 120 credits, or if they are studying at least 50 per cent of a full-time course.

Further, if a student is entitled to a student loan, s/he must have taken out a loan in the current academic year before being eligible for help from the hardship fund. (The student does not have to take out the additional student hardship loan if they are aged over 25, disabled or has dependants.) Institutions devise their own criteria and priorities for allocation within government guidelines, although this is currently under review. Some students' unions/guilds/associations are actively involved in the administration. The overall purpose of hardship funds is to provide financial help to students whose access to higher education might be limited by financial constraints, or who face financial hardship. Hardship funds are not payable to students who receive a non-means-tested NHS bursary or who are salaried NHS employees.

Advisers can assist students to make successful applications in certain ways:

- By ascertaining the criteria and priorities of a particular institution's funds, and providing evidence or a supporting letter to show how the particular student meets these criteria. Although institutions generally devise their own priorities, hardship funds are specifically required to assist students who meet certain criteria. These are: part-time undergraduate students who lose their job after beginning their course, or who are in receipt of certain benefits (IS, income-based JSA, HB or CTB), tax credits or whose family income is below the threshold for receiving IS, and are eligible to have their fees waived through assistance from access funds. (Hardship funds cannot be used for fee remission for full-time students.) Students whose net annual income is at broadly the same level as tax credit recipients (£11,543 in 2002/03) (even if the student is not actually receiving tax credits) will also be considered for fee waivers. The Foyer Federation is a charity that works with young homeless, and the bursary payable (the suggested amount is £1,000 for each year of the course) is mainly to help meet accommodation costs outside of term time but can be used for general course costs and living costs. Foyer students will be included as a priority from 2002 and local foyers should bring the student to the attention of the institution. Foyer bursary commitments should be given for the duration of the course. Hardship funds may be used for emergency payments/loans to help students who have not yet received their loan cheque at the start of the year.

- By encouraging enquirers to make applications even if they are outside the application dates, although being aware that the fund is cash-limited and funds are likely to be low/exhausted at certain times of the year.

Many hardship fund administrators will make emergency grants or interest-free loans where appropriate. Institutions are encouraged to set aside money to assist with financial difficulties arising during the summer vacation.

Hardship funds are required to have an appeal procedure. Thus, if a student has been refused a payment, or paid too little, advisers should assist her/him to use this procedure. Even successful applicants should be advised to re-apply if their circumstances change during the year, as further assistance could be forthcoming.

Many hardship fund administrators have a great deal of discretion in deciding or recommending grants, and have to process vast numbers of applications. Intervention by an adviser on behalf of a student could be most effective in improving her/his prospects.

Hardship fund administrators have the power to make third party payments, including payments direct to creditors. Creditors who are pressing for payment are often willing to allow more time where a payment is to be made directly by an institution of higher education.

For the purpose of means-tested benefits, payments from the hardship fund are treated as voluntary and charitable payments (see CPAG's *Welfare Benefits Handbook*).

Access bursaries

These bursaries are available to full-time student parents (or part-time students studying to be teachers) who need help with the cost of childcare. They are administrated by the institution and should be applied for before starting a course. Access bursaries are paid to those students with children who are eligible for a dependant's grant, childcare grant or both. Payments are up to a set level (£500 in 2002/03), although the institution has the discretion to give a higher bursary if it considers it appropriate. As well as covering childcare costs the bursaries can be used to pay for course-related costs, such as books or travel not met by the books and travel grant, or for educational expenses for their children – eg, school uniform, sports kit, school trips and so on. They may also be used for other child-related expenses if provided as a single payment. Continuing students who received a bursary in their previous year should be considered for a bursary and unless their circumstances have changed these should be awarded at the same level of support as the previous year.

Opportunity bursaries

Opportunity bursaries are intended for young students from low-income families who have had little or no experience of higher education. They are paid in three instalments over their course (in 2002/03 this is £1,000 in the first year and £500 in each of the next two years). To be eligible:

- the pupil must be studying in a state school or college in an Excellence in Cities (EiC) Phase 1 or 2 /education action zone;
- the pupil must be a home student;
- the pupil must be from a family with little or no experience of higher education; *and*
- the pupil must be in receipt of an education maintenance allowance which is above or equivalent to the amount payable where the family income is below £20,000; *or*
- her/his family has a gross income of £20,000; *or*
- the family must be in receipt of either IS, HB, income-based JSA or incapacity benefit.

Working families' tax credit/disabled families' tax credit is not an automatic qualification for an opportunity bursary, as family income may still exceed the £20,000 threshold. Where the family's sole income is from welfare benefits and they receive any of the following non-means-tested benefits:

- incapacity benefit;
- severe disablement benefit;
- disability living allowance;

then they meet the criteria for an opportunity bursary; however, the family income will still need to be below the £20,000 threshold.

All full-time higher education undergraduate courses in England that attract student support are eligible for these bursaries.

Additional funds to assist students

Most institutions and some students' unions/guilds/associations and religious groups at the institution have a number of small funds available to meet specific circumstances, as well as general hardship funds. Some funds will make grants, others will make interest-free loans available. Students should consult the student services department or students' union/guild/association at their own institution for advice.

Employment

See also the section on benefits (pp354 to 356) for the impact of working on students claiming benefits and p360 for information on tax refunds.

Traditionally, undergraduate students have worked during their vacation periods; many now work part time through the term time as well. Income from part-time or casual work is disregarded for the purposes of assessing student support. Advisers need to warn students of the danger of relying on vacation work to supplement their mainstream income. Annual budgeting based on the expectation of an income from vacation work will falter if a job fails to materialise or is offered for fewer hours or weeks than anticipated.

More full-time students are now taking employment during term time. Increasingly, institutions and students' unions provide information regarding jobs available to students. Most students' unions host Jobshops and there is a national organisation called NASES which has grown out of the volume of these types of services up and down the country. The institution may have regulations restricting the number of hours students are allowed to work. Aside from these, advisers need to assist clients balance their time between employment and study, and to check that the student is profiting financially from the work after travel expenses, etc, are taken into account.

Tax refunds

A student who has been working prior to her/his course, or for part of the year, should be advised to claim a refund of income tax when the employment ceases. S/he can apply on a form P50. These are usually available from students' unions/guilds or tax offices. The form should be submitted to the tax office of her/his last employer, along with the student's P45.

Tax concessions

In order to gain the maximum benefit from term-time and vacation employment, a student who is working and earning under the appropriate tax allowance can arrange that no income tax be deducted from her/his wages. The student will need to declare that her/his total taxable income in the whole of that financial year will not exceed her/his personal allowance for the same period. For vacation employment the employer needs to complete Form P38S and submit it to the tax office. At any other time a P46 will need to be completed.

6. Dealing with priority debts

See Chapter 7.

Deciding on priority debts to the institution

Certain debts to the institution may need to be treated as priority debts because of the consequences of non-payment. Wherever non-payment carries a legitimate threat of loss of accommodation, the debt should be treated as a priority (as outlined in Chapter 7). However, in addition, there are some cases where the legitimate threat of not being able to continue with study or to be allowed to graduate will lead to prioritisation. See p343 for those debts that could lead to this.

Notes

1. **Introduction**
   1 For the extract of the judgment, see Notes for Guidance, Education (Student Support) Regulations 1999

5. **Maximising income**
   2 *The Times Higher Education Supplement* 22/02/02; NUS, 'Students Would be Better off on Benefits' based on figures from a Unite report.

Appendix 1

· ·

Relevant legislation

This appendix includes some of the most frequently used legislation in money advice, and which is referred to in this *Handbook*. This is contained, with detailed notes, in the *Civil Court Practice* (the Green Book) – reproduced with the permission of the Controller of Her Majesty's Stationery Office. For details of publications, see Appendix 6. The selection contained here is not intended as a substitute for these books. Post-1987 legislation not included here can be found at www.hmso.gov.uk.

The section contains:

Administration of Justice Act 1970
Part IV: Actions by mortgagees for possession
s40   Punishment for unlawful harassment of debtors

Administration of Justice Act 1973
8. Extension of powers of court action by mortgagee of dwelling-house

Charging Orders Act 1979

Consumer Credit Act 1974
Part II: Credit agreements, hire agreements and linked transactions
Part III: Licensing of credit and hire business
Part VI: Matters arising during currency of credit or hire agreements
Part IX: Judicial control

Council Tax (Administration and Enforcement) (Amendment) (No.2) Regulations 1993 (as amended 1998)

County Courts Act 1984
Transfer of proceedings
Interest on debts and damages
Judgments and orders
Enforcement of judgments and orders
Administration orders
Responsibility and protection of officers

· · · ·

The County Court (Interest on Judgment Debts) Order 1991

Distress for Rent Rules 1988

The High Court and County Courts Jurisdiction Order 1991 (as amended 1993, 1994, 1995 and 1999)

Administration of Justice Act 1970

Part IV: Actions by mortgagees for possession

Additional powers of court in action by mortgagee for possession of dwelling-house

36.–(1) Where the mortgagee under a mortgage of land which consists of or includes a dwelling-house brings an action in which he claims possession of the mortgaged property, not being an action for foreclosure in which a claim for possession of the mortgaged property is also made, the court may exercise any of the powers conferred on it by subsection (2) below if it appears to the court that in the event of its exercising the power the mortgagor is likely to be able within a reasonable period to pay any sums due under the mortgage or to remedy a default consisting of a breach of any other obligation arising under or by virtue of the mortgage.

(2) The court:

(a) may adjourn the proceedings; or

(b) on giving judgment, or making an order, for delivery of possession of the mortgaged property, or at any time before the execution of such judgment or order, may:

    (i) stay or suspend execution of the judgment or order; or

    (ii) postpone the date for delivery of possession, for such period or periods as the court thinks reasonable.

(3) Any such adjournment, stay, suspension or postponement as is referred to in subsection (2) above may be made subject to such conditions with regard to payment by the mortgagor of any sum secured by the mortgage or the remedying of any default as the court thinks fit.

(4) The court may from time to time vary or revoke any condition imposed by virtue of this section.

(5) This section shall have effect in relation to such an action as is referred to in subsection (1) above begun before the date on which this section comes into force unless in that action judgment has been given, or an order made, for delivery of possession of the mortgaged property and that judgment or order was executed before that date.

(6) In the application of this section to Northern Ireland, 'the court' means a judge of the High Court in Northern Ireland, and in subsection (1) the words from 'not being' to 'made' shall be omitted.

Administration of Justice Act 1973

Extension of powers of court in action by mortgagee of dwelling-house

8.–(1) Where by a mortgage of land which consists of or includes a dwelling-house, or by any agreement between the mortgagee under such a mortgage and the mortgagor, the mortgagor is entitled or is to be permitted to pay the principal sum secured by instalments or otherwise to defer payment of it in whole or in part, but provision is also made for earlier payment in the event of any default by the mortgagor or of a demand by the mortgagee or otherwise, then for purposes of section 36 of the Administration of Justice Act 1970 (under which a court has power to delay giving a mortgagee possession of the mortgaged property so as to allow the mortgagor a reasonable time to pay any sums due under the mortgage) a court may treat as due under the mortgage on account of the principal sum secured and of interest on it only such amounts as the mortgagor would have expected to be required to pay if there had been no such provision for earlier payment.

(2) A court shall not exercise by virtue of subsection (1) above the powers conferred by section 36 of the Administration of Justice Act 1970 unless it appears to the court not only that the mortgagor is likely to be able within a reasonable period to pay any amounts regarded (in accordance with subsection (1) above) as due on account of the principal sum secured, together with the interest on those amounts, but also that he is likely to be able by the end of that period to pay any further amounts that he would have expected to be required to pay by then on account of that sum and of interest on it if there had been no such provision as is referred to in subsection (1) above for earlier payment.

(3) Where subsection (1) above would apply to an action in which a mortgagee only claimed possession of the mortgaged property, and the mortgagee brings an action for foreclosure (with or without also claiming possession of the property), then section 36 of the Administration of Justice Act 1970 together with subsections (1) and (2) above shall apply as they would apply if it were an action in which the mortgagee only claimed possession of the mortgaged property, except that:

    (a)   section 36(2)(b) shall apply only in relation to any claim for possession; and

    (b)   section 36(5) shall not apply.

38A. This Part of this Act shall not apply to a mortgage securing an agreement which is a regulated agreement within the meaning of the Consumer Credit Act 1974.

Punishment for the unlawful harassment of debtors

40.–(1) A person commits an offence if, with the object of coercing another person to pay money claimed from the other as a debt due under a contract, he:

(a) harasses the other with demands for payment which, in respect of their frequency or the manner or occasion of making any such demand, or of any threat or publicity by which any demand is accompanied, are calculated to subject him or members of his family or household to alarm, distress or humiliation;

(b) falsely represents, in relation to the money claimed, that criminal proceedings lie for failure to pay it;

(c) falsely represents himself to be authorised in some official capacity to claim or enforce payment; or

(d) utters a document falsely represented by him to have some official character or purporting to have some official character which he knows it has not.

(2) A person may be guilty of an offence by virtue of subsection (1)(a) above if he concerts with others in the taking of such action as described in that paragraph, notwithstanding that his own course of conduct does not by itself amount to harassment.

(3) Subsection (1)(a) above does not apply to anything done by a person which is reasonable (and otherwise permissible in law) for the purpose:

(a) of securing the discharge of obligation due, or believed by him to be due, to himself or to persons for whom he acts, or protecting himself or them from future loss; or

(b) of the enforcement of any liability by legal process.

(4) A person guilty of an offence under this section shall be liable on summary conviction to a fine of not more then [level 5 on the standard scale].

Charging Orders Act 1979

Charging orders

Charging orders

1.–(1) Where, under a judgment or order of the High Court or a county court, a person (the 'debtor') is required to pay a sum of money to another person (the 'creditor') then, for the purpose of enforcing that judgment or order, the appropriate court may make an order in accordance with the provisions of this Act imposing on any such property of the debtor as may be specified in the order a charge for securing the payment of any money due or to become due under the judgment or order.

(2) The appropriate court is:

(a) in a case where the property to be charged is a fund in court, the court in which that fund is lodged;

(b) in a case where paragraph (a) above does not apply and the order to be enforced is a maintenance order of the High Court, the High Court or a county court;

(c) in a case where neither paragraph (a) nor paragraph (b) above applies and the judgment or order to be enforced is a judgment or order of the High Court for a sum exceeding the county court limit, the High Court or a county court; and

(d) in any other case, a county court.

In this section 'county court limit' means the county court limit for the time being specified in an Order in Council under section 145 of the County Courts Act 1984 as the county court limit for the purpose of this section and 'maintenance order' has the same meaning as in section 2(a) of the Attachment of Earnings Act 1971.

(3) An order under subsection (1) above is referred to in this Act as a 'charging order'.

(4) Where a person applies to the High Court for a charging order to enforce more than one judgment or order, that court shall be the appropriate court in relation to the application if it would be the appropriate court, apart from this subsection, on an application relating to one or more of the judgments or orders concerned.

(5) In deciding whether to make a charging order the court shall consider all the circumstances of the case and, in particular, any evidence before it as to:

(a) the personal circumstances of the debtor; and

(b) whether any other creditor of the debtor would be likely to be unduly prejudiced by the making of the order.

Property which may be charged

2.–(1) Subject to subsection (3) below, a charge may be imposed by a charging order only on:

(a) any interest held by the debtor beneficially:
   (i) in any asset of a kind mentioned in subsection (2) below; or
   (ii) under any trust; or

(b) any interest held by a person as trustees of a trust ('the trust'), if the interest is in such an asset or is an interest under another trust and:
   (i) the judgment or order in respect of which a charge is to be imposed was made against that person as trustee of the trust; or
   (ii) the whole beneficial interest under the trust is held by the debtor unencumbered and for his own, benefit; or

(iii) in a case where there are two or more debtors all of whom are liable to the creditor for the same debt, they together hold the whole beneficial interest under the trust unencumbered and for their own benefit.

(2) The assets referred to in subsection (1) above are:

(a) land;

(b) securities of any of the following kinds:

   (i) government stock;

   (ii) stock of any body (other than a building society) incorporated within England and Wales;

   (iii) stock of any body incorporated outside England and Wales or of any state or territory outside the United Kingdom, being stock registered in a register kept at any place within England and Wales; or

(c) funds in court.

(3) In any case where a charge is imposed by a charging order on any interest in an asset of a kind mentioned in paragraph (b) or (c) of subsection (2) above, the court making the order may provide for the charge to extend to any interest or dividend payable in respect of the asset.

Provisions supplementing sections 1 and 2

3.–(1) A charging order may be made either absolutely or subject to conditions as to notifying the debtor or as to the time when the charge is to become enforceable, or as to other matters.

(2) The Land Charges Act 1972 and the Land Registration Act 1925 shall apply in relation to charging orders as they apply in relation to other orders or writs issued or made for the purpose of enforcing judgments.

(3) In section 49 of the Land Registration Act 1925 (protection of certain interests by notice) there is inserted at the end of subsection (1) the following paragraph:

'(g) charging orders (within the meaning of the Charging Orders Act 1979) which in the case of unregistered land may be protected by registration under the Land Charges Act 1972 and which, notwithstanding section 59 of this Act, it may be deemed expedient to protect by notice instead of by caution.'

(4) Subject to the provisions of this Act, a charge imposed by a charging order shall have the like effect and shall be enforceable in the same courts and in the same manner as an equitable charge created by the debtor by writing under his hand.

(5) The court by which a charging order was made may at any time, on the application of the debtor or of any person interested in any property to which the order relates, make an order discharging or varying the charging order.

(6) Where a charging order has been protected by an entry registered under the Land Charges Act 1972 or the Land Registration Act 1925, an order under

subsection (5) above discharging the charging order may direct that the entry be cancelled.

(7) The Lord Chancellor may by order made by statutory instrument amend section 2(2) of this Act by adding to, or removing from, the kinds of asset for the time being referred to there, any asset of a kind which in his opinion ought to be so added or removed.

(8) Any order under subsection (7) above shall be subject to annulment in pursuance of a resolution of either House of Parliament.

Stop orders and notices

Stop orders and notices

5.–(1) In this section:

'stop order' means an order of the court prohibiting the taking, in respect of any of the securities specified in the order, of any of the steps mentioned in subsection (5) below;

'stop notice' means a notice requiring any person or body on whom it is duly served to refrain from taking, in respect of any of the securities specified in the notice, any of those steps without first notifying the person by whom, or on whose behalf, the notice was served; and

'prescribed securities' means securities (including funds in court) of a kind prescribed by rules of court made under this section.

(2) The power to make rules of court under section 84 of the Supreme Court Act 1981 shall include power by any such rules to make provision:

(a) for the court to make a stop order on the application of any person claiming to be entitled to an interest in prescribed securities;

(b) for the service of a stop notice by any person claiming to be entitled to an interest in prescribed securities.

(3) The power to make rules of court under section 75 of the County Courts Act 1984 shall include power by any such rules to make provision for the service of a stop notice by any person entitled to an interest in any securities by virtue of a charging order made by a county court.

(4) Rules of court made by virtue of subsection (2) or (3) above shall prescribe the person or body on whom a copy of any stop order or a stop notice is to be served.

(5) The steps mentioned in subsection (1) above are:

(a) the registration of any transfer of the securities;

(b) in the case of funds in court, the transfer, sale, delivery out, payment or other dealing with the funds, or of the income thereon;

(c) the making of any payment by way of dividend, interest or otherwise in respect of the securities; and

(d) in the case of units of a unit trust, any acquisition of or other dealing with the units by any person or body exercising functions under the trust.

(6) Any rules of court made by virtue of this section may include such incidental, supplemental and consequential provisions as the authority making them considers necessary or expedient, and may make different provisions in relation to different cases or classes of case.

Supplemental

Interpretation

6.–(1) In this Act:

'building society' has the same meaning as in the Building Societies Act 1986;

'charging order' means an order made under section 1(1) of this Act;

'debtor' and 'creditor' have the meanings given by section 1(1) of this Act;

'dividend' includes any distribution in respect of any unit of a unit trust;

'government stock' means any stock issued by Her Majesty's government in the United Kingdom or any funds of, or annuity granted by, that government;

'stock' includes shares, debentures and any securities of the body concerned, whether or not constituting a charge on the assets of that body;

'unit trust' means any trust established for the purpose, or having the effect, of providing, for persons having funds available for investment, facilities for the participation by them, as beneficiaries under the trust, in any profits or income arising from the acquisition, holding, management or disposal of any property whatsoever.

(2) For the purposes of section 1 of the Act references to a judgment or order of the High Court or a county court shall be taken to include references to a judgment, order, decree or award (however called) of any court or arbitrator (including any foreign court or arbitrator) which is or has become enforceable (whether wholly or to a limited extent) as if it were a judgment or order of the High Court or a county court.

(3) References in section 2 of this Act to any securities include references to any such securities standing in the name of the Accountant General.

Consumer Credit Act 1974

Part II: Credit agreements, hire agreements and linked transactions

Consumer credit agreements

8.–(1) A personal credit agreement is an agreement between an individual ('the debtor') and any other person ('the creditor') by which the creditor provides the debtor with credit of any amount.

(2) A consumer credit agreement is a personal credit agreement by which the creditor provides the debtor with credit not exceeding £15,000.

(3) A consumer credit agreement is a regulated agreement within the meaning of this Act if it is not an agreement (an 'exempt agreement') specified in or under section 16.

Meaning of credit

9.–(1) In this Act 'credit' includes a cash loan, and any other form of financial accommodation.

(2) Where credit is provided otherwise than in sterling it shall be treated for the purposes of this Act as provided in sterling of an equivalent amount.

(3) Without prejudice to the generality of subsection (1), the person by whom goods are bailed or (in Scotland) hired to an individual under a hire-purchase agreement shall be taken to provide him with fixed-sum credit to finance the transaction of an amount equal to the total price of the goods less the aggregate of the deposit (if any) and the total charge for credit.

(4) For the purpose of this Act, an item entering into the total charge for credit shall not be treated as credit even though time is allowed for its payment.

Running-account credit and fixed-sum credit

10.–(1) For the purposes of this Act:

(a) running-account credit is a facility under a personal credit agreement whereby the debtor is enabled to receive from time to time (whether in his own person, or by another person) from the creditor or a third party cash, goods and services (or any of them) to an amount or value such that, taking into account payments made by or to the credit of the debtor, the credit limit (if any) is not at any time exceeded; and

(b) fixed-sum credit is any other facility under a personal credit agreement whereby the debtor is enabled to receive credit (whether in one amount or by instalments).

(2) In relation to running-account credit, 'credit limit' means, as respects any period, the maximum debit balance which, under the credit agreement, is allowed to stand on the account during that period, disregarding any term of the agreement allowing that maximum to be exceeded merely temporarily.

(3) For the purposes of section 8(2), running-account credit shall be taken not to exceed the amount specified in that subsection ('the specified amount') if:

(a) the credit limit does not exceed the specified amount; or

(b) whether or not there is a credit limit, and if there is, notwithstanding that it exceeds the specified amount:

(i) the debtor is not enabled to draw at any one time an amount which, so far as (having regard to section 9(4)) it represents credit, exceeds the specified amount; or

(ii) the agreement provides that, if the debit balance rises above a given amount (not exceeding the specified amount), the rate of the total charge for credit increases or any other condition favouring the creditor or his associate comes into operation; or

(iii) at the time the agreement is made it is probable, having regard to the terms of the agreement and any other relevant considerations, that the debit balance will not at any time rise above the specified amount.

Restricted-use credit and unrestricted-use credit

11.–(1) A restricted-use credit agreement is a regulated consumer credit agreement:

(a) to finance a transaction between the debtor and the creditor, whether forming part of that agreement or not; or

(b) to finance a transaction between the debtor and a person (the 'supplier') other than the creditor; or

(c) to refinance any existing indebtedness of the debtor's, whether to the creditor or another person;

and 'restricted-use credit' shall be construed accordingly.

(2) An unrestricted-use credit agreement is a regulated consumer credit agreement not falling within subsection (1), and 'unrestricted-use credit' shall be construed accordingly.

(3) An agreement does not fall within subsection (1) if the credit is in fact provided in such a way as to leave the debtor free to use it as he chooses, even though certain uses would contravene that or any other agreement.

(4) An agreement may fall within subsection (1)(b) although the identity of the supplier is unknown at the time the agreement is made.

Debtor-creditor-supplier agreements

12. A debtor-creditor-supplier agreement is a regulated consumer credit agreement being:

(a) a restricted-use credit agreement which falls within section 11(1)(a); or

(b) a restricted-use credit agreement which falls within section 11(1)(b) and is made by the creditor under pre-existing arrangements, or in contemplation of future arrangements, between himself and the supplier; or

(c) an unrestricted-use credit agreement which is made by the creditor under pre-existing arrangements between himself and a person (the 'supplier') other than the debtor in the knowledge that the credit is to be used to finance a transaction between the debtor and the supplier.

Debtor-creditor agreements

13. A debtor-creditor agreement is a regulated consumer credit agreement being:

(a) a restricted-use credit agreement which falls within section 11(1)(b) but is not made by the creditor under pre-existing arrangements, or in contemplation of future arrangements, between himself and the supplier, or

(b) a restricted-use credit agreement which falls within section 11(1)(c), or

(c) an unrestricted-use credit agreement which is not made by the creditor under pre-existing arrangements between himself and a person (the 'supplier') other than the debtor in the knowledge that the credit is to be used to finance a transaction between the debtor and the supplier.

Credit-token agreements

14.–(1) A credit-token is a card, check, voucher, coupon, stamp, form, booklet or other document or thing given to an individual by a person carrying on a consumer credit business, who undertakes:

(a) that on the production of it (whether or not some other action is also required) he will supply cash, goods, and services (or any of them) on credit; or

(b) that where, on the production of it to a third party (whether or not any other action is also required), the third party supplies cash, goods and services (or any of them), he will pay the third party for them (whether or not deducting any discount or commission), in return for payment to him by the individual.

(2) A credit-token agreement is a regulated agreement for the provision of credit in connection with the use of a credit-token.

(3) Without prejudice to the generality of section 9(1), the person who gives to an individual an undertaking falling within subsection (1)(b) shall be taken to provide him with credit drawn on whenever a third party supplies him with cash, goods or services.

(4) For the purposes of subsection (1), use of an object to operate a machine provided by him giving the object or a third party shall be treated as the production of the object to him.

Consumer hire agreements

15.–(1) A consumer hire agreement is an agreement made by a person with an individual (the 'hirer') for the bailment or (in Scotland) the hiring of goods to the hirer, being an agreement which:

(a) is not a hire-purchase agreement; and

(b) is capable of subsisting for more than three months; and

(c) does not require the hirer to make payments exceeding £15,000.

(2) A consumer hire agreement is a regulated agreement if it is not an exempt agreement.

Small agreements

17.–(1) A small agreement is:

(a) a regulated consumer credit agreement for credit not exceeding [£50], or other than a hire-purchase or conditional sale agreement; or

(b) a regulated consumer hire agreement which does not require the hirer to make payments exceeding [£50], being an agreement which is either unsecured or secured by a guarantee or indemnity only (whether or not the guarantee or indemnity is itself secured).

(2) Section 10(3) applies for the purposes of subsection (1) as it applies for the purposes of section 8 (2).

(3) Where:

(a) two or more small agreements are made at or about the same time between the same parties; and

(b) it appears probable that they would instead have been made as a single agreement but for the desire to avoid the operation of provisions of this Act which would have applied to that single agreement but, apart form this subsection, are not applicable to the small agreements;

this Act applies to the small agreements as if they were regulated agreements other than small agreements.

(4) If, apart from this subsection, subsection (3) does not apply to any agreements but would apply if, for any party or parties to any of the agreements, there were substituted an associate of that party, or associates of each of those parties, as the case may be, then subsection (3) shall apply to the agreements.

Linked transactions

19.–(1) A transaction entered into by the debtor or hirer, or a relative of his, with any other person ('the other party'), except one for the provision of security, is a linked transaction in relation to an actual or prospective regulated agreement (the 'principal agreement') of which it does not form part if:

(a) the transaction is entered into in compliance with a term of the principal agreement; or

(b) the principal agreement is a debtor-creditor-supplier agreement and the transaction is financed, or to be financed, by the principal agreement; or

(c) the other party is a person mentioned in subsection (2), and a person so mentioned initiated the transaction by suggesting it to the debtor or hirer, or his relative, who enters into it:

   (i) to induce the creditor or owner to enter into the principal agreement; or

   (ii) for another purpose related to the principal agreement; or

   (iii) where the principal agreement is a restricted-use credit agreement, for a purpose related to a transaction financed, or to be financed, by the principal agreement.

(2) The persons referred to in subsection (1)(c) are:

(a) the creditor or owner, or his associate;

(b) a person who, in the negotiation of the transaction, is represented by a credit-broker who is also a negotiator in antecedent negotiations for the principal agreement;

(c) a person who, at the time the transaction is initiated, knows that the principal agreement has been made or contemplates that it might be made.

(3) A linked transaction entered into before the making of the principal agreement has no effect until such time (if any) as that agreement is made.

(4) Regulations may exclude linked transactions of the prescribed description from the operation of subsection (3).

Part III: Licensing of credit and hire business

Licensing principles

Businesses needing a licence

21.–(1) Subject to this section, a licence is required to carry on a consumer credit business or consumer hire business.

(2) A local authority does not need a licence to carry on a business.

(3) A body corporate empowered by a public general Act naming it to carry on business does not need a licence to do so.

Licensee to be a fit person

25.–(1) A standard licence shall be granted on application of any person if he satisfies the Director that:

(a) he is a fit person to engage in activities covered by the licence; and

(b) the person or names under which he applies to be licensed is or are not misleading or otherwise undesirable.

(2) In determining whether an applicant for a standard licence is a fit person to engage in any activities, the Director shall have regard to any circumstances appearing to him to be relevant, and in particular any evidence tending to show that the applicant, or any of the applicant's employees, agents or associates (whether past or present) or, where the applicant is a body corporate, any person appearing to the Director to be a controller of the body corporate or an associate of any such person, has:

(a) committed any offence involving fraud or other dishonesty, or violence;

(b) contravened any provisions made by or under this Act, or by or under any other enactment regulating the provision of credit to individuals or other transactions with individuals;

[(bb)] contravened any provisions in force in an EEA State which corresponds to a provision of the kind mentioned in paragraph (b);]

(c) practised discrimination on grounds of sex, colour, race or ethnic or national origins in, or in connection with, the carrying on of any business; or

(d) engaged in business practices, appearing to the Director to be deceitful or oppressive, or unfair or improper (whether lawful or not).

Offences against Part III

39.–(1) A person who engages in any activities for which a licence is required when he is not a licensee under a licence covering those activities commits an offence.

(2) A licensee under a standard licence who carries on business under a name not specified in the licence commits an offence.

(3) A person who fails to give the Director or a licensee notice under section 36 within the period required commits an offence.

Enforcement of agreements made by unlicensed trader

40.–(1) A regulated agreement, other than a non-commercial agreement, if made when the creditor or owner was unlicensed, is enforceable against the debtor or hirer only where the Director [General of Fair Trading] has made an order under this section which applies to the agreement.

(2) Where during any period an unlicensed person (the 'trader') was carrying on a consumer credit business or consumer hire business, he or his successor in title may apply to the Director for an order that regulated agreements made by the trader during that period are to be treated as if he had been licensed.

(3) Unless the Director determines to make an order under subsection (2) in accordance with the application, he shall, before determining the application, by notice:

(a) inform the applicant, giving his reasons, that, as the case may be, he is minded to refuse the application, or to grant it in terms different from those applied for, describing them; and

(b) invite the applicant to submit to the Director representations in support of his application in accordance with section 34.

(4) In determining whether or not to make an order under subsection (2) in respect of any period the Director shall consider, in addition to any other relevant factors:

(a) how far, if at all, debtors or hirers under regulated agreements made by the trader during that period were prejudiced by the trader's conduct;

(b) whether or not the Director would have been likely to grant a licence covering that period on an application by the trader; and

(c) the degree of culpability for the failure to obtain a licence.

(5) If the Director thinks fit, he may in an order under subsection (2):

(a) limit the order to specified agreements, or agreements of a specified description or made at a specified time;

(b)   make the order conditional on the doing of specified acts by the applicant.

Part V: Entering into credit and hire agreements

Withdrawal from prospective agreement

57.–(1) The withdrawal of a party from a prospective regulated agreement shall operate to apply this Part to the agreement, any linked transaction and any other thing done in anticipation of the making of the agreement as it would apply if the agreement were made and then cancelled under section 69.

(2) The giving to a party of a written or oral notice which, however expressed, indicates the intention of the other party to withdraw from a prospective regulated agreement operates as a withdrawal from it.

(3) Each of the following shall be deemed to be the agent of the creditor or owner for the purpose of receiving a notice under subsection (2):

(a)   a credit-broker or supplier who is the negotiator in antecedent negotiations; and

(b)   any person who, in the course of a business carried on by him, acts on behalf of the debtor or hirer in any negotiations for the agreement.

(4) Where the agreement, if made, would not be a cancellable agreement, subsection (1) shall nevertheless apply as if the contrary were the case.

Form and content of agreements

60.–(1) The Secretary of State shall make regulations as to the form and content of documents embodying regulated agreements, and the regulations shall contain such provisions as appear to him appropriate with a view to ensuring that the debtor or hirer is made aware of:

(a)   the rights and duties conferred or imposed on him by the agreement;

(b)   the amount and rate of the total charge for credit (in the case of a consumer credit agreement);

(c)   the protection and remedies available to him under this Act; and

(d)   any other matters which, in the opinion of the Secretary of State, it is desirable for him to know about in connection with the agreement.

(2) Regulations under subsection (1) may in particular:

(a)   require specified information to be included in the prescribed manner in documents, and other specified material to be excluded;

(b)   contain requirements to ensure that specified information is clearly brought to the attention of the debtor or hirer, and that one part of a document is not given sufficient or excessive prominence compared with another.

Signing of agreement

61.–(1) A regulated agreement is not properly executed unless:

(a) a document in the prescribed form itself containing all the prescribed terms and conforming to regulations under section 60(1) is signed in the prescribed manner both by the debtor or hirer and by or on behalf of the creditor or owner; and

(b) the document embodies all the terms of the agreement, other than implied terms; and

(c) the document is, when presented or sent to the debtor or hirer for signature, in such a state that all its terms are readily legible.

(2) In addition, where the agreement is one to which section 58(1) applies, it is not properly executed unless:

(a) the requirements of section 58(1) were complied with; and

(b) the unexecuted agreement was sent, for his signature, to the debtor or hirer by post not less than seven days after a copy of it was given to him under section 58(1); and

(c) during the consideration period, the creditor or owner refrained from approaching the debtor or hirer (whether in person, by telephone or letter, or in any other way) except in response to a specific request made by the debtor or hirer after the beginning of the consideration period; and

(d) no notice of withdrawal by the debtor or hirer was received by the creditor or owner before the sending of the unexecuted agreement.

(3) In subsection (2)(c), 'the consideration period' means the period beginning with the giving of the copy under section 58(1) and ending:

(a) at the expiry of seven days after the day on which the unexecuted agreement is sent, for his signature, to the debtor or hirer; or

(b) on its return by the debtor or hirer after signature by him, whichever first occurs.

(4) Where the debtor or hirer is a partnership or an unincorporated body of persons, subsection (1)(a) shall apply with the substitution for 'by the debtor or hirer' or 'by or on behalf of the debtor or hirer'.

Duty to supply copy of unexecuted agreement

62.–(1) If the unexecuted agreement is presented personally to the debtor or hirer for his signature, but on the occasion when he signs it the document does not become an executed agreement, a copy of it, and of any other document referred to in it, must be there and then delivered to him.

(2) If the unexecuted agreement is sent to the debtor or hirer for his signature, a copy of it, and of any other document referred to in it, must be sent to him at the same time.

(3) A regulated agreement is not properly executed if the requirements of this section are not observed.

Duty to supply copy of executed agreement

63.–(1) If the unexecuted agreement is presented personally to the debtor or hirer for his signature, and on the occasion when he signs it the document becomes an executed agreement, a copy of the executed agreement, and of any other document referred to in it, must be there and then delivered to him.

(2) A copy of the executed agreement, and of any other document referred to in it, must be given to the debtor or hirer within the seven days following the making of the agreement unless:

(a) subsection (1) applies; or

(b) the unexecuted agreement was sent to the debtor or hirer for his signature and, on the occasion of his signing it, the document became an executed agreement.

(3) In the case of a cancellable agreement, a copy under subsection (2) must be sent by post.

(4) In the case of a credit-token agreement, a copy under subsection (2) need not be given within the seven days following the making of the agreement if it is given before at the time when the credit-token is given to the debtor.

(5) A regulated agreement is not properly executed if the requirements of this section are not observed.

Duty to give notice of cancellation rights

64.–(1) In the case of a cancellable agreement, a notice in the prescribed form indicating the right of the debtor or hirer to cancel the agreement, how and when that right is exercisable, and the name and address of a person to whom notice of cancellation may be given:

(a) must be included in every copy given to the debtor or hirer under section 62 or 63; and

(b) except where section 63(2) applied, must also be sent by post to the debtor or hirer within the seven days following the making of the agreement.

(2) In the case of a credit-token agreement, a notice under subsection (1)(b) need not be sent by post within the seven days following the making of the agreement if either:

(a) it is sent by post to the debtor or hirer before the credit-token is given to him; or

(b) it is sent by post to him together with the credit-token.

(3) Regulations may provide that except where section 63(2) applied a notice sent under subsection (1)(b) shall be accompanied by a further copy of the executed agreement, and of any other document referred to in it.

(4) Regulations may provide that subsection (1)(b) is not to apply in the case of agreements such as are described in the regulations, being agreements made by a particular person, if:

(a) on an application by that person to the Director, the Director has determined that, having regard to:

(i) the manner in which antecedent negotiations for agreements with the applicant of that description are conducted; and

(ii) the information provided to debtors or hirers before such agreements are made, the requirement imposed by subsection (1)(b) can be dispensed with without prejudicing the interests of debtors or hirers; and

(b) any conditions imposed by the Director in making the determination are complied with.

(5) A cancellable agreement is not properly executed if the requirements of this section are not observed.

Consequences of improper execution

65.–(1) An improperly-executed regulated agreement is enforceable against the debtor or hirer on an order of the court only.

(2) A retaking of goods or land which a regulated agreement relates is an enforcement of the agreement.

Notice of cancellation

69.–(1) If within the period specified in section 68 the debtor or hirer under a cancellable agreement serves on:

(a) the creditor or owner; or

(b) the person specified in the notice under section 64(1); or

(c) a person who (whether by virtue of subsection (6) or otherwise is the agent of the creditor or owner;

a notice (a 'notice of cancellation') which, however expressed and whether or not conforming to the notice given under section 64(1) indicates the intention of the debtor or hirer to withdraw from under the agreement, the notice shall operate:

(i) to cancel the agreement, and any linked transaction; and

(ii) to withdraw any offer by the debtor or hirer, or his relative, to enter into a linked transaction.

(2) In the case of a debtor-creditor-supplier agreement for restricted-use credit financing:

(a) the doing of work or supply of goods to meet an emergency; or

(b) the supply of goods which, before service of the notice of cancellation, had by the act of the debtor or his relative become incorporated in any land or thing not compromised in the agreement or any linked transaction;

subsection (1) shall apply with the substitution of the following for paragraph (i):

"(i) to cancel only such provisions of the agreement and any linked transaction as:

(aa) relate to the provisions of credit; or

(bb) require the debtor to pay an item in the total charge for credit; or

(cc) subject the debtor to any obligation other than to pay for the doing of the said work, or the supply of the said goods".

(3) Except so far as is otherwise provided, references in the Act to the cancellation of an agreement or transaction do not include a case within subsection (2).

(4) Except as otherwise provided by or under this Act, an agreement or transaction cancelled under subsection (1) shall be treated as if it had never been entered into.

(5) Regulations may exclude linked transactions of the prescribed description from subsection (1)(i) or (ii).

(6) Each of the following shall be deemed to be the agent of the creditor or owner for the purpose of receiving a notice of cancellation:

(a) a credit-broker or supplier who is the negotiator in antecedent negotiations; and

(b) any persons who, in the course of a business carried on by him, acts on behalf of the debtor or hirer in any negotiations for the agreement.

(7) Whether or not it is actually received by him, a notice of cancellation sent by post to a person shall be deemed to be served on him at the time of posting.

Cancellation: recovery of money paid by debtor or hirer

70.–(1) On the cancellation of a regulated agreement, and of any linked transaction:

(a) any sum paid by the debtor or hirer, or his relative, under or in contemplation of the agreement or transaction, including any item in the total charge for credit, shall become repayable; and

(b) any sum, including any item in the total charge for credit, which but for the cancellation is, or would or might become, payable by the debtor or hirer, or his relative, under the agreement or transaction shall cease to be, or shall not become, so payable; and

(c) in the case of a debt-creditor-supplier agreement falling within section 12(b), any sum paid on the debtor's behalf by the creditor to the supplier shall become repayable to the creditor.

(2) If, under the terms of a cancelled agreement or transaction, the debtor or hirer, or his relative, is in possession of any goods, he shall have a lien on them for any sum repayable to him under subsection (1) in respect of that agreement or transaction, or any other linked transaction.

(3) A sum repayable under subsection (1) is repayable by the person to whom it was originally paid, but in the case of a debtor-creditor-supplier agreement falling within section 12(b) the creditor and the supplier shall be under a joint and several liability to repay sums paid by the debtor, or his relative, under the agreement or under a linked transaction falling with section 19(1)(b) and accordingly, in such a case, the creditor shall be entitled, in accordance with rules

of the court, to have the supplier made a party to any proceedings brought against the creditor to recover any such sums.

(4) Subject to any agreement between them, the creditor shall be entitled to be indemnified by the supplier for loss suffered by the creditor in satisfying his liability under subsection (3) including costs reasonably incurred by him in defending proceedings instituted by the debtor.

Part VI: Matters arising during currency of credit or hire agreements

Liability of creditor for breaches by supplier

75.–(1) If the debtor under a debtor-creditor-supplier agreement falling within section 12(b) or (c) has, in relation to a transaction financed by the agreement, any claim against the supplier in respect of a misrepresentation or breach of contract, he shall have a like claim against the creditor, who, with the supplier, shall accordingly be jointly and severally liable to the debtor.

(2) Subject to any agreement between them, the creditor shall be entitled to be indemnified by the supplier for loss suffered by the creditor in satisfying his liability under subsection (1), including costs reasonably incurred by him in defending proceedings instituted by the debtor.

(3) Subsection (1) does not apply to a claim:

(a) under a non-commercial agreement; or

(b) so far as the claim relates to any single item to which the supplier has attached a cash price not exceeding £100 or more than £30,000. [1983]

(4) This section applies notwithstanding that the debtor, in entering into the transaction, exceeded the credit limit or otherwise contravened any term of the agreement.

(5) In an action brought against the creditor under subsection (1) he shall be entitled, in accordance with rules of court, to have the supplier made a party to the proceedings.

Duty to give information to debtor under fixed-sum credit agreement

77.–(1) The creditor under a regulated agreement for fixed-sum credit, within the prescribed period after receiving a request in writing to that effect from the debtor and payment of a fee of 50 new pence, shall give the debtor a copy of the executed agreement (if any) and of any other document referred to in it, together with a statement signed by or on behalf of the creditor showing, according to the information to which it is practicable for him to refer:

(a) the total sum paid under the agreement by the debtor;

(b) the total sum which has become payable under the agreement by the debtor but remains unpaid, and the various amounts comprised in that total sum, with the date when each became due; and

(c)   the total sum which is to become payable under the agreement by the debtor, and the various amounts comprised in that total sum, with the date, or mode of determining the date, when each becomes due. [1983]

(2) If the creditor possesses insufficient information to enable him to ascertain the amounts and dates mentioned in subsection (1)(c), he shall be taken to comply with that paragraph if his statement under subsection (1) gives the basis on which, under the regulated agreement, they would fall to be ascertained.

(3) Subsection (1) does not apply to:

(a)   an agreement under which no sum is, or will or may become, payable by the debtor; or

(b)   a request made less than one month after a previous request under that subsection relating to the same agreement was complied with.

(4) If the creditor under an agreement fails to comply with subsection (1)

(a)   he is not entitled, while the default continues, to enforce the agreement; and

(b)   if the default continues for one month he commits an offence.

(5) This section does not apply to a non-commercial agreement.

Duty to give information to debtor under running-account credit agreement

78.–(1) The creditor under a regulated agreement for running-account credit, within the prescribed period after receiving a request in writing to that effect from the debtor and payment of a fee of 50 new pence, shall give the debtor a copy of the executed agreement (if any) and of any other document referred to in it, together with a statement signed by or on behalf of the creditor showing, according to the information to which it is practicable for him to refer:

(a)   the state of the account; and

(b)   the amount, if any, currently payable under the agreement by the debtor to the creditor; and

(c)   the amounts and due dates of any payments which, if the debtor does not draw further on the account, will later become payable under the agreement by the debtor to the creditor. [1983]

(2) If the creditor possesses insufficient information to enable him to ascertain the amounts and dates mentioned in subsection (1)(c), he shall be taken to comply with that paragraph if his statement under subsection (1) gives the basis on which, under the regulated agreement, they would fall to be ascertained.

(3) Subsection (1) does not apply to:

(a)   an agreement under which no sum is, or will or may become, payable by the debtor; or

(b)   a request made less than one month after a previous request under that subsection relating to the same agreement was complied with.

(4) Where running-account credit is provided under a regulated agreement, the creditor shall give the debtor statements in the prescribed form, and with the prescribed contents:

(a) showing according to the information to which it is practicable for him to refer, the state of the account at regular intervals of not more than twelve months; and

(b) where the agreement provides, in relation to specified periods, for the making of payments by the debtor, or the charging against him of interest or any other sum, showing according to the information to which it is practicable for him to refer the state of the account at the end of each of those periods during which there is any movement in the account.

(5) A statement under subsection (4) shall be given within the prescribed period after the end of the period to which the statement relates.

(6) If the creditor under an agreement fails to comply with subsection (1):

(a) he is not entitled, while the default continues, to enforce the agreement; and

(b) if the default continues for one month he commits an offence.

(7) This section does not apply to a non-commercial agreement, and subsections (4) and (5) do not apply to a small agreement.

Part VII: Default and Termination

Need for default notice

87.–(1) Service of a notice on the debtor or hirer in accordance with section 88 (a 'default notice') is necessary before the creditor or owner can become entitled, by reason of any breach by the debtor or hirer of a regulated agreement:

(a) to terminate the agreement; or

(b) to demand earlier payment of any sum; or

(c) to recover possession of any goods or land; or

(d) to treat any right conferred on the debtor or hirer by the agreement as terminated, restricted or deferred; or

(e) to enforce any security.

(2) Subsection (1) does not prevent the creditor from treating the right to draw upon any credit as restricted or deferred, and taking such steps as may be necessary to make the restriction or deferment effective.

(3) The doing of an act by which a floating charge becomes fixed is not enforcement of a security.

(4) Regulations may provide that subsection (1) is not to apply to agreements described by the regulations.

Contents and effect of default notice

88.–(1) The default notice must be in the prescribed form and specify:

(a) the nature of the alleged breach;

(b) if the breach is capable of remedy, what action is required to remedy it and the date before which that action is to be taken;

(c) if the breach is not capable of remedy, the sum (if any) required to be paid as compensation for the breach, and the date before which it is to be paid.

(2) A date specified under subsection (1) must not be less than seven days after the date of service of the default notice, and the creditor or owner shall not take action such as is mentioned in section 87(1) before the date so specified or (if no requirement is made under subsection (1)) before those seven days have elapsed.

(3) The default notice must not treat as a breach failure to comply with a provision of the agreement which becomes operative only on breach of some other provision, but if the breach of that other provision is not duly remedied or compensation demands under subsection (1) are not duly paid, or (where no requirement is made under subsection (1)) if the seven days mentioned in subsection (2) have elapsed, the creditor or owner may treat the failure as a breach and section 87(1) shall not apply to it.

(4) The default notice must contain information in the prescribed terms about the consequences of failure to comply with it.

(5) A default notice making a requirement under subsection (1) may include a provision for the taking of action such as is mentioned in section 87(1) at any time after the restriction imposed by subsection (2) will cease, together with a statement that the provision will be ineffective if the breach is duly remedied or the compensation duly paid.

Recovery of possession of goods or land

92.–(1) Except under an order of the court, the creditor or owner shall not be entitled to enter any premises to take possession of goods subject to a regulated hire-purchase agreement, regulated conditional sale agreement or regulated consumer hire agreement.

(2) At any time when the debtor is in breach of a regulated conditional sale agreement relating to land, the creditor is entitled to recover possession of the land from the debtor, or any person claiming under him, on an order of the court only.

(3) An entry in contravention of subsection (1) or (2) is actionable as a breach of statutory duty.

Interest not to be increased on default

93. The debtor under a regulated consumer credit agreement shall not be obliged to pay interest on sums which, in breach of the agreement, are unpaid by him at a rate:

(a) where the total charge for the credit includes an item in respect of interest, exceeding the rate of that interest; or

(b) in any other case, exceeding what would be the rate of the total charge for credit if any items included in the total charge for credit by virtue of section 20(2) were disregarded.

Right to complete payments ahead of time

94.–(1) The debtor under a regulated consumer credit agreement is entitled at any time, by notice to the creditor and the payment to the creditor of all amounts payable by the debtor to him under the agreement (less any rebate allowable under section 95), to discharge the debtor's indebtedness under the agreement.

(2) A notice under subsection (1) may embody the exercise by the debtor of any option to purchase goods conferred on him by the agreement, and deal with any other matter arising on, or in relation to, the termination of the agreement.

Part IX: Judicial control

Enforcement of certain regulated agreements and securities

Enforcement orders in cases of infringement

127.–(1) In the case of an application for an enforcement order under:

(a) section 65(1) (improperly executed agreements); or
(b) section 105(7)(a) or (b) (improperly executed security instruments); or
(c) section 111(2) (failure to serve copy of notice on surety); or
(d) section 124(1) or (2) (taking of negotiable instruments in contravention of section 123), the court shall dismiss the application if, but subject to subsections (3) and (4) only if it considered it just to do so having regard to:
  (i) prejudice caused to any person by the contravention in question, and the degree of culpability for it; and
  (ii) the powers conferred on the court by subsection (2) and sections 135 and 136.

(2) If it appears to the court just to do so, it may in an enforcement order reduce or discharge any sum payable by the debtor or hirer, or any surety, so as to compensate him for prejudice suffered as a result of the contravention in question.

(3) The court shall not make an enforcement order under section 65(1) if section 61(1)(a) (signing of agreements) was not complied with unless a document (whether or not in the prescribed form and complying with regulations under section 60(1)) itself containing all the prescribed terms of the agreement was signed by the debtor or hirer (whether or not in the prescribed manner).

(4) The court shall not make an enforcement order under section 65(1) in the case of a cancellable agreement if:

(a) a provision of section 62 or 63 was not complied with, and the creditor or owner did not give a copy of the executed agreement, and of any other document referred to in it, to the debtor or hirer before the commencement of the proceedings in which the order is sought; or
(b) section 64(1) was not complied with.

(5) Where an enforcement order is made in a case to which subsection (3) applies, the order may direct that the regulated agreement is to have effect as if it did not include a term omitted from the document signed by the debtor or hirer.

Extension of time

Time orders

129.–(1) If it appears to the court just to do so:

(a) on application for an enforcement order; or

(b) on an application made by a debtor or hirer under this paragraph after service on him of:

   (i)   a default notice; or

   (ii) a notice under section 76(1) or 98(1); or

(c) in an action brought by a creditor or owner to enforce a regulated agreement or any security, or recover possession of any goods or land to which a regulated agreement relates,

the court may make an order under this section (a 'time order').

(2) A time order shall provide for one or both of the following, as the court considers just:

(a) the payment by the debtor or hirer or any surety of any sum owed under a regulated agreement or a security by such instalments, payable at such times, as the court, having regard to the means of the debtor or hirer and any surety, considers reasonable;

(b) the remedy by the debtor or hirer of any breach of a regulated agreement (other than non-payment of money) within such period as the court may specify.

Supplemental provisions about time orders

130.–(1) Where in accordance with rules of court an offer to pay any sum by instalments is made by the debtor or hirer and accepted by the creditor or owner, the court may in accordance with rules of court make a time order under section 129 (2) (a) giving effect to the offer without hearing evidence of means.

(2) In the case of a hire-purchase or conditional sale agreement only, a time order under section 129 (2) (a) may deal with sums which, although not payable by the debtor at the time the order is made, would if the agreement continued in force become payable under it subsequently.

(3) A time order under section 129 (2) (a) shall not be made where the regulated agreement is secured by a pledge if, by virtue of regulations made under section 76 (5), 87 (4) or 98 (5), service of a notice is not necessary for enforcement of the pledge.

(4) Where, following the making of a time order in relation to a regulated hire-purchase or conditional sale agreement or a regulated consumer hire agreement, the debtor or hirer is in possession of the goods, he shall be treated (except in the case of a debtor to whom the creditor's title has passed) as a bailee or (in Scotland) a custodier of the goods under the terms of the agreement, notwithstanding that the agreement has been terminated.

(5) Without prejudice to anything done by the creditor or owner before the commencement of the period specified in a time order made under section 129 (2) (b) ('the relevant period'):

(a) he shall not while the relevant period subsists take in relation to the agreement any action such as is mentioned in section 87 (1);

(b) where:

    (i) a provision of the agreement ('the secondary provision') becomes operative only on breach of another provision of the agreement ('the primary provision'); and

    (ii) the time order provides for the remedying of such a breach of the primary provision within the relevant period, he shall not treat the secondary provision as operative before the end of that period;

(c) if while the relevant period subsists the breach to which the order relates is remedied it shall be treated as not having occurred.

(6) On the application of any person affected by a time order, the court may vary or revoke the order.

Protection of property pending proceedings

Protection orders

131. The court, on the application of the creditor or owner under a regulated agreement, may make such orders as it thinks just for protecting any property of the creditor or owner, or property subject to any security, from damage or depreciation pending the determination of any proceedings under this Act, including orders restricting or prohibiting use of the property or giving directions as to its custody.

Hire and hire-purchase, etc, agreements

Financial relief for hirer

132.–(1) Where the owner under a regulated consumer hire agreement recovers possession of goods to which the agreement relates otherwise than by action, the hirer may apply to the court for an order that:

(a) the whole or part of any sum paid by the hirer to the owner in respect of the goods shall be repaid; and

(b) the obligation to pay the whole or part of any sum owed by the hirer to the owner in respect of the goods shall cease, and if it appears to the court just to do so, having regard to the extent of the enjoyment of the goods by the hirer, the court shall grant the application in full or in part.

(2) Where in proceedings relating to a regulated consumer hire agreement the court makes an order for the delivery to the owner of goods to which the agreement relates the court may include in the order the like provision as may be made in an order under subsection (1).

••

Hire-purchase, etc, agreements: special powers of court

133.–(1) If, in relation to a regulated hire-purchase or conditional sale agreement, it appears to the court just to do so:

(a) on an application for an enforcement order or time order; or

(b) in an action brought by the creditor to recover possession of goods to which the agreement relates;

the court may:

(i)   make an order (a 'return order') for the return to the creditor of goods to which the agreement relates;

(ii) make an order (a 'transfer order') for the transfer to the debtor of the creditor's title to certain goods to which the agreement relates ('the transferred goods'), and the return to the creditor of the remainder of the goods.

(2) In determining for the purposes of this section how much of the total price has been paid ('the paid-up sum'), the court may:

(a) treat any sum paid by the debtor, or owed by the creditor, in relation to the goods as part of the paid-up sum;

(b) deduct any sum owed by the debtor in relation to the goods (otherwise than as part of the total price) from the paid-up sum;

and make corresponding reductions in amounts so owed.

(3) Where a transfer order is made, the transferred goods shall be such of the goods to which the agreement relates as the court thinks just; but a transfer order shall be made only where the paid-up sum exceeds the part of the total price referable to the transferred goods by an amount equal to at least one-third of the unpaid balance of the total price.

(4) Notwithstanding the making of a return order or transfer order, the debtor may at any time before the goods enter the possession of the creditor, on payment of the balance of the total price and the fulfilment of any other necessary conditions, claim the goods ordered to be returned to the creditor.

(5) When, in pursuance of a time order or under this section, the total price of goods under a regulated hire-purchase agreement or regulated conditional sale agreement is paid and any other necessary conditions are fulfilled, the creditor's title to the goods vests in the debtor.

(6) If, in contravention of a return order or transfer order, any goods to which the order relates are not returned to the creditor, the court, on the application of the creditor, may:

(a) revoke so much of the order as relates to those goods; and

(b) order the debtor to pay the creditor the unpaid portion of so much of the total price as is referable to those goods.

(7) For the purposes of this section, the part of the total price referable to any goods is the part assigned to those goods by the agreement or (if no such assignment is made) the part determined by the court to be reasonable.

Evidence of adverse detention in hire-purchase, etc, cases

134.–(1) Where goods are comprised in a regulated hire-purchase agreement, regulated conditional sale agreement or regulated consumer hire agreement, and the creditor or owner:

(a) brings an action or makes an application to enforce a right to recover possession of the goods from the debtor or hirer; and

(b) proves that a demand for the delivery of the goods was included in the default notice under section 88(5), or that, after the right to recover possession of the goods accrued but before the action was begun or the application was made, he made a request in writing to the debtor or hirer to surrender the goods;

then, for the purposes of the claim, of the creditor or owner to recover possession of the goods, the possession of them by the debtor or hirer shall be deemed to be adverse to the creditor or owner.

(2) In subsection (1) 'the debtor or hirer' includes a person in possession of the goods at any time between the debtor's or hirer's death and the grant of probate or administration, or (in Scotland) confirmation.

(3) Nothing in this section affects a claim for damages for conversion or (in Scotland) for delict. Supplemental provisions as to orders.

Power to impose conditions or suspend operation of order

135.–(1) If it considers it just to do so, the court may in an order made by it in relation to a regulated agreement include provisions:

(a) making the operation of any term of the order conditional on the doing of specified acts by any party to the proceedings;

(b) suspending the operation of any term of the order either:

    (i) until such time as the court subsequently directs; or

    (ii) until the occurrence of a specified act or omission.

(2) The court shall not suspend the operation of a term requiring the delivery up of goods by any person unless satisfied that the goods are in his possession or control.

(3) In the case of a consumer hire agreement, the court shall not so use its powers under subsection (1) (b) as to extend the period for which, under the terms of the agreement, the hirer is entitled to possession of the goods to which the agreement relates.

(4) On the application of any person affected by a provision included under subsection (1), the court may vary the provision.

Power to vary agreements and securities

136. The court may in an order made by it under this Act include such provision as it considers just for amending any agreement or security in consequence of a term of the order.

Extortionate credit bargains

Extortionate credit bargains

137.–(1) If the court finds a credit bargain extortionate it may reopen the credit agreement so as to do justice between the parties.

(2) In this section and sections 138 to 140:

(a) 'credit agreement' means any agreement between an individual (the 'debtor') and any other person (the 'creditor') by which the creditor provides the debtor with credit of any amount; and

(b) 'credit bargain':

(i) where no transaction other than the credit agreement is to be taken into account in computing the total charge for credit, means the credit agreement; or

(ii) where one or more other transactions are to be so taken into account, means the credit agreement and those other transactions, taken together.

When bargains are extortionate

138.–(1) A credit bargain is extortionate if it:

(a) requires the debtor or a relative of his to make payments (whether unconditionally, or on certain contingencies) which are grossly exorbitant; or

(b) otherwise grossly contravenes ordinary principles of fair dealing.

(2) In determining whether a credit bargain is extortionate, regard shall be had to such evidence as is adduced concerning:

(a) interest rates prevailing at the time it was made;

(b) the factors mentioned in subsection (3) to (5); and

(c) any other relevant considerations.

(3) Factors applicable under subsection (2) in relation to the debtor include:

(a) his age, experience, business capacity and state of health; and

(b) the degree to which, at the time of making the credit bargain, he was under financial pressure, and the nature of that pressure.

(4) Factors applicable under subsection (2) in relation to the creditor include:

(a) the degree of risk accepted by him, having regard to the value of any security provided;

(b) his relationship to the debtor; and

(c) whether or not a colourable cash price was quoted for any goods or services included in the credit bargain.

(5) Factors applicable under subsection (2) in relation to a linked transaction include the question of how far the transaction was reasonably required for the protection of debtor or creditor, or was in the interest of the debtor.

Reopening of extortionate agreements

139.–(1) A credit agreement may, if the court thinks just, be reopened on the ground that the credit bargain is extortionate:

    (a)   on an application for the purpose made by the debtor or any surety to the High Court, county court or sheriff court; or

    (b)   at the instance of the debtor or a surety in any proceedings to which the debtor and creditor are parties, being proceedings to enforce the credit agreement, any security relating to it, or any linked transaction; or

    (c)   at the instance of the debtor or a surety in other proceedings in any court where the amount paid or payable under the credit agreement is relevant.

(2) In reopening the agreement, the court may, for the purpose of relieving the debtor or a surety from payment of any sum in excess of that fairly due and reasonable, by order:

    (a)   direct accounts to be taken, or (in Scotland) an accounting to be made, between any persons;

    (b)   set aside the whole or part of any obligation imposed on the debtor or a surety by the credit bargain or any related agreement;

    (c)   require the creditor to repay the whole or part of any sum paid under the credit bargain or any related agreement by the debtor or a surety, whether paid to the creditor or any other person;

    (d)   direct the return to the surety of any property provided for the purposes of the security; or

    (e)   alter the terms of the credit agreement or any security instrument.

(3) An order may be made under subsection (2) notwithstanding that its effect is to place a burden on the creditor in respect of an advantage unfairly enjoyed by another person who is a party to a linked transaction.

(4) An order under subsection (2) shall not alter the effect of any judgment.

(5) In England and Wales an application under subsection (1) (a) shall be brought only in the county court in the case of:

    (a)   a regulated agreement; or

    (b)   an agreement (not being a regulated agreement) under which the creditor provides the debtor with fixed-sum credit not exceeding the county court limit or running-account credit on which the credit limit does not exceed the county court limit. [1977, 1981, 1982]

Miscellaneous

141.–(1) In England and Wales the county court shall have jurisdiction to hear and determine:

    (a)   any action by the creditor or owner to enforce a related agreement or any security relating to it;

    (b)   any action to enforce any linked transaction against the debtor or hirer or his relative;

and such an action shall not be brought in any other court.

(2) Where an action or application is brought in the High Court which, by virtue of this Act, ought to have been brought in the county court it shall not be treated as improperly brought, but shall be transferred to the county court.

(3) In Scotland the sheriff court for the district in which the debtor or hirer resides or carried on business, or resided or carried on business at the date on which he last made a payment under the agreement, shall have jurisdiction to hear and determine any action falling within subsection (1) and such an action shall not be brought in any other court,

(4) In Northern Ireland the county court shall have jurisdiction to hear and determine any action or application falling within subsection (1).

(5) Except as may be provided by rules of court, all the parties to a regulated agreement, and any surety, shall be made parties to any proceedings relating to the agreement.

Part XI: Enforcement of the Act

Contracting-out forbidden

173.–(1) A term contained in a regulated agreement or linked transaction, or in any other agreement relating to an actual or prospective regulated agreement or linked transaction, is void if, and to the extent that, it is inconsistent with a provision for the protection of the debtor or hirer, or his relative or any surety contained in this Act or in any regulation made under this Act.

(2) Where a provision specified the duty or liability of the debtor or hirer or his relative or any surety in certain circumstances, a term is inconsistent with that provision if it purports to impose, directly or indirectly, an additional duty or liability on him in those circumstances.

(3) Notwithstanding subsection (1), a provision of this Act under which a thing may be done in relation to any person on an order of the court or the Director only shall not be taken to prevent its being done at any time with that person's consent given at that time, but the refusal of such consent shall not give rise to any liability.

Service of documents

176.–(1) A document to be served under this Act by one person ('the server') on another person ('the subject') is to be treated as properly served on the subject if dealt with as mentioned in the following subsections.

(2) The document may be delivered or sent by post to the subject, or addressed to him by name and left at his proper address.

(3) For the purposes of this Act, a document sent by post to, or left at, the address last known to the server as the address of a person shall be treated as sent by post to, or left at, his proper address.

(4) Where the document is to be served on the subject as being the persons having any interest in land, and it is not practicable after reasonable inquiry to ascertain the subject's name or address, the document may be served by:

(a)   addressing it to the subject by the description of the person having that interest in the land (naming it); and

(b)   delivering the document to some responsible person on the land or affixing it, or a copy of it, in a conspicuous position on the land.

(5) Where a document to be served on the subject as being a debtor, hirer or surety, or as having any other capacity relevant for the purposes of this Act, is served at any time on another person who:

(a)   is the person last known to the server as having that capacity; but

(b)   before that time had ceased to have it;

the document shall be treated as having served at that time on the subject.

(6) Anything done to a document in relation to a person who (whether to the knowledge of the server or not) has died shall be treated for the purposes of subsection (5) as service of the document on that person if it would have been so treated had he not died.

(8) References in the preceding subsections to the serving of a document on a person include the giving of the document to that person.

Council Tax (Administration and Enforcement) (No.2) Regulations 1993 (as amended 1998)

Schedule 5: Charges connected with distress

1. The sum in respect of charges connected with the distress which may be aggregated under regulation 45(2) shall be as set out in the following Table –

(1)	(2)
Matter connected with distress	Charge
A For making a visit to premises with a view to levying distress (where no levy is made):	
(i) where the visit is the first or only such visit	£20
(ii) where the visit is the second such visit	£15
B For levying distress	The lesser of: (i) the amount of the costs and fees reasonably incurred; and (ii) the relevant amount calculated under paragraph 2(1) with respect to the levy.
C For one attendance with a vehicle with a view to the removal of goods (where, following the levy, goods are not removed)	Reasonable costs and fees incurred

D	For the removal and storage of goods for the purposes of sale	Reasonable costs and fees incurred
E	For the possession of goods as described in paragraph 2(2): (i) for close possession (the man in possession to provide his own board) (ii) for walking possession	 £12.50 per day £10
F	For appraisement of an item distrained, at the request in writing of the debtor	Reasonable fees and expenses of the broker appraising
G	For other expenses of, and commission on, a sale by auction: (i) where the sale is held on the auctioneer's premises (ii) where the sale is held on the debtor's premises	 The auctioneer's commission fee and out-of-pocket expenses (but not exceeding in aggregate 15 per cent of the sum realised), together with reasonable costs and fees incurred in respect of advertising The auctioneer's commission fee (but not exceeding $7\frac{1}{2}$ per cent of the sum realised), together with reasonable costs and fees incurred in respect of advertising
H	Where no sale takes place by reason of payment or tender in the circumstances referred to in regulation 45(4)	Either: (i) £20; or (ii) the actual costs incurred to a maximum of 5 per cent of the sum due, whichever is greater

2.–(1) In head B of the Table to paragraph 1, 'the relevant amount' with respect to a levy means:
(a) where the sum due at the time of the levy does not exceed £100, £20;
(b) where the sum due at the time of the levy exceeds £100, 20 per cent on the first £100 of the sum due, 4 per cent on the next £400, $21\frac{1}{2}$ per cent on the next £1,500, 1 per cent on the next £8,000 and $\frac{1}{4}$ per cent on any additional sum;

and the sum due at any time for these purposes means so much of the amount in respect or which the liability order concerned was made as is outstanding at the time.

(2) An authority takes close or walking possession of goods for the purposes of head E of the Table to paragraph 1 if it takes such possession in pursuance of an agreement:
(a) to which the debtor is a signatory;
(b) which is made at the time that the distress is levied; and

(c) (without prejudice to such other terms as may be agreed) which is expressed to the effect that, in consideration of the authority not immediately removing the goods distrained upon from the premises occupied by the debtor and delaying its sale or the goods, the authority may remove and sell the goods after a later specified date if the debtor has not by then paid the amount distrained for (including charges under this Schedule);

and an authority takes close possession of goods on any day for those purposes if during the greater part of the day a person is left on the premises in physical possession of the goods on behalf of the authority under such an agreement.

2A. No charge shall be payable under head F of the Table in respect of the appraisement of an item unless the debtor has been advised of the charge, and the manner of its calculation, before the appraisement is made.

3.–(1) Where the calculation under this Schedule of a percentage of a sum results in an amount containing a fraction of a pound, that fraction shall be reckoned as a whole pound.

(2) In the case of dispute as to any charge under this Schedule (other than a charge of a prescribed amount), the debtor or the authority may apply to the district judge of the county court for the district in which the distress is or is intended to be levied for the amount of the charge to be taxed.

(3) On any such application, the district judge may give such directions as to the costs of the taxation as he thinks fit; and any such costs directed to be paid by the debtor to the billing authority shall be added to the sum which may be aggregated under regulation 45(2).

(4) References in the Table to paragraph 1 to costs, fees and expenses include references to amounts payable by way of value added tax with respect to the supply of goods or services to which the costs, fees and expenses relate.

County Courts Act 1984

Transfer of proceedings

Transfer of proceedings to county court

40.–(1) Where the High Court is satisfied that any proceedings before it are required by any provision of a kind mentioned in subsection (8) to be in a county court it shall:

(a) order the transfer of the proceedings to a county court; or

(b) if the court is satisfied that the person bringing the proceedings knew, or ought to have known, of that requirement order that they be struck out.

(2) Subject to any such provision, the High Court may order the transfer of any proceedings before it to a county court.

(3) An order under this section may be made either on the motion of the High Court itself or on the application of any party to the proceedings.

(4) Proceedings transferred under this section shall be transferred to such county court as the High Court considers appropriate, having taken into account the convenience of the parties and that of any other persons likely to be affected and the state of business in the courts concerned.

(5) The transfer of any proceedings under this section shall not affect any right of appeal from the order directing the transfer.

(6) Where proceedings for the enforcement or any judgment or order of the High Court are transferred under this section:

    (a)   the judgment or order may be enforced as if it were a judgment or order of a county court; and

    (b)   subject to subsection (7), it shall be treated as a judgment or order of that court for all purposes.

(7) Where proceedings for the enforcement of any judgment or order of the High Court are transferred under this section:

    (a)   the powers of any court to set aside, correct, vary or quash a judgment or order of the High Court, and the enactments relating to appeals from such a judgment or order, shall continue to apply; and

    (b)   the powers of any court to set aside, correct, vary or quash a judgment or order of a county court and the enactments relating to appeals from such a judgment or order, shall not apply.

(8) The provisions referred to in subsection (1) and any made:

    (a)   under section 1 of the Courts and Legal Services Act 1990; or

    (b)   by or under any other enactment.

(9) This section does not apply to family proceedings within the meaning of Part V of the Matrimonial and Family Proceedings Act 1984. [1990]

Interest on debts and damages

Power to award interest on debts and damages

69.–(1) Subject to rules of court, in proceedings (whenever instituted) before a county court for the recovery of a debt or damages there may be included in any sum for which judgment is given simple interest, at such rate as the court thinks fit or as may be prescribed, on all or any part of the debt or damages in respect of which judgment is given, or payment is made before judgment, for all or any part of the period between the date when the cause of action arose and:

    (a)   in the case of any sum paid before judgment, the date of the payment; and

    (b)   in the case of the sum for which judgment is given, the date of the judgment. [1997]

(2) In relation to a judgment given for damages for personal injuries or death which exceed £200 subsection (1) shall have effect:

(a) with the substitution of "shall be included" for "may be included"; and

(b) with the addition of "unless the court is satisfied that there are special reasons to the contrary" after "given", where first occurring.

(3) Subject to rules of court, where:

(a) there are proceedings (whenever instituted) before a county court for the recovery of debt; and

(b) the defendant pays the whole debt to the plaintiff (otherwise that in pursuance of a judgment in the proceedings);

the defendant shall be liable to pay the plaintiff simple interest, at such rate as the court thinks fit or as may be prescribed, on all or any part of the debt for all or any part of the period between the date when the cause of action arose and the date of payment. [1997]

(4) Interest in respect of a debt shall not be awarded under this section for a period during which, for whatever reason, interest on the debt already runs.

(5) Interest under this section may be calculated at different rates in respect of different periods.

(6) In this section 'plaintiff' means the person seeking the debt or damages and 'defendant' means the person from whom the plaintiff seeks the debt or damages and 'personal injuries' includes any disease and any impairment of a person's physical or mental condition.

(7) Nothing in this section affects the damages recoverable for the dishonour of a bill of exchange.

(8) In determining whether the amount of any debt or damages exceeds that prescribed by or under any enactment, no account shall be taken of any interest payable by virtue of this section except where express provision to the contrary is made by or under that or any other enactment. [1990]

Judgments and orders

Finality of judgments and orders

70. Every judgment and order of a county court shall, except as provided by this or any other Act as may be prescribed, be final and conclusive between the parties.

Satisfaction of judgment and orders for payment of money

71.–(1) Where a judgment is given or an order is made by a county court under which a sum of money of any amount is payable, whether by way of satisfaction of the claim or counterclaim in the proceedings or by way of costs or otherwise, the court may, as it thinks fit, order the money to be paid either:

(a) in one sum, whether forthwith or within such period as the court may fix; or

(b) by such instalments payable at such times as the court may fix.

(2) If at any time it appears to the satisfaction of the court that any party to any proceedings is unable from any cause to pay any sum recovered against him

(whether by way of satisfaction of the claim or counterclaim in the proceedings or by way of costs or otherwise) or any instalment of such a sum, the court may, in its discretion, suspend or stay any judgment or order given or made in the proceedings for such time and on such terms as the court think fit, and so from time to time until it appears that the cause of inability has ceased.

Register of judgments and orders

73.–(1) A register of every:

(a) judgment entered in a county court;

(b) administration order made under section 112; and

(c) order restricting enforcement made under section 112A;

shall be kept in such a manner and such place as may be prescribed.

(2) The Lord Chancellor may, by statutory instrument, make regulations as to the keeping of the register, and in this section 'prescribed' means prescribed by those regulations.

(3) Regulations under this section may:

(a) prescribe circumstances in which judgments or orders are to be exempt from registration or in which the registration of any judgment or order is to be cancelled;

(b) provide for any specified class of judgments or orders to be exempt from registration.

(4) Regulations under this section shall be subject to annulment in pursuance of a resolution of either House of Parliament.

(5) The Lord Chancellor may, with the concurrence of the Treasury, fix the fees to be paid in respect of:

(a) the making of any information contained in an entry on the register available for inspection in visible and legible form;

(b) the carrying out of any official search of the register;

(c) the supply of a certified copy of any information contained in an entry in the register.

(6) The proceeds of the fees shall be applied in such manner as the Treasury may direct in paying the expenses incurred in maintaining the register, and any surplus, after providing for the payment of those expenses, shall be paid to the credit of the Consolidated Fund. [1990]

Interest on judgment debts etc.

74.–(1) The Lord Chancellor may by order made with the concurrence of the Treasury provide that any sums to which this subsection applies shall carry interest at such rate and between such times as may be prescribed by the order.

(2) The sums to which subsection (1) applies are:

(a) sums payable under judgments or orders given or made in a county court, including sums payable by instalments; and

(b) sums which by virtue of any enactment are, if the county court so orders, recoverable as if payable under an order of that court, and in respect of which the county court has so ordered.

(3) The payment of interest due under subsection (1) shall be enforceable as a sum payable under the judgment or order.

(4) The power conferred by subsection (1) includes power:

(a) to specify the descriptions of judgment or order in respect of which interest shall be payable;

(b) to provide that interest shall be payable only on sums exceeding a specified amount;

(c) to make provision for the manner in which and the periods by reference to which the interest is to be calculated and paid;

(d) to provide that any enactment shall or shall not apply in relation to interest payable under subsection (1) or shall apply to it with such modifications as may be specified in the order; and

(e) to make such incidental or supplementary provisions as the Lord Chancellor considers appropriate.

(5) Without prejudice to the generality of subsection (4), an order under subsection (1) may provide that the rate of interest shall be the rate specified in section 17 of the Judgments Act 1838 as that enactment has effect from time to time.

(5A) The power conferred by the subsection (1) includes power to make provision enabling a county court to order that the rate of interest applicable to a sum expressed in a currency other than sterling shall be such rate as the court thinks fit (instead of the rate otherwise applicable).

(6) The power to make an order under subsection (1) shall be exercisable by statutory instrument subject to annulment in pursuance of a resolution of either House of Parliament.

Enforcement of judgments and orders

Execution against goods

Execution of judgments or orders for payment of money

85.–(1) Subject to article 8 of the High Court and County Courts Jurisdiction Order 1991 a sum of money payable under a judgment or order of a county court may be recovered, in case of default or failure of payment, forthwith or at the time or times and in the manner thereby directed, by execution against the goods of the party against whom the judgment or order was obtained. [1991]

(2) The [district judge], on the application of the party prosecuting any such judgment or order, shall issue a warrant of execution in the nature of a writ of fieri facias whereby the [district judge] shall be empowered to levy or cause to be levied by distress and sale of the goods, wherever they may be found within the district

of the court, the money payable under the judgment or order and the costs of the execution.

(3) The precise time of the making of the application to the [district judge] to issue such a warrant shall be entered by him in the record prescribed for the purpose under section 12 and on the warrant.

(4) It shall be the duty of every constable within his jurisdiction to assist in the execution of every such warrant.

Execution of orders for payment by instalments

86.–(1) Where the court has made an order for payment of any sum of money by instalments, execution on the order shall not be issued until after default in payment of some instalment according to the order.

(2) County court rules may prescribe the cases in which execution is to issue if there is any such default and limit the amounts for which and the times at which execution may issue.

(3) Except so far as may be otherwise provided by county court rules made for those purposes, execution or successive executions may issue if there is any such default for the whole of the said sum of money and costs then remaining unpaid or for such part as the court may order either at the time of the original order or at any subsequent time; but except so far as may be otherwise provided by such rules, no execution shall issue unless at the time when it issues the whole or some part of an instalment which has already become due remains unpaid.

Execution to be superseded on payment

87.–(1) In or upon every warrant of execution issued from a county court against the goods of any person, the [district judge] shall cause to be inserted or endorsed the total amount to be levied, inclusive of the fee for issuing the warrant but exclusive of the fees for its execution.

(2) If the person against whom the execution is issued, before the actual sale of the goods, pays or causes to be paid or tendered to the [district judge] of the court from which the warrant is issued, or to the bailiff holding the warrant, the amount inserted in, or endorsed upon, the warrant under subsection (1), or such part as the person entitled agrees to accept in full satisfaction, together with the amount stated by the officer of the court to whom the payment or tender is made to be the amount of the fees for the execution of the warrant, the execution shall be superseded, and the goods shall be discharged and set at liberty.

Power to stay execution

88. If at any time it appears to the satisfaction of the court that any party to any proceedings is unable from any cause to pay any sum recovered against him (whether by way of satisfaction of the claim or counterclaim in the proceedings or by way of costs or otherwise), or any instalment of such a sum, the court may, in its discretion, stay any execution issued in the proceedings for such time and

on such terms as the court thinks fit, and so from time to time until it appears that the cause of inability has ceased.

Goods which may be seized

89.–(1) Every bailiff or officer executing any warrant of execution issued from a county court against the goods of any person may by virtue of it seize:

(a) any of that person's goods except:

    (i) such tools, books, vehicles and other items of equipment as are necessary to that person for use personally by him in his employment, business or vocation;

    (ii) such clothing, bedding, furniture, household equipment and provisions as are necessary for satisfying the basic domestic needs of that person and his family;

(b) any money, banknotes, bills of exchange, promissory notes, bonds, specialities or securities for money belonging to that person.

(2) Any reference to the goods of an execution debtor in this part of this Act includes a reference to anything else of his that may lawfully be seized in execution. [1990]

Custody of goods seized

90. Goods seized in execution under process of a county court shall, until sale:

(a) be deposited by the bailiff in some fit place; or

(b) remain in the custody of a fit person approved by the [district judge] to be put in possession by the bailiff; or

(c) be safeguarded in such other manner as the [district judge] directs.

Period to elapse before sale

93. No goods seized in execution under process of a county court shall be sold for the purpose of satisfying the warrant of execution until the expiration of a period of at least 5 days next following the day on which the goods have been seized unless:

(a) the goods are of a perishable nature; or

(b) the person whose goods have been seized so requests in writing.

Goods not to be sold except by brokers or appraisers

94. No goods seized in execution under process of a county court shall be sold for the purpose of satisfying the warrant of execution except by one of the brokers or appraisers appointed under this part of this Act.

Appointment of brokers, appraisers, etc

95.–(1) The [district judge] may from time to time as he thinks fit appoint such number of persons for keeping possession, and such number of brokers and appraisers for the purpose of selling or valuing any goods seized in execution under process of the court, as appears to him to be necessary.

(2) The [district judge] may direct security to be taken from any broker, appraiser or other person so appointed for such sum and in such manner as he thinks fit for the faithful performance of his duties without injury or oppression.

(3) The judge or [district judge] may dismiss any broker, appraiser or other person so appointed.

(4) There shall be payable to brokers and appraisers so appointed in respect of their duties, out of the produce of goods distrained or sold, such fees as may be prescribed by the fees order.

Power to appoint bailiffs to act as brokers and appraisers

96.–(1) The judge may appoint in writing any bailiff of the court to act as a broker or appraiser for the purpose of selling or valuing any goods seized in execution under process of the court.

(2) A bailiff so appointed may, without other licence in that behalf, perform all the duties which brokers or appraisers appointed under section 95 may perform under this Act.

Sales under executions to be public unless otherwise ordered

97.–(1) Where any goods are to be sold under execution for a sum exceeding £20 (including legal incidental expenses), the sale shall, unless the court from which the warrant of execution issued otherwise orders, be made by public auction and not by bill of sale or private contract, and shall be publicly advertised by the [district judge] on, and during three days next preceding, the day of sale.

(2) Where any goods are seized in execution and the registrar [district judge] has notice of another execution or other executions, the court shall not consider an application for leave to sell privately until the prescribed notice has been given to the other execution creditor or creditors, who may appear before the court and be heard upon the application.

Effect of warrants of execution

99.–(1) Subject:

(a) to subsection (2); and

(b) to section 103(2);

a warrant of execution against goods issued from a county court shall bind the property in the goods of the execution debtor as from the time at which application for the warrant was made to the [district judge] of the county court.

(2) Such a warrant shall not prejudice the title to any goods of the execution debtor acquired by a person in good faith and for valuable consideration unless he had at the time when he acquired his title:

(a) notice that an application for the issue of a warrant of execution against the goods of the execution debtor had been made to the [district judge] of a county court and that the warrant issued on the application either:

    (i)   remained unexecuted in the hands of the [district judge] of the court from which it was issued; or

    (ii)   had been sent for execution to, and received by, the [district judge] of another county court, and remained unexecuted in the hands of the [district judge] of that court; or

  (b)   notice that a writ of fieri facias or other writ of execution by virtue of which the goods of the execution debtor might be seized or attached had been delivered to and remained unexecuted in the hands of the sheriff.

(3) It shall be the duty of the [district judge] (without fee) on application for a warrant of execution being made to him to endorse on its back the hour, day, month and year when he received the application.

(4) For the purposes of this section:

  (a)   'property' means the general property in goods, and not merely a special property;

  (b)   'sheriff' includes any officer charged with the enforcement of a writ of execution; and

  (c)   a thing shall be treated as done in good faith if it is in fact done honestly whether it is done negligently or not.

Administration orders

Power to make administration order

112.–(1) Where a debtor:

  (a)   is unable to pay forthwith the amount of a judgment obtained against him; and

  (b)   alleges that his whole indebtedness amounts to a sum not exceeding the county court limit, inclusive of the amount for which the judgment was obtained,

a county court may make an order providing for the administration of his estate.

[(1) Where a debtor is unable to pay forthwith the amount of any debt owed by him, a county court may make an order providing for the administration of his estate.

(1A) The order may be made:

  (a)   on the application of the debtor (whether or not a judgment debt has been obtained against the debtor in respect of his debt, or any of his debts);

  (b)   on the application of any creditor under a judgment obtained against the debtor; and

  (c)   of the court's own motion during the course of, or on the determination of, any enforcement or other proceedings.]

(2) In this part of this Act:

'administration order' means an order under this section; and 'the appropriate court', in relation to an administration order, means the court has the power to make the order.

(3) Before an administration order is made, the appropriate court shall, in accordance with county court rules, send to every person whose name the debtor has notified to the appropriate court as being a creditor of his, a notice that that person's name has been so notified.

(4) So long as an administration order is in force, a creditor whose name is on the schedule to the order shall not, without the leave of the appropriate court, be entitled to present, or join in, a bankruptcy petition against the debtor unless:

(a)   his name was so notified; and

(b)   the debt by virtue of which he presents, or joins in, the petition, exceeds £1,500; and

(c)   the notice given under subsection (3) was received by the creditor within 28 days immediately preceding the day on which the petition is presented.

[(4A) Subsection (4) is subject to section 112A.]

[(5) An administration order shall not be invalid by reason only that the total amount of the debts is found at any time to exceed the county court limit, but in that case the court may, if it thinks fit, set aside the order.] [Prospectively repealed]

(6) An administration order may provide for the payment of the debts of the debtor by instalments or otherwise, and either in full or to such extent as appears practicable to the court under the circumstances of the case, and subject to any conditions as to his future earnings or income which the court may think just.

(7) The Secretary of State may by regulations increase or reduce the sum for the time being specified in subsection 4(b); but no such increase in the sum so specified shall affect any case in which the bankruptcy petition was presented before the coming into force of the increase.

(8) The power to make regulations under subsection (7) shall be exercisable by statutory instrument; and no such regulations shall be made unless a draft of them has been approved by resolution of each House of Parliament.

[(9) An administration order shall cease to have effect:

(a)   at the end of the period of three years beginning with the date on which it is made; or

(b)   on such earlier date as may be specified in the order.] [1990]

Notice of order and proof of debts

113. Where an administration order has been made:

(a)   notice of the order:

(i)   *[Repealed 1985];*

(ii)   shall be posted in the office of the county court for the district in which the debtor resides; and

(iii) shall be sent to every person whose name the debtor has notified to the appropriate court as being a creditor of his or who has proved;

(b) any creditor of the debtor, on proof of his debt before the [district judge], shall be entitled to be scheduled as a creditor of the debtor for the amount of his proof;

(c) any creditor may object in the prescribed manner to any debt scheduled, or to the manner in which payment is directed to be made by instalments;

(d) any person who, after the date of the order, becomes a creditor of the debtor shall, on proof of his debt before the [district judge], be scheduled as a creditor of the debtor for the amount of his proof, but shall not be entitled to any dividend under the order until the creditors who are scheduled as having been creditor before the date of the order have been paid to the extent provided by the order.

Effect of administration order

114.–(1) Subject to section 115 and 116, when an administration order is made, no creditor shall have any remedy against the person or property of the debtor in respect of any debt:

(a) of which the debtor notified the appropriate court before the administration order was made; or

(b) which has been scheduled to the order,

except with the leave of the appropriate court, and on such terms as that court may impose.

(2) Subject to subsection (3), any county court in which proceedings are pending against the debtor in respect of any debt so notified or scheduled shall, on receiving notice of the administration order, stay the proceedings, but may allow costs already incurred by the creditor, and such costs may, on application, be added to the debt.

(3) The requirement to stay proceedings shall not operate as a requirement that a county court in which proceedings in bankruptcy against the debtor are pending shall stay those proceedings.

Appropriation of money paid under order and discharge of order

117–(1) Money paid into court under an administration order shall be appropriated:

(a) first in satisfaction of the costs of administration (which shall not exceed 10 pence in the pound on the total amount of the debts); and

(b) then in liquidation of debts in accordance with the order.

(2) Where the amount received is sufficient to pay:

(a) each creditor scheduled to the order to the extent provided by the order;

(b) the costs of the plaintiff in the action in respect of which the order was made; and

(c) the costs of the administration,

the order shall be superseded, and the debtor shall be discharged from his debts to the scheduled creditors.

Responsibility and protection of officers

Liability of bailiff for neglect to levy execution

124.–(1) Where a baliff of a county court, being employed to levy any execution against goods, loses the opportunity of levying the execution by reason of neglect, connivance or omission, any party aggrieved thereby may complain to the judge of that court.

(2) On any such complaint the judge, if the neglect, connivance or omission is proved to this satisfaction, shall order the bailiff to pay such damages as it appears that the complainant has sustained by reason of it, not exceeding in any case the sum for which the execution issued.

Irregularity in executing warrants

125.–(1) No officer of a county court in executing any warrant of a court, and no person at whose instance any such warrant is executed, shall be deemed a trespasser by reason of any irregularity or informality:

(a)   in any proceedings on the validity of which the warrant depends; or

(b)   in the form of the warrant or in the mode of executing it;

but any person aggrieved may bring an action for any special damage sustained by him by reason of the irregularity or informality against the person guilty of it.

(2) No costs shall be recovered in such an action unless the damages awarded exceed £2.

The County Court (Interest on Judgment Debts) Order 1991

1.–(1) This Order may be cited as the County Court (Interest on Judgment Debts) Order 1991 and shall come into force on 1 July 1991.

(2) In this Order, unless the context otherwise requires:

'administration order' means an order under section 112 of the 1984 Act;

'given', in relation to a relevant judgment, means 'given or made';

'judgment creditor' means the person who has obtained or is entitled to enforce the relevant judgment and 'debtor' means the person against whom it was given;

'judgment debt' means a debt under a relevant judgment;

'relevant judgment' means a judgment or order of a county court for the payment of a sum of money of not less than £5,000 and, in relation to a judgment debt, means the judgment or order which gives rise to the judgment debt;

'the 1984 Act' means the County Courts Act 1984.

(3) Where in accordance with the provisions of this Order interest ceases to accrue on a specified day, interest shall cease to accrue at the end of that day.

(4) Nothing in this Order shall apply where the relevant judgment is given before 1 July 1991.

The general rule

2.–(1) Subject to the following provisions of this Order, every judgment debt under a relevant judgment shall, to the extent that it remains unsatisfied, carry interest under this Order from the date on which the relevant judgment was given.

(2) In the case of a judgment or order for the payment of a judgment debt, other than costs, the amount of which has to be determined at a later date, the judgment debt shall carry interest from that later date.

(3) Interest shall not be payable under this Order where the relevant judgment:

(a) is given in proceedings to recover money due under an agreement regulated by the Consumer Credit Act 1974;

(b) grants:

(i) the landlord of a dwelling-house; or

(ii) the mortgagee under a mortgage of land which consists of or includes a dwelling-house;

a suspended order for possession.

(4) Where the relevant judgment makes financial provision for a spouse or a child, interest shall only be payable on an order for the payment of not less than £5,000 as a lump sum (whether or not the sum is payable by instalments).

For the purposes of this paragraph, no regard shall be had to any interest payable under section 23(6) of the Matrimonial Causes Act 1973.

Interest where payment deferred

3. Where under the terms of the relevant judgment payment of a judgment debt:

(a) is not required to be made until a specified date; or

(b) is to be made by instalments;

interest shall not accrue under this Order:

(i) until that date; or

(ii) on the amount of any instalment, until it falls due;

as the case may be.

Interest and enforcement or other proceedings

4.–(1) Where a judgment creditor takes proceedings in a county court to enforce payment under a relevant judgment, the judgment debt shall cease to carry interest thereafter, except where those proceedings fail to produce any payment from the debtor in which case interest shall accrue as if those proceedings had never been taken.

(2) For the purposes of this article 'proceedings to enforce payment under a relevant judgment' include any proceeding for examining or summoning a judgment debtor or attaching a debt owed to him, but do not include proceedings under the Charging Orders Act 1979.

(3) Where an administration order or an attachment of earnings order is made, interest shall not accrue during the time the order is in force.

Rate of interest

5. Where a judgment debt carries interest, the rate of interest shall be the rate for the time being specified in section 17 of the Judgments Act 1838.

Appropriation of interest

6.–(1) Where the debtor is indebted to the same judgment creditor under two or more judgments or orders, money paid by him shall be applied to satisfy such of the judgments as the debtor may stipulate or, where no such stipulation is made, according to their priority in time.

(2) Money paid by the debtor in respect of any judgment debt shall be appropriated first to discharge or reduce the principal debt and then towards the interest.

Distress for Rent Rules 1988

Complaints as to fitness to hold a certificate

8.–(1) Any complaint as to the conduct of fitness of any bailiff who holds a certificate shall be made in Form 4 or, where the complainant has conducted a formal investigation into a complaint by a third party against the bailiff, in Form 5 to the court from which the certificate issued.

(2) Upon the receipt of any such complaint as is referred to in paragraph (1), the proper officer shall send written details of the complaint to the bailiff and require him to deliver a written reply to the court office within 14 days thereafter or within such longer time as the court may specify.

(3) If the bailiff fails to deliver the reply within the time specified, or if upon reading the reply the Judge is unsatisfied as to the bailiff's fitness to hold a certificate, the proper officer shall issue a notice to summon the bailiff to appear before the Judge on a specified date and show why his certificate should not be cancelled.

(3A) If upon reading the reply the Judge is satisfied as to the bailiff's fitness to hold a certificate, the court officer shall issue a notice to that effect and no further action shall be taken in respect of that complaint.

(4) The proper officer shall send a copy of the notice under paragraph (3) or (as the case may be) (3A) above to the complainant and any other interested party.

(4A) If, after a notice has been issued under paragraph (3) above, the complainant so applies in writing, and the application is received by the court no later than the date 14 days before the date set for the hearing, the court officer of the court receiving the complaint shall order that the complaint be heard in the issuing county court whose name appears in column 2 of the Table opposite the name of the complainant's home county court.

(4B) In the event of an order being made under paragraph (4A) above the court officer of the court receiving the complaint shall forthwith send:

(a) to the court officer of the court hearing the complaint:

    (i) certified copies of any relevant entries in the records of the court receiving the complaint; and

    (ii) copies of all other documents in his custody relating to the bailiff's certificate and to the complaint; and

(b) to the bailiff and any other interested party, notice of the order made under paragraph (4A) above.

(5) At the hearing:

    (i) the bailiff shall attend for examination and may make representations; and

    (ii) the complainant may attend and make representations.

(6) The procedure to be followed at the hearing including the calling of evidence, shall be such as the Judge considers just, and he may proceed with the hearing notwithstanding that the bailiff has failed to attend.

(7) If an order is made under paragraph (4A) above, the court officer of the court hearing the complaint shall, following the hearing, send to the court officer of the court which received the complaint certified copies of the order and all other documents in his custody relating to the bailiff's certificate and to the complaint, including the certified copies and copies sent under paragraph (4B)(a) above.

Cancellation of certificates

9.–(1) Following the hearing of any complaint under rule 8 the Judge may, whether he cancels the certificate or not, order that the security shall be forfeited whether wholly or in part, and that the amount or amounts directed to be forfeited shall be paid to any complainant by way of compensation for failure in due performance of the bailiff's duties, costs or expenses or where costs, fees and expenses have been incurred by the court, to Her Majesty's Paymaster General.

(2) Where an order for the forfeiture of the security, either wholly or in part, is made, but the certificate is not cancelled, the Judge may direct that fresh security under rule 6 shall be provided.

(3) Where a certificate is cancelled, the order of the Judge shall be in Form 6 and, subject to the provisions of this rule, the security shall be cancelled and the balance of the deposit returned to the bailiff.

(4) When a certificate is cancelled or expires it shall nevertheless continue to have effect for the purpose of any distress where the bailiff has entered into possession before the date of cancellation or expiry, unless the Judge otherwise directs.

(5) When a general certificate is cancelled or expires it shall be surrendered to the Judge, unless he otherwise directs.

(5A) When a bailiff holding a certificate ceases, for any reason, to carry on business as a bailiff he shall forthwith surrender his certificate to the Judge at the county court which issued the certificate, unless the Judge otherwise directs, and as from the date of the surrender the certificate shall be treated as if it had expired on that date.

(6) If a certificate is cancelled the proper officer shall publish a notice to that effect in an appropriate newspaper, and the costs of the notice shall be deducted from the security.

(7) References, in this rule, to the cancellation of a certificate shall not include the cancellation of a certificate upon the issue of a duplicate certificate, in accordance with rule 7A(4).

Fees, charges and expenses

10. No person shall be entitled to charge or recover from a tenant any fees, charges or expenses for levying a distress, or for doing any act or thing in relation thereto, other than those authorised by the tables in Appendix 1 to these Rules.

11.–(1) In the case of any difference as to the fees, charges and expenses between any of the parties, the fees, charges and expenses shall upon application be assessed by way of detailed assessment under Part 47 of the Civil Procedure Rules 1998 by the [district judge] of the county court of the district where the distress is levied, and he may make such order as he thinks fit as to the costs of the detailed assessment.

(2) Where the court in which the detailed assessment conducted is not the court in which the bailiff was granted his certificate and the [district judge] is of the opinion on the taxation that there has been overcharging of such magnitude as to call into question the fitness of a bailiff to hold a certificate, the proper officer shall send to the court in which the bailiff was granted his certificate a copy of the completed bill endorsed with a note of the [district judge's] opinion.

(3) The receipt of a bill under paragraph (2) shall be treated as a complaint under rule 8(1).

Appendix 1

Table of fees, charges and expenses

1. For levying distress –
   (i)   when the sum demanded and due does not exceeds £100, £12.50;

(ii) where the sum demanded and due exceeds £100, 12½% on the first £100, 4% on the next £400, 2½% on the next £1,500, 1% on the next £8,000 and ¼% on any additional sum.

2. For attending to levy distress where the levy is not made, the reasonable costs and charges for attending to levy, not exceeding the fees and charges which would have been due under paragraph 1 if the distress had been levied, the costs and charges are subject to taxation under rule 11.

3. For taking possession:

(i) where a man is left in physical possession, £4.50 per day;

(ii) where walking possession is taken, 45p per day.

Note: The charge for walking possession is payable only if a walking possession agreement in Form 8 has been concluded. A man left in possession must provide his own board in every case.

The possession fee is payable in respect of the day on which the distress is levied, but a fee for physical possession must not be charged where a walking possession agreement is signed at the time when the distress is levied.

4. For appraisement, at the request in writing of the tenant the reasonable fees, charges and expenses of the broker, subject to taxation under rule 11.

5. For attending to remove, the reasonable costs and charges attending the removal; the costs and charges are subject to taxation under rule 11.

6. For sale:

(i) where the sale is held on the auctioneer's premises, for commission to the auctioneer, an inclusive charge to include all out-of-pocket expenses of 15% on the sum realised, and the reasonable cost of advertising, removal and storage;

(ii) where the sale is held on the debtor's premises, for commission to the auctioneer, in addition to out-of-pocket expenses actually and reasonably incurred, 7½% on the sum realised.

7. Reasonable fees, charges and expenses, where distress is withdrawn or where no sale took place, and for negotiations between landlord and tenant respecting the distress, subject to taxation under rule 11.

8. For the purpose of calculating any percentage charges a fraction of £1 is to be reckoned as £1 but any fraction of a penny in the total amount of the fee so calculated is to be disregarded.

9. In addition to any amount authorised by this Table in respect of the supply of goods or services on which value added tax is chargeable there may be added a sum equivalent to the value added tax at the appropriate rate on that amount.

The High Court and County Courts Jurisdiction Order 1991 (as amended 1993, 1994, 1995 and 1999)

Allocation – commencement of proceedings

4. Subject to articles 4A, 5, 6 and 6A, proceedings in which both the county courts and the High Court have jurisdiction may be commenced either in a county court or in the High Court.

4A. Except for proceedings to which article 5 applies, a claim for money in which county courts have jurisdiction may only be commenced in the High Court if the financial value of the claim is more than £15,000. [1999]

5.–(1) Proceedings which include a claim for damages in respect of personal injuries may only be commenced in the High Court if the financial value of the claim is £50,000 or more. [1999]

(2) In this article 'personal injuries' means personal injuries to the claimant or any other person, and includes disease, impairment of physical or mental condition, and death.

(3) This article does not apply to proceedings which include a claim for damages in respect of an alleged breach of duty of care committed in the course of the provision of clinical or medical services (including dental or nursing services). [1999]

6. Applications and appeals under section 19 of the Local Government Finance Act 1982 and appeals under section 20 of that Act shall be commenced in the High Court. [1993]

6A. Applications under section 1 of the Access to Neighbouring Land Act 1992 shall be commenced in a county court. [1993]

Enforcement

8.–(1) Subject to paragraph (1A) a judgment or order of a county court for the payment of a sum of money which it is sought to enforce wholly or partially by execution against goods:

(a) shall be enforced only in the High Court where the sum which it is sought to enforce is £5,000 or more; and

(b) shall be enforced only in a county court where the sum which it is sought to enforce is less than £600; [1999]

(c) in any other case may be enforced in either the High Court or a county court. [1995]

(1A) A judgment or order of a county court by the Consumer Credit Act 1974 shall be enforced only in a county court. [1995]

(2) Section 85(1) of the County Courts Act 1984 is amended by the insertion, at the beginning of the subsection, of the words "Subject to article 8 of the High Court and County Courts Jurisdiction Order 1991". [1993]

Appendix 2

Standard letters

The following letters are designed for common debt advice situations. They can be adapted where desired and then customised for each debtor.

The letters are reproduced by kind permission of Stoke on Trent CABx.

To creditors, to withhold action and supply further information

Dear Madam/Sir

Re Mr and Mrs Smith
Account Number ....
Reference Number ....

Mr & Mrs Smith have approached us for assistance with their current financial problems. [Please find enclosed an authority form allowing me to deal with matters on behalf of the above named clients.*] We are writing to all their creditors in order to make a full evaluation of the situation. Could you therefore provide the following information:

1. Copies of the original agreement for supply of goods or finance.
2. Copies of any Default Notices issued.
3. Details of the amount outstanding, current contractual payments, current arrears and amount of interest being charged.
4. Date and amount of any court orders and details of subsequent payments.
5. A statement for the last 12 months.

As you will appreciate, the collection of this information from all creditors will take at least one month, and we are not in a position to make an offer of repayment until all the details have been received.

We therefore request that you take no further enforcement action and freeze all interest on the amount until at least .... when we will contact you again with our clients' offer.

We thank you for your consideration of this matter.

Yours faithfully

* Delete if appropriate and insert:
We are not enclosing a signed form of authorisation to act on our clients' behalf and request, instead, that you write directly to them, confirming your co-operation.

To ask unsecured creditors to write off the debt immediately where there is no available income

Dear Madam/Sir
[Name and address of debtor]

We are helping the above to deal with her/his finances as a whole.

A signed form of authorisation to act on her/his* behalf is enclosed.*
or
We do not enclose a signed form of authorisation to act on her/his* behalf and request, instead, that you write directly to her/him* confirming your co-operation in this matter.*

Please ensure when replying to us that you quote the name and address of our debtor.

Unfortunately, financial problems have now arisen.
[Enter
1) reasons for financial difficulties – eg, unemployment, ill health, relationship breakdown, collapse of business, low income, reduction of income, taking on loans to meet existing loans, personal difficulties, etc. Give as much relevant information as possible, including arrears of priority debts;
   and if no financial statement is enclosed:
2) details of income, and explain any high expenses (eg, mortgage).]

On the financial statement enclosed, we show suggestions for a realistic budget (including allowance for miscellaneous and unexpected expenditure). It also shows the amount of debt. Although the outgoings significantly exceed the income, these figures are based on levels of expenditure which have been found acceptable by the courts. As you can see, it is difficult to meet even basic needs.*
or
The state benefits received are intended to cover only very basic needs, so there is no spare money once such essentials have been met. Under these circumstances we have not enclosed a financial statement. We have enclosed a list of creditors.*

Thus, we are unable to make a constructive suggestion as to how an offer of repayment could be made.

In these circumstances, we would usually suggest that interest be frozen and payments suspended for a period of time. The position could then be reviewed and if there was still no prospect of payment at that stage, we would ask creditors to consider writing the debt off.

However, the position now and for the foreseeable future appears bleak. This is because [name's] income is unlikely to improve.

Even if circumstances improved, it is extremely unlikely that any offer would realistically be worth collecting.

Given these harsh circumstances we would ask that [name's] account be written off. We acknowledge this is an exceptional request, but were bankruptcy to be pursued, the financial outcome would be the same. It appears the Official Receiver would find no proceeds from realising her/his* few possessions. [The house is not owned.*] or [There is no real equity in the house.*]

Throughout the entire period all income would be protected, as there would be no surplus income to offer.

We would be grateful if you would confirm the account is written off. This would help remove the anxiety the debts are causing.

We thank you for your consideration of this matter.

Yours faithfully

* delete as appropriate

To ask unsecured creditors to suspend payments and to freeze interest for three to six months

Dear Madam/Sir
[Name and address of debtor]

We are helping the above to deal with her/his* finances as a whole.

A signed form of authorisation to act on her/his* behalf is enclosed.*
or
We do not enclose a signed form of authorisation to act on her/his* behalf and request, instead, that you write direct to her/him* confirming your co-operation in this matter.*

Please ensure when replying to us that you quote the name and address of our client.

[Enter
1) reasons for financial difficulties – eg, unemployment, ill health, relationship breakdown, collapse of business, low income, reduction of income, taking on loans to meet existing loans, personal difficulties, etc. Give as much relevant information as possible, including arrears of priority debts;
    and if no financial statement is enclosed:
2) details of income, and explain any high expenses (eg, mortgage).]

On the financial statement enclosed, we show suggestions for a realistic budget (including allowance for miscellaneous and unexpected expenditure). It also shows the amount of debt. Although the outgoings significantly exceed the income, these figures are based on levels of expenditure which have been found acceptable by the courts. As you can see, it is difficult to meet even basic needs.*
or
The state benefits received are intended to cover only very basic needs, so there is no spare money once such essentials have been met. Under these circumstances we have not enclosed a financial statement. We have enclosed a list of creditors.*

Thus, we are unable to make a constructive suggestion as to how an offer of repayment could be made.

Therefore, we suggest that payments on the account be suspended for [3 to 6] months and then the position can be reviewed. If interest is still being added to the account, we would appreciate it if this could be frozen to prevent the situation deteriorating any further. In addition, would you please confirm the balance and send a copy of the agreement.

We thank you for your consideration of this matter.

Yours faithfully

* delete as appropriate

To ask unsecured creditors to accept a token offer and freeze interest

Dear Madam/Sir
[Name and address of debtor]

We are helping the above to deal with her/his* finances as a whole.

A signed form of authorisation to act on her/his* behalf is enclosed. Please ensure when replying to us that you quote the name and address of our client.*
or
We do not enclose a signed form of authorisation to act on her/his* behalf and request, instead, that you write direct to her/him* confirming you cooperation in this matter.*

[Enter
reasons for financial difficulties – eg, unemployment, ill health, relationship breakdown, collapse of business, low income, reduction of income, taking on loans to meet existing loans, personal difficulties, etc. Give as much relevant information as possible, including arrears of priority debts.]

On the financial statement enclosed we show suggestions for a realistic budget (including allowance for miscellaneous and unexpected expenditure). It also shows the amount of debt. An offer of payment would not normally be made in such circumstances, but as a gesture of goodwill we suggest that our client offers £. . . . . per month [insert a figure for the token offer] and we would be grateful if you would accept this offer. We appreciate this is a low offer but believe it is the maximum amount that could be paid regularly.

We have also advised that payments start as soon as possible. Would you please supply a paying-in book or standing order/direct debit application form. If interest is still being added to the account, we would appreciate it if this could be frozen so that all of the payments made reduce the debt.

In addition, would you please confirm the balance and send a copy of the agreement.*

We thank you for your consideration of this matter.

Yours faithfully

* delete as appropriate

To ask unsecured creditors to accept equitable offers and freeze interest

Dear Madam/Sir
[Name and address of debtor]

We are helping the above to deal with her/his* finances as a whole.

A signed form of authorisation to act on her/his* behalf is enclosed.*
Unfortunately, financial problems have now arisen.*

[Enter
reasons for financial difficulties – eg, unemployment, ill health, relationship breakdown, collapse of business, low income, reduction of income, taking on loans to meet existing loans, personal difficulties, etc. Give as much relevant information as possible, including arrears of priority debts.*]
or
Now we have reviewed the situation and hope that the following information will prove useful.*

On the financial statement enclosed we show suggestions for a realistic budget (including allowance for miscellaneous and unexpected expenditure) and a payment proposal based on an equitable distribution of the available income. We appreciate that this is a significant reduction but believe it is a realistic amount that could be paid regularly. We have advised that this offer be increased should circumstances improve.

We have also advised that payments start as soon as possible. Would you please supply a paying-in book or standing order/direct debit application form. If interest is still being added to the account, we would appreciate it if this could be frozen so that all of the payments made reduce the debt.

We thank you for your consideration of this matter.

Yours faithfully

* delete as appropriate

. . . .

To ask unsecured creditors to agree to an administration order (and, if necessary, to write off the total balance or a proportion of the debt where the total indebtedness exceeds the maximum limit)

Dear Madam/Sir
[Name and address of debtor]

We are helping the above to deal with her/his* finances as a whole.

A signed form of authorisation to act on her/his* behalf is enclosed.*

Unfortunately, financial problems have now arisen.*
[Enter
reasons for financial difficulties – eg, unemployment, ill health, relationship breakdown, collapse of business, low income, reduction of income, taking on loans to meet existing loans, personal difficulties, etc. Give as much relevant information as possible, including arrears of priority debts.*]
or
Now we have reviewed the situation and hope that the following information will prove useful.*

On the financial statement enclosed we show suggestions for a realistic budget (including allowance for miscellaneous and unexpected expenditure). It also shows the amount of the debt. As some money is available once essential expenditure has been met and judgment has already been obtained by at least one creditor, an administration order would appear to be the best solution for making regular payments to creditors. This method should provide some security to creditors as payments are collected, monitored and reviewed under the control of the court.

However, as you can see, the total indebtedness exceeds the maximum amount for an administration order.

Compared with the total debt, the amount owed on the above account is small. The major creditors would not agree to accept any less than their fair share of the money available. It would greatly assist our client if you would agree to write off the balance so that an administration order can be applied for. We acknowledge this is an exceptional request but believe it is the only realistic solution. (We enclose a list of balances.)*
or
We are, therefore, writing to ask you to consider writing off a proportion of the money owed on condition that an administration order will be applied for. We enclose a list of proposed balances. We acknowledge this is an exceptional request but believe it is the only realistic solution.*

. . . .

We would be grateful if further action on the above account could be withheld to enable the application for an administration order to be made.

Yours faithfully

* delete as appropriate

. . . .

To ask unsecured creditors to suspend payments and freeze interest for a further three to six months

Dear Madam/Sir
[Name and address of debtor]

We are writing with reference to the above account. We have now reviewed the position and we hope you will find the following information helpful.

Unfortunately, the situation has [changed/worsened*].
This means there is still no possibility of an offer of payment.

We hope the following information will be helpful.*
[Add any additional new information about the debtor's circumstances, and position and summarise the creditors' responses that are helpful.]

Once again, we suggest that payments on the account be suspended for a further [three to six] months and that interest continues to be frozen. The position can be then reviewed in [three to six] months' time.

When replying to us, please ensure you quote the name and address of our client/your customer.*
or
We would be grateful if you would write directly to the customer confirming your agreement.*

We thank you for your consideration of this matter.

Yours faithfully

* delete as appropriate

To unsecured creditors where the first request to write off the debt has been refused

Dear Madam/Sir
[Name and address of debtor]

We are writing with reference to the above account.

As we have explained there is, unfortunately, no available income to offer and the realistic spending needs exceed the weekly income. The situation is unlikely to improve in the foreseeable future.

Even if [name/s] were in a position to make an equitable offer in the future, it is unlikely it would realistically be worth collecting. This is because any available income is likely to be limited, [and the amount owed is a relatively small proportion of the debt*].

We hope the following information will be helpful*:
[Add here additional new information about the debtor's circumstances, and summarise the creditors' responses that are helpful.]

Under these circumstances, we would be most obliged if the outstanding balance can now be written off.

We would be grateful if you would write directly to the client confirming your agreement.*
or
When replying to us please ensure you quote the name and address of our client/your customer.*

We thank you for your consideration of this matter.

Yours faithfully

* delete as appropriate

. . . .

To unsecured creditors where the first request to accept reduced payments and freeze interest has been refused

Dear Madam/Sir
[Name and address of debtor]

We are writing with reference to the above account.

As indicated in our last letter, unfortunately the offer of payment cannot be increased. In our experience, the county court would view this offer as reasonable. We hope that the reduced amount offered will now be accepted, and interest charges frozen.

We hope the following information will be helpful*:
[Add here additional new information about the debtor's circumstances, and summarise the creditors' responses that are helpful.]

As before, we would be grateful if you would write directly to the client confirming your agreement.*
or
When replying to us, please ensure you quote the name and address of our client/your customer.*

Once again, we thank you for your consideration of this matter.

Yours faithfully

* delete as appropriate

Appendix 3

Court forms

This appendix contains some of the most commonly used court forms and judgments. Apart from judgments, these and other court forms can be found at the websites www.courtservice.gov.uk (High Court and county court) and www.insolvency.gov.uk (bankruptcy). The forms are as follows.

High Court/County court

County court

Bankruptcy

General

Claim Form

In the

for court use only

Claim No.	—
Issue date	

Claimant

SEAL

Defendant(s)

Brief details of claim

Value

Defendant's name and address

	£
Amount claimed	
Court fee	
Solicitor's costs	
Total amount	

The court office at

is open between 10 am and 4 pm Monday to Friday. When corresponding with the court, please address forms or letters to the Court Manager and quote the claim number.

N1 Claim form (CPR Part 7) (01.02)

Printed on behalf of The Court Service

	Claim No.	

Does, or will, your claim include any issues under the Human Rights Act 1998? ☐ Yes ☐ No

Particulars of Claim (attached)(to follow)

Statement of Truth
*(I believe)(The Claimant believes) that the facts stated in these particulars of claim are true.
* I am duly authorised by the claimant to sign this statement

Full name _____

Name of claimant's solicitor's firm _____

signed _____ position or office held _____
*(Claimant)(Litigation friend)(Claimant's solicitor)   (if signing on behalf of firm or company)
*delete as appropriate

	Claimant's or claimant's solicitor's address to which documents or payments should be sent if different from overleaf including (if appropriate) details of DX, fax or e-mail.

Appendix 3: Court forms
Form N1A

Notes for claimant on completing a claim form
Further information may be obtained from the court in a series of free leaflets.

- Please read all of these guidance notes before you begin completing the claim form. The notes follow the order in which information is required on the form.
- Court staff can help you fill in the claim form and give information about procedure once it has been issued. But they cannot give legal advice. If you need legal advice, for example, about the likely success of your claim or the evidence you need to prove it, you should contact a solicitor or a Citizens Advice Bureau.
- If you are filling in the claim form by hand, please use black ink and write in block capitals.
- Copy the completed claim form and the defendant's notes for guidance so that you have one copy for yourself, one copy for the court and one copy for each defendant. Send or take the forms to the court office with the appropriate fee. The court will tell you how much this is.

Notes on completing the claim form

Heading

You must fill in the heading of the form to indicate whether you want the claim to be issued in a county court or in the High Court (The High Court means either a District Registry (attached to a county court) or the Royal Courts of Justice in London). There are restrictions on claims which may be issued in the High Court (see 'Value' overleaf).

Use whichever of the following is appropriate:

'In the ....County Court'
(inserting the name of the court)

or

'In the High Court of Justice........................Division'
(inserting eg. 'Queen's Bench' or 'Chancery' as appropriate)
'............................District Registry'
(inserting the name of the District Registry)

or

'In the High Court of Justice........................Division,
(inserting eg. 'Queen's Bench' or 'Chancery' as appropriate)
Royal Courts of Justice'

Claimant and defendant details

As the person issuing the claim, you are called the 'claimant'; the person you are suing is called the 'defendant'. Claimants who are under 18 years old (unless otherwise permitted by the court) and patients within the meaning of the Mental Health Act 1983, must have a litigation friend to issue and conduct court proceedings on their behalf. Court staff will tell you more about what you need to do if this applies to you.

You must provide the following information about yourself **and** the defendant according to the capacity in which you are suing and in which the defendant is being sued. When suing or being sued as:-

an individual:

All known forenames and surname, whether Mr, Mrs, Miss, Ms or Other (e.g. Dr) and residential address (**including** postcode and telephone number) in England and Wales. Where the defendant is a proprietor of a business, a partner in a firm or an individual sued in the name of a club or other unincorporated association, the address for service should be the usual or last known place of residence **or** principal place of business of the company, firm or club or other unincorporated association.

Where the individual is:

under 18 write '(a child by Mr Joe Bloggs his litigation friend)' after the name. If the child is conducting proceedings on their own behalf write '(a child)' after the child's name.

a patient within the meaning of the Mental Health Act 1983 write '(by Mr Joe Bloggs his litigation friend)' after the patient's name.

trading under another name

you must add the words 'trading as' and the trading name e.g. 'Mr John Smith trading as Smith's Groceries'.

suing or being sued in a representative capacity

you must say what that capacity is e.g. 'Mr Joe Bloggs as the representative of Mrs Sharon Bloggs (deceased)'.

suing or being sued in the name of a club or other unincorporated association

add the words 'suing/sued on behalf of' followed by the name of the club or other unincorporated association.

a firm

enter the name of the firm followed by the words 'a firm' e.g. 'Bandbox - a firm' and an address for service which is either a partner's residential address or the principal or last known place of business.

a corporation (other than a company)

enter the full name of the corporation and the address which is either its principal office **or** any other place where the corporation carries on activities and which has a real connection with the claim.

a company registered in England and Wales

enter the name of the company and an address which is either the company's registered office **or** any place of business that has a real, or the most, connection with the claim e.g. the shop where the goods were bought.

an overseas company (defined by s744 of the Companies Act 1985)

enter the name of the company and either the address registered under s691 of the Act **or** the address of the place of business having a real, or the most, connection with the claim.

N1A - w3 Notes for claimant (4.99)

Printed on behalf of The Court Service

Brief details of claim

Note: The facts and full details about your claim and whether or not you are claiming interest, should be set out in the 'particulars of claim' *(see note under 'Particulars of Claim').*

You must set out under **this** heading:

- a concise statement of the nature of your claim
- the remedy you are seeking e.g. payment of money; an order for return of goods or their value; an order to prevent a person doing an act; damages for personal injuries.

Value

If you are claiming a **fixed amount of money** (a 'specified amount') write the amount in the box at the bottom right-hand corner of the claim form against 'amount claimed'.

If you are not claiming a fixed amount of money (an 'unspecified amount') under 'Value' write "I expect to recover" followed by whichever of the following applies to your claim:

- "not more than £5,000" or
- "more than £5,000 but not more than £15,000"or
- "more than £15,000"

If you are **not able** to put a value on your claim, write "I cannot say how much I expect to recover".

Personal injuries

If your claim is for 'not more than £5,000' and includes a claim for personal injuries, you must also write "My claim includes a claim for personal injuries and the amount I expect to recover as damages for pain, suffering and loss of amenity is" followed by either:

- "not more than £1,000" or
- "more than £1,000"

Housing disrepair

If your claim is for 'not more than £5,000' and includes a claim for housing disrepair relating to residential premises, you must also write "My claim includes a claim against my landlord for housing disrepair relating to residential premises. The cost of the repairs or other work is estimated to be" followed by either:

- "not more than £1,000" or
- "more than £1,000"

If within this claim, you are making a claim for other damages, you must also write:

"I expect to recover as damages" followed by either:

- "not more than £1,000" or
- "more than £1,000"

Issuing in the High Court

You may only issue in the High Court if one of the following statements applies to your claim:-

"By law, my claim must be issued in the High Court. The Act which provides this is ....(specify Act)"
or
"I expect to recover more than £15,000"
or
"My claim includes a claim for personal injuries and the value of the claim is £50,000 or more"

or
"My claim needs to be in a specialist High Court list, namely...............................(state which list)".

If one of the statements does apply and you wish to, or must by law, issue your claim in the High Court, write the words "I wish my claim to issue in the High Court because" followed by the relevant statement e.g. "I wish my claim to issue in the High Court because my claim includes a claim for personal injuries and the value of my claim is £50,000 or more."

Defendant's name and address

Enter in this box the full names and address of the defendant receiving the claim form (ie. one claim form for each defendant). If the defendant is to be served outside England and Wales, you may need to obtain the court's permission.

Particulars of claim

You may include your particulars of claim on the claim form in the space provided or in a separate document which you should head 'Particulars of Claim'. It should include the names of the parties, the court, the claim number and your address for service and also contain a statement of truth. You should keep a copy for yourself, provide one for the court and one for each defendant. Separate particulars of claim can either be served

- with the claim form **or**
- within 14 days after the date on which the claim form was served.

If your particulars of claim are served separately from the claim form, they must be served with the forms on which the defendant may reply to your claim.

Your particulars of claim must include

- a concise statement of the facts on which you rely
- a statement (if applicable) to the effect that you are seeking aggravated damages or exemplary damages
- details of any interest which you are claiming
- any other matters required for your type of claim as set out in the relevant practice direction

Address for documents

Insert in this box the address at which you wish to receive documents and/or payments, if different from the address you have already given under the heading 'Claimant'. The address must be in England or Wales. If you are willing to accept service by DX, fax or e-mail, add details.

Statement of truth

This must be signed by you, by your solicitor or your litigation friend, as appropriate.

Where the claimant is a registered company or a corporation the claim must be signed by either the director, treasurer, secretary, chief executive, manager or other officer of the company or (in the case of a corporation) the mayor, chairman, president or town clerk.

Notes for defendant on replying to the claim form

Please read these notes carefully - they will help you decide what to do about this claim. Further information may be obtained from the court in a series of free leaflets

- If this claim form was received with the particulars of claim completed or attached, you must reply within 14 days of the date it was served on you. If the words 'particulars of claim to follow' are written in the particulars of claim box, you should not reply until after you are served with the particulars of claim (which should be no more than 14 days after you received the claim form). If the claim was sent by post, the date of service is taken as the second day after posting (see post mark). If the claim form was delivered or left at your address, the date of service will be the day after it was delivered.
- You may either
  - pay the total amount i.e. the amount claimed, the court fee, and solicitor's costs (if any)
  - admit that you owe all or part of the claim and ask for time to pay or
  - dispute the claim
- If you do not reply, judgment may be entered against you.
- The notes below tell you what to do.
- The response pack will tell you which forms to use for your reply. (The pack will accompany the particulars of claim if they are served after the claim form).
- Court staff can help you complete the forms of reply and tell you about court procedures. But they cannot give legal advice. If you need legal advice, for example about the likely success of disputing the claim, you should contact a solicitor or a Citizens Advice Bureau immediately.

Registration of Judgments: If this claim results in a judgment against you, details will be entered in a public register, the Register of County Court Judgments. They will then be passed to credit reference agencies which will then supply them to credit grantors and others seeking information on your financial standing. **This will make it difficult for you to get credit.** A list of credit reference agencies is available from Registry Trust Ltd, 173/175 Cleveland Street, London W1T 6QR.

Costs and Interest: Additional costs and interest may be added to the amount claimed on the front of the claim form if judgment is entered against you. In a county court, if judgment is for £5,000 or more, or is in respect of a debt which attracts contractual or statutory interest for late payment, the claimant may be entitled to further interest.

Your response and what happens next

How to pay

Do not bring any payments to the court - they will not be accepted.

When making payments to the claimant, quote the claimant's reference (if any) and the claim number.

Make sure that you keep records and can account for any payments made. Proof may be required if there is any disagreement. It is not safe to send cash unless you use registered post.

Admitting the Claim

Claim for specified amount

If you admit all the claim, take or send the money, including the court fee, any interest and costs, to the claimant at the address given for payment on the claim form, within 14 days.

If you admit all the claim and you are asking for time to pay, complete Form N9A and send it to the claimant at the address given for payment on the claim form, within 14 days. The claimant will decide whether to accept your proposal for payment. If it is accepted, the claimant may request the court to enter judgment against you and you will be sent an order to pay. If your

offer is not accepted, the court will decide how you should pay.

If you admit only part of the claim, complete Form N9A and Form N9B (see 'Disputing the Claim' overleaf) and send them to the court within 14 days. The claimant will decide whether to accept your part admission. If it is accepted, the claimant may request the court to enter judgment against you and the court will send you an order to pay. If your part admission is not accepted, the case will proceed as a defended claim.

Claim for unspecified amount

If you admit liability for the whole claim but do not make an offer to satisfy the claim, complete Form N9C and send it to the court within 14 days. A copy will be sent to the claimant who may request the court to enter judgment against you for an amount to be decided by the court, and costs. The court will enter judgment and refer the court file to a judge for directions for management of the case. You and the claimant will be sent a copy of the court's order.

If you admit liability for the claim and offer an amount of money to satisfy the claim, complete Form

N9C and send it to the court within 14 days. The claimant will be sent a copy and asked if the offer is acceptable. The claimant must reply to the court within 14 days and send you a copy. If a reply is not received, the claim will be stayed. If the amount you have offered is **accepted** -

• the claimant may request the court to enter judgment against you for that amount.

• if you have requested time to pay which is not accepted by the claimant, the rate of payment will be decided by the court.

If your offer in satisfaction is **not accepted** -

• the claimant may request the court to enter judgment against you for an amount to be decided by the court, and costs; and

• the court will enter judgment and refer the court file to a judge for directions for management of the case. You and the claimant will be sent a copy of the court's order.

Disputing the claim

If you are being sued as an individual for a specified amount of money and you dispute the claim, the claim may be transferred to a local court i.e. the one nearest to or where you live or carry on business if different from the court where the claim was issued.

If you need longer than 14 days to prepare your defence or to contest the court's jurisdiction to try the claim, complete the Acknowledgment of Service form and send it to the court within 14 days. This will allow you 28 days from the date of service of the particulars of claim to file your defence or make an application to contest the court's jurisdiction. The court will tell the claimant that your Acknowledgment of Service has been received.

If the case proceeds as a defended claim, you and the claimant will be sent an Allocation Questionnaire. You will be told the date by which it must be returned to the court. The information you give on the form will help a judge decide whether your case should be dealt with in the small claims track, fast track or multi-track. After a judge has considered the completed questionnaires, you will be sent a notice of allocation setting out the judge's decision. The notice will tell you the track to which the claim has been allocated and what you have to do to prepare for the hearing or trial. **Leaflets telling you more about the tracks are available from the court office.**

Claim for specified amount

If you wish to dispute the full amount claimed or wish to claim against the claimant (a counterclaim), complete Form N9B and send it to the court within 14 days.

If you admit part of the claim, complete the Defence Form N9B and the Admission Form N9A and send them both to the court within 14 days. The claimant will decide whether to accept your part admission in satisfaction of the claim (see under 'Admitting the Claim - specified amount'). If the claimant does not accept the amount you have admitted, the case will proceed as a defended claim.

If you dispute the claim because you have already paid it, complete Form N9B and send it to the court within 14 days. The claimant will have to decide whether to proceed with the claim or withdraw it and notify the court and you within 28 days. If the claimant wishes to proceed, the case will proceed as a defended claim.

Claim for unspecified amount/return of goods/non-money claims

If you dispute the claim or wish to claim against the claimant (counterclaim), complete Form N9D and send it to the court within 14 days.

Personal injuries claims:

If the claim is for personal injuries and the claimant has attached a medical report to the particulars of claim, in your defence you should state whether you:

• agree with the report **or**
• dispute all or part of the report **and** give your reasons for doing so **or**
• neither agree nor dispute the report **or** have no knowledge of the report

Where you have obtained your own medical report, you should attach it to your defence.

If the claim is for personal injuries and the claimant has attached a schedule of past and future expenses and losses, in your defence you must state which of the items you:

• agree **or**
• dispute **and** supply alternative figures where appropriate **or**
• neither agree nor dispute or have no knowledge of

Address where notices can be sent

This must be either your solicitor's address, your own residential or business address in England and Wales or (if you live elsewhere) some other address within England and Wales.

Statement of truth

This must be signed by you, by your solicitor or your litigation friend, as appropriate.

Where the defendant is **a registered company or a corporation** the response must be signed by either the director, treasurer, secretary, chief executive, manager or other officer of the company **or** (in the case of a corporation) the mayor, chairman, president or town clerk

Response Pack

You should read the 'notes for defendant' attached to the claim form which will tell you when and where to send the forms

Included in this pack are:

- either **Admission Form N9A**
  (if the claim is for a specified amount)
  or **Admission Form N9C**
  (if the claim is for an unspecified amount
  or is not a claim for money)

- either **Defence and Counterclaim Form
  N9B** (if the claim is for a specified amount)
  or **Defence and Counterclaim Form N9D**
  (if the claim is for an unspecified amount
  or is not a claim for money)

- **Acknowledgment of service**
  (see below)

Complete

If you admit the claim or the amount claimed and/or you want time to pay	the admission form
If you admit part of the claim	the admission form and the defence form
If you dispute the whole claim or wish to make a claim (a counterclaim) against the claimant	the defence form
If you need 28 days (rather than 14) from the date of service to prepare your defence, or wish to contest the court's jurisdiction	the acknowledgment of service
If you do nothing, judgment may be entered against you	

Acknowledgment of Service

Defendant's full name if different from the name given on the claim form

In the	
Claim No.	
Claimant (including ref.)	
Defendant	

Address to which documents about this claim should be sent (including reference if appropriate)

	if applicable
fax no.	
DX no.	
Ref. no.	
e-mail	

Tel. no.   Postcode

Tick the appropriate box

1. I intend to defend all of this claim ☐

2. I intend to defend part of this claim ☐

3. I intend to contest jurisdiction ☐

If you file an acknowledgment of service but do not file a defence within 28 days of the date of service of the claim form, or particulars of claim if served separately, judgment may be entered against you.

If you do not file an application within 28 days of the date of service of the claim form, or particulars of claim if served separately, it will be assumed that you accept the court's jurisdiction and judgment may be entered against you.

Signed		**Position or office held** (if signing on behalf of firm or company)		
(Defendant)(Defendant's solicitor) (Litigation friend)			**Date**	

The court office at

is open between 10 am and 4 pm Monday to Friday. When corresponding with the court, please address forms or letters to the Court Manager and quote the claim number.

N9 Response Pack (5.02)   *Printed on behalf of The Court Service*

Admission (specified amount)

- You have a limited number of days to complete and return this form
- Before completing this form, please read the notes for guidance attached to the claim form

When to fill in this form

Only fill in this form if:
- you are admitting all of the claim **and** you are asking for time to pay; or
- you are admitting part of the claim. (You should also complete form N9B)

How to fill in this form

- Tick the correct boxes and give as much information as you can. **Then sign and date the form.** If necessary provide details on a separate sheet, add the claim number and attach it to this form.
- Make your offer of payment in box 11 on the back of this form. **If you make no offer the claimant will decide how much and when you should pay.**
- If you are not an individual, you should ensure that you provide sufficient details about the assets and liabilities of your firm, company or corporation to support any offer of payment made in box 11.
- You can get help to complete this form at **any** county court office or Citizens Advice Bureau.

Where to send this form

- **If you admit the claim in full**
  Send the completed form to the address shown on the claim form as one to which documents should be sent.
- **If you admit only part of the claim**
  Send the form **to the court** at the address given on the claim form, together with the defence form (N9B).

How much of the claim do you admit?

☐ I admit the full amount claimed as shown on the claim form **or**

☐ I admit the amount of   £ _____

1   Personal details

Surname _____

Forename _____

☐ Mr ☐ Mrs ☐ Miss ☐ Ms

☐ Married ☐ Single ☐ Other *(specify)* ____

Age _____

Address _____

Postcode _____

Tel. no. _____

In the	
Claim No.	
Claimant (including ref.)	
Defendant	

2   Dependants   *(people you look after financially)*

Number of children in each age group

under 11 ☐   11-15 ☐   16-17 ☐   18 & over ☐

Other dependants *(give details)* _____

3   Employment

☐ **I am employed as a** _____
My employer is _____

Jobs other than main job *(give details)* _____

☐ **I am self employed as a** _____
Annual turnover is........................... £ ____

☐ **I am not** in arrears with my national insurance contributions, income tax and VAT

☐ **I am** in arrears and I owe........... £ ____

Give details of:
(a) contracts and other work in hand _____
(b) any sums due for work done _____

☐ **I have been unemployed for** ____ years ____ months

☐ **I am a pensioner**

4   Bank account and savings

☐ **I have a bank account**
☐ The account is in credit by........ £ ____
☐ The account is overdrawn by.... £ ____

☐ **I have a savings or building society account**
The amount in the account is.......... £ ____

5   Residence

I live in ☐ my own house   ☐ lodgings
☐ my jointly owned house   ☐ council accommodation
☐ rented accommodation

N9A Form of admission (specified amount) (11.01)

Printed on behalf of The Court Service

6 Income

	£	per
My usual take home pay (including overtime, commission, bonuses etc)	£	per
Income support	£	per
Child benefit(s)	£	per
Other state benefit(s)	£	per
My pension(s)	£	per
Others living in my home give me	£	per
Other income (give details below)		
	£	per
	£	per
	£	per
Total income	**£**	**per**

8 Priority debts *(This section is for arrears only. Do not include regular expenses listed in box 7.)*

	£	per
Rent arrears	£	per
Mortgage arrears	£	per
Council tax/Community Charge arrears	£	per
Water charges arrears	£	per
Fuel debts: Gas	£	per
Electricity	£	per
Other	£	per
Maintenance arrears	£	per
Others (give details below)		
	£	per
	£	per
Total priority debts	**£**	**per**

7 Expenses

(Do not include any payments made by other members of the household out of their own income)

I have regular expenses as follows:

	£	per
Mortgage (including second mortgage)	£	per
Rent	£	per
Council tax	£	per
Gas	£	per
Electricity	£	per
Water charges	£	per
TV rental and licence	£	per
HP repayments	£	per
Mail order	£	per
Housekeeping, food, school meals	£	per
Travelling expenses	£	per
Children's clothing	£	per
Maintenance payments	£	per
Others (not court orders or credit debts listed in boxes 9 and 10)		
	£	per
	£	per
	£	per
Total expenses	**£**	**per**

9 Court orders

Court	Claim No.	£	per

	£	per
Total court order instalments	**£**	**per**

Of the payments above, I am behind with payments to *(please list)*

10 Credit debts

Loans and credit card debts *(please list)*

	£	per
	£	per
	£	per
	£	per

Of the payments above, I am behind with payments to *(please list)*

11 Offer of payment

☐ I can pay the amount admitted on

or

☐ I can pay by monthly instalments of £

If you cannot pay immediately, please give brief reasons below

12 Declaration   I declare that the details I have given above are true to the best of my knowledge

Signed		Position or office held (if signing on behalf of firm or company)	
Date			

© Crown Copyright

Defence and Counterclaim (specified amount)

- Fill in this form if you wish to dispute all or part of the claim and/or make a claim against the claimant (counterclaim).
- You have a limited number of days to complete and return this form to the court.
- Before completing this form, please read the notes for guidance attached to the claim form.
- Please ensure that all boxes at the top right of this form are completed. You can obtain the correct names and number from the claim form. The court cannot trace your case without this information.

How to fill in this form

- Complete sections 1 and 2. Tick the correct boxes and give the other details asked for.
- Set out your defence in section 3. If necessary continue on a separate piece of paper making sure that the claim number is clearly shown on it. In your defence you must state which allegations in the particulars of claim you deny and your reasons for doing so. **If you fail to deny an allegation it may be taken that you admit it.**
- If you dispute only some of the allegations you must
  - specify which you admit and which you deny; and
  - give your own version of events if different from the claimant's.

In the

Claim No.	
Claimant (including ref.)	
Defendant	

- If you wish to make a claim against the claimant (a counterclaim) complete section 4.
- Complete and sign section 5 before sending this form to the court. Keep a copy of the claim form and this form.

Community Legal Service Fund (CLSF)

You may qualify for assistance from the CLSF (this used to be called 'legal aid') to meet some or all of your legal costs. Ask about the CLSF at any county court office or any information or help point which displays this logo.

1. How much of the claim do you dispute?

☐ I dispute the full amount claimed as shown on the claim form

or

☐ I admit the amount of £ [   ]

If you dispute only part of the claim you must **either**:

- pay the amount admitted to the person named at the address for payment on the claim form (see How to Pay in the notes on the back of, or attached to, the claim form). Then send this defence to the court

or

- complete the admission form **and** this defence form and send them to the court.

☐ I paid the amount admitted on (date) [   ]

or

☐ I enclose the completed form of admission (go to section 2)

2. Do you dispute this claim because you have already paid it? *Tick whichever applies*

☐ **No** (go to section 3)

☐ **Yes** I paid £ [   ] to the claimant

on [   ] (before the claim form was issued)

Give details of where and how you paid it in the box below (then go to section 5)

3. Defence

Defence (continued)

Claim No.

4. If you wish to make a claim against the claimant (a counterclaim)

If your claim is for a specific sum of money, how much are you claiming? £

My claim is for *(please specify nature of claim)*

- To start your counterclaim, you will have to pay a fee. Court staff will tell you how much you have to pay

- You may not be able to make a counterclaim where the claimant is the Crown (e.g. a Government Department). Ask at your local county court office for further information.

What are your reasons for making the counterclaim?
If you need to continue on a separate sheet put the claim number in the top right hand corner

5. Signed
(To be signed by you or by your solicitor or litigation friend)

*(I believe)(The defendant believes) that the facts stated in this form are true. *I am duly authorised by the defendant to sign this statement

*delete as appropriate

Position or office held (if signing on behalf of firm or company)

Date

Give an address to which notices about this case can be sent to you

Postcode

Tel. no.

if applicable

fax no.

DX no.

e-mail

Order for possession
(rented premises)
(suspended)

In the

Claim No.

Claimant

Defendant(s)

On   20 ,

sitting at

heard

SEAL

and the court orders that

1. The defendant give the claimant possession of

   on or before   20 .

2. The defendant pay the claimant £   for

3. The defendant pay the claimant's costs of the claim £   .

4. The defendant pay the total of £   to the claimant on or before   20 .

5. This order is not to be enforced so long as the defendant pays the claimant the rent arrears
   and the amount for use and occupation [and costs, totalling] £   by the payments set out below
   in addition to the current rent.

   Payments required

   [£   on or before   20   and]

   £   per   , the first payment being made on or before   20 .

To the defendant

The court has ordered that **unless you pay the arrears** and
costs at the rate set out above **in addition to your current
rent,** you must leave the premises.

Payments should be made to the claimant, not to the court.
If you need more information about making payments, you
should contact the claimant.

If you do not make the payments or leave the premises,
the claimant can ask the court, without a further hearing,
to authorise a bailiff or Sheriff to evict you. (In that case,
you can apply to the court to stay the eviction; a judge will
decide if there are grounds for doing so.)

*(If there is an order to pay money, made in a
county court)*

If you do not pay the money owed when it
is due and the claimant takes steps to enforce
payment, the order will be registered in the
Register of County Court Judgments. This may
make it difficult for you to get credit. Further
information about registration is available in a
leaflet which you can get from any county court
office.

Ref.

N28 Order for possession (rented premises)(suspended) (January 2002)

Judgment for Claimant
(in default)

In the	
	County Court
Claim No.	
Claimant (including ref)	
Defendant (including ref)	
Date	

To [Claimant] [Defendant] ['s Solicitor]

Seal

To the Defendant

You have not replied to the claim form.

It is therefore ordered that you must pay the claimant £   for debt [and interest to date of judgment] and £   for costs [less £   which you have already paid]

You must pay to the claimant a total of   £

[by instalments of   £   per [week][month]

[the first payment to reach the claimant] by   [and on or before this date each [week][month] until the debt has been paid]

Warning
If you ignore this order your goods may be removed and sold, or other enforcement proceedings may be taken against you. If this happens further costs will be added. If your circumstances change and you cannot pay, ask at the court office what you can do.

Notes for the defendant

If you did reply to the claim form and believe judgment has been entered wrongly in default, you may apply to the court office giving your reasons why the judgment should be set aside. An application form is available for you to use and you will need to pay a fee. A hearing may be arranged and you will be told when and where it will take place. If you live in, or your solicitor's business is in, another court's area, the claim may be transferred to that court.

This judgment has been registered on the Register of County Court Judgments. This may make it difficult for you to get credit. **If you pay in full within one month** you can ask the court to cancel the entry on the Register. You will need to give proof of payment. You can (for a fee) also obtain a Certificate of Cancellation from the court. If you pay the debt in full after one month you can ask the court to mark the entry on the Register as satisfied and (for a fee) obtain a Certificate of Satisfaction to prove that the debt has been paid.

If judgment is for £5,000 or more, or is in respect of a debt which attracts contractual or statutory interest for late payment, the claimant may be entitled to further interest.

How to pay

- **Payment(s) must be made to the person named at the address for payment, giving the claimant's reference and claim number**
- **DO NOT bring or send payments to the court - they will not be accepted**
- You should allow at least 4 days for your payment to reach the claimant or his representative
- Make sure that you keep records and can account for all payments made. Proof may be required if there is any disagreement. It is not safe to send cash unless you use registered post
- Leaflets on registered judgments, how to pay and what to do if you cannot pay are available from the court

———— Address for payment ————

The court office at

s open between 10 am and 4 pm Monday to Friday. When corresponding with the court, please address forms or letters to the Court Manager and quote the claim number.
N30

Order for possession
(mortgaged premises)
(suspended)

In the

Claim No.

Claimant

Defendant(s)

On   20 ,

sitting at

heard

SEAL

and the court orders that

1. The defendant give the claimant possession of

   on or before   20 .

2. The defendant pay the claimant £   being the amount outstanding under the mortgage
   on or before   20 .

3. [The defendant pay the claimant's costs of £   on or before   20 .]
   [The claimant's costs of the claim will be added to the amount owing under the mortgage.]

4. This order is not to be enforced so long as the defendant pays the claimant the unpaid instalments
   under the mortgage of £   by the payments set out below **in addition to** the future
   instalments under the mortgage.

Payments required

[£   on or before   20   and]

£   per   , the first payment being made on or before   20 .

To the defendant

The court has ordered that **unless you pay the arrears** under the mortgage at the rate set out above **in addition to your normal payments,** you must leave the premises.
Payments should be made to the claimant, not to the court.
If you need more information about making payments, you should contact the claimant.

If you do not make the payments or leave the premises, the claimant can ask the court, without a further hearing, to authorise a bailiff or Sheriff to evict you. (In that case, you can apply to the court to stay the eviction; a judge will decide if there are grounds for doing so.)

(If there is an order to pay money, made in a county court)
If you do not pay the money owed when it is due and the claimant takes steps to enforce payment, the order will be registered in the Register of County Court Judgments. This may make it difficult for you to get credit. Further information about registration is available in a leaflet which you can get from any county court office.

Ref.

N31 Order for possession (mortgaged premises)(suspended)(January 2002)

· ·

Application Notice

- You must complete Parts A **and** B, **and** Part C if applicable
- Send any relevant fee and the completed application notice to the court with any draft order, witness statement or other evidence
- It is for you (and not the court) to serve this application notice

In the	**High Court of Justice** **Queen's Bench Division** **Commercial Court** **Royal Courts of Justice**
Claim No.	
Warrant no. (if applicable)	
Claimant(s) (including ref.)	
Defendant(s) (including ref.)	
Date	

**You should provide this information
for listing the application**

Time estimate   (hours)   (mins)

Is this agreed by all parties? Yes ☐   No ☐

Please always refer to the Commercial Court Guide for details of how applications should be prepared and will be heard, or in a small number of exceptional cases can be dealt with on paper.

Part A

1. Where there is more than one claimant or defendant, specify which claimant or defendant

(The claimant)(The defendant)[1]

2. State clearly what order you are seeking (if there is room) or otherwise refer to a draft order (which must be attached)

intend(s) to apply for an order (a draft of which is attached) that[2]

3. Briefly set out why you are seeking the order. Identify any rule or statutory provision

because[3]

The court office at the Admiralty & Commercial Registry, Royal Courts of Justice, Strand, London WC2A 211

is open from 10am to 4.30 pm Monday to Friday. When corresponding with the court please address forms or letters to the Clerk to the Commercial Court and quote the claim number.

N244 (CC) - **w3** Application Notice (4.99)   *Printed on behalf of The Court Service*

Part B

(The claimant)(The defendant)[1] wishes to rely on: *tick one:*

the attached (witness statement)(affidavit) ☐   (the claimant)(the defendant)'s[1] statement of case ☐

evidence in Part C overleaf in support of this application ☐

Signed [   ]   **Position or**   [   ]
                                          office held
                                          (if signing on
(Applicant)('s litigation friend) ('s solicitor)   behalf of firm,
                                          company or
                                          corporation)

4. If you are Address to which documents about this claim should be sent (including reference if appropriate)[4]
not already a
party to the
proceedings,

		if applicable
you must provide an address for service of documents	Tel. no.	
	fax no.	
	DX no.	
Postcode	e-mail	

Part C

Claim No.

(Note: Part C should only be used where it is convenient to enter here the evidence in support of the application, rather than to use witness statements or affidavits)

(The claimant)(The defendant)[1] wishes to rely on the following evidence in support of this application:

Statement of Truth

*(I believe)(The applicant believes) that the facts stated in this application notice are true

*I am duly authorised by the applicant to sign this statement

Full name...

Name of*(Applicant)('s litigation friend)('s solicitor)

....

Signed

*(Applicant)('s litigation friend)('s solicitor)

Position or office held
(if signing on behalf of firm, company or corporation)

*delete as appropriate

Date

© Crown Copyright

Notice of Hearing of Application

In the	

To [Claimant][Defendant]['s solicitor]

Claim No.	
Claimant (including ref)	
Defendant (including ref)	
Date	

The hearing of the [claimant's][defendant's] application for

(see copy attached) will take place at   [am][pm] on the   of

at [   ]

The court office at

is open between 10 am and 4 pm Monday to Friday. When corresponding with the court, please address forms or letters to the Court Manager and quote the claim number.

N244A Notice of Hearing of Application

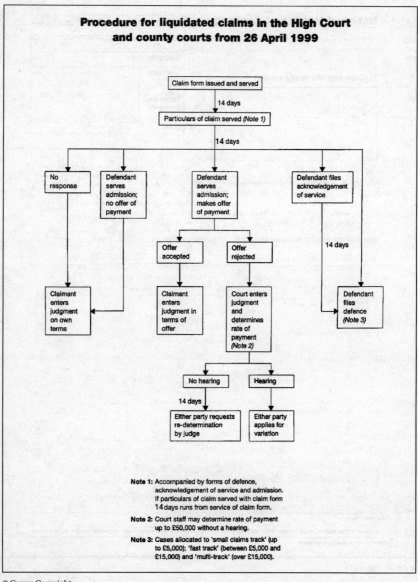

Procedure for liquidated claims in the High Court and county courts from 26 April 1999

Claim form issued and served

↓ 14 days

Particulars of claim served *(Note 1)*

↓ 14 days

- No response
- Defendant serves admission; no offer of payment
- Defendant serves admission; makes offer of payment
- Defendant files acknowledgement of service

Defendant serves admission; makes offer of payment →
- Offer accepted
- Offer rejected

Defendant files acknowledgement of service → 14 days

- Claimant enters judgment on own terms
- Claimant enters judgment in terms of offer
- Court enters judgment and determines rate of payment *(Note 2)*
- Defendant files defence *(Note 3)*

Court enters judgment and determines rate of payment →
- No hearing
- Hearing

- No hearing → 14 days → Either party requests re-determination by judge
- Hearing → Either party applies for variation

Note 1: Accompanied by forms of defence, acknowledgement of service and admission. If particulars of claim served with claim form 14 days runs from service of claim form.

Note 2: Court staff may determine rate of payment up to £50,000 without a hearing.

Note 3: Cases allocated to 'small claims track' (up to £5,000); 'fast track' (between £5,000 and £15,000) and 'multi-track' (over £15,000).

Notes for defendant on replying to the claim form (Consumer Credit Act claim)

Please read these notes carefully - they will help you decide what to do about this claim. You will have received a notice of hearing telling you when and where to come to court with the claim form. A leaflet is available from the court office about what happens when you come to a court hearing.

- You must reply to the claim form within 14 days of the date it was served on you. If the claim form was
  - sent by post, the date of service is taken as the second day after posting (see post mark)
  - delivered or left at your address, the date of service will be the day after it was delivered
  - handed to you personally, the date of service will be the day it was given to you
- You may either
  - pay the amount claimed
  - admit liability for the claim and offer to make payments to keep the goods
  - dispute the claim
- If you do not reply or attend the hearing, judgment may be entered against you.
- The notes below tell you what to do .
- Court staff can help you complete the forms of reply and tell you about court procedure. But they cannot give legal advice. If you need legal advice, for example about the likely success of disputing the claim, you should contact a solicitor or a Citizens Advice Bureau immediately.

Registration of Judgments: If this claim results in a judgment against you, details will be entered in a public register, the Register of County Court Judgments. They will then be passed to credit reference agencies which will then supply them to credit grantors and others seeking information on your financial standing. **This will make it difficult for you to get credit.** A list of credit reference agencies is available from Registry Trust Ltd, 173/175 Cleveland Street, London W1T 6QR.

Costs and Interest: Additional costs and interest may be added to the amount claimed on the front of the claim form if judgment is entered against you. In a county court, if judgment is for £5,000 or more, or is in respect of a debt which attracts contractual or statutory interest for late payment, the claimant may be entitled to further interest.

Your response and what happens next

How to pay

Do not bring any payments to the court - they will not be accepted.

When making payments to the claimant, quote the claimant's reference (if any) and the claim number.

Make sure that you keep records and can account for any payments made. Proof may be required if there is any disagreement. It is not safe to send cash unless you use registered post.

Admitting the Claim

If you admit liability for the claim and offer to make payments in order to keep the goods. Complete Form N9C and send it to the court within 14 days. **Remember** to keep a copy for yourself. The court will send a copy of your admission to the claimant and ask if your offer is acceptable.

If the claimant **accepts your offer** and asks the court to enter judgment before the date of the hearing, you will be sent a copy of the judgment and need not come to the hearing. If you do not hear from the court it is in your interests to attend the hearing.

If your offer is **not accepted**, you should attend the hearing. The court will treat your admission as evidence so remember to bring a copy of your admission with you to the hearing.

Disputing the claim

If you dispute the claim or wish to claim against the claimant (counterclaim), complete Form N9D and send it to the court within 14 days. **Remember** to keep a copy for yourself and to bring it with you to the hearing. The court will send a copy of your defence to the claimant. At the hearing the court may make a final order or judgment in the claim. If the court agrees that you have a valid defence (or counterclaim), it will tell you and the claimant what to do to prepare for a future hearing. If you send your defence to the court after the 14 days has expired, and you want to rely on it at the hearing, the court may take your failure to file it on time into account when deciding what order to make in respect of costs.

Statement of truth

This must be signed by you, by your solicitor or your litigation friend, as appropriate.

Where the defendant is **a registered company or a corporation** the response must be signed by either the director, treasurer, secretary, chief executive, manager or other officer of the company **or** (in the case of a corporation) the mayor, chairman, president or town clerk.

N1(FD) Consumer Credit Act claim (11.01)

Printed on behalf of The Court Service

· ·

Admission (unspecified amount, non-money and return of goods claims)

In the	
Claim No.	
Claimant (including ref.)	
Defendant	

- Before completing this form please read the notes for guidance attached to the claim form. If necessary provide details on a separate sheet, add the claim number and attach it to this form.
- If you are not an individual, you should ensure that you provide sufficient details about the assets and liabilities of your firm, company or corporation to support any offer of payment made.

In non-money claims only

☐ I admit liability for the whole claim
(Complete section 11)

In return of goods cases only

Are the goods still in your possession?

☐ Yes ☐ No

Part A Response to claim *(tick one box only)*

☐ I admit liability for the whole claim but want the court to decide the amount I should pay / value of the goods

OR

☐ I admit liability for the claim and offer to pay [ ] in satisfaction of the claim
(Complete part B and sections 1- 11)

Part B How are you going to pay the amount you have admitted? *(tick one box only)*

☐ I offer to pay on (date) [ ]

OR

☐ I cannot pay the amount immediately because *(state reason)*

[ ]

AND

I offer to pay by instalments of £ [ ]
per (week)(month)
starting *(date)* [ ]

1 Personal details

Surname [ ]

Forename [ ]

☐Mr ☐Mrs ☐Miss ☐Ms

☐Married ☐Single ☐Other *(specify)* [ ]

Age [ ]

Address [ ]

Postcode [ ]

Tel. no. [ ]

2 Dependants *(people you look after financially)*

Number of children in each age group

under 11 [ ] 11-15 [ ] 16-17 [ ] 18 & over [ ]

Other dependants
(give details) [ ]

3 Employment

☐ **I am employed as a** [ ]
My employer is [ ]

Jobs other than
main job *(give details)* [ ]

☐ **I am self employed as a** [ ]

Annual turnover is.......................... £ [ ]

☐ I am not in arrears with my national insurance contributions, income tax and VAT

☐ I am in arrears and I owe........... £ [ ]

Give details of:
(a) contracts and
   other work in hand
(b) any sums due
   for work done [ ]

☐ **I have been unemployed for** [ ] years [ ] months

☐ **I am a pensioner**

4 Bank account and savings

☐ **I have a bank account**

☐ The account is in credit by........ £ [ ]

☐ The account is overdrawn by.... £ [ ]

☐ **I have a savings or building society account**

The amount in the account is......... £ [ ]

5 Residence

I live in
☐ my own property ☐ lodgings
☐ jointly owned house ☐ rented property
☐ council accommodation

N9C - w3 Admission (unspecified amount and non-money claims) (8.99)   *Printed on behalf of The Court Service*

6 Income

My usual take home pay *(including overtime, commission, bonuses etc)*	£	per
Income support	£	per
Child benefit(s)	£	per
Other state benefit(s)	£	per
My pension(s)	£	per
Others living in my home give me	£	per
Other income *(give details below)*		
	£	per
	£	per
	£	per
Total income	£	per

8 Priority debts

(This section is for arrears only. Do not include regular expenses listed in section 7)

Rent arrears	£	per
Mortgage arrears	£	per
Council tax/Community Charge arrears	£	per
Water charges arrears	£	per
Fuel debts: Gas	£	per
Electricity	£	per
Other	£	per
Maintenance arrears	£	per
Others *(give details below)*		
	£	per
	£	per
Total priority debts	£	per

7 Expenses

(Do not include any payments made by other members of the household out of their own income)

I have regular expenses as follows:

Mortgate *(including second mortgage)*	£	per
Rent	£	per
Council tax	£	per
Gas	£	per
Electricity	£	per
Water charges	£	per
TV rental and licence	£	per
HP repayments	£	per
Mail order	£	per
Housekeeping, food, school meals	£	per
Travelling expenses	£	per
Children's clothing	£	per
Maintenance payments	£	per
Others *(not court orders or credit debts listed in sections 9 and 10)*		
	£	per
	£	per
	£	per
Total expenses	£	per

9 Court orders

Court	Claim No.	£	per
Total court order instalments		£	per

Of the payments above, I am behind with payments to *(please list)*

10 Credit debts

Loans and credit card debts *(please list)*

	£	per
	£	per
	£	per

Of the payments above, I am behind with payments to *(please list)*

11 Declaration

I declare that the details I have given above are true to the best of my knowledge

Signed ___

Position or office held *(if signing on behalf of firm or company)* ___

Date ___

© Crown Copyright

● ●

Judgment for Delivery of Goods
(suspended)

Claimant

Defendant

In the

Court

Claim No.	
Claimant's Ref.	
Defendant's Ref.	

Seal

(1) delete regulated or judgments made under the Hire - Purchase Act 1965

District Judge has ordered that, the defendant having failed to comply with the terms of a (regulated) hire - purchase agreement (or regulated conditional sale agreement) dated the day of [19][20] made between the claimant and the defendant(s)(2)

(2) or as the case may be

the claimant do recover against the defendant (3) the following goods of the claimant, being goods subject to the agreement and wrongfully detained by the defendant, namely:

(3) insert name of hirer

and do recover against the defendant the sum of £ for costs (or his costs of this action to be assessed)

(4) specify the goods which the court decides have been detained

District Judge has ordered that unless the defendant(s) fulfill the conditions of the suspension, the defendant(3) do return the goods to the claimant by

And that the operation of this order be suspended on condition that the unpaid balance of the hire - purchase price, namely £ , is paid to the claimant by instalments of £ for every calendar month, the first instalment to reach the claimant by

(5) add any further conditions imposed by the court

(5)

And that the terms of the above - mentioned agreement be modified in the following respects: no sum except the above - mentioned instalments shall be payable to the claimant in respect of the agreement during the suspension

(6)

(6) state any other respects in which the agreement is to be modified

And also that the defendant do pay the sum of £ for costs (or the amount of the costs when assessed) to the claimant by instalments of £ for every calender month, the first instalment to be paid one calender month after the last instalment of the hire - purchase price is paid

Dated

─── **Take Notice** ───

To the defendant

If you do not pay in accordance with this order your goods may be removed and sold or other enforcement proceedings may be taken against you. If circumstances change and you cannot pay, ask at the court office about what you can do.

This judgment has been registered in the Register of County Court Judgments. This may make it difficult for you to get credit. If you pay in full within one month you can ask the court to cancel the entry on the Register. You will need to give proof of payment. You can (for a fee) also obtain a Certificate of Cancellation from the court. If you pay the debt in full after one month you can ask the court to mark the entry on the Register as satisfied and (for a fee) obtain a Certificate of Satisfaction to prove that the debt has been paid.

─── **Address for Payment** ───

─── **How to Pay** ───

• **PAYMENT(S) MUST BE MADE to the person named at the address for payment quoting their reference and the court case number.**
• **DO NOT bring or send payments to the court. THEY WILL NOT BE ACCEPTED.**
• You should allow at least 4 days for your payment to reach the claimant or his representative.
• Make sure that you keep records and can account for all payments made. Proof may be required if there is any disagreement. It is not safe to send cash unless you use registered post.
• A leaflet giving further advice about payment can be obtained from the court.
• If you need more information you should contact the claimant or his representative.

The court office at

is open between 10 am and 4 pm Monday to Friday. When corresponding with the court, please address forms to the Court Manager and quote the claim number.

N32(2)HP/ CCA Judgment for delivery of goods

© Crown Copyright

Form for Replying to an Attachment of Earnings Application

In the	**County Court**
Claim Number	
Application No.	
Claimant *(including ref.)*	
Defendant	

- Read the notes on the notice of application before completing this form.

- Tick the correct boxes and give as much information as you can. The court will make an order based on the information you give on this form. You must give full details of your employment and your income and outgoings. Enclose a copy of your most recent pay slip if you can.

- *Make your offer of payment in box 10. You will get some idea of how much to offer by adding up your expenses in boxes 6, 7, 8 and 9 and taking them from your total income (box 5).*

- Send or take this completed and signed form immediately to the court office shown on the notice of application.

- You should keep your copy of the notice of application unless you are making full payment. (This does not apply to maintenance applications).

- For details of where and how to pay see notice of application.

3 Employment

I am
- [ ] employed as a _____
- [ ] self employed as a _____
- [ ] unemployed
- [ ] a pensioner

a. employment

My employer is _____

Employer's address _____

Address of employer's head office *(if different from above)* _____

My works number and/or pay reference is _____

Jobs other than main job *(give details)* _____

b. self employment
Length of time self employed _____ years _____ months

c. unemployment
Length of time unemployed _____ years _____ months

Give details of any outstanding interviews _____

1 Personal details

Surname _____

Forename _____

- [ ] Mr [ ] Mrs [ ] Miss [ ] Ms
- [ ] Married [ ] Single [ ] Other *(specify)*

Age _____

Address _____

Postcode _____

2 Dependants *(people you look after financially)*

Children *(under 19)*   Others *(give details)*
   Age   Date of Birth

(If more continue on a separate sheet)

4 Bank account and savings

- [ ] I have a bank account
  - [ ] The account is in credit by . . . £ _____
  - [ ] The account is overdrawn by . . . £ _____
- [ ] I have a savings account or building society account
  - The amount in the account is . . . £ _____

N56 - w3 Statement of means-attachment of earnings (4.99)   *Printed on behalf of The Court Service*

• •

5 Income

	£	per
My usual take home pay *(including overtime, commission, bonuses etc.)*	£	per
My husband's or wife's usual take home pay	£	per
Income support	£	per
Child benefit(s)	£	per
Other state benefit(s)	£	per
My pension(s)	£	per
Others living in my home give me	£	per
Other income *(give details below)*	£	per
....	£	per
....	£	per
Total income	£	per

7 Priority debts

(This section is for arrears only. Do not include regular expenses listed in box 6)

		£	per
Rent arrears		£	per
Mortgage arrears		£	per
Council Tax/Community charge arrears		£	per
Water charges arrears		£	per
Fuel debts:	Gas	£	per
	Electricity	£	per
	Other	£	per
Maintenance arrears		£	per
Others *(give details below)*			
....		£	per
		£	per
Total priority debts		£	per

6 Expenses

(Do not include any payments made by other members of the household out of their own income)

I have regular expenses as follows:

	£	per
Mortgage *(including second mortgage)*	£	per
Rent	£	per
Council Tax	£	per
Gas	£	per
Electricity	£	per
Water charges	£	per
TV rental and licence	£	per
HP repayments	£	per
Mail order	£	per
Housekeeping, food, school meals	£	per
Travelling expenses	£	per
Children's clothing	£	per
Maintenance payments	£	per
Others *(not court orders or credit debts listed in boxes 8 and 9)*		
....	£	per
....	£	per
	£	per
Total expenses	£	per

8 Court orders

Court	Claim No.	£	per
Total court order instalments		£	per

Of the payments above, I am behind with payments to *(please list)*

9 Credit debts

Loans and credit card debts *(please list)*

	£	per
	£	per
	£	per

Of the payments above, I am behind with payments to *(please list)*

10 Offer of Payment

I offer to have £ .... week/month deducted from my pay

● If you want an opportunity to pay voluntarily without your employer being ordered to make deductions from your pay you should ask for a suspended order. Tick the box below and give your reasons.

☐ I would like a suspended order because

12 Declaration

I declare that the details I have given above are true to the best of my knowledge

Signed .... Date ....

Application for suspension of a warrant and/or variation of an order

- *Read these notes carefully before completing the form.*

- *Tick the correct boxes and give as much information as you can. It will help the court make a fair decision about how much you can afford to pay if the plaintiff refuses your offer.*

- *If you do not complete all the details and sign the form, the court will not be able to deal with your application.*

- *The court will send you an order giving details of how and when to pay or will tell you when to come to court. You will be informed of the court's decision.*

- *You will have to pay a fee for your application. You can get details of the fee to pay and information about what to do if you cannot pay all or part of a fee from any county court office*

In the	
	Court
Claim Number	
Warrant No.	**Local No.**
Claimant *(including ref.)*	
Defendant	

For court use only	**Date copy sent to claimant**	

I cannot pay the amount ordered and

I wish to apply for

☐   suspension of the warrant

   and/or

☐   a reduction in the instalment order

1 Personal details

Surname

Forename

☐ Mr   ☐ Mrs   ☐ Miss   ☐ Ms

☐ Married   ☐ Single   ☐ Other *(specify)*

Age

Address

Postcode

2 Dependants *(people you look after financially)*

Children *(under 19)*		Others *(give details)*
Age	Date of Birth	

(If more continue on a separate sheet)

3 Employment

☐   **I am employed as a**

   My employer is

   Jobs other than
   main job *(give details)*

☐   **I am self employed as a**

   Annual turnover is . . . . £

     ☐   I am **not** in arrears with my national insurance contributions, income tax and VAT

     ☐   I am in arrears and I owe . . . £

     Give details of:
     (a) contracts and
        other work in hand
     (b) any sums due
        for work done

☐   **I have been unemployed for**   years   months

☐   **I am a pensioner**

4 Bank account and savings

☐   **I have a bank account**

     ☐   The account is in credit by   £

     ☐   The account is overdrawn by   £

☐   **I have a savings account or building society account**

     The amount in the account is   £

5 Property

I live in   ☐ my own property   ☐ lodgings

       ☐ jointly owned property   ☐ council property

       ☐ rented property

N245 - w3 - Form for applying for suspension of warrant of execution or reduction of instalment order (4.99)   *Printed on behalf of The Court Service*

··

6 Income

	£	per
My usual take home pay *(including overtime, commission, bonuses etc.)*	£	per
Income support	£	per
Child benefit(s)	£	per
Other state benefit(s)	£	per
My pension(s)	£	per
Others living in my home give me	£	per
Other income *(give details below)*		
....	£	per
....	£	per
....	£	per
Total income	£	per

8 Priority debts

(This section is for arrears only. Do not include regular expenses listed in box 7)

		£	per
Rent arrears		£	per
Mortgage arrears		£	per
Council tax arrears		£	per
Water charge arrears		£	per
Fuel debts:	Gas	£	per
	Electricity	£	per
	Other	£	per
Maintenance arrears		£	per
Others *(give details below)*			
....		£	per
....		£	per
Total priority debts		£	per

7 Expenses

(Do not include any payments made by other members of the household out of their own income)

I have regular expenses as follows:

	£	per
Mortgage *(including second mortgage)*	£	per
Rent	£	per
Council tax	£	per
Gas	£	per
Electricity	£	per
Water charges	£	per
TV rental and licence	£	per
HP repayments	£	per
Mail order	£	per
Housekeeping, food, school meals	£	per
Travelling expenses	£	per
Children's clothing	£	per
Maintenance payments	£	per
Others *(not court orders or credit debts listed in boxes 9 and 10)*		
....	£	per
....	£	per
....	£	per
Total expenses	£	per

9 Court orders

Court	Claim No.	£	per

Total court order instalments	£	per

Of the payments above, I am behind with payments to *(please list)*

10 Credit debts

Loans and credit card debts *(please list)*

	£	per
	£	per
	£	per

Of the payments above, I am behind with payments to *(please list)*

11 Offer of Payment

• *If you take away the totals of boxes 7, 8 and 9 and the payments you are making in box 10 from the total in box 6, you will get some idea of the sort of sum you should offer. The offer you make should be one you can afford.*

I can pay	£	a month
(and I enclose	£	)
I also enclose the fee of	£	

12 Declaration

I declare that the details I have given above are true to the best of my knowledge

Signed		Date	

IN THE	COUNTY COURT
	Claim no.

IN THE MATTER OF AN APPLICATION FOR A TIME ORDER

Between _____ **Applicant**
(Insert your full name in block capitals)

and _____ **Respondent**
(insert the full name in block capitals of the company to whom you make your payments)

1. *I (Name)*
_____

of (Address)

apply to the court for a time order

2. The following are the details of the regulated agreement in respect of which I am asking for a time order.

a. The agreement is dated _____

and the reference number is _____

b. The names and addresses of the other parties to the agreement are:

c. The name and address of the person (if any) who acted as surety

is _____

of _____

d. *(Delete if not applicable)* The rights and duties of the party named _____

at b. above passed to the respondent
on _____ when *(here give the reasons why you now regard the respondent as your creditor)*

His address is

e. I signed the agreement at *(here give the address of the shop or other place where you signed the agreement)*

f. I agreed to pay instalments
of £ _____ a week [ ] a month [ ]

g. [ ] The unpaid balance due under the agreement is £ _____

or [ ] I do not know the unpaid balance

h. [ ] I am £ _____ in arrear with my payments.

or [ ] I do not know how much the arrears are.

N440 Notice of application for time order by debtor or hirer (4.99)

The Court Service Publications Unit

● ●

i. On _____ the Respondent served on me:

☐ a default notice

☐ a notice given under section 76(1)

☐ a notice given under section 98(1)

or I attach a copy of the notice which the Respondent served on me on

j. *You should complete this section if you are applying for time to pay, if not cross it out.*

My proposals for payment are £ _____

to clear the arrears (if any) and then by instalments of £ _____

k. *You should complete this section if you have failed to comply with the agreement in any other respect.*

I am in breach of the following provisions of the agreement:

And my proposals for remedying the breach(es) are as follows:

3. I have answered the questions about my financial circumstances set out in the schedule to this application.

4. The names and addresses of the persons to be served with this application are: *(You must include any sureties)*

5. My address for service is:

6. Signed _____

(Solicitor for the) Applicant.

Dated _____

Rule 6.37   Form 6.27

Debtor's Bankruptcy Petition
(Title)

(a) Insert full name,
address and
occupation (if any) of
debtor

I

(a)_____

_____

_____

(b) Insert in full any
other name(s) by
which the debtor is or
has been known

also known as

(b)_____

(c) Insert former
address or addresses
at which the debtor
may have incurred
debts or liabilities still
unpaid or unsatisfied

[lately residing at

(c)_____

_____

(d) Insert trading
name (adding "with
another or others", if
this is so), business
address and nature of
the business

[and carrying on business as (d) _____

_____

_____]

(e) Insert any former
trading names
(adding "with
another or others", if
this is so), business
address and nature of
the business in
respect of which the
debtor may have
incurred debts or
liabilities still unpaid
or unsatisfied

[and lately carrying on business as (e) _____

_____

_____

_____

_____]

(f) Delete as
applicable

request the court that a bankruptcy order be made against me and say as follows:-

1. (f) [My centre of main interests has been][I have had an establishment] at

_____

OR

I carry on business as an insurance undertaking; a credit institution; investment undertaking providing services involving the holding of funds or securities for third parties; or a collective investment undertaking as referred to in Article 1.2 of the EC Regulation.

OR

My centre of main interests is not within a Member State

Under the EC Regulation
(i) Centre of main interests should correspond to the place where the debtor conducts the administration of his interests on a regular basis.
(ii) Establishment is defined in the Council Regulation (No 1346/2000) on insolvency proceedings as "any place of operations where the debtor caries out a non-transitory economic activity with human means and goods"

2. I have for the greater part of six months immediately preceding the presentation of this petition (f) [resided at] [carried on business at]_____

_____

(g) Insert name of court

within the district of (f) [this court] [(g)   county court]. I am presenting my petition to this court, as it is the nearest full-time county court to (g) county court, for the following reasons:

(h) State reasons

(h)

3. I am unable to pay my debts.

4. (f) That within the period of five years ending with the date of this petition:-

(j) Insert date

(i) I have not been adjudged bankrupt

(k) Insert name of court

OR

I was adjudged bankrupt on (j)   in the (k)

(l) Insert number of bankruptcy proceedings

Court No. (l)

(ii) I have not (f) [made a composition with my creditors in satisfaction of my debts] or (f) [entered into a scheme of arrangement with creditors] (S16 BA1914)

OR

On (j)   I (f) [made a composition] [entered into a scheme of arrangement] with my creditors.

(iii) I have not entered into a voluntary arrangement

OR

On (j)   I entered into a voluntary arrangement

(iv) I have not been subject to an administration order under Part VI of the County Courts Act 1984

OR

On (j)   an administration order was made against me in the (l)   county court.

5. A statement of my affairs is filed with this petition.

Date_____

Signature_____

Complete only if petition not heard immediately

Endorsement

This petition having been presented to the court on _____ it is ordered that the petition shall be heard as follows:-

Date _____

Time _____ hours

Place _____

• •

Form 6.28
(Rule 6.L1)

Statement of Affairs (Debtor's Petition)
Insolvency Act 1986

NOTE:
These details will
be the same as
those shown at the
top of your
petition

In the HIGH COURT OF JUSTICE

In Bankruptcy

NO_____of 200_____

Re _____

The 'Guidance Notes' Booklet tells you how to complete this form easily and
correctly

Show your current financial position by completing all the pages of this form
which will then be your Statement of Affairs

AFFIDAVIT

This Affidavit must be sworn by a Solicitor or Commissioner of Oaths or an
officer of the court duly authorised to administer oaths when you have
completed the rest of this form

Insert full name
and occupation

1 (a)_____

Insert full address

of (b)_____

_____

Make oath and say that the several pages marked

and contained in the exhibit marked "Z"

are to the best of my knowledge and belief a full, true and complete statement
of my affairs at today's date.

Sworn at   Thomas More Building
                        (2nd Floor), Royal Courts of Justice
                        Strand, London WC2A 2LL

Dated this_____day of_____200__ Signature(s)_____
Before me_____

A Solicitor or Commissioner of Oaths or Duly authorised officer

Before swearing the affidavit, the Solicitor or Commissioner is particularly
requested to make sure that the full name, address and description of the
deponent are stated, and to initial any crossing-out or other alterations in the
printed form. A deficiency in the affidavit in any of the above respects will
mean it will be refused by the court, and will need to be re-sworn.

● ●

IN THE HIGH COURT OF JUSTICE   No   of 200

IN BANKRUPTCY

Re

This is the exhibit marked "Z" referred to in the annexed affidavit of

sworn on the   day of   200

Before me

Officer appointed to administer oaths

A

LIST OF SECURED CREDITORS

Is anyone claiming something of yours to clear or reduce their claim?

If **'YES'** give details below:

Tick Box
YES   NO
☐   ☐

Name of creditor	Address (with postcode)	Amount owed to creditor £	What of yours is claimed and what is it worth?
1.			
2.			
3.			
4.			

Signature _____

Date _____

B

LIST OF UNSECURED CREDITORS

No.	2 Name of creditor or claimant	3 Address (with postcode)	4 Amount the creditor says you owe him/her £	5 Amount you think you owe £

Signature_____ Date_____

C1

ASSETS

	Tick Box	
	Yes	No
Do you have any bank accounts or an interest in one? If **'YES'** state where they are, how much is in them and how much is your share.	☐	☐

_____

_____

_____

_____

_____

	Yes	No
Do you have any business bank accounts, including joint accounts? If **'YES'** state the name of the accounts, where they are and how much is in them.	☐	☐

_____

_____

_____

	Yes	No
Do you have any building society accounts or an interest in one? If **'YES'** state where they are and how much is in them and how much is your share.	☐	☐

_____

_____

_____

_____

_____

_____

Signature _____ Date _____

- -

C2

ASSETS

	Tick Box	
	Yes	No
Do you have any other savings?	☐	☐
If **'YES'** give details		

_____

_____

_____

_____

_____

	Yes	No
Do you use a motor vehicle?	☐	☐
If **'YES'** who owns it and what is it worth?		

_____

_____

_____

_____

	Yes	No
Have you an interest in any other motor vehicles?	☐	☐
If **'YES'** give details and their value.		

_____

_____

_____

_____

_____

_____

Signature _____   Date _____

C3

ASSETS

Now show anything else of yours which may be of value:	£
a) Household furniture and belongings_____	
b) Life policies_____	
c) Money owed to you_____	
d) Stock in trade_____	
e) Other property (see Guidance Notes) –_____	
	TOTAL

Signature _____ Date _____

D

State the name, age (if under 18), and relationship to you of your dependants

1. _____ 6. _____
2. _____ 7. _____
3. _____ 8. _____
4. _____ 9. _____
5. _____ 10. _____

Has distress been levied against you by or on behalf of any creditor?
If 'YES' give details below:-

Tick Box

Yes   No
☐   ☐

Name of creditor	Amount of claim £	Date Distress levied	Description and estimated value of property seized
_____	_____	_____	_____
_____	_____	_____	_____
_____	_____	_____	_____
_____	_____	_____	_____
_____	_____	_____	_____
_____	_____	_____	_____
_____	_____	_____	_____
_____	_____	_____	_____
_____	_____	_____	_____

Signature _____   Date _____

E

---

3. At the date you present your bankruptcy petition, is any court judgement or other legal process outstanding against you that has been made by any court in England and Wales?

If '**YES**' give details below:-

Tick Box

Yes   No

☐   ☐

Name of creditor	Amount of claim £	Type and date of process issued	Description and estimated value of property involved
_____	_____	_____	_____
_____	_____	_____	_____
_____	_____	_____	_____
_____	_____	_____	_____
_____	_____	_____	_____
_____	_____	_____	_____
_____	_____	_____	_____
_____	_____	_____	_____
_____	_____	_____	_____

4. At the date you present your bankruptcy petition, is any attachment of earnings order in force against you?

If '**YES**' give details below:-

Tick Box

Yes   No

☐   ☐

Name of creditor	Date of order	Court	Amount of instalment payable under order (per month/week)	Total amount paid under order	Date order expires (if applicable)
_____	_____	_____	£_____	£_____	_____
_____	_____	_____	_____	_____	_____
_____	_____	_____	_____	_____	_____
_____	_____	_____	_____	_____	_____

Signature _____ Date _____

F

5(a) Have you, before you presented your petition, tried to come to any agreement with your creditors generally for payment of your debts?

Tick Box

Yes   No

☐   ☐

(b) If the answer to 5(a) is 'YES', what terms were offered to the creditors:-

   (1) Time for repayment_____

_____

   (2) Total pence in £ receivable by creditors_____

_____

   (3) When was the offer made?_____

_____

(c) Did the attempt fail because the creditors refused to accept the terms offered?

Tick Box

Yes   No

☐   ☐

If 'NO' why did it fail?_____

_____

_____

_____

6. Do you think that you will be able to introduce a voluntary arrangement to your creditors under Part VIII of Insolvency Act 1986, which is likely to be acceptable to them?

Tick Box

Yes   No

☐   ☐

If 'YES', give brief details:

_____

_____

_____

_____

Signature_____ Date_____

G

STATEMENT OF MEANS

(List below all items of regular "monthly" income and expenditure)

Items of income	£	Items of expenditure	£

This page shows that I will now not be able to pay creditors £ _____ a month.

Signature _____   Date _____

Witness statement in support of application to set aside judgment

IN THE SHIRE COUNTY COURT   Defendant: Bilbo Baggins: 1st: 14.08.02

Between   Goblin Supplies Ltd   Claimants
                 and
                 Bilbo Baggins   Defendant

Witness Statement of Bilbo Baggins

1. My name is Bilbo Baggins and I now live at 3 Hobbit Place, The Shire. I am unemployed. I
    am the defendant in this action. Except as otherwise stated, the statements contained
    herein are made from my own knowledge.

2. I understand from the Court Office that on 12 June 2002 the claimants obtained a
    judgment in default against me for immediate payment and subsequently applied for a
    warrant of execution. The Court Office informs me that the Claim Form was sent to me at
    9 Gollum Road, The Shire. I moved from that address to my present address six months
    ago and consequently had no knowledge of this claim until a county court bailiff called at
    my home to execute the warrant.

3. The bailiff advised me to obtain advice from my local Citizens Advice Bureau. I admit that
    I received goods from the claimants that I ordered from their catalogue through the post
    and for which I paid weekly by postal order which I sent to the claimants by post. I lost my
    job about a year ago and was unable to continue the payments. The Bureau wrote to the
    claimants on my behalf asking for a copy of my agreement with them. The claimants sent
    a blank pro forma agreement and said that was what I would have signed. I refer to the
    Bureau's letter (marked 'BB1'), the claimants' response (marked 'BB2') and the pro forma
    agreement (marked 'BB3'), copies of which are attached. I have never seen this
    agreement before and I never signed it or any other document. The Bureau then wrote to
    the claimants again and asked them if they would agree to set aside the judgment
    because:
    (a) there was no signed agreement; and
    (b) I had not received the claim form.

    They refused and said I owed them for the goods they had sent me from the catalogue. I
    refer to the Bureau's letter (marked 'BB4') and the claimants' reply (marked 'BB5'), copies
    of which are attached.

4. I understand from the Bureau that I have a defence to this claim on the following grounds:
   (a) Even though the claim relates to goods sold and delivered to me, because they were sold on credit, the agreement is regulated under s8 of the Consumer Credit Act 1974 (CCA 1974) and does not fall within any of the exemptions in s16 CCA 1974 or under the Consumer Credit (Exempt Agreements) Order 1989.
   (b) Under s61(1)(a) CCA 1974 a regulated agreement is not properly executed unless a document in the prescribed form itself containing all the prescribed terms and conforming to the regulations under s60(1) is signed in the prescribed manner both by the debtor or hirer and by or on behalf of the creditor or owner.
   (c) Under s65(1) CCA 1974 an improperly executed regulated agreement is enforceable against the debtor on an order of the court only.
   (d) Under s127(3) CCA 1974 the court shall not make an enforcement order under s65(1) if s61(1)(a) (signing of agreements) was not complied with, unless a document (whether or not in the prescribed form and complying with the regulations under s60(1) itself containing all the prescribed terms of the agreement) was signed by the debtor or hirer (whether or not in the prescribed manner).
   (e) I have signed no written agreement or document of any kind. The claimant has failed to comply with the requirements of s61 CCA 1974. The regulated agreement is improperly executed under s127(3) CCA 1974 and cannot be enforced by the court.

5. I, therefore, submit that I have a complete defence to the claimants' claim and I ask the court to set aside the judgment and the warrant of execution on the ground that I have a realistic prospect of success in this action and, in the meantime, to stay any enforcement proceedings against me until further order. I further submit that any delay in making this application was reasonable due to the Bureau needing to investigate this matter and then attempting to persuade the claimants to agree to the judgment being set aside.

I believe that the facts stated in this witness statement are true.

Appendix 4

Standard debt advice forms

The following forms assist the debt adviser in the most frequent data collection or calculation exercises.

Form 1 Example of completed financial statement (p471)
Form 2 Example of completed creditor list (p472)
Form 3 Equitable distribution calculation sheet (p473)
Form 4 Authorisation slip for enquirers to sign (p474)

Stoke CAB - DEBT SYSTEM

BUREAU FINANCIAL STATEMENT   Completed On: 2/7/71   Checked by: B

Name: _SMITH, STACEY AND JOHN_

Address: _172 HOVERINGHAM DRIVE, GREENWOOD, STAFFS_

Members of Household: _STACEY-UNMARRIED 23 JOHN-MARRIED 26, NICOLA 5_
(say what they do, and give ages): _NICHOLAS 4, TASON 7_

Amount of savings: £ _____   (say nil if none)

WEEKLY INCOME (state Wages as net, include all income from benefits, pensions, maintenance, lodgers etc).

SOURCE	DRAFT Amount £	FINAL Amount £
JOHNS WAGE		121.00
CHILD BENEFIT / FAMILY CREDIT		38.45
TOTAL INCOME		**159.45**

WEEKLY EXPENDITURE	DRAFT Amount £	FINAL Amount £
HOUSING COSTS		
Mortgage		23.23
Mortgage Endowment		1.60
House Insurance Mortgage Protection ____ Buildings ____ Contents ____		1.12
Other Mortgages		
Rent (after Housing benefit)		
Board & Lodgings		
Council Tax (after benefit) (monthly x 10 divide by £2)		12.05
Repairs & maintenance (Tenants up to £3 per wk. Owners up to £12)		3.00
FUEL AND WATER CHARGES		
Gas (Say if token meter / direct payment)		9.20
Electricity (say if token meter / direct payment)		7.20
Water Charges (monthly x 8 divide by £2)		4.05
Other Fuels (say which):		

Date: 10 April 1997   File: FINSTA2.WPD   ISO ref: 4.9   Rev: 1.0

page 1

Stoke CAB - DEBT SYSTEM

TRAVEL COSTS

Fares to work / school / general / jobhunting

Car / Motorbike costs : Petrol _____
Tax   £2.69
HP/Conditional Sale _____
Insurance _____
Repairs etc. _____

Total   2.50

OTHER BILLS AND COMMITMENTS

T.V. Licence: £1.71 (Colour) £0.56 (b/w)
T.V. rental   £ 3.92   Total   3.92
Maintenance Payments
Magistrate Court Fines
Pension Contributions (not deducted from wages and Life Insurance
Telephone

OTHER EXPENSES

Food, Household Items & Toiletries ($12 to $30 per person)   50.00
School Dinners / Pocket Money   5.00
Clothing (allow £3 to $8 per person)   1.00
Childcare
Launderette Costs
Furniture & Bedding (allow up to $5 per person)   4.50
Health Costs (prescription/dental/optical)   3.00

ADDITIONAL EXPENSES
List any other expenses here:
....
....
....
....
....

TOTAL EXPENDITURE	$	164.71
AVAILABLE INCOME	$	159.46

NO AVAILABLE INCOME

NOTES:

Date: 10 April 1997   File: FINSTA2.WPD   ISO ref: 4.9   Rev: 1.0

page 2

TAKING STEPS
CREDITOR LIST

INSTRUCTIONS
- Please use one column for each of your creditors
- Fill in as much detail as you can – leave a blank if you don't know the answer
- Include everyone you owe money to even if you are not behind with payments – make sure you include:

PRIORITY DEBTS
- ✔ mortgages & secured loans
- ✔ rent arrears
- ✔ rates, poll tax, council tax
- ✔ unpaid fines
- ✔ gas, water & electricity bills
- ✔ maintenance arrears
- ✔ TV licence debt
- ✔ hire purchase & conditional sale
- ✔ guaranteed loans
- ✔ telephone bill
- ✔ tax, national insurance & VAT

NON-PRIORITY DEBTS
- ✔ bank debts & overdrafts
- ✔ debts to door callers & moneylenders
- ✔ catalogues
- ✔ credit cards & store cards

Creditor's name	
Creditor's address	
Account/ref number	
If creditor is using a solicitor or collection agency – solicitor/agency's name	
Solicitor's/agency's address	
Reference number	
Who signed the agreement? (ring one) (partner means husband/wife/cohabitee/etc)	me I my partner I me & partner other – who? –
How much is owed now?	approx Y/N
What payments did you agree to make when you signed the agreement?	per wk/mth
How far are you behind with payments?	Please don/t fill in
Approx date began	
Reason for debt (eg, to buy cooker)	
Type of debt (see list to the left)	
Have you checked the agreement?	
Date and amount of last payment	
How is payment made (book/cash/direct debit)?	
Insurance – state type – eg sickness/redund./death	
Warning letter/red bill	Received Payment date
Default notice/threat of disconnection or distraint/notice to quit/other	Received Type Payment due
Summons received (state type – eg default/ possession/magistrates court/High Court	Type Received
Which court (eg Stoke)?	
Court case number	
Hearing dte	
Judgment	Amount for – Date made / / Instalments – £ : / in full
Enforcement action (state type – eg bailiffs/ attachment/charging order/statutory demand	Type Date action due / /
Other details (eg suggestions made/agreed)	
Action to be taken by enquirer	
Action to be taken by CAB	

Taking Steps Self Help Debt Pack

EQUITABLE DISTRIBUTION CALCULATION SHEET

NAME

ADDRESS

AVAILABLE INCOME (get from MY BUDGET sheet) £............... a week – use only the pounds figure – no pence.

a) Write NAMES and the AMOUNT OWED to each creditor – use only the pounds figure – no pence

b) Add up all the individual AMOUNTS OWED to get a total owed figure

c) For each creditor –

1) Divide the AMOUNT OWED by the TOTAL OWED – this gives the PROPORTION OWED figure which should always be between 0 and 1 (eg. 0.14 or 0.675 would be correct figures, 3.63 or 21.06 are not). If any of your figures are bigger than 1 try calculating again!

2) Next multiply (times) the PROPORTION OWED figure by the AVAILABLE INCOME figure – the answer is the EQUITABLE OFFER per week.

3) To get a MONTHLY OFFER figure multiply the EQUITABLE OFFER per week by 52, and then divide by 12 to give the MONTHLY OFFER.

4) Round the offers to the nearest 10p (for example, £3.57 would be rounded up to £3.60, £5.34 would be rounded down to £5.30).

CREDITOR'S NAME	AMOUNT OWED	PROPORTION OWED = AMOUNT OWED divided by TOTAL BALANCE	EQUITABLE OFFER = PROPORTION times AVAIL INCOME/wk	MONTHLY OFFER = EQUITABLE OFFER times 52, then divided by 12
add up all AMOUNTS OWED to give TOTAL BALANCE =	£	Check total equals 1.00		

IF YOU HAVE TROUBLE DOING THIS CALCULATION – FILL IN YOUR AVAILABLE INCOME, ALL THE CREDITORS' NAMES AND ALL THE AMOUNTS OWED, THEN SEND OR BRING US THE FORM – WE WILL WORK OUT THE FIGURES AND SEND THE COMPLETED FORM BACK TO YOU.

CITIZENS ADVICE BUREAU

I agree to the above agency acting on my behalf. I authorise you to give to them any relevant information you may have about me.

NAME............................. ADDRESS..

....

SIGNATURE ....

DATE ....

Appendix 5

Useful organisations

Trade bodies

Arts and Humanities Research Board
Whitefriars
Lewins Mead
Bristol BS1 2AE
Tel 01179 876 500
www.ahrb.ac.uk

Association of British Insurers
51 Gresham Street
London EC2V 7HQ
Tel 020 7600 3333
www.abi.org.uk

Association of Civil Enforcement Agencies
Chesham House
150 Regent Street
London W1B 5SJ
Tel 020 7432 0366
www.acea.org.uk

Biotechnology and Biological Sciences Research Council
Polaris House
North Star Avenue
Swindon SN2 1UH
Tel 01793 413 200
www.bbsrc.ac.uk

British Insurance and Investment Brokers' Association
Beeber House
14 Bevis Marks
London EC3A 7NT
Tel 020 7623 9043
www.biba.org.uk

Certified Bailiffs Association
Ridgefield House
14 John Dalton Street
Manchester M2 6JR
Tel 01618 397 225
www.bailiffs.org.uk

The Chartered Association of Certified Accountants
29 Lincolns Inn Fields
London WC2A 3EE
Tel 020 7242 6855
www.accaglobal.com

Consumer Credit Association
Queen's House
Queen's Road
Chester CH1 3BQ
Tel 01244 312 044
www.ccauk.org

**Consumer Credit Trade
Association**
Suite 8
The Wool Exchange
10 Hustlergate
Bradford BD1 1RE
Tel 01274 390 380
www.ccta.co.uk

Council for Mortgage Lenders
3 Saville Row
London W1X 1AF
Tel 020 7437 0075
www.cml.org.uk

**Economic and Social Research
Council**
Polaris House
North Star Avenue
Swindon SN2 1UJ
Tel 01793 413 000
www.esrc.ac.uk

**Engineering and Physical Sciences
Research Council**
Polaris House
North Star Avenue
Swindon SN2 1UJ
Tel 01793 444 000
www.epsrc.ac.uk

Finance & Leasing Association
Imperial House
15-19 Kingsway
London WC2B 6UN
Tel 020 7836 6511
www.fla.org.uk

**Insolvency Practitioners'
Association**
52-54 Gracechurch Street
London
EC3V OEH
Tel 020 7623 5108
www.insolvency-practioners.org.uk

**Institute of Chartered Accountants
in England and Wales**
Gloucester House
399 Silbury Boulevard
Central Milton Keynes MK9 2HL
Tel 01908 248 100
www.icaew.co.uk

**Insurance Brokers' Registration
Council**
Tyne Business Centre
Midland Road, Higham Ferrers
Northants NN10 8DW
Tel 01933 359 083

Medical Research Council
20 Park Crescent
London W1B 1AL
Tel 020 7636 5422
www.mrc.ac.uk

**Natural Environment Research
Council**
Polaris House
North Star Avenue
Swindon SN2 1UJ
Tel 01793 411 500
www.nerc.ac.uk

**Particle Physics and Astronomy
Research Council**
Polaris House
North Star Avenue
Swindon SN2 1UJ
Tel 01793 442 000
www.pparc.ac.uk

Sheriff's Officers Association
c/o John Marston & Sons
5 Poplar Drive
Witton
Birmingham B6 7AD

Ombudsman and regulatory bodies

The Commission for Local Administration in England (Local Government Ombudsman)
21 Queen Anne's Gate
London SW1H 9BU
Tel 020 7915 3210
www.lgo.org.uk

The Commission for Local Administration in Wales
Derwen House
Court Road
Bridgend
Mid-Glamorgan CF31 1BN
Tel 01656 661 325
www.ombudsman-wales.org

Department for Education and Skills
Tel 08700 012 345
www.dfes.gov.uk

Financial Ombudsman Services
South Quay Plaza
183 Marsh Wall Street
London E14 9SR
Tel 08450 801 800
www.financial-ombudsman.org.uk

Financial Services Authority
25 The North Colonnade
Canary Wharf
London E14 5HS
Tel 020 7676 1000
Helpline 08456 061 234
www.fsa.gov.uk

The Law Society (England and Wales)
113 Chancery Lane
London WC2A 1PL
Tel 020 7242 1222
www.lawsociety.org.uk

Northern Ireland Assembly
Public Information Office
Parliament Buildings
Belfast BT4 3XX
Tel 028 9052 1333
www.ni-assembly.gov.uk

Office of the Data Protection Registrar
Wycliffe House
Water Lane, Wilmslow
Cheshire SK9 5AF
Tel 01625 545 745
www.dataprotection.gov.uk
(for complaints concerning out-of-date or inaccurate personal information)

Office of Fair Trading (OFT)
2-6 Salisbury Square
London EC4Y 8GX
Tel 020 7211 8000
www.oft.gov.uk

Office of Gas and Electricity Markets (Ofgem)
9 Millbank
London SW1P 3GE
Tel 020 7901 7000
www.ofgem.gov.uk

● ●

**Office of the Legal Services
Ombudsman**
3rd Floor
Sunlight House
Quay Street
Manchester M3 3JZ
Tel 01618 397 262
Lo Call No: 08456 010 794 (charged
at local rates, available nationally)

**Office of the Ombudsman for
Health and the Parliamentary
Commissioner (England)**
Millbank Tower
Millbank
London SW1P 4QP
Tel 08450 154 033
www.ombudsman.org.uk

**Office of the Pensions
Ombudsman**
11 Belgrave Road
London SW1V 1RB
Tel 020 7834 9144
www.pensions-ombudsman.org.uk

**Office for the Supervision of
Solicitors**
Victoria Court
8 Dormer Place
Leamington Spa
Warwickshire CV32 5AE
Tel 01926 820 082
Helpline 08456 086 565
www.lawsociety.org.uk

**Office of Telecommunications
(Oftel)**
Export House
50 Ludgate Hill
London EC4M 7JJ
Tel 020 7634 8888
www.oftel.gov.uk

Office of Water Services (Ofwat)
Centre City Tower
7 Hill Street
Birmingham B5 4UA
Tel 01216 251 300
www.ofwat.gov.uk

Revenue Adjudicator's Office
3rd Floor Haymarket House
28 Haymarket
London SW1Y 4SP
Tel 020 7930 2292
www.adjudicatorsoffice.gov.uk

Welsh Assembly
Tel: 02920 898 200
www.publicinformation.wales.
gov.uk

Organisations giving advice or representing advice networks

**Association of British Credit
Unions Ltd**
Holyoak House
Hanover Street
Manchester M60 0AS
Tel 01618 323 694
www.abcul.org

Education and Learning Wales
Tel 08456 088 066
www.elwa.ac.uk

**Federation of Information and
Advice Centres**
12th Floor
New London Bridge House
25 London Bridge Street
London SE1 9ST
Tel 020 7489 1800
www.fiac.org.uk

Law Centres Federation
Duchess House
18-19 Warren Street
London W1P 5DB
Tel 020 7387 8570
www.lawcentres.org.uk

Money Advice Association
Room 109-110
Bridge House
181 Queen Victoria Street
London EC4V 4DZ
Tel 020 7489 7707
www.moneyadvicetrust.org

Money Advice Scotland
Suite 306
Pentagon Centre
36 Washington Street
Glasgow G3 8AZ
Tel 01415 720 237
www.moneyadvicescotland.org.uk

National Association of Citizens Advice Bureaux
Myddelton House
115-123 Pentonville Road
London N1 9LZ
Tel 020 7833 2181
www.nacab.org.uk

National Consumer Council
20 Grosvenor Gardens
London SW1W 0DH
Tel 020 7730 3469
www.ncc.org.uk

National Union of Students
Nelson Mandela House
461 Holloway Road
London N7 6LJ
Tel 020 7272 8900
www.nusonline.co.uk

TaxAid
Room 304
Linton House
164-180 Union St
London SE1 0LH
Tel (advisers only; 9am-5pm)
020 7803 4950
Tel (clients; 10am-12pm Mon-Thurs)
020 7803 4959
www.taxaid.org.uk

UKCOSA: The Council for International Education
7-17 St Albans Place
London N1 0NX
Tel 020 7226 3762
www.ukcosa.org.uk

Appendix 6
Useful publications

A debt adviser should have access to the latest edition of most of the following books:

Debts

Consumer Law and Practice, Robert Lowe and Geoffrey Woodroffe, Sweet & Maxwell

Consumer Credit Law, R Goode, Butterworths

Tolleys Tax Guide, Tolley Publishing Company Ltd

* *Council Tax Handbook,* CPAG

* *Fuel Rights Handbook,* CPAG

Manual of Housing Law, Arden and Hunter, Sweet & Maxwell

* *Rights Guide for Home Owners,* CPAG/Shelter

Increasing resources

* *Welfare Benefits Handbook,* CPAG

* *Child Support Handbook,* CPAG

* *Social Security Legislation Volume I: Non Means Tested Benefits,* Bonner, Hooker and White, Sweet & Maxwell

* *Social Security Legislation Volume II: Income Support, Jobseeker's Allowance, Tax Credits and the Social Fund,* Mesher, Wood et al, Sweet & Maxwell

* *Social Security Legislation Volume III: Administration, Adjudication and the European Dimension,* Rowland and White, Sweet & Maxwell

* *CPAG's Housing Benefit and Council Tax Benefit Legislation* (Findlay/ Ward), Poynter and Stagg, CPAG

* *Child Support: the legislation,* Jacobs and Douglas, Sweet & Maxwell

* *Disability Rights Handbook,* Disability Alliance

A Guide to Grants for Individuals in Need, The Directory of Social Change

Voluntary Agencies Directory, available from Harper Row Distribution Ltd, Estover Road, Plymouth PL6 7PZ

Charities Digest, Family Welfare Enterprises Ltd

Tolley's Employment Law Handbook, Slade and Giffin, Tolley Publishing Company Ltd

* *Guide to Training and Benefits for Young People,* Centre for Economic & Social Inclusion

Student Loans: a guide for students, available from Student Loans Company Ltd, 100 Bothwell Street, Glasgow G2 7JD

Courts and the law

Anthony & Berryman's Magistrates' Court Guide, Butterworths

The Civil Court Practice 2002 (The Green Book), Butterworths

Winfield & Jolowicz on Tort, W Rogers, Sweet & Maxwell

Mosley & Whitley's Law Dictionary, Saunders, Butterworths

Defending Possession Proceedings, Luba, Madge, McConnell, LAG

Bankruptcy Law & Practice, Berry and Bailey, Butterworths

Personal Insolvency: A Practical Guide, Grier and Floyd, Sweet & Maxwell

Judicial Review Proceedings, Jonathan Manning, LAG

Manual of Housing Law, Andrew Arden et al, Sweet & Maxwell

The Law of Seizure of Goods: debtors' rights and remedies, J Kruse, Barry Rose Law Publishers

Skills

Client Interviewing for Lawyers, Avrom Cherr, Sweet & Maxwell

* Indicates that books are available from CPAG (in some cases for CPAG members only). For a full publications list write to CPAG, 94 White Lion Street, London N1 9PF.

Appendix 7

· ·

Abbreviations used in the notes

AC	Appeal Cases
All ER	All England Reports
BGA	British Gas Authorisation
CA	Court of Appeal
CCLR	Consumer Credit Law Reports
CCR	County Court Rules *or* Rules of the County Court
CPR	Civil Procedure Rules
Cr App R	Criminal Appeal Reports
DMG	*Debt Management Guidance,* Office of Fair Trading 366, December 2001
DRR	Distress for Rent Rules 1988
ESL	Electricity Suppliers' Licence
FSA	Financial Services Authority
GSL	Gas Suppliers' Licence
HL	House of Lords
HLR	House Law Reports
IR	Insolvency Rules 1986
JP	Justice of the Peace
LAG	Legal Action Group
MCR	Magistrates' Courts Rules
para	paragraph
PD	Practice Direction
QB	Queen's Bench Reports
QBD	Queen's Bench Division
reg	regulation
RSC	Rules of the Supreme Court
s	Section
ss	Sections
Sch	Schedule
WLR	Weekly Law Reports

· · · ·

Acts of Parliament

AEA 1971	Attachment of Earnings Act 1971
AJA 1970	Administration of Justice Act 1970
AJA 1973	Administration of Justice Act 1973
CAA 1995	Criminal Appeals Act 1995
CCA 1974	Consumer Credit Act 1974
CCA 1984	Consumer Credit Act 1984 as amended
CJA 1982	Criminal Justice Act 1982
COA 1979	Charging Orders Act 1979
CoCA 1984	County Court Act 1984
CLSA 1990	Courts and Legal Services Act 1990
DPMCA 1978	Domestic Proceedings and Magistrates' Court Act 1978
DRA 1689	Distress for Rent Act 1689
EA 1989	Electricity Act 1989
GA 1986	Gas Act 1986
GA 1995	Gas Act 1995
HA 1985	Housing Act 1985
HA 1988	Housing Act 1988
HA 1996	Housing Act 1996
IA 1986	Insolvency Act 1986
IAA 1999	Immigration and Asylum Act 1999
ICTA 1988	Income and Corporation Taxes Act 1988
JA 1838	Judgments Act 1838
JSA 1995	Jobseekers Act 1995
LA 1980	Limitation Act 1980
LGFA 1988	Local Government Finance Act 1988
MCA 1980	Magistrates' Court Act 1980
MEA 1991	Maintenance Enforcement Act 1991
MOA 1958	Maintenance Orders Act 1958
PCCA 1973	Powers of Criminal Courts Act 1973
RA 1977	Rent Act 1977
SCA 1981	Supreme Court Act 1981
SGA 1979	Sale of Goods Act 1979
SGSA 1982	Sale of Goods and Services Act 1982
SSA 1986	Social Security Act 1986
SSAA 1992	Social Security Administration Act 1992
SSCBA 1992	Social Security Contributions and Benefits Act 1992
TCA 1999	Tax Credits Act 1999
TLATA 1996	Trusts of Land and Appointment of Trustees Act 1996
TMA 1970	Taxes Management Act 1970

Regulations

CB & SS(FAR) Amdt Regs	The Child Benefit and Social Security (Fixing & Adjustment of Rates) (Amendment) Regulations 1998
CC(AE) Regs	The Community Charge (Administration and Enforcement) Regulations 1989
CC(CNCD) Regs	Consumer Credit (Cancellation Notices and Copies of Documents) Regulations
CC(IJD)O 1991	County Court (Interest on Judgment Debts) Order 1991
CC(RES) Regs	Consumer Credit (Rebate on Early Settlement) Regulations 1983
CT(AE) Regs	Council Tax (Administration and Enforcement) Regulations 1992
CTB Regs	The Council Tax Benefit (General) Regulations 1992
DWA Regs	The Disability Working Allowance (General) Regulations 1991

DWA is now disabled person's tax credit but the name of the regs has not changed.

FC Regs	The Family Credit (General) Regulations 1987

Family credit is now working families tax credit but the name of the regs has not changed.

HB (Gen) Regs 1987	Housing Benefit (General) Regulations 1987
HCCCJO 1991	High Court and County Courts Jurisdiction Order 1991
IS Regs	The Income Support (General) Regulations 1987
HB Regs	The Housing Benefit (General) Regulations 1987
JSA Regs	The Jobseeker's Allowance Regulations 1996
SFCWP Regs	The Social Fund Cold Weather Payments (General) Regulations 1988
SFM&FE Regs	The Social Fund Maternity and Funeral Expense(General) Regulations 1987
SFWFP Regs	The Social Fund Winter Fuel Payment Regulations 2000
SS(BTWB) Regs	The Social Security (Back to Work Bonus) Regulations 1996
SS(CMB) Regs	The Social Security (Child Maintenance Bonus) Regulations 1996
SS(CMPMA) Regs	The Social Security (Child Maintenance Premium and Miscellaneous Amendments) Regulations 2000 No.3176
SS(C&P) Regs	The Social Security (Claims and Payments) Regulations 1987 No. 1968
SS(WB&RP) Regs	The Social Security (Widow's Benefit & Retirement Pensions) Regulations 1979
UTCC Regs	Unfair Terms in Consumer Contracts Regulations 1994

Index